1999
The Supreme Court Review

1999
The

"Judges as persons, or courts as institutions, are entitled to
no greater immunity from criticism than other persons
or institutions . . . [J]udges must be kept mindful of their limitations and
of their ultimate public responsibility by a vigorous
stream of criticism expressed with candor however blunt."
—*Felix Frankfurter*

". . . while it is proper that people should find fault when
their judges fail, it is only reasonable that they should recognize the
difficulties. . . . Let them be severely brought to book,
when they go wrong, but by those who will take the trouble
to understand them."
—*Learned Hand*

THE LAW SCHOOL

THE UNIVERSITY OF CHICAGO

Supreme Court Review

EDITED BY

DENNIS J. HUTCHINSON

DAVID A. STRAUSS

AND GEOFFREY R. STONE

THE UNIVERSITY OF CHICAGO PRESS

CHICAGO AND LONDON

INTERNATIONAL STANDARD BOOK NUMBER: 0-226-36317-1

LIBRARY OF CONGRESS CATALOG CARD NUMBER: 60-14353

THE UNIVERSITY OF CHICAGO PRESS, CHICAGO 60637

THE UNIVERSITY OF CHICAGO PRESS, LTD., LONDON

© 2000 BY THE UNIVERSITY OF CHICAGO, ALL RIGHTS RESERVED, PUBLISHED 2000

PRINTED IN THE UNITED STATES OF AMERICA

The paper used in this publication meets the minimum requirements of American National Standard for Information Sciences–Permanence of Paper for Printed Library Materials, ANSI Z39.48-1984. ♾

TO

CHARLES ALAN WRIGHT

Teacher, Scholar, Public Citizen
for a Half-Century

CONTENTS

PREFACE

In 1959, Phil Kurland approached Edward Levi, Dean of the Law School, with a novel proposition: Phil would edit an annual journal dedicated to analysis of the work of the Supreme Court of the United States, not simply its doctrinal output, although that would be central, but also the history, impact, and behavior, in the broadest sense, of the Court. At the time, there was no professional journal that focused exclusively on the Court, and no regular law journal edited by the faculty. Phil thought both novelty and topic merited institutional support, at least to the extent of publishing subventions and stipends for contributors. Edward's response, as Phil later recalled it, was characteristic: *If what you produce is good enough, it will support itself.* In other words, no subvention, no stipends, but a secretary—part-time—could be made available. The incident can be read in multiple ways—evidence of a rough and ready academic egalitarianism, belief in an intellectual market, hard-headed decanal protection of the institutional fisc, and so on. Phil accepted the challenge, and you now hold the fortieth volume in the series, a fitting testament to the optimism which Edward disguised at the time as unsubsidized equality of intellectual opportunity.

The Supreme Court Review is the product of Edward Levi's stringent patronage, just as The Law School bears his hallmarks—from its intellectual convictions to its architecture—and just as the University he so loved and shaped bears his enduring imprint. If academic institutions are what we have come to call intentional communities, no individual imposed his vision on The University of Chicago more than Edward Levi—student, teacher, Dean of the Law School, Provost, and President. He believed that the domains of human knowledge were not the provinces of departments or other fiefdoms, so he insured that all of the social sciences were brought to bear on the study of the law, from statistics and economics to psychology and sociology; he believed that scholars should engage in earnest conversations across disciplinary lines and departmental affiliations, so he taught in the Law School, the College, and the Committee on Social Thought; he believed that the legal academy was responsible not only to its immediate clientele but also to the wider community of which it was a part, so he inaugurated one of the first clinical education programs, to serve both student and neighborhood. Edward Levi will be remembered by all who know the University of Chicago for his extraordinary energy and courage in reorganizing and revitalizing every corner of the institution. He seemed to personify the University—a product of its Lab School, College, and Law School—and its culture of relentless intellectual rigor. He was also a man of profound faith. He believed in reason, in uncompromising standards, and, even when it was most unfashionable, in the idea of the rule of law.

In many respects, the coda to Edward Levi's career is captured in two moments, a quarter-century apart. In 1949, he published *An Introduction to Legal Reasoning*, which presented itself as a careful description of the operation of legal analysis in the realms of common law, statutory construction, and constitutional adjudication. In some measure it was what it purported to be, but in fact, the slim essay was a patient and sustained response to the darker strains of American legal realism. Edward argued that customary legal systems developed a logic of their own—not rigid or geometric—which was accessible and consistent but nonetheless capable of adapting to changing conditions. All human institutions are subject to the human frailty of their governors, but to Edward that was the challenge to the profession, and to the institutions he dedicated his careers to, not a refutation of their legitimacy. In 1975, at an age when most men would be planning their retirement, especially after such a distinguished career, Edward accepted President Gerald Ford's call to be Attorney General of the United States. His charge was grave—to restore the integrity of the office and the confidence of the populace in the authority of the United States Department of Justice. For someone who avoided the lapidary turn of phrase, his remarks when he was sworn in memorably acknowledged the stakes of his stewardship: "We have lived in a time of change and corrosive skepticism and cynicism concerning the administration of justice. Nothing can more weaken the quality of life or more imperil realization of the goals we all hold dear than our failure to make clear by word and deed that our law is not an instrument for partisan purposes and it is not an instrument to be used in ways which are careless of the higher values within all of us."

None can doubt his fidelity, his achievement, nor that his final act of public service was entirely of a piece with his character and lifelong convictions. When he left the Attorney-Generalship in 1977, he returned to the College and the Law School as teacher, colleague, and friend. He is terribly missed but his impact is abiding, from the smallest to the largest detail of our work.

DENNIS J. HUTCHINSON
DAVID A. STRAUSS
GEOFFREY R. STONE

ERNEST A. YOUNG

STATE SOVEREIGN IMMUNITY AND
THE FUTURE OF FEDERALISM

The states are winning more federalism cases at the Supreme
Court these days than at any time since the New Deal. Important decisions have reinvigorated limits on the federal commerce
power,[1] imposed clear statement rules for a variety of congressional
impositions on state authority,[2] and crafted new limits on the ability of the federal government to "commandeer" state instrumentalities.[3] But the Court's most persistent and aggressive efforts have
focused on the arcane doctrine of state sovereign immunity.[4] In

Ernest A. Young is Assistant Professor, University of Texas School of Law.

AUTHOR'S NOTE: Many thanks to Lynn Baker, Stuart Benjamin, Heather Gerken, Calvin
Johnson, Ellen Katz, Douglas Laycock, Adrian Vermeule, Louise Weinberg, and Jonathan
Zasloff for helpful comments and suggestions, to Kelly Trish for excellent research assis-
tance, and to Allegra Young for everything else.

[1] *United States v Lopez*, 514 US 549 (1995). The Court has also recognized limits on
Congress's power to enforce the Fourteenth Amendment. See *City of Boerne v Flores*, 521
US 507 (1997).

[2] *Gregory v Ashcroft*, 501 US 452 (1991); *Will v Michigan Dept. of State Police*, 491 US
58 (1989). The most important of these "clear statement" rules—the presumption against
preemption of state regulatory authority—is not new, having been around since the New
Deal. See, e.g., *Rice v Santa Fe Elevator Corp.*, 331 US 218 (1947); Stephen A. Gardbaum,
The Nature of Preemption, 79 Cornell L Rev 767, 805–07 (1994).

[3] *Printz v United States*, 521 US 898 (1997).

[4] In addition to the cases cited in notes 1–3, see also *Idaho v Coeur d'Alene Tribe*, 521
US 261 (1997) (holding that the Eleventh Amendment barred a suit for declaratory and
injunctive relief against state officials based on a claim of ownership of certain submerged
lands); *Regents of the University of California v Doe*, 519 US 425 (1997) (holding that the
federal government's obligation to indemnify a state agency did not divest the agency of
Eleventh Amendment immunity). Not all the Court's recent Eleventh Amendment decisions have gone in favor of the states. See, e.g., *Wisconsin Dept. of Corrections v Schacht*, 524
US 381 (1998) (presence of claims barred by Eleventh Amendment did not divest federal
court, upon removal, of jurisdiction to hear remaining claims); *California v Deep Sea Research*,
523 US 491 (1998) (Eleventh Amendment did not bar federal jurisdiction over an *in rem*

1996, the Court rejected the then-prevailing view that Congress, when acting pursuant to its Article I powers, may abrogate the states' Eleventh Amendment immunity from suit in federal court.[5] Last Term, in *Alden v Maine*,[6] the Court took the next step by holding that Congress likewise could not abrogate state sovereign immunity in the states' *own* courts. And the two companion *College Savings Bank* decisions—handed down the same day as *Alden*—took a narrow view of the Congress's only remaining abrogation power under Section 5 of the Fourteenth Amendment.[7]

Concluding the last full Supreme Court Term of the century with the Eleventh Amendment has a certain aesthetic appeal; after all, the Court's other most notable forays into state sovereign immunity were likewise fin de siècle phenomena.[8] But one does not have to be a nationalist to think that the Rehnquist Court's state sovereign immunity jurisprudence marks an unfortunate turn for federalism doctrine. Even those of us who consider ourselves federalism "hawks"—who applauded *United States v Lopez*,[9] for example, for reinvigorating the idea of limited federal powers, and who look to the Court for some restoration of a federal-state balance thrown badly out of joint by the New Deal—need not think that all protections for states' rights are equally helpful. And sovereign immunity, to put it plainly, is a poor way to protect state prerogatives in a federal system.[10]

It may help to start with a framework for comparing different federalism doctrines. The federalism cases of the last half century can usefully be grouped into three rough models of federalism jurisprudence:

---

admiralty suit where the state did not possess the res in question); *Hess v Port Authority Trans-Hudson Corp.*, 513 US 30 (1994) (bi-state railway created by interstate compact was not entitled to Eleventh Amendment immunity). But these cases do illustrate the Court's apparent fascination with the Eleventh Amendment.

[5] *Seminole Tribe of Florida v Florida*, 517 US 44 (1996), overruling *Pennsylvania v Union Gas Co.*, 491 US 1 (1989).

[6] 119 S Ct 2240 (1999).

[7] *College Savings Bank v Florida Prepaid Postsecondary Education Expense (CSB I)*, 119 S Ct 2219 (1999); *Florida Prepaid Postsecondary Education Expense v College Savings Bank (CSB II)*, 119 S Ct 2199 (1999).

[8] See *Hans v Louisiana*, 134 US 1 (1890); *Chisolm v Georgia*, 2 US (2 Dall) 419 (1793).

[9] 514 US 549 (1995).

[10] For a similar view, see Charles Fried, *Supreme Court Folly*, New York Times A17 (July 6, 1999).

- "Process" federalism, which relies upon the states' representation in Congress as the primary means of protecting state sovereignty, and envisions judicial intervention only to ensure that this process is functioning properly;[11]
- "Power" federalism, which seeks to articulate substantive limits on federal power, particularly on Congress's power to supplant state regulatory authority by regulating private conduct directly;[12] and
- "Immunity" federalism, which protects state governments themselves from direct molestation at the hands of the federal government, but does little to protect the ability of the states to act as authoritative regulatory entities in their own right.[13]

These categorical distinctions are not perfectly clean. The anti-commandeering cases,[14] for example, partake of more than one model. But these categories do provide a useful tool for assessing the Court's federalism priorities.

The Rehnquist Court's federalism jurisprudence, I contend, displays a misplaced and potentially counterproductive propensity toward immunity federalism. As James Madison recognized in *The Federalist* 45 and 46, the states' ultimate security lies in the confidence of the people. That confidence expresses itself through the political process (hence the importance of process federalism) but ultimately turns upon the continuing relevance of state governmental institutions to the day-to-day lives of the citizenry. The greatest danger to federalism, therefore, is that the expanding regulatory concerns of the national government will leave the states with nothing to do.

With this core interest firmly in mind, we can evaluate federalism models in general and last Term's federalism decisions in particular. In terms of the sheer volume of state regulatory "turf" at stake, the biggest federalism case of last year was not *Alden*, not *College Savings Bank*, but *AT&T Corp. v Iowa Utilities Board*,[15] which

---

[11] See, e.g., *Garcia v San Antonio Metro. Transit Auth.*, 469 US 528 (1985); *Gregory v Ashcroft*, 501 US 452 (1991).

[12] See, e.g., *United States v Lopez*, 514 US 549 (1995).

[13] See, e.g., *Seminole Tribe of Florida v Florida*, 517 US 44 (1996).

[14] See *Printz v United States*, 521 US 898 (1997); *New York v United States*, 505 US 144 (1992).

[15] 119 S Ct 721 (1999).

interpreted the Telecommunications Act of 1996 to oust state regulatory authority over local telephone service—a core state regulatory function for the past 100 years. Although the case was a close one on the merits, it could easily have gone the other way based on familiar process federalism doctrines, such as the presumption against preemption of state law. That "might have been" illustrates the continuing—but neglected—potential of process theory to make meaningful contributions to federalism doctrine.

The cases that the Court did decide on federalism grounds—*College Savings Bank* and *Alden*—were both sovereign immunity cases. But *College Savings Bank* was primarily about the scope of Congress's legislative power under Section 5 of the Fourteenth Amendment (a legitimate exercise of that power being a prerequisite for valid abrogation of state sovereign immunity after *Seminole Tribe*). By rejecting Congress's attempt to support the Lanham and Patent Acts under Section 5, the Court ensured that the Fourteenth Amendment's protection of property rights could not be leveraged into a virtually unlimited tool for regulating commercial interests. *College Savings Bank* is thus best thought of as a "power federalism" decision that directly protects state regulatory prerogatives.

Alden, on the other hand, was a pure immunity case. And immunity federalism does little to ensure the states' continuing relevance. It is nice not to be subject, say, to private copyright suits, but it seems unlikely that many states have plans to set up a bootleg recording operation. And because the states remain subject to the commands of federal law, through its moral suasion, through suits against state officers for prospective relief, and the possible threat of a direct suit brought by the United States, the ultimate benefits of immunity seem limited at best.

Immunity may, on the other hand, be counterproductive in at least three ways: First, immunity decisions striking down federal attempts to subject the states to private suit may squander the Court's political capital, thereby undermining its ability to pursue a (more useful) process or power federalism model. Second, recognition of immunity from private suit may encourage Congress to subject the states to other, more intrusive means of ensuring compliance with federal law. Third, reducing state accountability to federal requirements may reduce Congress's inclination to devolve significant regulatory authority to state governments, much in the same way that elimination of the legislative veto threatened to undermine Congress's willingness to delegate authority to administrative agencies.

A final reason to worry about the Rehnquist Court's direction on federalism issues is the Court's inability to forge a consensus that can attract more than five votes. In many ways, we seem to be seeing "payback" for the *Garcia* decision in 1986, in which five liberal Justices dramatically cut back on judicial review of federalism issues over the vigorous dissent of four more conservative Justices who vowed not to accept that result as legitimate. Now the four Justices whom it seems fair to characterize as "nationalist"— Justices Stevens, Souter, Ginsburg, and Breyer—essentially refuse to accept the result in *Seminole Tribe*, promising another dramatic shift in the event of a fifth nationalist appointment to the Court. What is totally lacking is any effort, by either side, to construct a reasoned middle ground that could, by attracting support from both camps, hope to serve as a stable framework for federalism despite the inevitable future shifts in court personnel. This failure is particularly unfortunate because the uncertain outcome of the next presidential election provides a temporary "veil of ignorance" behind which each side ought to recognize incentives to compromise.

In this article, I offer a critique of the Court's state sovereign immunity decisions from a perspective that is highly sympathetic to states' rights and interests. It is important, however, to be clear at the outset as to several things that I am *not* attempting to do:

First, I am not mounting a general defense of federalism. Although the notion that federalism is worth reviving, preserving, or extending is certainly not uncontroversial,[16] one cannot manageably fight every battle in one article. For today, I wish to focus on a narrower question: Assuming that federalism is a good idea, is the Court's state sovereign immunity jurisprudence a sensible strategy for advancing federalist values?

---

[16] Compare, e.g., Edward L. Rubin and Malcolm Feeley, *Federalism: Some Notes on a National Neurosis*, 41 UCLA L Rev 903 (1994) (just like it sounds), with Vicki C. Jackson, *Federalism and the Uses and Limits of Law: Printz and Principle?* 111 Harv L Rev 2180, 2217–23 (1998) (refuting the Rubin and Feeley position).

Second, my focus is not primarily on the *merits* of the Court's sovereign immunity decisions. While those issues are fascinating, many of them have been rather thoroughly vetted elsewhere—not least in the comprehensive opinions of the Justices themselves.[17] The primary question here is one of strategy and of the relation of means to ends. Which broad model of federalism doctrine, in other words, makes the most sense as a vehicle for strengthening the states' role in the system?

Third, while I argue for a power-based model of federalism (complemented by process doctrines insofar as they also protect state regulatory power), I do not seek to advance a general theory for implementing and defining such a model here. I do suggest, in the last part, that a dual sovereignty theory might both support a reasonable set of federalism priorities and attract a centrist coalition of Justices. But the scope of the present project does not permit anything more than a tentative suggestion.

My exploration of these issues proceeds in six parts. Part I surveys the Court's sovereign immunity jurisprudence, focusing on the Court's recent decisions in *Alden* and *College Savings Bank*. Part II develops a framework for evaluating federalism doctrine by elaborating three distinct categories or approaches: process federalism, power federalism, and immunity federalism. Parts III, IV, and V focus on the Court's recent endeavors in each of these categories. In particular, I argue that process and power federalism are more promising than immunity federalism, and that for this reason *Alden* is likely to be unhelpful to the states, while *College Savings Bank* offers some promise. Finally, Part VI surveys the unfortunate cycle of the Court's federalism jurisprudence and the prospects for a lasting compromise.

---

[17] The essential literature on the general issue of abrogation includes Daniel J. Meltzer, *The Seminole Decision and State Sovereign Immunity*, 1996 Supreme Court Review 1; Lawrence Marshall, *Fighting the Words of the Eleventh Amendment*, 102 Harv L Rev 1342 (1989); Vicki Jackson, *The Supreme Court, the Eleventh Amendment, and State Sovereign Immunity*, 98 Yale L J 1 (1988); Akhil Reed Amar, *Of Sovereignty and Federalism*, 96 Yale L J 1425 (1987); William Fletcher, *A Historical Interpretation of the Eleventh Amendment: A Narrow Construction of an Affirmative Grant of Jurisdiction Rather Than a Prohibition Against Jurisdiction*, 35 Stan L Rev 1033 (1983); John J. Gibbons, *The Eleventh Amendment and State Sovereign Immunity: A Reinterpretation*, 83 Colum L Rev 1889 (1983). On sovereign immunity in state court, see Ellen D. Katz, *State Judges, State Officers, and Federal Commands After Seminole Tribe and Printz*, 1998 Wis L Rev 1465; Carlos M. Vazquez, *What Is Eleventh Amendment Immunity?* 106 Yale L J 1683 (1997). On the general history of state sovereign immunity, see John Orth, *The Judicial Power of the United States: The Eleventh Amendment in American History* (1987).

I. State Sovereign Immunity at Millennium's End

The Court's state sovereign immunity jurisprudence is frequently convoluted, contradictory, and obscure. It is, in other words, something only a law professor could love. Because my purpose here is to situate the Court's immunity jurisprudence in the broader context of federalism doctrine rather than to offer a doctrinal critique, I will attempt only a brief outline of how we arrived at our present troubles.

A. WHAT HAD GONE BEFORE

The Eleventh Amendment was ratified in 1795 as a response to the Court's decision in *Chisolm v Georgia*.[18] *Chisolm* held that Article III's provision for federal diversity jurisdiction over suits between a state and a citizen of another state had effectively abrogated the sovereign immunity from suit that the states had enjoyed at common law. Based on this reasoning, the Court exercised jurisdiction over a suit brought by a private individual against the State of Georgia to collect a debt. At this time many, if not all, the states were heavily indebted on loans arising from the Revolutionary War, and the *Chisolm* decision accordingly aroused widespread and ferocious opposition.[19] The resulting constitutional amendment firmly rejected *Chisolm*'s holding by providing that "[t]he Judicial power of the United States shall not be construed to extend to any suit in law or equity, commenced or prosecuted against one of the United States by Citizens of another State, or by Citizens or Subjects of any Foreign State."[20]

One might plausibly take either of two positions on what this text means. Most commentators—and apparently all the members of the current Court—have accepted the "diversity" view, that is, that the text of the Eleventh Amendment simply repeals the state-citizen diversity clause of Article III for all cases in which the state is a defendant.[21] Others have advanced a "plain meaning" theory,

---

[18] 2 US (2 Dall) 419 (1793).

[19] See Orth, *The Judicial Power of the United States* at 7 (cited in note 17); Fletcher, 35 Stan L Rev at 1058 (cited in note 17).

[20] US Const Amend XI.

[21] See, e.g., *Seminole Tribe of Florida v Florida*, 517 US 44, 54 (1996); *Pennsylvania v Union Gas Co.*, 491 US 1, 31 (1989) (Scalia concurring in part and dissenting in part); and Jackson, 98 Yale L J at 44–51; Fletcher, 35 Stan L Rev at 1035–37; Amar, 96 Yale L J at 1481–82 (all cited in note 17).

under which the Eleventh Amendment would bar federal jurisdiction wherever state-citizen diversity exists, regardless of whether some other ground—such as a federal question in the suit—might also support jurisdiction in the case.[22] Under the diversity theory, the Eleventh Amendment would never bar federal jurisdiction in federal question suits. Under the plain meaning theory, in-staters could bring federal question suits against states but out-of-staters could not.[23]

This debate over the proper reading of the Eleventh Amendment's text is interesting but largely academic. The real action in this area has concerned the Court's steady and relatively candid expansion of state sovereign immunity beyond the Amendment's textual scope. The most important step in this saga occurred in *Hans v Louisiana*,[24] in which the Court held a state immune from suit on a Contract Clause claim—a federal question claim, arising under the Federal Constitution—brought by an in-stater. *Hans* rested in part on the apparent anomaly of allowing out-of-staters to bring federal question suits against a state but not in-staters, and in part on a generalized principle of sovereign immunity based on scattered comments from the Framers and the immunity doctrines of English common law. As the Court later explained in *Principality of Monaco v Mississippi*,

> Manifestly, we cannot rest with a mere literal application of the words of § 2 of Article III, or assume that the letter of the Eleventh Amendment exhausts the restrictions upon suits against non-consenting States. Behind the words of the constitutional provisions are postulates which limit and control. There is the essential postulate that the controversies, as contemplated, shall be found to be of a justiciable character. There is also the postulate that States of the Union, still possessing attributes of sovereignty, shall be immune from suits, without their consent, save where there has been "a surrender of this immunity in the plan of the convention."[25]

---

[22] See Marshall, 102 Harv L Rev at 1346 (cited in note 17).

[23] See generally *Seminole Tribe of Florida v Florida*, 517 US 44, 109–16 (1996) (Souter dissenting) (discussing the two competing textual theories).

[24] *Hans v Louisiana*, 134 US 1 (1890).

[25] 292 US 313, 322–23 (1934) (quoting Federalist 81, at 487). *Monaco* implemented this understanding by holding that the states' immunity extends to suits by foreign sovereigns (not simply by their "citizens" or "subjects"), id at 330, and the Court followed up by extending the immunity beyond suits "in law or equity" to cover suits in admiralty in *Ex parte New York*, 256 US 490 (1921). See also *Blatchford v Native Village of Noatak*, 501 US 775 (1991) (extending the immunity to suits brought by Indian tribes).

Monaco's "postulates which limit and control" had assumed such a dominant role in Eleventh Amendment doctrine by 1996 that Chief Justice Rehnquist was able to dismiss an argument grounded in the text as a "straw man."[26]

The extension of state sovereign immunity to federal question cases threatened drastically to curtail the enforceability of federal rights against state governments. *Hans* and its progeny thus inspired three sets of cases designed to ease this threat.[27] The first group of cases, beginning with the Court's landmark decision in *Ex parte Young*, recognized that the state's sovereign immunity would not bar a suit against a state officer alleged to be acting in violation of federal law.[28] The doctrine that a suit against a state officer is not equivalent to a suit against the state itself has frequently been described as a "fiction," because court orders issued against officers frequently block state policy, and the state frequently defends such suits itself or reimburses damage awards entered against officers sued in their individual capacity.[29] Nonetheless, this "fiction" went hand in hand with the doctrine of sovereign immunity at common law, and it seems doubtful that the latter doctrine would have taken the broad form that it took absent the moderating influence of the officer remedy.[30] Subsequent cases have limited the officer remedy, however, by making

---

[26] *Seminole Tribe of Florida v Florida*, 517 US 44, 69 (1996). But see id at 116 n 13 (Souter dissenting) (replying that "plain text is the Man of Steel in a confrontation with 'background principle[s]' and 'postulates which limit and control'").

[27] Contemporaneously with *Hans*, the Court had recognized another important limit on the scope of state sovereign immunity by refusing to extend that immunity to local governments. See *Lincoln County v Luning*, 133 US 529 (1890).

[28] 209 US 123 (1908). The Court had recognized that the sovereign immunity of the United States would not bar a suit against a federal officer even earlier, in *United States v Lee*, 106 US 196 (1882).

[29] See *Idaho v Coeur d'Alene Tribe*, 521 US 261, 272 (1997) (plurality opinion); Laurence H. Tribe, 1 *American Constitutional Law* § 3–27, at 558 (Foundation Press, 3d ed 2000) (describing the distinction between suits against states and suits against officers as "unsatisfactory and conceptually unruly").

[30] See, e.g., *Coeur d'Alene*, 521 US at 308 (Souter dissenting); Tribe, 1 *American Constitutional Law* § 3–27, at 557–58 (cited in note 29) (describing the historical lineage and practical necessity of the *Young* doctrine); Richard H. Fallon, Daniel J. Meltzer, and David L. Shapiro, *Hart and Wechsler's The Federal Courts and the Federal System* 1015–16 (Foundation Press, 4th ed 1996) ("*Hart & Wechsler*") (suggesting that, in light of the historic availability of officer suits, the real "fiction" may be the proposition "that there ever existed a broad doctrine of sovereign immunity that, outside of a few specific areas, barred relief at the behest of individuals complaining of government illegality").

clear that only *prospective* relief may be had against state officials sued in their official capacity.[31]

The second set of cases—which actually predated *Hans*—held that a state may waive its sovereign immunity to suit notwithstanding the fact that the Eleventh Amendment itself is phrased as a limitation on federal subject matter jurisdiction.[32] The doctrine permitting express waiver has been relatively uncontroversial, although the Court has limited that doctrine by requiring that waivers be unmistakably clear[33] and by holding that a state may waive its immunity in its own courts without also waiving immunity to federal court suits.[34] The Court's "constructive waiver" cases have been more contested. Under the constructive waiver doctrine, a state that engages in an activity regulated by federal law waives its immunity to suits brought under the federal regulatory scheme.[35] The Court had already narrowed this doctrine considerably by the time it revisited the issue in *CSB I*.[36]

The final set of cases—and the ones which have preoccupied the Court in recent years—involve Congress's authority to abrogate the states' sovereign immunity and subject them to suit under federal law. The two landmarks are *Fitzpatrick v Bitzer*,[37] which held that Congress could subject the states to federal court suits when Congress acts pursuant to its power to enforce the Reconstruction Amendments, and *Pennsylvania v Union Gas Co.*,[38] which recognized a similar abrogation power when Congress acts under its general Commerce Clause authority. Abrogation is a counterintuitive proposition; indeed, the proposition that Congress *cannot* abrogate constitutional restrictions on its power is the very founda-

---

[31] See *Edelman v Jordan*, 415 US 651 (1974). Individual officers may be sued for damages in their personal capacity, but a plaintiff may not reach the state treasury through such a suit. See *Hart & Wechsler* at 1124 (cited in note 30).

[32] See, e.g., *Clark v Barnard*, 108 US 436, 447–48 (1883). Subject-matter limitations are not ordinarily subject to waiver by the parties to a suit. See *Mansfield, Coldwater & Lake Michigan Ry. v Swan*, 111 US 379 (1884).

[33] *Atascadero State Hosp. v Scanlon*, 473 US 234, 241 (1985); *Pennhurst State School and Hosp. v Halderman*, 465 US 89, 99 (1984).

[34] See *Smith v Reeves*, 178 US 436, 441–45 (1900).

[35] See *Parden v Terminal Railway*, 377 US 184 (1964).

[36] See *CSB I*, 119 S Ct 2219, 2226–27 (1999) (surveying the post-*Parden* case law).

[37] 427 US 445 (1976).

[38] 491 US 1 (1989).

tion of constitutional law. The Court's abrogation cases have explained this anomaly in two quite different ways.

The *Fitzpatrick* approach emphasized the unique nature of Congress's power under Section 5 of the Fourteenth Amendment. "When Congress acts pursuant to § 5," the Court said, "not only is it exercising legislative authority that is plenary within the terms of the constitutional grant, it is exercising that authority under one section of a constitutional Amendment whose other sections by their own terms embody limitations on state authority."[39] This somewhat ambiguous language might be taken to mean (*a*) that the ratification of the Fourteenth Amendment in 1868 amended the Eleventh Amendment simply because it was later in time, (*b*) that the broad intent of the Reconstruction Amendments was to create a general exception to federalism limitations on federal power, or (*c*) that Section 5's specific textual grant of power to "enforce" federal civil rights necessarily includes the power to impose a damages remedy. But regardless of which rationale one prefers, the important point is that *Fitzpatrick*'s approach is not generalizable to congressional action under other enumerated powers.

Union Gas took a broader approach. Although Justice Brennan's plurality opinion attempted to track *Fitzpatrick* by analogizing the commerce power to the Section 5 power,[40] that reasoning drew few adherents.[41] The more persuasive rationale was offered in Justice Stevens's concurrence, which began with the observation that we have "two Eleventh Amendments."[42] The first is the textual provision itself, while the second is the broader immunity recognized by the Court in *Hans v Louisiana*. Justice Stevens suggested that the latter sort of immunity must be a form of federal common law—a default rule which would bar suit in most cases but which

---

[39] *Fitzpatrick*, 427 US at 456.

[40] See 491 US at 19–20 (plurality opinion).

[41] Justice White, who provided the fifth vote in *Union Gas*, said that "I agree with the conclusion reached by Justice Brennan . . . , that Congress has the authority under Article I to abrogate the Eleventh Amendment immunity of the States, although I do not agree with much of his reasoning." Id at 57 (White concurring in the judgment in part and dissenting in part). Unfortunately, Justice White chose not to explain what rationale he found convincing. The dissenters in *Seminole Tribe* made no attempt to revive Justice Brennan's rationale or—given Justice White's eccentric performance—to rely on *Union Gas* as a matter of stare decisis.

[42] 491 US at 23 (1989) (Stevens concurring).

Congress could necessarily override by duly enacted legislation.[43] On this theory, abrogation would not involve the "override" of any constitutional restriction on Congress's power, but rather the uncontroversial proposition that judge-made federal common law rules are subject to modification at Congress's discretion.[44]

The Court's 1996 decision in *Seminole Tribe v Florida* rejected this reasoning and held that the immunity recognized in *Hans*, although broader than the text of the Eleventh Amendment itself, was nonetheless of constitutional stature. The Court thus overruled *Union Gas* and held that Congress may not abrogate state sovereign immunity when Congress acts pursuant to its general Article I powers. *Seminole Tribe* set the stage for last Term's decisions in *Alden* and *College Savings Bank* by appearing to leave open at least two methods of abrogating state sovereign immunity. First, Chief Justice Rehnquist's majority opinion in *Seminole Tribe* expressly reaffirmed the Court's earlier holding in *Fitzpatrick* (also authored by then-Justice Rehnquist) that Congress may abrogate state sovereign immunity when it acts pursuant to its enforcement power under Section 5 of the Fourteenth Amendment. *College Savings Bank* would deal with the contours of that remaining abrogation power. Second, *Seminole Tribe* did little to cast doubt on the assumption that Eleventh Amendment doctrine implicates only the *federal* courts—the Amendment's text, after all, discusses only the "Judicial power of the United States." As Carlos Vazquez noted at the time, however, there was language in *Seminole Tribe* indicating that the majority saw the Amendment as recognizing a broad-based immunity from suit, rather than constituting a mere forum-selection clause.[45] Professor Vasquez's prediction came true in *Alden*, where the same majority extended *Seminole Tribe*'s nonabrogation principle to suits in state court.[46]

---

[43] See id at 25 (describing immunity in federal question cases as resting "on a prudential interest in federal-state comity and a concern for 'Our Federalism'").

[44] See, e.g., *Milwaukee v Illinois*, 451 US 304, 313 (1981) ("We have always recognized that federal common law is subject to the paramount authority of Congress.").

[45] Vazquez, 106 Yale L J at 1702–03 (cited in note 17). See also Katz, 1998 Wis L Rev at 1468 (cited in note 17) (making a similar observation).

[46] A third route around *Seminole Tribe*—suits against state officers for injunctive relief under *Ex parte Young*—remains open. Although *Seminole Tribe* included ominous signs for *Ex parte Young*, see generally Vicki Jackson, *Seminole Tribe, The Eleventh Amendment, and the Potential Evisceration of Ex Parte Young*, 72 NYU L Rev 495 (1997), and a subset of the Court's conservative majority did try significantly to cut back on *Ex parte Young* in *Idaho v Coeur d'Alene Tribe*, 521 US 507 (1997), the officer remedy has come through the latest

B. COLLEGE SAVINGS BANK AND THE SECTION 5 POWER

The two *College Savings Bank* opinions both arose out of a dispute between College Savings Bank, a private bank that marketed specialized certificates of deposit designed to finance the cost of a college education, and the Florida Prepaid Postsecondary Education Expense Board, an arm of the State of Florida that administered a similar program. College Savings Bank sued Florida Prepaid under both the Patent Act[47] (the bank had patented its methodology for administering the CDs) and the Lanham Act[48] (for allegedly making misstatements about Florida's own tuition savings plans in its brochures and annual reports).

The Court dealt with these two claims separately in opinions by Justice Scalia and Chief Justice Rehnquist.[49] In the Lanham Act case, *College Savings Bank I*, Congress had specifically subjected the states to suit in federal court under the Trademark Remedy Clarification Act (TRCA).[50] As required by the Court's abrogation precedents, the TRCA included a clear statement providing that state defendants "shall not be immune, under the eleventh amendment . . . or any other doctrine of sovereign immunity, from suit in Federal Court."[51] Recognizing that *Seminole Tribe* had not questioned Congress's authority to abrogate state sovereign immunity when acting pursuant to Section 5 of the Fourteenth Amendment, Justice Scalia's majority opinion focused on the question whether the TRCA was a valid exercise of the Section 5 power.

Justice Scalia analyzed this question in light of the Court's decision two terms ago in *City of Boerne v Flores*.[52] That decision held that Congress's Section 5 power was limited to "remedial" legislation, meaning that "the object of valid § 5 legislation must be the

round of sovereign immunity decisions largely unscathed. See note 301. Congress may also seek in various ways to induce states to waive their sovereign immunity. See text accompanying notes 267–79.

[47] 35 USC § 271(a).

[48] 15 USC § 1125(a) (creating a private right of action against "[a]ny person" who uses false descriptions or makes false representations in commerce).

[49] The cases had been separated because, on appeal, the patent claims went to the Federal Circuit, see 28 USC § 1795(a)(1), while the 11th Circuit handled the Lanham Act claims.

[50] 106 Stat 3567.

[51] 15 USC § 1122. See, e.g., *Atascadero State Hosp. v Scanlon*, 473 US 234, 243 (1985) ("Congress must express its intention to abrogate the Eleventh Amendment in unmistakable language in the statute itself.").

[52] 521 US 507 (1997).

carefully delimited remediation or prevention of constitutional violations."[53] *City of Boerne* developed an essentially two-part test: First, the harm addressed by Congress must (in the Court's own view) be an actual constitutional violation.[54] Second, there must be "a congruence and proportionality between the injury to be prevented or remedied and the means adopted to that end."[55]

CSB I focused on the first part of the *City of Boerne* analysis. The bank sought to justify the TRCA as "enforcing" the protection of property rights in Fourteenth Amendment's Due Process Clause. The Court considered two property interests as candidates for such protection: "(1) a right to be free from a business competitor's false advertising about its own product, and (2) a more generalized right to be secure in one's business interests."[56] Neither of these asserted interests, Justice Scalia wrote, "qualifies as a property right protected by the Due Process Clause."[57] The Court rejected the first interest because a competitor's false advertising about its own product bore no relationship to the bank's right to exclude others from *its* property, a "hallmark of a protected property interest."[58] And while the bank's own business no doubt included traditional property interests—such' as the bank's assets—the Court found that the generalized interest in "the activity of doing business . . . is not property in the ordinary sense."[59] Because only this generalized interest was affected by a competitor's false advertising, the Court found no deprivation of property within the meaning of the Fourteenth Amendment.[60]

The Patent Act claims at issue in *CSB II*, on the other hand, clearly involved constitutionally protected property rights. As it had under the Lanham Act, Congress had passed specific legis-

---

[53] *College Savings Bank v Florida Prepaid Postsecondary Education Expense (CSB I)*, 119 S Ct 2219, 2224 (1999).

[54] *City of Boerne*, 521 US at 519.

[55] Id at 520.

[56] *CSB I*, 119 S Ct at 2224.

[57] Id.

[58] Id.

[59] Id at 2225.

[60] Id. The Court was careful to note, however, that the Lanham Act "may well contain [other] provisions that protect constitutionally cognizable property interests—notably, its provisions dealing with the infringement of trademarks, which are the 'property' of the owner because he can exclude others from using them." Id at 2224.

lation to abrogate state sovereign immunity for Patent Act suits. The bank likewise sought to defend this abrogation legislation, the Patent and Plant Variety Protection Remedy Clarification Act (PRCA),[61] as a valid exercise of Congress's Section 5 power. While acknowledging that "patents may be considered 'property' for purposes of our analysis," however, the Court again found that Congress had exceeded its remedial powers under Section 5.[62]

Chief Justice Rehnquist's conclusion for the majority rested on two major premises. First, Congress's "remedial" authority depends upon the existence of "a pattern of constitutional violations" by the states.[63] Second, patent infringement by a state government violates the Constitution "only where the State provides no remedy, or only inadequate remedies, to injured patent owners for its infringement of their patent."[64] Because the legislative record contained little evidence of either widespread patent violations by states or failures to provide adequate state law remedies for such violations, the Court concluded that "the Patent Remedy Act does not respond to a history of 'widespread and persisting deprivation of constitutional rights' of the sort Congress has faced in enacting proper prophylactic § 5 legislation."[65]

In addition to the abrogation arguments in both cases, the Court considered in *CSB I*—and rejected—an argument for constructive waiver of the state's Eleventh Amendment immunity. In *Parden v Terminal Railroad Co.*,[66] the Court had permitted employees of a

---

[61] 35 USC §§ 271(h), 296(a).

[62] *Florida Prepaid Postsecondary Education Expense v College Savings Bank (CSB II)*, 119 S Ct 2199, 2208 (1999).

[63] Id at 2207.

[64] Id at 2208 (citing *Parratt v Taylor*, 451 US 527, 529–31 (1981), and *Hudson v Palmer*, 468 US 517, 532–33 (1984)). The relationship of these two points demonstrates the extent to which the two parts of the *City of Boerne* analysis can run together. The absence of a pattern of constitutional violations seems to go to the second prong, by suggesting that the broad federal remedy was disproportionate to the underlying problem. But the second point—the absence of any showing that the states were failing to provide remedies—suggests that there may have been no constitutional violation in the first place. In light of this second point, *CSB II*'s "pattern" analysis might be read as dictum.

[65] Id at 2210 (quoting *City of Boerne v Flores*, 521 US 507, 526 (1997)). The Court concluded that, rather than responding to a widespread failure to provide adequate state remedies, the Patent Remedy Act was designed to preserve the uniformity of federal patent law by providing a single *federal* remedy. Id. The Court acknowledged that uniformity concerns would be a valid basis for legislation under Congress's Article I powers, but found that Section 5 required a higher level of justification. Id at 2210–11.

[66] 377 US 184 (1964).

state-owned railroad to sue the state in federal court under the
Federal Employees Liability Act. The Court reasoned that

> By enacting the [FELA] . . . Congress conditioned the right
> to operate a railroad in interstate commerce upon amenability
> to suit in federal court as provided by the Act; by thereafter
> operating a railroad in interstate commerce, Alabama must be
> taken to have accepted that condition and thus to have con-
> sented to suit.[67]

Similarly, the bank argued in *CSB I* that by engaging in the business of providing college savings accounts, Florida had construc-
tively waived its immunity for Lanham Act suits arising out of that
business.

By the time the Court sat to decide *CSB I*, the *Parden* doctrine
invoked by the bank was hanging by a thread. As Justice Scalia
observed, the Court had "never applied the holding of *Parden* to
another statute, and in fact [had] narrowed the case in every subsequent opinion in which it [had] been under consideration."[68] The
idea of constructive waiver, the Court pointed out, is in fundamental tension with cases holding that express waivers of sovereign
immunity must be unequivocal;[69] moreover, "constructive consent
is not a doctrine commonly associated with the surrender of constitutional rights."[70] In any event, *Parden*'s holding rested on "the
notion that state sovereign immunity is not constitutionally
grounded"—a notion repudiated in *Seminole Tribe*.[71] The Court
thus determined to "drop the other shoe" by expressly overruling
"[w]hatever may remain of our decision in *Parden*."[72]

Three primary principles emerge from the two *College Savings
Bank* opinions:

First, Congress's Section 5 power cannot be broadly invoked as
a substitute for the Article I powers—which will no longer support
abrogation of sovereign immunity after *Seminole Tribe*—by purporting to protect constitutionally protected "property" interests
wherever federal law provides for a pecuniary recovery.

---

[67] Id at 192.

[68] *CSB I*, 119 S Ct at 2228.

[69] Id (citing *Great Northern Life Ins. Co. v Read*, 322 US 47 (1944)).

[70] Id at 2229 (quoting *Edelman v Jordan*, 415 US 651, 673 (1974)).

[71] Id.

[72] Id at 2228.

Second, Section 5 "remedies" cannot be imposed in the absence of a widespread constitutional "problem" created by extant state constitutional violations. Where the constitutional violation is one of due process, moreover, the state must have failed to provide adequate remedies.[73]

Third, states can no longer be subjected to federal court suit based on *Parden*'s "constructive waiver" theory.

The first two of these principles amount to significant Eleventh Amendment holdings in that they narrow the only source of federal abrogation authority left standing after *Seminole Tribe*. But that significance is derivative of their primary import, which is their *substantive* limitations on the scope of Congress's Section 5 power. And the Court's unwillingness to read that power broadly had been foreshadowed in *City of Boerne v Flores* two terms back.[74]

The overruling of *Parden*, however, is arguably a significant Eleventh Amendment holding—but only arguably, as *Parden*'s constructive waiver approach had been doubted in theory and unused in practice for a number of years.[75] The recent proliferation of statutes like the TRCA and the Patent Remedy Act demonstrates that direct abrogation—not constructive waiver—had already become Congress's tool of choice in avoiding the Eleventh Amendment bar. *CSB I* and *CSB II* will make that tool incrementally more difficult to use; *Alden*, on the other hand, extended the abrogation debate to entirely new territory.

C. ALDEN AND THE STATES' IMMUNITY IN THEIR OWN COURTS

The underlying suit in *Alden* involved claims by state employees alleging violations of the Fair Labor Standards Act (FLSA), which was made applicable to state governments by amendments in 1974.[76] The employees, who sought compensation and liquidated

---

[73] As noted above, however, the "pattern of violations" aspect of this principle may not have been necessary to the decision in *CSB II*. See note 64.

[74] See *City of Boerne v Flores*, 521 US 507 (1997) (striking down the Religious Freedom Restoration Act).

[75] See *CSB I*, 119 S Ct at 226–28.

[76] 88 Stat 55, codified at 29 USC § 203. These amendments have been central to the history of federalism doctrine in the last quarter century: They were initially struck down in *National League of Cities v Usery*, in which case the Court recognized limits on Congress's ability to regulate state governments "in areas of traditional governmental functions." 426 US 833, 852 (1976). Then, in *Garcia v San Antonio Metropolitan Transit Authority*, the Court reversed *National League of Cities* and held that federalism-based limits on national power would henceforth be enforced primarily through the political process. 469 US 528, 556

damages under the Act, brought their suit initially in federal court, but that suit was dismissed in the wake of *Seminole Tribe*.[77] The employees then turned to state court, only to have their suit dismissed once again on the basis of sovereign immunity.[78] The Supreme Judicial Court of Maine affirmed the dismissal, holding that the provision of the FLSA purporting to subject the states to suit in their own courts was unconstitutional.[79]

In his opinion for the majority affirming this holding, Justice Kennedy squarely confronted the Eleventh Amendment's inconvenient text:

> [T]he fact that the Eleventh Amendment by its terms limits only "[t]he Judicial power of the United States" does not resolve the question. To rest on the words of the Amendment alone would be to engage in the type of ahistorical literalism we have rejected in interpreting the scope of the States' sovereign immunity since the discredited decision in *Chisolm* [*v Georgia*].[80]

The majority thus made clear that "sovereign immunity derives not from the Eleventh Amendment but from the structure of the original Constitution itself."[81] According to the Court, "it follows that the scope of the States' immunity from suit is demarcated not by the text of the Amendment alone but by fundamental postulates implicit in the constitutional design."[82]

Having dismissed the Eleventh Amendment itself, the majority relied heavily on historical evidence suggesting the acceptance of sovereign immunity as part of the legal background against which the Constitution was adopted.[83] Equally important support came from "the essential principles of federalism and . . . the special role of the state courts in the constitutional design."[84] Justice Ken-

---

(1985). I discuss the *Garcia* model of "process federalism" in the text accompanying notes 99–121.

[77] See *Mills v Maine*, 118 F3d 37 (1st Cir 1997) (affirming the district court's dismissal of the suit).

[78] See *Alden v Maine*, 715 A2d 172 (Me 1998). See also Katz, 1998 Wis L Rev at 1530 n 318 (cited in note 17) (collecting similar cases barring FLSA suits against the states in federal court).

[79] See 29 USC § 216(b) (Supp 1998) (subjecting the states to suit); *Alden*, 715 A2d at 173–74 (holding § 216(b) unconstitutional).

[80] *Alden v Maine*, 119 S Ct 2240, 2254 (1999).

[81] Id.

[82] Id.

[83] *Alden*, 119 S Ct at 2250–53.

[84] Id at 2263.

nedy began with "the indignity of subjecting a State to the coercive process of judicial tribunals at the instance of private parties."[85] While this indignity is bad enough when the suit is in a federal court, it is even worse in the state's own courts: To "press a State's own courts into federal service," Justice Kennedy argued, is "to turn the State against itself and ultimately to commandeer the entire political machinery of the State against its will and at the behest of individuals."[86] And practically speaking, such commandeering would permit judicial tribunals and private litigants to disrupt the basic resource allocation decisions of state governments.[87] Finally, the Court rejected the suggestion that Congress might have broader control over state sovereign immunity in the state's own courts than Congress has in the federal courts.[88]

The Court was at pains to note that recognition of state sovereign immunity would not "confer upon the State a concomitant right to disregard the Constitution or valid federal law."[89] Congress retains the power to abrogate state immunity when it acts pursuant to the Section 5 power, as well as means (such as conditional grants of federal funding[90]) to induce state consent to suit in other sorts of cases.[91] States remain subject to suits by the federal government or by other states, and both their individual officers and their political subdivisions may be sued by individuals.[92] In light of these principles, the Court concluded, "a federal power to subject nonconsenting States to private suits in their own courts is unnecessary to uphold the Constitution and valid federal statutes as the supreme law."[93]

The Court's efforts to downplay the significance of its holding

---

[85] Id at 2264. See also id ("Not only must a State defend or default but also it must face the prospect of being thrust, by federal fiat and against its will, into the disfavored status of a debtor, subject to the power of private citizens to levy on its treasury or perhaps even government buildings or property which the State administers on the public's behalf.").

[86] Id.

[87] Id. In so doing, the Court said, abrogation of state immunity would blur lines of political accountability for those allocation decisions. Id at 2265.

[88] Id (rejecting any suggestion that "Congress may in some cases act only through instrumentalities of the States").

[89] Id at 2266.

[90] See *South Dakota v Dole*, 483 US 203 (1987).

[91] *Alden*, 119 S Ct at 2267.

[92] Id.

[93] Id at 2268.

notwithstanding, *Alden* is an important extension of the immunity doctrines announced in *Seminole Tribe*. On one view of the matter, *Alden* is simply the logical implication of *Seminole Tribe*'s constitutionalization of the nontextual state sovereign immunity recognized in earlier cases. But it would also have been easy for the Court to draw a line between *Seminole Tribe* and *Alden*. The Eleventh Amendment has frequently been viewed as a forum selection provision—requiring states to be sued on their "home turf" rather than in federal court—rather than as a broad grant of substantive immunity in any forum.[94] And virtually all of the historical evidence cited by the Court in both *Seminole Tribe* and *Alden* concerned debates over the interaction of state sovereign immunity and the federal judicial power.[95]

Even if the Eleventh Amendment had been intended to signify a broader constitutional immunity than its text suggested, then, there is no reason to assume that this constitutional immunity limited anything other than the judicial power of the United States. State sovereign immunity in state courts would thus remain a creature of state common law, untouched by the Constitution, and therefore freely preemptible by Congress. And practical considerations would have supported a view that state court suits are simply less intrusive on state interests than suits in federal court. It is one thing, after all, to be hauled into the potentially unfriendly courts of another sovereign; quite another to be required to defend in the friendly confines of a state's own courts.

Alden's expansion of the states' constitutional immunity to state court suits is thus an important new addition to the Court's federalism jurisprudence. Whether this development is in the long-term interests of the states is a difficult question that forms the primary subject of this article. Before turning to that question, I seek to develop an analytical framework for distinguishing and evaluating various approaches to federalism doctrine.

---

[94] See, e.g., *Hart & Wechsler* at 1076 (cited in note 30) (suggesting that the Amendment may be viewed "as being, in effect, a forum choice provision, which merely permits the states to resist *federal court* jurisdiction over suits . . . seeking retrospective relief—while leaving the state courts obliged, under the Supremacy Clause, to provide such relief in suits under federal law").

[95] See Katz, 1998 Wis L Rev at 1479 (cited in note 17) (concluding that "even assuming counterfactually that the Framers of the Eleventh Amendment intend to enact the amalgam of rules the Court has held the Amendment to mandate, the historical record does not resolve whether they also meant to provide, or otherwise understood the states to enjoy, a constitutional immunity from claims arising under federal law brought in state court").

II. Three Models of Federalism

The doctrine of state sovereign immunity applied in *College Savings Board* and *Alden* derives not from constitutional text, but rather as an inference from constitutional structure. Not that there's anything wrong with that: As Charles Fried has observed, "[s]tructural arguments certainly have their place." But Professor Fried immediately goes on to recognize that such arguments "are slippery and easily overextended. One discipline on them is to ask that they make sense."[96] My primary task in this article is to ask whether the Court's structural arguments in *College Savings Bank* and *Alden* "make sense" as a strategy for protecting federalism, especially when viewed in the broader context of federalism doctrine as a whole.[97] In approaching this question, it may help more clearly to define three alternative models, or strategies, for protecting federalism that the Court has pursued over the last quarter century. All three have their merits, but they are not created equal. And to the extent that the Court's decision to pursue one strategy may trade off with its ability to pursue others, as I suggest below,[98] it is important to choose the right priorities.

A. PROCESS FEDERALISM

In *Garcia v San Antonio Metropolitan Transit Authority*,[99] the Court rejected a prior rule providing for substantive judicial protection of state autonomy in areas of "traditional government functions."[100] "[T]he fundamental limitation that the constitutional scheme imposes on the Commerce Clause," the Court said, "is one of process rather than one of result."[101] According to the Court, the states' direct representation in Congress and their critical role in electing the national executive is sufficient "to insulate the interests of the States."[102] The Court thus endorsed Herbert

---

[96] Fried, New York Times at A17 (cited in note 10).

[97] I consider *Alden*'s somewhat unusual approach to structural argument as a theory of constitutional interpretation in Ernest A. Young, *Alden v Maine and the Jurisprudence of Structure*, 41 Wm & Mary L Rev (forthcoming May 2000).

[98] See text accompanying notes 261–66.

[99] 469 US 528 (1985).

[100] *National League of Cities v Usery*, 426 US 833, 852 (1976).

[101] *Garcia*, 469 US at 554.

[102] Id at 550–51.

Wechsler's influential assertion that "the Court is on weakest ground when it opposes its interpretation of the Constitution to that of Congress in the interest of the states, whose representatives control the legislative process and, by hypothesis, have broadly acquiesced in sanctioning the challenged Act of Congress."[103] Wechsler's thesis in turn echoed James Madison's argument, in *The Federalist* 45, that "each of the principal branches of the federal government will owe its existence more or less to the favor of the State governments, and must consequently feel a dependence, which is much more likely to beget a disposition too obsequious than too overbearing towards them."[104]

The *Garcia*/Wechsler thesis has been challenged, most tellingly by those who point out that the Seventeenth Amendment's provision for direct election of senators drastically altered Madison's assumption that state governments would be directly represented in the federal political process.[105] Other commentators have come forward to suggest that other "political safeguards" have developed in the later twentieth century to take the place of those that have been superseded,[106] while still others have argued that a focus on the bipolar balance between federal and state governments ignores the extent to which coalitions of states may use the federal government to impose their preferences on less powerful states.[107] But

---

[103] Herbert Wechsler, *The Political Safeguards of Federalism: The Role of the States in the Composition and Selection of the National Government*, 54 Colum L Rev 543, 559 (1954). See also Jesse H. Choper, *Judicial Review and the National Political Process: A Functional Reconsideration of the Role of the Supreme Court* 171–259 (Chicago, 1980); Bruce La Pierre, *The Political Safeguards of Federalism Redux: Intergovernmental Immunity and the States as Agents of the Nation*, 60 Wash U L Q 779 (1982).

[104] Federalist 45 (Madison) in Clinton Rossiter, ed, *The Federalist Papers* 291 (Mentor, 1961). But see text accompanying notes 199–210 (explaining that Madison's argument ultimately rested on the authority of the states to regulate those subjects most immediate to the people's everyday lives).

[105] See, e.g., *Garcia*, 469 US at 565–66 n 9 (Powell dissenting); William W. Van Alstyne, *The Second Death of Federalism*, 83 Mich L Rev 1709, 1722–27 (1985); Andrzej Rapaczynski, *From Sovereignty to Process: The Jurisprudence of Federalism after Garcia*, 1985 Supreme Court Review 341, 392–93; Lewis Kaden, *Politics, Money, and State Sovereignty: The Judicial Role*, 79 Colum L Rev 847, 849 (1979). See also Larry Kramer, *Understanding Federalism*, 47 Vand L Rev 1485, 1503–14 (1994) (criticizing the political safeguards thesis as originally formulated).

[106] See, e.g., Kramer, 47 Vand L Rev at 1522–46 (cited in note 105) (discussing the roles of political parties and administrative agencies in protecting state prerogatives); Jenna Bednar and William N. Eskridge, Jr., *Steadying the Court's "Unsteady Path": A Theory of Judicial Enforcement of Federalism*, 68 S Cal L Rev 1447, 1485 (1995) (making similar arguments).

[107] See Lynn A. Baker, *Conditional Federal Spending after Lopez*, 95 Colum L Rev 1911, 1940 (1995) ("The problem . . . lies in the ability of *some states* to harness the federal

leaving this debate aside, both proponents and opponents of the *Garcia*/Wechsler thesis may have underestimated the potential of process federalism to move the law at least some distance away from the regime of no protection for state prerogatives that prevailed immediately after the New Deal.[108]

The Court might choose to enforce process federalism in a number of different ways, with varying degrees of doctrinal "bite." One method of choice has been the use of presumptions in interpreting federal statutes. The Court has long employed a presumption against preemption in construing the impact of federal legislation on state regulatory authority.[109] And the Court has employed stronger presumptions—"clear statement rules"—where federal statutes arguably regulate core state governmental functions,[110] impose conditions on federal funding,[111] or subject the states to suit in federal court pursuant to Congress's remaining Section 5 abrogation power.[112] The purpose of such rules is to make sure that the "political safeguards of federalism" are fully operational; as the Court explained in *Gregory v Ashcroft*,

---

lawmaking power to oppress *other states*. Not only can the state-based allocation of congressional representation not protect states against this use of the federal lawmaking power, it facilitates it."). Other critics have pointed out that the Court has not generally been willing to abandon substantive judicial review of separation of powers issues, despite the fact that political checks are at least as strong in that context as in the federalism area. See, e.g., *Garcia*, 469 US at 567 n 12 (Powell dissenting); Deborah Jones Merritt, *The Guarantee Clause and State Autonomy: Federalism for a Third Century*, 88 Colum L Rev 1, 18–19 & n 108 (1988).

[108] See, e.g., *Wickard v Filburn*, 317 US 111 (1942) (construing federal power *very* broadly); *United States v Darby*, 312 US 100 (1941) (same). Some commentators did immediately recognize process federalism's potential. See Rapaczynski, 1985 Supreme Court Review at 364–66 (cited in note 105).

[109] See, e.g., *Cipollone v Liggett Group, Inc.*, 505 US 504, 516 (1992); *Rice v Santa Fe Elevator Corp.*, 331 US 218, 230 (1947) ("[W]e start with the assumption that the historic police powers of the States were not to be superseded by the Federal Act unless that was the clear and manifest purpose of Congress."). An even more venerable form may be the familiar canon holding that statutes in derogation of the common law are disfavored. As David Shapiro has demonstrated, this canon frequently operates to protect state autonomy because so much of the common law background is state law. See David L. Shapiro, *Continuity and Change in Statutory Interpretation*, 67 NYU L Rev 921, 937 (1992).

[110] *Gregory v Ashcroft*, 501 US 452, 460–64 (1991).

[111] *Pennhurst State School & Hosp. v Halderman*, 451 US 1, 17 (1981).

[112] *Atascadero State Hosp. v Scanlon*, 473 US 234, 243 (1985). See also *Will v Michigan Dept. of State Police*, 491 US 58, 65 (1989) (applying clear statement rule to decide whether Congress subjected state officials in their official capacities to liability under 42 USC § 1983). For a general discussion of the Court's clear statement jurisprudence, see William N. Eskridge, Jr. and Philip P. Frickey, *Quasi-Constitutional Law: Clear Statement Rules as Constitutional Lawmaking*, 45 Vand L Rev 593 (1992). See also Rapaczynski, 1985 Supreme Court Review at 418 (cited in note 105) (anticipating this implication of process federalism).

[I]nasmuch as this Court in *Garcia* has left primarily to the
political process the protection of the States against intrusive
exercises of Congress' Commerce Clause powers, we must
be absolutely certain that Congress intended such an exercise. "[T]o give the state-displacing weight of federal law to
mere congressional *ambiguity* would evade the very procedure
for lawmaking on which *Garcia* relied to protect states'
interests."[113]

By demanding that the intent to impinge on state interests be clear
and obvious, in other words, the Court ensures that the states'
representatives in Congress have focused on the federalism issue
in the course of enacting the legislation in question.

A potentially more aggressive way of enforcing this political
check is to demand that federal legislation adversely affecting state
authority be supported by express congressional findings on the
federalism issue.[114] In *United States v Lopez*, for instance, one of
the factors cited by the Court in striking down the federal Gun
Free School Zones Act was the absence of any legislative findings
concerning the impact of guns in schools on interstate commerce.[115] While the extent to which the lack of congressional findings was dispositive in *Lopez* is unclear,[116] some academics have
endorsed this aspect of the Court's approach as a potential means
of avoiding the need to draw lines limiting the substantive extent of
Congress's authority.[117] Depending on whether or not boilerplate

[113] *Gregory*, 501 US at 464 (quoting Laurence H. Tribe, *American Constitutional Law* §
6–25, at 480 (Foundation Press, 2d ed 1988) ("*Second Edition*")).

[114] See generally Philip P. Frickey, *The Fool on the Hill: Congressional Findings, Constitutional
Adjudication, and United States v Lopez*, 46 Case W Res L Rev 695 (1996); Barry Friedman,
Legislative Findings and Judicial Signals: A Positive Political Reading of United States v Lopez,
46 Case W Res L Rev 757 (1996).

[115] 514 US 549, 561–63 (1995). See also Jackson, 111 Harv L Rev at 2239 & nn 254–
55 (cited in note 16) (discussing the state of the legislative record supporting the Act).

[116] Both the majority and the dissents denied that it was. See 514 US at 562 (majority
opinion); id at 613 (Souter dissenting); id at 617–18 (Breyer dissenting). The Fourth Circuit's decision striking down the federal Violence Against Women Act (VAWA), 42 USC
§ 13981, in *Brzonkala v Virginia Polytechnic Institute*, 169 F3d 820 (4th Cir 1999) (en banc),
cert granted, 1999 US LEXIS 4745, offers the Court an opportunity to clarify the relative
importance of legislative findings. While the VAWA suffers from several of the same weak-
nesses as the Gun Free School Zones Act—that is, it does not regulate commercial activity,
and the chain of causation linking it to interstate commerce is very long—the VAWA is
supported by extensive testimonial evidence and legislative findings concerning the impact
of violence against women upon the national economy. See id at 913–14 (Motz dissenting)
(cataloging these findings).

[117] See, e.g., Stephen Gardbaum, *Rethinking Constitutional Federalism*, 74 Tex L Rev 795,
823–26 (1996); Jackson, 111 Harv L Rev at 2237 (cited in note 16) (arguing that the Court
should consider "both the record before Congress and any formal legislative findings in

findings are held sufficient to sustain federal legislation,[118] this approach has the potential to be even more protective of state authority than the Court's clear statement rules.

A final, and frequently overlooked, form of process federalism is the framework of rules governing which actors in the national government are empowered to make federal law. By abandoning the idea of a general federal common law, for instance, *Erie Railroad v Tompkins* helped to ensure that lawmaking decisions that preempt state law (formally or in effect) would be made by Congress, in which the states are represented, and not by federal judges.[119] And by requiring that federal law be made through the cumbersome process provided by Article I, doctrines like *Erie* ensure that this gauntlet performs its intended function of cutting back on the volume of potentially preemptive federal law.[120] Conversely, the abandonment of the nondelegation doctrine and consequent dramatic expansion of federal lawmaking by executive agencies (who need not run the Article I gauntlet and are not directly representative of the states) represent a substantial erosion of process federalism values.[121]

---

order to determine whether the case had been made that the measure was 'necessary and proper' to carrying out enumerated powers").

[118] See, e.g., 104 PL 208, 110 Stat 3009, § 651 (1996) (amending the Gun Free School Zones Act to include congressional findings of an impact on interstate commerce). See also Matthew D. Adler and Seth F. Kreimer, *The New Etiquette of Federalism: New York, Printz, and Yeskey*, 1998 Supreme Court Review 71, 136 (arguing that the efficacy of a formal finding requirement may be short-lived if congressional staff learn to include boilerplate findings as a matter of course).

[119] See *Erie Railroad v Tompkins*, 304 US 64, 78 (1938) ("Except in matters governed by the Federal Constitution or by Acts of Congress, the law to be applied in any case is the law of the State. . . . There is no federal general common law."). Pre-*Erie* federal determinations of "general" common law did not, of course, preempt state law outside federal diversity suits, but the forum-shopping option provided by the pre-*Erie* regime did give many parties an ability to evade state law by filing in federal court.

[120] See Bradford R. Clark, *Ascertaining the Laws of the Several States: Positivism and Judicial Federalism after Erie*, 145 U Pa L Rev 1459, 1478–93 (1997). *Murdock v Memphis*, 87 US (20 Wall) 590, 633 (1874), plays a similar role by providing that, although Congress may preempt state law when it follows the difficult Article I procedure, Congress "may not have the power to authorize the Supreme Court to supplant state courts as the authoritative declarer of law within their jurisdictions by functioning as a court of last resort with respect to questions of state common law and state statutory law." Tribe, *Second Edition*. § 5–20, at 380 (cited in note 113).

[121] See, e.g., Merritt, 88 Colum L Rev at 10 (cited in note 107) (linking the Court's abandonment of nondelegation to a general expansion of federal regulatory authority at the expense of the States); Damien J. Marshall, Note, *The Application of Chevron Deference in Regulatory Preemption Cases*, 87 Geo L J 263 (1998) (highlighting the tension between federalism values and judicial deference to federal administrative agencies).

B. POWER FEDERALISM

Despite the potential of process federalism to offer significant protection for state authority, its requirements for expanding federal authority can always be surmounted by a sufficiently determined Congress. And no matter how many procedural hoops a fox must jump through to gain entry to the henhouse, it is still a fox.[122] In a political environment in which a state's federal representatives may often compete with state government officials for opportunities to gain the attention of their shared constituents, it is questionable how often members of Congress will place a high priority on protecting the prerogatives of state government.[123] For these reasons, among others, the Court has recently turned from the exclusive reliance on process federalism suggested by *Garcia*, to an attempt to delineate substantive limits on Congress's authority.

These lines, however, are notoriously hard to draw, and the Court has been burned before in attempting to draw them.[124] At least three distinct approaches show up in the recent cases and academic literature. The first is to identify certain enclaves of exclusive state authority that are immune from federal regulation.

---

[122] See, e.g., Bednar and Eskridge, 68 S Cal L Rev at 1473–74 (cited in note 106) (describing Congress's incentives to "cheat" on the federal arrangement by aggrandizing its own power at the expense of the states); Rapaczynski, 1985 Supreme Court Review at 388 (cited in note 105) (arguing that the federal government is likely to be influenced by well-established interest groups which have incentives to suppress the more diverse interests likely to be prevalent in the states). See also Michael B. Rappaport, *Reconciling Textualism and Federalism: The Proper Textual Basis of the Supreme Court's Tenth and Eleventh Amendment Decisions*, 93 Nw U L Rev 819, 866 (1999) ("[E]ven if the States were expert lobbyists, one may seriously question whether effective lobbying is really sovereignty.").

[123] See, e.g., Jackson, 111 Harv L Rev at 2226 n 206 (cited in note 16) (noting that "senators, like their colleagues in the House, are said to represent, not the interests of states as governments, but the interests of people in the states"); Merritt, 88 Colum L Rev at 15–16 (cited in note 107) (same); Kramer, 47 Vand L Rev at 1510–11 (cited in note 105) ("Federal politicians will want to earn the support and affection of local constituents by providing desired services themselves—through the federal government—rather than to give or share credit with state officials. State officials are rivals, not allies, a fact the Framers understood and the reason they made Senators directly beholden to state legislators in the first place.").

[124] See, e.g., *United States v Lopez*, 514 US 549, 604 (1995) (Souter dissenting) ("The modern respect for the competence and primacy of Congress in matters affecting commerce developed only after one of this Court's most chastening experiences, when it perforce repudiated an earlier and untenably expansive conception of judicial review in derogation of congressional commerce power."). See also Rapaczynski, 1985 Supreme Court Review at 351 (cited in note 105) (asserting that "even a moderately searching scrutiny of the powers of the federal government shows that the alleged existence of a residual category of exclusive state powers over any private, nongovernmental activity is in fact illusory").

Both the majority and dissenting justices in *Lopez*, for example, seemed to agree that the federal government generally has no power to regulate family law.[125] But such enclaves are exceptionally difficult to sustain because they frequently overlap with areas in which federal authority is unquestioned. Few would doubt, for instance, federal authority to provide remedies for delinquent child support payments where the offending parent lives in another state.[126] And it is woefully easy to reconstruct Justice Breyer's factually indisputable argument in *Lopez* that guns in schools have an impact on the national economy as an argument that family law has a similar effect: Surely family conditions have a greater impact on a child's education than the occasional presence of a gun, and the causal chain from education to jobs to productivity to the GNP flows smoothly from there.[127]

The recent execution of Angel Breard in Virginia provides another example.[128] If enclaves of exclusive state authority exist, then surely prescription of punishments for violations of state criminal law is one of them. Just as surely, the federal government has primary authority over foreign relations. So who should have the final say when a state's execution of a foreign national for a state law crime threatens to throw a wrench into American foreign policy? While the proper resolution of such cases is far from obvious, the one clear point is that both federal and state interests ought to count for something.[129] Our world, then, is one of largely *concurrent* power—one in which virtually any subject, depending on the circumstances, may (or may not) fall within the realm of legitimate federal authority.

The remaining two sorts of "power" federalism take account of this reality. One would simply increase the rigor with which the

---

[125] See *Lopez*, 514 US at 564 (majority opinion); id at 624 (Breyer dissenting).

[126] See Child Support Recovery Act of 1992, 18 USC § 228. Similarly, some have argued that the federal government may extensively regulate family law pursuant to the Treaty Power by ratifying and implementing the International Convention on the Rights of the Child. See, e.g., Susan Kilbourne, *The Convention on the Rights of the Child*, 5 Geo J Fighting Poverty 327 (1998).

[127] Compare *Lopez*, 514 US at 619–23 (Breyer dissenting).

[128] See *Breard v Greene*, 118 S Ct 1352 (1998) (per curiam).

[129] This recognition cuts both ways, to suggest that traditionally federal enclaves ought to be less exclusive than many have thought. See, e.g., Ernest A. Young, *Preemption at Sea*, 67 Geo Wash L Rev 273, 329–33 (1999) (demonstrating that the traditionally federal enclave of maritime law overlaps with areas of traditional state authority).

Court will examine the connection between a given federal action and an enumerated source of constitutional authority. So, for instance, the Court in *South Dakota v Dole* assumed that some nexus must exist between conditions placed on federal funding and the purposes of the spending program to which they are attached.[130] Similarly, in *Lopez*, the Court rejected the attenuated (if factually persuasive) chain of causation advanced by Justice Breyer linking guns in schools to interstate commerce[131] and instead seemed to suggest that Congress must regulate commercial transactions directly when acting under the Commerce Clause.[132]

The Court has imposed similar limits when Congress acts pursuant to Section 5 of the Fourteenth Amendment. *City of Boerne v Flores* insisted that Congress's power is strictly remedial—that is, Congress may act only to prevent or remedy an actual constitutional violation, and the federal cure must be proportionate to the state violation.[133] The *College Savings Bank* opinions tighten this analysis by narrowing the scope of "property" interests that may serve as a predicate for federal protection, and by insisting that the violations addressed by the federal law be widespread and unremedied by state governments.[134] This line of cases effectively restricts the circumstances in which Congress can use the possibility of state constitutional violations as a basis for preempting state efforts to regulate private conduct.[135]

---

[130] 483 US 203, 207–08 (1987). Because conditional spending offers a convenient "end run" around other restrictions on Congress's power, limits on the Spending Power may be the most critical aspect of power federalism. Baker, 95 Colum L Rev at 1914 (cited in note 107). At present, the doctrine as applied in *Dole* provides little meaningful constraint. For a proposal for tightening up the *Dole* test, see id at 1962–78. See also text accompanying notes 267–79.

[131] 514 US at 619–23 (Breyer dissenting).

[132] Id at 561 (majority opinion). A more limited reading would be that Congress's burden of justification is higher when it does not act upon commerce directly. Either version invites unfortunate comparisons to the old direct/indirect effects test employed by the Court during the *Lochner* period. See, e.g., *A.L.A. Schechter Poultry Corp. v United States*, 295 US 495, 545–48 (1935).

[133] *City of Boerne v Flores*, 521 US 507, 519 (1997). *City of Boerne* struck down the Religious Freedom Restoration Act, 42 USC § 2000bb et seq, which essentially mandated religious exemptions from generally applicable laws. Because subjecting religious practices to generally applicable laws was not unconstitutional in light of the Court's prior decision in *Employment Division v Smith*, 494 US 872 (1990), there was no adequate connection between the Religious Freedom Restoration Act and the enumerated basis of Congress's power. 521 US at 532.

[134] See text accompanying notes 63–65.

[135] See text accompanying notes 220–30.

A third approach asks whether, assuming that regulatory powers are *potentially* concurrent, the federal legislation responds to any actual need for national action on the particular problem at issue.[136] Donald Regan, for example, has suggested that this is the best way to read *Lopez*.[137] The Gun Free School Zones Act was unconstitutional, he argues, because it did not respond to any collective action problem or other circumstance that made it difficult to regulate guns in school at the state level.[138] The Chief Justice's opinion in *CSB II* arguably confirms this principle, as it imposes under the Section 5 power a requirement that Congress show an extant pattern of constitutional violations as a predicate to federal action—in other words, a "problem" requiring solution at the federal level.[139]

What all these approaches share is the mandate that the federal government simply cannot act on some subjects, at certain times or in certain circumstances, no matter what process it follows or how clearly it expresses its wish to do so. Because the remedy is so drastic, however, the Court has been most reluctant to impose these sorts of limits (at least in the post–New Deal era). The result is a set of doctrines that are far more embryonic at this point than those in the other two categories.

C. IMMUNITY FEDERALISM

While the Court has been hesitant to impose substantive limits on federal power, it has shown no such reluctance in a third category that I have called "immunity federalism." These cases involve protecting the states from being held accountable, in their own activities, to federal norms. The most obvious example, of course, is the Court's state sovereign immunity jurisprudence; others include doctrines barring federal interference with such basic

---

[136] See, e.g., Kramer, 47 Vand L Rev at 1499 (cited in note 105) (suggesting that courts could plausibly require Congress to demonstrate a need for federal action in order to eliminate externalities or protect local minorities, or to show that the states have already been given adequate time to experiment prior to the federal initiative); Bednar and Eskridge, 68 S Cal L Rev at 1469–70 (cited in note 106) (identifying collective action problems justifying federal intervention).

[137] See Donald H. Regan, *How to Think About the Federal Commerce Power and Incidentally Rewrite United States v Lopez*, 94 Mich L Rev 554, 555 (1995).

[138] Id at 569.

[139] *CSB II*, 119 S Ct at 2207–08.

governmental decisions as the location of the state capitol.[140] The immunity federalism model differs from "power" federalism in that it has nothing to do with the broad question of what level of government will regulate private conduct; rather, these cases are concerned with the federal government's ability to regulate the activities and conduct of state governments themselves. In many immunity federalism contexts, moreover, the rules announced by the Court do not even render federal norms nonbinding on state governments. Instead, they simply affect the ability of federal courts or private actors to enforce those norms directly against the states.

The state sovereign immunity cases are not the only example of immunity federalism. The category also includes the Court's extensive jurisprudence limiting federal court interference, through the writ of habeas corpus, with state court criminal prosecutions. The Burger and Rehnquist Courts have actively sought to limit the federal courts' ability to reopen state convictions through such means as limiting the application on habeas of "new" federal rules[141] and expanding the scope of procedural default and abuse of the writ.[142] These decisions do not modify the preemptive effect of federal constitutional and statutory rules on state regulation of private criminal conduct; federal constitutional rules on the permissible criteria for capital crimes,[143] for example, still supersede contrary state rules. Instead, more restrictive habeas rules serve in many cases to make the state courts the last word on federal claims,[144] "immune" from later revision in a federal habeas corpus proceeding.

My central argument is that, in the broad picture, expanding the immunity model of federalism is a poor way to protect the

---

[140] See *Coyle v Smith*, 221 US 559, 565 (1911). See also *Helvering v Gerhardt*, 304 US 405, 419–21 (1938) (recognizing some sphere of state governmental immunity from federal taxation).

[141] See *Teague v Lane*, 489 US 288 (1989).

[142] See *Wainwright v Sykes*, 433 US 72 (1977) (procedural default); *McCleskey v Zant*, 499 US 467 (1991) (abuse of the writ).

[143] See, e.g., *Lockett v Ohio* 438, US 586, 605 (1978) (plurality opinion) (requiring states to permit sentencing authority to consider mitigating factors in capital cases).

[144] See, e.g., *Wainwright*, 433 US at 90 (arguing that strict procedural default rules "will have the salutary effect of making the state trial on the merits the 'main event,' so to speak, rather than a 'tryout on the road' for what will later be the determinative federal habeas hearing").

states' role in our federal system.[145] I will try to make that case in Part V below. It will illuminate that discussion, however, to first explain how two of the Court's most recent efforts to develop judicially enforceable limits on federal authority—the "traditional governmental functions" jurisprudence of *National League of Cities v Usery*, and the anticommandeering principle of *New York* and *Printz*—fit into the tripartite scheme that I have laid out above.

D. HARD CASES

In *National League of Cities v Usery*,[146] the Court struck down the 1974 amendments to the Fair Labor Standards Act (FLSA)—the same amendments at issue in *Alden*—which had extended federal wage and hour regulations to cover most state and municipal employees.[147] Although the Court recognized that these amendments fell within the legitimate scope of the commerce power,[148] it held that general principles of state sovereignty forbade application of the FLSA to state governments. Subsequent opinions condensed the doctrine to a three-factor test: a federal law would be invalid if it (1) regulated the "States as States," (2) concerned matters that are "indisputably 'attribute[s] of state sovereignty,'" and (3) directly impaired states' ability "to structure integral operations in areas of traditional governmental functions."[149]

Although *National League of Cities* announced an affirmative and substantive limit on Congress's commerce power,[150] it operated as

---

[145] Federal habeas corpus doctrine may or may not be a special case, as it tends to involve a wide range of considerations—such as the accuracy and efficiency of criminal proceedings—not generally implicated in broader federalism debates. I therefore take no position here as to whether recent trends in habeas doctrine may be justified on grounds other than a general need to protect federalism by rendering the states less accountable to federal norms.

[146] 426 US 833 (1976).

[147] Prior to *National League of Cities*, "the conventional wisdom was that federalism in general—and the rights of states in particular—provided no judicially-enforceable limits on congressional power." Tribe, *Second Edition* § 5-20, at 378 (cited in note 113).

[148] See *National League of Cities*, 426 US at 841.

[149] *Hodel v Virginia Surface Mining & Reclamation Assn., Inc.*, 452 US 264, 287–88 (1981) (internal citations omitted). The cases also recognized "situations in which the nature of the federal interest advanced may be such that it justifies state submission." Id at 288 n 29.

[150] See Tribe, *Second Edition* § 5-22, at 386 (cited in note 113) (observing that the case "for the first time in our history created an outright override—a veto on otherwise authorized congressional legislation").

a protection for the states' right to structure their own internal governmental operations as they saw fit. Nothing in *National League of Cities* questioned Congress's authority to apply the FLSA to private employers, or to preempt state laws that regulated private wages and hours in a way inconsistent with federal directives. The *National League of Cities* doctrine thus fell within the category of immunity federalism. It allowed state governments to stand apart from a federal regulatory scheme, but did nothing to protect their own regulatory power over their citizens.[151]

The anticommandeering doctrine articulated in *New York v United States*[152] and *Printz v United States*[153] presents a more complicated picture. Like *National League of Cities*, the anticommandeering rule is also phrased as a substantive limit on Congress's power: "Even where Congress has the authority under the Constitution to pass laws requiring or prohibiting certain acts, it *lacks the power* directly to compel the States to require or prohibit those acts."[154] But as the quoted language makes clear, the anticommandeering rule—like the *National League of Cities* doctrine—does not go to the ultimate authority of Congress "to pass laws requiring or prohibiting certain acts." Congress remains free to regulate private conduct howsoever it chooses; it simply cannot employ state governmental entities as instruments of that regulation. In this sense, the anticommandeering rule follows the model of immunity federalism.[155]

Both the *New York* and *Printz* opinions, however, pay substantial

---

[151] See Rapaczynski, 1985 Supreme Court Review at 362 (cited in note 105) (observing that *National League of Cities* "did not protect the states as governmental institutions in the sense . . . of assuring their ability to impose the ultimate rules of conduct in any given area of extragovernmental activities"); Rappaport, 93 Nw U L Rev at 820 (cited in note 122) (characterizing *National League of Cities* as an immunity doctrine).

[152] 505 US 144 (1992) (holding that Congress may not require state legislatures to regulate pursuant to a federal regulatory scheme).

[153] 521 US 898 (1997) (holding that Congress may not require state executive officials to participate in implementing a federal regulatory scheme).

[154] *New York*, 505 US at 166 (emphasis added).

[155] See Rappaport, 93 Nw U L Rev at 819 (cited in note 122) (characterizing *New York* and *Printz* as articulating an immunity doctrine). It is somewhat imprecise to say that "the new jurisprudence of commandeering purports to define an area of total state . . . immunity from federal intervention." Adler and Kreimer, 1998 Supreme Court Review at 72 (cited in note 118). *New York* and *Printz* forbid Congress to use a particular *means* of regulation (requiring state personnel to implement federal directives) but do not wall off any substantive area (like family law) from federal regulation.

attention to questions of process. Both are concerned that allowing Congress to require state governmental institutions to carry out federal directives may blur lines of political accountability; disappointed gun license applicants, for example, may blame the state sheriff who carries out the background check rather than the Congress that imposed the requirement.[156] Because process federalism is ultimately rooted in the ability of the people to favor the institutions of government that are most responsive to their needs,[157] ambiguity as to political responsibility for programs and mandates can undermine the system.

A second aspect of process federalism that is largely implicit in the *New York* and *Printz* opinions, but explicit in the process federalism literature, is the need to ensure that the federal government internalizes the costs of its regulatory programs.[158] As long as costs are internalized, they will act as a constraint on Congress's ability to legislate in ways that may supersede state authority. If Congress can "commandeer" state enforcement resources, or force state legislatures to devote their time and attention to fleshing out federal regulatory mandates, Congress may be able to avoid much of the cost of its regulatory activity.[159] As Justice Scalia observed in *Printz*, "[t]he power of the Federal Government would be augmented immeasurably if it were able to impress into its service—and at no cost to itself—the police officers of the 50 States."[160]

The anticommandeering principle thus partakes of both immunity and process federalism. This fact demonstrates that my three types of federalism represent different approaches or strategies rather than mutually exclusive categories. Particular doctrinal tools may simultaneously pursue two or even all three approaches. Yet differentiating among these strategies may still clarify our thinking about the pros and cons of particular doctrines.

Distinguishing among these strategies accordingly highlights

---

[156] *Printz v United States*, 521 US at 930. See also Jackson, 111 Harv L Rev at 2200–05 (cited in note 16) (discussing the political accountability argument in *Printz*).

[157] See text accompanying notes 199–210.

[158] See La Pierre, 60 Wash U L Q at 988–89 (cited in note 103). The political accountability aspect of *New York* and *Printz* can be seen as a requirement that Congress internalize the political costs of the requirements that it imposes.

[159] See, e.g., La Pierre, 60 Wash U L Q at 1034 (cited in note 103); Bednar and Eskridge, 68 S Cal L Rev at 1473–74 (cited in note 106).

[160] 521 US at 922.

what the anticommandeering principle does *not* do: directly protect the regulatory authority of the states from federal encroachments. Indeed, one frequently remarked drawback of the anticommandeering rule is that it invites the federal government simply to supplant state authority altogether in a given field, expanding its own administrative rulemaking and enforcement apparatus as necessary to complete the job without state assistance.[161] I argue below that this threat—that federal activity may leave state governments with little or nothing to do—should be the focus of modern federalism doctrine.[162] The extent to which the Court's federalism decisions of last Term reflect this priority is the subject of the next three sections.

III. Process Federalism, Low Hanging Fruit, and the Biggest Federalism Decision of Last Term

One can never be sure about such things, but it seems unlikely that the Chief Justice has ever sat down in private conference with Justices O'Connor, Scalia, Kennedy, and Thomas to discuss what an ideal framework of federalism doctrines would look like or what the best strategy of case selection and decision would be to get there. Federalism doctrine is an incompletely theorized, common law sort of creature, and for this reason it is unrealistic to expect that doctrine to be perfectly coherent or strategic. In this section I discuss, first, why federalism doctrine tends to focus on targets of opportunity rather than a "master plan," and, second, why the process federalism of *Garcia* continues to present important opportunities despite its obvious limitations as a comprehensive vehicle for protecting state authority. In connection with the latter point, I risk a slight detour from state sovereign immunity to discuss last Term's decision in *AT&T Corp. v Iowa Utilities Board*,[163] a case whose significance for state authority surely dwarfs

---

[161] Id at 959 (Stevens dissenting); *New York*, 505 US at 210 (White dissenting). While requiring the federal government to foot the entire bill for such efforts will act as some constraint, the federal government's ultimate control over the national revenue base ensures that such constraints can be overcome if the requisite political will exists. Compare Lynn A. Baker, *The Revival of States' Rights: A Progress Report and a Proposal*, 22 Harv J L & Pub Pol 95, 104 (1998) (tracing much of the dramatic expansion in federal power to the Sixteenth Amendment's provision for a federal income tax).

[162] See text accompanying notes 199–210.

[163] 119 S Ct 721 (1999).

that of *Alden* and *College Savings Bank. Iowa Utilities Board* illustrates, in my view, the extent to which the Court's focus on immunity federalism may have caused it to overlook process federalism's significant potential.

A. THE COMMON LAW DEVELOPMENT OF FEDERALISM DOCTRINE

Justice O'Connor has frankly acknowledged that the Court's federalism decisions have followed an "unsteady path."[164] The commentators have been even less charitable.[165] Much of the doctrine's unsteadiness, however, is fairly traceable to more or less unavoidable characteristics of federalism as an issue and/or the Court as an institution. As a preface to evaluating whether the Court's sovereign immunity decisions make doctrinal and strategic sense as a means of protecting federalism, then, it is important to understand some of the inevitable limitations of the Court's enterprise.

Although the Court's five-member "conservative" majority has maintained a relatively united front on federalism issues—particularly in comparison to issues like substantive due process or equal protection[166]—this consensus nevertheless overlies a number of important cross-cutting differences on issues of both substance and method. The Court's approach to problems of conditional spending and conditional preemption, for example, has been dramatically shaped by the fact that while Justice O'Connor believes in the unconstitutional conditions doctrine,[167] the Chief Justice has adamantly opposed it across a wide range of doctrinal categories.[168]

---

[164] *New York v United States*, 505 US 144, 160 (1992).

[165] See, e.g., Bednar and Eskridge, 68 S Cal L Rev at 1447 (cited in note 106) (asserting that the Court's decisions have "waffled famously" and "flunk requirements of either good law or good policy"); Adler and Kreimer, 1998 Supreme Court Review at 72 (cited in note 118) (arguing that "[t]he area lacks a fabric of constitutional law sufficiently coherent and well-justified to last").

[166] See, e.g., *Planned Parenthood of Southeastern Pennsylvania v Casey*, 505 US 833 (1992) (O'Connor and Kennedy joining more liberal Justices to uphold expansive application of substantive due process); *Romer v Evans*, 517 US 620 (1996) (same with equal protection).

[167] See, e.g., *South Dakota v Dole*, 483 US 203, 213–15 (1987) (O'Connor dissenting).

[168] See, e.g., id at 210 (majority opinion); *Regan v Taxation with Representation*, 461 US 540, 549 (1983) (arguing that government "largesse" is "a matter of grace," even when conditioned on an agreement not to exercise constitutional rights). See also Baker, 95 Colum L Rev at 1915 n 13 (cited in note 107) (discussing the Chief Justice's attraction to the "greater power includes the lesser" argument).

Similarly, one hesitates to predict any revival of the *National League of Cities* analysis because, while Justices Kennedy and O'Connor may be willing to deal with the amorphousness of that analysis through case-by-case elaboration,[169] Justice Scalia's commitment to bright-line rules might prevent him from going along.[170] And while Justice Thomas has articulated what is essentially a compact theory of federalism,[171] Justices O'Connor and Kennedy are both on record in support of dual sovereignty.[172]

As Cass Sunstein has explained, building consensus among jurists whose substantive and methodological commitments differ in such ways frequently requires "incompletely theorized agreements" that do not aspire to complete coherence.[173] Because opinions must work to justify a result upon which the Justices agree while skirting the underlying fissures of potential disagreement, the writing Justice in each case has good reasons to avoid any attempt to articulate a comprehensive theory of federalism. The absence of such articulation, in turn, increases the likelihood that the next case, while not inconsistent in terms of its result, may rest on somewhat different theoretical premises. And the absence of any central textual provision in the Constitution—we have several clauses with important federalism implications, but no central "Federalism Clause"—increases the likelihood that the doctrine will evolve in this common law fashion.[174] Federalism doctrine,

---

[169] See, e.g., *Garcia v San Antonio Metropolitan Transit Auth.*, 469 US 528, 588–89 (1985) (O'Connor dissenting); Kathleen M. Sullivan, *The Supreme Court, 1991 Term—Foreword: The Justices of Rules and Standards*, 106 Harv L Rev 22, 115–21 (1992) (describing the preference of Justices O'Connor and Kennedy for standards over rules).

[170] Compare, e.g., Antonin Scalia, *The Rule of Law as the Law of Rules*, 56 U Chi L Rev 1175 (1989), with *Garcia*, 469 US at 538–39 (decrying the amorphous nature of the *National League of Cities* inquiry).

[171] See *U.S. Term Limits, Inc. v Thornton*, 514 US 779, 846 (1995) (Thomas dissenting) ("The ultimate source of the Constitution's authority is the consent of the people of each individual state, not the consent of the undifferentiated people of the nation as a whole.").

[172] See *Gregory v Ashcroft*, 501 US 452, 457–60 (1991) (O'Connor, J); *Term Limits*, 514 US at 838–39 (Kennedy concurring).

[173] See Cass R. Sunstein, *Incompletely Theorized Agreements*, 108 Harv L Rev 1733, 1746–47 (1995).

[174] Several scholars have tried to locate protection for state sovereignty in a particular clause of the Constitution. See, e.g., Merritt, 88 Colum L Rev 1 (cited in note 107) (Guarantee Clause); Rappaport, 93 Nw U L Rev 819 (cited in note 122) (relying on the meaning of "state" in various clauses). But in each case the central provision is so open-ended that it provides little unifying bite. See Young, *Jurisprudence of Structure*, 41 Wm & Mary L Rev (cited in note 97) (arguing that each textual theory merely imports larger theories about structure). Moreover, the very multiplicity of textual options, in conjunction with

perhaps even more than other doctrinal areas, has been characterized by a variety of adaptive and decentralized responses to changing institutional circumstances over time rather than any attempt
to discover the essential meaning of a particular constitutional
provision.[175]

The institutional characteristics of the Court also undermine its
ability to pursue a coherent strategy in advancing a particular federalism agenda. Social movements can often, to some extent at
least, formulate a sequenced litigation strategy that presents legal
questions in an order designed to bring about a coherent and favorable doctrine.[176] Despite the discretionary character of certiorari jurisdiction, however, the Court can select only among the
cases presented to it, and lower courts are frequently in a position
to force Supreme Court review whenever they decide against the
constitutionality of a federal statute.[177] More importantly, the
Court's actual or perceived political weakness has encouraged it
to begin with the "low hanging fruit"—the doctrinal advances that
can be achieved without entering into undue conflict with the political branches. It is probably no coincidence that the statutory
provisions invalidated in *Lopez*, *Seminole Tribe*, and *Printz*, for example, were relatively insignificant ones.

In light of these realities, it seems unfair to criticize the Court's
federalism doctrines for not being perfectly coherent or symmetrical. In an important recent article, for example, Matthew Adler

---

the theory of enumerated powers—which, by definition, relies primarily on the limits of
the various provisions of Article I—makes it difficult to base any grand unified theory of
federalism in the text.

[175] On the common law approach, see generally David Strauss, *Common Law Constitutional
Interpretation*, 63 U Chi L Rev 877 (1996); Ernest Young, *Rediscovering Conservatism:
Burkean Political Theory and Constitutional Interpretation*, 72 NC L Rev 619, 688–97 (1994).

[176] See, e.g., Jack Greenberg, *Crusaders in the Courts* (Basic Books, 1994) (chronicling the
NAACP Legal Defense Fund's legal strategy). The proliferation of interest groups using
litigation as an important part of their strategy may have made such coordination more
difficult of late.

[177] See, e.g., David Cole, *The Value of Seeing Things Differently: Boerne v Flores and Congressional Enforcement of the Bill of Rights*, 1997 Supreme Court Review 31, 62 (noting that
because the Court "is limited to deciding cases and controversies," it "is less free to set
its own agenda and to address an issue comprehensively"); Robert L. Stern et al., *Supreme
Court Practice* § 4.12, at 185 (7th ed 1993) ("Where the decision below holds a federal
statute unconstitutional . . . certiorari is usually granted because of the obvious importance
of the case."). Note that *Lopez*, *Seminole Tribe*, *Printz*, *CSB I*, and *Alden*—as well as the
Kimel, *Brzonkala*, and *Condon* cases that the Court has on its docket this Term, see text
accompanying notes 320–53—all are cases in which the invalidation of all or part of a
federal statute on federalism grounds occurred first in the lower courts.

and Seth Kreimer have criticized the anticommandeering doctrine because it seeks to protect values that remain subject to attack by other means.[178] But simply because other federal instruments such as preemption or conditional spending threaten federalism values quite as much as commandeering does not render a strict prohibition on the latter "arbitrary."[179] The asymmetry may reflect nothing more than the lack of a good case vehicle in recent years to tighten up the conditional spending doctrine. Or—more likely, in my view—the Court may feel more constrained in its ability aggressively to limit conditional spending without causing unwanted doctrinal reverberations elsewhere,[180] or to limit preemption without precipitating a direct conflict with Congress.[181] The anticommandeering doctrine, by contrast, is confined to the federalism area and strikes at a tool which Congress has never used very much. To recognize these realities is hardly "arbitrary." So long as the Court's pursuit of such "targets of opportunity" does not trade off with superior doctrinal strategies or prompt harmful responses from Congress,[182] it is not a persuasive criticism to observe that a given doctrine does not form part of a perfectly coherent or symmetrical structure.[183]

---

[178] Adler and Kreimer, 1998 Supreme Court Review 71 (cited in note 118).

[179] See id at 143 (characterizing the anticommandeering doctrine as "nothing more than some arbitrary rules of 'etiquette'").

[180] See text accompanying notes 275–79 (arguing that the Chief Justice's unwillingness to recognize an unconstitutional conditions doctrine on issues of speech or abortion blocks any tightening of the conditional spending doctrine).

[181] It is hard to imagine much in the way of a meaningful substantive limit on Congress's preemption authority that would remain faithful to the text of the Supremacy Clause. That is no doubt why preemption doctrine has generally pursued a process federalism model. See also Gardbaum, 79 Cornell L Rev at 807–12 (cited in note 117) (proposing to narrow the scope of federal preemption but working within the paradigm of implementing the preemptive intent of Congress).

[182] I argue below that the sovereign immunity decisions may in fact have these deleterious effects. See text accompanying notes 261–87. To the extent that the anticommandeering doctrine shares many characteristics of immunity federalism, see text accompanying notes 152–55, it may have similar liabilities. But these do not spring from the doctrinal asymmetries complained of by Adler and Kreimer.

[183] I do not wish to suggest that judges need not be principled in pursuing doctrinal targets of opportunity. (On a related point, see text accompanying notes 314–19.) But it is hardly unprincipled to recognize that the Constitution resists grand unified theories, see Adrian Vermeule and Ernest A. Young, *Hercules, Herbert, and Amar: The Trouble with Intratextualism*, 113 Harv L Rev 730, 749–57 (2000), or that law is sometimes best developed incrementally, see Young, *Rediscovering Conservatism*, 72 NC L Rev at 653–56, 680, 712 (cited in note 175).

B. PROCESS FEDERALISM'S UNTAPPED POTENTIAL

The point of the preceding discussion is to say that the Court need not always definitively choose among federalism models. Instead, it can and ought to proceed in an incremental, common law fashion—beginning, so to speak, with the "low hanging fruit" before moving on to more doctrinally aggressive steps. The Court's current focus on immunity federalism, however, may be causing it to miss the potential of process federalism doctrine significantly to protect state regulatory authority without requiring any aggressive doctrinal advances on the order of a *New York* or *Seminole Tribe*.

The Court's decision last Term in *Iowa Utilities Board* is a particularly dramatic example.[184] In the 1996 Telecommunications Act, Congress broadly sought to open up local telephone markets to competition by preempting state-law monopolies over local phone service and requiring incumbent monopolists to facilitate market entry by granting competitors access to their networks. Although the 1996 Act contained the broad outlines of the new competitive regime, it was less than crystal clear as to who would articulate the details. The primary question in *Iowa Utilities Board* was whether Congress had intended to delegate this authority to the Federal Communications Commission or to the various state utility commissions. Given the economic importance of local telephone service, as well as the fact that local communications had been a bastion of state regulatory authority for over a hundred years,[185] the stakes for the states could hardly have been higher.

In terms of practical impact on state power, it is surely fair to describe *Iowa Utilities Board* as the biggest federalism case of last Term. And it would have been relatively straightforward to write a classic process federalism opinion ruling against the FCC's jurisdiction. Although the Act's text was ambiguous as to who should have rulemaking authority under it,[186] one might have thought (and

---

[184] *AT&T Corp. v Iowa Utilities Bd.*, 119 S Ct 721 (1999).

[185] See 119 S Ct at 738 (noting that the issues implicated markets worth "tens of billions of dollars"); id at 741 (Thomas concurring in part and dissenting in part) (observing that "[s]ince Alexander Graham Bell invented the telephone in 1876, the States have been, for all practical purposes, exclusively responsible for regulating intrastate telephone service").

[186] See 119 S Ct at 738 (majority opinion) ("It would be gross understatement to say that the Telecommunications Act of 1996 is not a model of clarity. It is in many important respects a model of ambiguity or indeed even self-contradiction.").

one dissenter argued) that such ambiguity would trigger the presumption against preemption.[187] Even more compelling, the Communications Act of 1934 (into which Congress inserted the 1996 Act) contained an express provision that "nothing in this chapter shall be construed to apply or to give the Commission jurisdiction with respect to . . . intrastate communication service."[188] The Supreme Court had previously construed that provision as not only a "substantive jurisdictional limitation on the FCC's power," but also "a rule of statutory construction" requiring "unambiguous" and "straightforward" evidence before permitting a finding of FCC jurisdiction over intrastate matters.[189] It is hard to imagine a more Wechslerian instance of Congress voluntarily subordinating national power to state autonomy, and one would have expected a Court mindful of process federalism to enforce this concession strictly on the states' behalf, particularly as against an unrepresentative federal agency with bureaucratic incentives to maximize its own power.

To be sure, *Iowa Utilities Board* was a complicated and difficult case on the merits, and one critical characteristic of the presumption against preemption is that it can be overcome by an adequate showing of Congressional intent. I do not wish to argue definitively that the majority failed to make that showing; rather, the

---

[187] See id at 749–50 (Breyer concurring in part and dissenting in part) (citing *Cipollone v Liggett Group, Inc.*, 505 US 504, 518 (1992), and *Rice v Santa Fe Elevator Corp.*, 331 US 218, 230 (1947)). Justice Scalia's answer to this point for the Court was that the 1996 Act clearly did preempt the existing state regulatory regime, and that the presumption against preemption therefore did not extend to the issue of what regulatory authority the states might retain in the wake of that preemption. See 119 S Ct at 730 n 6. But this seems equivalent to the debate in *Cipollone* about whether the presumption applies to restrict the scope of preemption in a statute that includes an express preemption clause. See 505 US at 533 (Blackmun concurring in part and dissenting in part). Justice Scalia likewise argued there that the presence of an express preemption clause overcame and therefore exhausted any presumption against preemption, so that such a presumption could not require a narrow construction of the preemption clause itself. Id at 545 (Scalia concurring in the judgment in part and dissenting in part). But that view was expressly rejected in *Cipollone* by a majority of the Court. Id at 518; id at 533 (Blackmun concurring in part and dissenting in part). See also Tribe, 1 *American Constitutional Law* § 6-29, at 1195 n 74 (cited in note 29) (concluding that "there seems no reason to dissolve established presumptions against broad preemption of state regulation when interpreting *any* portion of a federal statute").

[188] 47 USC § 152(b).

[189] *Louisiana Public Service Comm'n v FCC*, 476 US 355, 372–73 (1986). The Eighth Circuit below had relied upon *Louisiana* and § 152(b) to reject FCC jurisdiction, concluding that § 152(b) erected a fence that is "hog tight, horse high, and bull strong, preventing the FCC from intruding on the states' intrastate turf." *Iowa Utilities Board v FCC*, 120 F3d 753, 800 (8th Cir 1997), rev'd, 119 S Ct 721 (1999).

important point is that plausible arguments were available for the states' position. In such circumstances, it is odd to see a majority opinion written by Justice Scalia (the author of *CSB I* and *Printz*) and joined by Justice Kennedy (the author of *Alden*) simply give the federalism arguments in the case the back of the hand.[190] Indeed, only Justice Breyer stuck up for the process federalism values inherent in the presumption against preemption.[191] Given the importance of the regulatory authority at issue to both the states and the federal government, surely the case warranted at least a more searching review of the federalism issues at stake.

It seems fair to characterize *Iowa Utilities Board* as a missed opportunity in the Court's continuing effort to develop a workable set of federalism doctrines. The majority's interpretation of the Telecommunications Act represents a considerably greater encroachment upon traditional state authority than other federal statutes that the Court has found unacceptable. As Justice Breyer observed, "[t]oday's decision does deprive the States of practically significant power, a camel compared with *Printz*'s gnat."[192] One explanation for this irony may be that, in cases like *Iowa Utilities Board*, issues of federalism become subordinated to different divisions—such as the debate over the appropriate level of deference to agency interpretations of law—that implicate wholly different coalitions on the Court.[193]

---

[190] Justice Scalia called the appeals to "States' rights" by Justices Thomas and Breyer in dissent "most peculiar" because even if the Act were interpreted to leave rulemaking authority with the states, that authority would have been subject to federal judicial review under federal statutory standards. See 119 S Ct at 730 n 6. But this argument is "peculiar" in its own right, since judicial review of agency rulemaking is typically narrow; cf. *Motor Vehicle Mfrs. Assn. of United States, Inc. v State Farm Mut. Automobile Ins. Co.*, 463 US 29 (1983), and the availability of federal judicial review is not typically thought of as eliminating all state regulatory interests in other areas (such a state criminal trials, which are subject to review by federal district courts on habeas corpus and by the U.S. Supreme Court on direct review).

[191] Justice Thomas (joined by the Chief Justice as well as Justice Breyer) went to great lengths to avoid invoking that presumption by relying instead on other statutory canons and the statutory interpretive rule in § 152(b). See 119 S Ct at 744 (Thomas concurring in part and dissenting in part). Justice O'Connor, the author of *Gregory*, did not participate in the case. The best way to explain Justice Breyer's position is probably his evident belief that, in this context, a regime offering diverse approaches accommodated to local conditions and the opportunity for experimentation in different states makes good practical sense. See id at 748 (Breyer concurring in part and dissenting in part).

[192] Id at 753.

[193] Compare, e.g., Stephen Breyer, *Judicial Review of Questions of Law and Policy*, 38 Admin L Rev 363, 373–82 (1986) (criticizing *Chevron* and urging a narrow reading), with Antonin

Another explanation might be that while the Court's conservatives were once willing (in *Gregory*, for example) to accept process federalism as half a loaf, they are now confident enough of their strength to abandon process federalism in favor of more aggressive models of federalism doctrine. That, in my view, would be a mistake. Process federalism has the important advantage of recognizing that, at the end of the day, the states must rely primarily—even if not exclusively—on the political process for protection of their authority. No one, after all, expects the Court to undertake a pre-1937-style frontal assault on federal power.[194] Process federalism also ought to have a sort of "least common denominator" acceptability to Justices who believe, for instance, that *Garcia* was rightly decided.[195] To the extent that process federalism retains the capacity to protect important spheres of state regulatory authority in particular cases—and *Iowa Utilities Board* demonstrates that it does—it ought to remain part of the Court's doctrinal repertoire.

IV. COLLEGE SAVINGS BANK AND THE VIRTUES OF POWER

If last Term's Court chose not to strike a blow for process federalism in *Iowa Utilities Board*, it made significant contributions to power federalism in the companion *College Savings Bank* opinions. At first glance, of course, *College Savings Bank* is an immunity decision. *College Savings Bank* applied the principles of *Seminole Tribe* to two important federal statutes and, therefore, may have rammed home *Seminole Tribe*'s significance for federal law generally.[196] But *College Savings Bank* made little new Eleventh Amendment law. The cases' major contribution is, instead, in narrowing the scope of Congress's substantive lawmaking power under Section 5 of the Fourteenth Amendment. The *College Savings Bank* opinions may thus have primary significance as "power federalism"

Scalia, *Judicial Deference to Administrative Interpretations of Law*, 1989 Duke L J 511, 516–21 (praising *Chevron* and arguing for a broad reading).

[194] See, e.g., *United States v Lopez*, 514 US at 555–57 (reaffirming the New Deal precedents reading the commerce power broadly); id at 573–74 (Kennedy concurring) (same). See also sources cited in note 232 (reading *Lopez* as a mere warning to Congress that *some* limits exist).

[195] In addition to Justice Breyer's dissent in *Iowa Utilities Board*, see *Gade v National Solid Wastes Mgt. Assn.*, 505 US 88, 116–17 (1992) (Souter dissenting) (applying a very strong version of the presumption against federal preemption).

[196] *Seminole Tribe* itself, after all, dealt with the rather obscure Indian Gaming Regulatory Act, 25 USC § 2710.

cases that limit Congress's power not only to subject the states to private suits, but also to supplant state regulatory authority over private conduct. As a result, *College Savings Bank* advances protection of core state interests in a way that, I will argue below, *Alden* does not.

A. STATE REGULATORY AUTHORITY AND THE REAL POLITICAL
   SAFEGUARDS OF FEDERALISM

States have a variety of interests that include, for example, maintaining autonomy over their internal structure and allocation of resources or preserving their dignity as "sovereign" entities. My central argument, however, is that the most important interest of the states lies in making sure that, despite the proliferation of federal activity, they retain something to *do*. This is true regardless of which underlying values federalism is thought to serve. If one chooses to emphasize the values of decentralized decision making—such as facilitating experimentation, diverse outcomes, or public participation[197]—then the importance of giving state governments meaningful decisions to make should be obvious. But even if one stresses the mere existence of state governments as an institutional counterweight to central authority,[198] state regulatory authority over private individuals is probably equally or even more important than the preservation of state governments' internal integrity.

The states' fundamental interest in regulating private conduct and providing benefits to private individuals traces back to Madison's original version of the "political safeguards of federalism."[199] Although Madison did place some weight upon the institutional "dependence" of federal officials on state governments,[200] his primary reliance was upon the loyalty of the people themselves. He thus rebuffed the antifederalist call for more explicit structural protection for state prerogatives:

---

[197] See, e.g., Merritt, 88 Colum L Rev at 7–9 (cited in note 107).

[198] See, e.g., id at 3–7.

[199] See *Garcia v San Antonio Metropolitan Transit Auth.*, 469 US 528, 571 (1985) (Powell dissenting) ("The Framers believed that the separate sphere of sovereignty reserved to the States would ensure that the States would serve as an effective 'counterpoise' to the power of the Federal Government . . . because they would attract and retain the loyalty of their citizens. The roots of such loyalty, the Founders thought, were found in the objects peculiar to state government.").

[200] See Federalist 45, at 291 (Madison).

> The adversaries of the Constitution seem to have lost sight of
> the people altogether in their reasonings on this subject. . . .
> They must be told that the ultimate authority . . . resides in
> the people alone, and that it will not depend merely on the
> comparative ambition or address of the different governments
> whether either, or which of them, will be able to enlarge its
> sphere of jurisdiction at the expense of the other. Truth, no
> less than decency, requires that the event in every case should
> be supposed to depend on the sentiments and sanction of their
> common constituents.[201]

Madison understood that federal representatives will protect the
interests of state governments only if and to the extent that their
own constituents are loyal to those governments and care about
the preservation of state prerogatives. This reliance on popular
loyalty should not worry the states, Madison argued, because
"[m]any considerations . . . seem to place it beyond doubt that
the first and most natural attachment of the people will be to the
governments of their respective States."[202] These included Madison's prediction that the states would have larger governmental
establishments than the central government, would therefore be
able to dispense more patronage, and would have closer ties to the
community as a result.[203]

   All of these predictions presuppose a viable and active state government—a government, so to speak, with a lot going on. They
thus emphasize the centrality of an additional consideration advanced by Madison: the fact that "[b]y the superintending care of
[state governments], all the more domestic interests of the people
will be regulated and provided for."[204] Madison had emphasized
this advantage of state governments in *The Federalist* 45 as well,
where he noted that

> The powers delegated by the proposed Constitution to the fed-
> eral government are few and defined. Those which are to re-
> main in the State governments are numerous and indefinite.
> The former will be exercised principally on external objects,
> as war, peace, negotiation, and foreign commerce. . . . The
> powers reserved to the several States will extend to all the ob-

---

[201] Federalist 46, at 294 (Madison).

[202] Id.

[203] Id at 294–95.

[204] Id.

jects which, in the ordinary course of affairs, concern the lives, liberties, and properties of the people, and the internal order, improvement, and prosperity of the State.[205]

The People will be loyal to the states, in other words, because it is the states that oversee and regulate the things that matter in the ordinary lives of individual citizens.[206] States build schools, enforce contracts, catch criminals.[207] In order to maintain loyalty, then, the states must continue to have primary authority to provide services to private individuals and regulate private conduct.[208]

Without such authority, the basis for political loyalty to state governments—and consequently the influence of state governments in the national political process—evaporates. Madison and the other federalists thus assumed, as Robert Nagel has observed, that "to be able to protect themselves in the political process states would need (and were assured under the proposed Constitution) the capacity to elicit loyalty by providing for the needs of their residents."[209] Even assuming that political safeguards are the primary check on federal power, then, process federalism is incomplete without some concern for preserving enough substantive state regulatory authority for state governments to remain a meaningful presence in the consciousness of their citizens.[210]

---

[205] Federalist 45, at 292–93 (Madison). Hamilton similarly observed that because state governments "regulat[e] all those personal interests and familiar concerns to which the sensibility of individuals is more immediately awake," the states are assured of possessing the "affection, esteem, and reverence" of their citizens. Federalist 17, at 120 (Hamilton).

[206] In fact, Madison argued, if the federal government did its job and kept the nation out of foreign trouble, it wouldn't have much to do at all. See id at 293.

[207] See, e.g., Kramer, 47 Vand L Rev 1504 (cited in note 105) (observing that "[t]he law that most affects most people in their daily lives is still overwhelmingly state law—except perhaps law professors, for whom it is easier to study one federal system than many state systems, and who may, therefore, have a somewhat warped perspective").

[208] See Robert F. Nagel, *Federalism as a Fundamental Value: National League of Cities in Perspective*, 1981 Supreme Court Review 81, 100 ("[T]he Federalists understood and emphasized that influence through electoral politics presupposes that state governments would exist as alternative objects of loyalty to the national government. Unless the residents of the states and their political representatives understand that states are entitled to claim governmental prerogatives and unless they perceive states as legitimate, separate governments, there will be no impulse to use political influence to protect the interests of states as governmental entities.").

[209] Id at 103.

[210] See Rapaczynski, 1985 Supreme Court Review at 404 (cited in note 105) ("Naturally, the vitality of the participatory state institutions depends in part on the types of substantive decisions that are left for the states. Should the federal government preempt them from most fields that touch directly on the life of local communities, the states would become but empty shells within which no meaningful political activity could take place.").

Madison's view comports with basic insights drawn from contemporary public choice theory.[211] Under the "economic theory of
regulation," politicians obtain political support from interest
groups in exchange for providing regulation that benefits those
groups.[212] It follows that political support will track regulatory authority. If state regulatory authority declines—especially in comparison with federal authority—one would expect interest groups
to shift their support to federal politicians.[213] The ability of state
governments to protect their own interests in the political process
by relying on the backing of private groups would correspondingly
decline as well.

One might plausibly suggest, in response to these sorts of arguments, that the states' basic regulatory responsibilities are so well
entrenched as to foreclose any significant threat to their political
support. Certainly state governments continue to have a great deal
to do, despite radical expansion of federal authority since the New
Deal.[214] But consider the following list of "standard day-to-day
public goods" offered by state governments: "education, roads,
some public utilities, trash collection, police and fire protection,
rules governing sexuality and families, zoning, and nuisance abate-
ment."[215] Almost every one of these "police powers" has recently
been subject to actual or proposed federal encroachment.[216] Surely

---

[211] A number of scholars have noted the "continuity [of public choice theory] with the
thought of the Framers." John O. McGinnis, *The Original Constitution and Its Decline: A
Public Choice Perspective*, 21 Harv J L & Pub Pol 195, 195 (1997). See also Michael W.
McConnell, *Federalism: Evaluating the Founders' Design*, 54 U Chi L Rev 1484, 1492 (1987)
(observing that public choice theory "lays the theoretical groundwork for an appreciative
appraisal of the founders' thought").

[212] See, e.g., Jonathan R. Macey, *Federal Deference to Local Regulators and the Economic
Theory of Regulation: Toward a Public-Choice Explanation of Federalism*, 76 Va L Rev 265, 269
(1990).

[213] Federal politicians may indeed seek to further their own interests by affirmatively promoting such a shift. See sources cited in note 105 (noting competition between state and
federal representatives).

[214] See Bednar and Eskridge, 68 S Cal L Rev at 1469 (cited in note 106) (noting a "constitutional cliché that ordinary 'police powers' are presumptively left to state and local
governments").

[215] Id at 1469 n 95.

[216] See, e.g., *AT&T Corp. v Iowa Utilities Board*, 119 S Ct 721 (1999) (upholding FCC
jurisdiction over local phone service); Defense of Marriage Act, 104 PL 199, 110 Stat 2419
(September 21, 1996) (articulating a federal definition of "marriage" to exclude homosexu-
als); Jeneba Jalloh, Comment, *Local Tower Siting Preemption*, 5 CommLaw Conspectus 113
(1997) (discussing federal preemption of local land use regulation under the 1996 Telecommunications Act); Michael Heise, *Goals 2000: Educate America Act: The Federalization and
Legalization of Educational Policy*, 63 Fordham L Rev 345 (1994) (discussing increasing federal

it would be difficult to claim today—as Wechsler did in 1954[217]—
that Congress gives much weight to any general presumption in
favor of state regulation. Excessive complacency about the future
of state regulatory authority thus seems as wrongheaded as the fear
that such authority will collapse tomorrow.[218]

Madison's understanding of the relationship between state and
federal politics suggests that any viable set of federalism doctrines
must develop and maintain meaningful limits on federal ability to
supplant state regulatory authority.[219] I will argue in Part V that
sovereign immunity holdings such as *Alden* are comparatively *un-*
important to this effort. *College Savings Bank*, however, addresses
not only the states' immunity but also the substantive limits of
Congress legislative authority under Section 5. I consider those
limits in the next section.

B. THE APPROPRIATE SCOPE OF SECTION 5

The relevance of the Section 5 power to state authority over
private conduct is not completely obvious. Unlike the commerce
power, Section 5 gives Congress no authority to regulate private
conduct itself; rather, it allows Congress to regulate the behavior
of other governmental bodies to enforce their compliance with the
Constitution.[220] If Congress believes that state governments are

---

role in education policy); Kilbourne, 5 Geo J Fighting Poverty 327 (cited in note 126)
(discussing proposed extensive federal regulation of family law under the International Convention on the Rights of the Child).

[217] See Wechsler, 54 Colum L Rev at 544 (cited in note 103) ("National action has . . .
always been regarded as exceptional in our polity, an intrusion to be justified by some
necessity, the special rather than the ordinary case.").

[218] As Professor Tribe famously observed in 1978, "no one expects Congress to obliterate
the states, at least in one fell swoop. If there is any danger, it lies in the tyranny of small
decisions—in the prospect that Congress will nibble away at state sovereignty, bit by bit,
until someday essentially nothing is left but a gutted shell." Laurence H. Tribe, *American
Constitutional Law* 302 (Foundation Press, 1st ed 1978).

[219] See *Garcia*, 469 US at 572 (Powell dissenting) (arguing that "by usurping functions
traditionally performed by the States, federal overreaching under the Commerce Clause
undermines the constitutionally mandated balance of power between the States and the
Federal Government").

[220] However, in the Violence Against Women Act (VAWA), 42 USC § 13981, Congress
appears to have taken the position that it may remedy unconstitutional state regulatory
behavior toward private parties by assuming the state's regulatory role for itself. The VAWA
responds to the alleged failure of state court systems adequately to respond to violence
against women by creating a federal remedy not against the supposedly deficient state judicial systems, but against the private perpetrators of the violence. The Court will consider
the constitutionality of the VAWA this term. See *Brzonkala v Virginia Polytechnic Institute*,
169 F3d 820 (4th Cir 1999) (en banc), cert granted, 1999 US LEXIS 4745.

regulating private conduct in an unconstitutional way, however, Section 5 confers the federal power to preempt that regulation or prescribe federal norms to which it must conform. If, for example, a state allocated land-use permits in a racially discriminatory fashion, Congress would have the power to preempt that permitting regime or prescribe federal requirements for its continued operation.[221]

In order to see the significance of *College Savings Bank* for limiting Congress's Section 5 powers, it helps to consider the alternatives to the Court's holding. The government's position in *College Savings Bank* threatened to unlimit the Section 5 power in two ways. First, the government argued that, because the Fourteenth Amendment protects property interests, Congress may legislate whenever a property interest is arguably at stake. The interest asserted by the bank—in securing its business from false advertising by others—was ephemeral at best. Had the Court accepted this theory, Congress would have a basis for preempting any state regulatory policy that, in Congress's view, imposed excessive burdens on commercial interests. While Congress could probably reach most such activity under the Commerce Clause, allowing Section 5 to become virtually coextensive with the commerce power would defeat any ongoing effort by the Court to articulate some sort of limits on the latter.[222]

The holding of *CSB II*—and therefore the implications of a ruling the other way—are somewhat more difficult to pin down. As I have discussed, *CSB II* may be read as holding that (1) Congress may "remedy" constitutional violations under Section 5 only after a demonstration that such violations are in fact widespread, or, more narrowly, that (2) Congress may remedy state deprivations of property only when the states have failed to provide an adequate

---

[221] A court, of course, could likewise prohibit such unconstitutional state practices by awarding injunctive relief in a suit challenging the practice. Section 5 arose in part out of suspicion that the courts would not reliably enforce Fourteenth Amendment guarantees on their own. See Douglas Laycock, *RFRA, Congress, and the Ratchet*, 56 Mont L Rev 145, 158–62 (1995). It is also clear that Congress's remedial authority extends somewhat further than the relief that a court might grant. See *City of Boerne v Flores*, 521 US 507, 517–18 (1997).

[222] Compare Cole, 1997 Supreme Court Review at 55 (cited in note 177) (acknowledging that "[t]he potential sweep of Section 5, when combined with the effects of incorporation, is dramatic").

remedy.[223] The alternative holdings in either event—that Congress could act to avert merely hypothetical constitutional violations, or to redress violations for which the states have already provided a remedy—would render Section 5 a far-reaching grant of power indeed. Congress could, for example, broadly preempt state land-use or environmental regulation (to prevent takings of property[224]), enact a national code governing punitive damages (to prevent substantive due process violations[225]), or even ban the death penalty for state crimes (to prevent the unconstitutional execution of someone who might actually be innocent[226]). This would be true, under the government's theory in *CSB II*, even though constitutional violations in each of these areas have generally been adjudged to be few and far between, and the states tend to provide procedures to deal with allegations of unconstitutionality.

College Savings Bank's requirement that Congress show that violations are widespread and/or unremedied by state procedures, as well as its somewhat narrow definition of protectable property rights, thus help to preserve significant areas of state regulatory authority from preemption under Section 5. Some of these areas may nonetheless fall within other enumerated powers, but it seems better to have a forthright debate over the proper scope, say, of the Commerce Clause than to allow Section 5 to evolve into a blank check available to avoid whatever commerce limits may exist. Moreover, such an interpretation may strengthen Section 5 as well by restricting invocations of that power that fall far from its core historical justification. The battles of the Civil War and Reconstruction, after all, were not fought to assert federal supremacy over false advertising.

It seems at least plausible, in this regard, that the breadth of the Section 5 power may ultimately trade off with its depth. The

---

[223] See text accompanying notes 63–65. Note that these two requirements are not mutually exclusive; the Court may be intending to require that both conditions be met.

[224] See *Lucas v South Carolina Coastal Council*, 505 US 1003 (1992) (recognizing that environmental or land-use regulation may violate the Takings Clause in particular instances); *Nollan v California Coastal Comm'n*, 483 US 825 (1987) (same).

[225] See *BMW of North America, Inc. v Gore*, 517 US 559 (1996) (recognizing that some punitive damages awards or procedures may violate the Due Process Clause); *Honda Motor Co., Ltd. v Oberg*, 512 US 415 (1994) (same).

[226] See *Herrera v Collins*, 506 US 390 (1993) (recognizing that the execution of someone who is actually innocent may be unconstitutional).

argument is analogous to Vincent Blasi's contention that the Free Speech Clause acts as a more effective check on real threats to core First Amendment values (such as political expression) if judicial protection is not extended to more controversial forms of expression that lie far from this core.[227] This argument has been controversial, and it may not translate perfectly to the context of legislative enforcement, but there are some reasons to think that Blasi's point may be germane to Section 5 doctrine. A critical current question concerning that doctrine, for example, is whether general federalism limits formulated in the Commerce Clause context, such as the anticommandeering principle, should limit Congress's power under Section 5.[228] It is much easier to hold that Section 5 is "special"—and therefore warrants an exception to *New York* and *Printz*—if the Section 5 is a narrow, focused power rather than a general grant of regulatory jurisdiction comparable to the commerce power in scope.[229] Similarly, *Fitzpatrick*'s holding that Congress may abrogate the states' sovereign immunity pursuant to Section 5 is much easier to defend in a post–*Seminole Tribe* world if Section 5 is not read as permitting a general end run around limits governing the commerce power. To the extent that *College Savings Board* helps maintain the narrowness and "specialness" of Section 5, then, that power may remain more effective with respect to its core purposes.[230]

V. ALDEN AND THE TROUBLE WITH IMMUNITY FEDERALISM

While the *College Savings Bank* opinions respond to the states' core interest in preserving their own regulatory authority,

---

[227] See Vincent Blasi, *The Pathological Perspective and the First Amendment*, 85 Colum L Rev 449 (1985).

[228] See Adler and Kreimer, 1998 Supreme Court Review at 119–33 (cited in note 118) (arguing that anticommandeering should not apply to Section 5). The question was noted, but not decided, in *Pennsylvania Department of Corrections v Yeskey*, 118 S Ct 1952 (1998).

[229] One way in which the Court has sought to enforce the "specialness" of Section 5 is by refusing to presume that Congress has invoked its Section 5 power absent a clear congressional statement to that effect. See *Pennhurst State School and Hosp. v Halderman*, 451 US 1, 16 (1981).

[230] The point may also work in reverse: If a pro-federalism Court is forced to recognize every extension of individual rights vis-à-vis state authority as also entailing a broadening of Congress's legislative power, the Court may be tempted to be more parsimonious in its articulation of rights.

the same cannot be said of *Alden*. The Court's argument in *Alden* relied not only on history and political theory, but also on a cluster of related points concerning the present needs of the states as actors in the federal system. These concerns included the impact on a state's "dignity" of being subjected to coercive judicial process, the threat of money damages to the "financial integrity" of the states, and the importance of ensuring that state governments and their constituents—not private litigants—remain in control of "the allocation of scarce resources among competing needs."[231] None of these arguments is wholly implausible; private lawsuits, no doubt, at times impose real hardships on state governments. But in attempting to insulate the states from outside interference in the form of private lawsuits, the Court is pursuing a model of federalism that ultimately promises little protection for the states' most fundamental interests.

A. HOW HELPFUL IS IMMUNITY?

The Court's decision in *Alden*, following on the heels of *Seminole Tribe* just three Terms back, may signify that immunity federalism is the Court's new strategy of choice for preserving, or reestablishing, some balance between state and nation. *Lopez* seems, for now at least, important mostly as a "warning shot across [Congress's] bow"—a reminder that substantive limits *do* exist on Congress's authority, but not necessarily a judicial commitment to enforce those limits aggressively.[232] And, as I have noted, one simply does not see the sustained and consistent effort to enforce process values (aside from their role in the anticommandeering cases) that characterizes the Court's immunity-based jurisprudence.[233] It is far from

---

[231] *Alden v Maine*, 119 S Ct 2240, 2264 (1999).

[232] Meltzer, 1996 Supreme Court Review at 63 (cited in note 17). A wide range of commentators have interpreted *Lopez* in this way. See also Bednar and Eskridge, 68 S Cal L Rev at 1484 (cited in note 106). We will know more about whether this view is correct when the Court revisits *Lopez* this term. See text accompanying notes 332–37 (discussing *Brzonkala v Virginia Polytechnic Institute*, 169 F3d 820 (4th Cir 1999) (en banc), cert granted, 1999 US LEXIS 4745, in which the Fourth Circuit struck down the Violence Against Women Act, 42 USC § 13981, on *Lopez* grounds, and *United States v Jones*, 178 F3d 479 (7th Cir), cert granted, 120 S Ct (1999), in which the Seventh Circuit rejected a *Lopez* challenge to the federal arson statute, 18 USC § 844(i)).

[233] See text accompanying notes 190–95. *Gregory v Ashcroft*, 501 US 452 (1991), for example, could have been read broadly to suggest that limits on federal authority would be enforced through statutory construction. But we have seen few cases extending *Gregory*. Frequently, the "clear statement" strategy illustrated in *Gregory* has been employed to prevent state governments from being held accountable to federal law. See, e.g., *Will v Michigan*

obvious, unfortunately, that the immunity model offers the best means for protecting federalism as we enter the next century.

The central problem with immunity federalism is that the Court's analysis begins by inquiring what state "sovereignty" might mean in isolation, then develops the proper relationship between the states and the federal government by inference from there. Andrzej Rapaczynski identified a similar problem with the *National League of Cities* doctrine over a decade ago, arguing that the Court should begin instead with "a functional analysis of the role of the states in the federal system."[234] The problem is that the classical concept of "sovereignty" has never described any institution of American government very well, and the extensive qualifications and adaptations that the term must suffer in order to apply here at all strip the concept of most of its explanatory power.[235]

In practice, discussions of "sovereignty" in immunity federalism cases frequently reduce to reliance on states' "dignitary" interests.[236] States have, of course, a wide range of interests and prerogatives not shared by individuals in our constitutional system. But these arise from the necessary functions performed by the states in service to the ultimate sovereign—the people.[237] As Justice Wil-

Dept. of State Police, 491 US 58, 65–66 (1989) (refusing to find, absent a clear statement of Congress's intent, that a state is a "person" liable under § 1983). And in other areas where the Court arguably *has* struck a blow for process federalism, the Court has not articulated that as a rationale for its decision. See, e.g., *Yamaha Motor Corp. v Calhoun*, 516 US 199 (1996) (holding that judge-made federal admiralty law did not preempt state tort remedies, but not relying on need to restrict preemptive lawmaking to Congress's own enactments); Ernest A. Young, *The Last Brooding Omnipresence: Erie Railroad Co. v Tompkins and the Unconstitutionality of Preemptive Federal Maritime Law*, 43 St Louis U L J 1349, 1354–55 (2000) (arguing that process federalism is sufficient to protect state interests vis-à-vis federal admiralty law).

[234] Rapaczynski, 1985 Supreme Court Review at 345 (cited in note 105). Rapaczynski's further point that such an analysis "would parallel the Court's jurisprudence in the area of separation of powers," id, is illuminating, although it must be qualified by the recognition of several separation of powers decisions of a more formalist cast. See, e.g., *Bowsher v Synar*, 478 US 714 (1986); *INS v Chadha*, 462 US 919 (1983).

[235] See Rapaczynski, 1985 Supreme Court Review at 346–59 (cited in note 105). Rapaczynski acknowledges that the Framers *did* think it important to have some theory of sovereignty and in fact located that sovereignty in the people themselves. See id at 357. See also sources cited in notes 237–38. But he rightly points out that a concept of *delegated* state sovereignty emanating from the people is so different from classical sovereignty theory as to severely undermine the classical theory's usefulness today. See id at 357–58.

[236] See, e.g., *Alden v Maine*, 119 S Ct 2240, 2264 (1999); *Idaho v Coeur d'Alene Tribe of Idaho*, 521 US 261, 268 (1997) (plurality opinion).

[237] On the ultimate sovereignty of the people, see, e.g., Federalist 49, at 339 (Madison) (asserting that "the people are the only legitimate fountain of power"); 1 *Pennsylvania and*

son, the primary architect of popular sovereignty, insisted in *Chisolm*, "[a] State; useful and valuable as the contrivance is, is the inferior contrivance of man; and from his native dignity derives all its acquired importance."[238] A state has an interest in preserving the integrity of its internal decision-making processes, for example, because that will insure that it remains responsive and accountable to its citizens and not to some other body.[239] It is simply an extraordinary statement, in our political tradition, to suggest that any governmental entity has a "dignity" intrinsically superior to that of the individual. There are no kings here.[240]

To be worthy of constitutional protection, then, surely a state's "dignitary" interest in avoiding private lawsuits must somehow be linked to its ability to carry out its governmental functions.[241] Perhaps, for example, dignity would be a credible interest if one could demonstrate that the sheer spectacle of the state appearing as defendant in a civil trial would decrease public respect for the state's efforts at governance. But this is an empirical demonstration of likely insurmountable difficulty, and to my knowledge it has never been attempted. "Dignity" therefore seems a relatively weak basis for striking down a duly enacted federal law.

Equally plausible arguments, moreover, suggest that "dignity"—defined as the credibility of public institutions—might cut

---

the Federal Constitution, 1787–1788, at 302 (J. McMaster and F. Stone, eds, 1888) (quoting James Wilson's insistence that sovereignty "resides in the PEOPLE, as the fountain of government"); Gordon Wood, *The Creation of the American Republic, 1776–1787*, at 530–32 (1969) (observing that Wilson's theory of the sovereignty of the people "would eventually become the basis of all Federalist thinking").

[238] *Chisolm v Georgia*, 2 US (2 Dall) 419, 455 (1793) (opinion of Wilson). Justice Souter echoed these sentiments in his *Alden* dissent:

> It would be hard to imagine anything more inimical to the republican conception, which rests on the understanding of its citizens precisely that the government is not above them, but of them, its actions being governed by law just like their own. Whatever justification there may be for an American government's immunity from private suit, it is not dignity.

Alden v Maine, 119 S Ct 2240, 2289 (Souter dissenting). See Gerald Neuman, *Human Dignity in United States Constitutional Law* (unpublished manuscript) (pointing out the juxtaposition of Justices Wilson and Souter).

[239] See Rappaport, 93 Nw U L Rev at 844 (cited in note 122) (arguing that state political systems must remain effective in order for states to check central authority).

[240] See *No More Kings*, in *Schoolhouse Rock! America Rock* (video) (25th Anniversary ed 1995).

[241] Private lawsuits may, of course, affect a state's governmental functions directly—by depleting the state's treasury, for instance. I discuss the states' interests in avoiding these sorts of impacts in the text accompanying notes 254–56. But the invocation of "dignity" is entirely superfluous to the identification and evaluation of these practical sorts of interests.

in favor of civil liability. In our constitutional tradition, confidence in the government arises rather directly from the proposition that the government is subject to the rule of law.[242] The earliest authorities on sovereign immunity knew this; that is why the ancient maxim that "the King can do no wrong" originally meant "that the king must not, was not allowed, not entitled to do wrong."[243] Legitimate government, in other words, is *accountable* government.

For a more prosaic example, one need only look as far as the state debt cases that dominated the jurisprudence of sovereign immunity in the eighteenth and nineteenth centuries. The Eleventh Amendment was enacted largely to prevent suits against the states to recover debts incurred during the Revolution.[244] And the late-nineteenth-century immunity cases culminating in *Hans* revolved around the massive debts incurred by Reconstruction-era state governments in the South.[245] In each of these episodes, assertions of immunity can only have hurt the states' "dignity" in the tangible sense of the credibility of the states' financial obligations.[246]

In any event, the dignitary argument is far from compelling when placed in the context of modern sovereign immunity doctrine. First, the continuing availability of private suits against state officers undermines any dignitary gains from barring direct suits

---

[242] See, e.g., Rapaczynski, 1985 Supreme Court Review at 357 (cited in note 105) (arguing that accountability of government institutions is more central to the American political tradition than classical notions of sovereignty).

[243] Louis L. Jaffe, *Suits Against Governments and Officers: Sovereign Immunity*, 77 Harv L Rev 1, 4 (1963) (quoting Ludwik Ehrlich, *Proceedings Against the Crown* (1216–1377), in 6 *Oxford Studies in Social and Legal History* 42 (P. Vinogradoff ed. 1921)). See also 1 William Blacksone, *Commentaries* *246 (interpreting the maxim to mean that "the prerogative of the crown extends not to do any injury"); *Seminole Tribe of Florida v Florida*, 517 US 44, 103 n 2 (1996) (Souter dissenting) (noting this aspect of the history). This idea that the sovereign must be accountable was realized, at common law, through the petition of right—the precursor to modern officer suits. As I argue at text accompanying notes 247–48, the continued existence of officer suits undermines any claim that the state's dignity is undermined by having to defend a private lawsuit.

[244] See *Cohens v Virginia*, 19 US (6 Wheat) 264, 407 (1821).

[245] See Orth, *The Judicial Power of the United States* at 53–57 (cited in note 17); Gibbons, 83 Colum L Rev at 1978–82 (cited in note 17).

[246] Madison, e.g., argued that the states' attempts to evade their debts by shifting to paper money "disgrace[d] Republican Govts in the eyes of mankind." James Madison, *Notes for a Speech for the Virginia Assembly Opposing Paper Money* (Nov 1, 1786), in 9 Papers of James Madison 158 (Robert A. Rutland et al, eds, 1975). Compare *United States v Winstar Corp.*, 518 US 839, 884 (1996) (plurality opinion) (observing that undermining remedies for the government's breach of its contracts would "produce the untoward result of compromising the Government's practical capacity to make contracts, which we have held to be of the essence of sovereignty itself") (internal quotation marks omitted).

against the state. The defendants in officer suits are frequently high-profile officials identified directly with the state by the public,[247] and the state frequently undertakes the defense of the suit even though it is not a named defendant.[248] Second, *Alden* surely presents the least compelling case for a dignitary injury. When the state is sued in its own courts, it has an opportunity to control the circumstances and atmospherics of the litigation in ways that are not available in federal court suits.[249] Third, a possible consequence of the Court's immunity cases—an increase in suits against the states brought by the United States as plaintiff—may be even more damaging to dignitary interests than private litigation.[250] Not only are such suits likely to be higher profile, but they also present the state as knuckling under to superior force, rather than graciously acceding of its own accord to the rule of law.[251]

Most importantly, the immunity model's focus on dignity does little to protect state interests defined in terms of state regulatory authority. "Dignity" is not part of Madison's equation; a meaningful sphere of state governmental responsibility is. While immunity federalism focuses on foreclosing federal interference with state government activity within the state's sphere of responsibility, immunity does not itself guarantee the continued existence or extent of that sphere. It would be quite consistent with *Alden* (and with *National League of Cities*, for that matter) for the federal government to allow state governments to pay their employees whatever the state wishes, while preempting every field of state governmen-

---

[247] In *Seminole Tribe*, e.g., the plaintiff tribe sought (unsuccessfully) to bring an officer suit against the governor of Florida. See 517 US at 73.

[248] For those inclined to think that the absence of the state from the complaint's caption makes a difference in terms of preserving institutional dignity, consider our most prominent recent suit against a governmental official in his individual capacity: *Clinton v Jones*, 520 US 681 (1997). I am inclined to think that the dignity of the executive institution is enhanced by affirming the president's accountability to law. But can anyone doubt that the suit affected the dignity of the presidency as an institution—for good or ill—regardless of the fact that the president was not sued in his official capacity?

[249] The state can control, for example, whether the proceedings are televised, or the venue in which they take place, by articulating such rules in its general procedures governing suits against the sovereign.

[250] See text accompanying notes 280–82 (discussing suits brought by the United States).

[251] Where the state's sovereign immunity is preempted (as the federal government argued in *Alden*), the state is, in fact, yielding to federal supremacy. But yielding to the binding force of federal law seems somehow more graceful than yielding only to an actual federal enforcement action brought by the federal executive.

tal activity in which those employees had formerly been occupied. A more realistic example is that the increasing deference to state courts shown by the Supreme Court's recent habeas jurisprudence does nothing to stop the drain of substantive responsibility from the state courts due to the federalization of crime.[252] Immunity federalism thus poses the same problem that Laurence Tribe has identified with respect to *Coyle v Smith*'s rule that the federal government may not dictate the location of a state capitol: Such limits "encompass little beyond the continued formal existence of separate and independent states. If states are to have any real meaning, Congress must also be prevented from acting in ways that would leave a state formally intact but functionally a gutted shell."[253]

The Court's sovereign immunity jurisprudence, of course, does considerably more to protect state prerogatives than *Coyle*; as the Court pointed out in *Alden*, immunity from suit does protect the state's ability to perform its basic responsibilities in important ways. Immunity protects the state treasury and ensures that state officials, not private litigants or courts, decide which claims merit the allocation of scarce public resources and which do not.[254] These benefits are real and have a direct relation to Madison's concerns about the ability of state governments to meet the needs of their citizens.[255] There are countervailing drawbacks, however. Immu-

---

[252] State courts, of course, currently have little cause to mourn any decrease in their criminal dockets resulting from federalization. But on the day that state governments cease to be seen by citizens as the primary guarantors of public safety, a considerable part of the predicate for loyalty that Madison deemed so essential will have ceased to exist. And of course the reason driving the federalization of crime is the wish of *federal* politicians to take credit for crime-fighting measures. See, e.g., Ann Althouse, *Enforcing Federalism After United States v Lopez*, 38 Ariz L Rev 793, 812–13 (1996).

[253] Tribe, *Second Edition* § 5–22, at 388 (cited in note 113). See also id at 395 (noting that the *National League of Cities* court erred by protecting "the state in its role as an employer and provider of services and not in its role as a lawmaker and regulator of private conduct").

[254] *Alden v Maine*, 119 S Ct 2240, 2264–65 (1999).

[255] See, e.g., Bednar and Eskridge, 68 S Cal L Rev at 1465 (cited in note 106) (observing that "[i]f Congress can capriciously foist increased costs onto the states . . . Congress can undermine local capacity for self-government"); Rappaport, 93 Nw U L Rev at 870 (cited in note 122) (arguing that costs of liability may interfere with states' ability to provide services). Professor Rapaczynski goes so far as to argue that protecting the states from federal interference with the internal mechanisms of state government is the most essential aspect of federalism. This is true, he says, because state governments are valuable primarily as an organizational force against federal tyranny. See Rapaczynski, 1985 Supreme Court Review at 389 (cited in note 105). See also id at 398–99 (stressing the importance of intermediary institutions generally). There is much validity to this analysis, but states can hardly be effective organizations without retaining the loyalty of their citizens, and this—as Madison knew—depends on their ability to regulate private conduct and provide private benefits.

nity from federal directives that continue to govern private citizens takes a state's interests out of alignment with those of its citizens, thereby undermining a crucial predicate of Madison's political safeguards. Moreover, uncertainty about the extent to which the state will honor basic federal requirements like, for example, wage and hour laws—and the inability to hold the state accountable if it does not—seems likely to breed distrust between state governments and their constituents. Madison cites the opportunity to seek state employment as a critical basis for citizen loyalty,[256] for example, but how attractive is such employment likely to be if citizens cannot rely on state adherence to federal employment statutes that have come to form many employees' baseline expectations of fair treatment?

In any event, it is important to remember that sovereign immunity only blurs the enforceability of federal statutes against the states at the behest of private individuals; it does not absolve the states of their obligation to follow federal law.[257] Unlike *National League of Cities, Alden* does not have the effect of rendering the FLSA unconstitutional as applied to the state government of Maine, and we ordinarily think of law as carrying an obligation to comply wholly apart from the ease with which it may be enforced against us.[258] Even if a state wishes to behave as a Holmesian "bad man," enforcement through a suit by the United States or a suit against a state officer for prospective relief is always lurking in the

---

See text accompanying notes 199–210. See also Macey, 76 Va L Rev at 269 (cited in note 212) (observing that, under the economic theory of regulation, politicians generally obtain political support in exchange for providing regulation). Rapaczynski admits the importance of a state's extragovernmental activity to maintaining the vitality of political participation at the state level, see Rapaczynski, 1985 Supreme Court Review at 404 (cited in note 105), but the point is equally true of maintaining a state government's organizational strength. In any event, being subject to private lawsuits hardly implicates the internal integrity of state governmental processes to the same degree as the direct regulation of those processes at issue in *National League of Cities* and *Garcia.*

[256] Federalist 46, at 294.

[257] I say "blurs" enforceability because many states will no doubt choose to waive their immunity to suit under provisions like the FLSA. But the effectiveness of such waivers as a means of preserving public trust will depend on the clarity of the states' waiver scheme.

[258] See H. L. A. Hart, *The Concept of Law* 86–88 (Oxford, 1961) (discussing the "internal aspect of rules," under which an actor obeys the law independently of the likelihood that a sanction will be imposed for noncompliance). One would expect this obligation to weigh especially heavily with a state government, which is itself a law-giving entity with a critical interest in voluntary compliance with state law by its citizens. Compare *Alden v Maine*, 119 S Ct 2240, 2266 (1999) ("We are unwilling to assume the States will refuse to honor the Constitution or obey the binding laws of the United States.").

background.[259] These means of enforcement ensure that states will never be truly free to allocate their own resources without having to heed federal requirements. And enforcement by the federal government, in particular, is only likely to further undermine citizen loyalty to the extent that state citizens come to look to the federal government as their "protector" against the depredations of state governments.

B. IMMUNITY'S DOWNSIDE

I argued in the preceding section that immunity federalism does little to promote the states' core interest in maintaining a robust authority over private conduct and benefits. In this sense, the Court's aggressive development of the immunity model may not be worth the candle. One might, however, view the Court's efforts to develop a model of immunity federalism as largely unhelpful to state interests without condemning them as counterproductive. It is not obvious, after all, that the Court must choose one model of federalism to the exclusion of the others.[260] I have already suggested some reasons to view the Court's state sovereign immunity jurisprudence as counterproductive. In this section, I want to focus on three more specific ways in which the Court's pursuit of immunity federalism risks actual harm to state governments.

1. *The opportunity cost of immunity rulings.* The first reason, and the simplest, is that the Court has limited political capital.[261] As Dean Choper has argued, "the federal judiciary's ability to persuade the populace and public leaders that it is right and they are wrong is determined by the number and frequency of its attempts

---

[259] See *Alden*, 119 S Ct at 2267 (noting that the states' immunity does not bar suits by the federal government or officer suits brought by individuals). For a somewhat extreme view, see Rapaczynski, 1985 Supreme Court Review at 346 n 21 (cited in note 105) (asserting that the possibility of suits by the United states or other states renders a state's sovereign immunity "irrelevant to the problems of federalism").

[260] Vicki Jackson, e.g., has argued that some occasional enforcement of "power" federalism may be necessary to make process federalism meaningful by "cueing" Congress to the existence of limits on its power. See Jackson, 111 Harv L Rev at 2226–27 (cited in note 116) ("[W]hile I agree that the national political process should be the primary mechanism for considering the interests of states, and its judgments should be entitled to substantial deference, the possibility of judicial review may be necessary (or at least helpful) to promote the likelihood that the political process in fact works in this way.").

[261] See, e.g., Choper, *Judicial Review and the National Political Process*, at 139 (cited in note 103) ("The people's reverence and tolerance is not infinite and the Court's public prestige and institutional capital is exhaustible.").

to do so, the felt importance of the policies it disapproves, and the perceived substantive correctness of its decisions."[262] There is thus likely to be, at some point, a limit on the Court's ability to continue striking down federal statutes in the name of states' rights.[263] To the extent that this limit exists, then the Court's extended adventure in aggressive enforcement of state sovereign immunity will trade off with its ability to develop a meaningful jurisprudence of process or power federalism. If protecting state authority to regulate private conduct is the key to a viable state/federal balance, then a considered reaffirmation, explanation, or extension of *Lopez* may do more good than another expansion of *Seminole Tribe.*

"Political capital," of course, is a pretty vague concept. It might be that the Court's ability to enforce federalism limits is more like muscles than money: it atrophies unless it is exercised regularly.[264] The *National League of Cities* story arguably illustrates this phenomenon, in that the Court's failure to apply the doctrine to check federal power in a series of subsequent cases may have helped lead to the outright rejection of the doctrine in *Garcia.*[265] The important point, however, is that the Justices who matter most on these issues tend to think in terms of limited capital and worry about judicial actions that may draw down the reserves.[266] Political capital

[262] Id.

[263] See also Bednar and Eskridge, 68 S Cal L Rev at 1481 (cited in note 106) (arguing that "the Court assumes institutional risks when it invalidates congressional enactments" and that "the Court is not likely to challenge national political equilibria very often"); Cass R. Sunstein, *Law and Administration after Chevron,* 90 Colum L Rev 2071, 2111 (1990) ("Because judicial invalidation of statutes is troublesome in a constitutional democracy, courts are properly reluctant to enforce the Constitution with the vigor that might be appropriate for institutions having a better electoral pedigree.").

[264] Compare Erwin Chemerinsky, *Cases Under the Guarantee Clause Should Be Justiciable,* 65 U Colo L Rev 849, 860 (1994) (arguing that "[t]here is no reason to believe that a series of controversial decisions under a particular constitutional provision will undermine the Court's credibility, lead to disobedience of judicial orders, and decrease the judiciary's power"); Peter M. Shane, *Rights, Remedies and Restraint,* 64 Chi Kent L Rev 531, 546 (1988) (suggesting that, in some cases, the Court may enhance its legitimacy through opposing the political branches). Professor Merritt has argued that the Court cannot, as Dean Choper had urged, see Choper, *Judicial Review and the National Political Process,* at 169 (cited in note 103), save up its political capital for individual rights cases by deferring to the political branches on structural issues. See Merritt, 88 Colum L Rev at 17–18 n 101 (cited in note 107). But it is one thing to say that political capital is not transferable across broad doctrinal categories, and quite another to deny that the Court will be more successful within the area of federalism doctrine if it picks its battles with some care.

[265] Compare Van Alstyne, 83 Mich L Rev at 1717 (cited in note 105) (arguing that "[s]everal Justices, respectfully, did not try to make [*National League of Cities*] work").

[266] Compare *Planned Parenthood of Southeastern Pennsylvania v Casey,* 505 US 833, 865–68 (1992) (joint opinion of O'Connor, Kennedy, and Souter) (discussing judicial legitimacy

is thus likely to function as an internal constraint on the Court's willingness repeatedly to confront Congress.

2. *Draconian federal alternatives.* A second problem is that Congress may not be simply willing to give up the federal norms that it had sought to enforce against the states by private lawsuits; instead, Congress may choose to enforce those strictures through means that are even more intrusive into state sovereignty. For instance, while the Court has aggressively limited Congress's ability to subject states to private suits, it has continued to recognize a broad congressional power to condition the grant of federal funds on state compliance with federal directives.[267] One can thus readily imagine, in response to cases like *Alden* and *College Savings Bank*, a proliferation of spending conditions designed to require state consent to private suits.[268]

Congress might require, for example, that states waive their immunity to patent suits, notwithstanding *CSB II*, as a condition attached to research grants to state universities. To the extent that the need to monitor compliance with such conditions creates additional day-to-day federal supervision of state activities (over and above the occasional private lawsuit), the states may be worse off than they were before *CSB II*. Similarly, some in Congress have already proposed amendments to the Patent Act and other federal intellectual property laws that would render state governmental entities ineligible to receive patents or other federal rights unless they first waive sovereign immunity for private lawsuits under those laws.[269] The same bill purports to create a new federal cause

in the related context of overruling prior decisions); Adler and Kreimer, 1998 Supreme Court Review at 139 (cited in note 118) (suggesting that the Court will be reluctant to push the anticommandeering doctrine so far as to overrule important federal regulatory regimes).

[267] See *South Dakota v Dole*, 483 US 203 (1987). See also Baker, 95 Colum L Rev at 1918 n 24 (cited in note 107) (noting dramatic growth in federal grants to state and local governments, both in absolute terms and as a proportion of revenue).

[268] See Meltzer, 1996 Supreme Court Review at 50–55 (cited in note 17). Indeed, the Court noted that this option remains open to Congress in *Alden* itself. See 119 S Ct at 2267.

[269] See the Intellectual Property Protection Restoration Act of 1999, S 1835, 106th Cong, 1st Sess (Oct 29, 1999). The states are already significant users of the patent system, and it seems likely that most would face substantial pressure to acquiesce in the proposed waiver. See id at § 2(a)(14) (finding that "[i]n recent years, states have increasingly elected to avail themselves of the benefits of the Federal intellectual property system by obtaining and enforcing Federal intellectual property rights").

of action against state governments that, if upheld, would appear to place states in a worse position than under the prior PRCA.[270] While such a proposal would not in itself appear to leave the states worse off than before *CSB II*, it might set a damaging precedent for denying the states equal access to federal rights in other contexts.

Similarly, the Court's rejection of *Parden*'s constructive waiver doctrine appears to leave open the option of coercing express waivers through conditional preemption. The Court has held, for example, that Congress may commandeer state legislative and administrative processes if it offers states the alternative of accepting preemptive federal regulation outright.[271] Although conditional preemption is generally employed where the right to regulate private conduct is at issue, there is no obvious impediment to using preemption to ban certain state activities unless the state accepts a federal condition—such as waiving its sovereign immunity for cases arising out of that activity.[272] So, for instance, Congress could prohibit the states from operating a railroad unless they waived their immunity for tort suits brought by injured employees.[273] Or Congress could bar the states from engaging in the sorts of commercial activity at issue in *College Savings Bank* without waiving immunity to intellectual property lawsuits.

Trading constructive waiver for conditional preemption may leave the states worse off because, while *Parden* had become a fairly narrow doctrine, conditional preemption remains quite broad. The version of *Parden* advanced by the government in *College Savings Bank* would have applied only to activities that fell outside the states' core governmental functions.[274] But there is no reason to expect Congress always to be similarly restrained when exercising the power of conditional preemption. At best, then, the states' rights benefits of overruling *Parden* are likely illusory; at worst, the

---

[270] Title II of the new bill creates a new remedy for "constitutional violations" that, inter alia, appears to shift the burden of proof against the state on some issues. See id at § 201.

[271] See *FERC v Mississippi*, 456 US 742 (1982).

[272] See, e.g., Katz, 1998 Wis L Rev at 1498 n 167 (cited in note 17) (characterizing the Driver's Privacy Protection Act, 18 USC § 2721(a)(d), in this way).

[273] Compare *Parden v Terminal Railway*, 377 US 184 (1964).

[274] See *CSB I*, 119 S Ct 2219, 2230–31 (1999).

Court's action may spur Congress to act in ways that leave the states less autonomy than before.

Conditional spending, patent grants, and preemption all implicate the unconstitutional conditions doctrine, which holds generally that the government may not condition receipt of a benefit on the surrender of a constitutional right.[275] But that doctrine has had remarkably little bite in the federalism context; so long as Congress can identify some minimal nexus between the purpose for which it has granted the benefit and the condition, the Court's opinion in *South Dakota v Dole*[276] "offered Congress a seemingly easy end run around any restrictions the Constitution might impose on its ability to regulate the states."[277] Some have suggested that closing this loophole is the logical next step on the Court's federalism agenda.[278] But this seems unlikely in the near term, given Chief Justice Rehnquist's authorship of *Dole* and his adamant opposition to the unconstitutional conditions doctrine in other contexts.[279]

Finally, Congress might accept another suggestion offered by the *Alden* Court: a new emphasis on suits brought on behalf of the United States.[280] Such suits are currently rare, but one can imagine an attempt to institutionalize the federal suit option by, say, creating a division of the Justice Department devoted to enforcing federal law against the states on behalf of private claimants.[281] Although the Court in *Alden* rightly pointed out that such

---

[275] See, e.g., *Speiser v Randall*, 357 US 513 (1958). See generally Kathleen M. Sullivan, *Unconstitutional Conditions*, 102 Harv L Rev 1413 (1989). Several scholars have questioned whether there is any such thing as a single, unified "unconstitutional conditions doctrine." See, e.g., Cass R. Sunstein, *Why the Unconstitutional Conditions Doctrine is an Anachronism (with Particular Reference to Religion, Speech, and Abortion)*, 70 BU L Rev 593 (1990). Even if the skeptics are correct, it may be possible to develop workable versions of the doctrine in particular contexts. See Lynn A. Baker, *The Prices of Rights: Toward a Positive Theory of Unconstitutional Conditions*, 75 Cornell L Rev 1185, 1196–97 (1990).

[276] 483 US 203 (1987).

[277] Baker, 95 Colum L Rev at 1914 (cited in note 107).

[278] Id.

[279] See, e.g., *Regan v Taxation with Representation*, 461 US 540 (1983).

[280] *Alden v Maine*, 119 S Ct 2240, 2267 (1999).

[281] A somewhat more doubtful option—allowing private parties to bring *qui tam* actions nominally on behalf of the United States—will be tested next term. See *United States ex rel. Stevens v State of Vermont Agency of Natural Resources*, 162 F3d 195 (2d Cir 1998), cert granted, 119 S Ct 2391 (1999). Even if upheld, this option would be of somewhat limited utility for the reason that the United States must be the real party in interest. See id at 202.

suits would "require the exercise of political responsibility for each suit prosecuted against a State,"[282] the power of this check would likely decline as such suits became more and more routine. And the development of a federal enforcement bureaucracy whose raison d'être is suing state governments would surely be both an irritant in federal-state relations and a step backward for state independence.

3. *Discouraging devolution.* The worst-case scenario is that erosion of the states' accountability to federal requirements may discourage the further devolution of federal authority to the state level. Rhetorically speaking, it may tend to blunt the force of arguments that power must be returned to more accountable state governments if those governments become, well, less accountable. More importantly, devolutions of authority are frequently accompanied by federal standards that must be observed in the exercise of the ceded power. If Congress must devote substantial federal enforcement resources to policing state compliance with such requirements, instead of employing the cheaper alternative of private attorneys general, that may discourage devolutionary impulses in general.

The Medicaid Act, for example, once required state agencies to reimburse health-care providers for the "reasonable cost" of hospital services actually provided, measured according to federal standards. The 1980 Boren Amendment substantially expanded the states' power to define reimbursement rates. This devolution of authority was accompanied, however, by the continuing requirement that the rates be reasonable and adequate to meet the providers' costs, and the Supreme Court held in 1990 that health-care providers were entitled to enforce this requirement directly through private suits under 42 USC § 1983.[283] The Boren Amendment thus demonstrates that Congress may seek to use private lawsuits as an enforcement tool to ensure the states' exercise of devolved authority conforms to federal standards. And while most such standards might be enforceable through suits for injunctive relief that may not be barred by state sovereign immunity, it is not unheard of to find cooperative federalism schemes that envi-

---

[282] *Alden*, 119 S Ct at 2267.

[283] *Wilder v Virginia Hospital Assn.*, 496 US 498 (1990).

sion private actions for money damages where state programs fail to meet federal requirements.[284]

Will devolution be less likely if it becomes more difficult to hold states accountable in these ways? The history of the legislative veto may be analogous. That veto is widely thought to have encouraged Congress to delegate power to administrative agencies by providing Congress with a convenient ex post means to ensure agency compliance with congressional directives.[285] When the Supreme Court struck down the legislative veto, it was feared that Congress would be less willing to delegate such authority[286] or would at least be forced to circumscribe its delegations much more narrowly.[287] Immunity federalism may present similar disincentives to delegate

---

[284] See, e.g., *Wright v Roanoke Redevelopment and Housing Authority*, 479 US 418 (1987) (upholding damages suit under § 1983 where state public housing authority had charged rents exceeding those permitted by the Federal Housing Act).

[285] See, e.g., Louis Fisher, *The Politics of Shared Power: Congress and the Executive* 91 (4th ed 1998). Dissenting from the Court's decision striking down the legislative veto, Justice White described it as "a central means by which Congress secures the accountability of executive and independent agencies." *INS v Chadha*, 462 US 919, 967–68 (1983) (White dissenting). As pressure to delegate greater authority to the executive mounted, "[t]he legislative veto offered the means by which Congress could confer additional authority while preserving its own constitutional role." Id at 969.

[286] See, e.g., *Chadha*, 462 US at 968 (White dissenting) (suggesting that, absent the legislative veto, Congress must either give up delegating authority to agencies, or give up any hope of holding those agencies accountable for their work); Tribe, *Second Edition* § 4-3, at 217 (cited in note 113) ("Without a legislative veto, some congressional delegations of power to the executive are probably out of the question.").

[287] See Tribe, *Second Edition* § 4-3, at 217 n 21 (cited in note 113) (noting that "the inability to rein in the executive branch by legislative veto may simply induce Congress to devote more care to circumscribing executive conduct *before* the fact through the imposition of nondiscretionary statutory duties"). At the end of the day, *Chadha* does not seem to have made a huge dent in Congress's willingness to delegate authority to administrative agencies. But cf. Sidney A. Shapiro and Robert L. Glickman, *Congress, the Supreme Court, and the Quiet Revolution in Administrative Law*, 1988 Duke L J 819, 877–78 (observing that a trend toward narrower, more specific delegations to agencies by Congress has coincided with a shift by the Supreme Court away from strict judicial review of agency decision making, but concluding that there may be no causal relationship between these two phenomena). *Chadha*'s impact, however, is likely to have been mitigated primarily by the continued availability of functional equivalents to the legislative veto, see Fisher (cited in note 285), at 99–104, as well as other more informal means of congressional oversight, see Jessica Korn, *The Power of Separation: American Constitutionalism and the Myth of the Legislative Veto* 47 (Princeton, 1996) (arguing that "empirical evidence reveals that the legislative veto shortcut authority was superfluous to the informal interbranch contacts and negotiations that serve as the real workhorse of congressional oversight power"). It is far from clear that Congress's means of enforcing limits on devolved authority against state governments would prove as robust if private lawsuits were removed from the mix.

by ceding authority to state governments, especially if it is difficult and costly to enforce the limits of the delegation.

Both these disincentives to devolve authority as well as Congress's use of more draconian enforcement mechanisms might be avoided if the states choose to waive the sovereign immunity for suits under particular federal statutory schemes. The Court has placed control over the scope of state accountability firmly in the hands of state governments, and one should not assume that those governments will be blind to immunity's downside potential. It is possible, at least in theory, to construct statutory regimes where states become eligible to receive devolved authority or avoid Justice Department enforcement actions once they waive their immunity to private lawsuits. This consideration surely mitigates the risks of immunity federalism for state governments to some degree.

I doubt, however, that waiver is a complete answer. Such waivers are unlikely to be uniform; some states may not waive at all, and some waivers may vary in scope. Congress may decide that evaluating such waivers on a case-by-case basis is not worth the trouble, especially if a federally imposed alternative must be established anyway for those states that do not participate. Congress might fear that some states might waive their immunity at the outset, then cancel such waivers later on, especially if a subsequent Congress seemed less likely to retaliate. And Congress might sensibly worry that a Court that has pushed immunity federalism as far as *Alden* might eventually turn its attention to limiting the validity of immunity waivers that seem coerced. All these factors might lead a Congress considering whether to devolve regulatory authority in a particular area to question the credibility of commitments by states to waive their immunity.

The Court will have done little to protect federalism if, in the end, the Court's expansion of state sovereign immunity encourages the development of new federal supervisory bureaucracies and stifles devolutionary impulses at the federal level. And these risks assume a greater importance when compared to immunity federalism's relatively modest benefits. One last risk remains to be considered, however: By aggressively pursuing its immunity agenda, the Court's conservative majority may be undermining prospects for a lasting consensus on federalism doctrine.

VI. Federalism and Distrust

The conservative wing of the Rehnquist Court's impressive string of victories has inspired commentators to speak of a "Federalist revival"[288] and even a new "constitutional moment."[289] But despite the mounting pile of pro-states precedent, the Court's current direction seems as fragile as the five-vote majority that has prevailed in most of the individual cases.[290] The latest round of cases shows signs of continuing the pendulum swings that have characterized the Court's federalism jurisprudence ever since *National League of Cities* in 1976.[291] If this cycle is to be broken, the Justices must begin to think seriously about the possible ingredients for a stable compromise on federalism issues.

A. "NEVER SAY DIE": DISSENT, REVENGE,
AND PRINCIPLED COMPROMISE

Certainly the dissenting Justices in the state sovereign immunity cases show no signs of accepting *Seminole Tribe* as settled law. Justice Breyer's dissent in *College Savings Bank*, joined by Justices Stevens, Souter, and Ginsburg, announced that "I am not yet ready to adhere to the propositions of law set forth in *Seminole Tribe*."[292] Likewise, Justice Stevens's dissent in the first of the present Term's sovereign immunity cases declared on behalf of the same four Justices that "[d]espite my respect for *stare decisis*, I am unwilling to

---

[288] See Jackson, 111 Harv L Rev at 2213 (cited in note 16). See also Baker, 22 Harv J L & Pub Pol at 95 (cited in note 161) (asserting that the Court's recent decisions have "signaled a willingness to resume its too-long-ignored duty to enforce the Constitution's protections for state autonomy").

[289] See Mark Tushnet, *Living in a Constitutional Moment? Lopez and Constitutional Theory*, 46 Case W Res L Rev 845, 869–75 (1995).

[290] The only cases that have not been 5–4 are *New York v United States*, *Gregory v Ashcroft*, and *City of Boerne v Flores*. In *New York* and *Gregory* Justice Souter joined the majority. See text accompanying notes 294, 302 (discussing Justice Souter's stance). In *City of Boerne*, the split over the continuing validity of the *Smith* decision obscured the precise lineup on the federalism issue.

[291] One might plausibly trace the pendulum swings further back to *Maryland v Wirtz*, 392 US 183 (1968), which first held that states could be subjected to generally applicable laws like the FLSA, to *NLRB v Jones & Laughlin*, 301 US 1 (1937), which announced a very broad view of the commerce power, or even further. The important point is that we are clearly swinging now, regardless of when we started.

[292] *CSB I*, 119 S Ct 2219, 2237 (1999) (Breyer dissenting).

accept *Seminole Tribe* as controlling precedent."[293] Justice Stevens concluded that *Seminole Tribe* was so far wrong that it "should be opposed whenever the opportunity arises."[294]

These sorts of statements by the dissenting Justices are eerily reminiscent of similar statements by the dissenters in *Garcia*. There, Justice O'Connor bitterly protested the Court's abdication of judicial review of federalism issues, but vowed in conclusion that "this Court will in time again assume its constitutional responsibility."[295] Then-Justice Rehnquist echoed this sentiment, stating that "I am confident [that the *National League of Cities* principle will] in time again command the support of a majority of this Court."[296] Individual Justices dissent all the time, but such vows to "never say die" are less common. And because the cycles of presidential politics tend to ensure (through the appointments process) that ideological majorities on the Court shift back and forth over time, what goes around often tends to come around. In a real sense, the current "federalist revival" is simply a fulfillment of the *Garcia* dissenters' promise.[297]

Garcia and *Seminole Tribe* are thus both cases where a five-vote majority of the Court pushed a portion of federalism doctrine all

---

[293] *Kimel v Florida Board of Regents*, 120 S Ct 631, 654 (2000) (Stevens dissenting).

[294] Id at *66. The dissents in *Seminole Tribe* itself struck much the same tone: Justice Stevens, in particular, expressed confidence that "the better reasoning in Justice Souter's far wiser and far more scholarly opinion will surely be the law one day." *Seminole Tribe of Florida v Florida*, 517 US 44, 99–100 (1996) (Stevens dissenting). Justice Souter, the principal dissenter in both *Seminole Tribe* and *Alden*, has generally avoided such statements, and may have a higher regard for stare decisis than some of his colleagues. See, e.g., *Planned Parenthood of Southeastern Pennsylvania v Casey*, 505 US 833, 854 (1992) (joint opinion of O'Connor, Kennedy, and Souter). On the other hand, his *Alden* dissent signaled nonacquiescence by relying primarily on arguments that would require reversal of *Seminole Tribe*, rather than attempting to distinguish the earlier case from *Alden*. See 119 S Ct at 2270–71 (arguing that state sovereign immunity cannot be of constitutional magnitude, whatever its source).

[295] *Garcia v San Antonio Metropolitan Transit Auth.*, 469 US 528, 589 (1985) (O'Connor dissenting).

[296] Id at 580 (Rehnquist dissenting).

[297] There are, in fact, aspects of *Alden* that suggest the Court might reverse *Garcia* if the question were squarely presented. Significantly, the sorts of interference with state autonomy cited by the Court to bar private lawsuits—for example, interference with the ability of state governments to make resource allocation decisions, see 119 S Ct at 2264–65—are exactly the same sorts of interference that the Court cited in *National League of Cities* to warrant a constitutional exemption from the requirements of federal law. See *National League of Cities v Usery*, 426 US 833, 845–52 (1976).

the way (or almost all the way) to one end of a possible spectrum of results—no substantive judicial review of federalism issues, virtually no Congressional abrogation power[298]—while the defeated minority refused to accept the outcome as legitimate and binding in future cases. The fact that the *Garcia* dissenters were able to make good on their threats suggests that their own victory may be no less secure, with the dissenters of *Seminole Tribe* (and *Lopez* and *Printz* and *Alden*) simply waiting for the appointments process to bring them one more vote.[299] No one (except law professors) benefits from such dramatic pendulum shifts in doctrine. Especially where basic questions of constitutional structure are at stake, we are entitled to demand of the Court a little continuity.

In order to build an edifice of federalism doctrine that will stand the test of time (and personnel changes), someone on the Court is going to have to come up with a general federalism framework that can attract at least six or seven votes.[300] Unfortunately, no one

---

[298] The Court could, I suppose, have gone even further in *Seminole Tribe* by stating that Congress would lack abrogation power even under Section 5 of the Fourteenth Amendment. But the pre-*Seminole Tribe* middle ground had been that Congress has abrogation power but only subject to an extremely strong clear statement rule. See *Atascadero State Hosp. v Scanlon*, 473 US 234, 243 (1985). *Seminole Tribe*, of course, took sovereign immunity doctrine far past this compromise position.

Although a thorough analysis of the Section 5 abrogation power is outside the scope of this discussion, the "extreme" position I have postulated does have a certain coherence to recommend it, assuming that *Seminole Tribe* is correct. After all, the text of Section 5 does nothing more than create another enumerated power; nothing in the Amendment suggests that this power is somehow more durable or extensive than, say, the commerce power. See, e.g., Tribe, *Second Edition* § 3-26, at 181 n 28 (cited in note 113) (noting that "*all* of the Constitution's affirmative grants of power to Congress should equally be viewed as in derogation of state sovereignty"). Given that Chief Justice Rehnquist authored both *Seminole Tribe* and *Fitzpatrick*, however, it seems unlikely that the present Court will adopt this position. And it may be that Section 5's grant of power to "enforce"—which the Court has understood to include providing a remedy, see *City of Boerne*, 521 US 507, 519 (1997)—can be read to encompass provision of a damages remedy against state governments without construing Section 5 as a "trump card" over federalism doctrines generally.

[299] The future of *College Savings Bank* in the event of another nationalist appointment or two may be more secure. Although the four nationalist justices dissented in both *College Savings Bank* appeals, they appear to have relied solely on *Parden* and the incorrectness of *Seminole Tribe* itself. Neither in *College Savings Bank* nor in *City of Boerne* itself did any of the nationalists question the majority's analysis under Section 5. No one, for example, has spoken up to defend the broadest of Justice Brennan's alternative readings of Section 5 in *Katzenbach v Morgan*, 384 US 641 (1966). See Tribe, 1 *American Constitutional Law* § 5-16, at 954–55 (cited in note 29). It is thus hard to tell how many votes there are for the majority's narrow reading of Congress's legislative power to enforce the Reconstruction Amendments.

[300] A less numerous coalition might prove equally stable if it were carved out of the Court's middle, rather than based in one of the ends of the Court's ideological spectrum.

seems particularly interested in compromise at present. The conservatives seem determined, for the most part, to press their advantage about as far as it can go across a broad range of issues—including the Commerce Clause, anticommandeering, and state sovereign immunity.[301] And the more nationalist Justices have been no more helpful. It hardly promotes compromise, for example, when Justice Souter asserts in *Lopez* that the attempt to discern *any* limits on federal authority will send the Court down a slippery slope to *Lochner*,[302] or when Justice Breyer offers a theory of "substantial effects" that will transparently justify federal regulation of anything at all.[303]

Justice Breyer's dissent in *College Savings Bank* likewise displays a disappointing lack of seriousness about developing a viable federalism doctrine. He suggests that "the details of any particular federalist doctrine" are unimportant and that, because "judicial rules that would allocate power are often far too broad," Congress should instead be trusted to determine the proper allocation of power.[304] And the only legitimate judicially enforceable federalism

---

[301] *Coeur d'Alene* is both a disturbing and reassuring example in this regard. Disturbing, because Justice Kennedy and the Chief Justice very aggressively sought to use the case as a vehicle to undermine *Ex parte Young*. See *Idaho v Coeur d'Alene Tribe*, 521 US 261, 274 (1997) (plurality opinion) (suggesting that *Young*'s applicability should turn on a balancing test involving, inter alia, whether a state forum is available to hear the claim). See also Vicki Jackson, *Coeur d'Alene, Federal Courts and the Supremacy of Federal Law: The Competing Paradigms of Chief Justices Marshall and Rehnquist*, 15 Const Comm 301, 314 (1998). Reassuring, because Justice O'Connor and the remaining members of the conservative majority (Justices Scalia and Thomas) refused to go that far. *Coeur d'Alene*, 521 US at 291 (O'Connor concurring in the judgment). See also Katz, 1998 Wis L Rev at 1484 n 86 (cited in note 17) (discussing the *Coeur d'Alene* opinions).

[302] *United States v Lopez*, 514 US 549, 605–09 (1995) (Souter dissenting). The roots of Justice Souter's unwillingness to acknowledge any limits on the commerce power may lie in the concern that the federalism limits articulated by the Court in other contexts have not been disciplined by intellectual rigor. See Young, *Jurisprudence of Structure*, 41 Wm & Mary L Rev (cited in note 97) (arguing that the Court's use of the common law background to demonstrate the scope and limits of state sovereign immunity may be legitimate in theory but insufficiently nuanced in practice). If one doubts that any principle can be found that will adequately constrain judges in administering Commerce Clause limits, one plausible response is to disavow the enterprise of enforcing such limits at all. But this response seems to assume that danger lies in only one direction: excessive and unfettered judicial invalidation of federal action. Surely total judicial abdication carries risks as well. And the idea that federalism limits on federal activity should be abandoned altogether seems unlikely to attract any sort of consensus on the Court in the foreseeable future.

[303] *Lopez*, 514 US at 619–23 (Breyer dissenting). See also text accompanying note 127 (demonstrating how Justice Breyer's approach would support federal regulation of family law—the one area which Justice Breyer asserted was clearly outside the reach of federal power).

[304] *CSB I*, 119 S Ct 2219, 2239 (1999) (Breyer dissenting). But see Cass R. Sunstein, *Interpreting Statutes in the Regulatory State*, 103 Harv L Rev 405, 446 (1989) ("The basic case

principle that he can think of is the dormant Commerce Clause, which of course limits the states' authority, not Congress's.[305] At this point, one would not be surprised to find a basic problem of distrust: The nationalist Justices may feel that any concession will simply snowball against them down the line, while the conservative Justices are equally unwilling to concede anything to national power until the nationalists accept the concept of limited government.[306]

How to break this impasse? The problem would not exist if these issues were not extremely difficult, and I am not so presumptuous as to offer a general and comprehensive framework of federalism doctrines here. I can only sketch the outlines of a possible middle ground, drawing on the Framers' political theory of dual sovereignty. As Justice O'Connor explained in *Gregory*, this theory begins "with the axiom that . . . the States possess sovereignty concurrent with that of the Federal Government, subject only to limitations imposed by the Supremacy Clause."[307] The model also contemplates, however, that "[a]s long as it is acting within the powers granted it under the Constitution, Congress may impose its will on the States."[308] Neither the state nor the federal sphere

---

for judicial review depends on the proposition that foxes should not guard henhouses."). In fairness, Justice Breyer's view of deference to Congress's need for flexibility does not appear to foreclose a set of process federalism interpretive presumptions that effectively raise the costs of shifting power away from the states. See note 191 and accompanying text (discussing Justice Breyer's position in *Iowa Utilities Board*).

[305] *CSB I*, 119 S Ct at 2234 (Breyer dissenting). Justice Stevens likewise signaled a complete retreat to *Garcia*'s minimalist version of process federalism this term. See *Kimel v Florida Bd of Regents*, 120 S Ct 631, 651–52 (2000) (Stevens dissenting). Such rhetoric suggests that the nationalist justices may refuse to accept the stare decisis legitimacy not only of *Seminole Tribe*, but of *New York*, *Printz*, and *Lopez* as well.

[306] The hardening of the battle lines is evident in this Term's decision in *Kimel*. See 120 S Ct at 643 (Justice O'Connor, observing that "the present dissenters' refusal to accept the validity and natural import of decisions like *Hans*, rendered over a full century ago by this Court, makes it difficult to engage in additional meaningful debate on the place of state sovereign immunity in the Constitution"). While Justice O'Connors' frustration with the dissenters' nonacquiescence is understandable, her observation betrays a continuing failure to understand that the dissenters' quarrel is not so much with *Hans* as with *Seminole Tribe*'s extension of *Hans* into the abrogation context. See *Seminole Tribe of Florida v Florida*, 517 US 44, 130 (1996) (Souter dissenting) (stating that "I would not, as a matter of *stare decisis*, overrule *Hans* today," but arguing against "taking *Hans* the further step of investing its rule with constitutional inviolability against the considered judgment of Congress to abrogate it").

[307] *Gregory v Ashcroft*, 501 US 452, 457 (1991) (quoting *Tafflin v Levitt*, 493 US 455, 458 (1990)).

[308] Id at 458.

may be neglected or overrun if the essential balance is to survive. As Justice O'Connor concluded, "[t]hese twin powers [the states and the federal government] will act as mutual restraints only if both are credible."[309]

Dual sovereignty thus provides a basis not only for protecting some sphere of state activity from federal interference, but also for rejecting claims for states' rights that intrude upon the federal sphere. Justice Kennedy, for example, relied on the dual sovereignty idea in *Term Limits*, his one defection from the pro-states majority. There, Justice Kennedy argued that dual sovereignty theory means that both state and national governments have their own direct and unmediated relationship with the people, with the necessary implication being that states may not interfere with the relationship between citizens and their federal representatives by imposing term limits.[310] Similarly, Justice Souter relied on the political theory of dual sovereignty in both *Seminole Tribe* and *Alden* to demonstrate why a state government could not possibly be "sovereign" as against a claim based on federal law.[311]

Gregory, *Term Limits*, and *Seminole Tribe* demonstrate not only that dual sovereignty theory provides a basis for upholding some federal actions while striking others, but also that this theory stands a good chance of attracting the centrist Justices necessary to any middle-ground coalition.[312] Such a middle ground would

---

[309] Id at 459.

[310] See *U.S. Term Limits, Inc. v Thornton*, 514 US 779, 838–41 (1995) (Kennedy concurring). The dual sovereignty theory, as elaborated in *Term Limits*, does create a certain tension with the process federalism of *Garcia*. *Garcia* relied heavily on the view that members of Congress represent state governments, not just people in the states. See *Garcia v San Antonio Metropolitan Transit Auth.*, 469 US 528, 550–54 (1985). *Term Limits*, on the other hand, rather clearly takes the position that state governments are not party to the relationship between citizens and their federal representatives. See 514 US at 803–04, 837–38 (majority opinion). But *Garcia*'s assumption was probably somewhat unrealistic anyway, see sources cited in notes 105, 107; in the end, the important aspect of process federalism is probably its tendency to force federal lawmaking into channels that reduce the overall output of federal law. See text accompanying notes 114–21.

[311] *Seminole Tribe of Florida v Florida*, 517 US 44, 150–55 (1996) (Souter dissenting); *Alden v Maine*, 119 S Ct 2240, 2287–88 (1999) (Souter dissenting). Justice Breyer's dissent in *CSB I* likewise invoked dual sovereignty. See 119 S Ct at 2238 (Breyer dissenting).

[312] Federalism may thus be an unusual counterexample to Cass Sunstein's theory of incompletely theorized agreements in the sense that, while the conservative majority that generally agrees on pro-states results may have to rely on such agreements, see text accompanying notes 166–72, a different, more centrist coalition might be able to fashion a compromise that *begins* with broad agreement on theory. For a somewhat related point, see Richard H. Fallon, *How to Choose a Constitutional Theory*, 87 Cal L Rev 535, 565–66 (1999) (suggesting that sometimes the more abstracted a constitutional theory is from particular

probably need to accept at least the following two principles: (1) the Constitution imposes some federalism-based limits on the permissible scope or nature of federal activity; but (2) the states are not sovereign as against any exercise of federal power within the scope of authority delegated by the Constitution.

The hard part, of course, will be agreeing on the nature of the limits entailed by the first of these principles, but two points are worth noting. First, these limits need not be in the nature of subject-matter "enclaves" which the federal government may not regulate. As I noted above, "power" federalism includes other tools— such as requiring a close connection to an enumerated federal power or some sort of argument for why federal action is necessary to fill a gap the states cannot fill on their own—that avoid the problem of defining exclusive enclaves.[313] And a strong version of process federalism might even suffice to guarantee that, practically speaking, a robust state sphere will remain, without the need to define its contours ex ante.

The second point is that merely accepting the proposition that federalism imposes some judicially enforceable limits on federal power—even defined in very general terms—forecloses the position taken by the nationalist Justices in *Lopez*. Such a concession would force those Justices to devote their considerable talents to the enterprise of developing workable federalism doctrines, rather than denying that such doctrines exist. And that would surely be an important first step in the development of a lasting federalism.

One might object that the very idea of "compromise" misunderstands the judicial function, which is to find "right answers" rather than cut deals.[314] But neither side's position on these issues seems rooted in intractable principle. Justice Souter's opposition to virtually all judicially enforceable limits on Congress's power, for example, does not appear to derive from a conviction that, in principle, the Constitution simply contains no such limits. Rather, he has emphasized prudential concerns about the judiciary's ability to for-

---

results, the greater is the likelihood that the theory may facilitate agreement—or at least good faith debate—on more specific issues).

[313] See text accompanying notes 130–39. See also Kramer, 47 Vand L Rev at 1498 (cited in note 105) (noting that "just because it's no longer possible to maintain a *fixed* domain of exclusive state jurisdiction it's not necessarily impossible to maintain a *fluid* one").

[314] See, e.g., Ronald R. Dworkin, *Hard Cases*, 88 Harv L Rev 1057 (1975) (arguing that judges can and must find "right answers" in hard cases).

mulate and enforce workable rules.[315] As Justice Souter has noted in other contexts, however, such concerns need not necessarily bar incremental, common law efforts to fashion administrable limits on government power.[316]

Similarly, the most persuasive argument for the conservative majority in cases like *Printz* and *Alden* is not so much that text, history, or political theory dictated the Court's conclusions,[317] but rather that preservation of functional balance in our present constitutional environment requires such doctrines.[318] The ultimate criterion, to return to Professor Fried's phrase, is that these doctrines "make sense."[319] To the extent that these doctrines—and *Alden* in particular—fail to protect the states' core interests, there ought not to be any principled objection to abandoning or limiting them.

B. THE CLOSING WINDOW OF OPPORTUNITY

The next act in this drama will come sooner rather than later. Although portentous grants of certiorari do not always lead to significant rulings, the 1999 Term has the makings of the most important year for federalism in recent memory. The Court has taken no less than eight cases with important implications for the balance of power between the nation and the states. And because

---

[315] See *United States v Lopez*, 514 US 549, 604–07 (Souter dissenting). The *Lopez* dissent thus differs in kind from Justice Souter's more narrow opposition to state sovereign immunity, which is clearly rooted in a conviction that *Seminole Tribe* arrived at the "wrong answer" to a question which constitutional text, history, and theory determinately resolves.

[316] See *Washington v Glucksberg*, 521 US 702, 767–73 (1997) (Souter concurring in the judgment).

[317] I can only assert this point here. A satisfactory demonstration would require a comprehensive review of the merits in these cases that is far beyond the scope of this article. In brief, I think that the historical arguments in *Printz* are close, and therefore most persuasive when combined with a translation-type argument. In *Alden*, I find Justice Souter's arguments on the text, history, and theory wholly persuasive. See Young, *Jurisprudence of Structure*, 41 Wm & Mary L Rev (cited in note 97).

[318] Compare Lawrence Lessig, *Translating Federalism: United States v Lopez*, 1995 Supreme Court Review 125 (arguing that *Lopez* itself is most defensible as an effort to "translate" the presuppositions of the Framers' constitutional regime into the modern context, rather than as a compelled reading of the Constitution's text). The other plausible argument for *Alden*'s result is that it is largely dictated by the Court's prior holding in *Seminole Tribe*. But this sort of common law elaboration almost always implicates a question of judgment as to whether the next step "makes sense."

[319] See text accompanying note 96.

the cases on the docket implicate a variety of doctrinal niches, they offer a significant opportunity to choose among federalism strategies.

The Court has two Eleventh Amendment cases, one of which has just come down as this article goes to press. In *Kimel v Florida Board of Regents*,[320] the Court held that the Age Discrimination in Employment Act did not validly abrogate the states' sovereign immunity pursuant to Section 5 of the Fourteenth Amendment.[321] Like *College Savings Bank*, *Kimel* primarily implicates the limits of the Section 5 power and is therefore best considered a power federalism case. *United States ex rel. Stevens v Vermont Agency of Natural Resources*,[322] on the other hand, concerns the scope of the exception to state sovereign immunity for suits by the United States. In *Stevens*, the Second Circuit held that *qui tam* suits brought by private plaintiffs in the name of the United States under the False Claims Act[323] are not subject to the Eleventh Amendment bar. *Stevens* thus falls squarely within the immunity category.

Two other cases primarily implicate an immunity model, although they do not involve sovereign immunity from suit. In *Condon v Reno*,[324] the Fourth Circuit struck down the Drivers Privacy Protection Act (DPPA),[325] which restricted state governments from releasing drivers license information concerning private individuals. The Fourth Circuit held that the DPPA violated the anticommandeering rule not because it required the states to regulate third parties—which would have implicated both immunity and process federalism concerns[326]—but because the law regulates only the

---

[320] 120 S Ct 631 (Jan 11, 2000), affirming 139 F3d 1426 (11th Cir 1998).

[321] See 29 USC § 630(b)(2) (including state governments within the definition of "employer" covered by the statute). In *Kimel*, one judge held that Congress had failed clearly to state its intent to abrogate the states' immunity, 139 F3d at 1433 (opinion of Edmondson), another found that Congress *had* spoken clearly and that the abrogation was valid, see id at 1436–40 (Hatchett concurring in part and dissenting in part), while the third judge avoided the clear statement issue by holding that in any event Congress lacked power under Section 5 to abrogate state sovereign immunity in this context, see id at 1445 (Cox concurring in part and dissenting in part).

[322] 162 F3d 195 (2d Cir 1998), cert granted, 119 S Ct 2391 (1999).

[323] 31 USC § 3729 et seq.

[324] 155 F3d 453 (4th Cir 1998), cert granted, 119 S Ct 1753 (1999).

[325] 18 USC §§ 2721–25.

[326] See text accompanying notes 152–60.

behavior of state governments.[327] *Condon* is thus exclusively concerned with the contours of Congress's authority to subject the states to federal directives. As this article goes to press, the Court has unanimously rejected the Fourth Circuit's position and upheld Congress's ability to regulate state governments in this way.[328]

Williams v Taylor[329] presents a different facet of immunity federalism: the extent to which state courts may be held accountable to federal constitutional norms through the federal writ of habeas corpus. Under Congress's amendments to the federal habeas statute in 1996, a federal court may grant habeas relief on a claim previously adjudicated on the merits in state court only if the state court's decision "resulted in a decision that was contrary to, or involved an unreasonable application of, clearly established Federal law, as determined by the Supreme Court of the United States."[330] The precise meaning of this new language is unclear, and the Supreme Court's initial construction of it in *Williams* may importantly affect the ability of federal courts to hold state tribunals accountable to federal norms.[331]

Two of this Term's cases have critical implications for power federalism insofar as they explore the limits of the Court's holding in *Lopez*. *United States v Jones*[332] concerns the federal arson statute,[333] which two circuits have held may not constitutionally be applied to arson of residential property.[334] Because the arson stat-

---

[327] See *Condon*, 155 F3d at 460–63. See also Jackson, 111 Harv L Rev at 2205 (cited in note 17) (observing that the DPPA does not " 'commandeer' in the sense of requiring state regulation of nongovernmental actors").

[328] *Reno v Condon*, 120 S Ct 666 (Jan 12, 2000). The Court purported to avoid the question whether Congress may regulate state governments without passing laws of "general applicability" that also regulate private parties, as it found at least some private parties covered by the DPPA. See id at 672. But the Court's view of what constituted a "generally applicable" law in *Condon* seems sufficiently capacious to largely obviate the broader question. See id.

[329] 189 F3d 421 (4th Cir), cert granted, 120 S Ct 395 (1999).

[330] 28 USC § 2254(d).

[331] See James S. Liebman and William F. Ryan, *"Some Effectual Power": The Quantity and Quality of Decisionmaking Required of Article III Courts*, 98 Colum L Rev 695, 866–84 (1998) (discussing § 2254(d)).

[332] 178 F3d 479 (7th Cir), cert granted, 120 S Ct 494 (1999).

[333] 18 USC § 844(i).

[334] See *United States v Pappadopoulos*, 64 F3d 522 (9th Cir 1995); *United States v Denali*, 73 F3d 328 (11th Cir), modified on other grounds, 90 F3d 444 (1996). In *Jones*, Judge Easterbrook upheld the statute's application to residential property. See 178 F3d at 481.

ute requires proof of a jurisdictional nexus to interstate commerce—that is, "that the torched property was 'used in interstate or foreign commerce or in any activity affecting interstate or foreign commerce' "[335]—*Jones* will require the Court to explore the extent of the connection to interstate commerce that the Constitution requires.

A different aspect of *Lopez* is at issue in *Brzonkala v Virginia Polytechnic Institute*,[336] which concerns the Violence Against Women Act's (VAWA)[337] provision of a federal cause of action for women injured by "bias-motivated violence." Unlike the Gun Free School Zones Act struck down in *Lopez*, the VAWA was supported by extensive hearings and formal findings by Congress on the impact of gender-motivated violence on interstate commerce; as in *Lopez*, however, the object of federal regulation is not commercial activity. *Brzonkala* will thus test the relative importance of these different aspects of *Lopez*'s analysis.

The Fourth Circuit also held in *Brzonkala* that the VAWA exceeded Congress's power to provide a remedy for gender discrimination under Section 5 of the Fourteenth Amendment.[338] *Brzonkala* and *Kimel* thus both offer important opportunities to further develop the Section 5 inquiry under *City of Boerne*. *Brzonkala* involves both the ability of Congress to use Section 5 to regulate private conduct[339]—a critical aspect of power federalism—and the proportionality aspect of *City of Boerne*.[340] *Kimel*, on the other hand, has already limited Congress's ability to provide remedies for discrimination against nonsuspect classes.[341]

Two significant preemption cases provide another opportunity for the Court to exploit the largely untapped potential of process federalism. *Geier v American Honda Motor Co.*[342] involves the preemption of state common law tort claims by the National Traffic

---

[335] *Jones*, 178 F3d at 480 (quoting 18 USC § 844(i)).

[336] 169 F3d 820 (4th Cir 1999) (en banc), cert granted, 1999 US LEXIS 4745.

[337] 42 USC § 13981.

[338] See 169 F3d at 913–14 (Motz dissenting).

[339] See id at 862–80.

[340] See id at 883–89.

[341] 2000 US LEXIS at *34–53.

[342] 166 F3d 1236 (DC Cir), cert granted, 120 S Ct 33 (1999).

and Motor Vehicle Safety Act and its accompanying regulations.[343] At its heart, *Geier* implicates the manner in which the presumption against preemption should be applied to conflict preemption, where the issue is not the clarity of statutory language but the degree of interference with federal policy.[344] Another important preemption issue arises in *International Ass'n of Independent Tanker Owners (Intertanko) v Locke*.[345] There, the Ninth Circuit held that neither the federal Oil Pollution Act nor various international navigation treaties preempted, in most respects, the State of Washington's ability to regulate operation of oil tankers in state waters.[346] Importantly, the Ninth Circuit also held that the Coast Guard exceeded its delegated authority by issuing regulations that purported to preempt the state mandates.[347] This latter holding raises a long-standing process federalism issue concerning Congress's ability to short circuit the Article I limits on its power by delegating preemptive authority to federal agencies.[348]

A final important case concerns not the scope of federal regulatory authority, but rather the implied preemption of state regulatory authority touching on foreign affairs. In *National Foreign Trade Council v Natsios*,[349] the First Circuit struck down a Massachusetts law restricting the ability of state agencies to purchase goods or services doing business with the foreign state of Burma.[350] The law was enacted as an expression of the state's disapproval of the human rights conditions under Burma's new government.[351] The First Circuit's opinion has a certain "kitchen sink" quality to it—relying alternatively on the federal foreign affairs power, the

---

[343] See 15 USC § 1381 et seq.; 49 CFR § 571.208 (1997).

[344] See 166 F3d at 1241–43 (holding that state common law claims were impliedly preempted despite the court's earlier holding that the presumption against preemption barred a finding of *express* preemption by the statutory language).

[345] 148 F3d 1053 (9th Cir 1998), cert granted, 120 S Ct 33 (1999).

[346] See id at 1060–67.

[347] See id at 1067–68.

[348] See generally Marshall, 87 Geo L J at 264 (cited in note 17) (noting an unresolved conflict between the presumption against preemption and the *Chevron* deference ordinarily accorded agency interpretations of law).

[349] 181 F3d 38 (1st Cir), cert granted, 120 S Ct 525 (1999).

[350] See Mass Gen Laws ch 7, §§ 22G-22M, 40F½ (West Supp 1998).

[351] See 181 F3d at 46–47.

Foreign Commerce Clause, and preemption under the Federal Burma Law[352]—and it is accordingly difficult to predict what doctrinal path the Supreme Court's resolution will take. It seems likely, however, that as the categorical distinction between "foreign" and "domestic" affairs continues to collapse,[353] decisions like *Natsios* will take an increasingly important place in the development of federalism doctrine.

Taken together, these varied federalism cases offer the Court an opportunity to choose among federalism models. Although the Court certainly could rule for the states in all the suits, I have suggested above that this strategy may not be sustainable forever, and that immunity rulings may in any event be counterproductive in terms of the Court's political capital and Congress's likely reactions. Such a strategy may also be counterproductive in the sense that a refusal by the conservative majority to moderate its positions on some federalism issues may harden the nationalist justices' views across the board. This Term will thus offer an important chance for the Court's conservative majority to realign its priorities and pursue a more lasting synthesis.

The results in *Kimel* and *Condon*, both decided just as this article goes to press, seem to offer at least some hope of establishing a sensible set of priorities. The Court upheld relatively strict limits on the Section 5 power in *Kimel*,[354] while rejecting invitations to formulate a broad new form of immunity doctrine in *Condon*.[355] And the ability of all nine Justices to agree in *Condon* suggests that consensus is not entirely out of the question, despite the frustration evident on both sides in *Kimel*.[356]

This term may be a particularly good time—and perhaps the last good time for a while—to think about compromise. Both the states' rights and nationalist camps surely appreciate that the situation is precarious; depending on the outcome of the next presidential election, either side could find itself with a fairly firm majority within the next several years. The impending election thus casts

---

[352] See id at 49–61 (foreign affairs power), 61–71 (Foreign Commerce Clause), 71–77 (federal Burma Law).

[353] See the discussion at text accompanying notes 128–29.

[354] See 120 S Ct at 645–50.

[355] See id at 672.

[356] See text accompanying notes 293–94 and note 306.

a sort of Rawlsian "veil of ignorance" over the future voting strength of each ideological bloc.[357] This ought to create an incentive to build a consensus that can survive significant personnel changes now, rather than wait in the hope that one's own side will soon have (or will keep) the strength to simply impose its will. But the opportunity may be fleeting; once the next president becomes a known quantity, the side likely to receive reinforcements will have little incentive to be reasonable.

VII. Conclusion

Ever since the first controversies over payment of state Revolutionary War debts, state sovereign immunity has been something of an odd world apart from the rest of constitutional law. Unfortunately, the Rehnquist Court's preoccupation with this world has gone awry in such a way as to threaten the current majority's worthy project of restoring some balance to the relationship between the states and the nation. That project, as the Court has already recognized this Term in *Condon*,[358] will not be threatened if the states fail to prevail in every single federalism case that comes before the Court. It *will* be undermined, however, if the bitter disputes over state sovereign immunity distort the methodology with which the Court approaches federalism cases, obscure the central importance of state interests that simply may not be implicated in the immunity cases, or prevent the compromises necessary to formulate a stable set of federalism doctrines that will last well into the new century.

---

[357] See John Rawls, *A Theory of Justice* 136–42 (Belknap, 1971).

[358] See text accompanying notes 324–28, 355–56.

MARK R. KILLENBECK

PURSUING THE GREAT EXPERIMENT: RESERVED POWERS IN A POST-RATIFICATION, COMPOUND REPUBLIC

In a series of remarkable opinions, a generally cohesive bloc of five Justices are offering intriguing perspectives on what is "perhaps our oldest question of constitutional law."[1] Believing firmly that "the states as states have legitimate interests which the national government is bound to respect,"[2] this group has embarked on a course of constitutional reformation whose ultimate boundaries

Mark R. Killenbeck is the Wylie H. Davis Professor of Law at the University of Arkansas, Fayetteville.

AUTHOR'S NOTE: The paper that provided the foundations for this article was prepared for and delivered at "The Concept of Reserved Powers in American Constitutional Law and History," a conference co-sponsored by the Jefferson Memorial Lecture Program, the Center for Law and Society, and the Boalt Hall School of Law, all of the University of California, Berkeley. I am grateful to the conference organizer, Dan Rodriguez, to my co-panelist, Jack Rakove, and the session commentators, Maeva Marcus and Shannon Stimson, whose comments on the original draft encouraged me to go forward with this project. Various individuals since then have offered a helpful combination of criticism and support. They include Bill Leuchtenburg, Harry Scheiber, Mark Brandon, Rick Hills, Evan Caminker, John Oakley, and Thornton Miller. I also want to thank the editors of the *Michigan Law Review*, who helped focus and clarify a small portion of the arguments made here, which appeared in substantially abbreviated form in Mark R. Killenbeck, *The Qualities of Completeness: More? Or Less?* 97 Mich L Rev 1629 (1999), and are reprinted with their permission.

[1] *New York v United States*, 505 US 144, 149 (1992). The five are Chief Justice Rehnquist and Justices O'Connor, Scalia, Kennedy, and Thomas. The group has voted together, albeit at times with varying views, in each of the cases that prompted this article but one, where Justice Kennedy's "defection" provided the critical fifth vote to strike state-imposed term limits on U.S. senators and representatives. See *United States Term Limits, Inc. v Thornton*, 514 US 779 (1995).

[2] *Garcia v San Antonio Metropolitan Transit Authority*, 469 US 528, 581 (1985) (O'Connor dissenting).

are becoming increasingly clear. The opinions themselves speak in largely measured terms, stressing the need for "great restraint"[3] and averring respect for "established federalism jurisprudence."[4] There is, nevertheless, every reason to believe that in their single-minded quest to protect the "'residuary and inviolable sovereignty'" of the states,[5] these Justices contemplate substantial revision, perhaps even wholesale reversal, of many of the assumptions that have guided American constitutional doctrine and public policy this century. Indeed, at least one of them, Justice Thomas, both expressly acknowledges this goal and, in his discussion of principles first articulated by the Marshall Court, intimates that the "mistakes" he longs to correct may well have been committed by Marshall himself.[6]

The cases themselves embrace three distinctive, yet complementary threads. One group invokes a notion of federalism per se. Grounded in a revitalized and robust Tenth Amendment, these opinions postulate a limiting principle that requires the Court to reject encroachments on state sovereignty by a misguided and meddlesome federal government.[7] A second set of decisions has expanded the jurisdictional curbs imposed by the Eleventh Amendment, denying to litigants both a federal and state judicial forum for questioning actions of the states themselves.[8] Finally, various opinions hint broadly that this respect for a newly robust federalism provides a context for a more appropriate understanding of a wide variety of issues, even as the Court relies on other, more

---

[3] *United States v Lopez,* 514 US 549, 568 (1995) (Kennedy concurring).

[4] *Seminole Tribe of Florida v Florida,* 517 US 44, 64 (1996).

[5] *Printz v United States,* 521 US 898, 919 (1997) (quoting Federalist 39 (Madison)).

[6] See, e.g., *Lopez,* 514 US at 601 (Thomas concurring) ("This extended discussion . . . does not *necessarily* require a wholesale abandonment of our more recent opinions.") (emphasis added), and id at 1646–48 (discussing *Gibbons v Ogden,* 9 Wheat 1 (1824)).

[7] These decisions include *Term Limits, Lopez, Printz, New York,* and, to a lesser extent, *Gregory v Ashcroft,* 501 US 452 (1991). For a discussion of the cases and their implications, see Matthew D. Adler and Seth F. Kreimer, *The New Etiquette of Federalism: New York, Printz, and Yeskey,* 1998 Supreme Court Review 71; Evan Caminker, *Printz, State Sovereignty, and the Limits of Formalism,* 1997 Supreme Court Review 199; Lawrence Lessig, *Translating Federalism: United States v Lopez,* 1995 Supreme Court Review 125.

[8] These cases include *Seminole Tribe v Florida,* 517 US 44 (1996), and, from the Court's most recent Term, *Alden v Maine,* 119 S Ct 2240 (1999), *College Savings Bank v Florida Prepaid Postsecondary Expense Board,* 119 S Ct 2219 (1999), and *Florida Prepaid Postsecondary Education Expense Board v College Savings Bank,* 119 S Ct 2199 (1999). See Daniel J. Meltzer, *The Seminole Decision and State Sovereign Immunity,* 1996 Supreme Court Review 1.

traditional principles for fashioning the specific rules and results embraced in these cases.[9] In each instance, the underlying message is clear: Court and Congress must acknowledge and respect certain "fundamental aspect[s] of the sovereignty which the States enjoyed before the ratification of the Constitution and which they retain today."[10]

My focus in this article is not on the policy implications of this quest, but rather on what are alleged to be its justifications. At every turn, these Justices have averred that this is, in effect, a relatively simple matter of returning to "first principles" that "every schoolchild learns."[11] They characterize this move toward the states and away from the federal government as a straightforward exercise in identifying the "federal balance the Framers designed . . . that this Court is obliged to enforce."[12] And they insist that the conclusions they reach are not driven by ideological perspectives or individual preferences, but rather by the need for steadfast adherence to "truths . . . so basic that, like the air around us, they are easily overlooked."[13]

These explanations strike me as problematic for any number of reasons, not the least of which is that virtually all of the members of the founding generation whose thoughts and words figure most prominently in this "original intent" jurisprudence understood that the Constitution they created sketched necessarily imprecise

---

[9] In its October 1998 Term, for example, various members of the Court raised the federalism flag in dissent as an additional ground for concern. See *Olmstead v LC ex rel Zimring*, 119 S Ct 2176, 2198 (Thomas dissenting) ("I fear the majority's approach imposes significant federalism costs"); *Davis v Monroe County Board of Education*, 119 S Ct 1661, 1691 (Kennedy dissenting) ("the most grave, and surely the most lasting, disservice of today's decision is that it ensures the Court's own disregard for the federal balance will soon be imparted to our youngest citizens"). Indeed, both sides in the basic dispute played that card. See *O'Sullivan v Boerckel*, 119 S Ct 1728, 1739 (1999) (Stevens dissenting) ("most ironically [the Court's decision] will undermine federalism by thwarting the interests of those state supreme courts that administer discretionary dockets").

[10] *Alden*, 119 S Ct at 2246–47.

[11] See *Term Limits*, 514 US at 846 (Thomas dissenting) ("Because the majority fundamentally misunderstands the notion of 'reserved' powers, I start with some first principles"); *Lopez*, 514 US at 552 ("We start with first principles."); *Gregory*, 501 at 457 ("As every schoolchild learns, our Constitution establishes a system of dual sovereignty between the States and the Federal Government.").

[12] *Lopez*, 514 US at 583 (Kennedy concurring). See also *New York*, 505 US at 157 (Court's task "consists not of devising our preferred system of government, but of understanding and applying the framework set forth in the Constitution").

[13] *New York*, 505 US at 187.

and frankly tentative boundaries of a radically new division of power. For these individuals, ratification marked the first stages in a "great experiment,"[14] the creation of a new, Compound Republic whose operational parameters would be ascertained only over time. This was especially the case when the issue was proper delineation of the respective authority of nation and states, a matter deliberately left "more or less obscure and equivocal, until [its] meaning be liquidated and ascertained by a series of particular discussions and adjudications."[15]

Those members of the Court arguing for state supremacy as a necessary corollary to the teachings of the Framers and Founders take, moreover, a strangely ahistorical approach to what is alleged to be an exercise in historical fidelity. Almost without exception, the opinions confine the history marshaled to a recitation of the words and events of the period between May 1787, when the Framers gathered in Philadelphia, and June 1788, when ratification by New Hampshire sealed the transition from confederacy to nation.[16] More tellingly, the precept that lies at the heart of these opinions—the belief that it is state sovereignty per se that matters, rather than any notion that the federal conduct complained of works a positive harm—seems, at least to me, at odds with both the impulses that led to the formation of our "more

---

[14] The allusion is taken from Jefferson, who spoke of complex and evolving questions to be "pursue[d] with temper and perseverance" as we struggle continuously to perfect "the great experiment which shall prove that man is capable of living in society, governing itself by laws self-imposed, and securing to its members the enjoyment of life, liberty, property and peace." Thomas Jefferson, *The solemn Declaration and Protest of the commonwealth of Virginia on the principles of the constitution of the US. of America and the violations of them*, in 3 James Morton Smith, ed, *The Republic of Letters: The Correspondence between Thomas Jefferson and James Madison 1776–1826*, 1944, 1946 (Norton, 1995) ("*Republic of Letters*"). For other uses of this metaphor, see George Washington, *Farewell Address*, Sept 17, 1796, in 1 James D. Richardson, ed, *A Compilation of the Messages and Papers of the Presidents*, at 213, 216 (Government Printing Office, 1897) ("Richardson") ("It is well worth a fair and full experiment."); Letter to John Adams, May 22, 1817, in 8 Gaillard Hunt, ed, *The Writings of James Madison* 390, 391 (G. P. Putnam's Sons, 1908) ("*Madison's Writings*") (the "proper division and distribution of power among different bodies" is a "great question" and "experiment").

[15] Federalist 37 (Madison), in Clinton Rossiter, ed, *The Federalist Papers* 229 (Mentor, 1961). It is in this particular sense that *M'Culloch* looms especially large.

[16] Indeed, in one telling instance, *Seminole Tribe of Florida v Florida*, 517 US 44 (1996), history is abandoned, confined to a single terse paragraph and footnote in Chief Justice Rehnquist's opinion for the Court in the face of Justice Souter's massive discussion of the applicable history. Compare id at 69 & n 12 with id at 100–85 (Souter dissenting).

perfect union" and the principles that animated the approach actually embraced.[17]

My primary task in this article, accordingly, will be to establish that much of the evidence adduced in support of this vigorous new, old federalism confirms only where one begins the analysis, rather than where, or how, it is properly concluded. In particular, I will argue that the recent federalism opinions undervalue the extent to which the Framers and Founders embraced certain constitutional precepts as necessary means for reaching appropriate ends, perhaps the most important of which was to curtail the sovereignty of the states. I will also maintain that these individuals understood that the text as ratified provided an important, but by design not necessarily a definitive matrix for analyzing sovereignty issues. And I will discuss how the founding generation "liquidated and ascertained" the parameters of state sovereignty over time in two particular instances. One is the familiar debate about the constitutionality of a Bank of the United States, which culminated in *M'Culloch v Maryland*.[18] A second— well known to historians, but largely *un*known and unremarked upon in most legal circles—is whether it was proper for the emerging nation to engage in a systematic program of "internal improvement."

My goal is to demonstrate why this particular vision of federalism more accurately characterizes the approach embraced by the Framers and Founders and is, accordingly, at odds with the emerging views of the Rehnquist Court. The exercise is, of necessity, limited in scope and tentative in its conclusions. I explore only two of the myriad constitutional issues that arose in the early years of the Republic, and have selected as my principal guides the thoughts and words of a very small number of the universe of individuals who might properly be characterized as Framers and

---

[17] I am very much aware that this, in itself, is deemed a harm by those who value state sovereignty for its own sake. What I dispute is the extent to which that position should control where, for example, as appears to be true of the result reached in *New York v United States*, the necessary price for recognizing state sovereignty is the destruction of what appears to have been the only practical solution to the intractable "not in my backyard" problem posed by the storage of nuclear waste. Certainly, as I argue in this article, Madison would have viewed that development with alarm.

[18] 4 Wheat 316 (1819).

Founders.[19] Arguably, by doing so I commit some of the same sins I ascribe to certain members of the Court. Nevertheless, what I have found strikes me as representative of a wider picture that the Court has to date largely ignored, and suggests that we should approach what we might call the brave *old* world of a vigorous, *new* federalism with skepticism and caution.[20]

I

> But let us not sacrifice the end to the means: let us not rush
> on certain ruin in order to avoid a possible danger. [Letter
> from James Madison to James Monroe, August 7, 1785][21]

If "first principles" are important in our constitutional regime— and they are—so too are ultimate objectives. The individuals who gathered in Philadelphia in the summer of 1787 were acutely aware of the importance of their task, and understood the need for a principled approach to the work before them. But they were also pragmatists who viewed their assignment, creating not the "ultimate" Union, but simply "a *more* perfect" one, as an exercise in blending means and ends.

This was especially true with regard to two fundamental questions. The first was whether the proposed system would be

---

[19] I am, for example, acutely aware of the dominant position my reading of Madison's views plays in my analysis. I take some solace in the fact that he figures just as prominently in the opinions of the Court and in the scholarship on the Constitution. The best of these, in my estimation, is Jack N. Rakove, *Original Meanings: Politics and Ideas in the Making of the Constitution* (Knopf, 1996). One might also profitably consult Lance Banning, *The Sacred Fire of Liberty: James Madison and the Founding of the Federal Republic* (Cornell University Press, 1995); Richard K. Matthews, *If Men Were Angels: James Madison and the Heartless Empire of Reason* (University Press of Kansas, 1995); William Lee Miller, *The Business of May Next: James Madison and the Founding* (University Press of Virginia, 1992); Gary Rosen, *American Compact: James Madison and the Problem of Founding* (University Press of Kansas, 1999).

[20] This is a matter of some importance, as, encouraged by what they read, litigants have pressed the Court to, for example, "'formally reconsider' and 'abando[n]' its negative Commerce Clause jurisprudence," an invitation declined in that instance "because the state did not make clear it intended to make this argument until it filed its brief on the merits." *South Central Bell Telephone Co. v Alabama*, 119 S Ct 1180, 1186 (1999) (quoting Brief for Respondent at 3, 28). For an argument that the real "support for [this] movement is not primarily coming from the Supreme Court," but rather from the political branches, see Jesse H. Choper, *Did Last Term Reveal "A Revolutionary States' Rights Movement Within the Supreme Court"?* 46 Case W Res L Rev 663 (1996).

[21] Robert A. Rutland and William M. E. Rachal, eds, 8 *The Papers of James Madison* 333, 334 (University Press of Virginia, 1973) ("*Madison's Papers*").

"strictly republican" since "it was evident that no other form would be reconcilable with the genius of the people of America."[22] Madison and his colleagues deemed a "republican" government to be one "which derives all its powers directly or indirectly from the great body of the people, and is administered by persons holding their offices during pleasure for a limited period, or during good behavior."[23] Jefferson in particular argued that "[t]he further the departure from direct and constant control by the citizens, the less has the government the ingredients of republicanism."[24] This undoubtedly means, as Justice Thomas argued recently, that "[o]ur system of government rests on one overriding principle: All power stems from the consent of the people."[25] But it is not enough to simply recognize this core precept and assume that where the text is silent or arguably unclear, "the people" rule. For one thing, while the people's consent gave the government legitimacy, their inevitably human impulses also posed substantial challenges in the day-to-day realities involved in fashioning a workable social enterprise. As Madison observed:

> If men were angels, no government would be necessary. If angels were to govern men, neither external nor internal controls on government would be necessary. In framing a government which is to be administered by men over men, the great difficulty lies in this: you must first enable the government to control the governed; and in the next place oblige it to control itself. A dependence on the people is, no doubt, the primary control on government; but experience has taught mankind the necessity of auxiliary precautions.[26]

More tellingly, theoretical principles were to tested against and understood in the light of the goals to be achieved. Consider, for

---

[22] Federalist 39 (Madison) at 240 (cited in note 15).

[23] Id at 241.

[24] Letter to John Taylor, May 28, 1816, in Paul Leicester Ford, ed, 11 *The Works of Thomas Jefferson* 527, 530 (G. P. Putnam's Sons, 1905) ("*Jefferson's Works*").

[25] *United States Term Limits, Inc. v Thornton*, 514 US 779, 846 (1995) (Thomas dissenting).

[26] Federalist 51 (Madison) at 322 (cited in note 15). Hamilton made much the same point when he asked, "Why has government been instituted at all? Because the passions of men will not conform to the dictates of reason and justice without constraint." Federalist 15 (Hamilton) at 110. This was a pervasive notion at the time. See, e.g., Bernard Bailyn, *The Ideological Origins of the American Revolution* 59 (Belknap, 1992) ("[w]hat made it so, what turned power into a malignant force, was not its own nature so much as the nature of man—his susceptibility to corruption and his lust for self-aggrandizement").

example, the analytic lodestar of Justice Thomas's *Term Limits* dissent, his frequent and often eloquent contention that "[t]he ultimate source of the Constitution's authority is the consent of the people of each individual State, not the consent of the undifferentiated people of the Nation as a whole."[27] For Justice Thomas, the separate and independent political identity retained by the citizens of each state meant that they enjoyed wide latitude in selecting and, by implication, determining the qualifications of those who will represent them in Congress. Leaving aside whether or not this is a proper reading of the text and its creation, there is considerable room to believe that many members of the founding generation would have viewed this sort of argument with polite skepticism. In 1835, for example, Madison seemed to address this precise point when he observed:

> The question, whether we the people means the people in their aggregate capacity, acting by numerical majy. of the whole, or by a majy. in each of all the States, the authy. being equally valid and binding, the question is interesting, but as an historical fact of merely speculative curiosity.[28]

What matters, Madison declared, is not "the mode of the grant, but the extent and effect of the powers granted."[29] And, as subsequent events would make quite clear, those powers granted to the federal government, while limited, were both "complete" and "supreme."

I do not for a moment argue that this single piece of evidence somehow conclusively proves Justice Thomas is wrong, although, for reasons I hope someday to make clear, I believe he is.[30] It does nevertheless illustrate the need to place principles in perspective,

---

[27] *Term Limits*, 514 US at 846 (Thomas dissenting).

[28] James Madison, *Notes on Nullification*, June 1835 ("*Nullification*"), in 9 *Madison's Writings* at 573, 603 (cited in note 14).

[29] Id at 604.

[30] I examined the term limits question in what I believed to be a neutral and disciplined manner prior to the Court's decision, and opined that neither the historical record nor the extant constitutional doctrines provided a conclusive answer. See Mark R. Killenbeck and Steve Sheppard, *Another Such Victory? Term Limits, Section 2 of the Fourteenth Amendment, and the Right to Representation*, 45 Hastings L J 1121 (1994). Having now read the various opinions, and having reread much, albeit not all, of the primary materials, I have come to the conclusion that the Framers did in fact intend the Qualifications Clauses as exclusive, federally prescribed criteria. Indeed, I don't think it's even a close call. But the detailed recounting necessary to establish this is well beyond the scope of this article.

an exercise requiring both a more complete historical analysis and more distinctive analytic approach than those evident in recent opinions of the Court.

A second threshold question for the Framers and Founders was whether the governmental structure reflected in the text, dependent on the people and sufficiently imbued with auxiliary precautions, "preserved the *federal* form, which regards the Union as a *Confederacy* of sovereign states," or was "a *national* government, which regards the Union as a *consolidation* of the States."[31] The founding generation compromised. Both theory and reality counseled that the creation of an appropriately republican government for the new nation would, of necessity, be "not [through] a *national* but a *federal* act," that is, undertaken in ways that treated "[e]ach State . . . as a sovereign body independent of all others, and only to be bound by its own voluntary act."[32] Once again, as Justice O'Connor in particular has argued vigorously, this means our Constitution recognizes that "the States *as States* have legitimate interests which the National Government is bound to respect even though its laws are supreme."[33] But there are, and must be, limits. Both the Constitution and the Union it outlined would be "in strictness, neither . . . national nor . . . federal . . . but a composition of both," one whose precise nature varied, depending on whether one probed foundations, sources and operation of powers, or modes of amendment.[34]

My point in recounting this is not to reveal startling new insights. This is indeed fundamental material, of the sort "every schoolchild" should learn, particularly those who either become or clerk for Supreme Court Justices. Rather, my objective is to stress that every principled assumption made about the meaning of the text as framed and ratified must also be tested against the objectives to be pursued. Consider, for example, an issue of extraordinary importance to those now concerned about the meaning and effect of the Tenth and Eleventh Amendments: the nature and

---

[31] Federalist 39 (Madison) at 243 (cited in note 15).

[32] Id at 243 and 244.

[33] *Garcia v San Antonio Metropolitan Transit Authority*, 469 US 528, 581 (1985). This rather grudging formulation seems to imply that the government should not act in some instances, and that if it does the action must nevertheless fail, a prophecy fulfilled in *New York v United States*.

[34] See generally Federalist 39 (Madison).

scope of the power of Congress to regulate commerce. As Justice Thomas has reminded us, the modern "aggregation" doctrine, characterized by decisions like *Wickard v Filburn*,[35] "is clever, but has no stopping point."[36] More tellingly, if the commerce power includes within its ambit the authority to regulate matters understood at ratification to "belong" to the states—much less the power to regulate the affairs of the states themselves—there is something to be said for his desire to "be true to a Constitution that does not cede a police power to the Federal Government."[37] Viewed in isolation, it is quite clear that today's expansive reading of the Commerce Clause yields results the Framers would have found "unimaginable."[38] As Madison emphasized in *The Federalist:*

> The powers delegated by the proposed Constitution to the federal government are few and defined. Those which are to remain in the State governments are numerous and indefinite. The former will be exercised principally on external objects, as war, peace, negotiation, and foreign commerce; with which the last the power of taxation will, for the most part, be connected. The powers reserved to the several States will extend to all objects which, in the ordinary course of affairs concern the lives, liberties, and properties of the people, and the internal order, improvement, and prosperity of the State.[39]

The Commerce Clause in particular had a limited and commonly understood meaning. Commerce was trade. More narrowly, it was the largely international exchange of the raw materials and manufactures necessary to the survival of the young nation. Thus, when Madison spoke of "the positive power of regulating trade and sundry other matters in which uniformity is proper,"[40] the focus was

---

[35] 317 US 111 (1942).

[36] *United States v Lopez*, 514 US 549, 600 (1995) (Thomas concurring).

[37] Id at 602.

[38] *New York v United States*, 505 US 144, 157 (1992) (characterizing certain government activities as "unimaginable to the Framers" both as to the nature of the function and its locus in the federal government).

[39] Federalist 45 (Madison) at 292–93 (cited in note 15).

[40] Letter from Madison to Jefferson, March 19, 1787, in 1 *Republic of Letters* at 469, 470 (cited in note 14). The bulk of the individual papers in The Federalist dealing with commercial issues came from the pen of Hamilton (nos. 6, 7, 11, 12, 17, 22, and 35), who viewed "commerce," quite narrowly defined, as "the most useful as well as the most productive source of national wealth." Federalist 12 (Hamilton) at 91 (cited in note 15). Madison largely deferred to Hamilton in this exposition, see Federalist 42 (Madison) at 266 ("The regulation of foreign commerce . . . has been too fully discussed to need additional proofs here of its being properly submitted to the federal administration."), a matter of some importance when assessing the essentially Hamiltonian cast of *M'Culloch* and the decisions that followed.

mainly on navigation,[41] often characterized as the "carrying trade."[42] There is nevertheless a great deal to be said for the Court's current views on matters commercial and their implications for state sovereignty. This is especially the case if we focus, as I suspect we must, not simply on what was said when the Commerce Clause was crafted and the Tenth and Eleventh Amendments ratified, but on how the members of the Founding generation implemented that Clause and understood its limitations.

The federal power to regulate commerce was, by design, "complete"[43] and, of necessity, supreme.[44] It was also, as virtually everyone at the time understood, a textual grant of authority that was imprecise in its expression and about to be invoked in radically altered circumstances. James Wilson, addressing concerns raised in the Pennsylvania Convention about the scope of the powers granted, observed:

> They have asserted that these powers are unlimited and undefined. These words are as easily pronounced as limited and defined. . . . [I]t is not pretended that the line is drawn with mathematical precision; the inaccuracy of language must, to a certain degree, prevent the accomplishment of such a desire. Whoever views the matter in a true light will see that the pow-

---

[41] See, e.g., *Gibbons v Ogden*, 9 Wheat 1, 190 (1824) ("[a]ll America understands and has uniformly understood the word commerce to comprehend navigation").

[42] For a discussion of the background and content of the policies that informed the text, see Joyce Appleby, *Capitalism and a New Social Order: The Republican Vision of the 1790s* (New York University Press, 1984); John E. Crowley, *The Privileges of Independence: Neomercantilism and the American Revolution* (Johns Hopkins University Press, 1993); Drew R. McCoy, *The Elusive Republic: Political Economy in Jeffersonian America* (University of North Carolina Press, 1980). Crowley notes, for example, that "the *Federalist Papers* made navigation the privileged sector in American commercial policy, as the precondition for economic autonomy and security in a world where the political hostility of nations shaped their economic competition." Crowley, at 123. For an argument that "the breakdown of taxation by the state governments [was] at the center of the story of the Constitution's genesis," see Ralph H. Brown, *Redeeming the Republic: Federalists, Taxation, and the Origins of the Constitution* (Johns Hopkins University Press, 1993).

[43] Charles Pinckney, *Observations of the Plan of Government Submitted to the Federal Convention*, May 28, 1787, in Max Farrand, ed, 3 *The Records of the Federal Convention of 1787*, at 106, 116 (Yale University Press, 1937 ("Farrand") ("The 7th article invests the United States, with the complete power of regulating the trade of the Union, and levying such imposts and duties . . . as shall, in the opinion of Congress, be necessary and expedient."). Pinckney's characterization is especially interesting, since it pairs the positive power to regulate with the collateral power "to make all Laws which shall be necessary and proper."

[44] See, e.g., Letter to James Monroe, Aug 7, 1785, in 8 *Madison's Papers* at 333, 333 (cited in note 21) (stating that the states "can no more exercise this power separately than they could separately carry on war, or separately form treaties of alliance and commerce").

ers are as minutely enumerated and defined as was possible, and will also discover that the general clause [Article I, section 8] . . . is nothing more than what was necessary to render effectual the particular powers that are granted.[45]

This meant, as Madison in particular subsequently emphasized, that those seeking an understanding of how each enumerated power might properly be exercised cannot simply rely on the words and understandings during debate and ratification. Indeed, Madison would stress that "[i]t ought to have occurred that the Govt. of the U.S. being a novelty & a compound, had no technical terms or phrases appropriate to it, and that old terms were to be used in new senses, explained by the context or by the facts of the case."[46] As a practical matter, it was incumbent on Congress to begin the process of assigning "new senses" to such "old terms" as the regulation of commerce by enacting measures that transformed constitutional theory into republican reality. This was not an easy task. As Madison observed early in the first session, "[a]mong other difficulties, the exposition of the Constitution is frequently a copious source, and must continue so until its meaning on all great points shall have been settled by precedents."[47] It was, however, a responsibility that Congress and nation embraced by enacting measures that did not regulate mere "selling, buying, and bartering, as well as transporting for these purposes,"[48] but were rather

---

[45] James Wilson (Dec 4, 1787), in Merrill Jensen, ed, 2 *The Documentary History of the Ratification of the Constitution* 493, 496 (State Historical Society of Wis, 1976) ("*Documentary History*"). See also Letter from the President of the Convention to the President of Congress (Sept 17, 1787), in 1 id 305, 305 ("President's Letter") ("It is at all times difficult to draw with precision the line between those rights which must be surrendered and those which may be reserved.").

[46] Letter to N. P. Trist, Dec 1831, in 9 *Madison's Writings* at 471, 475 (cited in note 14). For an insightful discussion of this problem, see Lawrence Lessig, *Understanding Changed Readings: Fidelity and Theory*, 47 Stan L Rev 395 (1995)

[47] Letter to Samuel Johnston, June 21, 1789, in 12 *Madison's Papers* at 250 (cited in note 21). See also 2 *Annals of Congress* 1962 (1789) (statement of Rep. Theodore Sedgwick) ("[T]he Constitution had expressly declared the ends of Legislation; but in almost every instance had left the means to the honest and sober discretion of the Legislature"). For a discussion of how Congress handled these issues, and the significance of what it accomplished, see David P. Currie, *The Constitution in Congress: The Federalist Period 1789–1801* (University of Chicago Press, 1997); Joseph M. Lynch, *Negotiating the Constitution: The Earliest Debates Over Original Intent* (Cornell University Press, 1999); Kent Greenfield, *Original Penumbras: Constitutional Interpretation in the First Year of Congress*, 26 Conn L Rev 79 (1993).

[48] *United States v Lopez*, 514 US 549, 585 (1995) (Thomas concurring).

constitutionally proper exercises of the enumerated power because the Congress seemed to believe that the objects of regulation had what is now referred to as a "'substantial effect' on [interstate] commerce."[49]

One of these was An Act for the Government and Regulation of Seamen in the Merchants Service,[50] which, among other things, structured numerous aspects of the day-to-day working lives of ordinary seamen. "Seamen or mariners" were obviously necessary participants in a continuum that would lead ultimately to an exchange of goods. However, it is difficult, if not impossible, to envision how Congress could require "an agreement in writing or in print, with every seaman or mariner on board" a ship "bound from a port in one state to a port in any other than an adjoining state,"[51] *unless* Congress believed the Commerce Clause authorized something more than simple regulation of "selling, buying, and bartering, as well as transporting for these purposes."[52] Indeed, two arguably essential elements of the Act posed fundamental concerns about the sanctity of state sovereignty. The first made penalties paid by delinquent seamen to ship owners "recoverable in any court, or before any justice or justices of any state, city, town or county within the United States" that had "congizance of debts of equal value."[53] The second "required" local justices of the peace to resolve controversies between owners and seamen over the seaworthiness of a vessel.[54]

---

[49] Id at 584.

[50] Act of July 20, 1790, ch 29, 1 Stat 131.

[51] Id § 1. The stricture applied only to a "ship or vessel of the burthen of fifty tons or upwards," id, much like modern requirements that trigger regulation only when an enterprise employs a specified minimum number of people or engages in a specified level of commercial activity. See, e.g., 42 USC § 2000e(b) (1994) (defining an "employer" for the purposes of Title VII of the Civil Rights Act of 1964).

[52] *Lopez*, 514 US at 585–86 (Thomas concurring) (citing 1 Samuel Johnson, *A Dictionary of the English Language* 361 (4th ed 1773)). The Act also regulated numerous matters that arguably fall outside the narrow strictures Justice Thomas proposes, including such matters as the requirement that ships bound overseas carry "a chest of medicines, put up by some apothecary of known reputation, and accompanied by directions for administering the same," § 8, 1 Stat at 134, and that there be, "well secured under deck, at least sixty gallons of water, one hundred pounds of salted flesh meat, and one hundred pounds of wholesome ship-bread" for each person aboard. Id § 9.

[53] § 2, 1 Stat at 132.

[54] § 3, 1 Stat at 132–33.

While not quite "federal regulation of the janitor of a State building,"[55] the 1790 Act is nevertheless far broader than any Justice Thomas would presumably tolerate if we take seriously the implications of his various opinions on these matters. The structuring of and strictures imposed on the relationship between employer and employee, for example, are precisely the sort of regulations that would presumably be condemned by a Court intent on enforcing a narrow view of the proper scope of the term "commerce." Indeed, speaking in ways that echo the approach taken by Justice Thomas, the Court did exactly that in *Adair v United States*[56] and *Railroad Retirement Board v Alton Railroad Company*.[57] These are, I suspect, some of the decisions Justice Thomas had in mind when he condemned "the Court's dramatic departure in the 1930's from a century and a half of precedent."[58] And, while the majority in *Printz* rejected the argument that the provisions of the 1790 Act reflected an assumption by the First Congress that it was free to "commandeer" the states,[59] it is difficult to see how that could be. The majority in *Printz* found the provisions unremarkable, believing the functions the Act imposed on state judges were not "executive" in nature, as were the tasks at issue in the case before it. It is unclear, however, why that distinction should matter if the core concern is for state sovereignty. It is one thing to provide that "[t]his Constitution, and the Laws of the United States which shall be made in Pursuance thereof . . . shall be the supreme Law of the Land,"[60] and expect state judges to enforce federal statutes in cases otherwise within their jurisdiction. It is quite another to posit that Congress may command state judges to entertain federally created causes of action. And that, of course, is precisely what the First Congress did, to no apparent dismay during the very period we are otherwise led to believe should be deemed dispositive in other interpretive instances.

---

[55] Raoul Berger, *Federalism: The Founders' Design* 130 (University of Oklahoma Press, 1987).

[56] 208 US 161, 179 (1908) (holding that because "interstate commerce" does not cover labor organizations, Congress had no power to prohibit the discharge of employees based on union membership).

[57] 295 US 330, 374 (1935) (holding that a pension plan thus imposed is in no proper sense a "regulation of the activity of interstate transportation").

[58] *Lopez*, 514 US at 599.

[59] *Printz v United States*, 521 US 898, 908 n 2 (1997).

[60] US Const, Art VI, cl 2.

The 1790 Act is then an example of the process of "liquidating and ascertaining" the meaning of the original text. That is the approach Madison described in *Federalist* 37, and it is one that the founding generation found both necessary and proper in giving meaning to a federal commerce power that was complete and supreme. The latitude afforded was not absolute. Congress could only exercise those powers specifically given, and the actions taken needed to be tied, in a meaningful way, to truly national interests.[61] For example, perhaps the most cogent and prescient contemporary criticism of *M'Culloch* was Madison's argument that the critical flaw in Marshall's reasoning was his apparent abandonment of any meaningful judicial check on Congress. The real danger, Madison believed, lay in the risk that Marshall's opinion would both encourage Congress to act precipitously and preclude effective judicial review of the resulting measures. He asked, pointedly:

> Does not the Court also relinquish by their doctrine, all controul on the Legislative exercise of unconstitutional powers? According to that doctrine, the expediency & constitutionality of means for carrying into effect a specified Power are convertible terms; and Congress are admitted to be the Judges of expediency. The Court certainly cannot be so; a question, the moment it assumes the character of mere expediency or policy, being evidently beyond the reach of Judicial cognizance.[62]

Madison himself would struggle with the practical implications of his position. His initial hostility to the creation of the Bank of the United States would, over time, yield in the face of the considered judgments of a wide variety of actors that this was constitutionally proper.[63] The important question was not, however, how Madison

---

[61] For a discussion of Lopez that makes this precise point, see Donald H. Regan, *How to Think About the Federal Commerce Power and Incidentally Rewrite United States v Lopez*, 94 Mich L Rev 554 (1995). For an argument that "the framers' expressed [a] desire that the national government in fact have a national perspective," see Mark R. Killenbeck, *A Matter of Mere Approval? The Role of the President in the Creation of Legislative History*, 48 Ark L Rev 239, 299–306 (1995).

[62] Letter to Spencer Roane, Sept 21, 1819, in 8 *Madison's Writings* at 447, 449 (cited in note 14). This is in effect a criticism of the Court's "rational basis review" doctrine, within which it seems that virtually any legislative rationale, no matter how silly, will suffice. Indeed, the reasons embraced by the Court need not even be those the legislature had in mind. I find these doctrines troubling and, to the extent they signal a move away from its sillier manifestations, believe that there is much to be said for the "robust" view of rational basis review evident in decisions like *Lopez*.

[63] See Part IV.

felt about this and many other matters in 1787, when he helped shape the text of the Constitution, or even in 1791, when the constitutionality of the First Bank was debated in Congress. It was, rather, how the question was to be viewed after full and careful examination over time by each of the many parties who quite properly had a role in liquidating and ascertaining the meaning of an inherently vague document.

There is, accordingly, a profound difference between an argument that Congress lacks certain powers because they were reserved expressly to the states,[64] and what I believe to be a more representative assessment of the founding generation's position, namely, that each specific exercise of the federal power should be assessed over time in the light of an original textual understanding leavened by the necessarily moderating influences of ultimate national objectives. In the specific context of "reserved powers," perhaps the most telling goal was a desire to curb the authority of the states, a constitutional consideration to which I now turn.

II

> I hold it for a fundamental point that an individual independence of the States, is utterly irreconcilable with the idea of an aggregate sovereignty. I think at the same time that a consolidation of the States into one simple republic is not less unattainable than it would be inexpedient. Let it be tried then whether any middle ground can be taken which will at once support a due supremacy of the national authority, and leave in force the local authorities so far as they can be subordinately useful. [Letter from James Madison to Edmund Randolph, April 8, 1787][65]

---

[64] See, e.g., *Lopez*, 115 US at 593–99 (Thomas concurring) (arguing that current Commerce Clause doctrines "contradict[] the federal balance the Framers designed and that this Court is obliged to enforce"); *Hodel v Virginia Surface Mining and Reclamation Ass'n*, 452 US 264, 307 (1981) (Rehnquist concurring) (arguing that "one of the greatest 'fictions' of our federal system is that Congress exercises only those powers delegated to it, while the remainder are reserved to the States or to the people"). Ironically, one of the most convincing arguments for a narrow originalist reading of the Commerce Clause is also one of the most compelling demonstrations that the Framers had no tolerance for state measures that interfered with or burdened commerce. See Albert S. Abel, *The Commerce Clause in the Constitutional Convention and in Contemporary Comment*, 25 Minn L Rev 432 (1941).

[65] 9 *Madison's Papers* at 369 (cited in note 21).

If current reserved powers opinions are deficient in their recognition of the need to strike a balance between means and ends, they also shortchange the extent to which the decisions made in the nation's formative years were motivated by and directed toward a pervasive desire to curtail the sovereignty of "subordinately useful" states. Obviously, the "Framers were not single-minded," and in drafting and ratifying the Constitution they were "animated by an array of intentions."[66] The truly remarkable thing about the story behind the creation of the text is not, however, the degree to which the Framers and Founders tried to preserve state " 'sovereignty concurrent with that of the Federal Government' "[67] in order to afford greater "protection of individuals."[68] It is, rather, the extent to which the transition from Articles of Confederation to Constitution was fueled by an overwhelming perception that state governments and their claims of "sovereignty" were a primary source of the problems that needed to be addressed.

The dominant concern in months prior to the Philadelphia Convention was the need to cure increasingly obvious defects in the structure created by the Articles of Confederation. The problems were legion, and the primary cause seemed clear: The Articles had fashioned a confederation, rather than a nation, a system of "government" in which an inherently weak Congress was dependent in virtually every instance on the whims of thirteen increasingly independent and "sovereign" states.[69] In theory, the national government had considerable authority. The Articles provided, for example, that "[e]very state shall abide by the determinations of the united states in congress assembled, on all questions which by this confederation are submitted to them."[70] But the requirement

---

[66] *Garcia v San Antonio Metropolitan Transit Authority*, 469 US 528, 581 (1985) (O'Connor dissenting).

[67] *Gregory v Ashcroft*, 501 US 452, 457 (1991) (quoting *Tafflin v Levitt*, 493 US 455, 458 (1990)).

[68] *New York v United States*, 505 US 144, 181 (1992).

[69] The best treatment of the period is Jack N. Rakove, *The Beginnings of National Politics: An Interpretive History of the Continental Congress* (Knopf, 1979). Other valuable discussions include Herman Belz, Ronald Hoffman, and Peter J. Albert, eds, *To Form a More Perfect Union: The Critical Ideas of the Constitution* (University Press of Virginia, 1992); Cathy D. Matson and Peter S. Onuf, *A Union of Interests: Political and Economic Thought in Revolutionary America* (University Press of Kansas, 1990); Peter S. Onuf, *The Origins of the Federal Republic: Jurisdictional Controversies in the United States 1775–1787* (University of Pennsylvania Press, 1983).

[70] Articles of Confederation, Art XIII, in 1 *Documentary History* at 86, 93 (cited in note 45).

that a given request be unanimously agreed to, coupled with the guarantee that "[e]ach state retains its sovereignty, freedom and independence,"[71] meant that the national government remained inherently weak.[72]

Numerous efforts at reform were undertaken, and various amendments, grants of power, and even the occasional truly constructive legislative measure emerged.[73] It became quite clear, however, that the corrective procedures contemplated by the Articles could not be relied on to produce the needed changes. As Monroe observed regarding the Articles Congress, "recommendations from that body are received with such suspicion by the States that their success however proper they may be is always to be doubted."[74] Something more was called for, both in form and substance. And that process of reform had its catalyst not in Philadelphia in May 1787, but rather in Annapolis in September 1786, when, at the insistence of Virginia, delegates from five states met to discuss whether federal authority over a particular national concern, commerce and trade, should be substantially strengthened.[75]

The final report that emerged from that meeting stressed that the defects in the Articles were "of a nature so serious, as, in the view of [the] Commissioners to render the situation of the United

---

[71] Articles, Art II, id at 86.

[72] For assessments of the Articles, see Merrill Jensen, *The Articles of Confederation: An Interpretation of the Social-Constitutional History of the American Revolution* 1774–1781 (University of Wisconsin Press, 1940); Jack P. Greene, *The Background of The Articles of Confederation*, 12 Publius 15 (1982); Donald S. Lutz, *The Articles of Confederation as the Background to the Federal Republic*, 12 Publius 55 (1982); Jack Rakove, *The Legacy of the Articles of Confederation*, 12 Publius 45 (1982).

[73] See generally 1 *Documentary History* at 140–74 (cited in note 45). Ironically, perhaps the most important accomplishment of the Article Congress, the Northwest Ordinance, was passed on July 13, 1787, as the Convention's deliberations were sealing the fate of the Articles. For discussions of the significance of the Ordinance, see Peter S. Onuf, *Statehood and Union: A History of the Northwest Ordinance* (Indiana University Press, 1987); Robert S. Hill, *Federalism, Republicanism, and the Northwest Ordinance*, 18 Publius 41 (1988).

[74] Letter from James Monroe to John Sullivan, Aug 16, 1786, in letter from James Monroe to the President of New Hampshire (John Sullivan), Aug 16, 1786, in 8 Edmund C. Burnett, ed, *Letters of Members of the Continental Congress*, 430, 430 (Peter Smith, 1963).

[75] See *Resolution of the Virginia Legislature, Jan 21, 1786*, in 1 *Documentary History* at 180 (cited in note 45). It is worth noting that individuals relying solely on recent opinions of the Court would have no idea that the Annapolis meeting ever took place, much less the extent to which the Framers and Founders understood that a "uniform system in their commercial regulations may be necessary to the[ ] common interests and . . . permanent harmony" of "the said States." Id.

States delicate and critical."[76] It also recognized that changes, in order to be effective, needed to be general.[77] For, as one skeptic noted even before the delegates met, "a partial reformation will be fatal; things had better remain as they are than not to probe them to the bottom."[78]

Congress "responded" to the Annapolis Report on February 21, 1787 with a call for a "convention of delegates" that would recommend "alterations" in the Articles sufficient to "render the federal constitution adequate to the exigencies of government and the preservation of the Union."[79] But that carefully couched declaration simply affirmed the inevitable: By the time Congress acted, six states had already elected and empowered delegates to act on their behalf "in May next."[80] And while each state action was predicated on the need to revisit and revise the Articles of Confederation, there was both an obvious sense of urgency and a general understanding that the approach embodied in the Articles was not likely to survive.[81] The otherwise reticent Washington wrote Madison in March 1787 and declared that it was "idle in my opinion to suppose that the Sovereign can be insensible of the inadequacy of the powers under which it acts—and that seeing, it should not recommend a revision of the Federal system, when it is considered by many as the *only* Constitutional mode by which the defects can be remedied."[82] He believed, moreover, that "a thorough reform of the present system is indispensable," especially the creation of

---

[76] *Proceedings and Report of the Commissioners at Annapolis, Maryland, 11–14 September 1786,* in 1 id at 181, 184.

[77] See, e.g., id ("the defects" have "been found greater and more numerous, than even" the acts of the states sending Commissioners "imply").

[78] Letter from William Grayson, May 28, 1786, in 9 *Madison's Papers* at 61, 64 (cited in note 21).

[79] *Resolution of the Confederation Congress,* Feb 21, 1787, in 1 *Documentary History* at 185, 187 (cited in note 45).

[80] They were New Jersey (Nov 23, 1786); Virginia (Dec 4, 1786); Pennsylvania (Dec 30, 1786); North Carolina (Jan 6, 1787); Delaware (Feb 3, 1787); and Georgia (Feb 10, 1787). Massachusetts initiated its process on February 22 and completed it March 10. The various acts and resolutions may be found in 1 id at 192–230.

[81] See, e.g., James Madison, *Notes on Debates,* Feb 21, 1787, in 9 *Madison's Papers* at 290, 291 (cited in note 21) ("It appeared from the debates & still more from the conversation among the members that [many] of them considered this resolution as a deadly blow to the existing Confederation.").

[82] Letter from George Washington, Mar 31, 1787, in 9 id at 342, 342.

a "Congress [that] will upon all proper occasions, exercise the powers with a firm and steady hand, instead of frittering them back to the Individual States where the members in place of viewing themselves in their National character, are too apt to be looking."[83]

Madison, encouraged by what Washington and others were telling him, sketched what he thought necessary in a series of letters and documents. The resulting work product was as politic as it was masterful, weaving together a compelling case for substantial inroads on state sovereignty even as Madison made appropriately empathetic statements about the value and importance of state government. In his *Vices of the Political System of the United States,* for example, Madison identified twelve specific categories of concern. Every one recounted, some more forcefully than others, problems caused by a structure that was "in fact nothing more than a treaty of amity of commerce and of alliance, between so many independent and Sovereign States."[84] Thus, while Madison would continue to cultivate the support of the same entities and actors whose conduct were a cause of concern,[85] the "middle ground" he sought was one within which the states, as states, were "subordinately useful,"[86] subject to a "national Government armed with a positive and compleat authority in all cases where uniform measures are necessary."[87]

The same themes infused his correspondence with Jefferson,

---

[83] Id at 343. For a general discussion of Washington's views, see Glenn A. Phelps, *George Washington and American Constitutionalism* (University Press of Kansas, 1993). As Phelps notes, Washington's experiences during the Revolution convinced him "that there was very little genius in federalism" and that "[t]he states . . . had demonstrated only that they could serve as breeding grounds for the tendentiousness and petty jealousies that continued to imperil the union." Id at 127.

[84] *Vices of the Political System,* April 1787, in 9 *Madison's Papers* at 348, 351 (cited in note 21).

[85] For example, in April 1787 he wrote Edmund Randolph, suggesting that "I think with you that it will be well to retain as much as possible of the old Confederation, tho' I doubt whether it may not be best to work the valuable articles into the new System, instead of engrafting the latter on the former." Letter to Edmund Randolph, April 8, 1787, in 9 id at 368, 369. Randolph had written Madison in December, agreeing that "Congress want additional powers," but indicating that "[I] can't suppress my fears of giving that of regulating commerce." Letter from Edmund Randolph, Dec 9, 1786, in id at 201, 202.

[86] Letter to Randolph, id at 369.

[87] Id at 370. He repeated this observation, virtually verbatim, in a subsequent letter to Washington, stressing that "the national Government should be armed with positive and compleat authority in all cases which require uniformity; such as the regulation of trade,

who expressed a desire "[t]o make us one nation as to foreign concerns, and keep us distinct in Domestic ones, gives the outline of the proper division of powers between the general and particular governments."[88] In his most extensive pre-Convention reply, sent before the Convention's decision to deliberate in secret sealed his lips,[89] Madison responded by listing the four principal objectives consistent with a "stable Government not infringing fundamental principles, as the only security against an opposite extreme of our present situation."[90] All were important, and all would ultimately factor into the document that would emerge. Two in particular, however, spoke directly to the paramount question of the proper role of the states: the need for "such a ratification by the people themselves of the several States as will render it clearly paramount to their Legislative authorities," and the need "to arm the federal head with a negative *in all cases whatsoever* on the local legislatures."[91]

As the Convention wound down, Madison would return to these issues. In September 1787 he wrote Jefferson and broke his substantive silence with a sketchy outline of the document that was emerging. He also felt compelled to "hazard an opinion nevertheless that the *plan should* it *be adopted* will neither effectually *answer* its *national object* nor prevent the local *mischiefs* which every where *excite disgusts* against the *state governments*."[92] That perception was not, however, rooted in any sense that the Convention had not formulated an arguably sensible approach. Rather, it reflected his deep ambivalence about the failure of the Convention to account, as forcefully as he had wished, for the corrosive influence of the states, as states.

---

including the right of taxing both exports and imports, the fixing the terms and forms of naturalization, &c &c." Letter to George Washington, April 16, 1787, in 9 id at 383, 383.

[88] Letter from Jefferson to Madison, Dec 16, 1786, in 1 *Republic of Letters* at 457, 458 (cited in note 14).

[89] See Letter from Madison to Jefferson, June 6, 1787, in 1 id at 477, 478 (completing the list of delegates and noting that "[i]n furnishing you with this list of names, I have exhausted all the means which I can make use of for gratifying your curiosity").

[90] Letter from Madison to Jefferson, March 19, 1787, in 1 id at 469, 470.

[91] Id. The third goal, "to change the principle of Representation in the federal system," id, was required in order to acknowledge the differing size and influence of the respective states. The fourth, "to organise the federal powers in such a manner as not to blend together those which ought to be exercised by separate departments," id at 471, was essential if both the powers and number of representatives were to be "enlarged."

[92] Letter from Madison to Jefferson, Sept 6, 1787, id at 490, 491.

The interplay between nation and states was summarized in Madison's justly famous October 24, 1787 letter to Jefferson. As Madison noted:

> Structurally, the federal and state conventions debated at some length the three precepts that lie at the heart of the current controversies: a general theory of allocating powers between federal and state actors; certain specific powers deemed essential for the survival of the national government; and the ultimate authority of whatever federal structure that might emerge.[93]

The "general theory of allocating powers" was, as indicated, one of a republican government neither wholly federal nor wholly national. The Constitution envisioned, rather, a "compound republic of America," within which

> the power surrendered by the people [wa]s first divided between two distinct governments, and then the portion allotted to each subdivided among distinct and separate departments. Hence a double security arises to the rights of the people. The different governments will control each other, at the same time that each will be controlled by itself.[94]

The states, as states, would remain. But the nature and scope of their residual sovereignty *as states* was fundamentally and permanently transformed by express recognition, in a national Constitution, of the people as the ultimate arbiters. The powers of the federal government were perhaps few and defined. But they were expressly declared supreme by a document to be submitted directly to and ratified by the people:

> It was generally agreed that the objects of the Union could not be secured by any system founded on the principle of a confederation of sovereign States. . . . Hence was embraced the alternative of a government which instead of operating, on the States, should operate without their intervention on the individuals composing them: and hence the change in the principle and proportion of representation.[95]

---

[93] Letter from Madison to Jefferson, Oct 24, 1787, id at 495, 495.

[94] Federalist 51 (Madison) at 323 (cited in note 15).

[95] Letter from Madison to Jefferson, Oct 24, 1787, in 1 *Republic of Letters* at 495, 496 (cited in note 14).

The governing structure that resulted, in turn, would be compound in multiple significant senses, precisely because of a need to insure proper control over state governments:

> Encroachments of the States on the general authority, sacrifices of national to local interests, interferences of the measures of different States, form a great part of the history of our political system. . . . In the American Constitution The general authority will be derived entirely from the subordinate authorities. The Senate will represent the States in their political capacity, the other House will represent the people of the States in their individual capacity. . . . This dependence of the General, on the local authorities seems effectually to guard the latter against any dangerous encroachments of the former: Whilst the latter within their respective limits, will be continually sensible of the abridgment of their power, and be stimulated by ambition to resume the surrendered portion of it.[96]

Ironically, Madison's greatest disappointment would arguably turn out to be the least problematic. In a pre-Convention letter to Jefferson he stressed:

> Over and above the positive power of regulating trade and sundry other matters in which uniformity is proper, to arm the federal head with a negative in *all cases whatsoever* on the local legislatures. Without this defensive power experience and reflection have satisfied me that however ample the federal powers may be made, or however Clearly their boundaries may be delineated, on paper, they will be easily and continually baffled by the Legislative sovereignties of the States. The effects of this provision would be not only to guard the national rights and interests against invasion, but also to restrain the States from thwarting and molesting each other, and even from oppressing the minority within themselves by paper money and other unrighteous measures which favor the interests of the majority.[97]

Jefferson rejected the idea: "Prima facie I do not like it. It fails in an essential character, that the hole and the patch should be commensurate. But this proposes to mend a small hole by covering the whole garment."[98] He assumed, arguably correctly given the understandings of the time, that only a small number of state acts would touch on national interests: "Not more than 1. out of 100.

---

[96] Id at 499.

[97] Letter from Madison to Jefferson, March 19, 1787, in 1 id at 469, 470.

[98] Letter from Jefferson to Madison, June 20, 1787, in 1 id at 480, 480.

state-acts concern the confederacy."[99] More importantly, he understood that definitional problems lurked, and speculated that the
appropriate course of correction was judicial: "Would not an appeal from the state judicatures to a federal court, in all cases where
the act of Confederation controuled the question, be as effectual
a remedy, and exactly commensurate to the defect."[100] And he an-
ticipated many of the seminal judicial controversies of the early
nineteenth century:

> A British creditor, e.g. sues for his debt in Virginia; the defen-
> dant pleads an act of the state excluding him from their courts;
> the plaintiff urges the Confederation and the treaty made un-
> der that, as controuling the state law; the judges are weak
> enough to decide according to the views of their legislature.
> An appeal to a federal court sets all to rights. It will be said
> that this court may encroach on the jurisdiction of the state
> courts. It may. But there will be a power, to wit Congress, to
> watch and restrain them. But place the same authority in Con-
> gress itself, and there will be no power above them to perform
> the same office. They will restrain within the due bounds a
> jurisdiction exercised by others much more rigorously than if
> exercised by themselves.[101]

Madison argued in response that "it is more convenient to prevent the passage of a law, than to declare it void after it is passed,"
and expressed fears about both the ability of private citizens to
pursue judicial recourse and the willingness of states to abide by
decisions against their interests.[102] These reservations were ultimately to prove misplaced. Much to Jefferson's chagrin, the Supreme Court would prove to be more than willing to both rule
against the States and to command their respect and acquiescence.[103] Indeed, the very success of the doctrine of judicial review

---

[99] Id. Given the limited scope envisioned for federal action, that estimate may have been
an accurate one. But it is clearly not appropriate in an era where expansive readings of the
Commerce and Spending Clauses make federal intrusions into matters Jefferson understood
to be state, rather than federal, the rule rather than the exception.

[100] Id at 480–81.

[101] Id at 481. One may profitably compare this passage with the views expressed in *Chisolm
v Georgia*, 2 Dall 419 (1793), the Eleventh Amendment, and, more recently, *Alden v Maine*,
119 S Ct 2240 (1999), and *Seminole Tribe of Florida v Florida*, 517 US 44 (1996).

[102] Letter from Madison to Jefferson, Oct 24, 1787, in 1 *Republic of Letters* at 495, 500
(cited in note 14).

[103] The two most obvious instances, both of which provoked strong negative reactions,
were *Martin v Hunter's Lessee*, 1 Wheat 304 (1816), and *M'Culloch v Maryland*, 4 Wheat
316 (1819).

as practiced by the Marshall Court would prove to be one of the most vexing facts of life for certain key members of the founding generation in their later years. Jefferson and his allies in particular would rail against the Court, arguing vigorously that "turn-coats and apostates"[104] were bringing the nation to "a crisis, when the first principles of the government and some of the dearest rights of the states are threatened with being utterly ground into dust and ashes."[105] But the success of the Court in "restrain[ing] within the due bounds a jurisdiction exercised by others,"[106] and in particular its affirmation of the supremacy of the national over the state governments, would ultimately prove to be the single most important element in the eventual realization of many of the objectives envisioned by those who participated in the great debates of 1787 and 1788.

The most important of these objectives was, it seems, the need to imbue the national government with powers and sovereignty sufficient to insure that it would never again be held hostage by the states. In a variety of fora and in various ways, the citizens were asked to deal with the "unequivocal experience of the inefficiency of the subsisting federal government,"[107] a "crisis" brought about by the "awful spectacle" of a "NATION, without a NATIONAL GOVERNMENT."[108] The ratification debates were therefore remarkable, not simply for the frequency and intensity with which these same citizens were apprized of the difficulties posed by excessive deference to notions of state sovereignty, but for the degree to which ratification affirmed an innovative approach that preserved the states while making the nation supreme in those matters properly entrusted to its exclusive care.

These beliefs were not universally shared, and it would be a mistake to discount the importance of the views of the group that collectively became known as the Anti-Federalists. These individuals generally supported the need for and notion of a stronger na-

---

[104] Spencer Roane, 1 *Hampden Essay*, June 11, 1819, in Gerald Gunther, *John Marshall's Defense of McCulloch v Maryland*, at 107, 113 (Stanford University Press, 1969) ("Gunther").

[105] John Taylor, *Construction Construed, and Constitutions Vindicated* ii (Sheppard & Pollard, 1820).

[106] Letter from Jefferson to Madison, June 20, 1787, in 1 *Republic of Letters* at 480, 480 (cited in note 14).

[107] Federalist 1 (Hamilton) at 33 (cited in note 15).

[108] Federalist 85 (Hamilton) at 527.

tional government. They believed, however, that the approach embraced in the text posed grave dangers to the states, as states. The Federal Farmer, for example, declared that "[o]ur object has been all along, to reform our federal system, and to strengthen our governments—to establish peace, order and justice in the community—but a new object now presents."[109] That object was the creation of "one consolidated government,"[110] crafted with "a view to collect all powers ultimately, in the United States into one entire government."[111] That, he believed, ran counter to the needs and interests of a free people, who might appropriately "consolidate the states as to certain national objects," but should "leave them severally distinct independent republics, as to internal police generally."[112] James Winthrop, writing as Agrippa, emphasized the primacy of the states as the fora within which essential local concerns would be respected, maintaining that "[t]o attempt to reduce all to one standard, is absurd in itself, and cannot be done but upon the principle of power, which debases the people, and renders them unhappy, till all dignity of character is put away."[113] And, in one of the most forceful attacks, Luther Martin alleged that the text reflected the impulses of "the favourers of monarchy, and those who wished the total abolition of State governments."[114] Martin conceded the need for a "*strong and energetic federal government.*"[115] But he believed that "the government we were forming was not in reality a *federal* but a *national* government, not founded on the principles of the *preservation*, but the *abolition* or *consolidation* of all *State governments.*"[116]

---

[109] 1 *Letter from a Federal Farmer*, Oct 8, 1787, in Herbert J. Storing, ed, 2 *The Complete Anti-Federalist* at 223, 226 (University of Chicago Press, 1981) ("Storing").

[110] Id.

[111] Id at 229–30.

[112] Id at 229.

[113] 12 *Letters of Agrippa*, Jan 11, 1788, in 4 id at 93, 93.

[114] Luther Martin, *The Genuine Information Delivered to the Legislature of State of Maryland Relative to the Proceedings of the General Convention Lately Held at Philadelphia*, in 2 id at 19, 34.

[115] Id at 40.

[116] Id at 45. For a general overview of the Anti-Federalist position, see Herbert J. Storing, *What the Anti-Federalists Were For*, in 1 id. More recent discussions include Saul Cornell, *The Other Founders: Anti-Federalism and the Dissenting Tradition in America, 1788–1828* (University of North Carolina Press, 1999), and Christopher M. Duncan, *The Anti-Federalists and Early American Political Thought* (Northern Illinois University Press, 1995).

These concerns were widely shared, and these individuals played an important role in shaping the text, the ratification dialogues, and, eventually, the drafting and ratification of what became the Tenth Amendment. Preserving state "sovereignty" was, accordingly, an operative and occasionally important founding principle. But that normative value was neither fashioned nor intended to operate in a vacuum. Indeed, as James Wilson stressed during the ratification debates in Pennsylvania, the Framers and Founders recognized that "the states, as governments, have assumed too much power to themselves, while they left little to the people."[117] Claims regarding that "first principle" must, accordingly, be assessed against the backdrop provided by a group of individuals determined to fashion a truly effective national government. We may, indeed, in many respects we must quibble about practical details of both the dialogue and the Constitution that the Framers and Founders fashioned. There is, however, no mistaking the contextual reality from which the text emerged, one that stressed the need to escape a "state of imbecility" that threatened the survival of even the states themselves.

III

> I find, from looking into the amendments proposed by the State conventions, that several are particularly anxious that it should be declared in the constitution, that the powers not therein delegated should be reserved to the several States. Perhaps words which may define this more precisely than the whole of the instrument now does, may be considered as superfluous. I admit they may be deemed unnecessary; but there can be no harm in making such a declaration. [Rep. James Madison, June 8, 1789][118]

Madison was correct. There was "no harm in the declaration" that "[t]he powers not delegated to the United States by the Constitution, nor prohibited to it by the States, are reserved to the States respectively, or to the people."[119] That was true, however, only because the individuals who crafted and ratified the Constitu-

---

[117] 2 *Documentary History* at 475 (cited in note 45).

[118] 1 *Annals of Congress* 458 (1789).

[119] US Const, Amend X.

tion understood exactly what they were doing. The formation of "a more perfect Union" required that the powers of the central government be expanded. Events and exchanges prior to the Convention made it quite clear, however, that this called for more than a simple increase in the scope of the government. It was also essential that whatever powers might be conferred be made, in a meaningful sense, superior to those reserved to state governments determined to pursue conflicting and conflicted objectives.

The necessity of a formal statement akin to what became the Tenth Amendment was evident from the moment the Convention finished its work. Indeed, the tone for the ensuing ratification debates was set by the three delegates who refused to sign the document, Edmund Randolph, George Mason, and Elbridge Gerry. Each of these individuals made it clear that the nature and extent of the shift in power, from states to nation, factored in their decision. Randolph condemned "the indefinite and dangerous power given by the Constitution to the Congress."[120] Mason "2ded. & followed Mr Randolph in animadversions on the dangerous power and structure of the Government, concluding that it would end either in monarchy, or a tyrannical aristocracy; which, he was in doubt, but one or other, he was sure."[121] Subsequently, he stressed that "[u]nder their own Construction of the general Clause at the End of the enumerated powers the Congress may . . . extend their Power as far as they think proper; so that the State Legislatures have no Security for the Powers now presumed to remain to them; or the People for their Rights."[122] And Gerry, while seemingly more circumspect in floor statements alluding to the "power[s] of Congress,"[123] would characterize the text as one within which "the several State Governments shall be so altered, as in effect to be dissolved."[124]

These concerns were echoed in every ratifying convention and

---

[120] 2 Farrand at 631 (cited in note 43).

[121] Id at 632.

[122] *Objections to the Constitution of Government formed by the Convention—(1787)*, in Storing at 11, 13 (cited in note 109).

[123] 2 Farrand at 632–33 (cited in note 43).

[124] *Hon. Mr. Gerry's objections to signing the National Constitution*, Oct 17, 1787, in 2 Storing at 6, 7 (cited in note 109).

were sufficiently pronounced that, even though ratification would eventually occur, each of the states that requested specific amendments as the "price" of ratification proposed something that expressed the tenets of what would become the Tenth Amendment. Massachusetts, for example, listed as its first condition a request "[t]hat it be explicitly declared that all Powers not expressly delegated by the aforesaid Constitution are reserved to the several States to be by them exercised."[125] Nevertheless, it does not necessarily follow that "[a]s far as the Federal Constitution is concerned, then, the States can exercise all powers that the Constitution does not [expressly] withhold from them."[126] Described variously through the years as simply a "truism"[127] or "tautology,"[128] the Tenth Amendment was in fact declaratory precisely because it captured in a single sentence the essential characteristics of a truly Compound Republic. As Justice Story noted, "[the Tenth] amendment is a mere affirmation of what, upon any just reasoning, is a necessary rule of interpreting the constitution."[129] It "does not profess, and, indeed, did not intend to confer on the states any new powers; but merely to reserve to them, what were not conceded to the government of the union."[130] The "propriety" of the Supremacy Clause, in turn, stemmed "from the very nature of the Constitution. If it was to establish a national government, that government ought, to the extent of its powers and rights, to be supreme."[131] For to do otherwise, by affording too great a respect to the "sovereignty" of the constituent parts, would render the result "a mere treaty, dependent upon the good faith of the parties,

---

[125] Amendment Proposed by the Massachusetts Convention, Feb 6, 1789, in Neil H. Cogan, ed, *The Complete Bill of Rights: The Drafts, Debates, Sources, and Origins* 674 (Oxford University Press, 1997) ("Cogan").

[126] *United States Term Limits, Inc. v Thornton*, 514 US 779, 847–48 (1995) (Thomas dissenting) (emphasis added). My focus here, quite obviously, is on the extent to which the force of this statement relies on the silent, but in this rendering, explicit, insertion of the term "expressly," a limitation the Framers and Founders deliberately left out of the Tenth Amendment.

[127] *United States v Darby*, 312 US 100, 124 (1941).

[128] *New York v United States*, 505 US 144, 157 (1992).

[129] Joseph Story, 3 *Commentaries on the Constitution of the United States* § 1900 (Hilliard, Gray & Co., 1833).

[130] 2 id § 625.

[131] 3 id § 1831.

and not a government, which is only another name for political power and supremacy."[132]

Both the states, as states, and the people to whom the task of ratification fell understood from the outset the nature and magnitude of the changes proposed. The formal letter transmitting the text to the Confederation Congress set the stage, stating "[i]t is obviously impracticable in the federal government of these States; to secure all rights of independent sovereignty to each, and yet provide for the interest and safety of all—Individuals entering into society, must give up a share of liberty to preserve the rest."[133] The powers of "the general government of the Union" were to be "fully and effectively vested" in that entity, consistent with "that which appears to us the greatest interest of every true American, the consolidation of our Union, in which is involved our prosperity, felicity, safety, perhaps our national existence."[134]

The importance of the letter cannot be underestimated, both as an expression of settled expectations and for what it made express regarding the nature and scope of "reserved" state powers. Approved unanimously by the Convention, and included with the text when it was "transmitted to the several state legislatures in order to be submitted to a convention of delegates chosen in each state by the people thereof,"[135] the letter arguably masked or glossed over significant conflicts in deliberations that would, for the time being, remain secret. But the united front on the question of state sovereignty was significant precisely because it expressed a collective bottom line: the determination to provide the new government

---

[132] Id. Throughout his career Story was a powerful and effective advocate of a strong central government. See, e.g., Gerald T. Dunne, *Justice Joseph Story and the Rise of the Supreme Court* (Simon & Schuster, 1970); James McClellan, *Joseph Story and the American Constitution: A Study in Political and Legal Thought* (University of Oklahoma Press, 1971).

[133] President's Letter at 305 (cited in note 45). The letter was signed by Washington, which presumably added to its significance, independent of the fact that he did so in his capacity as president of the Convention. For a detailed and insightful discussion of the letter and its significance, see Daniel A. Farber, *The Constitution's Forgotten Cover Letter: An Essay on the New Federalism and the Original Understanding*, 94 Mich L Rev 615 (1995).

[134] President's Letter at 305 (cited in note 45).

[135] Resolution, Sept 28, 1787, in 1 *Documentary History* at 340 (cited in note 45). One of the interesting side issues presented by this is, of course, the strict "legality" of what transpired. For a "dialogue" on the issues, compare Bruce Ackerman and Neal Katyal, *Our Unconventional Founding*, 62 U Chi L Rev 475 (1995), with Akhil Reed Amar, *The Consent of the Governed: Constitutional Amendment Outside Article V*, 94 Colum L Rev 457 (1994) and Akhil Reed Amar, *Philadelphia Revisited: Amending the Constitution Outside Article V*, 55 U Chi L Rev 1043 (1988).

with meaningful, express powers, and to do so at the acknowledged expense of the states.

This does not mean that the document forwarded to the people for their consideration answered every possible question with absolute clarity and precision. As I have already noted, those portions of the text describing the proposed division of authority were, both of necessity and by design, unclear. Indeed, the letter itself stressed that "[i]t is at all times difficult to draw with precision the line between those rights which must be surrendered, and those which may be reserved," a task made especially tenuous in this instance "by a difference among the several states as to their situation, extent, habits, and particular interests."[136] More tellingly, a necessarily imprecise initial understanding would itself be subject to interpretive change, "depend[ent] as well on situation and circumstance, as on the object to be obtained."[137] The ultimate goal, however, remained singularly evident: Individual state interests that might prove "particularly disagreeable or injurious to others" were deemed expendable in light of "our most ardent wish" to promote "the lasting welfare of that country so dear to us all, and secure her freedom and happiness."[138]

Moreover, this sense of latitude, of conferring on the national sovereign not simply necessary but sufficient power, was reinforced by the reality that the Tenth Amendment as ratified did not contain a significant qualification, the notion that the powers allocated to the United States were confined to those "expressly" enumerated. Various attempts to add this or similar limiting terms were made. Each was rejected, largely on the strength of the argument that such a limitation would prove unduly restrictive. Madison's response to an attempt by Thomas Tudor Tucker to have the amendment read "[t]he powers not expressly delegated by this constitution" was typical. Madison declared that

> because it was impossible to confine a Government to the exercise of express powers; there must necessarily be admitted powers by implication, unless the constitution descended to recount every minutiae. He remembered the word "expressly" had been moved in the convention of Virginia, by the oppo-

---

[136] President's Letter at 305 (cited in note 45).

[137] Id.

[138] Id at 306.

nents to the ratification, and, after full and fair discussion, was given up by them, and the system allowed to retain its present form.[139]

Roger Sherman agreed, stressing that "corporate bodies are supposed to possess all powers incident to a corporate capacity, without being absolutely expressed."[140]

The extent to which the Tenth Amendment was simply a "more precise definition" of an approach to sovereign relations understood and agreed to was also reinforced by the reality that the text adopted spoke not simply of the states, but of the states *and* the people. Interestingly, none of the proposed amendments suggested by the ratifying states included "the people" within their formulation of this precept,[141] and Madison's initial recommendation embraced this same form, stating that "[t]he powers not delegated by this constitution, nor prohibited by it to the states, are reserved to the states respectively."[142] All of them, however, included parallel declarations expressing the primacy of the people, and the proposed amendment that emerged from Congress and was sent to the states for ratification ultimately made clear the fundamental "sovereignty" of both the states and the people.

This is a matter of considerable significance. Obviously, there is nothing in the text, either of the Constitution proper or the Tenth Amendment, that suggests that either the nature or extent of the federal powers conferred varied depending on the entity over which sovereignty was exercised. Moreover, parallel realities at the state level made it quite clear that of the two, the people were arguably the more important. The states undeniably have a "separate and independent existence."[143] But so do the people. Indeed, under the revised system, theirs is primary, a principle state constitutions at the time of the framing made quite clear. In Virginia, for example, the fundamental text stressed that "[a]ll power is vested in, and consequently derived from, the people; . . . magis-

---

[139] 1 *Annals of Congress* 790 (Aug 18, 1789).

[140] Id. See also id at 199, where an attempt by Elbridge Gerry to add the word "expressly" was defeated.

[141] The various proposed amendments may be found in Cogan at 674–75 (cited in note 125).

[142] Id at 663.

[143] *Lane County v Oregon*, 7 Wall 71, 76 (1869).

trates are their trustees and serveants, and at all times amenable to them."[144] The people of Massachusetts expressed their relationship with the Union as one that passed directly from them to the national government, bypassing the state entirely:

> The people of this Commonwealth have the sole and exclusive right of governing themselves as a free, sovereign, and independent state; and do, and forever hereafter shall, exercise and enjoy every power, jurisdiction, and right, which is not, or may not hereafter, be by them expressly delegated to the United States of America, in Congress assembled.[145]

James Wilson, who while one of the more important Framers is seldom cited or quoted, made the same point near the beginning of his opinion in *Chisolm v Georgia:* "To the Constitution of the United States, the term SOVEREIGN, is totally unknown."[146] "A *State*," Wilson stressed, might be a "useful and valuable . . . contrivance," but it was also "the *inferior* contrivance of *man;* and from his *native* dignity derives all its *acquired* importance."[147]

This perspective is largely absent from the opinions of those Justices exploring "the benefits of this federal structure."[148] For example, Justice O'Connor's opinions evidence an extraordinary fixation on a Tenth Amendment within which the only apparent value is its affirmation of the primacy of state government. That is, she argues that there is some compelling, but largely unexplained, normative value served by elevating institutional autonomy to a preeminent role. Thus, in *New York v United States* she speaks of a division of power "among sovereigns and among branches of government" in ways that seems to treat the " 'residuary and inviolable sovereignty' " of the states as a matter beyond the reach of even the people themselves.[149] This is, however, a Bowdlerization of the Amendment, one that tends to read "the people" out of the

---

[144] Virginia Bill of Rights, in Francis Newton Thorpe, ed, 7 *The Federal and State Constitutions, Colonial Charters, and Other Organic Laws* 3812, 3813 (Government Printing Office, 1909).

[145] *Constitution or Form of Government for the Commonwealth of Massachusetts,* 1780, Part I, Art IV, in 3 id at 1888, 1890.

[146] 2 Dall 419, 454 (1793).

[147] Id at 455.

[148] *New York v United States,* 505 US 144, 157 (1992).

[149] Id at 187 and 188 (quoting Federalist 39 (Madison)).

text, or at least relegate them to what I deem an inappropriate secondary role.

More fundamentally, this reading denies, or at least burdens significantly, the ability of the people writ large to make binding pronouncements through their representatives in Congress. This is a matter of no small importance in a system in which one aspect of the compound structure, the division of Congress into a House and Senate, was clearly intended to afford one of the "auxiliary precautions" that would allow the various competing sovereigns to exercise oversight and control.[150] Admittedly, the Seventeenth Amendment altered the calculus by transferring the power to select senators from the state legislatures to the people of the states. The essence of the Great Compromise remains, however, in the equal voting power afforded each state in the Senate, one of the few provisions of the text made effectively permanent by its guarantee that no state may be denied such equal representation without its consent.[151] This tracks in certain important respects the "process" approach articulated in *Garcia*, a primary virtue of which is that it preserves the roles of the various, multiple actors in the Compound Republic.[152] Indeed, if anything, numerous recent events affirm the continuing power of individual states and senators even now to block needed reforms, an enduring legacy of a structure that may well in some instances be too solicitous of "states as states."[153]

Justice Thomas, at least in his *Term Limits* dissent, addresses one aspect of this by focusing on the people. Or at least he seems to. But his enumeration of "principles" is not so delimited. For Justice Thomas the critical "fact" is that "[t]he ultimate source of the Constitution's authority is the consent of the people of each

---

[150] See generally William H. Riker, *The Senate and American Federalism*, 49 Am Pol Sci Rev 452 (1955); Vik D. Amar, Note, *The Senate and the Constitution*, 97 Yale L J 1111 (1988).

[151] US Const, Art V.

[152] The classic statement of this approach remains Jesse H. Choper, *Judicial Review and the National Political Process: A Functional Reconsideration of the Role of the Supreme Court* (University of Chicago Press, 1980).

[153] The legislative history of the measure at issue in *New York* makes clear, for example, that many of the peculiarities of the Low-Level Radioactive Waste Policy Amendments of 1985 were the direct result of problems posed by the ability of individual states, through their senators, to flex their political muscles. It is also worth noting that the State of New York itself initially agreed with the approach taken in the federal legislation, and became a litigating party only after various political subdivisions in the state objected vehemently to its provisions.

individual State, not the consent of the undifferentiated people of the Nation as a whole."[154] This is true, but only so far as it goes. The fact that the Constitution "did not bind the people of North Carolina until they accepted it"[155] tells us nothing about the consequences that follow from ratification. After first refusing to do so, the people of North Carolina ceased "'whoring after Strange Gods,'"[156] and, in November 1789, became the twelfth state to both "adopt and ratify the said Constitution" and accept its "form of government."[157] Having done so, they became constituent members of "a more perfect Union" within which the predominant voice was that of an undifferentiated people acting together through Congress.

Madison in particular understood that in certain important instances "[i]f Congress have not the power it is annihilated for the nation."[158] He recognized that one of the primary virtues of congressional action was the ability to fashion a "uniform & practical sanction" in the face of dangers posed by competing or contradictory state regimes.[159] And he understood the importance of not

---

[154] *United States Term Limits, Inc. v Thornton,* 514 US 779, 846 (1995) (Thomas dissenting). This is not a new thought:

> So far from the Constitution being the work of the American people collectively, no such political body, either now or ever, did exist. In that character the people of this country never performed a single political act—nor indeed can, without an entire revolution in all our political relations.

Letter to James Hamilton, Jr., Aug 28, 1832, in Clyde N. Wilson, ed 11 *The Papers of John C. Calhoun* at 613, 615 (University of South Carolina Press, 1978). Similar statements are found throughout the works of the main apologists for the Confederacy. See, e.g., Jefferson Davis, 1 *The Rise and Fall of the Confederate Government* 103 (D. Appleton, 1881) (stating that the Constitution "was never submitted to 'the people of the United States in the aggregate,' or *as a people*" and asserting that "no such political community of the people of the United States in the aggregate exists this day or ever did exist"); Alexander H. Stephens, 1 *Constitutional View of the Late War Between the States* 125 (National Publishing Co., 1868) ("it is a Government instituted *by* States and *for* States").

[155] *Term Limits,* 514 US at 846 (Thomas dissenting).

[156] Letter from Jeremiah Hill to George Thatcher, Aug 29, 1788, quoted in Robert A. Rutland, *The Ordeal of the Constitution* 281 (University of Oklahoma Press, 1966).

[157] *Ratification Instrument of the State of North Carolina,* Aug 1, 1778, in Charles C. Tansill, ed, *Documents Illustrative of the Formation of the Union of the American States* 1044, 1051 (Library of Congress, 1927). For an account of North Carolina's struggle, see Michael Lienesch, *North Carolina: Preserving Rights,* in Michael Allen Gillespie and Michael Lienesch, eds, *Ratifying the Constitution* 343 (University Press of Kansas, 1989).

[158] Letter to Joseph C. Cabell, Sept 18, 1828, in 9 *Madison's Writings* at 316, 330 (cited in note 14).

[159] Id at 332–33. See also id at 334–35 (position consistent with the holding in *Brown v Maryland,* 12 Wheat 419 (1827)).

elevating an abstract principle, even one as important as state sovereignty, in ways that contravened the very purposes for which the Constitution was fashioned. Speaking expressly of the taxing power, for example, Madison addressed the need for a fundamental balance between principles and objectives when he observed that "[t]o refer a State therefore to the exercise of a power reserved to her by the Constitution, the impossibility of exercising which was an inducement to adopt the Constitution is, of all remedial devices the last that ought to be brought forward."[160] And in his *Notes on Nullification*, he indicated that he did not view matters of the sort raised in *New York* as ones fit for determination by a single state:

> There cannot be different laws in different states on subjects within the compact without subverting its fundamental principles, and rendering it as abortive in practice as it would be incongruous in theory. A concurrence & co-operation of the States in favor of each, would have the effect of preserving the necessary uniformity in all, which the Constitution so carefully & so specifically provided for in cases where the rule might be in most danger of being violated.[161]

Madison recognized that treating matters of this sort as grist for the legislative mill of all parties to the federal compact might leave individual states vulnerable within a national political process. But he stressed that the states were hardly helpless:

> However deficient a remedial right in a *single State* might be to preserve the Constn. against usurped power an ultimate and adequate remedy wd. always exist in the rights of the *parties* to the Constn. in whose hands the Const. is at all times but clay in the hands of the potter, and who could apply a remedy by explaing. amendg., or remakg. it, as the one or the other mode might be the most proper remedy.[162]

Indeed, he recognized that this process was one within which the focal point remained with the states and people:

---

[160] Id at 336. See also id at 337 (quoting Virginia resolutions stressing "'*uniformity* in their commercial regulations as the *only* effectual policy'").

[161] James Madison, *Nullification* at 577 (cited in note 28). Madison's argument here anticipates in important respects the Court's holding in *Cooley v Board of Wardens of the Port of Philadelphia*, 12 How 299 (1851), and the "dormant" Commerce Clause rulings that would emerge in the 1930s and 1940s.

[162] *Nullification* at 583.

If, at this time, the powers of the Genl. Govt. be carried to unconstitutional lengths, it will be the result of a majority of the States & of the people, actuated by some impetuous feeling, or some real or supposed interest, overruling the minority, and not of successful attempts by the Genl. Govt. to overpower both.[163]

Madison's focus on "fundamental principles" tracks closely the "first principles" rhetoric of the New Federalism opinions, with one important exception: his emphasis on a national bottom line in those instances in which the states did not in fact offer their "concurrence & co-operation." Madison was alert to the danger of the "General Govt." undertaking "subversive encroachments on the rights & authorities of the States."[164] But he also understood that the states themselves posed problems,[165] and observed "[n]or do I think that Congress, even seconded by the Judicial Power, can, without some change in the character of the nation, succeed in *durable* violations of the rights & authorities of the States."[166]

IV

[F]rom a conviction . . . that a National Bank is an institution of primary importance to the prosperous administration of the finances, and would be of the greatest utility in the operations connected with the support of the public credit, [my] attention has been drawn to devising the plan of such an institution, upon a scale which will entitle it to the confidence, and be likely to render it equal to the exigencies of the public. [Alexander Hamilton, *Report on a National Bank*, December 13, 1790][167]

---

[163] Letter to John G. Jackson, Dec 21, 1821, in 9 *Madison's Writings* at 70, 76 (cited in note 14).

[164] Letter to Spencer Roane, May 6, 1821, in 9 id at 55, 56–57.

[165] See id at 57–58, where he states

encroachments of the [National Legislature] are more to be apprehended from impulses given to it by a majority of the States seduced by expected advantages, than from the love of Power in the Body itself, controuled as it is *now* by its responsibility to the Constituent Body.

[166] Id at 58.

[167] 2 *Annals of Congress* 2082, 2082 (1790). Two early compilations are especially useful in dealing with the bank, and contain virtually all of the original source material. See M. St. Claire Clarke and D. A. Hall, eds, *Legislative and Documentary History of the Bank of the United States, Including the Original Bank of North America* (Gales & Seaton, 1832); R. K. Moulton, *Legislative and Documentary History of the Banks of the United States, from the Time of Establishing the Bank of North America, 1781, to October 1834* (G. & C. Carvill & Co., 1834). The Clark and Hall volume was reprinted in 1967 and is widely available.

Hamilton's belief that his proposal would "entitle it to the confidence . . . of the public" was, arguably, not misplaced. It certainly comported with his own expansive reading of the Constitution, and with his conviction that it was the duty of those to whom he submitted the *Report* "to do good to mankind,"[168] at least as Hamilton would define that good. The proposal to establish a bank would, nevertheless, quickly become one of the most important and controversial of the many issues that arose in the early years of the Republic.

Hamilton's *Report* did not express any concern about the constitutional issues that would soon threaten to engulf his proposals. His extensive discussion and justifications were directed at objections to banks per se, not to the constitutionality of the bank itself, an issue to which he never alluded. This is hardly surprising given Hamilton's expansive reading of the text, which, given his predominant role in describing the commercial dimensions of the document in *The Federalist*, he presumably believed was entitled to respect. It seems, nevertheless, at least curious that an advocate as accomplished and insightful as Hamilton would advance a proposal with no mention of what would ultimately become its most important feature.

Initially referred to a committee on December 23, 1790, a bill adopting Hamilton's recommendations was reported to the full Senate on January 3, 1791,[169] taken up on January 10, and ultimately approved on January 20. Since the Senate met in secret until 1794, accounts of its debates are necessarily sketchy. There is, nevertheless, little evidence that anyone in the Senate thought that this otherwise quite controversial measure was unconstitutional. In his diary entries for the period, for example, William

---

[168] 3 *Publius Letters*, in Harold C. Syrett and Jacob E. Cooke, eds, 1 *The Papers of Alexander Hamilton* at 580, 581 (Columbia University Press, 1961) ("*Hamilton's Papers*"). Specifically, he argued that a legislator should be "[a] man of virtue and ability" who would "esteem it not more the duty, than the privilege and ornament of his office, to do good to mankind" and "look down with contempt upon every mean or interested pursuit." Id. For a discussion of Hamilton's ideas and ideals, see Gerald Stourzh, *Alexander Hamilton and the Idea of Republican Government* (Stanford University Press, 1970).

[169] This timeline tells us one of two things: Either the work ethic was more pronounced, or the task was performed in a cursory manner. It is worth noting that the five were Caleb Strong of Massachusetts, Robert Morris of Pennsylvania, Philip Schyler of New York, Pierce Butler of South Carolina, and Oliver Ellsworth of Connecticut, 2 *Annals of Congress* 1782 (1990), and that of the five, all but Schyler, who was Hamilton's father-in-law, had served in Philadelphia.

Maclay refers to the bank debates several times, but never once mentions questions about the constitutionality of the measure.[170] Indeed, his entry on the day the measure was introduced stated simply: "This day the Bank bill reported, It is totally in Vain to oppose this bill. the only Useful part I can Act is to try to make it of some Benefit to the public, which reaps none from the existing Banks."[171]

The Senate, then, which arguably represented the interests of the State, found little to object to in the Bank Bill. That was not, however, the case in the "people's" House, where the question of constitutionality came to the fore almost immediately. Formal debate commenced on February 1, and several speakers mentioned constitutional concerns.[172] The most extensive and important discussion arose the next day, when Madison took the floor to explain why, after discussing the merits of the bill, he felt compelled to "deny Congress the authority to pass it."[173]

Madison's initial reservation arose from a matter on which he presumed to speak with considerable authority, the argument that the government lacked the power to grant charters of incorporation. During the Convention Madison moved that a motion by Franklin to amend the "post roads" clause also include "a power to provide for cutting canals where deemed necessary."[174] Responding, Madison had

> suggested an enlargement of the motion into a power "to grant charters of incorporation where the interest of the U.S. might require & the legislative provisions of individual States may be incompetent." His primary object was however to secure an

---

[170] See Kenneth R. Bowling and Helen E. Veit, eds, *The Diary of William Maclay and Other Notes on Senate Debates (March 4, 1789–March 3, 1791)* at 359–66 (Johns Hopkins University Press, 1988).

[171] Id at 355.

[172] See, e.g., 2 *Annals of Congress* 1891 (1791) (James Jackson (Ga.), "urg[ing] the unconstitutionality of the plan" and "call[ing] it a monopoly" that "contravenes the spirit of the Constitution"); id at 1892 (John Laurence (N.Y.) arguing that the measure was constitutional); id at 1893 (Hugh Williamson (N.C.), "explain[ing] the clause respecting monopolies as referring altogether to commercial monopolies").

[173] Id at 1896. Madison's remarks may also be found in 13 *Madison's Papers* at 372–88 (cited in note 21).

[174] 2 Farrand at 615 (cited in note 43) (Franklin motion to amend Art I, § 8, cl 7). Franklin's belief that such an amendment was necessary foretells much of the debate about the constitutionality of federal programs of internal improvement, which I discuss in Part V of this article.

easy communication between the States which the free intercourse now to be opened, seemed to call for – The political
obstacles being removed, a removal of the natural ones as far
as possible ought to follow.[175]

Franklin's motion was so modified but ultimately failed, gaining
the support of only three states: Pennsylvania, Georgia, and (ironically, as subsequent events would establish) Virginia. The accounts
of this debate are sketchy. But, significantly, one factor in the negative decision was apparently the very issue Hamilton now
broached, the spectre of "establishment of a Bank."[176]

That history reinforced the first, obvious step in Madison's analysis: There was no express power to incorporate, much less incorporate a bank.[177] He then examined in detail those clauses that
might support an inference that Congress had the power. He
found in the measure before Congress no indication that the bank
would either tax or borrow money, at least as those terms could
properly be understood. This left the Necessary and Proper
Clause, which Madison declared "must, according to the natural
and obvious force of the terms and the context, be limited to
means *necessary* to the *end*, and *incident* to the *nature*, of the specified powers."[178] He averred that the establishment of a bank would
not be "direct and incidental," but instead simply "conducive to
the successful conducting of the finances."[179] This went too far:
"If implications, thus remote and thus multiplied, can be linked
together, a chain may be formed that will reach every object of
legislation, every object within the whole compass of political
economy."[180] Both the terms of the Constitution and the realities

---

[175] 2 id at 615.

[176] See 2 id at 616, where Rufus King of Massachusetts observed that "[t]he states will
be prejudiced and divided into parties by it–In Philada. & New York, It will be referred
to the establishment of a Bank, which has been a subject of contention in those Cities."
Jefferson's diary contained a similar observation. See Paul Leicester Ford, ed, 1 *The Works
of Thomas Jefferson* 278, 278 (G. P. Putnam's Sons, 1904) (recounting a conversation between Abraham Baldwin and James Wilson regarding the corporate power and noting that
banks in particular had been a politically divisive issue).

[177] 2 *Annals of Congress* at 1896.

[178] Id at 1898. The italicized words are as they appear in the version printed in *Madison's
Papers*. See 13 *Madison's Papers* at 372, 376 (cited in note 21).

[179] 2 *Annals of Congress* at 1898.

[180] Id at 1899. This is, of course, the situation we arguably now find ourselves in, given
the Court's expansive reading of the Commerce Clause and spending power.

attendant to its ratification counseled against this course, which implicated the promise "that the powers not given were retained" and violated the "fundamental principle that the terms necessary and proper gave no additional powers to those enumerated."[181]

The bill passed, and while there are compelling reasons to believe that the debate on, and disposition of, the bank bill was influenced as much by personal and regional concerns as it was by considered judgment about the constitutional propriety of the measure,[182] there is little doubt that all parties eventually took the constitutional question quite seriously. This certainly seems to have been true of President Washington, who, while arguably not immune to the political machinations that lurked in the background,[183] requested formal opinions on its constitutionality from his attorney general, Edmund Randolph, and from his secretary of state, Jefferson.[184]

Randolph, like Madison, began with the "obvious," that "the power of creating corporations is not *expressly* given to Congress."[185] He then explained at some length why a power by implication must be rejected, tying his analysis to both an examination of those powers actually conferred and to the "real difference between the rule of interpretation, applied to a law & a constitution."[186] A constitution, he maintained, is "simply a summary of matter" and "is therefore to be construed with a discreet liberality," while laws are the "detail," to be examined "with a closer adherence to the literal meaning."[187] He found it necessary, never-

---

[181] Id at 1901. Madison spoke again on February 8, but that statement added little to this analysis. See id at 1956–60. It was the final significant speech in the debate, for when Gerry "rose to reply . . . the House discovering an impatience to have the main question put, after a few remarks, he waived any further observations." Id at 1960.

[182] The final votes in both houses followed predictable regional and political lines, and various irregularities were either open or just beneath the surface. See generally Bray Hammond, *Banks and Politics in America from the Revolution to the Civil War* (Princeton University Press, 1957) ("Hammond").

[183] For example, it is likely that his preferences in the divisive debate about the location of the national capitol factored into the equation. See Kenneth R. Bowling, *The Bank Bill, the Capital City and President Washington*, 1 Cap Studies 59 (1972).

[184] All of the opinions are printed in Clarke and Hall (cited in note 167). I will, however, use more commonly available sources.

[185] Edmund Randolph, Opinion (Feb 12, 1791), in Walter Dellinger and H. Jefferson Powell, *The Constitutionality of the Bank Bill: The Attorney General's First Constitutional Law Opinions*, 44 Duke L J 110, 122 (1994).

[186] Id at 123.

[187] Id.

theless, to read the enumerated powers according to "common sense and common language,"[188] and rejected an expansive reading of those powers as one likely to "stretch the arm of Congress into the whole circle of state legislation."[189] "The phrase, 'and proper,'" he concluded, could not be read that way, for "if it has any meaning, [it] does not enlarge the powers of Congress, but restricts them."[190]

Jefferson weighed in three days later. Consistent with his views on the question of state sovereignty, he began with a discussion of the reserved powers question:

> I consider the foundation of the Constitution as laid on this ground that "all powers not delegated to the U.S. by the Constitution, not prohibited by it to the states, are reserved to the states or to the people" [XIIth. Amendment]. To take a single step beyond the boundaries thus specifically drawn around the powers of Congress, is to take possession of a boundless field of power, no longer susceptible of any definition.[191]

He then examined each of the various powers that had been expressly conferred on the national government that might support such an action, and found them wanting. His attack on the invocation of the "necessary and proper clause" was especially sharp, turning on his sense that there was a profound difference between "the means which are 'necessary'" and "those which are merely 'convenient' for effecting the enumerated powers."[192] Drawing on his pronounced belief that the proposed measure would invade areas reserved to the states, Jefferson argued that it was essential to limit drastically exercises of implied federal powers: "Nothing but a necessity invincible by any other means, can justify such a pros-

---

[188] Id at 124.

[189] Id at 126.

[190] Id at 127.

[191] Thomas Jefferson, *Opinion on the Constitutionality of the Bill for establishing a National Bank*, Feb 15, 1791, in Julian P. Boyd and Ruth W. Lester, eds, 19 *The Papers of Thomas Jefferson* at 275, 276 (Princeton University Press, 1974) ("*Jefferson's Papers*" and "*Opinion*"). Jefferson apparently enclosed a copy of Madison's remarks on the floor of the House with his opinion. See id at 280 (note on the manuscript). His reference to what we now know as the Tenth Amendment (a "XIIth Amendment") reflects the reality that Congress had in fact sent twelve amendments to the states for their consideration, one of which has never been ratified and one of which became the Twenty-Seventh Amendment two hundred years later.

[192] Id at 278.

tration of laws which constitute the pillars of our whole system of jurisprudence."[193]

Washington then turned to Hamilton.[194] In his lengthy response, Hamilton examined in detail each of the arguments against the constitutionality of a bank, maintaining at the outset "that principles of construction like those espoused by the Secretary of State and the Attorney General would be fatal to the just & indispensable authority of the United States."[195] The linchpin in his argument was his expansive reading of the nature of sovereign powers, an interpretive gloss that not coincidentally echoed in important respects the arguments raised by Madison and others when debating the Tenth Amendment. Hamilton argued that a

> general principle is inherent in the very definition of Government and essential to every step of the progress to be made by that of the United States; namely—that every power vested in a Government is in its nature sovereign, and includes by force of the term, a right to employ all the means requisite, and fairly applicable to the attainment of the ends of such power; and which are not precluded by restrictions & exceptions specified in the constitution; or not immoral, or not contrary to the essential ends of political society.[196]

For Hamilton, a bank had "a natural relation to . . . the acknowledged objects [and] lawful ends of the government."[197] And Jefferson's limited take on how the term "necessary" should be defined was inappropriate, since both "the grammatical" and "the popular sense" of the term supported the construction that a given act needed simply to be that "which the interests of the government or person require, or will be promoted, by the doing of this or that thing."[198] The determinative constitutional criterion thus became

---

[193] Id at 279.

[194] Letter from George Washington, Feb 16, 1791, 8 *Hamilton's Papers* at 50, 50 (cited in note 168).

[195] Alexander Hamilton, *Final Version of an Opinion on the Constitutionality of an Act to Establish a Bank*, Feb 23, 1791, in 8 id at 97, 97 ("*Final Version*").

[196] Id at 98. Hamilton's reference to matters "immoral" is interesting. As Professor Rakove has noted, a sense of moral outrage may well have colored Madison's reaction to the bank bill. See Jack N. Rakove, *James Madison and the Creation of the American Republic* 94–95 (Harper Collins, 1990) (noting Madison's "disgust" with "fevered speculation in public securities and bank notes").

[197] *Final Version* at 100 (cited in note 195).

[198] Id at 102.

the *end* to which the measure relates as a *mean*. If the end be clearly comprehended within any of the specified powers, & if the measure have an obvious relation to that end, and is not forbidden by any particular provision of the constitution—it may safely be deemed to come within the compass of the national government.[199]

These views prevailed. Washington signed the bill,[200] and twenty-eight years later the Court would affirm the constitutionality of the institution in a magisterial opinion by Chief Justice Marshall that reads, in large measure, as a simple restatement of Hamilton's position. It is worth noting, of course, that acceptance of the notion that Congress had the power to establish a bank was gradual and grudging. The bank's initial charter, for example, expired in 1811 after a new round of debate during which many of the same arguments against the constitutionality of the institution were broached.[201] The Second Bank, in turn, came into being only after renewed debate, and would itself eventually fall victim to the objections of President Andrew Jackson, who argued vehemently that "some of the powers and privileges possessed by the existing bank are unauthorized by the Constitution, subversive of the rights of the States, and dangerous to the liberties of the people."[202]

Madison's role and views during this protracted process are especially interesting. As president, it was Madison who vetoed the first serious attempt at renewal. In his veto message, however, he

---

[199] Id at 107. Ironically, Hamilton's invocation of the "means/ends" calculus tracked closely an earlier declaration by Madison that "[n]o axiom is more clearly established in law, or in reason, than whenever the end is required, the means are authorized; whenever a general power to do a thing is given, every particular power necessary for doing it is included." Federalist 44 (Madison) at 585 (cited in note 15).

[200] There were no "signing statements" then, and my research to date does not show how Washington felt about the constitutional issue. Given his views on the veto power, it is entirely possible that any inclination he might have had to heed Jefferson's invitation to veto the bill, *Opinion* at 279–80 (cited in note 191), was undermined by Jefferson's own admonition that "if the pro and con hang so even as to balance his judgment, a just respect for the wisdom of the legislature would naturally decide the balance in favor of their opinion." Id at 280.

[201] See generally Hammond at 209–26 (cited in note 182). Hammond notes that Clarke and Hall reprinted thirty-nine speeches on the charter renewal, thirty-five of which mentioned constitutional questions. Id at 214. He then observes, "[i]t is entirely credible that some of the speakers were sincerely concerned about constitutionality, but one feels some skepticism when arguments that had been made by James Madison . . . were now offered with great earnestness" by certain individuals in circumstances where political and economic considerations seemed to be the dominant concerns. Id.

[202] *Veto Message*, July 10, 1832, in 2 Richardson at 576, 576 (cited in note 14).

confined his observations on the issue of constitutionality of a bank to a single, terse passage, in which he

> [w]aiv[ed] the question of the constitutional authority of the Legislature to establish an incorporated bank as being precluded in my judgment by repeated recognitions under varied circumstances of the validity of such an institution in acts of the legislative, executive, and judicial branches of the Government, accompanied by indications, in different modes, of a concurrence of the general will of the nation.[203]

Madison would eventually concede the apparent inconsistency between his position in 1791 and the one he embraced as president.[204] His views were, however, more nuanced than his critics alleged. He adhered to his original view that, in his estimation, Congress did not have the authority to create a bank. But that was, as a constitutional matter, secondary, as there was "an evidence of the Public Judgment necessarily superseding individual opinions."[205] This was not a new position, conjured up by an elder statesman looking back on his career and attempting to justify his actions. In his May 1821 letter to Spencer Roane, Madison had observed:

> In resorting to legal precedents as sanctions to power, the distinctions should ever be strictly attended to, between such as take place under transitory impressions, or without full examination & deliberation, and such as pass with solemnities and repetitions sufficient to imply a concurrence of the judgement & the will of those, who having granted the power, have the ultimate right to explain the grant.[206]

---

[203] *Veto Message*, Jan 30, 1815, in 8 *Madison's Writings* at 327, 327 (cited in note 14). For a discussion of the process and events, see Hammond at 227–33 (cited in note 182). Hammond notes that Madison's "objections were wholly practical," id at 232, and that "[t]he question of constitutionality, which had so much sincere prominence in 1791 and so much insincere prominence in 1811, had none at all in these debates of 1814, 1815, and 1816." Id at 233.

[204] Letter to N. P. Trist, Dec 1831, in 9 *Madison's Writings* at 471, 471 (cited in note 14).

[205] Id at 477. It is worth noting that Madison's actual grounds for the veto were a gap between the professed intentions and the actual mechanics.

[206] Letter to Spencer Roane, May 6, 1821, in 9 id at 55, 61. See also id at 62 ("A liberal & steady course of practice can alone reconcile the several provisions of the Constitution literally at variance with each other."). Madison insisted, however, that this process required broad participation. In the sentences immediately following, he stressed that purely "Legislative precedents are frequently of a character entitled to little respect, and that those of Congress are sometimes liable to peculiar distrust." Id.

There are striking parallels between this position and the one taken by Marshall in *M'Culloch*. Most proponents of an expansive reading of the text draw primary support from Marshall's axiom that "[i]n considering this question . . . we must never forget, that it is *a constitution* we are expounding."[207] The sentence is clearly critical to the opinion. It falls at the end of the paragraph in which Marshall stressed the refusal of the individuals who framed the Tenth Amendment to include the limiting term "expressly," and emphasized that the enumerated powers sections of the text simply provided a "great outline" within which "important objects [were] designated" while "the minor ingredients which compose those objects" remained to "be deduced from the nature of the objects themselves."[208] Marshall would subsequently indicate, however, that this interpretive gloss needed to be read with care.

Speaking as "A Friend of the Constitution," Marshall emphasized that the interpretive powers vested in the Court did not give that body "a right to change that instrument."[209] That did not signal, however, any sense that Marshall believed the text had a definite, fixed meaning at the point of ratification. Echoing Madison's precise argument, Marshall had stressed at the outset of his opinion that whether

> Congress [has the] power to incorporate a bank . . . can scarcely be considered as an open question, entirely unprejudiced by the former proceedings of the nation respecting it. The principle now contested was introduced at a very early period of our history, has been recognized by many successive legislatures, and has been acted upon by the judicial department, in cases of peculiar delicacy, as a law of undoubted obligation.[210]

In a clear reference to the debates between Madison, Jefferson, Randolph, and Hamilton, Marshall stressed that the measure creating the First Bank was "resisted, first in the fair and open field of debate, and afterwards in the executive cabinet, with as much persevering talent as any measure has ever experienced, and being

---

[207] *M'Culloch v Maryland*, 4 Wheat 316, 407 (1819).

[208] Id.

[209] John Marshall, 8 *A Friend of the Constitution* (July 15, 1819), in Gunther at 200, 209 (cited in note 104).

[210] *M'Culloch*, 4 Wheat at 401.

supported by minds as pure and intelligent as this country can boast, it became a law."[211]

This reading of *M'Culloch* does not do violence to the great lesson of *Marbury*, that "[i]t is emphatically the province and duty of the judicial department to say what the law is."[212] Rather, it suggests that both Marshall and Madison understood the role that each branch and the people play in the dynamic process of ascribing meaning to a necessarily imprecise document. In particular, it supports Madison's considered judgment that he should respect a course of interpretation and conduct, acceded to over time by individuals in a unique position to determine what the text should mean. Accordingly, the language and holding of *M'Culloch* seem to be precisely, and unmistakably, an exercise in "liquidating and ascertaining" a reading of the Constitution within which an initial textual grant gained substantive meaning only over time, one that Madison would characterize as "pass[ed] with solemnities and repetitions sufficient to imply a concurrence of the judgment & the will of those, who having granted the power, have the ultimate right to explain the grant."[213]

V

> A general power over internal improvement, if it be exercised by the Union, would certainly be cumbersome to the government, and of no utility to the people. But, to the extent you recommend it, it would be productive of no mischief, and of great good. I despair, however of the adoption of such a measure. [Letter from John Marshall to James Monroe, June 13, 1822][214]

A second, equally controversial matter during the early years of the Republic was the question of whether the federal government could engage in a systematic program of "internal improvement," principally the construction of roads, canals, and other public works projects that would facilitate the development of a rapidly

---

[211] Id at 404.

[212] *Marbury v Madison*, 1 Cranch 137, 177 (1803).

[213] Letter to Spencer Roane, May 6, 1821, in 9 *Madison's Papers* at 55, 61 (cited in note 21).

[214] Monroe Papers, Library of Congress, quoted in Noble E. Cunningham, *The Presidency of James Monroe* 166 (University Press of Kansas, 1996).

changing nation.[215] There was, understandably, virtually no serious opposition to such projects. As the Court itself would subsequently observe, "[t]he spirit of internal improvement pervades the whole country. There is perhaps no state in the Union, where important public works, such as turnpike roads, canals, rail roads, bridges, & c. are not either contemplated, or in a state of rapid progression."[216] And there was wide understanding that if undertaken, internal improvement projects were best left to government. For, as Jefferson explained with regard to a proposal to build a particular canal in Virginia, it was "much better that these [works] should be done at public than private expence."[217]

What did provoke dispute was the level of government at which the projects should be undertaken, for such matters posed in a much more direct manner than did the bank compelling questions about federal intrusions into traditionally local concerns.[218] Indeed, disputes about the constitutional propriety of such measures surfaced regularly, and the arguments against the exercise of federal powers seemed compelling. No enumerated power, with the possible exception of the power to establish post roads,[219] seemed to contemplate the sort of activities that fell within the general ambit

---

[215] For an especially valuable discussion, albeit one that traces later developments, see Charles Sellers, *The Market Revolution: Jacksonian America 1815–1846* (Oxford University Press, 1991). See also Carter Goodrich, *Government Promotion of American Canals and Railroads 1800–1890* (Columbia University Press, 1960); Louis Hartz, *Economic Policy and Democratic Thought: Pennsylvania, 1776–1860* (Harvard University Press, 1948); Curtis P. Nettles, *The Emergence of a National Economy 1775–1815* (Holt Rinehart & Winston, 1962); George Rogers Taylor, *The Transportation Revolution 1815–1860* (Holt Rinehart & Winston, 1951).

[216] *Proprietors of the Charles River Bridge v Proprietors of the Warren Bridge*, 11 Pet 420, 583 (1837).

[217] Letter to George Washington, May 10, 1789, in 15 *Jefferson's Papers* at 117, 117 (cited in note 191).

[218] For a general discussion of the history and issues, see especially two articles by Harry N. Scheiber: *The Transportation Revolution and American Law: Constitutionalism and Public Policy*, in *Transportation and the Early Nation* (Indiana Historical Society, 1982) ("*Transportation*"), and *Federalism and the American Economic Order, 1789–1910*, 10 Law & Soc'y Rev 57 (1975). Other valuable discussions include Douglas E. Clanin, *Internal Improvements in National Politics, 1816–1830*, in *Transportation*; Joseph H. Harrison, Jr., *Sic Et Non: Thomas Jefferson and Internal Improvement*, 7 J Early Repub 335 (1987); John Lauritz Larson, *"Bind the Republic Together": The National Union and the Struggle for a System of Internal Improvements*, 74 J Am Hist 363 (1987); E. C. Nelson, *Presidential Influence on the Policy of Internal Improvements*, 4 Iowa J Hist & Pol 3 (1906).

[219] US Const, Art I, § 8, cl 7. Even this power was subject to debate. Jefferson, for example, maintained that it was limited to the simple designation of preexisting roads as post roads. Letter to James Madison, Mar 6, 1796, in 8 *Jefferson's Works* at 223, 227 (cited in note 24).

of internal improvement. More tellingly, by their very nature such projects entailed substantial intrusions on matters traditionally reserved to the states and localities. If built and maintained by the federal government, a road or canal would of necessity involve a physical entry into and control over state property. And while simply funding such projects might cure some of the problems associated with this, fears of indirect federal control and of federal interference with the state's right to control its internal "police" counseled against such actions.[220]

As I have already noted, however, political and public support for a federal system was intense, a reality that would have profound implications for those who engaged in the constitutional debate. Jefferson, for example, conceded the appeal and value of such projects in his *Sixth Annual Message*, characterizing the application of an emerging public revenue surplus to "the great purposes of the public education, roads, rivers, canals, and other such objects of public improvement" as a "patriotic" objective.[221] Indeed, it was an appropriate national goal precisely because "[b]y these operations new channels of communication will be opened between the States, the lines of separation will disappear, their interests will be identified, and their union cemented by new and indissoluble ties."[222] Such measures would become appropriate in his estimation, however, only if "it may be thought proper to add to the constitutional enumeration of Federal powers."[223]

Madison tended to agree, although his opposition was not as pronounced. In 1796, for example, Madison would propose a survey for the construction of a national post road from Maine to Georgia, an action for which Jefferson would chide him. But that criticism was not couched in terms of constitutionality per se, although that consideration was present. Rather, Jefferson feared that such measures would become "a source of boundless patron-

---

[220] See, e.g., 7 *Essays of Brutus*, Jan 3, 1788, in 2 Storing at 400 (cited in note 109), where the author discusses at length his belief that under the Constitution "every source of revenue is under the controul of the Congress" and advances his "[o]wn opinion . . . that the objects from which the general government should have authority to raise a revenue, should be of such nature, that the tax should be raised by simple laws, with few officers, with certainty and expedition, and with the least interference with the internal police of the states." Id at 400 and 404.

[221] 1 Richardson at 405, 409 (cited in note 14).

[222] Id.

[223] Id. Similar strains were evident in his Second Inaugural Address. See id at 379.

age to the executive, jobbing to members of Congress and their friends, and a bottomless abyss of public money."[224] This struck a responsive chord in the mind of an individual who premised much of his original constitutional vision on the need to curb the pernicious influence of "faction,"[225] and both Jefferson and Madison would raise the spectre of "pork-barrel" politics in numerous subsequent discussions of internal improvement. Both would, nevertheless, occasionally accede to measures that seemed to run counter to their constitutional principles.[226] Jefferson, for example, approved one of Albert Gallatin's many proposals for internal improvement and signed the measures authorizing the construction of the Cumberland Road.[227] And once Madison assumed the presidency, he too would occasionally lean in the direction of such measures, even as he continued to express constitutional reservations. In 1811 he praised New York for the constructing the Erie Canal and alluded obliquely to the need for Congress to also authorize such projects by "proper" means.[228] And in his *Seventh Annual Message* he spoke glowingly of internal improvement: "No objects within the circle of political economy so richly repay the expense bestowed on them [and] there are none the utility of which is more universally ascertained and acknowledged."[229]

Some aspects of this fell in various "mode[s] which the Constitution itself has providently pointed out."[230] Ultimately, however,

---

[224] Letter from Jefferson to Madison, Mar 6, 1796, in 2 *Republic of Letters* at 922, 923 (cited in note 14).

[225] See generally Federalist 10 (Madison).

[226] A reality that led one critic to observe that "[t]heir opinions were thus reduced to practice, which was the best evidence in the world—'By their fruits ye shall know them.'" Thomas B. Searight, *The Old Pike: A History of the National Road* 51 (author published, 1894).

[227] See An Act to regulate the laying out and making a road from Cumberland, in the state of Maryland, to the state of Ohio, Ch 19, 2 Stat 357 (1806). The foundations for the 1806 Act were laid earlier as part of the compact for admission of Ohio as a state. See Ch 40, § 7(3), 2 Stat 173, 175 (1802) (creating the "two percent fund" from sales of public lands in Ohio for the construction of public roads). Albert Gallatin's *Report of the Secretary of the Treasury on the Subject of Roads and Canals* (R. C. Weightman, 1808) would become both a sensible blueprint for what was to come and an invitation to politicians to pursue such projects, arguably "for the public good."

[228] James Madison, *Letter to the Senate and House of Representatives*, Dec 23, 1811, in 1 Richardson at 497, 497 (cited in note 14).

[229] 1 id at 562, 567.

[230] 1 id at 568. These were, primarily, exercises of the post road power and spending power.

Madison continued to believe that full realization of an appropriate program of internal improvement required constitutional amendment.[231] Madison would, accordingly, veto Calhoun's Bonus Bill, a measure that included substantial authorizations of and funds for a general system of internal improvement. Madison stressed that he was "not unaware of the great importance of roads and canals," and believed "a power in the National Legislature to provide for them might be exercised with signal advantage to the general prosperity."[232] But "such a power is not expressly given by the Constitution," and could not in Madison's estimation be inferred "without an inadmissible latitude of construction" that would violate a clear and definite "partition of powers between the General and the State Governments."[233]

Monroe continued in this vein once he assumed the presidency. In his *First Inaugural Address* he stressed the value and importance of such projects:

> The improvement of our country by roads and canals, proceeding always with a constitutional sanction, holds a distinguished place. By thus facilitating the intercourse between the States we shall add much to the convenience and comfort of our fellow-citizens, much to the ornament of the country, and, what is of greater importance, we shall shorten distances, and, by making each part more accessible to and dependent on the other, we shall bind the Union more closely together.[234]

But his concern for constitutional propriety proved dispositive. In the *Annual Message* that followed Monroe expressed

> a settled conviction in my mind that Congress do not possess the right. It is not contained in any of the specified powers granted to Congress, nor can I consider it incidental to or a necessary means, viewed on the most liberal scale, for carrying into effect any of the powers which are specifically granted.[235]

Like his predecessors, Monroe "suggest[ed] to Congress the propriety of recommending to the States the adoption of an amendment . . . which shall give to Congress the right in question."[236] And

---

[231] See, e.g., Madison's *Eighth Annual Message*, Dec 3, 1816, in 2 id at 573, 576.

[232] James Madison, *Veto Message*, Mar 3, 1817, in id at 584, 585.

[233] Id.

[234] James Monroe, *First Inaugural Address*, Mar 4, 1817, in 2 id at 4, 8.

[235] James Monroe, *First Annual Message*, Dec 2, 1817, in id at 11, 18.

[236] Id.

also like them, he would find himself "forced" to veto a measure, the 1822 "'act for the preservation and repair of the Cumberland road.'"[237] The bill enjoyed wide support, a fact reflected in Monroe's decision to transmit with the veto message an extensive and unprecedented statement, *Views of the President of the United States on the Subject of Internal Improvements.*[238] Monroe believed, however, that a federal *power* to undertake such actions "can not be derived from" the expressed powers singly, "nor from all of them united, and in consequence it does not exist."[239] He found, nevertheless, support for the idea that simply funding such projects was a proper exercise of the federal power, provided such funds were appropriated and expended for "great national purposes, and for those only."[240]

Perhaps the most intriguing debate about these matters, at least for the purposes of this article, took place toward the end of Jefferson's life, precipitated in large measure by President John Quincy Adams's *First Annual Message to Congress.* In his *Inaugural Address,* Adams had intimated that he would reopen the internal improvement debate. Speaking of Monroe, he averred that

> [t]o the topic of internal improvement, emphatically urged by him at his inauguration, I recur with peculiar satisfaction. It is that from which I am convinced that the unborn millions of our posterity who are in future generations to people this continent will derive the most fervent gratitude to the founders of the Union; that in which the beneficent action of its Government will be most deeply felt and acknowledged.[241]

In December 1825, he did so, stressing that "[r]oads and canals, by multiplying and facilitating the communications and intercourse

---

[237] James Monroe, *Veto Message,* May 4, 1822, in id at 142, 142.

[238] Id at 144–83.

[239] Id at 143.

[240] *Views of the President* at 167. The Court as a whole seemed to accede to this notion in a remarkable letter from Justice Johnson to Monroe, in which he indicated that "they are all of the opinion that the decision on the Bank question completely commits them on the subject of internal improvement, as applied to Postroads and Military Roads," and that "[o]n the other points, it is impossible to resist the lucid and conclusive reasoning contained in the argument." Letter from William Johnson to James Monroe (nd), reprinted in 2 Charles Warren, *The Supreme Court in United States History* 56, 56 (Little, Brown, 1923).

[241] *Inaugural Address,* Mar 4, 1825, in 2 Richardson at 294, 298 (cited in note 14). For a general discussion of these matters, see John Lauritz Larson, *Liberty by Design: Freedom, Planning, and John Quincy Adams's American System,* in Mary O. Furner and Barry Supple, eds, *The State and Economic Knowledge: The American and British Experiences* (Cambridge University Press, 1990).

between distant regions and multitudes of men, are among the most important means of improvement."[242]

Adams's invocation of Monroe's discussion of these matters was, at best, disingenuous. Monroe clearly believed in the value of internal improvement, and would by the close of his administration signal a grudging approval of certain types of projects by signing an appropriation to repair the Cumberland Road. But Monroe never retreated from his firm belief that Congress lacked the power to undertake such measures, and argued consistently for amendment as the only sure manner in which to proceed. More tellingly, Adams himself appeared to concede the force of the constitutional arguments by treating them in dismissive manner. He conceded that "[t]he Constitution under which you are assembled is a charter of limited powers" and that if Congress believed "the enactment of laws for effecting them would transcend the powers committed to you by that venerable instrument which we are all bound to support, let no consideration induce you to assume the exercise of powers not granted to you by the people."[243] But he refused to address directly the reservations expressed by his predecessors. Instead, he simply listed the entire array of express powers and declared that "to refrain from exercising them for the benefit of the people themselves would be to hide in the earth the talent committed to our charge—would be treachery to the most sacred of trusts."[244]

Any hopes Adams might have harbored that his approach would assuage past concerns was clearly misplaced, especially as they might have related to Jefferson, who was, predictably, appalled by Adams's proposals.[245] In a letter to Madison he characterized the

---

[242] John Quincy Adams, *First Annual Message*, Dec 6, 1825, in 2 Richardson at 299, 311 (cited in note 14).

[243] Id at 315.

[244] Id at 316.

[245] Adams may have thought that tying his discussion of traditional internal improvements to a recommendation for a new university would appeal to Jefferson and Madison, who were deeply involved in the development of the University of Virginia at the time. He stressed that "[a]mong the first, perhaps the very first, instrument for the improvement of the condition of men is knowledge, and to the acquisition of much of the knowledge adapted to the wants, the comforts, and enjoyments of human life public institutions and seminaries of learning are essential." Id at 311–12. He alluded to the success of the military academy at West Point, and suggested that Washington "in surveying the city which has been honored with his name he would have seen the spot of earth which he had destined and bequeathed for to the use and benefit of his country as the site for an university still bare and barren." Id at 312

"question of Internal Improvement as desperate," fearing that "[t]he torrent of general opinion sets so strongly in favor of it as to be irresistible."[246] And he enclosed his draft of *The Solemn Declaration and Protest of the commonwealth of Virginia on the principles of the constitution of the US. of America and of the violations of them*,[247] which he suggested might be forwarded to the Virginia delegation for their use. Jefferson characterized the *Declaration* as one way by which like-minded individuals might "pursue with temper and perseverance the great experiment which shall prove that man is capable of living in society, governing itself by laws self-imposed, and securing to its' members the enjoyment of life, liberty property and peace."[248] And he repeated themes championed throughout his life, in particular, the sovereign character of the states[249] and the dangers of the federal government becoming "a complete government, without limitation of powers" if Adams's construction of the text were acceded to.[250]

The Declaration itself was ultimately suppressed, "written [when] all was gloom" and rendered "premature" by both subsequent developments and Madison's sage advice.[251] Madison's primary points were found in a letter to Thomas Ritchie, a copy of which he enclosed when he responded to Jefferson. In it, he began by stressing that

> [i]n seeking a remedy for these aberrations, we must not lose sight of the essential distinction, too little heeded, between assumptions of power by the General Government, in opposition to the Will of the Constituent Body, and assumptions by the Constituent Body through the Government as the Organ of its will.[252]

The former, Madison believed, could be corrected by simply "rous[ing] the attention of the people," for then "a remedy ensues

---

[246] Letter from Jefferson to Madison, Dec 24, 1825, in 3 *Republic of Letters* at 1943 (cited in note 14).

[247] Id at 1944–47.

[248] Id at 1946.

[249] Id at 1944 (the states "retained at the same time, each to itself the other rights of independent government comprehending mainly their domestic interests").

[250] Id at 1945.

[251] Letter from Jefferson to Madison, Jan 2, 1826, id at 1961.

[252] Letter from Madison to Thomas Ritchie, Dec 18, 1825, in id at 1949.

thro' the forms of the Constitution."[253] The latter, however, required something more, an appeal to "the recollections, the reason, and the conciliatory spirit of the Majority of the people agst. their own errors; with a persevering hope of success, and an eventual acquiescence in disappointment unless indeed oppression should reach an extremity overruling all other considerations."[254]

Madison clearly seems to counsel a prudent, longitudinal assessment. As was the case in his treatment of the issues posed by the bank, he believed matters of constitutional concern were subject to various interpretations by a variety of parties. Viewed in the abstract, there was for him little difference between the bank and internal improvement. Both represented exercises of federal authority not expressly authorized in the text, and the constitutionality of each depended, accordingly, on an ability to find implied authorization. And in each instance, implementation would invade areas arguably reserved to the states.

Unlike the bank controversy, however, internal improvement had as yet not gained "repeated recognitions under varied circumstances of . . . validity . . . in acts of the legislative, executive, and judicial branches."[255] That is, Madison could not find "a course of authoritative, deliberate, and continued decisions, such as the Bank could plead [as] evidence of the Public Judgment, necessarily superseding individual opinions."[256] He believed, for example, that actions like the approval and construction of the Cumberland Road were of dubious value as precedents, as "the question of Constitutionality was but slightly if at all examined" by Congress and Jefferson's "Executive assent was doubtingly or hastily given."[257] In particular, the Court had not found a federally administered program of internal improvement to be an appropriate extension of an enumerated power.[258] Thus, while the Justices seemed to have expressed general support for the approach outlined by Monroe

---

[253] Id. He offered as an example of this the public response to and subsequent repudiation of the Alien and Sedition Acts.

[254] Id.

[255] *Veto Message* (Jan 30, 1815), in 8 *Madison's Writings* at 327 (cited in note 14).

[256] Letter to N. P. Trist, Dec 1831, in 9 id at 471, 477.

[257] Letter to James Monroe, Dec 27, 1817, in 8 id at 403, 404–05.

[258] See, e.g., id at 476 (stressing his consistent recognition of the need for "the supremacy of the Judicial power on questions occurring in the course of its functions, concerning the boundary of the Jurisdiction between the U.S. & individual States").

in private correspondence, the Court itself had had no occasion to pass judgment on an expansive federal initiative. This seemed to settle matters, at least in a system in which the actual "division and depositories of pol. power, as laid down in the constl. charter,"[259] understood over time and assessed with an appreciation of the ends to be attained, were and should be seen as more important than "theoretical guides and technical language."[260]

The debate about internal improvement would continue virtually unabated for the next several years. President Jackson in particular would express strong opposition to any improvement program undertaken by the federal government, maintaining that "[t]he great mass of legislation relating to our internal affairs was intended to be left where the Federal Convention found it—in the State governments."[261] Ultimately, however, the constitutional controversy faded away as Congress crafted increasingly sophisticated measures that would achieve by indirection that which had been denied them by a consistent stream of presidential opposition and judicial silence. Indeed, Jackson would himself point the way for much of what would ensue in his veto of the Maysville Road bill, noting the ability of "the simple right to appropriate money from the National Treasury in aid of such works when undertaken by State authority, surrendering the claim of jurisdiction."[262] The story of how these programs evolved into a massive federal presence in many matters the founding generation believed more properly the province of the states is, however, beyond the scope of this article. It is enough for current purposes to stress that the resolution of these questions does not turn only on the interpretation of the words and actions of the Framers and Founders during the actual process of debate and ratification. It requires, rather, that we consider these matters over time, and resolve them, if at all, in the light of the practicalities encountered by a nation that experimented continuously as it sought the best and most effective constitutional means for "fully and effectively vest[ing] in the general government of the Union" those powers necessary

[259] James Madison, *Sovereignty*, 1835, in 9 id at 568, 569.

[260] Id at 569.

[261] *First Annual Message*, Dec 8, 1829, in 2 Richardson at 442, 452 (cited in note 14).

[262] *Veto Message*, May 27, 1830, in id at 483, 484.

to its "prosperity, felicity, safety, perhaps [even its] national existence."[263]

CONCLUSION

> When man emerged from a state of nature, he surely did not reserve the natural right of being the judge of his wrongs and the executioner of the punishments he might think they deserved. A renunciation of such rights is the price he paid for the blessings of good government; and for the same reason, state sovereignty . . . is as incompatible with the federal Union, as the natural rights of human vengeance is with the peace of society. [Plain Truth: Reply to an Officer of the Late Continental Army, November 10, 1787][264]

Two themes seem to emerge from the recent federalism opinions: Reverence for the states as states, and the notion that what really matters, textually speaking, is what the individuals who crafted and ratified the text had to say, at that time, and at virtually no other.[265]

The first of these is an arguably proper gloss, provided one understands and appreciates the full implications of the contexts within which this particular Compound Republic was created. I, obviously, believe there is a great deal more to that story than is evident in the various opinions extolling the "New Federalism." The founding generation viewed the Compound Republic as an enterprise that was simultaneously a creature born of principles and a structural mechanism designed to attain certain important national ends. Jefferson and his allies would, for example, argue strenuously on any number of occasions that there must be a strict separation between matters deemed fit for the federal and state governments, and in particular that the states should be accorded a virtually unchecked primacy in internal matters.[266] And, while his

---

[263] President's Letter at 305 (cited in note 45).

[264] 2 *Documentary History* at 216, 218 (cited in note 45).

[265] One important exception is, of course, the Court's willingness to cite its own decisions parsing the text.

[266] See, e.g., Letter Jefferson to Madison, Dec 16, 1786, in 1 *Republic of Letters* at 457, 458 (cited in note 14) ("[t]o make us one nation as to foreign concerns, and keep us distinct in Domestic ones, gives the outline of a proper division of powers between the general and particular governments"). For an interesting discussion of the Jefferson's influence, see H. Jefferson Powell, *The Compleat Jeffersonian: Justice Rehnquist and Federalism*, 91 Yale L J 1317 (1982). Jefferson's rhetoric, especially in his later years, was of course often at odds with the actions he took as president. The best and most extensive treatment of Jefferson's

subsequent actions as president would undermine the force of the observation, it was Jefferson who warned, regarding the First Bank, that "[t]o take a single step beyond the boundaries thus specially drawn around the powers of Congress, is to take possession of a boundless field of power, no longer susceptible of any definition."[267] It was, however, Madison's perspective that prevailed. That vision stressed twin precepts: ratification by the people, in a manner that made their supremacy to the states evident,[268] and a textual commitment to a system in which the national government exercised necessary and necessarily supreme powers.[269]

The second major theme in current federalism debate, the importance of the views of the Framers and Founders, poses in turn particular problems for the explication of a text crafted by individuals who understood that the meaning of the Constitution was not fully determined in 1789, not simply because the Court had not yet offered definitive glosses, but because the interpretive process required careful action over time by a multitude of actors. My reading of the record suggests that many, perhaps even most, of the precepts now championed by the conservative wing of the Court are clearly "true" only if our frame of reference is the intent of the Framers, measured in an intellectual, political, and historical vacuum. That approach is, as I have suggested, at odds with the manner in which many of the Framers and Founders both spoke about and implemented the text at the very time deemed critical by those Justices championing a robust vision of the rights and sovereignty of the states. And it is certainly belied by the particular manner in which the people and their government resolved, and understood the implications of, two seminal constitutional contro-

---

views may be found in David N. Mayer, *The Constitutional Thought of Thomas Jefferson* (University Press of Virginia, 1994). Other valuable works include Lance Banning, *The Jeffersonian Persuasion: Evolution of a Party Ideology* (Cornell University Press, 1978); Richard K. Matthews, *The Radical Politics of Thomas Jefferson: A Revisionist View* (Kansas, 1984), Garrett Ward Sheldon, *The Political Philosophy of Thomas Jefferson* (Johns Hopkins University Press, 1991).

[267] *Opinion* at 276 (cited in note 191).

[268] Letter from Madison to Jefferson, March 19, 1787, 1 *Republic of Letters* at 469, 470 (cited in note 14) ("the foundation of the new system in such a ratification by the people themselves of the several States as will render it clearly paramount to their Legislative authorities").

[269] Letter from Madison to Jefferson, Oct 24, 1787, 1 id at 495, 496 ("the objects of the Union could not be secured by any system founded on the principle of a confederation of sovereign States").

versies: whether the central government had the power to charter a bank, and whether it could itself engage in a systematic program of internal improvement.

My case is not free from doubt. This is both the oldest question in constitutional law and one of the oldest in American history and politics. A full and just appreciation requires, accordingly, much more thought and a wider range of inquiry than I have been able to offer in this relatively brief treatment.[270]

Certainly Jefferson disagreed, vigorously, with the notion that an expansive reading of both the Commerce and Spending powers justified broad exercises of federal power. But he also understood that "[t]he moment a person forms a theory his imagination sees in every object only the traits which favor that theory."[271] In his particular case, a theory of reserved powers was colored by his conviction that "our governments will remain virtuous for many centuries, as long as they are chiefly agricultural; and this will be as long as there shall be vacant lands in any part of America."[272] That is most assuredly not the nation that exists today, and it is perhaps possible that Jefferson himself would see the wisdom in allowing the Union more latitude than he was willing to tolerate given the conditions that prevailed in his lifetime. Jefferson did, after all, note with regard to Shay's Rebellion that "[t]hose states have suffered by the stoppage of the channels of their commerce, which has not yet found other issues."[273] It is arguably not all that great a leap from his understanding of the seriousness of those threats to a recognition that the powers conferred by the Com-

---

[270] One could, for example, spend many profitable hours delving into the lessons contained in Willi Paul Adams, *The First American Constitutions: Republican Ideology and the Making of State Constitutions in the Revolutionary Era* (University of North Carolina Press, 1980); Samuel H. Beer, *To Make a Nation: The Rediscovery of American Federalism* (Belknap, 1993); Stanley Elkins and Eric McKitrick, *The Age of Federalism: The Early American Republic, 1788–1800* (Oxford University Press, 1993); Jack P. Greene, *Peripheries and Center: Constitutional Development in the Extended Politics of the British Empire and the United States 1607–1788* (University of Georgia Press, 1986); Edmund S. Morgan, *Inventing the People: The Rise of Popular Sovereignty in England and America* (Norton, 1988); James Roger Sharp, *American Politics in the Early Republic: The New Nation in Crisis* (Yale University Press, 1993). I am quite certain I have not done justice to the insights gleaned from these and many other works.

[271] Letter to Charles Thomson, Sept 20, 1787, in 5 *Jefferson's Works* at 342 (cited in note 24).

[272] Letter from Jefferson to Madison, Dec 20, 1787, in 1 *Republic of Letters* at 511, 514 (cited in note 14).

[273] Letter from Jefferson to Madison, Jan 30 and Feb 5, 1787, in 1 id at 460, 461.

merce Clause can and should now extend to matters he would have once deemed inappropriate.

Then again, perhaps not. Many of the principles for which Jefferson and Madison stood reveal fears that have been more than fulfilled by the realities of an expansive reading. For example, there is reason to believe that both would express at least reservations about, and in Jefferson's case, hostility to, the expansive reading the Court has given the Commerce Clause. And the manner in which Congress has exercised the spending power, with its strong overtones of pork-barrel politics, conjures up images of the fears many members of the founding generation shared as they made their case against a general power of internal improvement.

Ultimately, the question is not whether my judgments about what the founding generation deemed appropriate and constitutional are correct, but whether the record the Framers and Founders would find fit for judicial scrutiny is more expansive than the Court has led us to believe. I at least sense that many of the figures whose thoughts and words figure prominently in the reserved powers catechism championed by the conservative wing of the Court would be puzzled to find themselves numbered among its adherents. In particular, I believe they would be mystified by the notion that the entire meaning of the text is to be divined from whatever evidence we might marshal from the words and events of the 1780s. And I suspect they would be among the first to suggest that the Court consider more carefully the validity and implications of the course on which it has embarked.

DEBRA LIVINGSTON

GANG LOITERING, THE COURT, AND SOME REALISM ABOUT POLICE PATROL

When the Supreme Court voted to review the decision of the Illinois Supreme Court holding Chicago's "gang loitering" ordinance invalid on federal constitutional grounds, it seemed plausible that *City of Chicago v Morales*[1] would be the occasion for a major statement from the Court on a set of complex issues—issues including not only the nature of the police officer's authority to maintain order in public places, but also the relative roles of politics and judicial decision making in delineating both the limits on this authority and the latitude left to police to employ discretion in its exercise. After all, communities today are experimenting with a broad variety of new policing styles.[2] Some of these experiments have emphasized the importance of a neighborhood's public spaces to the health of its community and have involved police in efforts to improve the "quality of life" in such spaces. Police have seen to the removal of trash and abandoned cars along streets where children play. There has been a revival of interest in the enforcement of statutes and ordinances aimed at low-level public disorder. In some places, this local experimentation has produced a new con-

---

Debra Livingston is Associate Professor, Columbia University School of Law.

AUTHOR'S NOTE: I am grateful to John Manning, John McEnany, and Rick Pildes for many helpful comments.

[1] 119 S Ct 1849 (1999).

[2] For a general description of this phenomenon, see Debra Livingston, *Police Discretion and the Quality of Life in Public Places: Courts, Communities, and the New Policing*, 97 Colum L Rev 551, 562–84 (1997).

fidence among community residents in the ability of police to contribute to the well-being of the neighborhoods they serve. Elsewhere, however, police initiatives directed at crime and disorder
have generated concern, anxiety, and outright anger about police
intrusiveness, particularly as directed at minority populations.

In *Morales*, a coalition that ultimately included prominent scholars, community activists, and the Solicitor General (not to mention
various city attorneys, state attorneys general, and law enforcement
groups) attacked the decision of the Illinois Supreme Court for
being badly out of touch both with the legitimate aspiration of
inner city residents to reclaim control over their neighborhoods
and with the capacity of these residents, freed from the ineffective
attempts of courts to restrain unreasonable police actions, themselves to impose meaningful political controls over the conduct of
police.[3] Others, meanwhile, fiercely contended that the Chicago
ordinance was a frank invitation to arbitrary and discriminatory
police enforcement; they called upon the Supreme Court to resist
the siren song of "community" and "neighborhood empow-
erment" and to hold the line against a serious threatened erosion
in constitutional liberties.[4] *Morales*, then, seemed to advocates on

---

[3] This argument was presented most powerfully in several articles by Tracey Meares and
Dan Kahan, as well as in an amicus brief before the Supreme Court that they helped to
draft. See, e.g., Dan M. Kahan and Tracey L. Meares, *Foreword: The Coming Crisis of Criminal Procedure*, 86 Geo L J 1153, 1171–80 (1998); Tracey L. Meares and Dan M. Kahan,
The Wages of Antiquated Procedural Thinking: A Critique of Chicago v. Morales, 1998 U Chi
Legal F 197, 209–14; *Chicago v Morales*, No 97-1121, Brief Amicus Curiae of the Chicago
Neighborhood Organizations in Support of Petitioner, at 1–5. The United States and approximately thirty-one states, as well as various community groups, governmental associations, and law enforcement organizations, also submitted briefs arguing that the Chicago
ordinance represented a constitutionally appropriate response to the plague of gang violence
besetting some Chicago neighborhoods. See, e.g., Brief for the United States as Amicus
Curiae Supporting Petitioner, at 8–11 ("Brief for the United States Supporting Petitioner");
Brief Amicus Curiae of Ohio, et al, in Support of the Petitioner, at 1–6; Brief of the Center
for the Community Interest as Amicus Curiae in Support of Petitioner, at 7–27; Brief of
the U.S. Conference of Mayors, et al, as Amici Curiae in Support of Petitioner, at 2–7;
Brief of Amici Curiae Natl Dist Attorneys Association and Intl Association of Chiefs of
Police in Support of Petitioner, at 2–5.

[4] See, e.g., David Cole, *Foreword: Discretion and Discrimination Reconsidered: A Response to
the New Criminal Justice Scholarship*, 87 Geo L J 1059, 1067 (1999). See also Albert W.
Alschuler and Stephen J. Schulhofer, *Antiquated Procedures or Bedrock Rights? A Response to
Professors Meares and Kahan*, 1998 U Chi Legal F 215, 216. This argument was also pressed
in amicus briefs submitted by various civil rights organizations, law enforcement associations, and lawyers' groups. See, e.g., Brief of Amici Curiae Natl Black Police Association,
et al, in Support of Respondents, pp 7–14; Brief Amicus Curiae of the Natl Association
of Criminal Defense Lawyers in Support of the Respondents, pp 5–9; Brief of Chicago
Alliance for Neighborhood Safety, et al, as Amici Curiae in Support of Respondents, pp
12–18 ("Chicago Alliance Brief in Support of Respondents").

both sides the proper occasion for a significant Supreme Court pronouncement—a pronouncement either reaffirming and clarifying the application of existing constitutional doctrines to the host of loitering ordinances, curfews, and other "order maintenance" laws recently adopted in many local communities or, instead, setting the nation's courts on a new course with regard to the review of such laws.

Viewed from this perspective, *Morales* must be deemed disappointing to everyone. In Justice Stevens's lead opinion, which was joined in full by only two Justices and in part by three others, six Justices agreed, narrowly, that Chicago's gang loitering ordinance was impermissibly vague in its authorization to police to disperse gang members and those accompanying them whenever these people were found "loitering" (defined in the ordinance to mean "remain[ing] in any one place with no apparent purpose") in public spaces.[5] Despite arguments by supporters of the ordinance that such a holding would do little to realize the principal ambition the Court has articulated for its vagueness doctrine—namely, setting meaningful limits on the opportunity for arbitrary and discriminatory law enforcement—the Court failed to clarify the rationale for this doctrine or to explain how its application to the Chicago ordinance would promote the wise use of discretion by Chicago police.[6] At the same time, the Court's parsimonious holding did not offer opponents of the ordinance anything like a robust defense of vagueness doctrine nor of its application to public order laws.

It may be too hasty, though, simply to dismiss *Morales* as yet another case in which the Court has evaded—or at least failed to come to grips with—important issues concerning the relationship between local police and their communities. After all, the issue in the background of *Morales*—namely, the proper role for police patrol in a community—is extraordinarily complex, implicating, as it does, not only the law enforcement role of police, but also the role of police officers as peacekeepers and providers of a multitude of community services. Should patrol officers seek to deter crime and ameliorate disorder largely through their visible, uniformed

---

[5] *Morales*, 119 S Ct at 1861–62.

[6] For a statement by the Court that the facial vagueness doctrine is animated principally by a concern with limiting the potential for arbitrary enforcement, see *Kolender v Lawson*, 461 US 352, 357–58 (1983).

presence in public places, or should they adopt a more proactive posture? If they should be more proactive, what should they do? Enforce laws? Mediate conflicts? Serve as ombudsmen to address a broad variety of problems in the provision of governmental services? And if we are to authorize a significant category of *coercive* encounters between patrol officers and people found in public places, how do we guard against the abuse of this authority? How do we ensure that the grant of authority to police to serve as a useful support for the common use of public spaces does not become, instead, an instrument for the surveillance and harassment of disfavored individuals or groups? Even the Warren Court, which spoke with significant resolve in articulating the procedures to be followed in the investigation of serious crime, was remarkably tentative in *Terry v Ohio,*[7] the principal case in which that Court confronted everyday aspects of police patrol: "[W]e approach the issues in this case mindful of the limitations of the judicial function in controlling the myriad daily situations in which policemen and citizens confront each other on the street."[8]

It is increasingly apparent, moreover, that answers to the many questions posed today about the appropriate role of police in communities—questions not only about the proper scope of police patrol authority, but also about the best means for assuring police accountability—are likely to emanate not from national judicial pronouncements, but from the accumulated wisdom deriving from local experimentation. And in this regard, the *Morales* opinions as a whole are perhaps greater than the sum of their parts. These opinions, read together, do not foreclose, but in an important way expand the opportunity for further experimentation with laws regulating public disorder—even as the Court retains for itself a good deal of room to step in and limit this experimentation, if necessary, at some future point. In this sense, *Morales* is quite different from *Papachristou v City of Jacksonville*[9]—that most dramatic of the facial vagueness cases that collectively remade the law applicable to public order in the 1960s and 1970s—even though in both cases the

---

[7] 392 US 1 (1968).

[8] Id at 12.

[9] 405 US 156 (1972).

Court invalidated a public order law.[10] The unanimous Court in
Papachristou self-confidently, even eagerly, pronounced Jacksonville, Florida's vagrancy ordinance an archaic law that threatened
both fundamental rule-of-law values and central tenets of the
American constitutional system.[11] In contrast, the Court in *Morales*
groped anxiously for narrow grounds. Even the Justices in the majority felt constrained to empathize with the efforts of Chicago
communities to deal with the serious gang problems afflicting
them, to "characterize . . . clearly the narrow scope" of the Court's
holding, and most importantly, to suggest alternative means by
which Chicago might constitutionally regulate the loitering of
gang members.[12]

Still, even acknowledging a special need for judicial humility in
this fluid area, the *Morales* Court could at least have begun to define a framework within which future experimentation with new
forms of police patrol might be assessed. The Court made precious
little progress on this more modest front. Indeed, there is a strong
case to be made that the majority in *Morales* did more harm than
good to the project of placing reasonable constraints on police.
The Court invalidated Chicago's ordinance on the ground that the
ordinance granted too much discretion to police, thus creating an
undue risk that it would be arbitrarily employed;[13] the Court's de-

---

[10] For a description of the application of facial vagueness doctrine to a broad variety of
"street order" laws in the 1960s and 1970s, see Livingston, 97 Colum L Rev at 595–601
(cited in note 2).

[11] *Papachristou*, 405 US at 161–62, 168–71. The text of the Jacksonville ordinance provided in relevant part as follows:

> Rogues and vagabonds, or dissolute persons who go about begging, common gam-
> blers, persons who use juggling or unlawful games or plays, common drunkards,
> common night walkers, thieves, pilferers or pickpockets, traders in stolen property,
> lewd, wanton and lascivious persons, keepers of gambling places, common railers
> and brawlers, persons wandering or strolling around from place to place without
> any lawful purpose or object, habitual loafers, disorderly persons, persons neglect-
> ing all lawful business and habitually spending their time by frequenting houses
> of ill fame, gaming houses, or places where alcoholic beverages are sold or served,
> persons able to work but habitually living upon the earnings of their wives or
> minor children shall be deemed vagrants and, upon conviction in the Municipal
> Court shall be punished as provided for Class D offenses.

405 US at 158 n 1 (quoting ordinance).

[12] See, e.g., *Morales*, 119 S Ct at 1863 (opinion of Stevens, joined by Souter and Ginsburg); id at 1864–65 (O'Connor concurring in part and concurring in the judgment, joined
by Breyer).

[13] See *Morales*, 119 S Ct at 1861–63.

cision, however, may well point localities in the direction of *ex-panding* the scope of police discretion in subsequent legislation. Similarly, the facial vagueness doctrine that was the basis for the decision addresses the concern that imprecise laws delegate basic policy matters to police officers on patrol, thus promoting ad hoc and capricious police enforcement.[14] But *Morales* does not encourage localities and their police departments frankly to acknowledge police discretion and to develop means of using it in an accountable way for the positive good of communities. Instead, the decision is more likely to drive discretion underground and to suppress the open discussion of considerations regarding its appropriate exercise.

The result in *Morales* was arrived at through the highly technical parsing of nine words in Chicago's gang loitering ordinance.[15] The majority opinion resulting from this exercise is not only unconvincing on its own terms; it is also disturbingly detached from serious consideration of both the nature of police patrol discretion and the efficacy of the Court's attempts to influence its character. Because no law can be entirely precise and because there is "no yardstick of impermissible indeterminacy" to be used in the review of challenged legislation,[16] vagueness doctrine as employed by the *Morales* majority confers on courts considerable discretion to second-guess the efforts of localities to regulate public conduct in an effort to enhance the common use of public spaces. At the same time, however, the majority's methodology—its narrow focus on the language of Chicago's gang loitering ordinance—deprives judges employing the doctrine of any real ability to promote the positive use of police discretion for a community's good. Thus, the *Morales* majority may foster an illusion of judicial competence in this arena. But the realities of street-level policing remain unchanged and may even have been influenced for the worse.

This article offers an analysis of the Court's situation and a modest proposal for reform. I argue that the Court will make little

---

[14] See *Grayned v City of Rockford*, 408 US 104, 108–09 (1972).

[15] The majority in *Morales* concluded after parsing its language that the Chicago ordinance's loitering definition (which defined loitering to mean "remain[ing] in any one place with no apparent purpose") was impermissibly vague. See *Morales*, 119 S Ct at 1861–62.

[16] John Calvin Jeffries, Jr., *Legality, Vagueness, and the Construction of Penal Statutes*, 71 Va L Rev 189, 196 (1985).

progress on the project of constraining arbitrary police enforcement of newly enacted public order laws until it imports some
realism into its doctrinal framework. Realism about police patrol
discretion, moreover, points in the direction of a vagueness test
that is not focused exclusively on the words of this new generation
of public order laws. Rather, the Court should consider more
broadly whether the exercise of police discretion contemplated in
new legislation will take place under conditions that provide reasonable assurances of police accountability.

Part I briefly describes both the context in which the *Morales*
ordinance was enacted and the *Morales* opinions themselves. Part
II then delves into the confusion in the Court's vagueness analysis.
This part argues that the *Morales* Court's approach to vagueness
does not meaningfully constrain the opportunity for arbitrary police action because it has no application to many contexts in which
this opportunity is present—in the enforcement of traffic laws, for
instance, or in the area of stop and frisk. Moreover, the *Morales*
majority's narrow focus on the language of Chicago's gang loitering ordinance may encourage legislators searching for precise
terms to broaden the enforcement authorization given to police
and thus to augment, rather than narrow, the scope of police discretion. The majority thus focused on factors of little importance
to the restraint of police arbitrariness. It also ignored aspects of
the Chicago law that might actually have promoted the judicious
use of discretion by Chicago police. Indeed, the majority's disregard of significant innovations in the Chicago ordinance is likely
to retard efforts at promoting police accountability. Part III con-
cludes with a sketch of a more realistic vagueness jurisprudence in
the area of public order policing.

I. The Case and Its Context

A. THE CHICAGO ORDINANCE

Chicago's gang loitering ordinance was enacted in 1992, during
a period when the number of Chicago homicides deemed to be
gang related by the Chicago Police Department was in the midst
of a fivefold increase—from approximately fifty-one such homicides in 1987 to around 132 in 1991, and then to a high of about

240 in 1994 (a number representing 26.2 percent of all Chicago homicides for that year).[17] Street gang homicide tends to increase and decrease in spurts, but the huge spurt in the early 1990s broke all previous records in Chicago and dramatically increased the risk of being killed in a street gang-related homicide for, in particular, African-American males and Latinos aged fifteen to nineteen years.[18] Of course, because Chicago gangs tend to concentrate in particular geographical areas, neither this risk nor any of the other risks associated with gang activity fell uniformly across Chicago's neighborhoods. Indeed, one prominent study of Chicago gangs found that for the three-year period from 1987 to 1990, the rate of street-gang motivated crime in the two most dangerous parts of Chicago was seventy-six times that of the two safest areas.[19] Moreover, even in high-crime neighborhoods (some of which echoed with gunfire almost nightly during this period), gang-related crime "[was] not monolithic, but rather diverse, affecting different neighborhoods in different ways."[20] In those neighborhoods where competition among rival street gangs for constricted turf was intense, for example, buildings of all sorts were often covered with multiple layers of graffiti; neighborhoods in other parts of Chicago, however, were remarkably free of graffiti even though inundated with gang members simply because a given gang "was so much in command that [it] did not need many physical markers to identify [its] turf."[21] The potentially most lethal street gang situations in Chicago at this time involved turf-related violence—violence that researchers found to be primarily "expressive" (meaning that it was undertaken principally for purposes like defense and glorification of the gang) rather than "instrumental" (motivated primarily by the desire to acquire money or property from, for

---

[17] See Carolyn Rebecca Block, et al, *Research Bulletin: Street Gangs and Crime* 4 (Ill Criminal Justice Information Authority, Sept 1996) ("*Street Gangs and Crime*"). The Chicago Police Department designates an offense as street gang related when a preponderance of the evidence indicates "that the offense grew out of an street gang function." Id at 2. The gang membership of a perpetrator or victim is not alone enough to establish gang relatedness. Id.

[18] See id at 5, 8. See also Carolyn Rebecca Block and Richard Block, *Street Gang Crime in Chicago* 4 (Natl Institute of Justice, Dec 1993) ("*Street Gang Crime in Chicago*").

[19] See *Street Gang Crime in Chicago* at 1 (cited in note 18).

[20] *Street Gangs and Crime* at 23 (cited in note 17).

[21] *Street Gang Crime in Chicago* at 4 (cited in note 18).

instance, the possession or sale of drugs).[22] The Chicago Police
Department estimated in 1992 that more than forty major street
gangs were active in Chicago.[23] The most violent gangs tended to
be those smaller gangs that controlled only a few fiercely defended
blocks.[24]

The effort to enact a gang loitering law in Chicago can be traced
to 1991, when a number of Chicago neighborhood groups concerned about the rising violence associated with street gangs began
negotiating with city officials to develop anti-gang legislation.[25]
These negotiations led to hearings before the Chicago City Council in the spring of 1992 during which testimony was elicited concerning a proposal for enactment of an ordinance regulating loitering by gang members in public places. Many concerned citizens
testified poignantly about the disruption that the latest wave of
gang violence had worked in their lives. A mother of four, for instance, attested that in her neighborhood, children no longer
played hopscotch or jacks in the street: "I wish you could see the
rust that has accumulated because they cannot ride [their] bikes."[26]
Eighty-eight-year-old Susan Mary Jackson spoke forcefully of the
fear she experienced in public spaces: "'We used to have a nice
neighborhood. We don't have it anymore. . . . I am scared to go
out in the daytime . . . . you can't pass because they are standing.
I am afraid to go to the store.'"[27] City Council members, however,
also heard warnings that loitering ordinances were both unconstitutional and prone to abuse: "[V]ague laws . . . based on the concept of loitering . . . have historically been subject to massive abuse
by law enforcement, both in this city and other cities."[28] They
heard from a representative of the police department who affirmed

---

[22] See id at 8. See also *Street Gangs and Crime* at 20 (cited in note 17).

[23] See *Street Gang Crime in Chicago* at 2, n 6 (cited in note 18).

[24] See *Street Gangs and Crime* at 20 (cited in note 17).

[25] See Alschuler and Schulhofer, 1998 U Chi Legal F at 217 (cited in note 4). See also
Editorial, *Anti-Gang Law Isn't the Answer*, Chi Tribune 16 (May 20, 1992).

[26] Transcription of Proceedings before the Committee on Police and Fire of the Chicago
City Council 168–69 (May 18, 1992) (statement of Desiree Davidson) ("*May 18
Transcript*").

[27] *Morales*, 119 S Ct at 1880 (Thomas dissenting, joined by Rehnquist and Scalia) (quoting
Transcription of Proceedings before the Committee on Police and Fire of the Chicago
City Council 93–95 (May 15, 1992)).

[28] *May 18 Transcript* at 99 (statement of Harvey Grossman, Legal Director of the American Civil Liberties Union of Illinois) (cited in note 26).

that a loitering ordinance would be a viable tool for use in dealing with gang problems, but who also cautioned that no ordinance, standing alone, could substitute for a more comprehensive approach to these problems.[29]

The proposed ordinance "drew both support and opposition from Chicago citizens of all backgrounds."[30] The City Council debate on the ordinance reflected this division and was described by the *Chicago Tribune* as "one of the most heated and emotional council debates in recent memory."[31] Much of the debate centered on the concern that the proposed ordinance would have a disparate impact on racial minorities—a concern that was most passionately expressed by several of the eight African-American aldermen who ultimately voted against the new law.[32] These alderman charged that the ordinance was "'drafted to protect the downtown area and the white community' at the expense of innocent blacks."[33] At the same time, however, the ordinance received critical support from aldermen representing over a dozen high-crime, predominantly African-American and Latino wards.[34] Alderman Ed Smith, an African American representing a heavily minority district with severe crime problems, was particularly outspoken in his support: "This doesn't allow the police to go hog wild. But we're tired of seeing the rights of gangbangers get protected when . . . a mother can't send her children outside for fear of them getting shot to death in a drive-by shooting."[35] On June 18, 1992, the City Council enacted the proposed ordinance by a wide margin of thirty-one

---

[29] Id at 175, 185–86 (statement of Gerald Cooper, Assistant Deputy Superintendent, Chicago Police Department).

[30] Chicago Alliance Brief in Support of Respondents at 4 (cited in note 4).

[31] Robert Davis, *New Police Arrest Power Light City Council Fuse*, Chi Tribune A1 (June 18, 1992).

[32] See id. See also Alschuler and Schulhofer, 1998 U Chi Legal F at 220 (cited in note 4) (noting that eight African-American aldermen voted against the ordinance).

[33] Fran Spielman, *Loitering Ban Passes: Aldermen Bitterly Split on Anti-Gang Measures*, Chi Sun-Times 1 (June 18, 1992) (quoting remarks of Ald. John Steele). See also id (remarks of Ald. Dorothy Tillman and Ald. Allan Streeter).

[34] See Tracey L. Meares and Dan M. Kahan, *Black, White and Gray: A Reply to Alschuler and Schulhofer*, 1998 U Chi L F 245, 249–50. See also Jan Crawford Greenburg, *Top Court Ruling Shows Way to a Legal Anti-Loitering Law*, Chi Tribune 1 (June 11, 1999) (noting that "ordinance had widespread support in many communities plagued by gang violence, putting some activists at odds with the ACLU—a traditional ally").

[35] John Kass, *Old Tactic Sought in Crime War*, Chi Tribune A1 (May 15, 1992). See also Meares and Kahan, 1998 U Chi Legal F at 247–48 (cited in note 34).

to eleven.[36] At the end of the debate, six of the city's eighteen African-American aldermen voted in favor of the ordinance; as noted previously, eight African-American aldermen voted against the new law.[37]

The City Council issued findings based on the evidence presented at the Council hearings that were included in the text of the ordinance to explain the reasons for its enactment. The council found that Chicago was experiencing an increasing murder rate, as well as an increase in violent and drug-related crime, and that both were largely attributable to criminal street gang activity.[38] The members determined that in many parts of Chicago, street gangs had, in effect, "taken over" entire neighborhoods by intimidating residents into retreating from parks, sidewalks, and other public spaces that the gangs then occupied as their turf. "One of the methods by which criminal street gangs establish control over identifiable areas," the council found, "is by loitering in those areas and intimidating others from entering. . . ."[39] The members determined that loitering in such places by gang members created "a justifiable fear for the safety of persons and property in the area because of the violence, drug-dealing and vandalism often associated with such activity."[40] Aggressive action was necessary, the council determined, "to preserve the City's streets and other public places so that the public [might] use such places without fear."[41]

The Chicago ordinance accordingly authorized police to order any group of two or more people found loitering in public places to move along on pain of arrest, so long as at least one of the group was reasonably believed to be a member of a criminal street gang. The law specifically provided as follows:

> Whenever a police officer observes a person whom he reasonably believes to be a criminal street gang member loitering in any public place with one or more other persons, he shall

---

[36] See Davis, *New Police Arrest Power Lights City Council Fuse*, Chi Tribune at A1 (cited in note 31).

[37] Alschuler and Schulhofer, 1998 U Chi Legal F at 220 (cited in note 4). Four African-American aldermen did not vote. Id & n 33.

[38] See *Chicago v Morales*, 177 Ill 2d 440, 445, 687 NE2d 53 (1997) (quoting the ordinance's findings in full).

[39] Id.

[40] Id.

[41] Id.

order all such persons to disperse and remove themselves from the area. Any person who does not promptly obey such an order is in violation of this section.[42]

Drafted in a manner analogous to that employed in the federal Racketeer Influenced Corrupt Organizations Act,[43] the Chicago ordinance was replete with prolix definitions of each of its key terms. Thus the ordinance defined a "criminal street gang" to mean any ongoing organization, association in fact, or group of three or more persons having as one of its substantial activities the commission of certain specified crimes (like murder, drug dealing, and armed violence), and whose members individually or collectively were engaged in or had engaged in a pattern of criminal gang activity.[44] "Criminal gang activity" was further defined to mean the commission, attempted commission, or solicitation of a lengthy list of offenses "by two or more persons, or by an individual at the direction of, or in association with, any criminal street gang, with the specific intent to promote, further, or assist in any criminal conduct by gang members."[45] A "pattern" of such activity simply denoted two or more acts of criminal gang activity, provided that at least two of these acts must have been committed within five years of each other and at least one such act must have occurred after the effective date of the ordinance.[46]

"Loitering" was also a defined term in the Chicago ordinance. It referred to "remain[ing] in any one place with no apparent purpose."[47] Notably, the law was drafted so that gang members and those loitering with them did not violate the ordinance simply by loitering together, but only by thereafter defying a police order "to disperse and remove themselves from the area."[48] The ordinance further provided as an affirmative defense "that no person who was observed loitering was in fact a member of a criminal street gang."[49] Violations of the law were punishable by a fine of

---

[42] Municipal Code of Chicago, § 8-4-015(a).

[43] 18 USC §§ 1961–68.

[44] Municipal Code of Chicago, § 8-4-015(c)(2) & (3).

[45] Id at § 8-4-015(c)(3).

[46] See id at § 8-4-015(c)(4).

[47] Id at § 8-4-015(c)(a).

[48] Id at § 8-4-015(a).

[49] Id at § 8-4-015(b).

up to $500, imprisonment for not more than six months, and the requirement to perform up to 120 hours of community service.[50]

Within two months of the ordinance's enactment, the Chicago Police Department promulgated General Order 92-4, a police regulation which set forth specific guidelines to govern enforcement of the new law for the purpose of ensuring that the ordinance was not enforced in an arbitrary or discriminatory way.[51] The order required each police district and each area unit of the department's Gang Crime Section to maintain a file for the purpose of identifying those groups and individuals active in a given district who constituted "criminal street gangs" and "criminal street gang members" as defined in the ordinance.[52] Identification of a gang as a criminal street gang was to be based on factors like the analysis of crime pattern data, interviews with gang members or witnesses, and information from reliable informants.[53] The order specified that dispersal orders should issue only on probable cause to believe that criminal street gang members were loitering with each other or with other people in a given area. Probable cause of a person's membership in a criminal street gang, the order stated, might be established by evidence such as the individual's admission of membership, his use of signals distinctive of a specific gang, or the wearing of emblems, tattoos, or similar markings that could not reasonably be expected to be displayed by anyone except a member of a particular gang.[54] The order specifically cautioned that gang membership could not be established solely on the basis of clothing worn by the individual but available for sale to the general public.[55]

On its face, Chicago's gang loitering ordinance applied citywide. In practice, the Chicago Police Department limited its application in General Order 92-4 to public places designated by the department as areas in which the presence of gang members had resulted in "a demonstrable effect on the activities of law abiding persons in the surrounding community."[56] Examples of areas ap-

---

[50] See id at § 8-4-015(e).

[51] See Chicago Police Department, General Order No 92-4 at §§ I, II.

[52] See id at § III.A.

[53] See id at § IV.

[54] See id at § V.

[55] See id at § V.B.

[56] Id at § VI.A.1.

propriate for such designation, according to police, included "locations near schools used for criminal street gang recruiting" or "locations near businesses where criminal street gang activity [has] adversely affect[ed] the patronage of those businesses."[57] Designations were to be made by district commanders based on consultations with relevant police personnel, local officials, leaders of community organizations, and other citizens able to provide reliable information.[58]

In addition, General Order 92-4 specified that only specially designated police personnel—like members of the Gang Crime section or the district tactical units—could arrest individuals for violating the gang loitering law.[59] These police officers were required to familiarize themselves with the information maintained by the department concerning criminal street gangs active in the areas in which the officers worked.[60] Officers making arrests pursuant to the gang loitering law were also required to prepare written reports which, among other things, fully described the circumstances giving rise to probable cause to arrest.[61]

The Chicago Police Department began enforcing the new law in August 1992 and stopped enforcing it in December 1995, when it was held invalid by an Illinois appellate court.[62] During that time, the police issued over 89,000 dispersal orders and arrested over 42,000 people for violating the ordinance.[63] Enforcement was "overwhelmingly concentrated on the City's high-crime neighborhoods."[64]

When the ordinance was first enacted, Chicago Mayor Richard Daley (one of the law's ardent supporters) had sarcastically offered that "the Police Department might not enforce the new law in the wards of those aldermen who voted against it. . . ."[65] No City

---

[57] Id.

[58] See id.

[59] See id at § III.C.

[60] See id at § VI.C.1.

[61] See id at § VI.C.3.c.

[62] See *Morales*, 119 S Ct at 1855, n 6.

[63] See id at 1855. Police made 5,251 arrests under the ordinance in 1993, 15,660 in 1994, and 22,056 in 1995. See id, n 7.

[64] Meares and Kahan, 1998 U Chi Legal F at 252 (cited in note 34).

[65] Robert Davis, *Special Units to Police Loiterers: City Wants to Make New Anti-Gang Law Hold Up in Court*, Chi Tribune 3 (June 19, 1992).

Council member attempted to take the mayor up on this proposal during the three years that the law was enforced. In fact, there is little evidence that support for the ordinance among City Council members in any way diminished once the ordinance had actually been employed. In May 1998, the City Council passed a resolution urging the U.S. Supreme Court to uphold the ordinance. The resolution passed by a vote of twenty-five to eight—and now, incidentally, with the support of a majority of those voting aldermen representing predominantly African-American wards.[66]

The gang loitering law fared considerably less well in the courts. At the trial level, three judges of the Circuit Court of Cook County upheld the ordinance (and one judge held it constitutional as applied to people whom the police reasonably believed to be gang members), but twelve judges, in separate cases, declared the ordinance invalid on its face.[67] The Appellate Court of Illinois concluded that the ordinance impermissibly impaired the freedom of assembly of non-gang members in violation of the First Amendment, that it was unconstitutionally vague, that it infringed upon Fourth Amendment rights, and that it improperly criminalized status rather than conduct.[68] The Supreme Court of Illinois held that the gang loitering law violated due process because it was "impermissibly vague on its face and an arbitrary restriction on personal liberties."[69] The U.S. Supreme Court affirmed the Illinois Supreme Court's judgment on the ground that Chicago's gang loitering ordinance was void for vagueness in that the ordinance failed to set sufficiently specific limitations on the enforcement discretion of Chicago police.

B. THE MORALES OPINIONS

1. *The holding.* The void-for-vagueness doctrine is one of several devices by which judges may avoid making difficult constitutional

---

[66] Alschuler and Schulhofer, 1998 U Chi Legal F at 220, n 35 (cited in note 4). Only thirteen of the nineteen African-American aldermen were present at this vote. The majority of those present, however, voted in favor of the resolution, and four of the six not present had voted in favor of the ordinance's passage in 1992. Based on the assumption that each of the six missing aldermen would not have changed his vote if present, Professors Meares and Kahan suggest that by 1998, a majority of African-American aldermen supported the ordinance. See Meares and Kahan, 1998 U Chi Legal F at 250, n 24 (cited in note 34).

[67] Alschuler and Schulhofer, 1998 U Chi Legal F at 237 (cited in note 4).

[68] *Chicago v Youkhana*, 277 Ill App 3d 101, 106–14, 660 NE2d 34 (1995).

[69] *Morales*, 177 Ill 2d at 447.

decisions while deciding the controversy before them—in the case
of the vagueness doctrine, by invalidating a constitutionally suspect
law as overly vague while leaving open the possibility that a clearer
version of the law might be upheld.[70] Professor Sunstein has shown
that the current Supreme Court has a special fondness for such
devices: that this Court not infrequently employs doctrines like
void-for-vagueness to "avoid[ ] clear rules and final resolutions"
and to "allow[ ] continued space for democratic reflection from
Congress and the states."[71] He terms this style of decision making
by courts "judicial minimalism."[72] "[K]now[ing] that there is much
that it does not know" and "intensely aware of its own limitations," a minimalist court seeks "to decide cases on narrow
grounds."[73] And this Supreme Court, according to Professor
Sunstein, "embraces minimalism."[74]

The Supreme Court's holding in *Morales* could be termed an
exercise in judicial minimalism. Indeed, even by minimalist standards, the majority's holding would have to be characterized as
unusually narrow. Traditionally, penal laws are said to be unconstitutionally vague when they fail to "define the criminal offense with
sufficient definiteness that ordinary people can understand what
conduct is prohibited" and to establish guidelines for enforcement
that are sufficiently concrete so as not to "encourage arbitrary and
discriminatory [law] enforcement."[75] The *Morales* majority found
that Chicago's gang loitering ordinance failed to satisfy the second
of these two requirements.[76] Six Justices concluded that the ordinance's definition of loitering ("to remain in any one place with
no apparent purpose") was so vague that it in effect entrusted police with lawmaking authority and thus created a grave risk of capricious enforcement decisions.[77]

The majority's vagueness holding was thus limited to one aspect
of the vagueness doctrine—the role of that doctrine in demanding

---

[70] See Cass R. Sunstein, *One Case at a Time* 110 (Harv U Press, 1999).

[71] Id at ix–x.

[72] Id at ix.

[73] Id.

[74] Id at xi.

[75] *Kolender*, 461 US at 357–58.

[76] See *Morales*, 119 S Ct at 1861–62.

[77] See id.

that enforcement discretion be appropriately constrained—and to a single phrase in Chicago's lengthy and complex loitering law. Justice Stevens's analysis for the majority, moreover, was nothing if not succinct. In deciding that the ordinance's loitering definition was impermissibly vague, the majority proceeded on the assumption that *every* person loitering in a public place manifests some purpose—if only the purpose to loiter. Police charged with dispersing gang members and their associates loitering "with no apparent purpose," then, were in effect tasked with choosing among the purposes manifested by these individuals—purposes which police could legitimate by acquiescing in the behavior or condemn through orders to disperse. In the Court's words:

> Presumably an officer would have discretion to treat some purposes—perhaps a purpose to engage in idle conversation or simply to enjoy a cool breeze on a warm evening—as too frivolous to be apparent if he suspected a different ulterior motive. Moreover, an officer conscious of the city council's reasons for enacting the ordinance might well ignore its text and issue a dispersal order, even though an illicit purpose [was] actually apparent.[78]

The majority professed to be bound by the Illinois Supreme Court's conclusion that the Chicago ordinance's loitering definition clothed officers with "'absolute discretion . . . to determine what activities constitute loitering.'"[79] Even setting aside any deference to this statement as a construction of local law, however, the majority found "[t]he 'no apparent purpose' standard" to be "inherently subjective."[80] And such a subjective standard, in the majority's view, impermissibly left lawmaking "'to the moment-to-moment judgment of the policeman on his beat.'"[81]

2. *Other issues.* The majority's holding, then, was decidedly limited. But Justice Stevens addressed several additional issues in those portions of his opinion joined only by Justices Souter and Ginsburg. First, he elaborated on the vagueness doctrine's "fair notice" requirement and its application to the Chicago ordinance. In the view of the plurality, the gang loitering law also violated the

---

[78] Id at 1862.

[79] Id at 1861 (quoting *Morales*, 177 Ill 2d at 457).

[80] Id at 1862.

[81] Id at 1861 (quoting *Kolender*, 461 US at 359).

vagueness prohibition by leaving the public uncertain as to the nature of the conduct the law prohibited:

> It is difficult to imagine how any citizen of the city of Chicago standing in a public place with a group of people would know if he or she had an "apparent purpose." If she were talking to another person, would she have an apparent purpose? If she were frequently checking her watch and looking expectantly down the street, would she have an apparent purpose?[82]

The plurality rejected the argument that police dispersal orders could serve to inform citizens of the nature of the prohibited conduct for two reasons. First, the plurality concluded that Chicago's citizens were entitled to advance notice regarding the loitering prohibited by the ordinance so that these citizens might avoid ever being ordered to disperse.[83] Second, the Justices in the plurality agreed that the dispersal orders contemplated in the new law (requiring gang members and their associates "to disperse and remove themselves from the area") had the effect of compounding the inadequacy of the notice afforded by the ordinance's definition of loitering.[84] In Justice Stevens's words, "After such an order issues, how long must the loiterers remain apart? How far must they move? If each loiterer walks around the block and they meet again at the same location, are they subject to arrest or merely to being ordered to disperse again?"[85]

The plurality also explicitly addressed the issue whether loitering is a constitutionally protected activity and determined that the freedom to loiter for innocent purposes *is* an attribute of personal liberty protected by the Due Process Clause: "Indeed, it is apparent that an individual's decision to remain in a public place of his choice is as much a part of his liberty as the freedom of movement inside frontiers that is 'a part of our heritage.'"[86] Notably, how-

---

[82] Id at 1859 (opinion of Stevens, joined by Souter and Ginsburg).

[83] See id at 1860.

[84] See id.

[85] Id.

[86] Id at 1857–58 (quoting *Kent v Dulles*, 357 US 116, 126 (1958)). The plurality rejected the view that Chicago's gang loitering ordinance violated First Amendment rights for two reasons. First, the ordinance's prohibition on loitering "with no apparent purpose," the plurality said, did not interfere with the First Amendment rights of those loitering for the apparent purpose of communicating ideas. Second, the ordinance, by not reaching associations for the purpose of engaging in core First Amendment activities or intimate human associations, failed to implicate any right protected by the right of association. See id at 1857.

ever, Justice Stevens did not analyze whether the impact of Chicago's gang loitering ordinance on this liberty interest would itself support a facial challenge to the ordinance: "There is no need . . . to decide whether the impact of the Chicago ordinance on constitutionally protected liberty alone would suffice to support a facial challenge under the overbreadth doctrine. For it is clear that the vagueness of this enactment makes a facial challenge appropriate."[87]

Justices O'Connor, Breyer, and Kennedy—the other three Justices in the majority—did not join in those portions of the Stevens opinion dealing with the notice issue,[88] nor did they address the issue whether loitering for innocent purposes is an activity protected by the Due Process Clause. Each wrote separately. In the most significant of these opinions concurring in part and concurring in the judgment, Justice O'Connor, joined by Justice Breyer, went to some lengths to explain that despite the invalidation of Chicago's gang loitering law, "there remain open to Chicago reasonable alternatives to combat the very real threat posed by gang intimidation and violence."[89] She underscored the majority's conclusion that an ordinance limited to loitering by gang members that had "an apparently harmful purpose" would no doubt satisfy the vagueness prohibition.[90] So, too, she said, would a loitering ordinance that restricted its criminal penalties to gang members or that defined loitering to mean "'remain[ing] in any one place with no apparent purpose other than to establish control over identifiable areas, to intimidate others from entering those areas, or to conceal illegal activities.'"[91] Laws incorporating limits on the area and manner in which they might be enforced, she suggested, should also be distinguished from Chicago's gang loitering law.[92]

3. *The dissents.* Justice Scalia dissented in a separate opinion, as

---

[87] Id at 1858 (citations omitted).

[88] In a brief opinion concurring in part and concurring in the judgment, Justice Kennedy did note that he shared many of the plurality's concerns about the sufficiency of the notice provided by the ordinance. See id at 1865 (Kennedy concurring in part and concurring in the judgment).

[89] Id at 1864 (O'Connor concurring in part and concurring in the judgment, joined by Breyer).

[90] See id.

[91] Id at 1864–65.

[92] See id at 1864.

did Justice Thomas, in an opinion joined by both Chief Justice Rehnquist and Justice Scalia. Justice Scalia's dissent began by questioning whether federal courts even have the power to declare laws void in all their applications rather than as applied.[93] Acknowledging that the Court has exercised such a power "for some of the present century," he next argued that except in free-speech cases subject to the overbreadth doctrine, the Court should at least confine this power to those cases where a law is unconstitutional in all its applications.[94] Justice Scalia relied heavily on *United States v Salerno*, in which the Court purported to disfavor facial challenges and noted that they are "the most difficult challenge to mount successfully, since the challenger must establish that no set of circumstances exists under which the Act would be valid."[95] Despite Justice Scalia's impassioned treatment of this issue, however, the majority in *Morales* did not address the rationale for entertaining a facial challenge to Chicago's ordinance, while the plurality expressly declined to "resolve the viability of [*Salerno*'s] dictum."[96] The plurality asserted simply that when vagueness permeates a law like Chicago's gang loitering ordinance—a criminal law that the plurality characterized as containing no mens rea requirement and infringing on constitutionally protected rights—a facial attack should be entertained: "Since we, like the Illinois Supreme Court, conclude that vagueness permeates the ordinance, a facial challenge is appropriate."[97]

---

[93] See id at 1867–72 (Scalia dissenting).

[94] Id at 1869–71.

[95] 481 US 739, 745 (1987).

[96] Morales, 119 S Ct at 1858, n 22 (opinion of Stevens, joined by Souter and Ginsburg).

[97] Id. In his opinion concurring in part and concurring in the judgment, Justice Breyer similarly suggested that facial invalidation for vagueness is proper whenever a law delegates so much discretion to police that it can fairly be said that "*every* application of the ordinance represents an exercise of unlimited discretion." Id at 1866 (Breyer concurring in part and concurring in the judgment) (emphasis added). He argued that in this sense, facial invalidation for vagueness is unlike those cases in which the Court has entertained a facial challenge for overbreadth in the First Amendment context. In the latter cases, "a defendant whose conduct clearly falls within the law and may be constitutionally prohibited can nonetheless have the law declared facially invalid to protect the rights of others (whose protected speech might otherwise be chilled)." A law permeated with vagueness, in contrast, confers so much unchecked discretion on enforcement authorities that it is "invalid in all its applications." Accordingly, the right that defendants assert in facial vagueness cases—namely, "the right to be free from the officer's exercise of unchecked discretion"—is, in Justice Breyer's view, "more clearly their own." Id.

Not surprisingly, both Justice Scalia and Justice Thomas strongly disagreed with the characterization of Chicago's gang loitering ordinance as vague. Justice Scalia argued that even if the appropriate circumstances for a facial challenge extend more broadly than *Salerno* would suggest, Chicago's gang loitering law would still pass muster because the law is not vague "in most or even a substantial number of applications."[98] He took issue with the notion that loiterers are always manifesting some apparent purpose for remaining in any one place and argued, instead, that loiterers often display no apparent purpose for their behavior for the simple reason that they have no *actual* purpose in so behaving: "Remaining at rest will be a person's normal state, unless he has a purpose which causes him to move."[99] Justice Scalia concluded that in the bulk of cases, Chicago police could easily perceive the difference between those remaining in a place for an apparent reason and those remaining there without such a reason: "The criteria for issuance of a dispersal order under the Chicago Ordinance could hardly be clearer."[100] Justice Thomas's dissent was (if possible) even more emphatic: "[T]he Court's conclusion that the ordinance is impermissibly vague because it " 'necessarily entrusts lawmaking to the moment-to-moment judgment of the policeman on his beat,' " cannot be reconciled with common sense, longstanding police practice, or this Court's Fourth Amendment jurisprudence."[101]

Addressing the plurality, the dissenters similarly rejected the argument that a law hinging arrest on the refusal to obey a clear and explicit police order might nevertheless provide inadequate

---

[98] Id at 1875 (Scalia dissenting).

[99] Id at 1877, n 11.

[100] Id at 1876.

[101] Id at 1885 (Thomas dissenting, joined by Rehnquist and Scalia) (quoting majority's citation to *Kolender*, 461 US at 359). Both dissents similarly chastised the majority for purporting to be bound by the Illinois Supreme Court's statement that the "apparent purpose" standard "provides absolute discretion to police officers" to decide what constitutes loitering. See id at 1876 (Scalia dissenting); id at 1887, n 11 (Thomas dissenting, joined by Rehnquist and Scalia). In the words of Justice Scalia, the Illinois Supreme Court's statement was nothing more than a characterization of the ordinance's language in light of that court's refusal to read any limitations into it: "It [was] not a construction of the language (to which we are bound) but a legal conclusion (to which we most assuredly are not bound)." Id at 1876 (Scalia dissenting).

notice to the citizen as to the nature of the prohibited conduct: in Justice Thomas's words, "[t]here is nothing 'vague' about an order to disperse."[102] Justice Scalia chided the plurality for perceiving vagueness problems in police orders "to disperse and remove . . . from the area." He noted that this analysis, if adopted by the Court, "would render unconstitutional for vagueness many . . . Presidential proclamations," including President Eisenhower's command that all persons obstructing the court-ordered enrollment of black students in the Little Rock, Arkansas public schools "'cease and desist therefrom, and . . . disperse forthwith.'"[103] The dissenters also cited a lengthy history in which loitering has been criminalized to argue that loitering is not a fundamental right "'deeply rooted in this Nation's history and tradition,'" and thus properly characterized as a liberty interest protected by the Fourteenth Amendment's Due Process Clause.[104] Despite the plurality's insistence on a "Fundamental Freedom to Loiter," Justice Scalia noted, "there is not the slightest evidence for the existence of [such] a genuine constitutional right. . . ."[105]

Justice Thomas's dissent also detailed at some length the human costs exacted in many cities by the presence of criminal street gangs. "Gangs fill the daily lives of many of our poorest and most vulnerable citizens with a terror [to which] the Court does not give sufficient consideration," he said.[106] He noted that in 1998, "in an effort to curb plummeting attendance, the Chicago Public Schools hired dozens of adults to escort children to school"—children "too terrified of gang violence to leave their homes alone."[107] Justice Thomas quoted the testimony of one Chicago resident before the City Council to the effect that "'only about maybe one or two percent of the people in the city [are] causing these problems maybe, but it's keeping 98 percent of us in our houses and off the

---

[102] Id at 1886 (Thomas dissenting, joined by Rehnquist and Scalia). See also id at 1875–76 (Scalia dissenting).

[103] Id at 1875 (Scalia dissenting).

[104] Id at 1881–83 (Thomas dissenting, joined by Rehnquist and Scalia) (quoting *Washington v Glucksberg*, 521 US 702, 721 (1997) (citation omitted)). See also id at 1872–73 (Scalia dissenting).

[105] Id at 1872 (Scalia dissenting).

[106] Id at 1880 (Thomas dissenting, joined by Rehnquist and Scalia).

[107] Id.

streets and afraid to shop.'"[108] In a ringing conclusion to his dissent, Justice Thomas noted that "the Court focuses extensively on the 'rights' of gang members and their companions. It can safely do so—the people who will have to live with the consequences of today's opinion do not live in our neighborhoods."[109] He charged that the Court, by focusing exclusively on the 2 percent, had "denied our most vulnerable citizens the very thing that Justice Stevens elevates above all else—the 'freedom of movement.'"[110]

II. Some Clarity about Vagueness

The *Morales* opinions explicitly raise numerous significant issues and implicitly touch upon even more. It is with the Court's vagueness analysis, however, that one must begin in assessing the failure of the *Morales* majority to illuminate significant current issues regarding police patrol. The problems in this analysis are not apparent from a superficial reading of the *Morales* opinions. Such a reading discloses that the Court has reached no agreement as to those circumstances in which the facial vagueness doctrine should apply. This, however, is nothing new.[111] Such a reading demonstrates, as well, that the Justices vehemently disagree among themselves as to whether the "apparent purpose" language in Chicago's gang loitering ordinance is even vague. This fact alone does not constitute an indictment of their work. As Justice Frankfurter noted many years ago, unconstitutional indefiniteness "is itself an indefinite concept."[112] With the recent revival of statutes and ordinances aimed at improving the quality of life in public places, it is

---

[108] Id at 1887.

[109] Id.

[110] Id.

[111] See Richard H. Fallon, Jr., et al, *The Federal Courts and the Federal System* 212–13 (Foundation Press, 4th ed 1996) (noting mixed signals sent by Court as to when facial invalidation for vagueness is appropriate). Compare *Village of Hoffman Estates v Flipside, Hoffman Estates, Inc.*, 455 US 489, 494–95 (1982) ("[A]ssuming the enactment implicates no constitutionally protected conduct," a court should entertain a facial vagueness challenge "only if the enactment is impermissibly vague in all of its applications"), with *Kolender*, 461 US at 359, n 8 (permitting party to attack statute on ground that it would be impermissibly vague as applied to someone else and asserting that "[n]o authority cited by the dissent" supports argument that facial vagueness challenges are permitted only when statute is vague in all its applications).

[112] *Winters v New York*, 333 US 507, 524 (1948) (Frankfurter dissenting).

not altogether surprising that the Justices might come to different conclusions about whether any one of these newly enacted laws is sufficiently precise so as to reasonably confine the opportunity for abusive enforcement by police.

Looking no further than the four corners of the void-for-vagueness doctrine as it has been traditionally understood, then, it is possible to cast the *Morales* opinions as instances of reasonable disagreement among the Justices within a framework of overall doctrinal coherence. On closer inspection, however, *Morales* evinces a deeper problem—a real inability on the part of the majority to offer even a facially plausible account of the role that the vagueness doctrine actually plays in constraining the opportunity for arbitrary and discriminatory law enforcement by local police. To bring this aspect of *Morales* to the surface, I first explore the degree to which the *Morales* holding is in tension with other aspects of the legal environment in which public order policing occurs—and in ways that deprive the majority of the ability credibly to maintain that this holding represents a significant constraint on the opportunity for abusive police enforcement. I then argue that the majority focused its attention on matters of little relevance to the constraint of police discretion and ignored aspects of the Chicago law that could have promoted the judicious use of discretion by officers on patrol. Overall, this part contends that the majority's inability to articulate a workable framework for its vagueness doctrine threatens to deprive communities of the ability to enact legitimate laws that might assist in the amelioration of pressing social problems—and in what amounts to an illusory effort to constrain police.

A. THE LEGAL ENVIRONMENT FOR PUBLIC ORDER POLICING

The judicial invalidation of local public order laws as facially vague transformed the legal regime governing public order that was in place in this country into the 1960s and 1970s—a legal regime characterized by loitering, disorderly conduct, and vagrancy laws that were so vague in terminology and so broad in scope that they had the effect, in practice, of "'legally' authoriz[ing] the police to arrest virtually anyone."[113] The vagueness

---

[113] Robert Force, *Decriminalization of Breach of the Peace Statutes: A Nonpenal Approach to Order Maintenance*, 46 Tulane L Rev 367, 399 (1972). For a more detailed description of

cases from this period, though formally concerned that laws be sufficiently clear both to inform people what conduct is prohibited and to confine the discretion of enforcement authorities, were in fact animated most strongly by the latter concern—that laws should provide adequate guidelines for enforcement so as to limit the opportunity for the arbitrary and discriminatory application of legal prohibitions.[114] By the time *Kolender v Lawson* was decided in 1982, it was explicitly settled that the most important aspect of the vagueness doctrine is its role in requiring that a legislature establish minimal guidelines to govern law enforcement.[115] It was also settled (albeit implicitly) that the facial vagueness doctrine has a special application to local public order laws directed at various forms of public nuisance.[116] During the period leading up to *Kolender*, the exercise of police discretion pursuant to such laws was increasingly seen to evade any meaningful review in the criminal courts.[117] The decisions facially invalidating public order offenses as void for vagueness, then, were designed in large part to help secure a simple principle—that individuals should not walk public streets, as the Court said, "'only at the whim of . . . police officer[s].'"[118]

Morales, then, is but the latest in a line of Supreme Court cases in which the Court has employed the facial vagueness prohibition supposedly to constrain the potential for harsh and arbitrary law enforcement by local police. The assumption in all these cases— an assumption expressed quite clearly in *Morales*—is that courts

---

these laws and their invalidation in the 1960s and 1970s, see Livingston, 97 Colum L Rev at 595–601 (cited in note 2).

[114] For an explicit expression of this concern, see *Papachristou*, 405 US at 170 (noting that imprecise terms of ordinance "permit[ ] and encourage[ ] an arbitrary and discriminatory enforcement of the law").

[115] *Kolender*, 461 US at 358 (quoting *Smith v Goguen*, 415 US 566, 575 (1974)).

[116] See Jeffries, 71 Va L Rev at 215–16 (cited in note 16) (noting that vagueness doctrine is more commonly invoked against "street-cleaning" statutes than against laws criminalizing more serious conduct).

[117] The lack of meaningful judicial review in this area was seen as particularly troublesome because of ongoing civil rights struggles in the South. Indeed, many of the cases pressing facial challenges to public order laws in the 1960s involved the use of such laws to suppress peaceful sit-ins and civil rights demonstrations in Southern states. For a more detailed discussion of the historical context in which these cases were decided, see Livingston, 97 Colum L Rev at 598–601 (cited in note 2).

[118] *Kolender*, 461 US at 358 (quoting *Shuttlesworth v City of Birmingham*, 382 US 87, 90 (1965)).

significantly contribute to the reasonable restraint of capricious police enforcement when they facially invalidate those public order ordinances that afford "too much discretion to the police."[119] This assumption regarding the street-level efficacy of the facial vagueness doctrine seemed eminently plausible in the 1960s and 1970s, given both the panoply of broad and ill-defined public order laws to be found in the legal codes of many municipalities and the relative lack of empirical knowledge about the nature of police discretion.[120] Because police today are (and are understood to be) vested with a considerable degree of discretion that is beyond the scope of traditional vagueness doctrine, however, this assumption is significantly less plausible as applied to recently enacted laws like the one at stake in *Morales*.

This point can be most easily established by focusing on three characteristics of the current legal regime that, together, create substantial opportunities for police arbitrariness that do not raise traditional vagueness concerns. First is the significant potential for abusive enforcement that exists pursuant to broad but clear laws— such as the juvenile curfews that have become increasingly popular over the last ten years.[121] The most aggressive employment of the facial vagueness doctrine does not constrain the opportunity for police misuse of such laws and, indeed, may even encourage municipalities to enact them. Next, the prevalence in certain domains of numerous narrow and specific, but commonly violated, low-level statutes and ordinances likewise creates opportunities for abusive police enforcement. These opportunities, too, lie beyond the scope of traditional vagueness doctrine and thus challenge the *Morales* majority's assumption that the void-for-vagueness doctrine represents a meaningful check on police. Finally, the Court's own Fourth Amendment jurisprudence—its endorsement of warrantless police actions premised on admittedly nebulous concepts like probable cause—vests police with a significant degree of street-level discretion that is hard to reconcile with the *Morales*

---

[119] *Morales*, 119 S Ct at 1863 (opinion of Stevens, joined by Souter and Ginsburg).

[120] For an account of how discretion in criminal justice administration was only "discovered" beginning in the late 1950s and how thereafter it became better understood, see Samuel Walker, *Taming the System* 6–12 (Oxford U Press, 1993).

[121] See William Ruefle and Kenneth Mike Reynolds, *Curfews and Delinquency in Major American Cities*, 41 Crime & Delinquency 347, 353 (1995) (noting recent popularity of juvenile curfews).

majority's condemnation of the discretion involved in applying Chicago's gang loitering ordinance.

1. *Broad, clear laws and the vagueness prohibition.* A brief hypothetical can demonstrate not only that traditional vagueness doctrine fails to address the opportunity for abusive police enforcement created by broad but clear laws, but that vagueness doctrine may even encourage legislators to expand the reach of legal prohibitions. Consider the finding of the Chicago City Council that in many Chicago neighborhoods in 1992, criminal street gangs loitered in identifiable areas so as to establish control over these areas "and intimidat[e] others from entering" them.[122] Based on this finding, a council member in 1992 might well have proposed an ordinance authorizing police to order any person reasonably believed to be a gang member to depart from any neighborhood in which he might be found loitering so as to intimidate others from using public spaces. This formulation was essentially endorsed in Justice Stevens's opinion for the majority in *Morales*.[123] Thus, even as the Court invalidated Chicago's gang loitering ordinance on the ground that the "no apparent purpose" language in that law's loitering definition was unconstitutionally vague, the Court reached out to opine that an ordinance limited to loitering by gang members that "had an apparently harmful . . . effect" would "no doubt be sufficient" to satisfy vagueness concerns.[124]

But could our council member in 1992 have been reasonably confident that such a law would survive facial vagueness review? In an opinion offering only the most summary analysis, the Supreme Court in 1971 facially invalidated a law prohibiting three or more people from assembling on any sidewalk and conducting themselves in a manner annoying to passersby, noting that a city may not enact and enforce an ordinance "whose violation may entirely depend upon whether or not a policeman is annoyed."[125] Our hypothetical legislator, then, would have needed to address the question whether an ordinance authorizing police to move

---

[122] See *Morales*, 177 Ill 2d at 445 (quoting City Council's findings).

[123] It has also received some support in the academic literature. See, e.g., Peter W. Poulos, Comment, *Chicago's Ban on Gang Loitering: Making Sense of Vagueness and Overbreadth in Loitering Laws*, 83 Cal L Rev 379, 340 (1995).

[124] *Morales*, 119 S Ct at 1862.

[125] *Coates v Cincinnati*, 402 US 611, 614 (1971).

along loiterers who are acting so as to intimidate others is any less vague than an ordinance directed at conduct that annoys. Even prior to the majority's dicta in *Morales*, a court might have answered this question in the affirmative. But this answer was certainly not clear-cut in 1992.

So what would our legislator have done next? He might have suggested a law prohibiting those reasonably believed to be criminal street gang members from loitering in public places with the specific intent of intimidating others from entering these places. He might have pointed out that the Court has on occasion suggested that a specific intent requirement ameliorates vagueness concerns.[126] But on further consideration, he would probably have concluded that even this revision was inadequate to ensure the constitutionality of the legislation he intended to propose. The Supreme Court's observations about specific intent have not prevented several state supreme courts from invalidating public order laws reasonably read to include such an element as void for vagueness.[127]

Such invalidations, moreover, may in fact make sense—at least to the extent that the vagueness doctrine's chief concern is the potential for arbitrary police enforcement. The specific intent element has traditionally been said to address the vagueness doctrine's mandate that penal laws provide adequate notice to the public about the nature of prohibited conduct—not its concern that police might misuse an overly ambiguous law.[128] It is easy to understand, moreover, how including a specific intent element among those facts which must be shown at trial works (at least in theory) to cure notice difficulties. As the Court has said, to hold someone liable for violating a law containing a specific intent element, a fact finder must conclude that the defendant at the time of the alleged offense "[was] aware that what he [did was] precisely that which the statute forbids."[129] Such a conclusion, of course, substantially

---

[126] See, e.g., *Papachristou*, 405 US at 163.

[127] See, e.g., *E.L. v State*, 619 S2d 252, 253 (Fla 1993) (invalidating drug loitering ordinance as vague); *Wyche v State*, 619 S2d 231, 236 (Fla 1993) (invalidating prostitution loitering ordinance for vagueness); *City of Akron v Rowland*, 67 Ohio St 3d 374, 381–86, 618 NE2d 138 (Ohio 1993) (invalidating drug loitering ordinance as vague).

[128] See *Screws v United States*, 325 US 91, 103–04 (1945).

[129] Id at 104.

ameliorates any concern that because of the vagueness in a legal prohibition, the defendant had no notice of what the law required.

It is less easy to perceive, however, how a specific intent requirement meaningfully constrains the potential for arbitrary police enforcement on the street. In this context, the vagueness doctrine's demand for adequate specificity in statutes and ordinances is designed to ensure that officers do not capriciously employ ambiguous laws to charge people in light of the officers' own "personal predilections."[130] But our conscientious legislator in 1992 was already worried about the vagueness in a law authorizing police to disperse those gang members loitering in such a way as to intimidate others, objectively speaking. Could he honestly conclude that police receive significantly more guidance from a law directing them to move along those gang members loitering so as to intimidate others—but now from each gang member's *subjective* perspective? In reality, an officer would rely on the very same observable conduct to make judgments about the loiterer's internal mental state that he would have used to determine whether this loiterer was acting in a manner reasonably likely to have harmful effects on others.

Our legislator could not be blamed at this juncture for taking yet another tack to minimize any vagueness in his proposed ordinance. He might have noticed that most street gang offenses in Chicago have historically been committed by young people between the ages of fifteen and nineteen.[131] Why not enact a law prohibiting at least the juveniles in this group from loitering in public places? Or better yet, from being in public places, except for carefully specified purposes? By removing from police the necessity of distinguishing intimidating or purposefully harmful loitering from harmless loitering, this approach does substantially ameliorate vagueness concerns. But it does so only by broadening the category of people subject to the law to a group defined by age—an attribute offering the advantage that it can be specified (at least comparatively) with a substantial measure of rulelike precision.

This is not what happened in Chicago in 1992. There is evidence, however, that something very much like this hypothetical

---

[130] *Goguen*, 415 US at 575.

[131] See *Street Gangs and Crime* at 7 (cited in note 17).

happened in many other municipalities in the 1990s. In cities across the country, many legislators concerned with public order issues proposed and then enacted laws very similar to the one just discussed—namely, juvenile curfews.[132] These legislators, moreover, were not out of the mainstream in any sense. In the 1990s, curfews became "the norm in major American cities."[133] As of 1995, they existed in 77 percent of those cities with 1992 populations of 200,000 or more; half of all such cities either enacted new curfews or revised existing ones between the years 1990 and 1994.[134]

Curfews have also been upheld by several appellate courts. Indeed, within one week of the Court's decision in *Morales* invalidating Chicago's gang loitering law, the U.S. Court of Appeals for the District of Columbia Circuit, in an en banc decision, upheld the constitutionality of the District of Columbia's juvenile curfew—a law "which bars juveniles 16 and under from being in a public place unaccompanied by a parent or without equivalent adult supervision from 11:00 p.m. on Sunday through Thursday to 6:00 a.m. the following day" and from midnight on Friday and Saturday night to 6:00 a.m. the following morning.[135] The law was enacted "to protect the welfare of minors by reducing the likelihood that minors will perpetrate or become victims of

---

[132] See Livingston, 97 Colum L Rev at 556, n 15 (cited in note 2) (juvenile curfews now in effect in nearly three-quarters of the nation's largest cities).

[133] Ruefle and Reynolds, 41 Crime & Delinquency at 353 (cited in note 121).

[134] See id.

[135] *Hutchins v District of Columbia*, 188 F3d 531, 534 (DC Cir 1999). As the D.C. Circuit Court noted, by its terms, the curfew is not violated if the minor is:

(1) accompanied by the minor's parent or guardian or any other person 21 years or older authorized by a parent to be a caretaker for the minor; (2) on an errand at the direction of the minor's parent, guardian, or caretaker, without any detour or stop; (3) in a vehicle involved in interstate travel; (4) engaged in certain employment activity, or going to or from employment, without any detour or stop; (5) involved in an emergency; (6) on the sidewalk that abuts the minor's or the next-door neighbor's residence, if the neighbor has not complained to the police; (7) in attendance at an official school, religious, or other recreational activity sponsored by the District of Columbia, a civic organization, or another similar entity that takes responsibility for the minor, or going to or from, without any detour or stop, such an activity supervised by adults; or (8) exercising First Amendment rights, including free exercise of religion, freedom of speech, and the right of assembly.

Id at 535.

crime. . . ."[136] Similarly, the Fourth Circuit easily rejected a vagueness challenge to Charlottesville, Virginia's juvenile curfew, noting that the search for clarity in a criminal code "can be a receding mirage" which cannot be permitted to " 'convert into a constitutional dilemma the practical difficulties in drawing [appropriate] criminal statutes. . . .' "[137]

Juvenile curfews have both supporters and detractors.[138] But whatever their merits, it is perverse that vagueness decisions supposedly emanating from a concern with the potential for arbitrary police enforcement may well have tilted localities in the direction of enacting curfews as opposed to gang loitering, disorderly conduct, or other similar public order laws. Curfews may or may not be a better way of reducing crime and improving the quality of life in public spaces, but there is little to suggest that curfews are preferable from the standpoint of limiting the opportunity for arbitrary and discriminatory police enforcement.

At least within the hours of their operation, curfews have the practical effect of authorizing police to approach and detain *any* person who appears young enough to trigger their prohibitions. This is an extremely broad category of people—and incidentally, the very category of people who are already among the most likely to be approached by police in a public place.[139] Curfews, moreover, are often enacted as "quick-fix" solutions to concerns about community violence—and without any consideration of the police resources needed to enforce them evenhandedly.[140] Such laws may not be vague, but the manner in which they are (or are not) em-

---

[136] Id at 541.

[137] See *Schleifer v City of Charlottesville*, 159 F3d 843, 853 (4th Cir 1998) (quoting *Colten v Kentucky*, 407 US 104, 110 (1972)). See also *Qutb v Strauss*, 11 F3d 488, 492 (5th Cir 1993) (rejecting equal protection challenge to a juvenile curfew). But see *Nunez v City of San Diego*, 114 F3d 935, 940–52 (9th Cir 1997) (holding that juvenile curfew was unconstitutionally vague and overbroad, and that curfew violated equal protection and parents' fundamental right to rear children without undue governmental interference).

[138] See Robert Hanley, *Authorities Turn to Curfews to Clear the Streets of Teen-Agers*, NY Times B1 (Nov 8, 1993) (citing critics of curfews). See also Todd S. Purdum, *Clinton Backs Plan to Deter Youthful Violence*, NY Times A20 (May 31, 1996) (noting President Clinton's endorsement of juvenile curfews).

[139] See Egon Bittner, *Aspects of Police Work* 98 (Northeastern U Press, 1990) (noting that "young people in general" are "preferred targets of special police concern").

[140] See Hanley, *Authorities Turn to Curfews to Clear the Streets of Teen-Agers*, NY Times at B1 (cited in note 138).

ployed can in practice still subject a large number of people to spotty, erratic—and even arbitrary—enforcement efforts.

All this escapes traditional vagueness analysis. In evaluating whether a given law is impermissibly vague, courts do not routinely consider the alternatives to this law. They never consider that the overall effect of a body of decisions invalidating laws in a given subject area as overly vague may be paradoxical: that in future efforts to avoid vagueness and imprecision in defining a law's core concepts (like any ordinance addressed to "gang members" who adopt "turf" and "annoy," "harass," or "intimidate" others), legislators searching for precise terms may end up broadening the enforcement authorization given to police and thus adding to, rather than narrowing, the scope of enforcement discretion. The potential correlation between breadth and clarity in public order legislation, however, creates serious analytic difficulties for the *Morales* majority's assumption that traditional vagueness doctrine can be meaningfully employed to limit the potential for arbitrary exercises of police patrol discretion.

2. *Vagueness and the prevalence of frequently violated rules.* Vagueness doctrine is concerned with the *potential* for arbitrary enforcement posed by a given law. No one in the least familiar with current controversies involving police, however, can be unaware of the principal arena in which police today have been charged with *actual* arbitrariness and discrimination in enforcement—namely, traffic stops. The Justice Department and New Jersey officials, for instance, are even now in the process of implementing a consent decree that mandates changes in the operation of the New Jersey State Police to address long-standing charges of racial discrimination against minority motorists by personnel within this law enforcement agency—charges, parenthetically, that the governor of New Jersey has conceded to be true.[141] The admittedly small number of empirical studies on this subject, moreover, together with a much more substantial body of anecdotal evidence, strongly indicate that the problem of racial discrimination in traffic enforcement extends well beyond New Jersey. It is clear that mi-

---

[141] See Jerry Gray, *New Jersey Plans to Forestall Suit on Race Profiling*, NY Times A1 (Apr 30, 1999) (noting negotiations between Justice Department and New Jersey officials). See also Robert Cohen, *Whitman Vows to Root Out Racial Profiling*, Star-Ledger 24 (Apr 15, 1999) (reporting on statement by Governor Christine Whitman).

nority motorists around the country "are pulled over far more frequently than whites."[142] African Americans, in particular, "almost universally describe[ ] . . . as an everyday reality . . . the familiar roadside detention for 'Driving While Black.'"[143]

The grievances of minority motorists stopped by police represent an important challenge for law enforcement officials dedicated to overcoming the estrangement that has not infrequently characterized the relationship between police and minority communities. For our purposes here, however, the immediate significance of these grievances lies in the light they shed on the limited ability of the Court materially to influence the opportunity for arbitrariness in police enforcement through the invalidation of vague laws. Traffic rules regulating speed, lane changing, and the like are among the most precise regulations to be found in state and local legal codes. These laws, by traditional standards, are simply not vague. Despite the specificity of such laws, however, no one could deny that the opportunity for their arbitrary and discriminatory enforcement is huge—whatever one believes about the frequency with which police actually engage in the capricious exercise of enforcement authority. Low-level traffic offenses (like most laws regulating minor misconduct) are not invariably enforced, even when the evidence of their violation is clear. Because almost everyone violates traffic rules sometimes, moreover, the police, "if they are patient, can eventually pull over anyone they are interested in questioning . . . ."[144] In effect, clear and precise traffic laws empower police to pursue their own predilections in targeting people for enforcement *in precisely the manner condemned by the vagueness prohibition.*

But this point is obscured in traditional vagueness analysis. Lower courts do not routinely consider the claim that in fields of human endeavor that are heavily and minutely regulated with rules that are invariably broken at least part of the time, the judiciary's demand for specificity does not significantly reduce the opportunity for arbitrary law enforcement. Nor has the Supreme Court

---

[142] David A. Sklansky, *Traffic Stops, Minority Motorists, and the Future of the Fourth Amendment,* 1997 Supreme Court Review 271, 313.

[143] Id at 312. See also Henry L. Gates, Jr., *Thirteen Ways of Looking at a Black Man,* New Yorker 59 (Oct 23, 1995) (noting that "[t]here's a moving violation that many African-Americans know as D.W.B.: Driving While Black").

[144] Sklansky, 1997 Supreme Court Review at 298–99 (cited in note 142).

ever accepted the argument that the Due Process Clause's demand
for reasonable specificity in statutes and ordinances might also require that enforcement policies be adequately precise.[145] The Court's
continued skepticism with regard to such an argument, moreover, can probably be safely inferred from its recent unanimous
decision in *Whren v United States*.[146] There, the Court outright
rejected the claim that the Fourth Amendment might impose obligations on police to adhere to reasonably well-specified enforcement policies (above and beyond that Amendment's mandate that
probable cause exist to support arrest) merely because of the abun-
dance of commonly violated regulations within a given sphere.

Whren was, in fact, a "traffic" case. The incident giving rise to
the suppression motion in that case began when plainclothes vice-
squad officers in the District of Columbia who were patrolling a
"high drug area" in an unmarked vehicle observed a dark Pathfinder truck stopped at an intersection.[147] Their suspicions somewhat aroused by the behavior of the truck's youthful occupants, the
officers observed the Pathfinder turn without signaling and then
proceed at an "unreasonable" speed. They stopped the truck—
apparently in violation of local police regulations permitting plainclothes officers in unmarked cars to enforce traffic laws only in
the case of violations so grave as to pose an immediate threat to
the safety of others.[148] An officer testified that he approached the
Pathfinder to give the driver a warning about traffic violations.[149]
Drawing up to the driver's window, however, he observed plastic
bags of crack cocaine in the hands of the passenger, Whren. Both
Whren and Brown, the driver of the Pathfinder, were arrested,
and quantities of several types of illegal drugs were retrieved from
the truck.[150]

The petitioners in *Whren* had a simple argument. They contended that probable cause that a driver has violated a civil traffic

---

[145] This is despite the urging of Kenneth Culp Davis, who argued that "the vagueness
of the enforcement policy is at least as important as the vagueness of a statute or ordinance,
for it just as much permits and encourages arbitrary and discriminatory enforcement of the
law." Kenneth Culp Davis, *Police Discretion* 137 (West, 1975).

[146] 517 US 806 (1996).

[147] Id at 808.

[148] See id at 808, 815.

[149] See id at 809.

[150] See id at 808–09.

regulation should not without more be adequate to justify a traffic stop for the very reason that ". . . a police officer will almost invariably be able to catch any given motorist in [some] technical violation."[151] To guard against racially discriminatory traffic stops, as well as the pretextual use of traffic regulations as a tool for investigating other law violations, the petitioners contended that courts judging the reasonableness of a traffic stop for Fourth Amendment purposes should ask "whether the officer's conduct deviated materially from usual police practices, so that a reasonable officer in the same circumstances would not have made the stop for the reasons given . . . ."[152] The Court emphatically—and unanimously—rejected this argument:

> [W]e are aware of no principle that would allow us to decide at what point a code of law becomes so expansive and so commonly violated that infraction itself can no longer be the ordinary measure of the lawfulness of enforcement. And even if we could identify such exorbitant codes, we do not know by what standard (or what right) we would decide, as petitioners would have us do, what particular provisions are sufficiently important to merit enforcement.[153]

Consider the ramifications of this result. There is no question that police employ the maze of traffic regulations proactively to investigate or to prevent other law violations. Indeed, in many cities plagued by things like "gang activity, illegal guns . . . and drive-by shootings," police officials have observed that "saturating an area with traffic patrol shuts down these illegal operations."[154] The phenomenon of enforcing commonly violated, low-level regulations to pursue broader law enforcement goals, moreover, is not limited to traffic enforcement. In New York City, for example, police enforcing precise but often violated laws regulating public drinking, littering, and the like have admitted that one purpose in stepping up enforcement in such areas is to remove weapons from the street.[155] Police managers there have even claimed that such

---

[151] Id at 810.

[152] Id at 814.

[153] Id at 818–19.

[154] Earl M. Sweeney, *Traffic Enforcement: New Uses for an Old Tool*, Police Chief 45 (July 1996).

[155] See, e.g., Eric Pooley, *One Good Apple*, Time 54, 56 (Jan 15, 1996) (noting observation by one New York City police official that enforcement of public drinking law often permits officers to locate weapons on the people stopped).

enforcement serves generally to *deter* weapons possession in public places. In the words of one New York City police adminis-
trator, the vigorous enforcement of low-level offenses is important precisely because it makes people leave their guns at home,
"know[ing] they might get stopped."[156]

The aggressive enforcement of low-level offenses to serve
broader law enforcement goals may be broadly supported in a
community. It may, in fact, help to address more serious crime.
The experiences of many minority motorists, however, attest that
police do not always exercise discretion in this area with wisdom—
or sometimes with any sensitivity to the communities they serve.
Even more important for our purposes, moreover, is the undeni-
able fact that it is *police* who make these important discretionary
judgments concerning the resources to be put into the enforcement of low-level offenses and the broader goals to which this
enforcement should be directed. The vagueness prohibition has
never been interpreted to constrain the exercise of such discretion—despite the fact that the opportunity for police arbitrariness
in this context is at least as significant as the opportunity created
by ordinances like Chicago's gang loitering law.[157]

3. *The Fourth Amendment and the vagueness principle.* Finally, the
Court has repeatedly held that it is consistent with the Fourth
Amendment for officers on the street, without prior judicial authorization, to apply concepts like "probable cause" and "reasonable
suspicion" even as the Court has acknowledged that it is impossible to articulate "precisely what [these concepts] mean."[158] The
tolerance shown in *Whren* to affording police even extremely

---

[156] See Ruben Castaneda, *As D.C. Police Struggle On, Change Pays Off in New York*, Washington Post A1 (Mar 30, 1996) (quoting New York City Deputy Police Commissioner).

[157] This is not to say that police may exercise their discretion in a manner that discriminates on the basis of factors like race. As the Court has said, "the constitutional basis
for objecting to intentionally discriminatory application of laws is the Equal Protection
Clause. . . ." *Whren*, 517 US at 813. It is impossible to view the Court's selective enforcement doctrine, however, as a robust control over the arbitrary exercise of police discretion.
First, this doctrine addresses actual and intentional discrimination, rather than the potential
for arbitrary and discriminatory enforcement that a given legal regime may create. Second, defendants bear an "extremely heavy burden of proof" to overcome the presumption
of regularity that attaches to criminal law enforcement. Wayne R. LaFave, *Arrest* 163
(Little, Brown, 1965). See also *United States v Armstrong*, 517 US 456, 465 (1996) (to dispel
presumption that law enforcement authorities have not violated equal protection, "a criminal defendant must present 'clear evidence to the contrary'") (quoting *United States v Chemical Foundation, Inc.*, 272 US 1, 14–15 (1926)).

[158] *Ornelas v United States*, 517 US 690, 695 (1996).

broad street-level discretion, then, is not limited to the exceptional
Fourth Amendment case. Indeed, the Court has broadly endorsed
the notion in its Fourth Amendment jurisprudence that officers
can fairly employ "commonsense, nontechnical conceptions" to
deal with the practical realities of street patrol.[159] This idea exists
in considerable tension, however, with the *Morales* majority's assumption that a substantial degree of technical clarity in the language to be applied by patrol officers is necessary to the effective
constraint of police discretion.

A few examples can illustrate this point. First, the bulk of felony
arrests in this country take place pursuant to the conclusion of an
officer that probable cause exists to believe that a crime has been
committed by the person being arrested. Such arrests generally do
not require prior judicial authorization, nor is such authorization
sought in most circumstances.[160] Similarly, officers may in most
cases search automobiles and containers within automobiles based
on a street-level assessment that probable cause supports the
search.[161] They may enter homes to pursue fleeing suspects or to
seize evidence in the process of being destroyed—again without a
warrant, and based on their on-the-scene determinations regarding
the existence of probable cause.[162] All these activities have been
held to be reasonable for Fourth Amendment purposes despite the
Court's acknowledgment that probable cause itself—the central
concept that police must accurately employ to act within Fourth
Amendment constraints—is a "fluid" legal construct "not readily . . . reduced to a neat set of legal rules."[163]

Terry v Ohio, however, may be the Court's single most important
Fourth Amendment case in terms of its role in constituting a legal
environment broadly supportive of the street-level discretion of

---

[159] Id.

[160] See *United States v Watson*, 423 US 411, 414–24 (1976) (holding that warrantless felony
arrests in public places are consistent with the Fourth Amendment).

[161] See *California v Acevedo*, 500 US 565, 580 (1991) (holding police with probable cause
to believe evidence will be found in an automobile may search any container in automobile
in which said evidence might be located); *California v Carney*, 471 US 386, 30 (1985) (holding that a motor home falls within "automobile exception" and may be searched without
a warrant upon a finding of probable cause).

[162] See *Warden v Hayden*, 387 US 294, 298–99 (1967) (discussing "hot pursuit"); *Johnson
v United States*, 333 US 10, 15 (1948) (discussing threat of destruction of evidence).

[163] *Illinois v Gates*, 462 US 213, 232 (1983).

officers on patrol.[164] Police acting under the authority of the
Court's decision in *Terry* and subsequent cases may generally detain people based on reasonable suspicion to believe that these
people may be committing or about to commit a crime.[165] Individuals may be frisked when there is reasonable suspicion to believe
they may be armed and dangerous.[166] Once again, these detentions
and frisks take place without prior judicial authorization. In the
great majority of cases, moreover, there is no subsequent judicial
review of the officer's judgment about the propriety of his actions.

No one could deny that patrol officers employ significant street-
level discretion in this context, nor that the proper exercise of this
discretion is of tremendous importance both to communities and
to police. Indiscriminate street stops and searches, after all, were
blamed by the Kerner Commission for helping to foster the "deep
hostility between police and ghetto communities" that contributed
to numerous tragic riots between 1964 and 1968.[167] And even when
properly employed, aggressive use of stop and frisk can alienate
and estrange communities in ways that ultimately detract from,
rather than contribute to, the maintenance of a vibrant civil order.

But these considerations have not led the Court to attempt more
stringently to regulate the area of stop and frisk. The Court has
found both street detentions and frisks based on reasonable suspicion to be consistent with Fourth Amendment principles despite
its recognition that such encounters are not trivial, but are often
"annoying," "frightening," and even "humiliating" to the persons
involved.[168] The Court has upheld the stop-and-frisk authority
even though police departments vary widely in the degree to which
they train and oversee officers so as to minimize its abuse. It has
done so, moreover, irrespective of its recognition that the standard
by which officers have to judge the propriety of their actions in
detaining and frisking an individual cannot be stated in clear and
readily understandable language:

---

[164] 392 US at 1.

[165] Reasonable suspicion that a person has committed a crime in the past will also legitimate a *Terry* detention, at least in some circumstances. See *United States v Hensley*, 469 US
221, 227–29 (1985). For a general description of *Terry* and its progeny, see Wayne R.
LaFave and Jerold H. Israel, *Criminal Procedure* § 3.8 at 202–14 (West, 2d ed 1992).

[166] See *Terry*, 392 US at 12.

[167] See *Report of the Natl Advisory Commission on Civil Disorders* 157–59 (1968).

[168] *Terry*, 392 US at 25.

Courts have used a variety of terms to capture the elusive concept of what cause is sufficient to authorize police to stop a person. Terms like "articulable reasons" and "founded suspicion" are not self-defining; they fall short of providing clear guidance dispositive of the myriad factual situations that arise. But the essence of all that has been written is that the totality of the circumstances—the whole picture—must be taken into account.[169]

Compare the holding in *Morales*. There, the majority concluded that the loitering definition in Chicago's gang loitering ordinance afforded police an intolerable amount of discretion—so much discretion that the ordinance in effect entrusted police with lawmaking authority.[170] The Chicago law and its implementing regulations, however, at least facially limited the authority granted to officers and carefully defined the circumstances in which this authority might be employed—authorizing only designated officers, for example, in the first instance not to arrest *or even to detain*, but only to issue "move along" orders to those gang members and their associates remaining in specified public places with no apparent reason. The *Morales* majority made no effort to answer the dissenters' charge that its condemnation of the Chicago ordinance was simply inconsistent with the Court's Fourth Amendment case law and the trust placed in police there to detain, to search, and even to arrest based upon "spur-of-the-moment determinations about amorphous legal standards such as 'probable cause' and 'reasonable suspicion'. . . ."[171] The Court's Fourth Amendment jurisprudence, however, substantially undercuts the persuasiveness of the majority's position that the "no apparent purpose" language in Chicago's ordinance conferred on police a "vast discretion" too extravagant to be endured.[172]

B. SHORTCOMINGS IN THE COURT'S VAGUENESS ANALYSIS

One response to all this could well be, "So what?" Perhaps the Court has been too willing to tolerate the expansive street-level

---

[169] *United States v Cortez*, 449 US 411, 417 (1981). See also *Terry*, 392 US at 12 (noting "limitations of the judicial function in controlling the myriad daily situations in which policemen and citizens confront each other on the street").

[170] *Morales*, 119 S Ct 1861 (characterizing ordinance).

[171] Id at 1885 (Thomas dissenting, joined by Rehnquist and Scalia).

[172] Id at 1861 (majority opinion).

discretion conferred on police by broad, clear laws regulating minor misconduct, by the plethora of narrow (and commonly violated) regulations that characterize the legal environment in some spheres of human activity, and even by the Court's own Fourth Amendment case law. This is no reason to abandon whatever limited judicial control over arbitrary and capricious police enforcement that the facial vagueness doctrine represents.

Indeed, this doctrine may play an important role in disciplining police discretion even if there are contexts in which it has little or no application. The threat of facial invalidation may help prevent outright delegations to police to preserve order in public places in any way they choose. It may condition police and the lawyers who assist them to take administrative steps to monitor or restrain the exercise of discretion—thereby ameliorating the problems posed by laws embodying some degree of vagueness in their terms.[173] Finally, even if traditional vagueness doctrine can play at best a limited role in addressing arbitrary police enforcement, this in no way deprives the doctrine of its symbolic or expressive dimensions. It may be important, and very simply so, that the Supreme Court retains the authority to denounce the constitutional vice in laws that say that a person's use of public spaces is subject to the whim of police officers on patrol.[174]

Nevertheless, these observations speak generally to the existence of the facial vagueness doctrine and not to the question of how frequently it should be invoked—or whether its invocation in *Morales* was appropriate. Despite the claims of some advocates opposing Chicago's gang loitering law, the questions it presented to the Supreme Court were neither easy nor clear-cut. Granted, it is an open question whether laws like the one at stake in *Morales* will prove to be effective in addressing gang violence and the neighborhood disintegration it can effect.[175] Many cities like Chicago, how-

---

[173] This point draws upon and profits from Peter Strauss's more extended discussion of the role of the delegation and void-for-vagueness doctrines in the context of administrative law. See Peter L. Strauss, *Legislative Theory and the Rule of Law: Some Comments on Rubin*, 89 Colum L Rev 427, 441–45 (1989).

[174] See *Shuttlesworth*, 382 US at 90 (quoting *Cox v Louisiana*, 379 US 536, 579 (1965)).

[175] For an argument that law enforcement efforts directed specifically at gangs are often counterproductive because they have the unintended effect of transforming loosely associated groups of young people into more solidly bonded (and threatening) criminal organizations, see Malcolm W. Klein, *Street Gang Cycles*, in James Q. Wilson and Joan Petersilia, eds, *Crime* 217, 235 (ICS Press, 1995).

ever, are seriously experimenting with new methods of addressing violence in their communities while at the same time attempting appropriately to limit the power of police. The *Morales* majority's approach to vagueness may frustrate at least some of this experimentation while doing little, in reality, to restrain the discretion of patrol officers. Indeed, this approach may even contribute to police abuse—both by fostering an illusion of judicial competence in this arena that saps energy from other efforts at police reform and by depriving police of lawful authority to deal with community problems they are expected to handle.

It is important, then, that the Court begin to articulate a framework within which the real issues at stake might be addressed. This framework cannot limit courts assessing the vagueness of new public order laws to consideration of the text of such laws alone; it must be based upon a realistic assessment of the nature of police patrol discretion and the efficacy of the Court's efforts to influence its character. Caught up in the abstract parsing of the Chicago law's text, the *Morales* majority failed to grapple realistically with the issue of police discretion in many different ways. Four principal shortcomings in the *Morales* majority's opinion, in particular, point in the direction of a new framework for facial vagueness review.

1. *Hypertextualism.* First is the Court's hypertextualism. The majority's parsing of the Chicago ordinance's loitering definition at best provides a less than persuasive rationale for the Court's holding. More problematically, this hypertextual approach to vagueness may result in replacing one strategy for addressing gang loitering with others that present greater risks of police abuse. The majority claimed to have no choice in its interpretation of the Chicago ordinance, saying that it was bound by the Illinois Supreme Court's statement that the ordinance's loitering definition " 'provides absolute discretion to police officers to determine what activities constitute loitering.' "[176] Fairly read, however, this single sentence in the Illinois Supreme Court's decision was not a construction of the Chicago ordinance to which the Court was bound. Rather, it was a characterization of what the ordinance's language achieved in light of the Illinois court's refusal to read any limitations into it.[177] As both Justice Scalia and Justice Thomas argued in their

[176] *Morales*, 119 S Ct at 1861 (quoting *Morales*, 177 Ill 2d at 457).

[177] See *Wisconsin v Mitchell*, 508 US 476, 484 (1993) (noting that Court is not bound by such characterizations).

dissents, such characterizations are not binding on the Court: "[This was] not a construction of the language (to which we are bound) but a legal conclusion (to which we most assuredly are not bound)."[178]

The majority's analysis in fact hinged on its own characterization of how the "apparent purpose" language in the Chicago ordinance (as construed by the Illinois court) would be applied by officers on patrol. The majority reached its conclusion that the Chicago ordinance's loitering definition conferred a "vast discretion" on police only by assuming that virtually *all* loiterers have an apparent purpose for "remain[ing] in any one place"—so that officers applying the law were required in effect to come up with their own definition of prohibited loitering. This assumption, however, is unpersuasive for the simple reason that it renders Chicago's prohibition on remaining in one place with no apparent purpose utterly meaningless. In the Solicitor General's words, such a law "would prohibit nothing at all."[179] But once this assumption is set aside, the judgment whether the Chicago ordinance's language is sufficiently definite becomes considerably more difficult—and precisely because the law would seem to have many clear applications. Two women with neither umbrellas nor raincoats who stand in a doorway anxiously observing a downpour do manifest an apparent purpose for remaining in that doorway—namely, the purpose to stay out of the weather. Just as clearly, "a group that is talking or smoking while remaining in one place would not ordinarily have an apparent purpose, since it would rarely be apparent to an observer that the group's purpose for remaining in that place—rather than walking or moving elsewhere—was to talk or smoke."[180]

The conclusion that the Chicago law has a substantial number of clear applications, moreover, is at least implicitly supported by the record in *Morales*. There is little in that record to suggest that during the period the Chicago law was enforced, police had any trouble distinguishing between those gang members and their associates who remained in one place with an apparent purpose and those loitering without any discernible reason for doing so. As the

---

[178] *Morales*, 119 S Ct at 1876 (Scalia dissenting). See also id at 1887 n 11 (Thomas dissenting, joined by Rehnquist and Scalia).

[179] Brief for the United States Supporting Petitioner at 13 (cited in note 3).

[180] Id at 12.

petitioner in *Morales* pointed out, "after the many thousands of arrests under the ordinance, [the] record reflects not a single instance in which anyone . . . was arrested, or even ordered to move on, while engaged in political canvassing, planning a demonstration, . . . or doing anything else protected by the First Amendment."[181] The respondents could not even identify a single case in which clearly harmless loitering (admittedly falling within the statutory language) had been constrained—as, for instance, might have occurred if a social worker, minister, or other responsible adult found talking to gang members for the purpose of advising them to change their ways had been ordered to move along.[182]

The very difficulty of the judgment demanded in *Morales* suggests the importance in cases like this of considering not only the text of the law under review, but also alternative ways in which police might deal with the problem to which a given public order law is addressed. Thus, the *Morales* Court should have considered whether Chicago's gang loitering law might be preferable to alternatives like juvenile curfews precisely because police discretion in the gang loitering law is more clearly restrained. It should not have overlooked the possibility that Chicago's ordinance might pose fewer problems of arbitrary enforcement than another alternative that police have used to address the problems presented by a gang's turf occupation—namely, the employment of a menu of commonly violated (but admittedly clear) rules specifically to target gang members hanging out in public places.

The Court's neglect of these alternatives is troubling because the choice between Chicago's ordinance and these other approaches to gang loitering has serious implications for the core ambition the Court has articulated for its vagueness jurisprudence—namely, limiting the opportunity for arbitrary law enforcement. In the absence of a gang loitering law, patrol officers in a neighborhood afflicted by gang violence might turn to jaywalking, public littering, and juvenile curfew ordinances to suppress gang activity. An enforcement effort employing laws formally applicable to many people but directed narrowly at gang members, however, could well result in complaints about harassment—complaints to which police management would likely respond by citing the po-

---

[181] *Chicago v Morales*, No 97-1121, Brief for the Petitioner, at 22.

[182] See US S Ct Official Tr, *Chicago v Morales*, No 97-1121 (Dec 9, 1998), at 20–21.

lice department's responsibility for enforcing the law.[183] Such exchanges between police managers and community residents are not uncommon, but they have baleful effects on the project of reasonably restraining the potential for arbitrary enforcement. This is because such exchanges obscure rather than illuminate the issues surrounding the discretionary use of police authority—and in ways simply not possible when, as in the case of Chicago's gang loitering ordinance, a law is the subject of intense public scrutiny and is employed more precisely to deal with the problem for which it was enacted.

This is not to suggest that the vagueness question in *Morales* was simple, nor that Chicago's gang loitering ordinance was clearly preferable to other available approaches for dealing with a gang's occupation of turf. If the Court's vagueness jurisprudence is to have an effect on the realities of street-level policing, however, it is important that the Court move beyond its narrow focus on the text of the public order laws it reviews. The Court must recognize that the facial invalidation of public order laws that are imprecise to some degree can itself promote arbitrary law enforcement—by pushing police to employ admittedly clear laws for purposes other than those for which they were enacted, and in contexts where the exercise of police discretion is concealed.[184] The vagueness doctrine's traditional concern is to avoid the potential for arbitrariness that arises when imprecise laws delegate basic policy matters to police officers on patrol.[185] Realism demands an acknowledgment, however, that such delegation can occur even when laws are very precise—and in ways that can make the political control of discretion more difficult than when an admittedly imprecise law is employed.

2. *The "move along" provision.* The *Morales* majority next erred by neglecting to consider that the risk that Chicago's gang loitering law would be misused was mitigated by the law's limited reach—to gang loitering only when accompanied by the refusal to comply with a police order to move along, and not to gang loitering alone. The majority treated this aspect of the Chicago law dismissively, and as if it was wholly irrelevant to the ordinance's po-

---

[183] See Herman Goldstein, *Policing a Free Society* 105 (Ballinger, 1977).

[184] See id at 72.

[185] See *Grayned*, 408 US at 108–09.

tential to be used in an arbitrary and capricious way: "[T]hat the ordinance does not permit an arrest until after a dispersal order has been disobeyed," the majority concluded, "does not provide any guidance to the officer deciding whether such an order should issue."[186] In reality, however, this feature of the ordinance was of substantial importance to the question whether Chicago's law reasonably restrained police.

This is partly because the arrest power threatens individuals with serious consequences—like an arrest record—that are simply not presented by an order to "move along." Indeed, by not at least commenting favorably on this aspect of the Chicago ordinance, the *Morales* majority missed an opportunity to point municipalities in the direction of less punitive approaches to public order problems. This is unfortunate because such approaches are clearly preferable in many contexts: when the primary interest in enacting a new ordinance is not so much to prohibit an activity entirely, as to aid police in regulating it; when behaviors (like loitering) pose serious problems in communities but do not bear the traditional hallmarks of blameworthiness associated with criminal violations; and when it is difficult for legislators to define in the abstract precisely what behaviors they wish to proscribe.[187] The Court recognized in *Village of Hoffman Estates v The Flipside* that the need for clarity in a law depends in part on the severity of the penalties that flow from its violation.[188] In *Morales*, however, the majority overlooked an analogous point—that the potentially harmful effects of legislative imprecision are ameliorated when public order laws limit the arrest authority to cases involving defiance of a police command.

The significance of the Chicago ordinance's "move along" feature to the reasonable restraint of police discretion, moreover, is not limited to its role in softening the consequences that flow from the law's enforcement. By hinging the arrest authority on defiance of a police command rather than on simple loitering by gang mem-

---

[186] *Morales*, 119 S Ct at 1861–62.

[187] For a general theoretical discussion of factors influencing the choice between more or less punitive sanctions, see John C. Coffee, *Paradigms Lost: The Blurring of the Criminal and Civil Law Models—and What Can Be Done About It*, 11 Yale L J 1875, 1886 (1992).

[188] *Village of Hoffman Estates*, 455 US at 498–99 (expressing more tolerance for vagueness in laws with civil rather than criminal penalties "because the consequences of imprecision are qualitatively less severe").

bers and their associates, the Chicago ordinance also severed, to some degree, the connection between the "order maintenance" and "law enforcement" activities of police. This severance lessened the potential for arbitrary enforcement of the gang loitering law in a manner that should also have been considered by the *Morales* Court.

As is now well understood, police serve an order maintenance role that is distinct from their law enforcement role in two important ways. First, police invoking a public order law in service of order maintenance ends are often less interested in "enforcing the law" than in "maintaining a pattern of public order"—in putting an end to conditions or behaviors that threaten the public peace.[189] As a result, many order maintenance problems are handled on the street and informally, without any need for citation or arrest. Second, order maintenance, properly performed, is generally less adversarial than the ferreting out of serious crime.[190] This is partly because the maintenance of public order is often negotiated and thus does not place officers in frankly confrontational relations with people on the street. In addition, order maintenance does not feed the competitive, "crime fighting" self-image of many patrol officers.[191]

The potential interaction between the order maintenance and law enforcement roles of police, however, complicates any analysis of the ways in which patrol officers commonly employ discretion in the performance of order maintenance tasks. Police usually request that citizens desist from behaviors threatening the public order against the backdrop of a law criminalizing the underlying conduct that is the subject of the request. Patrol officers invoking such laws, then, are often tempted to employ them in the same way that traffic regulations are frequently employed—not to encourage people to desist from problematic conduct, but to pursue broader law enforcement goals. An officer may elect to make a "public order" arrest, for instance, without attempting to negotiate an end to troublesome conduct. This is because his real motivation is not

---

[189] Albert J. Reiss, Jr., *Consequences of Compliance and Deterrence Models of Law Enforcement for the Exercise of Police Discretion*, L & Contemp Probs, Autumn 1984, at 83, 84 n 3. See also James Q. Wilson, *Varieties of Police Behavior* 16 (Harv U Press, 1968).

[190] See *Johnson*, 333 US at 14 (discussing "competitive" nature of law enforcement).

[191] See Samuel Walker, *The Police in America* 61–63 (McGraw-Hill, 2d ed 1992) (noting prevalence of "crime fighting" self-image among police in traditional departments).

order maintenance at all. Instead, the officer wants to arrest so that he can conduct a search incident to arrest in the hope that this search will reveal evidence of more serious crime.

Because police at least generally expect their commands to be followed, however, limiting police authority in the first instance to the issuance of a "move along" order lessens the temptation on the part of police to employ a low-level public order law simply to gain the authority to search.[192] This is a significant advantage. The ferreting out of serious crime is an intensely competitive enterprise that poses a substantial risk of excessive police zeal.[193] Order maintenance, properly performed, is altogether different. By partially disentangling police measures that are principally directed at promoting and maintaining public order from the more adversarial business of investigating serious crime, then, the Chicago ordinance's "move along" feature at least reduced the risk of arbitrary and capricious enforcement.

3. *Administrative measures.* The next area in which the *Morales* majority failed to grapple realistically with the subject of police discretion concerns the Court's treatment of the Chicago Police Department's efforts to regulate and to monitor enforcement of the gang loitering law. The Court dismissed the Chicago Police Department's attempt to impose administrative controls on the use of Chicago's gang loitering ordinance, noting simply that the provision in General Order 92-4 limiting enforcement of the ordinance to designated areas in Chicago "would not provide a defense to a loiterer who might be arrested elsewhere."[194] This and other provisions in General Order 92-4, however, if implemented carefully, had the capacity substantially to ameliorate potential problems with the discretionary enforcement of Chicago's gang loiter-

---

[192] It is impossible entirely to separate order maintenance from law enforcement motives in policing as it is presently constituted. By approaching gang members in public places to issue "move along" orders, for example, police may thereby gain the ability to conduct legitimate *Terry* frisks for safety purposes—frisks that may uncover evidence to be used in the prosecution of serious crime. See, e.g., Pooley, *One Good Apple*, Time at 56 (cited in note 155) (noting observation of New York City police official that enforcement of public drinking law in New York has permitted officers to locate weapons carried by people stopped on the street). The formulation of Chicago's gang loitering law, however, ameliorates the problem posed by the interaction of order maintenance and law enforcement responsibilities in ways that should have been considered by the Court.

[193] See *Johnson*, 333 US at 14.

[194] *Morales*, 119 S Ct at 1862.

ing law—and regardless whether disregard of these provisions constituted a defense at trial.

Thus, it is important that police managers in Chicago at least limit the group of officers authorized to enforce Chicago's gang loitering ordinance to specially trained police knowledgeable about the gangs and gang members operating in their neighborhoods.[195] Indeed, to the extent that a police department structures its work to ensure that officers develop significant community-specific knowledge about the problems they are addressing, the exercise of police discretion is likely to be both better informed and more judicious. This reduces the potential for capricious exercises of police discretion to a significant degree.

Consider, for example, the position of the roving, citywide tactical team that last year confronted Amadou Diallo in his New York City foyer. Those officers approached Diallo, a local street peddler, based on their suspicion that he had committed a serious crime. But the officers had little connection to the neighborhood they were patrolling and little community-specific knowledge to draw upon in making the street-level judgment that Diallo was a likely suspect.[196] The results in that case were tragic: Diallo, an immigrant with no connection to the crime the officers were investigating, ended up "dead from a hail of bullets" and perhaps simply because "he acted furtively when confronted . . . by a band of plain-clothed armed men."[197]

Incidents involving officers confronting strange neighborhoods and people they do not know rarely end as tragically as in the Diallo case. Surely it makes a difference, however, that General Order 92-4 did not contemplate sending officers into unfamiliar neighborhoods for the purpose of "rounding up" gang members and their associates. The order limited enforcement of the ordinance to designated police personnel who were required to familiarize themselves with information regarding the criminal street gangs active in the neighborhoods in which these officers worked.[198] Further, enforcement of Chicago's gang loitering ordi-

---

[195] See Chicago Police Department, General Order No 92-4 at §§ III.C, VI.C.1 (cited in note 51).

[196] See Wesley G. Skogan, *Everybody's Business*, Boston Rev 15, 16 (Apr/May 1999).

[197] Id at 15.

[198] See Chicago Police Department, General Order No 92-4 at §§ III.C, VI.C.1 (cited in note 51).

nance was limited to areas designated in advance as places where
gang loitering had significantly affected the surrounding community. Such designations were to derive at least in part from some
measure of community consultation.[199] The overall thrust of these
provisions, then, was to encourage police to analyze a neighborhood's problems and to determine in advance the need to employ
the gang loitering law in that neighborhood. Properly implemented, these provisions in General Order 92-4 had the capacity
to influence the exercise of police discretion in profound and beneficial ways.

Other provisions of Chicago's police regulations were likewise
relevant to the question whether police discretion was reasonably
restrained. The requirement that officers making arrests pursuant
to the gang loitering law prepare written reports describing the
circumstances giving rise to probable cause to arrest, for instance,
represented a potentially significant constraint on the opportunity
for arbitrary enforcement.[200] Records of this type facilitate public
review of exercises of police discretion and also provide police
managers with helpful information about the behavior of their officers.[201] General Order 92-4 also contemplated that the department's records regarding gang members would be regularly up-
dated in ways designed to help ensure that officers exercising
discretion in the enforcement of the gang loitering law would be
acting on the basis of accurate information. Thus, these records
were to contain "only the names of individuals the Department
ha[d] concluded that it ha[d] probable cause to believe [were]
members of criminal street gangs."[202] The order provided for reg-

---

[199] See id at § VI.A.1. In oral argument, at least one Justice seemed to discount this
administrative requirement because the police regulations did not provide for *public* designation of those parts of the city determined to be places where the public presence of gang
members had resulted in "a demonstrable effect on the activities of law abiding persons in
the surrounding community." See US S Ct Official Tr, *Morales* at 22–23 (cited in note
182). Even internal administrative requirements, however, can help constrain the potential
for arbitrary police enforcement—and in this case without imposing the costs on borderline
neighborhoods that would likely flow from any formal public designation of their gang-
infested status.

[200] See Chicago Police Department, General Order No 92-4 at § VI.C.3 (cited in note
51).

[201] For a fuller discussion of the role of record keeping in enhancing police accountability,
see Debra Livingston, *Police Reform and the Department of Justice: An Essay on Accountability*,
2 Buff Crim L Rev 815, 846–52 (1999).

[202] Chicago Police Department, General Order No 92-4 at § VI.A.5 (cited in note 51).

ular deletion of the names of individuals apparently no longer actively involved in gang activity.[203]

Perhaps Chicago's police regulations were implemented badly.
Perhaps as implemented these regulations were even inadequate
to the task of restraining the discretion of Chicago police. For the
purpose of the majority's analysis in *Morales*, however, it was a
matter of no significance whatsoever that Chicago's police managers did much more than simply encourage widespread enforcement of the gang loitering law. This approach to vagueness is simply wrong. As the Court said in *Ward v Rock Against Racism*, the
administrative interpretation and implementation of a law are
"highly relevant" to facial vagueness analysis.[204] By *not* focusing on
this aspect of the case, the Court missed an opportunity to provide
both legislators and police managers with the incentive to experiment with innovative administrative approaches to the reasonable
restraint of police.

4. *Proposed changes to Chicago's gang loitering law.* Perhaps the shortcomings in the *Morales* majority's approach to vagueness, however,
are most evident not upon consideration of what the majority opinion omits, but upon consideration of what the Justices in the majority chose to say. Both Justice Stevens, writing for the majority, and
Justice O'Connor, in her concurring opinion, empathized with the
efforts of Chicago communities to address the serious gang problems afflicting them. Unusually, they even suggested ways in which
Chicago might constitutionally regulate the loitering of gang members. But the very changes to Chicago's gang loitering ordinance
that these Justices proposed attest to the failure of the Court to
grapple realistically with the issue of police discretion. Indeed, they
demonstrate that the majority has failed to fash-ion a framework
for its vagueness analysis that represents an effective response to
the potential for arbitrary and capricious police enforcement.

Consider first the majority's conclusion that a law prohibiting
only loitering having an "apparently harmful purpose or effect"
would "no doubt" satisfy vagueness review.[205] It is impossible to
conclude, as the majority blithely does, that officers charged with
dispersing loiterers remaining in a place for an "apparently harm-

---

[203] See id at § VI.A.6.a.

[204] 491 US 781, 795–96 (1989).

[205] *Morales*, 119 S Ct at 1862.

ful purpose" are significantly more constrained in the exercise of their discretion than officers acting to disperse those loiterers remaining for "no apparent purpose" whatsoever. Indeed, as the dissenters urged, an ordinance requiring officers to ascertain whether a group of loiterers has "an apparently harmful purpose" would seem to require these officers to exercise more discretion—more judgment in the law's application—than a law directing them to disperse loiterers hanging out for no apparent purpose at all.[206] Similarly, a mandate to officers to identify those loiterers remaining in any one place with "apparently harmful effects" would seem to require a substantial amount of judgment in its application. At least in the absence of some legislative specification of what these effects might be, such a law seems no better than the law enacted in Chicago.

Indeed, the Court ignores significant sociological research showing that patrol officers invoking public order laws in the service of order-maintenance ends do not consider these laws and then apply them to the facts in the manner of a law student taking an exam. Rather, police officers blend legal knowledge, "common sense," and various behavioral norms in using such laws to deal with problems they are called upon to handle.[207] In the words of one scholar:

> I am not aware of any descriptions of police work on the streets that support the view that patrolmen walk around, respond to service demands, or intervene in situations, with the provisions of the penal code in mind, matching what they see with some title or another, and deciding whether a particular infraction is serious enough to warrant being referred to further process.[208]

If police do not invoke the law in the manner of a law student taking an exam, however, the subtle differences in language discussed by the majority in *Morales* are unlikely to make any difference to the behavior of officers on patrol. Such subtle differences are also unlikely to affect the potential for police arbitrariness. The majority's approach to the reform of Chicago's gang loitering law is thus unpersuasive when viewed in light of the available empirical evidence about the behavior of police.

---

[206] See id at 1885 (Thomas dissenting, joined by Rehnquist and Scalia).

[207] See David Dixon, *Law in Policing* 278 (Clarendon, 1997).

[208] Bittner, *Aspects of Police Work* at 245 (cited in note 139).

This approach, moreover, is also unpersuasive when examined entirely on its own terms. Consider yet another modification to Chicago's gang loitering law discussed by the Court. The *Morales* majority suggested (without explicitly affirming) that limiting the criminal penalties in Chicago's gang loitering law to gang members alone might well cure the vagueness problem identified in the ordinance.[209] Justice O'Connor, in her concurrence, was definite on this point: "[L]imitations that restricted the ordinance's criminal penalties to gang members," she said, "would avoid the vagueness problems of the ordinance as construed by the Illinois Supreme Court."[210]

This position, however, undercuts entirely the stated rationale for the Court's holding. If the problem with the Chicago ordinance is really the one identified by the majority (namely, that the vagueness permeating the law creates too great an opportunity for its arbitrary enforcement), it makes little sense to argue that limiting the criminal penalties in Chicago's gang loitering law to gang members alone "solves" the problem. In Justice Scalia's words:

> [I]f "remain[ing] in one place with no apparent purpose" is so vague as to give the police unbridled discretion in controlling the conduct of non-gang-members, it surpasses understanding how it ceases to be so vague when applied to gang members alone. Surely gang members cannot be decreed to be outlaws, subject to the merest whim of the police as the rest of us are not.[211]

To a significant degree, then, it is fair to conclude that the majority in *Morales* both failed to consider factors truly relevant to a realistic approach to police discretion and focused on factors of little account. The result is a majority opinion that does not persuade and cannot assist localities in developing meaningful restraints on arbitrary and capricious law enforcement. This is not to say that a more realistic jurisprudence can render judgments like the one called for in *Morales* simple and clear-cut. Such a jurisprudence, however, could encourage localities to experiment with

---

[209] See *Morales*, 119 S Ct at 1862.

[210] Id at 1865 (O'Connor concurring in part and concurring in the judgment, joined by Breyer).

[211] Id at 1879 (Scalia dissenting).

approaches to the policing of public order that might more meaningfully constrain the opportunity for police arbitrariness.

III. A Realistic Vagueness Jurisprudence

So how might a more realistic vagueness jurisprudence
look? At the start, such a jurisprudence would be rooted in a recognition of both the breadth of police enforcement discretion and
the necessity for such discretion if police are adequately to perform
their jobs. Police discretion, especially in the enforcement of low-
level offenses, is a necessary consequence of limited resources and
the need to prioritize. Beyond these factors, moreover, it is also
a natural outgrowth of other variables: the recognition that not all
problems faced by police are best addressed through law enforcement, and that not all communities can or will tolerate full enforcement of laws specified by the legislature. This may seem obvious to informed observers today. As Justice O'Connor stated in
her concurrence, "some degree of police discretion is necessary
to allow the police 'to perform their peacekeeping responsibilities
satisfactorily.'"[212] As recently as forty years ago, however, "the
prevalent assumption of both the police and the public was that
the police had no discretion—that their job was to function in
strict accordance with the law."[213] And this notion that police are
ministerial officers—an idea that police have sometimes encouraged—still pervades much of the public discourse about law enforcement in ways detrimental to the reasonable restraint of arbitrary and capricious police behavior.

That said, it is equally important to affirm that police can be
held reasonably accountable for the exercise of enforcement discretion. Much of the discussion here has emphasized the degree
to which the void-for-vagueness doctrine creates an illusory sense
of formal accountability in its command that laws be sufficiently
precise so as to reasonably constrain enforcement discretion. Indeed, the doctrine has been cast in the worst of all possible lights:
as an ineffective constraint on abusive police conduct *that may even
contribute to such abuse* by casting officers left without lawful author-

---

[212] Id at 1863 (O'Connor concurring in part and concurring in the judgment, joined by
Breyer) (quoting id at 1885 (Thomas dissenting, joined by Rehnquist and Scalia)).

[213] Goldstein, *Policing a Free Society* at 93 (cited in note 183).

ity to address real community problems in the role of "dirty workers" who furtively bend rules or employ inappropriate laws to deal effectively with the situations they are called upon to handle.[214]

The vagueness doctrine, however, is but one small part of the legal and sociopolitical context in which police operate. Granted, there are police departments in which enforcement discretion, if not explicitly denied by police managers, is still exercised in a sub rosa and ad hoc fashion. There are also police departments, however, in which effective constraints on the opportunity for arbitrary and discriminatory enforcement have already emerged—in which a substantial effort is made to acknowledge enforcement discretion, to seek input from communities about its exercise, and to learn from experimentation within the department with different methods or styles of law enforcement. The differences between these two types of police department, moreover, translate into significantly different potentials for the arbitrary and capricious exercise of enforcement authority—and regardless of any differences in the clarity of the laws that they enforce.

A realistic vagueness jurisprudence, then, should work to stimulate local police departments to experiment with new and promising methods of promoting accountability in the exercise of police discretion. Admittedly, this is no easy task. The objectives behind the rules and procedures set by courts are always at least partially transformed by their interaction with the subcultural rules of police, the police organization's internal structure, and the practical exigencies of policing.[215] My colleague Michael Dorf's model of "provisional adjudication," however, outlines a way in which courts might focus more attention on the likely consequences of their decisions in order to find workable solutions to the problems they must address.[216] This form of adjudication is premised on the recognition that courts sometimes need to learn from experimentation with varied approaches to such problems. Professor Dorf's work suggests how courts might import some measure of realism

---

[214] For a discussion of how police not provided with "explicit authority to deal effectively with the problems they encounter" often become "dirty workers" who furtively " '[do]what has to be done' through the exercise of their discretion," see George L. Kelling and Catherine M. Coles, *Fixing Broken Windows* 167 (Free Press, 1996).

[215] See Dixon, *Law in Policing* at 267–68 (cited in note 207).

[216] See Michael C. Dorf, *Foreword: The Limits of Socratic Deliberation*, 112 Harv L Rev 4, 51–79 (1998).

into their facial vagueness assessments without thereby assuming the impossible burden of providing one-shot, definitive answers to empirical and policy questions concerning the best way in which to restrain police.

Simply stated, courts addressing difficult vagueness questions should consider whether the exercise of police discretion contemplated in challenged public order legislation will take place under conditions that provide reasonable assurances that the relevant police department will be accountable for the way in which it employs this discretion. Such assurances will not derive solely from the clarity of the statutory text, however, but from a more realistic assessment of the ways in which a public order law will be used. This approach to facial vagueness would both permit and stimulate experimentation with different methods of promoting police accountability. By tolerating some measure of disagreement among state and lower federal courts regarding the reasonableness of such methods, the Supreme Court might further encourage this experimentation. The Court might also maximize its own ability over time to make at least some judgments about the relative efficacy of these various methods of ensuring that the exercise of police discretion is reasonably constrained.

This approach to vagueness thus differs sharply from that endorsed by Kenneth Culp Davis, one of the early writers on the void-for-vagueness doctrine and its role in restraining police. Professor Davis recognized the limited effects of the vagueness doctrine on the scope of police enforcement discretion and proposed that the Court should extend the vagueness principle beyond the face of legislation to address vagueness in police enforcement policies:

> The Court [in *Papachristou v City of Jacksonville*] quite properly responded to the problem before it in asserting that lack of standards in the ordinance is unconstitutional. But I think the fundamental [point] may be broader—that vagueness of law or of enforcement policy is unconstitutional because it permits or encourages arbitrary and discriminatory enforcement of the law. . . . I do predict that the time will come when courts will generally hold that unnecessary or undue vagueness in an enforcement policy is unconstitutional, because of the reasons the unanimous Supreme Court stated in the *Papachristou* opinion.[217]

---

[217] Davis, *Police Discretion* at 137–38 (cited in note 145) (italics added).

The Court never adopted this proposal, for what seem in retrospect to be good and sufficient reasons. As Professor Davis himself admitted, the task for the Court of working out the limits and applications of his idea was truly "enormous."[218] It would have required courts across the country to determine for thousands of far-flung police agencies whether "unnecessary or undue vagueness" in their enforcement policies rendered these policies unconstitutional—a difficult job for generalist courts lacking knowledge about both internal law enforcement practices and the public order problems faced by police.[219] Even more fundamentally, Davis's work on police discretion did not grapple fully with the difficulties of drafting enforcement rules both sufficiently precise to establish accountability in the terms he contemplated and still flexible enough to achieve tolerably adequate results in terms of the problems with which police must deal.[220] Nor did Davis fully explore the question whether the mere elaboration of enforcement policies could even meaningfully constrain police in their routine encounters with citizens on the street.

Davis's insight was important: that courts concerned about reducing the potential for arbitrary and discriminatory police enforcement needed to focus more attention on the ways in which police actually employ laws regulating low-level misconduct. But his proposal demanded too much and too little at the very same time. The inadequacies of Davis's proposal, however, contain lessons that point in the direction of the alternative approach outlined here. This approach does not require courts to take on the task of passing on all enforcement policies. It does not lock police departments into overly rigid administrative rules that frustrate accomplishment of the substantive ends of policing while at the same time failing in their objective to constrain police.

This is not the place to specify all the features in a given law or its implementing plan that a more realistic approach to vagueness might take into account. Like all tests premised on reasonableness, the one articulated here will permit many factors to be

---

[218] Id at 137–38.

[219] See id at 138.

[220] For a provocative theoretical account of the general conflict between accountability and the flexibility required for effectiveness in bureaucratic administration—as well as a proposal for transcending this conflict—see Michael C. Dorf and Charles F. Sabel, *Drug Treatment Courts and Emergent Experimentalist Government*, Vand L Rev (forthcoming 2000).

considered. We can articulate some principles, however, that might guide the overall analysis of the question whether police enforcement discretion has been reasonably constrained.[221] The articulation of these principles, moreover, can serve as prelude to some final consideration of a more realistic approach to vagueness in the area of public order policing.

A. THREE PRINCIPLES OF A REALISTIC VAGUENESS JURISPRUDENCE

1. *Openness.* First is the principle of openness. As I have suggested, the healthy evolution of police organizations has long been stymied by the failure of police departments frankly to acknowledge the broad scope of police discretion and to explain the rationale for its exercise in different ways. Accountability is simply not possible when discretion is exercised furtively and with an air of illegitimacy. There are few reasons, moreover, for the secrecy that has often surrounded the formulation and implementation of enforcement policies involving public order problems. The goal of enforcement in this context is not the detection and punishment of offenders (a goal that may require that enforcement rationales remain unexplained), but compliance with legislated behavioral norms. Indeed, the public discussion of a public order problem and the police department's proposed response may help ameliorate the problem before enforcement ever takes place. And there is much to be gained from openness about enforcement discretion in terms of limiting the opportunity for its abuse.

Courts evaluating whether the admitted vagueness in a given public order law is tolerable, then, should consider whether the police department implementing this law is participating in a process in which it explains its reasons for employing the law in a given way and also reports on its results in a manner that permits evaluation of the efficacy and propriety of the strategy it has chosen.[222] In the case of Chicago's gang loitering law, for instance, it is certainly relevant that General Order 92-4, even without public designation of the specific places in which the law would be enforced, did specify the criteria for designating a given area in Chi-

---

[221] This analysis builds upon, but also partly departs from, my earlier work on this subject in Livingston, 97 Colum L Rev at 667–70 (cited in note 2).

[222] For a general discussion of this approach to accountability, see Dorf and Sabel, Vand L Rev (cited in note 220).

cago for gang loitering enforcement. It is likewise relevant that
the law required the preparation of written reports each time an
arrest was made. Standing alone, these measures might not be
enough to render a given public order law constitutional. Such
measures point in the right direction, however—toward the open
acknowledgment of enforcement discretion and the provision of
adequate information to ensure that exercises of discretion can be
appropriately reviewed within a community.

2. *Monitoring.* As a second principle of accountability, courts examining a public order law that might be vulnerable to facial
vagueness invalidation should also consider whether this law is being employed in such a way as to provide for effective monitoring
of its enforcement. Monitoring mechanisms can take a variety of
forms. Monitoring might be performed by a legislative oversight
committee armed with the rich information about enforcement
that a reasonably constrained police department could be required
to provide. Courts might participate in this role through their consideration of "as applied" challenges and their review of the sufficiency of the evidence in individual cases.

Perhaps most promisingly, the monitoring function might also
arise from the premises of community policing. In a police department that has implemented the principles of this substantive policing theory, neighborhood residents are involved in identifying
local public order problems and prioritizing among them "in
a constructive dialogue with one another and with police officers
who work in their immediate area."[223] In Chicago, this effort at
police-community partnership occurs at monthly public meetings
held in each of the city's 279 small police beats.[224] In theory, when
police and citizens meet together "to report on what they have
accomplished since the last meeting, and what they will work on
next," this form of cooperation can itself play an important role
in monitoring police order maintenance activities.[225] Certainly
when the implementation of a challenged public order law is built
into such an organizational framework—a framework dedicated to
"securing month-in, month-out accountability to residents for

---

[223] Skogan, *Everybody's Business*, Boston Rev at 15 (Apr/May 1999) (cited in note 196).

[224] See id.

[225] Id.

what beat officers are doing"—this is a relevant factor to consider in assessing the likelihood that this law will be employed in an arbitrary and capricious way.[226]

3. *Limited police authority.* Third and finally, courts evaluating whether the measure of indeterminacy in a given public order law is acceptable should consider whether reasonable efforts have been made to limit police authority. This is simply an extension of traditional vagueness review. In employing the facial vagueness doctrine, courts already purport to limit police authority by forcing legislatures to define prohibited conduct more carefully so that patrol officers cannot arbitrarily employ overly ambiguous laws. The principle at work here is precisely the same—that reasonable constraints on enforcement authority are beneficial because they reduce the opportunity for police abuse. In a more realistic approach to vagueness, however, such constraints need not derive solely from clarity in an ordinance's text.

Thus, courts might consider whether a police department, in ways analogous to an administrative agency, has given a law's restrictions "more precise shape" in advance of "subject[ing] citizens to penalties for unwanted behavior."[227] They might take into account both provisions for warnings before arrest and regulations like the one in General Order 92-4 limiting enforcement authority to specially designated officers. Even things like sunset provisions, surprisingly, might count in this fuller analysis—as imposing a time limitation within which a given degree of police enforcement authority will be tolerated and also at least potentially attesting to a good faith effort on the part of the legislative body to ensure a periodic reassessment whether police are implementing a public order law in a fair and equitable way.

B. A REALISTIC VAGUENESS JURISPRUDENCE REASSESSED

The constitutional test outlined here does not constitute a radical departure for the vagueness doctrine, even if the adjudication of facial vagueness challenges pursuant to this test might require hearings and the amassing of an evidentiary record in ways not

---

[226] Id at 16.

[227] See generally Strauss, 89 Colum L Rev at 445 (cited in note 173).

often deemed necessary in the traditional approach. This is because the test does not reject the central premise of the Court's
vagueness jurisprudence—namely, that courts bear some constitutional responsibility for limiting the opportunity for the arbitrary
application of legal prohibitions. Instead, the test seeks to transcend the limitations of the doctrine as employed in *Morales*, and
in ways that offer the reasonable prospect that courts might actually—as opposed to symbolically—promote the accountability of
police.

The test has two concrete advantages. First, this test avoids the
false choice evident in the *Morales* opinions. These opinions seem
to proffer only two options for courts employing the facial
vagueness doctrine. First is the majority's approach: an approach to
facial vagueness that authorizes courts to second-guess community
preferences about the regulation of public order in what is at best
an illusory response to the problems posed by unconstrained police. Second is the dissenters' approach. Admittedly, this approach
avoids even the appearance that courts are engaged in the ad hoc
review of public order legislation. It avoids this appearance, however, only by so limiting the facial vagueness doctrine as to essentially repudiate any role for this doctrine in contributing to the
reasonable constraint of police. The present test, in contrast, focuses courts on a realistic assessment of the ways in which public
order laws will be used. This focus guides judicial decision making
so that opinions in this area can be both persuasive and effective
in the terms in which they are written.

Second, the constitutional test outlined here stimulates those
actors best able to devise and then to experiment with new and
effective approaches to the reasonable constraint of police—
namely, legislatures and police departments. The incentives set by
current vagueness doctrine send these actors off on a chimerical
quest for ever greater standards of clarity in the public order laws
they propose. A realistic approach to vagueness doctrine, in contrast, enlists them in experiments that will have real-world consequences for the ways in which police employ public order laws on
the street. This approach thus promotes police accountability. But
it does not impose on generalist courts the impossible task of fully
defining the conditions pursuant to which accountability can be
achieved.

One objection to this analysis might be that it proposes what amounts to a one-way ratchet. Thus, some public order laws now vulnerable to facial vagueness review might be upheld pursuant to this approach. Relatively clear laws could not be challenged for vagueness, however, despite the opportunity for arbitrary enforcement they present. This "realistic" approach to the void-for-vagueness doctrine, then, in effect expands police power. This objection, however, ignores both the benefits that would accrue from the realistic approach and the detriments that now flow from sometimes denying police legitimate authority to deal with problems they are expected to handle.

The benefits of the realistic approach could be considerable. By encouraging police departments to adopt measures that open up police enforcement discretion to monitoring and that reasonably constrain the scope of police authority, courts may generate changes not only in the area of order maintenance, but in other areas of police work as well. Police may come to recognize that they have much to gain from the favorable review of monitoring authorities. They may begin to appreciate the value of openness as a way in which more generally to enlist community support for enforcement efforts.

Even if the realistic approach to vagueness has no ripple effects on other contexts in which police exercise discretion, however, this approach is still preferable to the *Morales* majority's approach. Courts do no service to the project of police reform when they enunciate tests that create an illusion of constraint that does not in fact exist. Nor do they promote police accountability by denying police legitimate authority to address community problems. The realistic approach offers a better way in which to assess whether the vagueness in a public order law truly threatens to promote arbitrariness on the street. Moreover, it brings courts closer to realizing the aspiration that courts themselves have articulated for the facial vagueness doctrine.

* * *

The majority in *Morales* made little progress in illuminating pressing issues concerning the relationship between police and communities. I should acknowledge in conclusion, however, that the Court's failure to shed light on these issues may be only partly attributable to the way in which the *Morales* majority approached the subject of police discretion. Indeed, the majority's suggestion that Chicago's gang loitering ordinance might be valid if applied to gang members alone raises the possibility that it was Chicago's regulation of "innocent conduct," rather than concerns about police discretion, that really drove the result in this case.[228] It is not my purpose in this conclusion to address the substantive dimensions of vagueness review. But a brief observation on the substantive undercurrents to *Morales* is in order.

The facial vagueness doctrine is sometimes employed by courts embracing Professor Sunstein's "judicial minimalism" to avoid difficult substantive issues—as when a potentially suspect law is invalidated for vagueness, leaving open the question whether this law was unconstitutional on other, substantive grounds. Admittedly, there are often good reasons for the judicial reticence that this substantive use of vagueness permits. Such reticence, however, is not always to be applauded. And perhaps it should not be applauded here.

If the problem whether Chicago's gang loitering ordinance infringed fundamental rights is complex, so too is the problem faced by communities seeking both to restrain their police and to confer on them those reasonable powers that might be of help in dealing with pressing problems of crime and disorder. Granted, realism about police patrol cannot illuminate the question whether activities like public loitering are protected by the Due Process Clause. Such realism, however, can help communities to better regulate their police. This article has suggested that the police need to deal forthrightly with communities in acknowledging their exercise of discretion and in seeking terms of accountability. If this is true for police, however, it may also be true for the Court. To the extent that substantive considerations are important to the outcome of cases like *Morales*, the Court may help communities by at least focusing them on the issues truly at stake in the regulation of public order. Perhaps it is time for the Justices, like police, to speak clearly.

---

[228] See *Morales*, 119 S Ct at 1862.

DAVID COLE

HANGING WITH THE WRONG CROWD: OF GANGS, TERRORISTS, AND THE RIGHT OF ASSOCIATION

> "History should teach us . . . that in times of high emotional excitement minority parties and groups which advocate extremely unpopular social or governmental innovations will always be typed as criminal gangs and attempts will always be made to drive them out."[1]

The freedom of association vies with privacy and state sovereign immunity as one of the most potentially capacious and least textually based rights that the Supreme Court has ever found in the Constitution. On the one hand, it is impossible to imagine a democratic society—much less the First Amendment rights of speech, assembly, religion, and petition—without a corresponding right of association, so it is not surprising that the absence of any explicit mention of association in the Constitution has proven little barrier to recognition of the right. But, on the other hand, virtually all conduct is at least potentially associational, presenting serious challenges to crafting a coherent jurisprudence. As a matter of democratic theory, the right of association is something we cannot live

David Cole is Professor, Georgetown University Law Center, and Volunteer Staff Attorney, Center for Constitutional Rights.

AUTHOR'S NOTE: I would like to thank for their helpful comments and input my colleagues Nancy Chang, Dennis Hutchinson, Gerald Neuman, Stephen Schulhofer, and Steven Shapiro, and my research assistants Jessica Attie, Ellis Johnston, and Allen Pegg. I am or was involved in litigating three cases discussed herein: *Texas v Johnson*, 491 US 397 (1989); *Reno v American-Arab Anti-Discrimination Comm.*, 119 S Ct 936 (1999), and *Humanitarian Law Project, Inc. v Reno*, 9 F Supp 2d 1176 (CD Cal 1998).

[1] *Barenblatt v United States*, 360 US 109, 150–51 (1959) (Black, J, dissenting).

without; but as a matter of social governance, the right, if uncontained, is something we cannot live with.

The Supreme Court has sought to navigate these shoals in recent years by adopting a categorical approach, treating associations as either protected or unprotected depending on their character. The approach is founded on the proposition that associational rights derive from other constitutional rights, and therefore should be protected only when those other rights are at risk. On this view, the right of association is protected by the First Amendment when it serves an "expressive" function, and by the Fifth Amendment's right of privacy when it is "intimate." Association that is neither expressive nor intimate, however, is categorically excluded from constitutional protection.[2]

Two Supreme Court decisions last term reflect this categorical approach. In *City of Chicago v Morales*,[3] the Court rejected in a single sentence a "right of association" challenge to a Chicago loitering ordinance that criminalized public association with gang members. The Court simply asserted that there is no right of social association, apparently assuming without discussion that gangs are neither expressive nor intimate associations. Moreover, the Court suggested that the real problem with the Chicago ordinance was that it reached non-gang-members, and suggested that if the ordinance had been exclusively targeted at gang members, it might have withstood constitutional scrutiny.[4] The same term, in *Reno v American-Arab Anti-Discrimination Comm.*,[5] the Court dismissed a First Amendment challenge to selective enforcement of the immigration laws against alleged members of a terrorist organization. Lower courts had found a First Amendment violation because the government had selectively targeted eight aliens for deportation based on their political associations, without regard to whether the aliens had furthered any illegal conduct of the terrorist group with which they were allegedly connected. The Supreme Court's rationale focused on the problems with recognizing any selective enforcement defense to deportation, whether the selection were predicated on politics, race, or religion. But the Court simulta-

---

[2] See *Roberts v United States Jaycees*, 468 US 609, 617–23 (1984).

[3] 119 S Ct 1849 (1999).

[4] Id at 1862; id at 1864 (O'Connor concurring in part and concurring in judgment).

[5] *Reno v American-Arab Anti-Discrimination Comm.*, 119 S Ct 936 (1999).

neously if cryptically acknowledged that some (unstated) bases for selection might justify a selective enforcement defense, while asserting without explanation that selection based on membership in a terrorist organization certainly would not.[6]

The federal government has advanced a related categorical approach in other associational rights cases, in which it seeks to distinguish regulation of association per se from regulation of associational *conduct*. The government has argued that a restriction on financial contributions to a political group or individual should not be viewed as a direct restraint on association, subject to rigorous scrutiny, but as regulation of conduct that only incidentally affects the right of association, and therefore subject to relaxed scrutiny under *United States v O'Brien*.[7] This term, the Solicitor General urged the Supreme Court to adopt that view with respect to the regulation of political campaign contributions.[8] The government advances the same contention in defending the 1996 Antiterrorism and Effective Death Penalty Act (AEDPA), which criminalizes material support of the *lawful* activities of "foreign terrorist organizations." Here, too, the government argues that the law regulates the conduct of material support, not association per se, and should therefore be subject only to relaxed scrutiny.[9]

These developments threaten to erode constitutional protection of the right of association, and warrant a reconsideration of the right's purpose in a democratic society. The Court's and the federal government's categorical approaches to the right of association are unsatisfactory for three principal reasons. First, they require courts to engage in incoherent line-drawing. Under these approaches, judges must ask whether associations are sufficiently "expressive" to warrant protection, and whether acts of association should be viewed as "association" or "conduct." But most, if not all, association is expressive to one degree or another, and one cannot distinguish conduct from association without reducing the right to a meaningless formality.

---

[6] Id at 947.

[7] 391 US 367 (1968).

[8] Brief Amicus Curiae of the United States in *Shrink Missouri Government PAC v Nixon*, No 98-963, 1998 US Briefs (LEXIS) 963, at *25 n 12.

[9] 18 USC § 2339A; 8 USC § 1189(a); *Humanitarian Law Project, Inc. v Reno*, 9 F Supp 2d 1176 (CD Cal 1998) (upholding in part AEDPA provisions making it a crime to provide humanitarian support to lawful activities of designated "foreign terrorist organizations"); Brief for the Appellees/Cross-Appellants in *Humanitarian Law Project, Inc. v Reno*, No 98-56062 (9th Cir pending), at 30–54.

Second, these categorical approaches cannot explain a central feature of the right of association—its prohibition on guilt by association. That principle insists on individual culpability, and in no way turns on whether the association for which an individual is punished is expressive or intimate, nor on whether the punishment turns on associational conduct or association per se.

Finally, the categorical approaches used by the Court and advanced by the government are insufficiently protective of association, which deserves recognition not merely as a derivative right, but as an independent constitutional right, and which if it is to be a meaningful right must protect associational conduct as well as association in the abstract. Association, no less than speech, plays a central role in both the political process and personal development, and deserves protection analogous to, but not limited to, that afforded speech.

Part I will sketch the current contours of the right of association, a right limited to "expressive" and "intimate" association, and will describe the government's attempts to extend this categorical approach by limiting associational protection still further to membership per se. Part II will argue that the Court's limitation of associational rights to expressive and intimate associations and the government's attempt to distinguish association from conduct are unworkable, inconsistent with the Court's own precedents, and fail to reflect the normative reasons for protecting the right of association. Part III will offer an alternative framework for addressing the right of association, borrowing from the Court's jurisprudence with respect to another potentially limitless but critical constitutional right, the right of symbolic speech. I will argue that the focus of a jurisprudence of association ought to be on *association*, not expression or intimacy, and that it should protect association in its physical manifestations as well as its abstract essence. The critical inquiry should not be whether an association is expressive or intimate, nor whether the individual affected is engaged in conduct or pure association, but rather whether the government's regulation arises from or is targeted at the associational character of the conduct. Where government seeks to regulate conduct without regard to its associational character, its actions should be subject to relaxed review, but where government seeks to regulate conduct because of its associational character, its actions must satisfy heightened scrutiny. Only that approach, which mirrors the

Court's jurisprudence of symbolic expression, does justice to the freedom of association.

I. Contours of the Right of Association

The right of association was born in the civil rights movement and crystallized in the crucible of the Cold War. The Court's first decisions expressly relying on a right of association protected the NAACP from harassment by southern states by barring compelled disclosure of its membership lists.[10] But the right took definitive shape—and certainly played its most important role in American life to date—in a series of decisions from the 1960s condemning a variety of anti-Communist measures for imposing guilt by association.[11] Since then, the Court has confronted assertions of the right in a wide range of settings, from objections to compulsory union dues,[12] to challenges to campaign finance regulation,[13] to defenses against the application of nondiscrimination provisions.[14] While the Court has never seriously questioned its initial recognition of a right of association, it has been less than clear about what the right entails. As Judge Frank Easterbrook has stated, "We have never had a principled theory of the appropriate scope of regulation of non-economic association."[15]

---

[10] See, e.g., *NAACP v Alabama ex rel Patterson*, 357 US 449 (1958); *Bates v City of Little Rock*, 361 US 516 (1960). As early as 1937, the Court invalidated the conviction of a man for participating in a meeting held under Communist Party auspices, but its decision rested on the right of assembly, not the right of association. *De Jonge v Oregon*, 299 US 353 (1937). *NAACP v Alabama* was the first time the Court explicitly relied on the right of association.

[11] See *United States v Robel*, 389 US 258, 262 (1967) (invalidating ban on Communist Party members working in defense facilities); *Keyishian v Board of Regents*, 385 US 589, 606 (1967) (invalidating statute barring employment in state university system to Communist Party members); *Elfbrandt v Russell*, 384 US 11, 19 (1966) (invalidating oath requiring state employees not to join Communist Party); *Scales v United States*, 367 US 203, 221–22 (1961) (construing Smith Act, which barred membership in organization advocating violent overthrow of government, to require showing of "specific intent" to further group's illegal ends); *Noto v United States*, 367 US 290, 299–300 (1961) (same).

[12] *Abood v Detroit Bd of Educ.*, 431 US 209 (1977).

[13] *Buckley v Valeo*, 424 US 1 (1974).

[14] *Roberts v United States Jaycees*, 468 US 609 (1984); *Runyon v McCrary*, 427 US 160, 175–76 (1976) (rejecting private school's assertion that right of association barred application of 42 USC § 1981 to its racially exclusive admission policy); *Hishon v King & Spalding*, 467 US 69, 78 (1984) (rejecting law firm's assertion of right of association as defense to Title VII sex discrimination claim).

[15] Frank H. Easterbrook, *Implicit and Explicit Rights of Association*, 10 Harv J L & Pub Pol 91, 98 (1987).

In its most recent applications of the doctrine, the Supreme Court has sought to limit the right of association categorically, maintaining that the Constitution protects only expressive and intimate association.[16] The theory underlying this approach is that association is only a means of protecting other rights—speech and privacy—and therefore ought to receive protection only where the association serves one of those rights.

On this view, expressive association derives its protection from the First Amendment. Association is not mentioned in the First Amendment, the Court reasons, but deserves protection (at least where it is not intimate) because it is a necessary means to the ends that are expressly mentioned—speech, assembly, petition, and religion. The right to petition or to assemble, for example, would be meaningless if one did not have the right to associate with others for these ends. The practice of religion is almost always group based. And without the right to join with others for speech purposes, the right to speak would be largely ineffectual. Because non-intimate association is but a means to these expressly protected ends, however, it does not deserve constitutional protection where it fails to serve those ends.[17] Thus, a private St. Patrick's Day parade organization cannot be required to include a gay and lesbian contingent in its parade, because the parade is an act of expressive association whose message would be altered by the compelled inclusion of the unwanted group.[18] But the Jaycees and the Rotary Club can be required to admit women against their will, because, the Court concluded, women's admission would not seriously alter these groups' *expressive* activities.[19]

Professor Thomas Emerson advocated a similar approach to as-

---

[16] *Roberts v United States Jaycees*, 468 US 609.

[17] Id at 618 ("the Court has recognized a right to associate *for the purpose of engaging in those activities protected by the First Amendment*—speech, assembly, petition for the redress of grievances, and the exercise of religion") (emphasis added); *Abood v Detroit Board of Education*, 431 US 209, 233 (1977) ("Our decisions establish with unmistakable clarity that the freedom of an individual to association *for the purpose of advancing beliefs and ideas* is protected by the First and Fourteenth Amendments.") (emphasis added); *Bates v City of Little Rock*, 361 US at 522–23 (Constitution protects "freedom of association *for the purpose of advancing ideas and airing grievances*") (emphasis added).

[18] *Hurley v Irish-American Gay, Lesbian and Bisexual Group of Boston*, 515 US 557 (1995).

[19] *Roberts v United States Jaycees*, 468 US 609 (1984); *Board of Directors of Rotary Int'l v Rotary Club of Duarte*, 481 US 537 (1987); *New York State Club Assn, Inc. v City of New York*, 487 US 1 (1988).

sociation, maintaining, much as he did in the free speech area, that
the Court should draw a sharp line between expression and action,
protecting the former absolutely and the latter only minimally. In
Emerson's view, it is "essential to determine in each [right of association] case—in most cases it is the critical issue—whether the
conduct involved is properly classified as 'expression,' and hence
fully protected, or is classifiable as 'action,' and hence subject to
a greater measure of government regulation."[20] On Emerson's
view, as on the Court's view, association deserves First Amendment protection where it is "expressive," but not otherwise.

Under the Court's current jurisprudence, nonexpressive association warrants constitutional protection only where it is "intimate,"
and then the source of its protection is not the First Amendment
but the right of privacy. This right protects "highly personal relationships" and extends to such matters as "marriage; childbirth;
the raising and education of children; and cohabitation with one's
relatives."[21] As Kenneth Karst has defined it, "intimate association" describes "a close and familiar personal relationship with another that is in some significant way comparable to a marriage or
family relationship."[22] Intimate associations, which serve a range
of deep human needs, are an integral part of the private decision
making that the Constitution protects from state interference. The
right of "intimate association," however, is dependent on the association being private and intimate, and therefore does not extend
to large nonintimate associations such as the Jaycees or the Rotary
Club.

Under this approach, which might be called the "labeling" theory of the right of association, an association that is neither intimate nor expressive lacks any constitutional protection. In *Dallas
v Stanglin*,[23] for example, the Court reasoned that social association
in a dance hall was neither intimate nor expressive, and therefore
concluded that its regulation did not implicate the right of association. Last term, the Court relied on *Stanglin* to reject in a single
sentence an associational rights objection to a Chicago ordinance

---

[20] Thomas I. Emerson, *Freedom of Association and Freedom of Expression*, 74 Yale L J 1, 24 (1964).

[21] *Roberts*, 468 US at 618, 619 (internal citations omitted).

[22] Kenneth L. Karst, *The Freedom of Intimate Association*, 89 Yale L J 624, 629 (1980).

[23] 490 US 19, 25 (1989).

that made it a crime to stand in public without an apparent purpose with a gang member, even though the law selectively imposed criminal penalties on gang members and those associated with them.[24]

Thus, the Court's approach to the right of association is, at least at first glance, a fairly simple one. Association is protected where it serves free speech or privacy aims, but not otherwise. The right of association is, in this view, less a right in itself than an implicit corollary to other rights, worthy of protection only where those other rights are at risk.

The federal government's approach to the right of association builds on the Court's "labeling" theory, but seeks to introduce still another categorical threshold inquiry. On its view, the right of association should trigger stringent scrutiny only when a government regulation penalizes association qua association. Thus, a law that penalized members of disfavored groups would be subjected to strict scrutiny. If, by contrast, a law penalizes not membership per se, but associational conduct, the government maintains, the law should trigger only relaxed scrutiny. Thus, a limit on financial contributions to political candidates, or a prohibition on material support to a terrorist organization, it has argued, should not be analyzed as a direct restraint on association triggering strict scrutiny, but as a regulation of *conduct* that only incidentally affects association, requiring only relaxed review.[25] The campaign finance regulation allows people to associate with the candidate in ways other than by making financial contributions, and the material support prohibition permits individuals to join terrorist organizations, the government argues, and therefore they should not be viewed as regulations of association, but of particular forms of conduct.

Borrowing from the Supreme Court's limitation of First Amendment protection to "expressive association," the government argues further that where a law regulates associational conduct and does so not to restrict expression, but to serve some other legitimate end, there is no basis for subjecting it to strict scrutiny. Campaign finance restrictions are designed to limit corruption, and the material support provision is designed to limit terrorism,

---

[24] *Morales*, 119 S Ct at 1857.

[25] See notes 8 and 9.

the government maintains. Because these interests are unrelated to expression, it reasons, the laws should not be subjected to strict scrutiny. On this view, because nonintimate association is protected only where it serves expressive purposes, the regulation of nonintimate associational conduct should not trigger heightened review unless the regulation is a ruse for controlling or penalizing speech.

What the government's and the Court's approaches have in common is a search for limiting categorical principles. The Court's approach seeks to delimit the range of protected association at the threshold, by extending protection to association only where it serves expressive or privacy goals. The government's approach similarly seeks to treat a wide range of associational action as presumptively regulable conduct rather than presumptively protected association. Each of these categorical approaches has the benefit of limiting an otherwise capacious right. But, as I will argue below, each approach carves off far more than is warranted by the search for a limiting principle, and ends by sacrificing valuable associational rights.

II. The Constitutional Values of Association

The Court's modern-day limitation of the right of association to "expressive" and "intimate" association, and the federal government's attempt to extend that categorical approach still further, fail for three reasons. First, the lines these approaches would have courts draw are largely unworkable. Second, the restrictive reading of associational rights that they imply does not account for a central tenet of the right—namely, the prohibition on guilt by association. And third, these approaches shortchange association by treating it as a merely derivative right, in the face of a strong normative case for independent constitutional protection, grounded in the right of assembly and the structure of the Constitution.

A. DRAWING UNWORKABLE LINES

There is much to be said for adopting categorical approaches to constitutional law issues. Bright lines are easier to administer and enforce, and can give much needed breathing room to otherwise delicate constitutional freedoms. Nowhere is this more important than in the area of political rights—the right to speak and associate with whom one pleases—because the chilling effect of uncertainty is so powerful there.[26] Accordingly, the Court has sought to establish bright-line rules to govern many speech issues, including the advocacy of illegal conduct,[27] sexual speech,[28] and libel.[29] But if a bright-line rule is to be effective, it must both pose a workable set of questions and carefully track the normative values of the right it is designed to protect. The Court's "labeling" approach to association—protecting only expressive and intimate association—and the government's extension of that approach fail both requirements. In this section, I will address whether these "labeling" approaches are administrable. In the next two sections, I will argue that even if the rules were workable, they do not serve the values underlying the right of association.

The Court's current approach to association establishes an incoherent inquiry. Asking whether association is expressive, and therefore deserving of First Amendment protection, is akin to asking whether a given action should be treated as "conduct" or "expression," an approach long rejected in free speech jurisprudence. Neither conduct nor association is usefully divided into "expressive" and "nonexpressive" categories. All association, like all conduct, is at least potentially expressive.[30] At a minimum, the act of associating with a group expresses something about one's relationship to other members of the group. In most instances, it will also express something about one's values and self-image. Even a purely social association—joining a bridge club, for example, or choosing which bar or dance club to frequent—is expressive of one's interests, likes

---

[26] *NAACP v Button*, 371 US 415, 433 (1963) (because First Amendment "freedoms are delicate and vulnerable," and "need breathing space to survive, government may regulate in the area only with narrow specificity"); *Reno v American Civil Liberties Union*, 117 S Ct 2329, 2344–45 (1997).

[27] *Brandenburg v Ohio*, 395 US 444 (1969).

[28] *Miller v California*, 413 US 15 (1973).

[29] *New York Times v Sullivan*, 376 US 254 (1964).

[30] Kenneth Karst has argued that:
   [a]lmost everything we do is expressive in one way or another, and thus to say that the First Amendment is a generalized presumptive guarantee of liberty to do anything that has expressive aspects would be much like saying that the constitutional right of privacy guarantees "the right to be let alone." The First Amendment would, in short, be stretched to cover all our constitutional freedoms.
Kenneth Karst, 89 Yale L J at 654 (cited in note 22).

and dislikes, and character. In a social world, we are defined, and we define ourselves, by the relationships we have with others, from the most intimate to the most public.

By expressive association, the Court seems to mean an association whose purpose is to express a point of view or idea. Thus, the ACLU is an expressive association because its very purpose is to gather like-minded people together to express their common views about the importance of protecting civil liberties. The local dance hall obviously has no such advocacy purpose. But it is not clear why choosing to go to the local dance hall is less expressive for the individual who makes that choice than choosing to go to an ACLU meeting is for an ACLU member. The dancer may well be expressing the view that companionship, camaraderie, drinking beer with friends, and physical expression are more important than defending individual liberties, for example.

In any event, if there is such a thing as nonexpressive association, it is far from clear how courts are to go about distinguishing it from expressive association. The question whether an association is expressive might turn either on the individual's subjective experience or on an objective assessment of the association from the standpoint of the reasonable observer. If the inquiry is subjective, wherever it matters individuals will likely claim that their association is expressive. Can courts realistically reject an individual's claim that she experienced her act of association as expressive?

An objective test fares little better. From an objective standpoint, all associations are expressive, even if they are not intended to express a particular point of view. All acts of association inevitably communicate something about the interests, character, or likes and dislikes of the actor. Even secret societies, which if truly secret do not communicate anything to the outside world, are expressive vis-à-vis other members of the secret society, and may well serve an expressive purpose for the individual. Thus, it makes little sense to ask whether a given association is "expressive," because in some sense all probably are.

At first blush there is undoubtedly a commonsense difference between the ACLU on the one hand and Standard Oil or the Mafia on the other. The ACLU's purpose is almost exclusively expressive, while the principal purpose of Standard Oil or the Mafia is to make as much money as possible, through licit and/or illicit means. But for many if not most of those who associate with Standard Oil or the Mafia, their association is nonetheless expressive in some way of who they are and what they believe, just as are their associations with family, church, friends, and neighbors. Even business associations provide a sense of identity and meaning to the lives of those who choose to associate themselves with them. And if the line between the ACLU and Standard Oil seems clear, how should we characterize the *New York Times*, Working Assets, or Benneton, for-profit businesses that seek to maximize profits but whose purpose includes the expression of certain points of view?

The Court's other threshold inquiry asks whether an association is sufficiently "intimate" to warrant protection of the Due Process Clause. Here again, the lines are extremely difficult to draw. What gives a heterosexual couple a right of intimate association but not a homosexual couple, for example? Here the threshold inquiry is identical to the question of whether there is a substantive right. This category, however, is less susceptible to the critique that it is incoherent in all settings. It is relatively noncontroversial, for example, to claim that joining the Rotary Club is not an act of "intimate" association. While the location of the line between "intimate" and "nonintimate" can never be precise, it at least operates as a rough principle of exclusion. The problem with the limitation to "intimate" association is less its manageability than its normative justification, a point to which I turn in the following sections.

The government's proposal that the Court distinguish regulation of mere association from regulation of associational conduct is also incoherent. The government's suggestions would resurrect in the jurisprudence of association the approach Justice Black sought to take with respect to speech. Justice Black believed that speech should be protected absolutely, but in order to render this principle acceptable he drew a sharp distinction between "speech" and "action."[31] Professor Thomas Emerson advocated a variant of that approach,[32] but no one else on the Court has ever been convinced, and for good reason. The attempt to distinguish speech from action is futile. As Louis Henkin wrote, "Speech *is* conduct,

---

[31] See, e.g., *Konigsberg v State Bar*, 366 US 36, 60–76 (1961) (Black dissenting); *Barenblatt v United States*, 360 US 109, 134, 140–53 (1958) (Black dissenting); Hugo Black, *The Bill of Rights*, 35 NYU L Rev 865, 874–81 (1960).

[32] Thomas I. Emerson, *The System of Freedom of Expression* 8–9 (1970).

and actions speak. There is nothing intrinsically sacred about wagging the tongue or wielding a pen; there is nothing intrinsically more sacred about words than other symbols."[33] Similarly, John Hart Ely has pointed out that the inquiry is incoherent because expressive conduct is simultaneously 100 percent conduct and 100 percent expressive.[34]

The same is true of association. All association takes the form of conduct, even if the conduct is simply showing up at a meeting, obtaining a membership card, paying dues, signing onto a mailing list, or clicking a mouse. One cannot associate with others without taking action. There is no association without conduct. Drawing a distinction between pure association and conduct undertaken for associative purposes, therefore, is as futile as distinguishing between speech and conduct.[35]

B. BEYOND EXPRESSIVE AND INTIMATE ASSOCIATION — GUILT BY ASSOCIATION

Even if one could overcome the incoherence problems with limiting protection to expressive, intimate, or "pure" association, these bright-line rules fail the more important test of normative fit. First, they cannot be squared with the doctrine's bedrock principle—namely, that guilt must be personal, and that guilt by association is forbidden.

A simple example illustrates the point. Under modern doctrine, one has no constitutional right to be a member of a social country club, because the club would likely be treated as neither expressive nor intimate, and there is no right of social association.[36] Yet a statute making it a crime to be a member of any country club that obtains illegal kickbacks from a vendor would plainly be unconstitutional, absent a requirement that the prosecutor prove that the

---

[33] Louis Henkin, *Foreword: On Drawing Lines*, 82 Harv L Rev 63, 79–80 (1968).

[34] John Hart Ely, *Flag Desecration: A Case Study in the Rules of Categorization and Balancing in First Amendment Analysis*, 88 Harv L Rev 1482, 1494–96 (1975).

[35] This is not to suggest that no distinctions can be made between regulation of the associational and the nonassociational aspects of conduct. As I will maintain later, courts can and should ask whether the government's regulation of conduct derives from the associational character of the conduct, or derives from an interest in regulating the conduct irrespective of its associational character. But that is very different from asking whether a given action is conduct or association, when it will almost always assuredly be both.

[36] *Dallas v Stanglin*, 490 US 19, 25 (1989); *City of Chicago v Morales*, 119 S Ct at 1857.

individual member specifically intended to further the club's illegal conduct. Such a statute would violate the right of association in the most direct sense of the term, by imposing guilt by association. Similarly, while it is surely constitutional to criminalize the use of legitimate business activities as a cover or laundering operation to further illegal activity, as the Racketeer Influenced and Corrupt Organizations Act (RICO) does,[37] it would surely be unconstitutional to prohibit mere association with the Mafia.

The principle of individual culpability, captured doctrinally in the "specific intent" requirement, was developed at a time when the right of association was most at risk in this country—during the McCarthy era, when thousands of Americans were targeted, investigated, blacklisted, harassed, and driven from public employment or office on charges that they were members of or fellow travelers with the Communist Party. The Court's early treatments of anti-Communist initiatives did not demonstrate much backbone,[38] but in time the Court developed a bright-line rule that effectively halted such efforts: the government may not impose criminal or civil disabilities on an individual because of his association with a group that engages in legal as well as illegal activities unless it proves that he specifically intended to further the group's illegal ends.

Anti-Communist initiatives almost by definition took the form of guilt by association: they punished Communist Party members and supporters because the Communist Party had engaged in illegal activities, regardless of whether the individual had supported those illegal activities. In a series of cases, the Court consistently rejected that rationale as a basis for imposing either civil or criminal disabilities, and instead required a showing of individual specific intent to further the Party's illegal ends.[39]

---

[37] Racketeer Influenced and Corrupt Organizations Act, 18 USC §§ 1961–68.

[38] See, e.g., *Dennis v United States*, 341 US 494 (1951); *Communist Party v Subversive Activities Control Bd.*, 367 US 1 (1961).

[39] See *United States v Robel*, 389 US 258, 262 (1967) (invalidating ban on Communist Party members working in defense facilities absent showing of "specific intent"); *Keyishian v Board of Regents*, 385 US 589, 606 (1967) ("[m]ere knowing membership without a specific intent to further the unlawful aims of an organization is not a constitutionally adequate basis" for barring employment in state university system to Communist Party members); *Elfbrandt v Russell*, 384 US 11, 19 (1966) (invalidating oath requiring state employees not to join Communist Party because "[a] law which applies to membership without the 'specific intent' to further the illegal aims of the organization infringes unnecessarily on protected freedoms"); *Scales v United States*, 367 US 203, 221–22 (1961) (construing Smith Act, which

The Court's most extensive discussion of the principle came in its first assessment of the Smith Act's membership provisions, which made it a crime to be a member of the Communist Party. In *Scales v United States*, the Court interpreted that statute narrowly in order to avoid the imposition of guilt by association, which it said would violate both the Fifth Amendment Due Process Clause and the First Amendment. With respect to the Fifth Amendment, the Court reasoned:

> In our jurisprudence guilt is personal, and when the imposition of punishment on a status or on conduct can only be justified by reference to the relationship of that status or conduct to other concededly criminal activity (here advocacy of violent overthrow), that relationship must be sufficiently substantial to satisfy the concept of personal guilt in order to withstand attack under the Due Process Clause of the Fifth Amendment.[40]

The due process principle recognized here is substantive, not procedural. It forbids the imposition of guilt by association no matter how clear the notice and no matter how fair the hearing. The point is that guilt must be "personal" in order to be consistent with due process. To punish A for the acts of B, without showing any connection between A and the illegal acts of B other than A's general connection to B, is fundamentally unfair. It is to punish a moral innocent. The "specific intent" requirement that the Court read into the Smith Act, and which it has subsequently held must be satisfied whenever the government seeks to penalize an individual for the acts of his associates, responds to the substantive due process problem by tying the imposition of guilt to an individually culpable act.

The guilt-by-association principle, and its doctrinal corollary, the requirement of "specific intent," also rest on the First Amendment. The Court in *Scales* noted that "[i]f there were a similar

---

barred membership in organization advocating violent overthrow of government, to require showing of "specific intent"); *Noto v United States*, 367 US 290, 299–300 (1961) (First Amendment bars punishment of "one in sympathy with the legitimate aims of [the Communist Party], but not specifically intending to accomplish them by resort to violence").

[40] *Scales*, 367 US at 224–25: Long before *Scales*, Justice Murphy made the same point, concurring in *Bridges v Wixon*, 326 US 135, 163 (1945):

> The doctrine of personal guilt is one of the most fundamental principles of our jurisprudence. It partakes of the very essence of the concept of freedom and due process of law. . . . It prevents the persecution of the innocent for the beliefs and actions of others.

blanket prohibition of association with a group having both legal and illegal aims, there would indeed be a real danger that legitimate political expression or association would be impaired."[41] Thus, in order to save the Smith Act, the Court interpreted it to require a showing of specific intent to further the illegal ends of the Communist Party.[42] When interpreted to require "clear proof that a defendant 'specifically intend[s] to accomplish [the aims of the organization] by resort to violence,'" the Court reasoned, the statute did not unnecessarily infringe on lawful associational activity.[43]

Significantly, the Court in the Communist Party cases never questioned Congress's findings that the Party was engaged in illegal activity, including terrorism and espionage, toward the end of overthrowing the United States by force and violence. Nor did the Court ever question that protecting the nation against such threats was a compelling interest. But even accepting that government interest, the Court insisted that "[a] law which applies without the 'specific intent' to further the illegal aims of the organization infringes unnecessarily on protected freedoms" and relies on "'guilt by association,' which has no place here."[44] Under the First Amendment, then, the "specific intent" standard is necessary to tailor the government's regulation to the harms it may legitimately regulate and to minimize the infringement of lawful association. It is, in effect, the result of the application of strict scrutiny to a regulation of association: it identifies the only narrowly tailored way to punish individuals for group wrongdoing (essentially by requiring evidence of *individual* wrongdoing), just as the *Brandenburg* test sets forth the narrowly tailored way to respond to advocacy of illegal conduct.

In the wake of *Scales*, the Court consistently applied the "specific intent" standard to a range of anti-Communist statutes, including many that imposed only a civil disability.[45] While the principle of individual culpability is strongest where criminal sanctions are sought, it plainly extends to civil disabilities as well. The point is

---

[41] *Scales*, 367 US at 229.

[42] Id at 221–30.

[43] Id at 229 (quoting *Noto v United States*, 367 US at 299).

[44] *Elfbrandt v Russell*, 384 US 11, 19 (1966).

[45] Note, *Civil Disabilities and the First Amendment*, 78 Yale L J 842 (1969).

that individuals should not be sanctioned for the bad acts of others, but only for their own bad acts. Whether the sanction is criminal or civil in nature is not determinative.[46]

The guilt-by-association principle quite plainly does not turn on the association being expressive, intimate, or "pure." Its twin rationales are that guilt must be personal, and that legitimate associations should not be sacrificed in the name of deterring illegitimate associations. Both rationales would apply to the hypothetical country club statute noted above. To punish a member who had no connection to the illegal kickbacks would be to punish a moral innocent, and therefore would contravene the due process principle that guilt must be personal. And to punish a member who had no intent to further the club's illegal conduct would be to deter legitimate association. Nor would the analysis be different if the statute punished the payment of dues to the country club as opposed to membership; it would still be imposing a penalty not for the culpable acts of the individual but for his or her wholly legitimate associational activity. Thus, the guilt-by-association principle, the cornerstone of the right of association, cannot be squared with the Court's limitation of the right to expressive and intimate association, nor with the federal government's suggestion that the right protects only membership itself.

While today's Court has never explicitly questioned its holdings in the Communist Party cases, its swift dismissal of the right-of-association claim in *Morales* suggests that the Court has lost sight of this principal feature of the right. The Chicago ordinance at issue imposed a criminal disability on gang members that did not apply to other citizens. Other citizens were free to stand on street

---

[46] The Court has continued to adhere to the prohibition on guilt by association, and to extend it to noncriminal settings. In *Healy v James*, 408 US 169 (1972), the Court held that a public university could not deny use of meeting rooms to a student group on the ground that it was affiliated with a national organization, Students for a Democratic Society, that had engaged in illegal violent activity. The Court stated that "[i]t has been established that 'guilt by association alone, without [establishing] that an individual's association poses the threat feared by the Government,' is an impermissible basis upon which to deny First Amendment rights." Id at 186 (quoting *United States v Robel*, 389 US at 265). Similarly, in *NAACP v Claiborne Hardware*, 458 US 886 (1982), the Court held that civil liability could not constitutionally be imposed on leaders of the NAACP on the ground that a boycott led by the NAACP had resulted in violence, absent evidence that the leaders specifically intended the violence. The Court stated that "guilt by association is a philosophy alien to the traditions of a free society and the First Amendment itself." Id at 932 (internal citations omitted).

corners with no apparent purpose to their hearts' content. But gang members who engaged in the same activity (and those who did so with them) could be ordered to move on and arrested. The definition of "gang member," moreover, required no evidence that an individual had engaged in or sought to further any illegal activity, but only that the *gang* engaged in illegal activity.[47] The ordinance was a classic instance of guilt by association.

The Court's one-sentence response to the associational claim— that the right of association does not encompass "social contact between gang members and others"[48]—misses the point altogether. The associational problem with the Chicago ordinance was that it hinged criminal disability on gang *membership* without any showing that the individual sought to further the gang's illegal activities. Such a law might not violate the right of association if the gang engaged in exclusively illegal activity, but few if any gangs do, and in any event that was neither an allegation in the case nor a prerequisite to application of the ordinance.

The Court's failure to recognize the guilt-by-association feature of the *Morales* case went even further, as the Court affirmatively suggested that the ordinance's infirmity might have been cured had Chicago adopted a more extreme version of guilt by association. Justice Stevens, speaking for the majority, invalidated as unconstitutionally vague the ordinance's definition of loitering as standing with "no apparent purpose," but added in dicta that the ordinance would "possibly" be constitutional "if it only applied to loitering by persons reasonably believed to be criminal gang members."[49] Justices O'Connor and Breyer, concurring, agreed that "no appar-

---

[47] The Chicago ordinance provided in relevant part:

> Whenever a police officer observes a person whom he reasonably believes to be a criminal street gang member loitering in any public place with one or more other persons, he shall order all such person to disperse and remove themselves from the area. Any person who does not promptly obey such an order is in violation of this section. Gang Congregation Ordinance, Chicago Municipal Code § 8-4-015(a), quoted in *Morales*, 119 S Ct at 1854 n 2.

The ordinance defines "loiter" to mean "to remain in any one place with no apparent purpose." Id at § (c)(1). And it defines "criminal street gang" to mean any group "having as one of its substantial activities the commission of one or more of the criminal acts enumerated in paragraph (3), and whose members individually or collectively engage in or have engaged in a pattern of criminal gang activity." Id at § (c)(2).

[48] *Morales*, 119 S Ct at 1857.

[49] Id at 1862.

ent purpose" was vague, but twice said that if the law were limited to gang members, it "would avoid the vagueness problems of the ordinance as construed by the Illinois Supreme Court."[50]

This suggestion is a non sequitur. Limiting the scope of persons subject to the law would do nothing whatsoever to respond to the vagueness of the term "no apparent purpose." The term is equally vague whether it applies to a million citizens or a single citizen. As Justice Scalia explained:

> if "remain[ing] in one place with no apparent purpose" is so vague as to give the police unbridled discretion in controlling the conduct of non-gang-members, it surpasses understanding how it ceases to be so vague when applied to gang members. Surely gang members cannot be decreed to be outlaws, subject to the merest whim of the police as the rest of us are not.[51]

Justice Thomas echoed that critique in a separate dissent.[52]

That the majority did not even offer a response to Justices Scalia and Thomas on this point only reveals how blind the majority was to the guilt-by-association problem. But beyond the logical fallacy pointed out by the dissenters, the majority had it exactly backward. Narrowing the ordinance to gang members would make the statute worse, not better, for it would exacerbate the law's reliance on guilt by association. The Court's suggestion that what cannot be done constitutionally to ordinary citizens might be done constitutionally to gang members, simply by virtue of their gang membership, is directly contrary to the lessons of the Court's Communist Party cases.

The majority was evidently motivated by concern about gangs, which undeniably pose a serious threat to the health and well-being of inner-city communities across the country. Gangs engage in criminal activity, fight over turf, and intimidate law-abiding citizens. They enforce antisocial norms, encouraging youth to engage in crime. And many young people growing up in poverty-stricken high-crime neighborhoods report that they feel compelled to join gangs for protection. Gangs play a particularly destructive role be-

---

[50] Id at 1865 (O'Connor concurring); see also id at 1864.

[51] Id at 1879 (Scalia dissenting).

[52] Id at 1885 (Thomas dissenting) (challenging logic of suggestion that ordinance might be cured by limiting it to gang members).

cause they often provide one of the few sources of peer support and guidance in communities decimated by poverty and crime.

But it is undoubtedly the rare gang that engages exclusively in illegal behavior. Gangs also provide social activities and networks of support to their members. For better or worse, peer groups are a central part of virtually every young person's upbringing; gangs are simply one particularly urban and usually lower class form of peer group. They provide for their members much as fraternities, sororities, basketball leagues, the Boy Scouts, and the Moose Lodge do.[53] Some gangs engage in political activity, working for community development, voter registration, and civil rights.[54]

Accordingly, for analytical purposes, most gangs are like the Communist Party—they engage in both legal and illegal activity. Antigang laws impermissibly impose guilt by association to the extent that they hinge adverse treatment of individuals (criminal or civil) on their gang membership, without evidence that the individual specifically intended to further the illegal ends of the gang.

This becomes clear in the Chicago case if one simply substitutes Communist Party for gang. If the Chicago ordinance had selectively authorized police to order loitering Communist Party members and their associates to move under penalty of arrest, the law's infirmity on associational grounds would have been self-evident, and it would certainly have been no response to assert that the right to social encounters on street corners is not protected by the First Amendment. There is no need to prove that the "activity" targeted is constitutionally protected where the law discriminates on its face on the basis of association. A law that criminalized gum chewing by Communist Party members would not be saved from constitutional attack by the fact that the Constitution does not protect the chewing of gum. There is no constitutional right to

---

[53] Terence R. Boga, *Turf Wars: Street Gangs, Local Governments, and the Battle for Public Space*, 29 Harv CR-CL L Rev 477, 487–88 (1994); Jeffrey J. Mayer, *Individual Moral Responsibility and the Criminalization of Youth Gangs*, 28 Wake Forest L Rev 943, 949 (1993) ("Gangs are, and always have been, groups of youths formed for many of the same motives that youths have always organized themselves—friendship and social identity as well as the pursuit of delinquent or criminal activities"); Felix M. Padilla, *The Gang as an American Enterprise* 9–10, 91–117 (1992).

[54] See, e.g., Don Terry, *Chicago Gangs, Extending Turf, Turn to Politics*, NY Times (Oct 25, 1993), at A12 (gang involvement with health care, education, voter registration, and supporting of candidates); *Gang Summit Ends with Call for Jobs*, LA Times (May 3, 1993), at A13 (noting gang summit policy positions on employment and civil rights); George Papajohn, *Gangs Aren't Rookies in City Politics*, Chicago Tribune (March 31, 1995), sec 1 at 1.

work in defense facilities, yet in *United States v Robel*[55] the Court recognized that when the government denied the opportunity to work on the basis of Communist Party membership, without the requisite showing of specific intent, it violated the right of association. Thus, even if there is no right to hang out on a street corner, a law that selectively bars gang members from hanging out while permitting all others to do so imposes guilt by association.

The Court's insensitivity to guilt by association is also reflected in its offhand treatment of the associational claim in *Reno v American-Arab Anti-Discrimination Comm.*[56] The lower courts in that case had found that the government had selectively targeted eight aliens for deportation on the basis of their alleged political associations with the Popular Front for the Liberation of Palestine (PFLP), a constituent group within the Palestine Liberation Organization. The government called the PFLP a "terrorist organization," but did not dispute that it engaged in a wide range of perfectly legitimate and lawful activity, from the provision of health care and day care to political and cultural activities. Nor did the government ever allege that the eight aliens had intended to support any of the PFLP's unlawful activities. The lower courts enjoined the deportations on a showing that the INS had not sought to deport similarly situated aliens, and had targeted these aliens for deportation based on their political associations without any evidence of specific intent to further the PFLP's illegal ends.[57]

The Supreme Court's principal holding in *American-Arab Anti-Discrimination Comm.* involved a jurisdictional issue. It concluded that a provision of the Illegal Immigration and Immigrant Responsibility Act of 1996 had effectively stripped the federal courts of jurisdiction to consider the aliens' selective-enforcement claims. It then confronted the question whether this interpretation raised constitutional concerns by depriving the federal courts of jurisdiction to hear a constitutional claim. The Court concluded that it did not, essentially because the Constitution does not recognize selective enforcement as a defense to deportation. The Court's analysis studiously avoided discussion of the First Amendment, fo-

[55] 389 US 258 (1967).

[56] 119 S Ct 936 (1999).

[57] *American-Arab Anti-Discrimination Comm. v Reno*, 70 F3d 1045 (9th Cir 1995), 119 F3d 1367 (9th Cir 1998), rev'd, 119 S Ct 936 (1999).

cusing instead on the problems that any selective-enforcement claim would present, and thus the decision can be read as having little or no implications for the doctrinal question of whether aliens have First Amendment rights.[58] But the Court did expressly leave open the possibility that *some* "outrageous" grounds for selective deportation might violate the Constitution, while asserting without explanation that selective deportation for being a "member of an organization that supports terrorist activity" was not sufficiently outrageous.[59]

The fact that the Court felt no need to explain why the grounds for selection in *Reno v American-Arab Anti-Discrimination Comm.* were not outrageous again illustrates its blindness to guilt by association.[60] In other contexts, the Court has stated that guilt by association "has no place here"[61] and "is a philosophy alien to the traditions of a free society and the First Amendment itself."[62] Infringements on the right of association generally trigger as stringent scrutiny as infringements on the freedom of speech or violations of equal protection. Thus, it is not clear why a selective deportation motivated by race would be more "outrageous" than one motivated by association. Nor, if the guilt-by-association principle stands, is it clear why selective deportation triggered by association with the Democratic Party would be more "outrageous" than one motivated by association with the PFLP. Yet the Court evidently felt the point to be so obvious that it needed no explanation.

---

[58] See Gerald L. Neuman, *Terrorism, Selective Deportation and the First Amendment after Reno v AADC,* forthcoming Georgetown Immig L J (2000); David Cole, *Damage Control? A Comment on Professor Neuman's Reading of Reno v AADC,* forthcoming Georgetown Immig L J (2000).

[59] 119 S Ct at 946–47.

[60] Justice Stevens, concurring, implied that the guilt-by-association principle was not triggered here because the government was not "punishing" innocent members, but merely selecting whom to deport among otherwise deportable aliens. 119 S Ct at 952 (Stevens concurring in part). But that view requires a rejection of the legion of cases applying the guilt-by-association principle to the imposition of civil disabilities and civil liabilities. See notes 45 and 46. If it violates guilt by association to deny a student group access to university meeting rooms on the basis of their association, surely it violates guilt by association to target an alien for deportation on that basis. On Justice Stevens's view, it would presumably be constitutional for the Internal Revenue Service to announce a policy of targeting for tax fraud investigations and prosecutions members of the Democratic Party, because it would not be "punishing" innocent members, but only those guilty of tax fraud.

[61] *Elfbrandt v Russell,* 384 US at 19.

[62] *NAACP v Claiborne Hardware,* 458 US at 932 (internal citations omitted).

The problem may be that it is always easier to recognize guilt by association in hindsight. It is no accident that the Court's approach to anti-Communist laws developed as the Communist threat waned. Our fears today are directed not at Communists but at "gangs" and "terrorists." The Court's inability to recognize the guilt-by-association problem in *Morales* and *American-Arab Anti-Discrimination Comm.* may be attributed to the blinders of today's hysteria. But it is precisely when those fears are greatest that constitutional protection is most needed.

The Court's early right-of-association decisions make clear that the constitutional right of association cannot be limited, as the Court's more recent decisions suggest, to expressive and intimate association. The right extends to all associations, including the nonexpressive and nonintimate, at least inasmuch as it forbids the imposition of disabilities on individuals merely because of their ties to a group, absent proof of specific intent to further some illegal activity. The specific intent standard distinguishes individual culpability from guilt by association, and because it serves that independent purpose, applies even if the association charged is neither intimate nor expressive.

C. ASSOCIATION AS AN END, NOT A MEANS — THE RIGHT TO WEAR A HAT

In addition to ignoring the lessons of its own decisions condemning guilt by association, the Court's modern jurisprudence of association also fails adequately to reflect the normative reasons for protecting the right of association. It treats the right of association as derivative, protected only to the extent that it serves other constitutional rights. But the constitutional case for protecting association extends beyond the right's derivative functions, and supports protecting association not merely as a means to protecting other rights, but as an independent right in itself. The guilt-by-association cases discussed in the preceding section demonstrate one way in which the right warrants protection independent of the concern for expression or privacy. But the normative case for constitutionally protecting association is even stronger, and ultimately justifies an independent jurisprudence of association, modeled on free speech jurisprudence, but not limited to expressive instances of association.

First, while the right of association is not literally mentioned in the Constitution, it nonetheless finds solid textual support in the First Amendment as the modern-day manifestation of the right of assembly. One of the Court's early right-of-association cases, *Bates v City of Little Rock*,[63] treated the rights of assembly and association interchangeably, albeit without explanation,[64] and the Court's right-of-association cases have relied on *De Jonge v Oregon*, an early right-of-assembly case.[65] That intuitive connection between the rights of assembly and association deserves more explicit recognition.

When the Constitution was drafted, association and assembly were virtually synonymous. In the absence of modern communications, it was difficult, if not entirely impossible, to associate effectively without physically assembling. While correspondence by messenger and primitive mail delivery made association and coordinated action marginally conceivable without physical assembly, the shortcomings of such avenues in a period without a national postal service or telephones were self-evident. If one asks why the Framers protected the right of assembly, the reasons would have little to do with the physical act of gathering together in a single place, and everything to do with the significance of coordinated action to a republican political process. Today we are connected by telephones, faxes, modems, and the internet, and association can and more often than not does take place without any physical "assembly." This is not to denigrate the value of face-to-face encounters and public demonstrations and meetings, but simply to acknowledge that what was sought to be furthered by protecting assembly was not assembly for its physical sake, but for the *association* and collective action that it made possible. Thus, just as the

---

[63] 361 US 516 (1960).

[64] The Court stated:

> Like freedom of speech and a free press, the right of peaceable assembly was considered by the Framers of our Constitution to lie at the foundation of a government based upon the consent of an informed citizenry—a government dedicated to the establishment of justice and the preservation of liberty. And it is now beyond dispute that freedom of association for the purpose of advancing ideas and airing grievances is protected by the Due Process Clause of the Fourteenth Amendment from invasion by the States.

Id at 522 (internal citations omitted).

[65] See, e.g., *NAACP v Claiborne Hardware*, 458 US at 908; *NAACP v Alabama*, 357 US at 460.

Court famously adapted the Fourth Amendment to the modern era by interpreting it to protect against searches by electronic wiretaps despite the absence of a physical invasion of property,[66] so the First Amendment "right of assembly" is best understood today as protecting the right of association irrespective of whether a physical meeting actually takes place.[67]

The right of association also finds support in the intent of the Framers of the Constitution. The centrality of collective action to a republican government was so accepted by the Framers that the only objection to including the right to assemble in the First Amendment was that the right was so obvious that it did not need to be mentioned. Representative Theodore Sedgwick proposed deleting the reference to the right to assemble on the ground that "it is a self-evident, inalienable right which the people possess; it is certainly a thing that never would be called in question."[68] He argued that "[i]f people freely converse together, they must assemble for that purpose," and sarcastically likened protecting the right to assemble to declaring that "a man should have the right to wear his hat if he pleased; that he might get up when he pleased, and go to bed when he pleased."[69] John Page of Virginia replied, however, that precisely because the right of assembly was so fundamental, it needed to be expressly protected: "If the people could be deprived of the power of assembly under any pretext whatsoever, they might be deprived of every other privilege contained in the clause."[70] Sedgwick's motion "lost by a considerable majority."[71] Thus, everyone agreed on the importance and purpose of the right of assembly; the only disagreement was whether something so fundamental as to be obvious needed to be mentioned in the Bill of Rights.

In its first extensive discussion of the right to assembly, the Su-

---

[66] *Katz v United States*, 389 US 347 (1967).

[67] As Glenn Abernathy has argued:

> Freedom to assemble need not be artificially narrowed to encompass only the physical assemblage in a park or meeting hall. It can justifiably be extended to include as well those persons who are joined together through organizational affiliation.

M. Glenn Abernathy, *The Right of Assembly and Association* 173 (2d ed 1981)

[68] 1 *Annals of Congress* 731–32 (1789).

[69] Id.

[70] Id.

[71] Id.

preme Court in effect agreed that the right was so basic that it did not need to be mentioned in the Constitution. In *United States v Cruikshank*, the Court stated that the right of assembly was implicit in the structure of our government, and that the First Amendment merely confirmed a pre-existing right: "The very idea of a government, republican in form, implies a right on the part of its citizens to meet peaceably for consultation in respect to public affairs and to petition for a redress of grievances."[72] If the right of assembly is implicit in a republican government, so too is the right of association, since the very reason assembly was considered implicit was that it made association possible.

Thus, the right of association finds textual and historical support in the right of assembly, a right considered so fundamental that it would find constitutional protection even if never mentioned in the Bill of Rights, and a right that was protected not for its physical attributes but because without it collective action would be largely impossible. The right of association is simply the modern-day manifestation of the right to assembly.

An independent constitutional right of association also finds strong normative support. Indeed, all of the arguments traditionally advanced to justify protecting speech also apply to association, and not only to expressive association. As the Supreme Court acknowledged in *Cruikshank*, the freedom to associate, no less than the freedom to speak, is a critical element of a democratic government. Just as speech is critical to self-government,[73] so is association. Indeed, the central metaphor in Alexander Meiklejohn's famous argument for protecting speech is a town meeting, a simultaneous confluence of speech, assembly, and association. There can be no politics without association. Politics in a democratic society requires collective action. If the government were free to restrict association, it could effectively close off the avenues for political change. As the Supreme Court recognized in *De Jonge v Oregon*,

---

[72] 92 US 542, 552 (1876). The Court elaborated:

> The right of the people peaceably to assemble for lawful purposes existed long before the adoption of the Constitution of the United States. In fact, it is, and always has been, none of the attributes of citizenship under a free government. . . . It is found wherever civilization exists.

Id at 551.

[73] Alexander Meiklejohn, *Free Speech and Its Relation to Self-Government* (1948); Alexander Meiklejohn, *The First Amendment Is an Absolute*, 1961 Supreme Court Review 245.

free assembly is critical "in order to maintain the opportunity for free political discussion, to the end that government may be responsive to the will of the people and that changes, if desired, may be obtained by peaceful means."[74]

Like the freedom of speech, the freedom of association also performs a checking function on the power of the state.[75] Voluntary associations can and often have become important independent sources of authority that mediate and limit the effective power of the state. Indeed, in today's world of "interest group politics," the state in a very real sense must be responsive to private groups, rather than vice versa. Our tax code encourages the creation of such mediating institutions, and these institutions play a very important role in society. As Arthur Schlesinger has described, "[t]raditionally, Americans have distrusted collective organization as embodied in government while insisting upon their own untrammeled right to form voluntary associations."[76] It was this feature of associations as mediating structures of authority that led Alexis de Tocqueville, the philosophical father of the right of association, to call association "a necessary guarantee against the tyranny of the majority."[77] Laurence Tribe has similarly warned that "to destroy the authority of intermediate communities and groups . . . destroys the only buffer between the individual and the state."[78]

A defender of the Court's "labeling" theory of the right of association might respond to the link between association and democratic self-governance and the checking function of mediating institutions by maintaining that protecting association when undertaken *for expressive purposes* fully serves these normative goals. And, indeed, the centrality of association to the democratic process does justify extending heightened protection to association for political purposes, just as speech doctrine accords extra scrutiny to regulation of political speech. But even if the link between association and the democratic process were the only normative justifica-

---

[74] 299 US 353, 364–65 (1876).

[75] Vincent Blasi, *The Checking Value in First Amendment Theory*, 1977 Am Bar Found Res J 521.

[76] Arthur M. Schlesinger, *Paths to the Present* 23 (1949).

[77] 1 Alexis de Tocqueville, *Democracy in America* 194–95 (Bradley ed 1948) (cited below as "Tocqueville").

[78] Laurence H. Tribe, *American Constitutional Law* 1313 (2d ed 1988).

tion for protecting speech and association, and it is not, protection for association should extend beyond expressive association. First, it is difficult and perhaps impossible to draw a clear line between political and nonpolitical association, just as it is difficult to distinguish political from nonpolitical speech.[79] Are fraternities, sororities, country clubs, or corporations nonpolitical? Many of their most adamant critics would certainly argue otherwise. Second, nonpolitical association plays a critical role in making political association possible, by forging links that are then used to unite individuals and groups around issues of governance. Friendships forged on street corners and golf courses, and in dance halls and country clubs, are essential to making political association possible. Social ties often provide the seeds for more overtly political association.

In addition, as with speech, the reasons for protecting association are not limited to its political uses. Choosing with whom to associate is as central to personal development and self-realization as are the freedoms of speech and belief.[80] We define ourselves in relation to others, and our associations simultaneously shape and reflect our sense of self. The freedom to choose one's associates is therefore fundamental to self-realization. Again, Tocqueville writes:

> The most natural privilege of man, next to the right of acting for himself, is that of combining his exertions with those of his fellow creatures and of acting in common with them. The right of association therefore appears to me almost as inalienable in its nature as the right of personal liberty.[81]

On this view, mediating institutions are important not only for their checking function, but because they foster civic virtue in indi-

---

[79] See Chafee, *Book Review*, 62 Harv L Rev 891, 899–900 (1949) (arguing that the most serious weakness in Meiklejohn's defense of political speech is the difficulty of drawing lines between public and private speech); Harry Kalven, *The Metaphysics of the Law of Obscenity*, 1960 Supreme Court Review 1, 15–16 (same).

[80] Martin Redish, *Freedom of Expression: A Critical Analysis* 11 (1984) (arguing that protection of free speech serves "individual self-realization," encompassing both an individual's development of his or her abilities, and an individual's control over his or her own destiny by making "life-affecting decisions"). Thomas Emerson, *The System of Freedom of Expression* 6 (1970) (speech is necessary to "assuring individual self-fulfillment").

[81] Tocqueville at 196.

viduals.[82] Association's role in furthering self-realization, self-fulfillment, and civic virtue is not limited to expressive or intimate
association. Membership in a country club or sorority, or social
association at the local bar, can and often will play a role in defining who we are and how we act as much as membership in the
Republican or Communist parties. As Amy Gutmann writes:

> Freedom of association is valuable for far more than its instru-
> mental relationship to free speech. . . . Freedom of association
> is increasingly essential as a means of engaging in charity, com-
> merce, industry, education, health care, residential life, reli-
> gious practice, professional life, music and art, and recreation
> and sports. . . . associational freedom is not merely a means
> to other valuable ends. It is also valuable for the many qualities
> of human life that the diverse activities of association routinely
> entail. By associating with one another, we engage in camara-
> derie, cooperation, dialogue, deliberation, negotiation, com-
> petition, creativity, and the kinds of self-expression and self-
> sacrifice that are possible only in association with others. In
> addition, we often simply enjoy the company.[83]

Finally, like the freedom of speech, the right of association
serves as a safety valve; allowing persons to join with like-minded
others makes it less likely that individuals and groups will go underground and adopt violent means.[84] Thus, the Supreme Court
in *DeJonge v Oregon*,[85] unanimously reversing a conviction for participation in a Communist Party meeting, stated that "the security
of the Republic, the very foundation of constitutional government"
lies in preserving the right of assembly "to the end that government may be responsive to the will of the people and that changes,
if desired, may be obtained by peaceful means."[86] Again, Tocqueville concurs: "In countries where associations are free, secret soci-

---

[82] See, for example, Robert Bellah, Richard Madsen, William Sullivan, Ann Swidler, and
Steven Tiptson, *Habits of the Heart* (1984); Ernest Gellner, *Conditions of Liberty: Civil Society
and its Rivals* (1994); Robert Putnam, *Bowling Alone Revisited*, 5 Resp Comm 18 (Spring
1995); Michael Sandel, *Democracy's Discontent: America in Search of a Public Philosophy* (1996).

[83] Amy Gutmann, *Freedom of Association: An Introductory Essay*, in Amy Gutmann, ed,
Freedom of Association 3–4 (1998).

[84] *Whitney v California*, 274 US 357, 375 (1927) (Brandeis concurring) ("the path of safety
lies in the opportunity to discuss freely supposed grievances and proposed remedies");
Thomas Emerson, *The System of Freedom of Expression* 7 (1970) (same).

[85] 299 US 353 (1937).

[86] Id at 364–65.

eties are unknown. In America there are factions, but no conspirac-
ies."[87] Here, too, social associations that are not explicitly
expressive in the Court's sense of the term serve an important
function in allowing otherwise alienated persons to find social
support.

Thus, the reasons for protecting association closely parallel
those for protecting free speech. Moreover, they are in no way
dependent upon association as a mere instrument to speech or privacy, but rest on the independent significance of association as a
mechanism for participating in democratic politics, checking state
power, achieving self-realization, and providing a safety valve for
individuals unhappy with the status quo.[88] If these normative claims
are persuasive, the right of association should receive constitutional
protection on its own terms, without a threshold inquiry into
whether it is expressive or intimate.

The Court's efforts to cabin the right of association are understandable, even if they are ultimately unsatisfactory. The right of
association is potentially limitless. Virtually everything we do in
society involves some degree of association with someone else.
Only the mythical self-supporting hermit could go through life
without associations with others. At the same time, society must
impose limits on associational freedom: the state enforces obligations to children and family, imposes restraints on association in
workplace environments and public accommodations, assigns children to schools and classrooms, and establishes voting districts, all
of which affect our freedom of association. The very act of governing a society requires the regulation of individuals' ability to associate. The Court's efforts to limit the right, then, can be seen as
efforts to avoid constitutionalizing all social regulation. More specifically, the right of association, and particularly its negative corollary, the right not to associate, have been advanced as objections
to some of the nation's most important goals, in particular,
desegregation.[89]

But much the same can be said of speech. Like association, ex-

---

[87] Tocqueville at 202–03.

[88] See George Kateb, *The Value of Association*, in Amy Gutmann, ed, *Freedom of Association*
35 (1998).

[89] Herbert Wechsler, *Toward Neutral Principles of Constitutional Law*, 73 Harv L Rev 1
(1959); Robert Bork, *Civil Rights—A Challenge*, New Republic (Aug 31, 1963).

pression can be found in virtually everything that a person does, particularly once it is accepted that conduct can be as expressive as verbal or written speech. At the same time, for a society to operate, it must limit speech in many settings—a teacher in a classroom, a judge in a courtroom, an employer in a workplace, and a police officer on a street corner all have to exercise the authority to limit speech, and could not effectively do their jobs without that power. And the right of free speech, like the right of association, can be used to hinder important social goals.[90]

What is needed is a more coherent approach to association. The Court's current approach—ignoring guilt by association, treating association as a second cousin to expression and privacy, and denying any protection for nonintimate and nonexpressive association—fails adequately to reflect the normative reasons for protecting association under our Constitution, and requires the drawing of incoherent and unpersuasive lines. In the following section, I propose an alternative framework.

III. An Alternative Framework

A jurisprudence of association is conceptually challenging for some of the same reasons that a jurisprudence of "symbolic speech" is challenging. As we have seen, just as virtually all conduct can be expressive, so virtually all conduct can be associational. Even a murderer may be expressing a point of view or acting in association with others. Thus, extending constitutional protection to association or symbolic speech potentially brings all conduct within the ambit of the First Amendment, much of it unworthy of protection and obviously subject to regulation. Yet a great deal of valuable expression takes the form of conduct other than speech, including music, dance, sculpture, photography, and marching, and accordingly it is unacceptable to hold that the First Amendment protects only verbal and written speech. Similarly, association would be an empty formality without the conduct that brings people together—meeting, raising funds, engaging in volunteer work, and the like—and therefore to limit the right of association to the formal act of joining a group would eviscerate the right.

---

[90] See Charles Lawrence, Mari Matsuda, et al, *Words That Wound* (1993).

As I have sought to demonstrate above, the Court's attempt to limit the scope of the right by protecting association only when it is expressive or intimate does not solve the problem. Nor does the federal government's attempt to classify human action as "association" or "conduct," and to treat regulation of anything but membership per se as a regulation of conduct only indirectly affecting associational rights. The alternative approach I propose here abjures the unrealistically rigid categories of "expressive," "intimate," "conduct," and "association," at least as threshold inquiries, and instead maintains that heightened scrutiny should be triggered whenever the governmental interest in regulating particular activity arises in some measure from the activity's associational character. This approach finds strong precedent in the Court's treatment of symbolic speech, and therefore I will first describe that jurisprudence.

It is now well accepted that drawing a line between unprotected conduct and protected speech does not solve the dilemma of how to provide limited protection to symbolic speech without simultaneously constitutionalizing all regulation of human conduct.[91] There is no such line, because so much is expressed through conduct. Accordingly, in reviewing regulation of symbolic speech, the Court does not ask whether the *activity* regulated is speech or conduct, but instead focuses on the *government's purpose* in regulating the activity.[92] The Court has acknowledged that "[t]he Government generally has a freer hand in restricting expressive conduct than it has in restricting the written or spoken word."[93] This necessarily follows once one admits that virtually all conduct is potentially expressive. The mere fact that the government has prohibited conduct that is potentially expressive does not trigger heightened First Amendment scrutiny, because all conduct is potentially expressive. But where the government regulates conduct *because* it has expressive elements, its regulation is subjected to the same scrutiny accorded the regulation of speech itself. In the latter situation, the government does *not* have a "freer hand" in restricting expressive

---

[91] See text at notes 31–34.

[92] Purpose as used here is distinct from motive. It refers to the purposes evident from the face of the statute and the interests asserted by the government, but does not authorize an inquiry into the motives of legislators. *United States v O'Brien*, 391 US 367, 382–84 (1968); John Hart Ely, 88 Harv L Rev at 1496–97 (cited in note 34).

[93] *Texas v Johnson*, 491 US 397, 406 (1989).

conduct than it does in restricting speech itself; rather, its regulation must satisfy the same scrutiny applied to regulations of pure speech.

For example, an environmental ordinance banning all public burning would be subjected to minimal scrutiny, even though it would have the effect of barring persons from burning flags or crosses to express their point of view. On the other hand, a law selectively prohibiting cross-burning or flag-burning is subject to strict scrutiny, because the governmental purpose in narrowly regulating such conduct is necessarily to restrict what those types of burnings express.

This approach is captured in the familiar cases of *Texas v Johnson*[94] and *United States v O'Brien*.[95] In *O'Brien*, the Court subjected a law banning the destruction of draft cards to minimal scrutiny because it accepted as legitimate the government's objective of preserving all draft cards for purposes of administering the draft. On its face, the law prohibited the destruction of draft cards irrespective of any message such destruction might send; it applied to private as well as public destruction, for example. The government's purpose in preserving draft cards, the Court reasoned, would be undermined whether a draft card was destroyed for expressive or nonexpressive purposes. Thus, the provision regulated conduct—draft card destruction—without regard to its communicative effect, and was subject only to lenient review.[96]

The Court in *O'Brien* contrasted the draft card regulation it upheld to "one where the alleged governmental interest in regulating conduct arises in some measure because the communication allegedly integral to the conduct is itself thought to be harmful," which it illustrated with a cite to *Stromberg v California*.[97] In *Stromberg*, the Court struck down a ban on flag displays that expressed "opposition to organized government." By its terms, the law regulated

---

[94] 491 US 397.

[95] 391 US 367 (1968).

[96] *O'Brien* states that "a government regulation is sufficiently justified if it is within the constitutional power of the Government; if it furthers an important or substantial governmental interest; if the governmental interest is unrelated to the suppression of free expression; and if the incidental restriction on alleged First Amendment freedoms is no greater than is essential to the furtherance of that interest." *United States v O'Brien*, 391 US at 377. This test sounds more stringent than it really is. In practice, the application of *O'Brien* nearly always leads to a decision upholding the statute.

[97] 283 US 359 (1931).

conduct only when it expressed a particular message. In *Texas v Johnson*, the 1989 decision invalidating a Texas flag-burning statute, the Court reaffirmed that "we have limited the applicability of *O'Brien*'s relatively lenient standard to those cases in which 'the governmental interest is unrelated to the suppression of free expression.'"[98] The *Johnson* Court held *O'Brien* inapplicable because the government's interest in banning flag-burning could not be attributed to anything other than the message thought to be communicated by flag-burning.

The conclusion that a statute is targeted at the communicative impact of particular conduct is not necessarily fatal. It simply means that the law will be treated as a content-based regulation of speech and subjected to heightened scrutiny. If the government is able to identify a compelling state interest and means narrowly tailored to further that end, the regulation will be upheld.[99] Indeed, while the Court's First Amendment jurisprudence generally applies strict scrutiny to content-based regulation of speech,[100] the doctrine nonetheless permits a great deal of content-based regulation. The Court has in many settings applied strict scrutiny in categorical rather than case-by-case fashion, leading to doctrine that does not consistently use the strict scrutiny rubric but can often be understood as reflecting the end result of such analysis on a categorical level. Thus, the Court permits the regulation of speech advocating illegal conduct only where the speech is likely and intended to produce imminent lawless action, a test that identifies a narrowly tailored way to further the state's compelling interest in forestalling the illegal conduct.[101] Similarly, the "fighting words" doctrine, which permits the regulation only of direct face-to-face insults likely to provoke a fight, identifies a narrowly tailored way to further the government's interest in forestalling violence.[102]

In other areas, such as obscenity, commercial speech, and regu-

---

[98] *Texas v Johnson*, 491 US at 407 (quoting *O'Brien*, 391 US at 377).

[99] See, e.g., *Burson v Freeman*, 504 US 191 (1992) (upholding law prohibiting solicitation of voters within 100 feet of polling place); *Buckley v Valeo*, 424 US 1 (1976) (upholding limits on contributions to candidates for federal office).

[100] See *R.A.V. v City of St. Paul*, 505 US 377, 382 (1992); *Boos v Barry*, 485 US 312, 321 (1988).

[101] *Brandenburg v Ohio*, 395 US 444 (1969).

[102] *Texas v Johnson*, 491 US at 409; *Gooding v Wilson*, 405 US 518 (1972); *Cohen v California*, 403 US 15, 20 (1971).

lation of cable television, the Court permits regulation of speech on showings that are less than compelling and through means that are less than narrowly tailored.[103] But in all of its modern speech jurisprudence, the Court's categorical rules are the result of a careful balancing of government interests against private rights, rather than a simple denial that any speech interests exist. When the Court, for example, says that obscenity is "unprotected," it does not mean that obscene speech is not *speech*, but that as a categorical matter, the interests in regulating obscene speech outweigh its value.[104] Similarly, "fighting words" and "advocacy of imminent illegal conduct" are sometimes said to be unprotected, but that conclusion is not the result of a threshold determination that such expression is not speech, but the end result of a careful balancing of interests between the freedom of expression and the state's interest in forestalling imminent violence.

A similar inquiry should guide analysis of laws regulating association. Instead of attempting to characterize associations as categorically protected (expressive and intimate) or unprotected (nonintimate and nonexpressive) as a threshold matter, the Court should ask instead whether the government's purpose in regulating arises in some measure from the conduct's associational character, and whether the regulation is neutral or selective. If the state regulates conduct generally, the fact that the regulation may incidentally impede some conduct engaged in for associational purposes should not trigger heightened scrutiny. For example, while a juvenile curfew has the effect of impeding associational activity by juveniles during curfew hours, it is not targeted at association as such, but at the heightened risk of juvenile crime at night, whether engaged in individually or in groups. By contrast, a curfew imposed only on gang members would be targeted at gang membership, an act of association. Under the latter law, the same conduct—being out after hours—would be permitted when engaged in by non-gang-members, but prohibited when engaged in by members. As the law's trigger would be association, it would properly be reviewed as a direct regulation of association and "subject to the closest

---

[103] See, e.g., *Miller v California*, 413 US 15 (1973) (obscenity); *Central Hudson Gas v Public Service Comm'n*, 447 US 557 (1980) (commercial speech); *Denver Area Educational Telecommunications Consortium, Inc. v FCC*, 116 S Ct 2374 (1996) (cable television).

[104] See *R.A.V. v City of St. Paul*, 505 US at 386.

scrutiny,"[105] whether or not the gang were found to be "expressive" or "intimate."

On this analysis, the Chicago ordinance in *Morales* directly infringed First Amendment associational rights. The law regulated conduct—hanging out in public places without an apparent purpose—only when done in association with gang members. As such, the governmental interest in regulating "ar[ose] in some measure" from the associational character of the conduct; in fact, the government demonstrated no interest whatsoever in regulating loitering unless it was done in association with a gang member. As a result, the ordinance should have been treated as a regulation of association. Because it imposed a disability on an act of association with a gang member without any showing that the individual or the gang member specifically intended to further any illegal ends of the gang, the ordinance would not survive such First Amendment review.[106] In this setting, namely, where government seeks to impose a disability on an individual because of his association with a group, narrow tailoring requires proof of individual specific intent to further the illegal ends of the group.

The above analysis does not compel a case-by-case application of strict scrutiny. Regulation of association, like regulation of speech, comes in many forms, some more deserving of skepticism than others, and the regulation of association may be subject to categorical rules analogous to those that govern a great deal of speech regulation. In the speech setting, content-based regulations are more suspicious than content-neutral regulations, and viewpoint-based laws are the most dubious. So in the associational setting, regulations that selectively target particular associations are more suspicious than laws generally regulating association, particularly when the selectivity is based on the political identity of the group. Thus, a law generally limiting political campaign contributions is more problematic than a tax law regulating all gifts across the board, because the campaign finance law singles out political association. But a law selectively limiting contributions only to particular political parties would be even more problematic. The former campaign regulation would be, in associational terms, analo-

---

[105] *NAACP v Alabama*, 357 US at 461.
[106] *Elfbrandt v Russell*, 384 US at 19.

gous to a content-based regulation of speech, while the latter would be analogous to a viewpoint-based speech restriction.

Similarly, regulation of economic associations, such as corporations, is properly subject to less stringent scrutiny, much as commercial speech regulation triggers less stringent scrutiny under speech doctrine. Reasonable regulations of business associations and corporations designed to deter fraud and to protect consumers, shareholders, and employees would generally be acceptable, just as reasonable regulations requiring financial disclosures, constraining speech in the workplace, and prohibiting deceptive advertising generally pass First Amendment muster without the heightened justifications necessary for other sorts of regulation.

Thus, the fact that a law is targeted at association does not necessarily mean that it should be invalidated; like the right of free speech, the right of association is not absolute. I do not propose here to identify all of the rationales that might justify infringements on association. My purpose is more limited—to identify when associational rights have been infringed, and therefore when First and Fifth Amendment interests must be weighed in the balance. My principal claim is that given the centrality of association to both a democratic system of government and self-realization, the regulation of association should be subject to scrutiny akin to that accorded the regulation of speech, without regard to whether the association is itself expressive or intimate.[107]

On the approach I have outlined here, it may be that certain types of association, like certain types of speech, could be said to be "unprotected." But as in the speech area, such a categorical determination would have to be justified by an explicit balancing of interests after recognizing that associational interests have been infringed, rather than by a mere assertion that the right of association is not implicated ab initio. The Court has unfortunately

---

[107] On this view, constitutional protection is not limited to expressive and intimate association, but the presence of an expressive or intimate element in the governmental purpose may trigger additional constitutional concerns. A regulation that targets association because of its expressive nature, like a regulation that targets any conduct because of its expressive nature, would be treated as a regulation of speech, wholly apart from the right of association. And, similarly, a regulation targeted at intimate association would raise privacy concerns in addition to associational issues. Thus, the regulation of expressive and intimate association may raise *additional* constitutional objections, but the right of association is implicated simply by the targeting of association, whether or not the association targeted is expressive or intimate.

sought to carve out categories of unprotected association simply by definitional fiat, without a careful weighing of the state's interests against associational freedoms. In *Dallas v Stanglin*, for example, the Court upheld a Dallas law limiting entry to certain youth dance halls to persons between the ages of fourteen and eighteen. The Court reasoned that while dance hall congregations "might be described as 'associational' in common parlance," they have no First Amendment protection because "this activity qualifies neither as a form of 'intimate association' nor as a form of 'expressive association.'"[108] To support its conclusion, the Court noted that the dance halls held as many as 1,000 persons on any given night, that the youth who came together there were not members of any particular "organized association," and that the patrons did not "take positions or public questions.'"[109]

If, as I have argued, association should be protected in its own right, not merely incident to the protection of speech and privacy, this analysis is wrong.[110] It would be difficult to imagine a more concrete example of assembly or association than the decision by a number of citizens to gather together in a large hall for an evening. The dance hall is not an assembly for the purpose of petitioning for the redress of grievances, of course, but the Court has long since rejected such a narrow reading of the right.[111]

This is not to say that the Court should have reached a different bottom line in *Dallas v Stanglin*. But a more sound basis for the result would have been to acknowledge that the regulation infringed on association as such, and then to uphold it as the associational equivalent of a content-neutral time, place, and manner re-

---

[108] *Dallas v Stanglin*, 490 US 19, 25 (1989).

[109] Id at 24–25.

[110] Indeed, even accepting the Court's limitation of association to intimate and expressive associations, its reasoning is unpersuasive. Many intimate associations are initiated on the floors of dance halls. Dance itself is a traditional form of expression. And the exchange of ideas that takes place in a social setting may be just as valuable from a speech perspective as that which takes place on the floor of a political convention or academic conference.

[111] Compare *NAACP v Alabama*, 357 US at 460–61 ("it is immaterial whether the beliefs sought to be advanced by association pertain to political, economic, religious or cultural matters") with *United States v Cruikshank*, 92 US at 552 (noting that the right of the people to assemble "for the purpose of petitioning Congress for a redress of grievances, or for any thing else connected with the powers or the duties of the national government, is an attribute of national citizenship, and as such, under the protection of, and guaranteed by, the United States").

striction on speech.[112] The Dallas ordinance did not prohibit association between youth and adults, but merely reserved certain times and places for youth to associate among themselves, much as states commonly do in the context of schools, organized youth activities, and organized adult activities. The city's interest in maintaining a safe environment for children was indisputably reasonable. The Dallas ordinance did not target any particular organizations, group identities, or ideologies. And it left youth and adults with plenty of other opportunities to associate with each other. The Court's simple assertion that "social association" is unprotected, however, does not adequately explain the result, for had Dallas forbade entry to the dance hall only to adult members *of certain gangs*, the law plainly would have violated the right of association.

The law in *Morales* could not similarly be viewed as a time, place, and manner restriction. Most importantly, it was not content-neutral, for it prohibited loitering *with gang members*. A law that forbade loitering by anyone in certain prescribed areas would be content-neutral, but this law selectively applied only to persons engaging in particular disfavored associations. Moreover, the ordinance barred loitering in any public place, and accordingly did not leave open ample alternative channels for association and assembly. Those who sought to loiter with gang members were effectively instructed to do so only in private.

The approach urged here might also require a different analysis, although not necessarily a different result, in the cases challenging the application of nondiscrimination laws to private groups. In *Roberts v United States Jaycees* and its progeny, the Court upheld the application of nondiscrimination provisions to private men-only clubs by finding that the expressive rights of members would not be undermined significantly by a requirement that they accept women. Applying its threshold analysis, the Court first concluded that the groups were not intimate because they were too large. The Court then acknowledged that the groups were expressive, but determined that the state's mandate that they include women

---

[112] See, e.g., *Ward v Rock Against Racism*, 491 US 781, 791 (1989); see also *Roberts v United States Jaycees*, 468 US at 634 (O'Connor concurring) (noting that expressive association may be subject to content-neutral time, place, and manner restrictions).

would not significantly affect their expressive rights. As many commentators have pointed out, this treatment is unsatisfactory; whatever else one might say about it, a state law dictating the terms of a private association's membership criteria clearly infringes on association.[113] Indeed, the Court admitted as much, stating in *Roberts* that "[t]here can be no clearer example of an intrusion into the internal structure or affairs of an association than a regulation that forces the group to accept members it does not desire."[114] But in turning to whether the state's interest in nondiscrimination justified the regulation, the Court asked only whether the group's *expressive* abilities would be affected, wholly ignoring any associational infringement that did not affect expression. A better account would have acknowledged that the nondiscrimination requirement infringed directly on members' rights of nonassociation, and would have forced the Court to confront more directly the competing interests at stake: when is it appropriate for the state to regulate private association in the name of furthering equality norms? Instead, the Court avoided that question by ignoring all associational rights not directly linked to expression.

The Court's prior treatment of the conflict between nondiscrimination principles and the right of association is no more satisfying. The Court has repeatedly rejected associational arguments as defenses to nondiscrimination laws in the business setting, albeit without much discussion.[115] In *Railway Mail Assn v Corsi*, for example, the Court upheld a New York civil rights law barring unions from discriminating on the basis of race. It did so principally because such a result "would be a distortion of the policy manifested in [the Fourteenth A]mendment, which was adopted to prevent state legislation designed to perpetuate discrimination on the basis

---

[113] See, e.g., William P. Marshall, *Discrimination and the Right of Association*, 81 Nw U L Rev 68 (1987); Douglas Linder, *Freedom of Association After Roberts v United States Jaycees*, 82 Mich L Rev 1878 (1984). George Kateb, *The Value of Association*, in Amy Gutmann, ed, *Freedom of Association* 35 (1998); Nancy L. Rosenblum, *Compelled Association: Public Standing, Self-Respect and the Dynamics of Exclusion*, in Amy Gutmann, ed, *Freedom of Association* 75 (1998).

[114] *Roberts*, 468 US at 623.

[115] *Hishon v King & Spalding*, 467 US 69, 78 (1984) (rejecting freedom-of-association objection to application of Title VII sex discrimination prohibition to law firm); *Runyon v McCrary*, 427 US 160, 175–76 (1976) (rejecting freedom-of-association objection to application of 42 USC § 1981 prohibiting discrimination in contracting to racially discriminatory private schools); *Railway Mail Assn v Corsi*, 326 US 88, 93–94 (1945) (rejecting freedom-of-association objection to New York antidiscrimination provision as applied to labor union).

of race or color."[116] It also reasoned that labor unions "function under the protection of the state," and that excluding minority employees from the union might deprive them of all means of protection from unfair treatment because the union's bargaining terms would apply to all employees.[117] Later cases simply assert that " 'the Court . . . places no value on discrimination,' " and that while " 'invidious private discrimination may be characterized as a form of exercising freedom of association protected by the First Amendment . . . it has never been accorded affirmative constitutional protection.' "[118]

But these rationales do not explain so much as announce a result. The Court has never fully confronted the tension between the nondiscrimination principle and the right of association, but has instead sought to deny the conflict. As Herbert Wechsler noted many years ago, nondiscrimination laws conflict with associational rights.[119] As anyone who has had a dinner party knows, the act of associating is an act of discrimination; to choose to associate with some is almost always a choice not to associate with others. The right of association would mean little if the right to choose one's associates could be overridden every time the state decides that a set of criteria are discriminatory. Yet the norm of equality would also mean little if all private entities were free to discriminate on the basis of race, sex, or any other criteria. How to balance these concerns is a difficult question, one beyond the scope of this article, and one not fully worked out by the Court itself. My only point is that the Court should not avoid the question by ignoring the associational interests at stake.[120]

---

[116] 326 US at 94.

[117] Id.

[118] *Runyon v McCrary*, 427 US at 176 (quoting *Norwood v Harrison*, 413 US 455, 470 (1973)).

[119] Herbert Wechsler, *Toward Neutral Principles of Constitutional Law*, 73 Harv L Rev 1 (1959).

[120] Justice O'Connor's concurrence in *Roberts* may come closer to confronting the issue, although her answer is also not ultimately satisfactory. She insists that associational rights are at stake, but suggests that associations organized essentially for commercial purposes are part of the public marketplace and thus more susceptible to regulation than noncommercial organizations. While the line between commercial and noncommercial is not an easy one to draw, it at least seeks to identify a public-private divide. The world of commerce is an inherently public and deeply regulated world, and government has a strong interest in ensuring nondiscriminatory access to that world, much as it has a strong interest in ensuring nondiscriminatory access to the vote. In both instances, that interest may justify the regulation of certain private entities that play a critical role in regulating such access. See *Terry v Adams*, 345 US 461 (1953) (invalidating as violation of the Fifteenth Amendment white-only preprimary election of private Democratic club, because of role it played as step toward

The federal government's proposed approach to associational rights cases is even more problematic than the Court's. It would draw a sharp dichotomy between conduct and association, maintaining that regulations of conduct, no matter how associational, should be subject only to lenient review, while reserving stringent review for regulations of association per se. Thus, it has argued that restrictions on financial contributions to political campaign candidates and foreign terrorist organizations should be treated as the regulation of conduct, subject to relaxed scrutiny, not the regulation of association, subject to stringent review. On this view, the right of association would demand stringent scrutiny only when a law expressly regulated membership or affiliation per se, leaving the government a free hand to regulate all other associational conduct.

The Solicitor General pressed this argument before the Supreme Court in *Nixon v Shrink Missouri Government PAC*,[121] a case revisiting the constitutionality of campaign contribution limits. In that case, the court of appeals struck down state campaign contribution limits virtually identical to the federal contribution limits upheld in *Buckley v Valeo*.[122] The Solicitor General, in an amicus brief supporting the state statute, invited the Supreme Court to reconsider *Buckley*, arguing that it had "applied an unduly stringent standard of review" to contribution limits, and that "[d]irect contributions of money to political candidates might be regarded as a form of expressive conduct subject (under *O'Brien* analysis) to significant regulation, so long as the regulation serves to advance governmental interests unrelated to suppression of the contributor's 'message.'"[123] This argument essentially resurrects the argument accepted by the court of appeals but rejected by the Supreme Court in *Buckley*, namely, that restrictions on political campaign contributions limit conduct—the giving and spending of money—rather than speech or association per se, and therefore should be subject only to lenient review.[124]

---

general public election); *Smith v Allwright*, 321 US 649 (1944) (same). But it does not follow that nondiscrimination principles are not also important in noncommercial settings, such as private schools

[121] 68 USLW 4102 (US Jan 24, 2000).

[122] 424 US 1 (1976).

[123] Brief Amicus Curiae of the United States in *Nixon v Shrink Missouri Government PAC*, No 98-963 (S Ct), 1998 US Briefs (LEXIS) 963, *25 n 12.

[124] See *Buckley v Valeo*, 424 US at 16–18 (discussing and rejecting court of appeals's reliance on *O'Brien*).

The Court in *Shrink Missouri Government PAC* correctly declined the Solicitor General's invitation, and reaffirmed that heightened scrutiny applies to regulation of political campaign contributions.[125] As the Supreme Court correctly noted in *Buckley* itself, distinctions between the expenditure of money and speech or association are inherently problematic, given the virtual impossibility of speaking or associating effectively without spending money. More importantly, however, the *Buckley* Court concluded that even if one could draw such a distinction in theory, campaign finance regulation would be subject to stringent scrutiny because the government's purpose in regulating campaign contributions and expenditures is necessarily related to the communicative effects of the expenditures and contributions.[126] The Court explained:

> The interests served by the Act include restricting the voices of people and interest groups who have money to spend and reducing the overall scope of federal election campaigns. Although the Act does not focus on the ideas expressed by persons or groups subjected to its regulations, it is aimed in part at equalizing the relative ability of all voters to affect electoral outcomes by placing a ceiling on expenditures for political expression by citizens and groups. Unlike [the situation in *O'Brien*], it is beyond dispute that the interest in regulating the alleged "conduct" of giving or spending money "arises in some measure because the communication allegedly integral to the conduct is itself thought to be harmful."[127]

Accordingly, the Court in *Buckley* applied heightened scrutiny to the regulation of both contributions and expenditures, upholding the former but invalidating the latter.

The decision to apply heightened scrutiny, reaffirmed in *Shrink Missouri Government PAC*, recognizes that the critical question is whether the government's regulation arises in some measure from the regulated conduct's communicative or associational character. This analysis sidesteps the impossible inquiry advanced by the gov-

---

[125] 68 USLW at 4104–05. The Court did suggest that contributions limits are subject to somewhat less rigorous scrutiny than expenditure limits, but nonetheless demanded that contribution limits be "'closely drawn' to match a 'sufficiently important interest.'" Id at 4105 (quoting *Buckley v Valeo*, 424 US at 30). Moreover, even this slightly less stringent scrutiny was justified by the fact that the regulation only placed a cap on, and did not prohibit altogether, contributions.

[126] *Buckley v Valeo*, 424 US at 16–17, 44–45; see also 68 USLW at 4104.

[127] Id at 17.

ernment, which would require dividing actions into "conduct" categories on the one hand and "speech" or "association" categories on the other, where virtually all actions are simultaneously both. Instead, the Court's inquiry focuses not on the objective or subjective character of the action, which is almost always going to be multifaceted, but on the government's purpose in regulating the action. When regulation is triggered by the action's communicative character, it is treated as a regulation of speech; when regulation is triggered by an action's associational character, it should be treated as a regulation of association.

On this view, lenient *O'Brien* scrutiny would apply to a general tax that regulated spending or contributions across the board and only incidentally affected spending and contributions for particular political or associational purposes. But campaign finance regulations by definition restrict spending and contributions only in association with a political campaign. A citizen is free to give money to his children, his church, or his local charity without restraint, but if he contributes money to a political candidate, the restrictions kick in. Similarly, citizens are generally free to spend money, subject only to general sales taxes, but their expenditures are limited when in furtherance of the election of a candidate. Such a law regulates the "conduct" of giving or spending money only when done in association with political candidates, and is therefore not a regulation of the general conduct of financial contributions or expenditures irrespective of their associational character.

The federal government makes a similar argument in defending the 1996 Antiterrorism and Effective Death Penalty (AEDPA) provisions criminalizing material support to "foreign terrorist organizations."[128] These provisions make it a crime, punishable by up to ten years in prison, to provide material support to the *lawful* activities of designated "foreign terrorist organizations."[129] Under the law, the Secretary of State is empowered to designate as a "foreign terrorist organization" virtually any foreign organization that has

---

[128] Pub L No 104-132, 110 Stat 1214, §§ 301–02 (1996), codified at 8 USC § 1189 and 18 USC § 2339A.

[129] "Material support or resources" is broadly defined as "currency or other financial securities, financial services, lodging, training, safehouses, false documentation or identification, communications equipment, facilities, weapons, lethal substances, explosives, personnel, transportation, and other physical assets, except medicine or religious materials." 18 USC § 2339A(b).

used or threatened illegal force, and it then becomes a crime to support the group's otherwise legal activities.[130] Under this law, it is a crime to send crayons to a day-care center or blankets to a health care facility run by a designated group, even if the donor can prove that he intended the crayons or blankets to be used for lawful purposes and that they were in fact so used. The law was designed to punish support of lawful activities, for pre-existing laws already made it a crime to support terrorist activity by foreign terrorist organizations.[131] AEDPA's proponents claimed that the law was necessary to cut off all support to terrorist groups because support is fungible; money that a terrorist group saves on donated crayons could be used to purchase bombs.

The federal government has defended this statute with arguments that parallel those it advanced in *Shrink Missouri Government PAC*. It claims that the statute targets the conduct of giving material support, not association with terrorist groups per se. Individuals are free to join the designated terrorist groups; they simply cannot offer the group any material support. As a result, the government contends, lenient *O'Brien* scrutiny ought to apply, and the interest in forestalling terrorism certainly justifies the limit on associational support.[132]

The government's argument rests on an insupportable distinction between association and material support. It distinguishes the many cases invalidating penalties imposed on Communist Party membership on the ground that they involved penalties imposed on association itself, while AEDPA permits association (i.e., mem-

---

[130] Under 8 USC § 1189(a)(1), "[t]he Secretary is authorized to designate an organization as a foreign terrorist organization . . . if the Secretary finds that—(*a*) the organization is a foreign organization; (*b*) the organization engages in terrorist activity (as defined at [8 USC § 1182(a)(3)(B)]); and (*c*) the terrorist activity of the organization threatens the security of United States nationals or the national security of the United States." Id. The term "terrorist activity" is broadly defined in 8 USC § 1182(a)(3)(B) to include, inter alia, the unlawful use of, or threat to use, an explosive or firearm against person or property, unless for mere personal monetary gain. "National security" is broadly defined in 8 USC § 1189(c)(2) to mean "national defense, foreign relations, or economic interests of the United States." Thus, the Secretary has broad discretion to designate any foreign group that has used or has threatened to use force, and whose activities the Secretary deems to be contrary to our national defense, foreign relations, or economic interests.

[131] See 18 USC § 2339A (1995) (making it a crime to provide material support or resources to any organization or individual for the purpose of furthering a comprehensive list of specified terrorist crimes, such as hostage taking and the killing of foreign officials).

[132] Brief for the Appellees/Cross-Appellants in *Humanitarian Law Project v Reno*, No 98-56062 (9th Cir pending), at 30–54.

bership) and bans only "material support." But just as speech and association cannot be meaningfully distinguished from expenditures and contributions in the political campaign setting,[133] so association with and support of a political group cannot be meaningfully distinguished. If the right of association did not include the right to contribute, it would be a meaningless formality. Groups cannot survive without the concrete support of their members. As the Supreme Court has said, "[t]he right to join together 'for the advancement of beliefs and ideas' . . . is diluted if it does not include the right to pool money through contributions, for funds are often essential if 'advocacy' is to be truly or optimally 'effective.'"[134] Moreover, if laws penalizing support of particular political groups are permissible where laws penalizing membership are not, all of the anti-Communist statutes the Supreme Court struck down could have been reenacted simply by rewriting them to target the payment of dues rather than membership itself. The government's attempt to draw this distinction exalts form over substance, and only underscores the futility of categorically dividing association from conduct.

In 1998, a district court agreed with the government and upheld AEDPA in major part.[135] While acknowledging that contribution of funds is a direct exercise of speech and association, the court nonetheless subjected the law to lenient scrutiny under *O'Brien*. It reasoned that the law was "content-neutral" because it proscribed aid to foreign groups "not . . . because the government disfavors the political speech" they promote, but because "the Secretary has determined that these organizations engage in terrorist activity that threatens the 'national defense, foreign relations, or economic interests of the United States.'"[136]

But this reasoning confuses the protection of association with the protection of speech. A law that imposes guilt by association is not saved simply because the government disapproves of the group for its illegal conduct rather than for its political ideas. If

---

[133] *Buckley v Valeo*, 424 US at 19.

[134] Id at 65–66 (quoting *NAACP v Alabama*, 357 US at 460).

[135] *Humanitarian Law Project, Inc. v Reno*, 9 F Supp 2d 1176 (CD Cal 1998), appeal pending (9th Cir). The district court struck down bans on the provision of "training" and "personnel" to foreign terrorist groups as unconstitutionally vague, but upheld the remainder of the challenged statute.

[136] 9 F Supp 2d at 1188.

that were the rule, the Communist Party cases would all have come out differently, because in those cases, as noted above, the Supreme Court accepted Congress's findings that the Party was engaged in terrorism, espionage, and other illegal conduct to the end of overthrowing the United States by force.[137] Yet the Court nonetheless applied heightened scrutiny and held that the only narrowly tailored way to further the compelling interest of national security was through application of the "specific intent" test. The pertinent question where the government seeks to punish an individual is not why did the government single out the *group*, but why did it single out the *individual* facing the sanction. If it has done so not for individual wrongdoing, but for the wrongdoing of those with whom he is associated, the guilt-by-association standard applies, and the government must prove individual specific intent.

Some restrictions on foreign-directed aid might be properly treated as the regulation of conduct subject to at most *O'Brien* scrutiny. Across-the-board currency or arms export restrictions, for example, would no doubt be constitutional, even as applied to a person who claimed that his export was an act of associational support. But this is because the governmental interest in such regulation would likely be unrelated to the associational character of the export. The same is true of restrictions on travel to particular countries; the fact that they may incidentally affect the ability of U.S. citizens to associate with persons or groups in the embargoed countries does not trigger stringent scrutiny, because the law on its face is directed at a nation, not a political association.[138]

---

[137] Act of September 23, 1950, Ch 1024, Title I, § 2, 64 Stat 987 (repealed 1993) (originally codified at 50 USC § 781).

[138] See, for example, *Regan v Wald*, 468 US 222 (1984) (upholding restriction on travel to Cuba); *Zemel v Rusk*, 381 US 1 (1965) (same). The Supreme Court has consistently struck down travel laws that target association with foreign political *organizations*. Thus, in *Regan v Wald*, the Court expressly distinguished two prior decisions, *Aptheker v Secretary of State*, 378 US 500 (1964), and *Kent v Dulles*, 357 US 116 (1958), in which it had invalidated decisions to deny passports to members of the Communist Party. As the *Regan* Court explained, the "Secretary of State in *Zemel*, as here, made no effort selectively to deny passports on the basis of political . . . affiliation, but simply imposed a general ban on travel to Cuba." *Regan*, 468 US at 241. In *Regan* and *Zemel*, the challenged laws were held not to implicate the "First Amendment rights of the sort that controlled in *Kent* and *Aptheker*" precisely because they were "across-the-board restriction[s]" not targeted at association with a political group. 468 US at 241. By contrast, AEDPA does not impose any across-the-board restriction, but selectively criminalizes "material support" *only when done in association with particular political groups*.

As a nation, our government routinely engages in nation-to-nation diplomacy, and must often take action specific to certain nations that limits what U.S. citizens may do. Targeting

AEDPA, however, is not an across-the-board regulation. The statute does not punish material support (or even arms export) generally, but only when it is provided to particular political organizations. Thus, AEDPA's very object is the suppression of associational activity with particular groups. Indeed, the case for treating AEDPA as an impermissible restriction on association is even stronger than the case for treating the Federal Election Campaign Act's contribution limits as restrictions on association. The Court in *Buckley* viewed the federal campaign law, as we have seen, as targeting association because it restricted financial contributions only when provided in connection with a political campaign. But AEDPA goes further and restricts contributions only when provided to particular political groups. A campaign finance law that limited contributions only to specific groups, to be designated annually by the commissioner of the FEC, would indisputably be invalid as an unconstitutional infringement of the right of association. AEDPA is of the same character.

Thus, a better approach to associational freedom would recognize that the right exists independently of privacy and expression, and would focus on the government's purpose in regulating. On this view, laws like AEDPA or the Chicago loitering ordinance in *Morales*, which selectively criminalize conduct only when done in association with certain identified groups, should receive the Court's most skeptical review. Laws like the campaign finance statute in *Buckley* sweep more broadly, and do not single out association with particular disfavored groups, but nonetheless target conduct for its associational character, and therefore also deserve heightened review.

IV. Conclusion

Few rights have garnered the encomiums that the right of association has. The Court has called it so fundamental to the structure of a republican government that it did not even need to be mentioned in the Bill of Rights.[139] Quoting Tocqueville, the Court has called the right of association "almost as inalienable in

---

a nation does not target political association as such. But the same is not true of targeting political organizations.

[139] *United States v Cruikshank*, 92 US at 552.

its nature as the right of personal liberty."[140] Without the right of association, politics itself would be impossible. And without freedom of association we would not be free to forge our own identities, identities that are necessarily formed in relation to fellow human beings. At the same time, however, few rights are as potentially limitless as the right of association. Again because we are social beings, virtually everything we do is in association with someone else. The problem, then, is how to protect the right without turning it into a veto power over all government regulation.

The solution the Court has adopted, at least for the moment, is to categorically define associations as protected or unprotected, depending on whether they further other rights, specifically the First Amendment right of free speech or the Fifth Amendment right of privacy.

This approach, which echoes Justice Black's ill-fated efforts to distinguish between protected "speech" and unprotected "action," should be abandoned, for much the same reasons that Justice Black's approach was rejected. It directs judges to conduct an incoherent inquiry, since all associations are likely expressive, and in any event there is no meaningful yardstick for distinguishing nonexpressive from expressive association. It fails to accord with the Court's own precedents, which have prohibited guilt by association for reasons wholly unrelated to whether the association is expressive or intimate. And most importantly, it fails to reflect the central role that association qua association plays in our daily lives and our constitutional structure.

I have proposed a different approach, one that draws heavily from the Court's approach to another important but potentially limitless right—the right of symbolic expression. In that setting, the Court has successfully distinguished those regulations of conduct that should raise heightened speech concerns from those that need not trigger skeptical review. The approach avoids the impossible task of dividing symbolic speech at the threshold into protected speech and unprotected conduct, and instead looks to the governmental purpose in regulating. If a regulation's purpose arises from the expressive character of the conduct, it is treated as a regulation of speech, and subjected to the same scrutiny that

---

[140] *NAACP v Claiborne Hardware*, 458 US at 933 n 80 (quoting 1 Alexis de Tocqueville, *Democracy in America* 203 (P. Bradley ed 1954)).

applies to regulations of "pure speech." So, too, I have argued, where the regulation of conduct arises from its associational character, it should be treated as a regulation of association and subjected to the same stringent scrutiny that generally governs regulations of "pure association."

This approach does not purport to answer all of the difficult questions presented by official regulation of association. It seeks only to get the inquiry off on the right foot, by identifying when the right of association is implicated. But that at least starts us down the road to a rational jurisprudence of association. And as recent anti-gang and anti-terrorist initiatives demonstrate, such a jurisprudence is sorely needed. If we are to learn from the lessons of the McCarthy era, we need to recognize guilt by association not only in hindsight, but at the moment that it is imposed.

LLOYD L. WEINREB

YOUR PLACE OR MINE? PRIVACY OF
PRESENCE UNDER THE FOURTH
AMENDMENT

The course of the Fourth Amendment in recent years has not run
smooth. Since the 1960s, when the Warren Court, empowered by
its decision in *Mapp v Ohio*,[1] expanded and solidified the rights
that the amendment protects, a more conservative Court has generally read it narrowly. In that respect, it is not so different from
other constitutional restraints on criminal investigation. The
Fourth Amendment, however, has been beset by an overload of
disagreement within the Court itself. The outcomes of cases all
too frequently have been determined by a divided, often 5–4, vote,
and the underlying jurisprudence has been shifting, vague, and
anything but transparent. Lately, there have been indications that
the disagreement is less and that the views of the Justices may be
converging toward some common ground, which perhaps creates
the appearance of a developing jurisprudence to restore coherence
to this troubled body of law. If so, the appearance is misleading.
There is convergence, but only around a variety of formulas that
have scant conceptual underpinning and are mostly the expression
of an attitude.

Much of the past disagreement has concerned the requirement

Lloyd L. Weinreb is Dane Professor of Law, Harvard Law School.

AUTHOR'S NOTE: Daniel Meltzer read the article in draft and gave me many helpful suggestions. Jacob Tyler helped greatly with the preparation of the final manuscript.

[1] 367 US 643 (1961).

of a warrant to search.[2] In these cases, textually the issue has been whether to prefer the first clause of the amendment, which prohibits "unreasonable searches and seizures," or the second clause, which provides in some detail for issuance of a search warrant.[3] With rare exceptions, the former clause has prevailed, with the effect that the provision for a warrant is less a hurdle to be overcome than a last resort if every other basis for a search fails. The practical significance of the issue is whether the authority to search should be regarded as within the general authority of the government or, rather, as an extraordinary authority reserved for special cases and specifically justified. Institutionally, the issue is whether, exercising the authority to search, the police should act spontaneously and forcefully as guardians of the peace or should ordinarily adopt a magisterial role and act only after deliberate reflection. In view of all that, it is unsurprising that the requirement of a warrant should occupy the Court's attention. Nevertheless, such cases reveal little about the nature of the interests that the Fourth Amendment protects or why it protects them. For it is conceded that the action of the police invades a protected interest, the only question being whether in the circumstances the police had authority (without a warrant) to do so.

The core of the Fourth Amendment is exposed in another line of cases, which appear superficially to raise a technical procedural matter: not whether the action of the police was lawful, but whether the particular defendant is allowed to challenge its legality by a motion to exclude evidence. Rights under the Fourth Amendment are personal and not delegable; a person has "standing," as it has been called, and is permitted to make such a challenge only if he claims that the police action violated his own rights. In some

---

[2] See, for example, *Maryland v Buie*, 494 US 325 (1990) (7–2) (protective sweep); *South Dakota v Opperman*, 428 US 364 (1976) (5–4) (automobile inventory search); *Chambers v Maroney*, 399 US 42 (1970) (7–1) (automobile search); *Chimel v California*, 395 US 752 (1969) (7–2) (search incident to arrest).

[3] One might argue that there is no occasion to prefer one to the other, because they provide for different circumstances, the Reasonableness Clause providing for a category of searches without a warrant and the Warrant Clause specifying what is required for issuance of a warrant, *if* a warrant is required. That is, in effect, how the Court reasons whenever it holds in a nonemergency situation that a search is reasonable and therefore requires no warrant. See, for example, *Buie*, 494 US 325; *Chambers*, 399 US 42. But such reasoning, in effect, prefers the Reasonableness Clause. The unqualified terms in which each clause is written and the conjunction "and" that joins them suggest that they are to be read together, not separately.

situations, the point is obvious. A criminal prosecution does not give the defendant a roving commission to examine how the police perform their duties. Although they may have carried out a flagrantly unlawful search at around the same time and in the same vicinity as the defendant's alleged crime, no one supposes that he can litigate the lawfulness of the search in the course of his own prosecution, if nothing seized in the search had anything to do with that crime or will be used as evidence against him. When persons' lives are intertwined and their interests intersect, the matter is more complex. Evidence may be found in a search that intrudes on the privacy of all, some, or even none of those whom it incriminates. Addressing the question of standing, a court fixes the boundaries of Fourth Amendment rights by asking directly whether this defendant in these circumstances had an interest that the amendment protects.

Minnesota v Carter[4] is such a case. Looking through a window, a police officer observed three persons packaging cocaine in an apartment that one of them occupied. They were subsequently prosecuted for narcotics offenses; part of the evidence against them was obtained in searches that were a consequence of the prior observation. As the case reached the Supreme Court, the two nonoccupants claimed that the officer had violated their rights under the Fourth Amendment when he observed them, and they argued that the evidence obtained thereby should be suppressed. The Court rejected their claim by a 6–3 vote, in which the majority was further split into four. The reasoning of the Justices in the various opinions, majority and dissenting, indicates how far we are still from achieving a coherent set of principles or even a clear understanding of the fundamental issues.

The divisions among the Justices make it difficult to predict how the decision in *Carter* will be deployed in future cases; but broadly or narrowly, it entrenches in the body of Fourth Amendment doctrine the astonishing proposition that someone who visits a friend or associate in the latter's home can have no expectation of privacy and, therefore, has no protection from governmental intrusion or surveillance while he is present there. Although this disregard of ordinary persons' wholly unexceptional conduct of their lives was foreshadowed in some prior cases, it has not before been stated

---

[4] 119 S Ct 469 (1998) (6–3).

so unequivocally and with such certitude as it is, by four Justices at least, in *Carter*. Although everyone will have his own candidate, the decision in *Carter* is possibly the most clearly mistaken and the underlying jurisprudence the most inadequate of all the cases decided under the Fourth Amendment in the past thirty years.

I

James Thielen, a police officer in Eagan, Minnesota, received a tip that his informant had seen people apparently packaging cocaine through the window of a ground-floor apartment. Thielen went to the apartment building and, looking in the window through a gap in the closed blinds, confirmed the tip. He notified police headquarters, which prepared affidavits for a search warrant. In the meantime, two men, Carter and Johns, who had been in the apartment, left and got into a car. Police stopped the car and arrested them. Police then went to the apartment and arrested its occupant, a woman named Thompson, to whom the apartment was leased. Evidence of the packaging operation was found in searches of the car and the apartment. Carter and Johns lived in Chicago and had come to the apartment solely to package the cocaine; in return for use of the apartment, they gave Thompson some cocaine. They had never been in the apartment before and were there for about two and a half hours. All three were tried and convicted of narcotics offenses.[5]

At their trial, Carter and Johns moved to suppress the evidence seized in the car and apartment as fruit of Thielen's observation through the window of the apartment, which, they claimed, was an unreasonable search in violation of the Fourth Amendment. The trial judge ruled that the men lacked standing to challenge Thielen's actions and that, in any event, his observation was not a search within the meaning of the Fourth Amendment. The Minnesota Court of Appeals affirmed.[6] The Minnesota Supreme Court

---

[5] The occupant of the apartment pleaded guilty. *State v Carter*, 569 NW 2d 169, 172 n 2 (1997). Cf. *Minnesota v Carter*, 119 S Ct at 483 n 1 (Ginsburg dissenting). Her conviction was not involved in the case before the Supreme Court.

[6] The Court of Appeals affirmed Carter's conviction on the basis that he lacked standing; it did not address the legality of the search. *State v Carter*, 545 NW 2d 695 (Minn Ct App 1996). In a separate appeal, the court affirmed Johns's conviction, without addressing the standing issue. *State v Johns*, No. C9-95-1765, 1996 WL 310305 (Minn Ct App, June 11, 1996), cited in *Minnesota v Carter*, 119 S Ct at 472.

reversed the convictions. It held that the men could contest the legality of Thielen's observation because they had "a legitimate expectation of privacy in the invaded place," and that the observation was an unreasonable search.[7]

The Supreme Court granted certiorari[8] and reversed. Chief Justice Rehnquist, writing for himself and four other Justices, concluded that Carter and Johns lacked standing and reinstated their convictions without considering the legality of Thielen's observation.[9] Justice Scalia, with whom Justice Thomas joined, and Justice Kennedy joined the majority opinion but also wrote separately, the former to pare down, if not eliminate, the protection that persons have in the premises of others, and the latter to affirm it, at least so far as "social guests" are concerned.[10] Justice Breyer also concurred; he agreed with the dissent that the men had standing but found that Thielen's observation through the window was not an illegal search.[11] Three Justices dissented. In an opinion by Justice Ginsburg, they concluded that the two men did have standing and indicated that they would have affirmed the state court's ruling without considering the merits.[12]

II

The ground for the decision in *Carter* was prepared and the seed sown in *Rakas v Illinois*,[13] decided twenty years earlier. In *Rakas*, the defendants were convicted of armed robbery. Evidence found during a search of a car in which they were passengers was used against them over their objection that the search was illegal. Acting on a radio call reporting a robbery and describing the getaway car, police officers had stopped the car carrying the defen-

---

[7] *State v Carter*, 569 NW 2d at 173–76 (standing, quoting *Rakas v Illinois*, 439 US 128, 143 (1978)); id at 176–79 (search).

[8] *Minnesota v Carter*, 118 S Ct 1183 (1998).

[9] 119 S Ct at 471. Justices O'Connor, Scalia, Kennedy, and Thomas joined the opinion.

[10] Id at 474 (Scalia); id at 478 (Kennedy).

[11] Id at 480. Examining the record for himself, Justice Breyer disagreed with some of the factual basis for the Minnesota Supreme Court's conclusion that Thielen's observation was an unreasonable search and concluded that it was reasonable.

[12] Id at 481.

[13] 439 US 128 (1978) (5–4).

dants and ordered them and the driver and another person out of the car. After they were out, the police searched the car and discovered a box of rifle shells in the glove compartment and a sawed-off rifle under the front passenger seat. At their trial for armed robbery, the defendants argued that the search was unlawful under the Fourth Amendment and moved to suppress the shells and rifle; but they did not claim that they owned them or that they had any interest in the car except as passengers at the time of the search.[14] The trial judge ruled that the defendants lacked standing to challenge the lawfulness of the search and denied the motion to suppress. The ruling was affirmed on appeal, and the convictions were affirmed.

The Supreme Court granted certiorari and used the occasion to reconsider generally the matter of standing to challenge an alleged violation of the Fourth Amendment. The defendants argued that anyone who was the "target" of a search, one against whom the search was directed, should have standing to challenge its legality and object to the use against him of evidence found in the search. Rejecting that argument, the Court adhered to the view that Fourth Amendment rights are personal and the lawfulness of a search can be challenged only by someone whose own rights were violated, whatever may have been the search's purpose or result.[15] The Court went on to say that the very concept of standing was unnecessary, because it simply reflected the substantive doctrine that determined whether a search had violated the rights of the person seeking to suppress its fruits.[16] On that basis, the Court turned to the question whether the search of the car had implicated the defendants' rights. The test, the Court said, derived from *Katz v United States*,[17] is "whether the person who claims the protection of the Amendment has a legitimate expectation of privacy

---

[14] In fact, one of the defendants had previously been married to the owner and driver of the car and may have had some connection with it. See id at 167 n 20 (White dissenting). The defendants' posture in the case was presumably dictated by their understanding of the law relating to standing before *Rakas* was decided.

[15] Id at 132–38.

[16] Oddly, although it indicated that the rubric of standing was superfluous and should generally be discarded, id at 139–40, elsewhere in its opinion, the Court continued to use it. See id at 135 & n 4.

[17] 389 US 347 (1967) (8–1).

in the invaded place."[18] Applying that test, the Court rejected the statement in *Jones v United States* (decided before *Katz*) that "anyone legitimately on premises where a search occurs may challenge its legality"[19]: "the fact that [the defendants] . . . were in the car with the permission of its owner is not determinative of whether they had a legitimate expectation of privacy in the particular areas of the automobile searched."[20] A mere passenger, that is to say, would not ordinarily have an expectation of privacy in the glove compartment or under the seat. And, in fact, the defendants had made no showing that they had any such expectation. Therefore, the Court concluded, they were not in a position even to raise the question whether the search was lawful.[21]

The factual predicate for the Court's conclusion—that mere passengers do not have an interest in the privacy of the glove compartment or under the seat—is obviously correct. In ordinary circumstances, were a hitchhiker—a "mere passenger"—to hop in and proceed to open the glove compartment and put his belongings inside or stuff them under the seat, the driver would surely be surprised and might well decide that the hitchhiker would be better off traveling by shank's mare. To conclude on that basis, however, that no protected interest of the defendants was affected by the police action is entirely to misconceive the issue. For the defendants were, after all, legitimately "on the premises" as passengers in the car. And unless the police had authority to *stop* the car and order the defendants out, their right to be where they were, uninterrupted by the police, was seriously infringed. Once they were *out of* the car—because the police had stopped it and

---

[18] *Rakas*, 439 US at 143. The phrase "legitimate expectation of privacy," which has become the shorthand rubric for this sort of Fourth Amendment right, is not used in the Court's opinion in *Katz*. The Court referred to the defendant in that case as "entitled to assume" that his words uttered into the telephone in a closed telephone booth would not be broadcast. 389 US at 352. Justice Harlan's concurring opinion in *Katz*, id at 360, is often cited as the source of the rubric, although, again, not the precise phrase. See *Carter*, 119 S Ct at 477 (Scalia concurring).

[19] 362 US 257, 267 (1960).

[20] *Rakas*, 439 US at 148.

[21] In fact, the search may well have been lawful. If the information that was communicated by radio gave the officers who stopped the car probable cause to believe that it was the getaway car used in the robbery, they were authorized to stop the car and search it. *Chambers v Maroney*, 399 US 42 (1970).

ordered them out—they, of course, had no interest in what was in the glove compartment or under the seat. But since the police could not have searched either place without stopping the car and ordering them out, the evidence found therein was directly the fruit of the police action that put their own right in issue.[22] For aught that appears from the opinion in *Rakas*, the police may stop cars at will and order passengers out, without even raising a question about the passengers' rights. That conclusion is plainly contrary to the understanding of ordinary persons and of the police themselves. It is contrary also to the Supreme Court's own understanding. In *Maryland v Wilson*,[23] decided in 1997, the court held that a police officer *making a lawful traffic stop* has authority to order a passenger out of the car. The basis of its holding was not that no protected interest of the passenger was at stake but that the potential danger to the officer was sufficient to justify the "intrusion on the passenger," which, the Court thought, "is minimal."[24] Had the Court applied its reasoning in *Rakas*, there would have been no need to consider the extent of the intrusion or the justification for it at all.

Although the Court's analysis in *Rakas* depended heavily on the concrete circumstances of passenger travel in an automobile, elsewhere in its opinion the Court indicated that its application of the "legitimate expectation of privacy" test was not so limited. Discussing the facts of *Jones v United States*,[25] in which the defendant had a key to his friend's apartment, where the search occurred, kept possessions there, and could come and go as he pleased, the Court observed that, in contrast with *Jones*, an occasional guest might not have any protected interest at stake if a search of prem-

---

[22] The Court's complete failure to address the legality of the stop is signaled by its posing the issue as whether the defendants had an "expectation of privacy *in the particular areas of the automobile searched.*" *Rakas*, 439 US at 148 (italics added).

Justice Powell concurring and Justice White dissenting noted that the defendants did not contest the legality of the stop. Id at 150 (Powell); id at 156, 160 n 5 (White). Although that may explain the Court's failure to discuss the merits of the issue, it does not explain the failure to mention it with respect to the defendants' *standing*, if only to state that the defendants conceded that the stop was lawful. Of course, had the Court done so, the entire discussion of standing would have been moot. Chief Justice (then Justice) Rehnquist was the author of the Court's opinion in *Rakas*. Any doubt about the significance of his (non)disposition of the stop issue in *Rakas* is eliminated by his opinion in *Carter*.

[23] 519 US 408 (1997) (7–2).

[24] Id at 415.

[25] 362 US 257 (1960).

ises occurred while he was present. Such a guest, it suggested, would be like a "mere passenger" in a car, lawfully present but not entitled to use the premises as his own.[26] That suggestion was reinforced in *Minnesota v Olson*,[27] in which police entered an apartment without a warrant to arrest the defendant. The Court concluded that since he was staying temporarily in the apartment, he had a legitimate expectation of privacy, which enabled him to challenge the police action. He had such an expectation, the Court said, not because he was present in the apartment when the police entered but because as an "overnight guest" he used it, albeit temporarily, in much the way that a person uses his own home:

> From the overnight guest's perspective, he seeks shelter in another's home precisely because it provides him with privacy, a place where he and his possessions will not be disturbed by anyone but his host and those his host allows inside. We are at our most vulnerable when we are asleep because we cannot monitor our own safety or the security of our belongings. It is for this reason that, although we may spend all day in public places, when we cannot sleep in our own home we seek out another private place to sleep, whether it be a hotel room, or the home of a friend.[28]

The overnight guest's expectation was legitimate because "[s]taying overnight in another's home is a longstanding social custom that serves functions recognized as valuable by society. . . . We will all be hosts and we will all be guests many times in our lives."[29]

There is a small but significant gap in the Court's reasoning. When the police entered the apartment, Olson was not asleep. Nor did the police action that Olson challenged have anything to

---

[26] Rejecting the statement in *Jones* that anyone "legitimately on the premises" when a search occurs has standing to challenge its legality, the Court said: "[A]pplied literally, this statement would permit a casual visitor who has never seen, or been permitted to visit, the basement of another's house to object to a search of the basement if the visitor happened to be in the kitchen of the house at the time of the search. Likewise, a casual visitor who walks into a house one minute before a search of the house commences and leaves one minute after the search ends would be able to contest the legality of the search. The first visitor would have absolutely no interest or legitimate expectation of privacy in the basement, the second would have none in the house, and it advances no purpose served by the Fourth Amendment to permit either of them to object to the lawfulness of the search." *Rakas*, 439 US at 142 (footnote omitted).

[27] 495 US 91 (1990) (7–2).

[28] Id at 99.

[29] Id at 98.

do with "his possessions"; it was simply an intrusion on him while he was present in a private place. So far as that is concerned, any invited guest in the apartment, even for a short time, would have the same interest as he. Evidently, the connection with the premises was enough to confer privacy on his presence, even though without that connection it was unprotected.

The full reach of the reasoning in *Rakas*, as endorsed in *Olson*, was not apparent before the decision in *Carter*. In *Rakas*, the contested evidence was property seized in a search after the defendants were (ordered by the police, to be sure) out of the "premises." In *Olson*, only the entry into the premises was at stake; the police did not observe and later testify about any activity that took place on the premises. In *Carter*, however, the issue was whether the defendants could challenge police observation of their *activities*, which they unquestionably intended to be private and believed were private. The Court's conclusion was that they did not have a legitimate expectation that their activities were private and, therefore, that no matter what the police had done in order to observe their activities, the defendants could not object. If the police secretly break into a house and conceal a microphone or a camera in it, no one except the occupants (or others who have the status of overnight guests or the equivalent) can object to what the microphone or camera discloses—neither guests at a dinner party, nor business associates discussing a new venture, nor a political candidate planning campaign strategy with volunteers, nor friends talking about themselves or others or about anything at all. If a man and a woman meet at a party and leave together, when one of them says, "Your place or mine?" the answer will determine which of them can count on what happens thereafter remaining beyond the scrutiny of the police—unless, at least, they make a night of it. Those consequences rest on the Court's assertion that none of those persons has a legitimate expectation of privacy in what is said or done in those circumstances.

The Court said in *Rakas*, and reaffirmed in *Carter*, that the legitimacy of an expectation of privacy cannot depend on Fourth Amendment jurisprudence itself, lest the test of Fourth Amendment rights be circular; rather, it must have "a source outside of the Fourth Amendment, either by reference to concepts of real or personal property law or to understandings that are recognized and permitted by society."[30] The Court asserts, then, that in all of the situations described above—that is to say, in the innumerable variety of private encounters that are a constant feature of ordinary life—society recognizes and permits no expectation of privacy, except for the persons on whose premises the encounter took place. The assertion is so plainly incorrect that one has to wonder not whether it is mistaken but only how the mistake can have been made. In any of those situations, were someone secretly to plant a microphone or camera—as at least four members of the Court allow the police to do with respect to any guest—the others who were present would protest strongly, precisely on the ground that their privacy had been violated. And they would, according to common understanding, be right.

How far the reasoning of *Carter* will be extended in the future is difficult to predict. Only four Justices asserted without qualification that social guests—those, at any rate, who do not attain a status akin to that of overnight guests—do not have a reasonable expectation of privacy. The firmness of the other Justices' resistance to that proposition is unclear. Justice Kennedy indicated in his separate concurring opinion that he would recognize the privacy of "almost all social guests."[31] His reasons for disallowing the defendants' claim in *Carter* are not reassuring. Their purpose in being there—"the mechanical act" of packaging cocaine[32]—he said, gave them only a "fleeting and insubstantial connection" with the apartment.[33] Nor was there a showing that while they were there they had engaged in "confidential communications" about the transaction.[34] But the defendants were in the apartment for more than two hours, hardly a "fleeting" visit. What made the defendants' actions "mechanical" and, if they were, why that deprived the defendants of an expectation of privacy, is not obvious. One might as well say that the purpose of a casual tryst—Your place or mine?—is the mechanical act of intercourse. As for confidential communications, Officer Thielen testified that when he

---

[30] *Rakas*, 439 US at 144 n 12, quoted in *Carter*, 119 S Ct at 472.

[31] Id at 478.

[32] Id at 479.

[33] Id.

[34] Id.

observed the three persons packaging cocaine, "[t]hey were talk-ing";[35] it would be surprising if none of the conversation were about what they were doing. But what does it matter whether the conversation was, in some manner that Justice Kennedy did not elaborate, "confidential"? It was private. Justice Kennedy observed that "most, if not all, social guests legitimately expect that, in ac-cordance with social custom, the homeowner will exercise her dis-cretion to include or exclude others for the guests' benefit."[36] And, he said, "where these social expectations exist—as in the case of an overnight guest—they are sufficient to create a legitimate ex-pectation of privacy, even in the absence of any property right to exclude others."[37] Why those propositions did not apply to the defendants is simply baffling. Did Justice Kennedy believe that they did not expect their hostess—"in accordance with social cus-tom"—to keep their activities private? Or was his point that, since they were not "social guests," the "social custom" is irrelevant? The former possibility is too obviously counterfactual to be enter-tained. And the latter opens a potentially large gap in the "general rule"[38] that Justice Kennedy posited. For his grounds for departing from the rule in this instance might similarly be applicable to any number of private encounters, certainly those among persons en-gaged in criminal activity, who are those most likely to seek the rule's coverage.

The conundrums that are raised by a straightforward reading of Justice Kennedy's opinion invite speculation that he intended to deny the protection of the Fourth Amendment only to those who, like the defendants, use the premises of another person exclusively for a criminal "business" purpose, without any other noncriminal or nonbusiness activity, and the invasion of whose privacy concerns only their criminal enterprise. Even so understood, his reasoning is not without difficulty;[39] but it captures a commonly felt sense that unmistakably criminal activity ought not have the shield of

---

[35] Petitioner's Brief on the Merits, Joint App G, *Minnesota v Carter*, 1998 WL 541976, at *14 aaaaaaa (May 14, 1998) (No 97–1147).

[36] 119 S Ct at 479.

[37] Id.

[38] Id.

[39] See text at note 66.

the Fourth Amendment and that little is sacrificed if it does not. Whether *Carter* will be confined to such cases, if that was Justice Kennedy's intention, remains to be seen.

In her dissenting opinion, Justice Ginsburg questioned Justice Kennedy's conclusion that the defendants' connection with the apartment was too insubstantial to give them a legitimate expectation of privacy. Saying that "[o]ur leading decision in *Katz* is key to my view of this case,"[40] she observed that persons who "engage in a common endeavor" in private premises have as reasonable an expectation of privacy as someone, like Katz, who makes a business call from a public telephone booth.[41] Her unelaborated reliance on *Katz*, however, leaves in some doubt her understanding of its import for cases involving the premises of others. There was no such issue in *Katz*, because the "premises" were the telephone booth occupied by Katz alone. So far as appears from her opinion, Justice Ginsburg's chief reason for protecting the guest was that the security of the host would otherwise be at risk, because police would often be tempted to invade a home illegally to look for evidence against a guest.[42] A comparable argument was made by the dissent in *Rakas*[43]; it was disregarded by the majority in that case,[44] as it was here. Justice Ginsburg appeared also to have believed that the guest himself has a protected interest, created by the host's invitation;[45] but, relying entirely on the precedents of

---

[40] 119 S Ct at 483.

[41] Id at 483–84.

[42] Id at 482. The requirement of standing always creates a risk of this kind, because the right and the remedy of exclusion of evidence may be separated. Justice Ginsburg evidently felt that putting a homeowner at risk was particularly to be avoided. See id. There is in fact a discontinuity between the Court's insistence that Fourth Amendment rights are personal, when it considers the matter of standing, and its insistence that the function of the exclusionary rule is not to vindicate the Fourth Amendment right that has been violated but to deter such violations in the future. For example, compare *Rakas*, 439 US at 133–34, with id at 137–38.

[43] 439 US at 156, 168–69 (White dissenting).

[44] The Court said only that since its holding was confined to areas of the car in which the defendants had no expectation of privacy, it was not necessarily depriving passengers of standing to protest a search of the vehicle, and, therefore, did not agree that its decision would encourage police to violate the Fourth Amendment. Id at 150 n 17. See also the concurring opinion of Justice Powell, id at 152 n 1. That, of course, took no notice of the stop of the car. See text at notes 22–24. *Carter*'s reliance on *Rakas* disposes of the Court's argument, in any event.

[45] See *Carter*, 119 S Ct at 482–83.

Katz and *Olson*,[46] she did not explain more particularly what that interest is.

III

The source of the Court's mistake in *Rakas*, now compounded in *Carter*, is its failure to consider concretely the nature of the privacy that one expects when he is present in a place that is the private premises of another person. Although it has said plainly that the privacy protected by the Fourth Amendment is built on people's ordinary understandings, the Court has signally ignored such understandings in this context. Treating privacy as one-dimensional and the homeowner's interest in the privacy of his home as paradigmatic, it has effectively denied to all of us protection for a different dimension of privacy that is just as fully acknowledged and confirmed and just as important for the conduct of our lives.

Privacy of place.[47] Most persons have some place that is their own: by title, lease, license, or any number of informal individual arrangements. The place may be as large as a house or as small as a room or portion of a room, like a closet or desk. It may be hers exclusively or shared with another person or persons: members of the family, roommates, short- or long-term invitees. The "privacy of place" that one acquires there is based on her continuing connection with that place and persists so long as the connection persists, whether she is present or absent. In that place, unlike elsewhere, she can extend her personality, by stamping it on the place: hanging her favorite pictures and photographs on the walls, putting her books on shelves, leaving love letters on the desk and last night's dishes in the sink; or being compulsively tidy. Having such privacy, a person is able to enlarge her self, to create and substantiate what is permanent about her, without exposing it to all the world.

---

[46] She said only that the "logic" of *Olson* "extends to shorter term guests as well," and, quoting *Olson*, that a short visit " 'serves functions recognized as valuable by society' " and short-term visitors "anticipate privacy in another's home, 'a place where [the guest] and his possessions will not be disturbed. . .' " 119 S Ct at 482, quoting *Olson*, 495 US at 98, 99.

[47] I used the phrases "privacy of place" and "privacy of presence" twenty-five years ago, in an article that explores this and some other issues. Lloyd L. Weinreb, *Generalities of the Fourth Amendment*, 42 U Chi L Rev 47, 52–54 (1974).

Privacy of presence. Were a person's privacy confined to the place(s) that are her own, it would be very limited. Although we do not expect to hang pictures or leave our clothes lying about in places not our own, everyone, except an occasional recluse, who is not involuntarily confined or physically incapacitated lives a considerable portion of her life away from her home, either in public or in the private places of others. The distinction between being "in public" and being "in private," although not in one's own private place, is a constant feature in the conduct of our lives, and it is well understood and acknowledged. The "privacy of presence" that one has when she is "in private" is based not on a continuing connection with that place but simply on one's presence there for the time being.[48] It is established by one's presence and continues for as long as, but no longer than, one is present. While a person is thus present and not in public, she can *be* in private and exercise her personality not only by trying out activities that are confidential, like a novel experiment or a political tactic, but also by doing any of the things that she would not do before all the world: play hard rock or chamber music with friends, love and be loved, sing off-key in the shower, strut before the mirror, wear odd clothes or none at all. Having such privacy, a person validates her self and gives it expression, without declaring it to the world.

Both kinds of privacy are prominent features of our lives, but they are different. The removal of either would disrupt the most ordinary features of most persons' lives. One's own home is a place where there is both privacy of place and privacy of presence; but if the latter were available only there, our lives would be sadly diminished. Imagine, on one hand, that there were no privacy of place. Whenever you are in a private place, your own or someone

---

[48] Accordingly, although one might imagine extravagant cases in which a *part* of one's body conferred privacy of presence, it is typically found only in places large enough for someone to be *in*. The privacy of a telephone conversation, which extends to both parties, is, of course, disembodied privacy of presence. In *Alderman v United States*, 394 US 165 (1969) (5–3), it was conceded that the parties to a conversation have standing to challenge the admission of evidence obtained by violating the privacy of that conversation. The majority held also, over the dissent of Justices Harlan and Stewart, id at 187, that the owner of the premises in which a conversation occurs also has standing, even though he was not a party to the conversation, id at 176–80. Although the court relied on *Alderman* extensively for other points in *Rakas*, 439 US at 133–34, 136–37, 138 n 6, it ignored the recognition in *Alderman* of privacy of presence. The same reasoning that gave nonoccupant parties to a conversation standing in *Alderman* should have given the defendants standing in *Rakas* (and *Carter*) as well.

else's, what you do and say is private. Other persons present with you have your privacy in their keeping; but no one else, without your or their consent, is aware of what transpires. Whenever you leave a place, including your own, however, your privacy in that place ends. While you are absent, other persons, including government officials, have access to the place and are free to come in and inspect whatever is there. Imagine, on the other hand, that privacy of place were preserved but there were no privacy of presence. Whatever you keep in your own home is private and whenever you are in your own home what you say and do is private. Others with whom you share the place have your privacy in their keeping; but no one else, without your or their consent, is aware of what you keep there. Anything that anyone else says or does in your home, however, and anything that you say or do anyplace except in your home, including the homes of others, is recorded and on camera, and available for other persons, including government officials, to see and hear.

Perhaps we should learn to ignore the exposure of our selves in the ways described and carry on just as before. More than likely, however, in the first instance, persons would alter their living spaces to make them less individual and more "neutral"; they would destroy personal letters, remove pictures and books that revealed their special tastes and replace them with "standard" works (Monet? Norman Rockwell? Charles Dickens?), hang up their pajamas, and so forth. One person's place would differ from another's, but only in ways that told little about them. Persons would likely be more idiosyncratic in their behavior and speech while they were in private; in place of their lost privacy of place, they would rely on privacy of presence to constitute and express themselves as individuals. In the second instance, the likely changes would be the reverse. Except in their own homes, persons would avoid saying or doing things that revealed much about themselves; they would behave in the homes of their friends and the offices of their business associates much as they do now on the public streets. At the same time, they would furnish and decorate their homes more idiosyncratically.

The point of these speculative scenarios is not to predict people's behavior were privacy of place or privacy of presence gone; they are both too much an ordinary part of our lives for us well to imagine their absence. It is rather to suggest how familiar and

uncontroversial they both are. Because both are so evidently included within the general notion of privacy, a society that protects
one is likely also to protect the other. If one had to choose, however, a strong case could be made that privacy of presence is the
more essential to the respect for the individual and individual responsibility that is a fundamental value of this country.

After *Carter*, the status of privacy of presence is, at best, inse-
cure. Four Justices would sustain it only as a kind of limited privacy
of place, which a person acquires by some continuing connection
with a place, like an overnight visit. A fifth, Justice Kennedy, has
stated that he would afford most social guests privacy of presence.
His dismissal of an equivalent claim by the defendants in *Carter*
suggests otherwise, however; and he would apparently not uphold
privacy of presence outside a social context.[49] Four Justices uphold
privacy of presence, without distinguishing it clearly from privacy
of place or, apparently, recognizing it explicitly. They uphold it
either by piggyback on the homeowner's privacy of place or in
reliance on precedent without further analysis.

Whatever protection may remain of a person's privacy when he
is a visitor on the premises of another, the treatment of privacy
of presence as a derivative or lesser version of privacy of place
strongly suggests that there is no protection at all when one is in
public. In a great many situations that are a feature of ordinary
life, persons stand or sit in a public place away from others and
lower their voices, to have a private conversation. Although they
have no protection against disclosure of the conversation if, even
unintentionally, they speak audibly within earshot of others, they
are generally thought to be protected against surreptitious eavesdropping by electronic devices that frustrate a "legitimate expectation of privacy."[50] The reasoning of none of the Justices in *Carter*

---

[49] Although Justice Kennedy did not explicitly exclude business invitees from the protection of the Fourth Amendment, his opinion strongly suggests that he would do so. He
referred repeatedly and apparently deliberately to "social guests" as well as to "social custom" and "social expectations," *Carter*, 119 S Ct at 478–79. Furthermore, even his dismissive characterization of the defendants' activities leaves no doubt that they qualified as
business guests, if not social guests.

[50] Cases are few. See, for example, *California v Ciraolo*, 476 US 207, 214 (1986) (5–4)
(observation from airplane by "naked eye" does not violate Fourth Amendment; use of
electronic devices distinguished); *Dow Chemical Co. v United States*, 476 US 227, 237 (1986)
(5–4) (conventional aerial surveillance and photography distinguished from "sophisticated
surveillance equipment"); cf. *United States v Agapito*, 620 F2d 324 (2d Cir 1980) (conversation in hotel room; eavesdropping with naked ear distinguished from electronic eaves-

supports such protection. For aught that appears, even in the dissenting opinion of Justice Ginsburg, police may now employ parabolic microphones and similar equipment to eavesdrop on conversations that the participants intend and expect to be private; for if a person is allowed no "legitimate expectation of privacy" in a private place unless he has some "connection" with the premises, he surely can have none in a public place. Of course, if that practice is permitted and becomes common, their expectation will no longer be reasonable or, therefore, legitimate. But who would approve such a change in the pattern of our lives?

In a concurring opinion, Justice Scalia, joined by Justice Thomas, asserted bluntly that the Fourth Amendment does not protect privacy of presence.[51] The text of the amendment, he said, protects the right of the people to be secure in "'*their* persons, houses, papers, and effects.'"[52] Since the word "their" modifies all the following nouns alike and it is "absurd" to suppose that someone could have a right to be secure in the "persons" of others, it follows that the right to be secure in "houses" also is a right to be secure only in one's own house.[53] That is, Justice Scalia would in effect add the word "respective" or "own" between the word "their" and the nouns that follow. It is, he said, "not linguistically possible" to read the amendment any other way.[54]

Justice Scalia's argument is vulnerable on its own terms. There is nothing linguistically impossible or even difficult about interpreting the security of one's own "person" to include respect for his privacy when he is in a private place. Justice Scalia's failure even to consider such an interpretation shows how much he starts from the premise that the Fourth Amendment has to do only with property, tangible things, and not with any other aspect of one's person.[55] But the argument bends the Fourth Amendment out of

---

dropping); *United States v Fisch*, 474 F2d 1071 (9th Cir 1973) (same). See Wayne R. La Fave, 1 *Search & Seizure* 441–49 (West, 1996).

[51] *Carter*, 119 S Ct at 474.

[52] Id (italics in original).

[53] Id at 474–75.

[54] Id at 474. In his opinion, Chief Justice Rehnquist indicated agreement with Justice Scalia's textual argument but acknowledged that the Court had departed from it in *Olson*. 119 S Ct at 473.

[55] Justice Scalia's blindered reading of the amendment in this respect gives point to Justice Ginsburg's observation that his opinion recalled Justice Black's dissenting opinion in *Katz*. See *Carter*, 119 S Ct at 484 n 3 (Ginsburg dissenting). Justice Black had argued that the

shape more fundamentally. The text of the first clause of the amendment, on which he relies, contains only twenty-four words; it is manifestly broad and general, not a detailed code. At the time when it was drafted, most forms of surveillance of persons in private premises required a physical entry. Does Justice Scalia seriously believe that the authors of the amendment thought it allowed government officials to break into a person's house or secretly to conceal themselves in a house, in order to observe what the proprietor's guests were up to? Does he seriously believe that "the right of the people to be secure in their persons, houses, papers, and effects" has nothing to say about such a practice? Since it is conceded that such an entry, if "unreasonable," is unlawful, does he seriously believe that the Fourth Amendment addresses the question whether a guest who is present rather than the proprietor can challenge the admission of evidence obtained in a search?[56] The conclusion to which Justice Scalia asserts we must all linguistically and logically be led is in fact a know-nothing refusal even to entertain the contrary, which depends on the interpretive premise that whatever is not explicitly affirmed is implicitly denied, any textual or contextual indications to the contrary notwithstanding.[57] It is not a constitution that he is expounding.

Aside from Justice Scalia's *parti-pris* exegesis of the Fourth

---

Fourth Amendment did not protect against wiretapping, because the words of the first clause "connote the idea of tangible things with size, form, and weight, things capable of being searched, seized, or both. . . . A conversation overheard by eavesdropping, whether by plain snooping or wiretapping, is not tangible and, under the normally accepted meanings of the words, can neither be searched nor seized." *Katz*, 389 US at 365.

[56] Compare the observation of Justice Black dissenting in *Katz:* "There can be no doubt that the Framers were aware of this practice [of eavesdropping], and if they had desired to outlaw or restrict the use of evidence obtained by eavesdropping, I believe that they would have used the appropriate language to do so in the Fourth Amendment." 389 US at 366.

[57] Justice Scalia referred to four comparable provisions in state constitutions when the Fourth Amendment was adopted. Two, he said, use the same ambiguous "their" that is used in the amendment. The other two avoided the ambiguity by using "his" instead of "their." This indicates, he suggested, that the ambiguity should be resolved as it was in the latter two. Were it not contrary to his purpose, he might as easily have argued that, with the latter example before them, the Framers' failure to follow that model indicates that they rejected it. In truth, such parsing of pronouns has little significance in any direction.

Justice Scalia extracted further support for his position from the maxim, well known in the eighteenth century, that a man's home is *his* castle and the rule that private premises provided no refuge from the law for "'a stranger, *or perhaps a visitor*'" (emphasis added). *Carter*, 119 S Ct at 476, quoting *Oystead v Shed*, 13 Mass 520, 523 (1816). What that aspect of the law of arrest has to do with the protection of privacy of persons not subject to arrest and lawfully on private premises is not apparent.

Amendment, several other factors may have obscured from the Court the full implications of its decisions in *Rakas* and now *Carter*. Doctrinally, it may have confused the question whether a person has an independent right to privacy while he is on the premises of another person with the quite different question whether he has a right to be on the premises. Unless a guest has the sort of continuing connection with the premises that the Court has said is important (and often even then), he is present only with the permission of the host and subject to withdrawal of that permission at any time. It may seem to follow that the guest's privacy is merely a reflection of the host's right to privacy; only the host, then, according to the general notion that Fourth Amendment rights are personal, would have standing to challenge its invasion. The fact that the host may bring his guest's privacy to an end is, however, no more dispositive of his privacy while he is present than is the fact that a lessee's privacy may be terminated at the end of the lease dispositive of the lessee's privacy while the lease is in force.[58] The permission of the host occupies the same position in the analysis of the guest's right as a title, lease, or license occupies in the analysis of the right of an owner, lessee, or licensee. It is a condition of his having the right, not a qualification of the right itself. More generally, the Fourth Amendment protects the privacy of persons who have access to private places. It does not, on one hand, guarantee access; nor, on the other hand, does it prefer one kind of access—title, lease, or invitation—to another, except insofar as it has a bearing on the expectation of privacy that is legitimate.[59]

In *Carter*, Chief Justice Rehnquist emphasized that the defendants were present in the apartment where they were observed "for a business transaction,"[60] and that "[p]roperty used for commercial purposes" has less protection under the Fourth Amendment than dwellings.[61] Justice Kennedy also apparently thought it

---

[58] The privacy of an overnight guest, as in *Olson*, is similarly subject to the host's continuing permission, which, presumably, may be withdrawn at any time.

[59] See Weinreb, 42 U Chi L Rev at 81–85 (cited in note 47).

[60] 119 S Ct at 473. Elsewhere he referred to "the purely commercial nature of the transaction engaged in here." Id at 474.

[61] Id. Chief Justice Rehnquist acknowledged that in this case the apartment was not a commercial establishment but a home; but, he added, "it was not [the defendants'] home." Id.

significant that the defendants' activities were "commercial." Throughout his opinion, he refers to "social guests" as the class of persons whose privacy is protected in the homes of others.[62] There is nothing in the amendment itself to support such a distinction.[63] Nor is there any doctrinal support. Occasionally, the Court has intimated that business activities rank lower in our concern for privacy than personal activities.[64] Although some particular social activities are commonly regarded as especially private, conventional understandings do not support the view that business activities in general are less private than social activities; the range and variety of both are too great for any such generalization. Many unexceptional private encounters have both business and social elements; it would be a difficult task to separate the elements of each or to characterize such an encounter as one or the other. Business activities and conversations are as likely to be private as social ones and, if the specific reasons for seeking privacy are different, they are not regarded generally as less worthy, as the Court well knows; it takes extensive steps to preserve the privacy of its own deliberations. Any effort of this kind to qualify some activities as more or less private than others for purposes of the Fourth Amendment is surely mistaken and ought strenuously to be resisted, even if it is no more than an aside. The right to privacy liberates us from precisely that sort of official "approval."

The business of the defendants in *Carter* was not, of course, any business; it was a serious crime.[65] There may be little impulse to protect sellers of narcotics or, as in *Rakas*, robbers; and the notion of a "legitimate" expectation of privacy may founder in that context. Justice Kennedy's dismissive characterization of the defen-

---

[62] Id at 478–79.

[63] One might argue that the reference to "houses" supports a distinction between homes and business establishments, although that is dubious in view of the generality and brevity of the amendment. But even if that were accepted, there is no support for a distinction between social and business *activities* in one kind of premises or another. Many business establishments are "open to the public" as homes rarely are, which may affect the authority of public officials to enter, although not to search.

[64] See, for example, *Lewis v United States*, 385 US 206, 211 (1966): "[W]hen, as here, the home is converted into a commercial center to which outsiders are invited for purposes of transacting unlawful business, that business is entitled to no greater sanctity than if it were carried on in a store . . . or on the street." Despite the suggestion to the contrary, the home in *Lewis* was not in any way open to the public.

[65] Justice Scalia, no doubt tongue in cheek, referred to it as "monkey-business." 119 S Ct at 477.

dants' activities in *Carter* suggests something of that sort.[66] As Justice Ginsburg pointed out, no rule regulating criminal investigation can be premised on the assumption that only crimes and criminals will be investigated. For innocent persons will rarely have the opportunity or occasion to protest; if the success of an investigation established its legality, that would almost always be the end of the matter, however many illegal investigations also had occurred.

The Court has correctly reasoned that the "security" protected by the Fourth Amendment is not self-defining and takes its meaning from reasonable expectations of privacy that the community's shared way of life sustains. Property law is relevant not because privacy is intrinsically tied to proprietorship but because it is the ground of much of the common understanding of when privacy may be expected. A large, altogether familiar part of that understanding is that being "in private" is not being "in public," and that when one is in private, he reasonably expects that what he says and does is, indeed, private. A guest's privacy is dependent on the willingness of the homeowner to have him as a guest; but it is the guest's own privacy that protects him from unauthorized surveillance.

The Court's statement in *Jones v United States* that "anyone legitimately on premises where a search occurs may challenge its legality,"[67] which it has since rejected, was a correct application of the governing principle that allows anyone whose own rights may have been infringed to do so. There is no basis for excluding guests who do not remain overnight, because it is only what they say and do while they are present that is protected. Nor is there any basis for distinguishing between social guests and business or other guests. Not only is the distinction often indeterminate; it also does not respond to our ordinary understanding, which takes it for granted that many nonsocial arrangements are and are meant to be private. Persons who use their privacy to package cocaine surely abuse the protection that the Fourth Amendment affords. But a

---

[66] Compare the plurality opinion of Justice White, formulating the appropriate protection against eavesdropping in relation to "the wrongdoer whose trusted accomplice is or becomes a police agent," with the dissenting opinion of Justice Harlan, considering the issue in relation to the "ordinary citizen," in *United States v White*, 401 US 745, 752 (White), 790 (Harlan) (1971).

[67] 362 US at 267. See note 19.

rule that excludes evidence only if there is no evidence to exclude is self-defeating. Even "classroom hypotheticals"[68] like a milkman or pizza deliverer are entitled to privacy of presence while they are present, although if they did nothing more than make a delivery, they would have little occasion to assert it.[69]

---

[68] *Carter*, 119 S Ct at 482 (Ginsburg dissenting).

[69] A pizza deliverer who took advantage of his momentary privacy in a customer's kitchen to display the tattoo on his buttock would probably have a brief tenure on the job. But who knows? His performance might be advertised along with extra anchovies. He is for the moment on private premises, at the invitation of the occupant. Were the occupant to respond to the performance by asking the deliverer to display the tattoo on his other buttock and secretly to transmit the view to the world at large, or were the police secretly to video-tape it, the deliverer might understandably complain that his privacy had been violated. His odd behavior violates what we ordinarily expect when we order a pizza, not what he as an, admittedly brief, guest in the house may expect while he is there.

It would be a limiting case if the pizza deliverer were to enter the premises, say, wearing a shirt that incriminated him. Were the police to break into the house while he was waiting for the occupant to pay for the pizza and to see the incriminating shirt, should he be able to assert that his privacy (of presence) had been violated? Perhaps not. But that conclusion depends on the fact that he has done nothing whatever to exercise his privacy; when the police broke in, he was wearing exactly what he had been wearing a moment before in public. It would be a different case if for some reason he had put on the incriminating garment only for the time that he was inside. The exception in this instance, and the reason for making it, confirm the rule.

RODERICK M. HILLS, JR.

POVERTY, RESIDENCY, AND FEDERALISM: STATES' DUTY OF IMPARTIALITY TOWARD NEWCOMERS

Must states provide the same benefits to new and long-term residents? The U.S. Supreme Court recently answered this question in *Saenz v Roe*,[1] holding that California cannot discriminate against recently arrived indigent residents by paying them lower welfare benefits than indigents who had resided in the state for more than one year. According to the Court, the Citizenship and Privileges or Immunities clauses of the Fourteenth Amendment categorically bar California from favoring long-term over newly arrived residents: once an individual becomes a bona fide resident, the state may not subject him or her to any further durational residence requirement to become eligible for state programs. The whole opinion had a brisk, matter-of-fact tone, as if Justice Stevens (its author) believed that he was not confronted with any deep interpretive ambiguities or tough policy dilemmas but rather was merely tidying up existing doctrine that was already pretty clear.

Despite its confident tone, however, Justice Stevens's opinion for the Court avoided the central and perplexing issue raised by

Roderick M. Hills, Jr., is Professor of Law, University of Michigan Law School.

AUTHOR'S NOTE: For their helpful comments on earlier versions of this article, I thank Evan Caminker, William Cohen, Daryl Levinson, Deborah Malamud, Rick Pildes, Larry Tribe, and the participants in the Legal Studies Workshop at the University of Virginia Law School. In the interest of full disclosure, I note that I wrote and filed an amicus brief on behalf of various professors of constitutional law in the *Saenz* case in favor of the respondents.

[1] 119 S Ct 1518 (May 17, 1999).

the case—the problem of defining when a new migrant to a state should be eligible for the state's redistributive programs. The Court avoided this question by assuming that all bona fide residents are equally eligible for all state programs, from reduced tuition at state universities to welfare benefits, regardless of how long they have been in the state. But this assumption ignores the possibility that the meaning of "bona fide residency" might properly change depending on whether the state program for which the new resident seeks eligibility is intended to redistribute wealth from one class of residents to another. If the state must provide redistributive benefits to anyone who relocates to a state, then there is a distinct danger that the state legislature will be deterred from providing sensible redistributive programs by the prospect of becoming a "magnet" to nonresidents who wish to reap the benefits—cheap university tuition, welfare benefits, and so on—of the current residents' tax effort. Such deterrence is a serious deadweight loss to society, if the sacrificed redistributive program would have served some socially beneficial purpose.

These considerations suggest that the test for residence might sensibly vary depending on whether residence determines eligibility for redistributive or allocative programs. But how should it vary? An unlimited power to discriminate against newcomers in redistributive programs might undermine the ideals of equal citizenship and invites old-timers to extract monopoly rents from newcomers by taxing immobile or unique resources for their own benefit. But, if states have no power to limit newcomers' access to redistributive programs, then states may likely cut back on useful redistributive programs to avoid an open-ended liability to newcomers who migrate to the state to reap the benefits of the program.

Bona fide residency, in short, is itself a puzzle rather than an answer. As I shall suggest in Part I of this article, this is a puzzle that the *Saenz* Court did not confront. Rather than explore how redistribution of wealth might change the meaning of residency, the Court treated residence as an empirical fact that could be easily identified and deployed to resolve the doctrinal conundra raised by *Shapiro v Thompson* and its progeny.[2]

---

[2] It would be unfair to criticize the Court for not providing a more complete account of what it means to establish state "residency." The state of California, after all, had conceded that the plaintiffs in *Saenz were* state residents. It is understandable that the Court

In Parts IB and IC, I will argue that the *Saenz* Court's textual and precedent-based arguments failed to answer the critical question raised by the relevant precedents and the Citizenship Clause of the Fourteenth Amendment—how the definition of "residency" (or state citizenship) might properly become more strict when the state redistributes wealth. The Fourteenth Amendment provides that all national citizens are also "citizens . . . of the State wherein they reside." It is also well settled that the Fourteenth Amendment requires some level of equality between new resident citizens and old-timer citizens in privileges and immunities of citizenship. But, as I suggest in Part IB, these propositions beg rather than answer the relevant question: What constitutes sufficient evidence that a new resident has the intent to become a "bona fide resident," and what constitutes sufficient equality among state citizens?

In Part II, I will offer a functional theory of residence requirements that (I hope) accommodates the Court's precedents, yet also makes sense of the fundamental problems of federalism that any sensible theory of residence requirements must solve. I will suggest that any such theory must squarely confront a dilemma. On one hand, one can argue that eligibility for a state's redistributive programs must be narrowly drawn to encourage states to make the efficient level of investment in such programs. On the other hand, any such restriction on state membership undermines the sense of national citizenship that, at least since the New Deal, has been the foundation for a mobile labor force and equality among newcomers and old-timers. If unconstrained, states' residence requirements create an orgy of class and race exclusion typical of the eighteenth- and nineteenth-century regime of "settlement and removal" of the indigent, a regime that the Court's "right-to-travel" precedents were supposed to eliminate.

With this dilemma in mind, I argue in Parts II and III that *Saenz* reaches the right result for the wrong reason. California's discrimination in *Saenz* is suspect because it involves discrimination in a means-tested redistributive program—welfare benefits. This sort of discrimination against indigent newcomers is suspect because, unlike restrictions on divorce decrees or college education, it is likely to be rooted in cultural animosity rather than fiscal self-de-

---

would seize on this concession as a way to avoid the thorny question of how to define state residency.

fense. Such cultural animosity is impermissible, I suggest in Part IIB, because states cannot aspire to be what I call "affective communities": they cannot attempt to make themselves into culturally or socially homogenous communities united by deep affective ties that exclude other persons from different social classes or cultures. Such state efforts to convert themselves into "affective communities" are so threatening to our sense of national citizenship that even Congress ought not to have the power to authorize them without the most careful explanation of their necessity.

I. Some Unanswered Questions about Text and Precedent: Who Are State "Residents," and How Much Equality Do They Get?

As the Court conceded in *Saenz*, its review of the right to travel "may be more categorical" than that articulated in *Shapiro v Thompson*,[3] "but it is certainly no less strict."[4] Both the strictness and the categorical nature of the Court's reshaped doctrine are welcome improvements on the notoriously uncertain analysis of *Shapiro*. Rather than attempt to distinguish "penalties" on interstate travel from other forms of discrimination against newcomers, *Saenz* effectively prohibits all classifications that burden bona fide residents on the basis of their length of state residency. This clean and simple nondiscrimination rule made resolution of *Saenz* easy. California's statute paid lower benefits to recently arrived bona fide residents than to long-term residents; it was, therefore, unconstitutional.

But, as I shall explain below, this simplicity is purchased by the price of interpretative unpersuasiveness. The Court's opinion places tremendous legal significance on the fact that a new resident is a bona fide resident without explaining either why bona fide residence is dispositive or what bona fide residence is.

A. SAENZ'S REINTERPRETATION OF SHAPIRO: NEWCOMERS AS A SUSPECT CLASS

Like the Connecticut, Pennsylvania, and District of Columbia laws that the Court held unconstitutional in *Shapiro*, the California

---

[3] 394 US 618 (1969).

[4] *Saenz*, 119 S Ct at 1527.

statute challenged in *Saenz*[5] discriminated against newcomers by requiring them to wait for a year before receiving the full Cal-WORKS assistance that other California residents receive. The main difference between California's waiting period statute and the durational residence requirements at issue in *Shapiro* was the extent of the deprivation: unlike the *Shapiro* statutes, the California statute did not deny all welfare benefits to recent immigrants, but instead gave them for one year the lower of either the California level of benefits or the welfare benefits that they would have received in the state where they formerly resided. Because California's welfare benefits were more generous than the benefits provided by most other states, this rule tended to give recently arrived immigrants lower benefits than the welfare enjoyed by other California residents.[6]

Should this distinction between a total and partial reduction in benefits be constitutionally relevant? According to *Shapiro*, the state laws that deprived new residents of welfare benefits for one year were unconstitutional burdens on the right to travel because they "serv[ed] to penalize the exercise of that right."[7] The *Shapiro* Court, however, never defined what it meant by an unconstitutional "penalty" beyond suggesting that such "penalties" had the purpose or the effect of deterring migration into the state.[8] Taken literally, this formulation would prohibit any state actions designed to reduce the incentives to move into the state, even when such action applied impartially to all residents of the state, new and old. For instance, if a state were to reduce welfare benefits for all of its citizens to the level of benefits provided by neighboring states, such a reduction could violate the right to travel under *Shapiro*'s "penalty" analysis, because the reduction would very likely have

---

[5] Welfare and Institutions Code § 11450.03. The relevant language of the statute provides that eligible families who have resided in the state for less than twelve consecutive months immediately before applying cannot receive CalWORKs assistance any higher than "the maximum aid payment that would have been received by that family from the state of prior residence." Cal Welf & Inst Code § 11450.03(a).

[6] Id.

[7] *Shapiro*, 394 US at 635.

[8] See, e.g., id at 631 ("[T]he purpose of deterring the in-migration of indigents cannot serve as justification for the classification created by the one-year waiting period, since that purpose is constitutionally impermissible").

both the purpose and effect of "deterring the in-migration of indigents."[9]

Saenz can be seen as an attempt to tame the confusion and extravagance of *Shapiro*. There had been earlier efforts. The earliest, suggested by Justice Marshall in *Memorial Hospital v Maricopa County*,[10] could be dubbed the "severe penalties" view. Under this view, *Shapiro* prohibited only those state laws that imposed a *severe* burden on interstate travel—for instance, loss of all welfare benefits for a year, as in *Shapiro*, or loss of medical care, as in the Arizona law overturned in *Maricopa County*. Under this theory, California's partial reduction of newcomers' welfare benefits might be distinguished from the laws held unconstitutional in *Shapiro*, because a partial reduction of benefits is less "severe" than a total reduction. Moreover, if the relevant consideration is whether interstate travel is "penalized"—that is, actually deterred—then one could argue that California's statute deterred no travel. After all, California's measure gave new residents the same benefits that they would have received in their state of origin, theoretically leaving them no worse off than if they had never exercised their constitutional right of travel—at least if one pays no attention to the higher cost of living in California.

The *Saenz* Court wisely ignored the "severe penalties" approach and opted for a second theory that can be dubbed the "nondiscrimination" rule.[11] Under the "nondiscrimination" theory, once a new resident demonstrates that he or she is a bona fide resident, then states are categorically barred from drawing distinctions that burden that new resident based on length of residence. If one assumes that the concept of "bona fide resident" is a self-defining notion, then this "nondiscrimination" view provides a crisp, clear

---

[9] Id at 632.

[10] 415 US 250 (1974).

[11] The "severe penalties" theory is almost as self-refuting as the broadest view of *Shapiro*, for it provides no baseline with which to distinguish "penalties" from "nonpenalties." Were newcomers to California entitled to the treatment that they received in their former state or the treatment that was generally provided in their new state? Either view leads to absurdity if the inquiry is defined by the "severity" of the deterrent to interstate travel. If there is an entitlement to the former state's level of benefits, then migrants from California to, say, Arkansas should be permitted to demand from the Arkansas government the higher level of payment afforded by California law, even though Arkansas pays all of its citizens a uniform low payment. If the new state provides the standard, then California should be barred from cutting its benefits "too much" for all state residents, because such cuts might deter migration from stingier neighbors.

alternative to the "severe penalties" theory. As Justice Stevens wrote, "[w]ere we concerned solely with actual deterrence to migration, we might be persuaded that a partial withholding of benefits constitutes a lesser incursion on the right to travel than an outright denial of all benefits. But since the right to travel embraces the citizen's right to be treated equally in her new State of residence, the discriminatory classification is itself a penalty."[12]

As I suggest below, the Court's justification of the "nondiscrimination theory" is unsatisfactory in two respects. First, the Court provides no convincing textual or other argument that the nondiscrimination rule should be a categorical rule barring all discrimination against newly arrived state residents. Second, the Court did not resolve the confusion in the precedents about the meaning of "bona fide residency."

B. SHOULD THERE BE ABSOLUTE EQUALITY BETWEEN NEW AND LONG-TERM RESIDENTS?

Saenz rested its categorical nondiscrimination rule on the first two clauses of the Fourteenth Amendment—the Citizenship Clause, which defines state citizenship, and the Privileges or Immunities Clause, which defines the rights of state and national citizenship. Although the Court grouped this nondiscrimination rule loosely with two other entitlements as an "aspect" of the right to travel,[13] Chief Justice Rehnquist's dissent was probably correct to note that the concept of interstate travel played no substantial role in the Court's analysis.[14] Instead, the Court essentially derived a new right from two clauses of the Fourteenth Amendment that the Court had previously virtually ignored.

How persuasive is this textual inference? To Justice Stevens's credit, he did not emulate the *Shapiro* Court's disdain for textual

---

[12] *Saenz*, 119 S Ct at 1527.

[13] These three rights are "the right of a citizen of one State to enter and to leave another State, the right to be treated as a welcome visitor rather than an unfriendly alien when temporarily present in the second State, and, for those travelers who elect to become permanent residents, the right to be treated like other citizens of that State."

[14] *Saenz* at 13 ("I cannot see how the right to become a citizen of another State is a necessary 'component' of the right to travel, or why the Court tries to marry these separate and distinct rights").

analysis[15] but made a plausible argument based on text and original understanding that the Fourteenth Amendment's first two clauses were intended to give newcomers some sort of equality with old-timers in state entitlements. To be sure, the Court may have over-stated the case when it declared that this strong nondiscrimination rule "is plainly identified in the opening words of the Fourteenth Amendment." As Douglas Laycock has noted, the Privileges or Immunities Clause of the Fourteenth Amendment (unlike the analogous clause of Article IV) does not specify the class against which discrimination is forbidden and therefore suggests a set of absolute rather than comparative rights.[16]

However, while Laycock's position is probably correct in part,[17] it is only part of the story. As John Harrison has shown in his careful and intelligent study of the Fourteenth Amendment's original understanding, the framers of the Amendment believed that the Privileges or Immunities Clause would also bar "arbitrary" discrimination in state-law entitlements.[18] Harrison concentrates on arbitrary *racial* distinctions, but there is evidence that the framers regarded distinctions based on a newcomer's state of origin as equally suspect. It is well known that Republican drafters of these two clauses intended them to reverse *Dred Scott v Sandford*,[19] a case

---

[15] *Shapiro*, 395 US at 630 ("We have no occasion to ascribe the source of this right to travel interstate to a particular constitutional provision"). After blandly dismissing the whole question of textual interpretation, the *Shapiro* Court had then proceeded to list in a footnote four different textual provisions that might serve as the textual hook on which the right to travel could be hung—the Privileges and Immunities Clause of Article IV, section 2; the Dormant Commerce Clause; the Privileges or Immunities Clause of the Fourteenth Amendment; and the Fifth Amendment's Due Process clauses.

[16] Douglas Laycock, *Equal Citizens of Equal and Territorial States: The Constitutional Foundations of Choice of Law*, 92 Colum L Rev 249, 263 (1992) ("Whatever these privileges and immunities [protected by the Fourteenth Amendment] are thought to be . . . they depend directly on federal law applicable to all and not on the rights of some reference group").

[17] Akhil Amar has persuasively indicated that the Fourteenth Amendment's Privileges or Immunities Clause was intended in part to incorporate the U.S. Constitution's Bill of Rights. See Akhil Amar, *The Bill of Rights* 137–214 (1998).

[18] See, e.g., John Harrison, *Reconstructing the Privileges or Immunities Clause*, 101 Yale L J 1385, 1457–58 (1992). Douglas Laycock argues that the Privileges or Immunities Clause of the Fourteenth Amendment cannot contain a comparative right, because it does not specify the groups between which equality is required. As a textual matter, Laycock is surely correct: unlike Article IV's Privileges and Immunities Clause, the Fourteenth Amendment's language seems to specify an absolute right. Harrison's argument, however, indicates that the framers assumed that the rights covered by the Privileges or Immunities Clause would be defined at least in part by state law.

[19] 60 US (19 How) 393 (1857).

in which a migrant intending to settle in a new state (i.e., Dred Scott) was denied the benefits of state citizenship (i.e., freedom from slavery) because he did not qualify for state citizenship.[20] Chief Justice Taney rejected the possibility of state citizenship for free Blacks under Article IV, section 2 precisely because he assumed that state citizenship would give "[free Blacks] the right to enter every other State whenever they pleased" under Article IV's Privileges or Immunities Clause, a conclusion that he found unacceptable.[21] The Republicans, by contrast, insisted on precisely this conclusion and drafted the Fourteenth Amendment's first two clauses to entrench it as constitutional law.

More generally, Republican ideology was strongly influenced by the Abolitionist argument that the southern states had egregiously violated Article IV, section 2 in their treatment of free Blacks and abolitionists who visited southern states.[22] The Citizenship and Privileges or Immunities clauses of the Fourteenth Amendment were intended to correct this underenforcement of Article IV, section 2, to act as a new constitutional confirmation of the Privileges and Immunities Clause of Article IV, section 2,[23] guaranteeing to all national citizens (in Senator Lyman Trumbull's words) the right to go into any state of the Union and to reside there.[24]

So far, so good: *Saenz* is almost certainly correct that the first

---

[20] See, e.g., *Sugarman v Dougall*, 413 US 634, 652 (1973) (Rehnquist, J, dissenting).

[21] Id at 417.

[22] Prior to the Civil War, southern states were notorious for their interference with interstate migration, excluding free Black citizens and abolitionists from their territory even when it was widely acknowledged that such exclusion interfered with the comity owed to northern states under Article IV, section 2, or the dormant commerce power of Congress. For instance, southern states imprisoned free Black seamen who entered southern ports with their ships, even in the teeth of Justice Johnson's decision in *Elkison v Deliesseline*, 8 F Cas 493 (CCDSC 1823) striking down such restrictions on free movement of both free Black northern citizens and foreign seamen as encroachments of Congress's power to regulate international commerce. For an account of the Negro Seamens Acts, see Paul Finkelman, *States Rights North and South in Antebellum America*, in Kermit Hall and James W. Ely, Jr., eds, *An Uncertain Tradition: Constitutionalism and the History of the South* 130–33 (1989). For an account of southern state courts' rejection of free Blacks' claims to freedom under northern liberty laws, see Paul Finkelman, *An Imperfect Union: Slavery, Federalism, and Comity* ch 7 (1981).

[23] Jacobus tenBroek, *Equal Under the Law* 232 (1965) ("The comity clause . . . was the particular provision of the existing Constitution, most speakers agreed, the systematic violation of which had made necessary a new constitutional confirmation").

[24] Lyman Trumbull's remarks are reported at Cong Globe, 29th Cong, 1st Sess 1757 (1866). The Republican consensus on Article IV, section 2 is discussed in Earl Maltz, *Civil Rights, the Constitution, and Congress, 1863–1869* at 55, 63–65, 97 (1990).

two clauses of the Fourteenth Amendment embody some sort of antidiscrimination rule designed to guarantee certain newcomers—bona fide state residents who are state citizens by the terms of the Fourteenth Amendment—some sort of parity with old-timers. But exactly what kind of parity, and which kinds of newcomers? Just because a clause bars many types of distinctions between two classes does not mean that it bars all such distinctions. Article IV, section 2 is a case in point. Article IV's Privileges and Immunities Clause specifies that discrimination against nonresidents is presumptively forbidden. But the Court allows such discrimination in contexts where no "fundamental right" is at stake.[25] By analogy, why not construe the Fourteenth Amendment's Privileges or Immunities Clause presumptively to forbid discrimination against recently arrived residents but allow such discrimination when it serves some valuable function—for instance, when it serves to preserve states' incentives usefully to redistribute wealth?

This is not to say that such an analogy with Article IV is decisive: there might be other differences between the two contexts that make discrimination against newcomers especially worse than discrimination against nonresidents. Perhaps anti–new resident discrimination is even more disruptive of the federal union than discrimination against nonresidents (although it is intuitively hard to see why this should be[26]). Or perhaps such discrimination is an affront to the idea of equality among state citizens (although any such theory would have to explain what it means to be a "state citizen" as opposed to a mere sojourner, and how one should best prove such domiciliary intent). Or perhaps discrimination against newcomers is simply inherently offensive—akin to racial discrimination—in a way that discrimination against nonresidents is not.[27] But these are questions that the Court could have more directly

---

[25] See, e.g., *Baldwin v Fish & Game Comm'n of Montana*, 436 US 371 (1978).

[26] Discrimination against nonresidents attacks a person who actually belongs to another state community: intuitively, one would think that this sort of direct attack on a specific state's citizen would inspire more interstate animosity than discrimination against a new resident who, after all, has abandoned his or her tie with some other state government and whose cause is unlikely to be espoused by that government.

[27] The *Shapiro* Court made such an analogy when it argued that, just as Congress could not "induce wider state participation in school construction" by "authorizing the use of joint funds for the building of segregated schools," so too, Congress cannot induce state expenditures by allowing states to discriminate on the basis of length of residence. *Shapiro*, 394 US at 641.

engaged: it begs the question simply to assert that "[p]ermissible justifications for discrimination between residents and nonresidents are simply inapplicable to [discrimination against newcomers]."

Instead of providing a functional analysis of discrimination against new residents who were recently nonresidents, the Court relied on dicta from *The Slaughterhouse Cases*.[28] *Saenz* quoted Justice Miller's assertion for the Court that one of the privileges conferred by this Clause "is that a citizen of the United States can, of his own volition, become a citizen of any State of the Union by a bona fide residence therein, *with the same rights* as other citizens of that State."[29] *Saenz* buttressed this quote with a longer one from Justice Bradley's dissent, in which Bradley stated that "[a] citizen of the United States has a perfect constitutional right to go to and reside in any State he chooses, and to claim citizenship therein, *and an equality of rights with every other citizen;* and the whole power of the nation is pledged to sustain him in that right."[30]

The italicized language from these opinions in *The Slaughterhouse Cases*, while better than nothing, is still a thin reed on which to hang the categorical theory: they are, after all, dicta, in an opinion that is not trying to mark out the rights in question with any precision. It would no doubt surprise both Justices Bradley and Miller to discover that their rhetoric entailed that states could not impose durational residence requirements as a condition for obtaining public assistance: such requirements were a standard part of welfare law throughout our history,[31] the sort of law that the Court had previously cited as an instance of an acceptable burden to place on new migrants to the state.[32]

In short, the text and precedent cited by *Saenz* does not provide sufficient support for its categorical rule. New residents are (by hypothesis) state citizens entitled to some sort of equality with other state citizens under the Fourteenth Amendment. But so what? Nonresidents are also entitled to some sort of equality with other citizens under Article IV: they nevertheless do not get im-

---

[28] 83 US 36 (1872).

[29] *Saenz*, 119 S Ct at 1526–27 (quoting *Slaughterhouse Cases* at 80) (emphasis added).

[30] Id (quoting *Slaughterhouse Cases* at 112–13).

[31] See notes 105–09 and accompanying text (discussing the regime of settlement and removal).

[32] See notes 110–12 and accompanying text.

munity from all disabilities based on their more tenuous attachment to the state. Why should state citizenship require absolute equality when national citizenship does not? The text and precedent cited by the Court do not answer this question. To evaluate the Court's rule, therefore, it is necessary to consult an additional source of authority.

C. WHAT EXACTLY IS "BONA FIDE RESIDENCY" AND HOW DOES ONE
    PROVE THAT ONE HAS IT?

It may be, of course, that the real source for *Saenz* is neither text nor *The Slaughterhouse Cases* but rather more recent precedents—*Shapiro* and its progeny. *Saenz* is the result of a long series of precedents in which the Court has grappled with the question of newcomers' eligibility for various state benefits—public assistance for the indigent,[33] emergency medical care,[34] the right to vote,[35] subsidized college education,[36] free public school education,[37] divorce decrees,[38] property tax exemptions,[39] and subsidies from a state mineral tax.[40]

In all but three of these decisions, the Court struck down either a durational residence requirement or a "fixed date" residence requirement for the benefit in question, invoking either the right to travel or the Equal Protection Clause. The residence requirements were upheld in only three contexts—divorce decrees, free public education, and reduced in-state college tuition—and the Court justified these exceptions by arguing that the residence requirements at issue served to insure that the new resident was, in fact, a "bona fide resident" of the state.

With these precedents in mind, it is not hard to regard *Saenz* as an easy case. To be sure, *Saenz* tidies up the doctrine by aban-

---

[33] *Shapiro v Thompson*, 394 US 618 (1969).

[34] *Memorial Hospital v Maricopa County*, 415 US 250 (1974).

[35] *Dunn v Blumstein*, 405 US 330 (1972).

[36] See *Vlandis v Kline*, 412 US 441 (1973); *Starns v Malkerson*, 401 US 985 (1971), aff'g without opinion 326 F Supp 234 (D Minn 1970).

[37] *Martinez v Bynum*, 461 US 321 (1983).

[38] *Sosna v Iowa*, 419 US 393 (1975).

[39] *Att'y Gen'l of NY v Soto-Lopez*, 476 US 898 (1986); *Hooper v Bernalillo County Assessor*, 472 US 612 (1985).

[40] *Zobel v Williams*, 457 US 55 (1982).

doning the pretense that the Court applies the "rational basis" test to such residence requirements and instead lodging the right under a distinct clause of the Fourteenth Amendment. But this was judicial housekeeping: the essential holding of *Saenz*—that residence requirements disadvantaging recently arrived bona fide residents are subject to strict scrutiny—has apparently been a solidly ensconced part of constitutional law for three decades.

This view of *Saenz* as an easy case, however, is mistaken: *Saenz* did not create a simple categorical nondiscrimination rule that reconciles conflicting precedent once and for all. This is so because *Saenz* sheds no light on what it means to be a bona fide resident, a concept that lies at the heart of *Saenz*'s nondiscrimination rule. Judging from the precedents, both the definition and the proof of "bona fide residence" are murky and controversial. Moreover, buried in these conflicting views of what bona fide residence is and how it is proven lies a deep conflict about the degree to which a state can protect its fisc from migrants who enter the state to take advantage of the state's redistributive programs. By overlooking the issue of how a migrant proves that he or she is indeed a bona fide resident, *Saenz* left open the critical question that was unresolved in the *Shapiro* line of cases: can migrants be bona fide residents if their migration is motivated by the prospect of reaping a subsidy from a state?

Shapiro seemed to have resolved this question, but this resolution turned out to be illusory. In justifying the durational residence requirements that they imposed on newcomers seeking welfare benefits, the defendants argued that the requirement of one year's residence "may be justified as a permissible state attempt to discourage those indigents who would enter the State solely to obtain larger benefits."[41] The *Shapiro* Court retorted that

> a State may no more try to fence out those indigents who seek higher welfare benefits than it may try to fence out indigents generally. Implicit in any such distinction is the notion that indigents who enter a State with the hope of securing higher welfare benefits are somehow less deserving than indigents who do not take this consideration into account. But we do not perceive why a mother who is seeking to make a new life for herself and her children should be regarded as less deserving

---

[41] *Shapiro*, 394 US at 632.

because she considers, among other factors, the level of a
State's public assistance. Surely such a mother is no less deserving than a mother who moves into a particular State in order
to take advantage of its better educational facilities.[42]

But *Shapiro* undermined the force of this egalitarian rhetoric in a
footnote in which the Court acknowledged that the case would be
different if it involved payments of benefits under a state insurance
program because states might "legitimately tie the amount of benefits to the individual's contributions."[43] It is not easy to square
Shapiro's insistence on equal treatment of new residents with this
acknowledgment that states have "legitimate" interests in insuring
that the payment of benefits is linked to contributions.

Four years later, *Vlandis v Kline*[44] cast further doubt on *Shapiro*'s
categorical statement that states could not legitimately discriminate against new residents to protect their fisc. At issue in *Vlandis*
was a state law defining the residential status of students at the
University of Connecticut. Under the law, students who had a legal address outside of Connecticut at any time within a year of
their application to the University of Connecticut were irrebutta-
bly presumed not to be bona fide residents of Connecticut during
their entire period of attendance at the University of Connecticut.
The practical effect of the law was that the students who were
deemed to be nonresidents were charged twice as much for their
tuition at the University of Connecticut as resident students. The
Court assumed for the sake of argument that the state could require nonresident students to pay more for tuition, but it struck
the statute down on the ground that it created an irrational irre-
buttable presumption about the students' residential status.[45]

Vlandis's holding, therefore, is consistent with *Shapiro*. But dicta
in *Vlandis* suggest that the Court distanced itself from *Shapiro*'s
assertion that a migrant's motive for coming to a state is irrelevant
to whether they should be entitled to a state-financed benefit. In
an effort to provide guidance to the State of Connecticut, Justice
Stewart's plurality opinion observed that "[o]ur holding today

---

[42] Id at 632–33.

[43] 395 US at 633 n 10.

[44] 412 US 441 (1973).

[45] For a sympathetic account of the doctrine, see Laurence Tribe, *American Constitutional Law* 1618–25 (2d ed 1988).

should in no wise be taken to mean that Connecticut must classify the students as residents for the purposes of tuition and fees just because they go [to the University of Connecticut]."[46] Justice Stewart stated that Connecticut could adopt more nuanced tests for bona fide residence that would not only be constitutional but also would "certainly [be] sufficient to prevent abuse of the lower, in-state rates by students who come to Connecticut *solely to obtain an education.*"[47] Justice Stewart made perfectly clear why such students were "abus[ing]" in-state rates: despite the fact that they planned to make the state their home for four years or so, these students were not bona fide residents of the state. "The state can establish such reasonable criteria as to make it virtually certain that students who are not, in fact, bona fide residents of the State, *but who have come there solely for educational purposes,* cannot take advantage of the in-state rates."[48]

In other words, even if a student was physically present within a state for the entire period needed to get a degree, that presence does not establish bona fide residence if the student entered the state "solely" to obtain the reduced in-state tuition. This definition of bona fide residence seems in tension with *Shapiro: Vlandis* states that states can deter nonresidents from entering the state in order to take advantage of a state subsidy program, while *Shapiro* says that they cannot. But the debate is smuggled into the apparently technical and innocuous issue of how to define and prove "bona fide residence." According to Stewart's plurality opinion in *Vlandis,* those who migrate to a state "solely for educational purposes" are simply not bona fide residents but "bad faith migrants."[49] Being a bona fide resident depended not only on how long you plan to stay, but also on why you came.[50]

Of course, Justice Stewart's remarks about bona fide residence were only dicta in a plurality opinion. But they were dicta that

---

[46] *Vlandis,* 412 US at 453 n 9.

[47] Id at 451–52 (emphasis added).

[48] Id at 453–54 (emphasis added).

[49] Id at 451.

[50] To be sure, *Vlandis* does not specifically say that a state may consider the migrant's motives for migrating to ascertain residential status. But *Vlandis* states that "students . . . are not in fact bona fide residents" if they "have come there solely for educational purposes." This seems to say that bona fide residence depends on the migrant's motive for coming to the state.

had the support of the Court.[51] Moreover, Justice Stewart offered his remarks as an account of why the Court had summarily affirmed Minnesota's one-year residence requirement for in-state tuition at its state universities.[52] In some sense, then, *Vlandis* has meaningful precedential force.

Sosna v Iowa[53] presented the Court with the next opportunity to clarify the law. Iowa barred persons from obtaining divorce decrees in Iowa courts unless they resided for a year or more in Iowa before they obtained the decree. The Court held that the residence requirement was a reasonable way of "[a]voiding intermeddling in matters which another state has a paramount interest and in minimizing the susceptibility of its own divorce decrees to collateral attack."[54] The Court's only hint that a state might discourage subsidy-motivated migration was the statement that "[a] state such as Iowa may reasonably decide it does not wish to become a divorce mill for unhappy spouses."[55] But the Court seemed to base its reasoning more on traditional choice-of-law considerations rather than on protection of the state's fisc from newcomers' raids (perhaps, one might speculate, because the fiscal cost of extending judicial services to newcomers either was negligible or was already internalized by court fees).

The confusion of *Shapiro*, *Vlandis*, and *Sosna* was only compounded by *Martinez v Bynum*,[56] in which the Court sidestepped the issue of whether states could discourage subsidy-motivated migration. At issue in *Martinez* was a Texas statute stating that children who live within a school district are not entitled to attend free public school if (1) they lived with a person other than their parent or legal guardian and (2) the "primary purpose" for this living arrangement was to attend public school in the district. On the basis of this statute, the McAllen School District barred Ro-

---

[51] Justice Rehnquist and Justice Douglas dissented on the ground that Connecticut could reasonably exclude children whose parents had not contributed to the University of Connecticut in the form of past tax payments. Id at 464–65. Given this embrace of fiscal justifications for exclusion, one can infer that they would *a fortiori* endorse the proposition that "bona fide residency" could be defined to exclude benefit-motivated migrants.

[52] *Vlandis*, at 453 n 9.

[53] 419 US 393 (1975).

[54] *Sosna*, 419 US at 407.

[55] Id.

[56] 461 US 321 (1983).

berto Morales from attending public school in the district unless he paid tuition. Morales lived in McAllen, Texas, with his older sister, Oralia Martinez; although he was a citizen of the United States, his parents were nonresident aliens living in Mexico, and the school district reasonably believed that his living arrangement with his sister was motivated primarily by his parents' (and his own) desire to attend McAllen's public schools. Accordingly, they insisted that he pay tuition.

The Court upheld this scheme—but it did so in a way that left the definition and proof of "bona fide residency" obscure. According to the Court, Texas's two-part requirement for free public schooling was nothing more than a requirement of bona fide residence not different in character from the residence requirements for reduced state university tuition that the Court had previously upheld in *Starns* and *Sturgis*.[57] In particular, the Court quoted approvingly from the University of Minnesota's motive-based residence requirement that, like Texas's statute, barred students from receiving reduced in-state tuition unless they had a domicile in the state "for other than educational purposes."[58] The Court seemed to be hinting that states could bar newcomers from receiving governmental services, if they migrated to the jurisdiction "primarily" to get a subsidy from existing taxpayers.

But this was only a hint—a hint from which the Court seemed to retreat as the opinion proceeded. In explaining the practical function of residence requirements that rested on the motives of the migrant for entering the jurisdiction, the Court was obscurely—and conveniently—tautological: "A bona fide residence requirement . . . furthers the substantial state interest in assuring that services provided for its residents are enjoyed only by residents."[59] The Court also noted that residence requirements somehow promoted the local control of schools without exactly explaining how.[60] But the Court never explained why Roberto Morales's likely time spent in McAllen—at least four years that were needed to graduate from high school—did not suffice to establish his residential status.

---

[57] Id at 321, 325–28, 328 n 6.

[58] Id.

[59] Id at 328.

[60] Id at 329.

Moreover, the Court seemed to shy away from Texas's likely reasons for enacting its motive-based residence requirement: Texas probably did not want to bear the cost of educating the children of outsiders who did not pay the property taxes necessary to fund the public schools.[61] Like the in-state tuition cases, this case involved a residence requirement that, on its face, was designed to prevent newcomers from free-riding on the tax effort of old-timers.

The Court was silent on whether this fiscal motivation was legitimate. Instead, the Court construed the Texas statute to codify the traditional test for domicile by conferring residential status on any student who "has a bona fide intention to remain in the school district indefinitely." As Justice Marshall noted in his dissent,[62] this was an odd interpretation of the state law, because the law did not refer to the future intentions of newcomers to stay in the jurisdiction but rather their past motivations for entering the jurisdiction. The Court accomplished this reconstruction of the statute, however, by assuming that, if a student intended to reside indefinitely in the school district, "he then would have a reason for being there other than his desire to attend school: His intention to make his home in the district."[63] The Court assumed without much textual basis that the Texas statute referred to the migrant's motive for entering the school district only because this was good evidence of the migrant's likelihood of staying in the district in the future.

But what if the "desire to make a new home [in the district]" is motivated solely by the desire to attend school? By the literal terms of the statute, such a student would be barred from attending public school for free, even if the student planned to live and die in McAllen, for their initial motive for entering the district placed them outside the terms of the statue's definition of bona fide residency. *Martinez* avoided the issue, noting only that Roberto Morales lacked standing to challenge this aspect of the statute, as he did not in fact "intend to make his home in McAllen, Texas."[64]

---

[61] For an account of how school districts aggressively try to exclude nonresidents' children from attending public school because their parents do not pay taxes into the school district, see Andy Newman, *Dangerous Crossing: Lying, Scheming, and Conniving to Get Into Public School*, New York Times Magazine (March 14, 1999) at 28–29.

[62] *Martinez*, 461 US at 335 (Marshall, J, dissenting).

[63] Id at 332.

[64] Id at 332 n 15.

But even *Martinez*'s central holding tends to undermine both *Shapiro* and *Saenz*. *Martinez* squarely holds that, as part of the test for domicile, a state could require a person to show that they had a reason to enter the state other than receipt of benefits from the state. Thus, in theory, California could require Brenda Roe to show that she had some reason to remain in California other than a desire to get higher welfare benefits—say, family members or a job or friends in California. *Martinez* leaves open the possibility that Brenda Roe could respond simply by saying that she really did want to make the state her home, in which case the issue of her domicile would depend on some sort of determination of credibility. *Saenz* did not resolve the multitude of questions surrounding how such a determination of domicile should be made (e.g., who should bear the burden of proof, what counts as acceptable evidence of a commitment to stay in the state, and so on) because, in *Saenz*, California conceded that Brenda Roe was in fact a bona fide resident of California. But both *Saenz* and *Martinez* leave open the possibility that states might require newcomers to bear the burden of showing that they migrated to the state for reasons other than a desire to obtain a government-financed benefit—a proof that might practically undo the holding of *Saenz* for many new arrivals in a state.[65]

In sum, the Court issued contradictory pronouncements in *Shapiro*, *Vlandis*, *Sosna*, and *Martinez* as to whether states can find that newcomers lack domiciliary intent when they enter the jurisdiction primarily to obtain a state-financed benefit. *Shapiro* says that this sort of exclusion is unconstitutional. *Vlandis* and *Sosna* hint that such exclusion is permissible. And *Martinez* suggests that states may infer that newcomers lack domiciliary intent to remain indefinitely in a state if the newcomer entered the state "primarily" to become eligible for a state-provided service of limited duration

---

[65] For a similar view of *Martinez*, see Laurence Tribe, *American Constitutional Law* 1457 n 15 (2d ed 1988) (noting that "*Martinez* . . . calls into question the premises behind the Court's statement in *Shapiro* that a mother who considers the level of public assistance when moving into a state 'is no less deserving than a mother who moves into a state to take advantage of its better educational facilities'"). Professor Tribe attempts to limit *Martinez* "to circumstances like those in *Martinez* where the excluded child has conceded his intention to leave after the state has provided a service of limited duration." Id. But Professor Tribe's description of *Martinez*'s holding might be overly narrow: there is no indication in the U.S. Supreme Court's opinion that domicile can be denied only when the person seeking it concedes that they lack domiciliary intent.

like education. But what about states that frankly wish to protect their fisc from newcomers? Can such states presume that the new-comers are not bona fide residents unless the newcomers prove that they have reasons for migrating to the state other than ob-taining a temporary benefit from the state's treasury? The Court's precedents seem unclear.

Saenz does little to resolve the ambiguity of these precedents. The Court in *Saenz* distinguishes *Sosna* and the instate tuition cases by noting that, unlike welfare, university diplomas and di-vorce decrees are "portable" assets from which the migrant can benefit even after leaving the state. In the Court's words,

> because whatever benefits they receive will be consumed while they remain in California, there is no danger that recognition of their claim will encourage citizens of other States to estab-lish residence for just long enough to acquire some readily por-table benefit, such as a divorce or a college education, that will be enjoyed after they return to their original domicile. [Citing *Sosna* and *Vlandis*.]

The Court may be correct that, unlike welfare benefits, diplomas and divorce decrees produce benefits outside of the state in which they are obtained. But so what? Why is this distinction constitu-tionally relevant?

The Court seems to say that there is a special "danger" that citizens will leave the state too soon if they can reap a tax-subsi-dized benefit like a college degree that will continue to benefit them even after they leave the state. But why is this risk of prema-ture departure greater when the state-subsidized benefit is "porta-ble" than when it is consumed directly in the state? To be sure, if a newcomer comes to the state only to obtain some subsidized service, then one would expect that such a migrant might stay no longer than necessary to secure the benefit. But this would be the case regardless of whether the benefit were "portable." If the state required recipients of the benefit to consume that benefit in the state, then presumably the resident who migrated to the state solely to obtain that benefit would stay only so long as he or she can continue to consume the benefit—five years in the case of welfare benefits.[66] If the benefit were portable, then the subsidy-

---

[66] Under the TANF block grant program authorized by the federal Personal Responsibil-ity and Work Opportunity Act, a 60-month limit applies to federal money funding welfare. 42 USC § 608 (Supp II 1996).

motivated migrant would stay only as needed to qualify for the benefit—four years for most undergraduate degrees, for instance. But, in either case, the migrant motivated solely by the prospect of obtaining subsidies would presumably have the same incentive to leave the state after he or she had extracted the maximum benefit from the state, regardless of whether the state program continued to produce benefits for the migrant after the migrant left.

I do not mean to suggest that "portability" is irrelevant to the constitutional issue: there are plausible functional arguments for considering "portability." For instance, portable benefits might present a greater risk that one state will "free ride" off the tax effort of another state, because "stingy" states that refuse to fund programs will get the benefit of those programs when migrants who obtain "portable" benefits from other more generous states migrate to the "stingy" states (perhaps to take advantage of the stingy state's low tax rates).[67]

The difficulty with such functional arguments for taking portability into account is that they are no different in kind than the functional arguments that the *Saenz* Court rejected as either "speculative" or "unequivocally impermissible."[68] A "free rider" problem also afflicts states that provide generous welfare benefits to their residents. Such states typically maintain that other stingier states "free ride" off of the more generous states' tax effort, by maintaining low benefit levels that induce the indigent residents of the stingier states to migrate to the more generous states.[69] If the Court can take into account the portability of benefits because

---

[67] For instance, absent a residence requirement for in-state tuition, a citizen of, say, Alaska (which lacks any state-subsidized law school) could attend, say, the tax-subsidized (and by hypothesis superb) University of California law schools, earn a law degree at the expense of California taxpayers, and then return to Alaska with a valuable professional credential. The law degree will earn the Alaskan resident a handsome living in Alaska, and it will also benefit Alaska's taxpayers (who will tax the lawyer's income), but no Alaskan taxpayers will have to bear the cost of the professional education. Under these circumstances, it is easy to see how the taxpayers and would-be lawyers of Alaska would have zero incentive to lobby the Alaska legislature to fund an Alaskan law school. Likewise, one can see why the incentives of California's taxpayers to bear the tax burden of educating residents from other states might diminish their enthusiasm for their public universities.

[68] *Saenz*, 119 S Ct at 1527–28.

[69] For a detailed account of how this "free-rider" argument became a theme of Tommy Thompson's successful campaign against then-Governor Earle of Wisconsin, see Paul Peterson and Mark Rom, *Welfare Magnets* 26–47 (1988). At the time, Wisconsin's welfare benefits were considerably more generous than those paid by Illinois. See also notes 84–87.

such portability gives rise to a problem of strategic behavior among states, then why cannot the Court take into account the analogous danger that states will reduce welfare payments in hopes that indigents migrate to more generous states? On the other hand, if some sort of "free rider" problem does not explain the relevance of benefits' "portability," then what does? The *Saenz* opinion's reliance on "portability" to distinguish earlier cases seems either arbitrary or self-contradictory.

Moreover, the Court's reliance on "portability" is not only unpersuasive but also ambiguous: it would seem to allow states to discriminate against newcomers with extra long residence requirements in a variety of contexts—vocational education, job training, drug rehab, and so on—where the state-subsidized benefit is portable. Chief Justice Rehnquist may be incorrect that welfare payments alone constitute a "portable" investment in human capital. But many other benefits are as "portable" as college degrees. If portability justifies the year-long residence requirements for instate tuition upheld in *Starns*, then the same portability ought logically to justify a myriad of distinctions burdening newcomers. Yet it is hard to believe that the Court would approve those sorts of distinctions after reaffirming *Shapiro*'s condemnation of efforts to fence out the indigent.

In sum, neither the *Saenz* Court nor the precedents that it attempts to reconcile provide an adequate account of what it means to be a bona fide resident of a state. The precedents suggest that the definition of state residence will vary with the particular program to which a new resident seeks access—suffrage is easier to get than reduced tuition at a state university—but the precedents do not explain why or how. *Vlandis* and *Martinez* suggest that the newcomers' motives for migrating to the state may be relevant to residential status—in particular, whether they are moving to take advantage of some state-subsidized service. But *Shapiro* and *Saenz* both emphasize that states cannot discourage the indigent from entering the state with stringent residence requirements. The precedents, in short, are in disarray. Nor will constitutional text resolve the definition of "bona fide residency": of course, the Citizenship Clause requires that all state "residents" be treated equally. But who exactly is a state resident? The text is silent on this question.

II. Figuring Out a Functional Theory of "Residency" and Local Responsibility for the Redistribution of Wealth

To answer this question, I think that it is essential to examine the practical function served by the concept of state residency. The Court sometimes seems to assume that this question is not worth asking because the answer is self-evident: with supreme circularity, *Martinez* asserts, "[a] *bona fide* residence requirement . . . furthers the substantial state interest in assuring that services provided for its residents are enjoyed only by residents."[70] I think, to the contrary, that some functional account of "bona fide residency" is necessary to make any headway in satisfactorily resolving the constitutional issues posed by cases like *Saenz*.

To summarize my argument, I suggest that the definition of bona fide residence should be rooted in a balance between two rival considerations. On the one hand, states cannot undermine our common national citizenship by trying to transform themselves into tightly cohesive or socially homogenous communities—what I call "affective communities." Therefore, the Court should be especially suspicious of state laws that treat newcomers as unwelcome strangers out of cultural or social hostility toward those newcomers. On the other hand, states have a legitimate interest in limiting eligibility for their redistributive programs[71] to those residents whose migration into the state was motivated by a purpose other than becoming eligible for the redistributive program. Otherwise, the newcomers who migrate to a state to take advantage of a redistributive subsidy—persons whom I shall call "subsidy-motivated migrants"—might undermine the state's incentives to maintain the redistributive programs that attracted the migrants to the state in the first place.

A. THE LEGITIMACY OF DETERRING BENEFIT-MOTIVATED MIGRATION

In *Shapiro* and *Saenz*, the Court seemed to indicate that a state cannot discriminate against subsidy-motivated newcomers as a way

---

[70] *Martinez*, 461 US at 328.

[71] Following Paul Peterson, I define "redistributive programs" negatively, as programs that are *not* designed to give government services to the taxpayer that are roughly equivalent in value to the taxes that the taxpayer pays. Paul Peterson, *The Price of Federalism* 64–67 (1995).

of limiting the financial exposure of the state. As I shall suggest below in Parts IIB and IIC, this view makes sense, if the argument is limited to state laws that deter the migration of indigents into a state. But if *Shapiro* and *Saenz* mean that states never seek to prevent subsidy-motivated migration that might undermine the state's spending programs, then the Court's position is not only inconsistent with precedents like *Martinez v Bynum* but also with the very purpose of bona fide residence as the Court itself has understood the concept.

Bona fide residence defines both the obligations of the states to provide service and the powers of the states to extract payment for those services. For states to provide public goods, these duties and powers cannot be radically decoupled: the power to extract payment must be roughly commensurate with the obligation to provide services, or else the state would risk going bankrupt. Therefore, contrary to the suggestion of *Shapiro*, states ought to have the power to limit access to their spending programs where those programs' popularity threatens to attract so many noncontributing consumers that taxpayers will refuse to support the taxes necessary to sustain the program.[72] Put another way, the state must be able to limit its redistributive duties so that they do not outstrip the states' powers of taxation. Otherwise, states would be deterred from providing redistribution to *anyone* by the possibility that they must extend such redistribution to *everyone*—a serious deadweight loss where such redistribution serves socially useful purposes.

One might object to these propositions on the ground that they rest on highly speculative assumptions. It is possible that there simply is no evidence that states are deterred from providing benefits by the prospect that those benefit programs will attract noncontributing migrants from other states. As I shall suggest below,[73] there is substantial (albeit controversial) evidence that state legislatures *are* deterred from spending as much as they otherwise would for the support of the indigent by the prospect that more indigent will be attracted to the state by such expenditures. But, before I summarize this evidence, it is important to note that the Court itself has recognized that states might plausibly be deterred from

---

[72] The same argument would suggest that states should be able to finance government services with user fees, special assessments, or benefits charges rather than general taxes.

[73] See notes 84–87 and accompanying text.

providing financial benefits to their citizens by the prospect that indigent persons would migrate to the state to obtain those benefits.

In *Helvering v Davis*,[74] the Court upheld the old age benefits provisions in Titles VIII and II of the Social Security Act in part by noting that "the laws of the separate states cannot deal with [poverty among the elderly] effectively." Writing for the majority, Justice Cardozo observed,

> A system of old age pensions has special dangers of its own, if put in force in one state and rejected in another. *The existence of such a system is a bait to the needy and dependent elsewhere, encouraging them to migrate and seek a haven of repose.* Only a power that is national can serve the interests of all.[75]

Faced with this prospect of attracting the needy from other states, Justice Cardozo argued that "states and local governments are at times reluctant to increase so heavily the burden of taxation to be borne by their residents for fear of placing themselves in a position of economic disadvantage as compared with neighbors or competitors."[76]

In short, the Court upheld New Deal spending programs by endorsing the assumption that states would be deterred from spending money on the needy by the prospect of attracting more of the needy. It seems, therefore, a little odd for *Saenz* or its defenders to dismiss this assumption as "speculative." If "Congress, at least, had a basis for that belief"[77] when enacting the Social Security Act, then why cannot Congress have an equally reliable basis for the same belief when it authorizes California to impose a durational residence requirement?

One might respond that the spending program upheld in *Helvering* did not burden anyone's right to travel and, therefore, deference to Congress's judgment on policy matters might be appropriate. But *Helvering* is not the only precedent in which the Court has recognized that state spending programs might be threatened by the migration that they attract. The Court has also

---

[74] 301 US 619 (1937).

[75] Id at 644.

[76] Id.

[77] Id.

recognized this threat in its decisions allowing states to discriminate in favor of residents and against nonresidents under the "market participant" exception to the Dormant Commerce Clause
doctrine.

The usual argument for the "market participant" exception is
that residents should receive priority over nonresidents in the distribution of state services because they pay the lion's share of
taxes.[78] This "reap-what-you-sow" argument has an element of
distributive justice and an element of allocational efficiency. Such
a nondiscrimination rule would be inefficient because it "would
discourage similar state projects."[79] Extending the same state-subsidized services to nonresidents and residents alike would also be
distributively unjust because, as Justice Blackmun declared in
Reeves, it would "rob [the state taxpayers] of the intended benefit
of its foresight, risk, and industry."[80] The problem of distributive
injustice can be restated as a free-rider problem. As Jonathan Varat
notes, if nonresidents could partake of state subsidies without paying the taxes necessary to fund such subsidies, then each state
would then tend to wait for neighboring states to provide subsidized services desired by their own residents in hopes that their
residents could obtain the desired services in other states without incurring the extra taxes needed to fund the service.[81] Those
states foolish enough to provide generous payments to nonresidents would reap the sucker's payoff: in effect, the state's taxpayers would be providing a subsidy to taxpayers in stingier states
by footing the bill for services provided to the other states'
residents.

In short, the Court has accepted the proposition that states can

---

[78] As Douglas Laycock argues, "States can generally restrict such services to their own
residents, or account for the subsidy in a higher user fee for non-residents. Otherwise,
individuals could benefit from subsidies without being subject to the taxes that pay the
subsidies." Douglas Laycock, *Equal Citizens of Equal and Territorial States: The Constitutional
Foundations of Choice of Law*, 92 Colum L Rev 249, 271 (1992). For similar arguments, see
Dan T. Coenen, *Untangling the Market Participant Exception to the Dormant Commerce Clause*,
88 Mich L Rev 395, 421–26 (1989).

[79] Id. For an endorsement of this "efficiency" argument, see Donald Regan, *The Supreme
Court and State Protectionism: Making Sense of the Dormant Commerce Clause*, 88 Mich L Rev
1091, 1194 (1986).

[80] *Reeves, Inc. v Stake*, 447 US 429, 446 (1980).

[81] See Jonathan Varat, *State "Citizenship" and Interstate Equality*, 48 U Chi L Rev 487,
522–23 (1980).

limit nonresidents' access to state spending programs in order to maintain the connection between revenues and expenditures necessary to sustain the state's programs. Just so long as a state's spending program is not intended to redistribute wealth, it is an easy matter to define bona fide residence to insure this revenue-expenditure connection: nonresidents become bona fide residents eligible to receive state services when they have contacts with the state sufficient to insure that they will pay the normal tax burden (e.g., *ad valorem* property taxes or income taxes) that other residents pay. By imposing this simple residence requirement, the state can have some crude assurance that the crucial link is maintained between revenues and expenditures.[82] This is because the nonresidents' decision to consume the state services by becoming a state resident will (at least in theory) also simultaneously be a decision to pay the average tax price of the service.[83]

But redistributive programs pose a special problem for matching revenues with expenditure, because the beneficiaries of such programs cannot be charged with the average cost of the program benefits without defeating the whole point of the program. Therefore, insisting that nonresidents become residents for the purposes of tax liability will not meaningfully ration access to the redistributive program: by becoming residents, the nonresident who becomes eligible for redistributive services will not pay the average cost of the service that he or she receives. This is not to say that the cost of migrating is zero. Sometimes migration can be extremely expensive: the migrant must sometimes uproot himself or herself from friends and family, pay transportation costs, find new

---

[82] For a more detailed discussion of why this "Wicksellian" link between revenues and expenditures constitutes the best definition of "efficiency" in the context of public finance, see Albert Breton, *Competitive Governments: An Economic Theory of Politics and Public Finance* 23–24 (1996).

[83] There are at least a couple problems with the revenue-expenditure link. The first problem is that migrants who purchase property or have incomes below the median property value or income of the median taxpayer will pay lower *ad valorem* property taxes or income taxes for the same level of state services. As Bruce Hamilton has famously argued, this will lead such "undertaxed" nonresidents to migrate to the jurisdiction in inefficiently high numbers. Bruce W. Hamilton, *Zoning and Property Taxation in a System of Local Governments*, 12 Urban Stud 205 (1975). Second, it might be the case that the new resident will add congestion costs to the community that will exceed the new resident's marginal cost of migrating to the community—again, causing an inefficiently large number of migrants to join the community. The first problem could be solved by financing state services with a lump-sum tax, while the second problem could be solved by some sort of growth management movement. I will discuss the former issue in more detail later in Part IIIA.

housing and a new community, and so on. However, unlike residence requirements for nonredistributive programs, there is no necessary link between these migration costs and the benefits that the migrant receives as a result of the move. The migrant who becomes a resident eligible for nonredistributive services pays a price for such eligibility—state taxes—that is linked to the benefits that he or she receives. The migrant who becomes a resident eligible for a redistribution of wealth pays a price—migration costs—that has nothing whatsoever to do with the benefits of residency. This price may sometimes be arbitrarily greater where migration costs are high (in, say, a move to Hawaii from New York) and sometimes the price may be arbitrarily trivial (in, say, a migration across the street from Arkansas to Texas within the City of Texarkana). But the crucial point is that the link between revenues and expenditures has been lost.

Once this link is broken, the "free-rider" problem discussed in *Reeves* reemerges. Stingy states have an incentive to cut redistributive spending in hopes of letting their indigent citizens receive support from more generous states. Those more generous states cannot effectively respond by requiring such migrants to become bona fide residents, because the newcomers' "bona fide residency" does not entail that they will pay the average costs of the benefits that they receive. If the cost of migration—forgoing the benefits provided by the previous state, bus fare, rental location, and so on—are lower than the benefits of the new state's proffered redistribution, then new migrants will choose to migrate to the new state in numbers that can threaten to overwhelm the very redistributive programs to which the migrants seek access.

Public assistance to needy families provides one of the most well-known—and controversial—examples of the way in which the possibility of migration can depress state incentives to redistribute wealth. According to one prominent theory, state governments compete with each other to reduce public assistance to the indigent in order to avoid attracting indigent persons. It is a hotly controverted question whether indigent migration is actually influenced by the level of welfare benefits in a state. Several studies of post-1970 data suggest that welfare levels do have a significant and positive (albeit modest) influence on indigent migration, although no scholar claims that the "magnetic" attraction of welfare

is overwhelming.[84] But, while the magnitude of the "welfare magnet" effect is uncertain, there is less doubt that state politicians
believe that such migration occurs and cut their welfare benefits
significantly as a result of this belief. Influenced by considerable
anecdotal evidence that generous benefits attract the indigent,[85]

---

[84] The scholarly literature that analyzed indigent behavior prior to 1970 generally found
little evidence that benefit levels influenced indigent migration. For two general surveys of
the studies of pre-1970 data, see Larry H. Long, *Poverty Status and Receipt of Welfare Among
Migrants and Non-Migrants in Large Cities*, 39 Am Soc Rev 46, 48 (1974), and Richard J.
Cebula, *A Survey of the Literature on the Migration-Impact of State and Local Government
Policies*, 1 Pub Finance 69 (1979). For an exceptional contrary report, see Lawrence South-
wick, Jr., *Public Welfare Programs and Recipient Migration*, 12 Growth & Change 22–32
(1981) (based on a 1967 survey of 66,577 AFDC families). For a more recent study finding
that welfare-induced migration is trivial in extent, see Russell L. Hanson and John T. Hart-
man, *Do Welfare Magnets Attract?* (U Wis, 1994).
    However, as Paul Peterson and Mark Rom pointed out in their 1988 landmark study,
most states required newcomers to wait 12 months before they could receive welfare prior
to *Shapiro v Thompson*, and one would expect such a waiting period to dampen indigent
incentives to migrate in order to get higher benefits. Paul Peterson and Mark Rom, *Welfare
Magnets: A New Case for a National Standard* 57–58 (Brookings, 1988). Later studies of post-
1970 data suggest that the effects of welfare on indigent migration are positive and statisti-
cally significant. Edward Gramlich and Deborah Laren, *Migration and Income Redistribution
Responsibilities*, 19 J Hum Resources 489 (1983); Rebecca M. Blank, *The Impact of State
Economic Differentials on Household Welfare and Labor Force Behavior*, 28 J Pub Econ 25 (1985);
Paul Peterson and Mark Rom, *Welfare Magnets* at 83; Robert Moffitt, *Incentive Effects of
the U.S. Welfare System: A Review*, 30 J Econ Literature 1, 34 (1992) (reviewing literature
and finding significant albeit inconclusive evidence that welfare levels significantly influence
indigents' migration decisions). As Peterson and Rom noted in 1988, there is no evidence
that "large numbers of poor people rush from one state to another with every modest
adjustment in state benefit levels." But Peterson and Rom reflect the views of a substantial
number of scholars in stating that "over time, as people make major decisions about whether
they should move or remain where they are, they take into account the level of welfare a
state provides and the extent to which the level is increasing. The poor do this roughly to
the same extent that they respond to differences in wages." Peterson and Rom, *Welfare
Magnets* at 83.

[85] For anecdotal evidence, see National Public Radio, *Transcript of All Things Considered*,
1997 WL 12832095 (Tuesday, August 19, 1997). In the course of exploring why Minneapo-
lis's indigent population grew during the 1980s, the interviewer noted that "Greg Owen
[a sociologist with a St. Paul nonprofit organization that surveys shelter residents] stated
that newcomers give many reasons for coming to Minnesota—jobs, better schools, safer
neighborhoods—but he says the safety net is a factor for some." According to Owen,
"Frankly, it's known outside of Minnesota that Minnesota provides a good shelter system—
good housing opportunities for lower income families. And a number of the responses that
we get relate to that specifically—'I thought I could get on my feet more easily here in
Minnesota.'" See also Dirk Johnson, *Rethinking Welfare: Interstate Migration—a Special Report: Larger Benefits Lure Chicagoans to Wisconsin*, NY Times A11 (May 8, 1995). Wisconsin
sought to discriminate against newcomers because it feared that it was attracting newcomers
from Illinois, where welfare benefits were 40% lower than in Wisconsin. According to one
consultant's survey, 29% of the migrants cited higher welfare benefits as a reason for their
migration to Wisconsin. Rogers Worthington, *Study Finds Evidence Some View Wisconsin as
a Welfare Magnet*, Chicago Trib (May 23, 1995) at 4.

state politicians campaign successfully against generous welfare on the theory that such an effect exists.[86]

This does not mean that states move their benefits in lockstep with each other or converge at a single point: on the contrary, states consistently maintain different levels of welfare spending even controlling for differences in the cost of living.[87] Nevertheless, fear of becoming a welfare magnet constrains state welfare policy: states do not race to the bottom, but they seem to edge nervously toward the center, not ever converging but also not getting too out of line with their neighbors. According to the recent study by Peterson, Schreve, and Rom, for every $100 change in the average benefit guarantee of contiguous states, a state adjusted its benefit level by approximately $27.[88]

The important point for this article's purposes is that these threats to redistributive programs from newcomers are not different in kind from the dangers from nonresidents that the Court identifies in *Reeves* and that scholars like Jonathan Varat identify in their commentary on such doctrine. Like consumption of government services by nonresidents, subsidy-motivated migration can discourage states from funding redistributive programs, and subsidy-motivated migration can lead to a "free-rider" problem. When migrants leave a state that provides stingy subsidies and migrate to a state with more generous subsidies, then the "receiving" state arguably provides a subsidy to the taxpayers of the "sending" state: the stingier state is relieved of the need (or political pressure) to provide the same redistributive subsidies to its ex-citizens. In

[86] See Peterson and Rom, *Welfare Magnets* 24–49 (1988) (describing Tommy Thompson's successful gubernatorial campaign against Anthony Earle, in which Thompson cited evidence that Wisconsin's generous benefits were attracting indigent from Illinois).

[87] F. H. Buckley and Margeret F. Brinig, *Welfare Magnets: The Race for the Top*, 5 S Ct Econ Rev 141, 159–64 (1997); Craig Olden, *Entrusting the States with Welfare Reform*, in John Ferejohn and Barry Weingast, eds, *The New Federalism: Can the States Be Trusted?* 74–76 (1997).

[88] Mark C. Rom, Paul E. Peterson, and Kenneth F. Schreve, Jr., *Interstate Competition and Welfare Policy*, 28 Publius 17, 37 (Summer 1998). Both Buckley/Brinig and Volden respond to Peterson by noting that there are persistent disparities between the welfare payments offered by rich and poor states. They conclude from this fact that there cannot be any race to the bottom (or even toward the middle). But this inference implicitly assumes that there is perfect interjurisdictional competition between the states. In reality, because it is costly for both taxpayers and the indigent to move between states, one would expect that large and rich states would be able to redistribute some level of wealth with impunity.

effect, state taxpayers who provide generous welfare benefits to their state residents provide an indirect subsidy to state taxpayers in stingy states. Knowing this, each state will make an effort to keep its welfare benefits in line with those of its neighbors. Unless each state can limit its redistribution of wealth to those residents who enter the state for reasons other than a desire to benefit from the redistribution, then all states may strategically avoid redistribution in which all would like to engage.

The *Reeves* Court has held that states can legitimately take measures to prevent these "free-rider" problems from overwhelming nonredistributive programs. The odd aspect of *Shapiro* and *Saenz* is that they seem to say that the states cannot legitimately accomplish precisely the same purpose with *redistributive* programs. In either case, the consumption of the state benefit by either new migrants or nonresidents tends to "discourage similar state [spending] projects"[89]—a deadweight loss that the Court seems to regard as *ceteris paribus* undesirable in the context of the "market participant" exception. Why can the state address this problem by discriminating against nonresidents but not by discriminating against newcomers who present precisely the same threat to state programs that nonresidents present—the threat of consuming state fiscal resources without paying for them?

Of course, one can question whether indigent migration really threatens state welfare programs, especially given the relative immobility of the indigent.[90] *Saenz* seems to do so, arguing that the danger of states' attracting indigent migrants through more generous welfare benefits is "speculative." But this judicial skepticism about the empirical assessments of politicians seems odd: why is the Court the appropriate branch to make these empirical judgments? This is not the role that the Court assumes when assessing state discrimination against nonresidents. The *Reeves* Court certainly cited no empirical evidence that South Dakota would be deterred from subsidizing cement factories by a "cement magnet" effect; nevertheless, the Court still upheld discrimination against nonresidents in *Reeves* on the theory that there was a nonfrivolous

---

[89] *Reeves*, 447 US at 446.

[90] On the relative immobility of the indigent, see Scott Allard, *Revisiting Shapiro: Welfare Magnets and State Residence Requirements in the 1990s*, 28 Publius 46–52 (Summer 1998).

possibility that nonresident consumption would discourage such state projects. The same possibility exists that states will be deterred from generous welfare spending by the prospect of becoming a "welfare magnet." Why not give the California legislature and Congress the same level of deference as the *Reeves* Court gave the South Dakota legislature?

The answer cannot be that California threatened the "right to travel," whereas South Dakota did not. According to *Saenz*, Article IV, section 2's rule barring discrimination against nonresidents is also an aspect of "the right to travel." By discriminating against nonresidents, South Dakota threatened this right by discriminating against nonresidents just as surely as California did by discriminating against new residents. (Indeed, Article IV's nondiscrimination rule is much more firmly ensconced in constitutional text than the rule enforced in *Saenz*.) One would think that judicial scrutiny of such discrimination would be at least as severe as judicial scrutiny in *Saenz*.

One also cannot argue that new residents pose less of a threat to the state fisc than do nonresidents because there are fewer of the former. Whether there will be few new residents depends, in part, on the costs and benefits of residential status. If the law makes acquisition of resident status easy when the benefits of being a resident are large, then one would think that the number of bona fide residents would increase as a result. Common sense, therefore, suggests that states should be able to tailor the definition and proof of residential status to the nature of the benefit for which residential status makes one eligible: the greater the benefit, the more difficult it should be to acquire residential status. Yet *Shapiro* and *Saenz* suggest that this calibration of the costs and benefits of residential status is somehow illegitimate.

As I suggest below in Part IIB, there are important reasons why such deference is inappropriate when states discriminate against indigent newcomers, because such discrimination presents a special risk of undermining our sense of national citizenship. But *Saenz*'s broad pronouncements condemning discrimination against newcomers go far beyond aid to the indigent: they would seem to apply even to state efforts to save *any* redistributive program from subsidy-motivated migration—for instance, state efforts to save tuition subsidies at state universities from subsidy-motivated applica-

tions of newcomers who become state residents solely to obtain a
subsidized college education. As Justice Rehnquist noted in his
Vlandis dissent, the purpose of stiff residence requirements for in-
state tuition is to prevent applicants from stingy states from free-
riding off of the tax effort of taxpayers who subsidize state universities.[91] This is precisely the sort of purpose that *Saenz* and *Shapiro*
declare to be illegitimate. While *Saenz* deploys the "portability"
argument to distinguish in-state tuition from welfare, neither
Saenz nor *Shapiro* provide any convincing functional argument for
why residence requirements for in-state tuition should not be
caught in the same net that sweeps up residence requirements for
welfare.

   Shapiro offers another argument against classifications that burden newcomers—the argument that such classifications implicitly
rest on an illegitimate belief that indigent newcomers who migrate
to a state to take advantage of a state's redistributive programs
"are somehow less deserving than indigents who do not take this
consideration into account."[92] This assertion, however, seems like
a groundless non sequitur. The fiscal justification for such discrimination does not depend on the premise that subsidy-motivated
indigent migrants are somehow "undeserving." Rather, the fiscal
argument depends only on the view that states ought not to be
deterred from expending resources by the prospect that other
states will "free ride" off of their tax effort.

   Saenz and *Shapiro* advise states worried about the fiscal security
of their redistributive programs to cut expenditures across the
board without discriminating against newcomers.[93] Such impartial
reductions, however, do not solve the "free-rider" problem but
succumb to it. When a generous state cuts its welfare payments
to match the welfare cuts of its stingier neighbors, then society
loses the benefit of the more generous state's tax effort. There may
be constitutional values that are worth this sacrifice, but neither
Saenz and *Shapiro* satisfactorily explains these values.

---

[91] *Vlandis*, 412 US at 459–60 ("It is not narrow provincialism for the State to think that
each State should carry its own educational burdens").

[92] *Shapiro*, 394 US at 393–94.

[93] Id at 633. ("We recognize that a State has a valid interest in preserving the fiscal
integrity of its programs. It may legitimately attempt to limit its expenditures, whether for
public assistance, public education, or any other program").

B. NATIONAL CITIZENSHIP AND THE PROHIBITION ON STATES
   ACTING LIKE AFFECTIVE COMMUNITIES

To better understand those constitutional values that might justify *Saenz* despite its costs, I turn now to the second factor in my
functional test for state residency: to what extent should the need
to preserve a common sense of national citizenship trump states'
efforts to preserve their redistributive programs by discriminating
against newcomers?

The best starting point for such an inquiry is the Court's three
opinions barring states from withholding financial benefits from
persons who arrived in a state after a specific date. In these decisions, the Court consistently invalidated "fixed date" residence requirements as inconsistent with the idea of equal state citizenship.
In *Hooper v Bernalillo County Assessor*, for instance, the Court held
that New Mexico could not provide a special reduction in property
tax liability only to Vietnam veterans who had resided in New
Mexico prior to May 6, 1976. According to the Court,

> [t]he State may not favor established residents over new resi-
> dents based on the view that the State may take care of "its
> own," if such is defined by prior residence. Newcomers, by
> establishing bona fide residence in the State, become the
> State's "own" and may not be discriminated against solely on
> the basis of their arrival in the State."[94]

In other words, New Mexico could not reward those residents who
had demonstrated long-term commitment to the state. Likewise,
in *Zobel v Williams*, the Court struck down Alaska's system of dis-
tributing its royalties from oil extraction under which persons
would receive a "dividend unit" for each year that they resided in
Alaska since statehood. Although the majority opinion was cryptic
about the basis for its decision, relying only on the Equal Protection Clause's "rational basis" test to strike down Alaska's fixed date
residence requirement, the concurrences by Justices Brennan and
O'Connor were more revealing. Justice Brennan opined that "[the
Citizenship clause of the Fourteenth Amendment] does not provide for, and does not allow for, degrees of citizenship based on
length of residence."[95] According to Justice Brennan, if a state

[94] 472 US 612, 623 (1985).
[95] 457 US 55, 69 (1982).

were to reward seniority within a state, then "the mobility so essential to the economic progress of our Nation, and so commonly accepted as a fundamental aspect of our social order, would not long survive," because state citizens would be deterred from migrating to a new state by the fear that they would lose their accrued seniority.[96]

Why have such a rule? As Professor Saul Levmore has noted, the Court's hostility toward seniority for old-timers seems a bit odd in light of the fact that private organizations routinely reward their most senior members simply for sticking around.[97] Trade unions and private corporations give greater job security and higher pay to their most senior employees, university faculties frequently give the most senior members the largest offices, and charitable organizations and clubs give plaques to members who have logged the most years with the group. The policies underlying these awards to long-term members are straightforward: it is widely believed that newcomers do not make the same contribution to the welfare of the organization as do old-timers. New members' initial contributions might not equal their consumption of the organization's resources: in the popular phrase, they have not "paid their dues." Old-timers also might contribute a special sort of stability or experience that the organization wants to encourage. Therefore, no one expects recent arrivals to law firms, churches, legislatures, bureaucracies, or most other organizations to get the same privileges as long-term members.

Why not give state governments the same right to reward long-term members' commitment to the state by giving them special privileges based on their seniority? I suggest that the Court's condemnation of seniority in state citizenship can best be explained by the idea that states should not be affective communities. By "affective communities," I mean groups of people held together by ties of mutual affection, special trust, or esprit de corps not extended to outsiders. Families are the epitome of the affective community, but other less personal groups—neighborhoods, military units, schools, churches, recreational clubs, trade unions, political parties, or towns—might also be affective communities, in

---

[96] Id at 68.

[97] Saul Levmore, *Interstate Exploitation and Judicial Intervention*, 69 Va L Rev 563 (1983).

that the members of the organization might be united by their shared experiences or common sense of mission.

Affective communities universally reward commitment to the organization, because merely logging time with the organization contributes to the close ties that sustain the group. The Court's refusal to tolerate such rewards for long-term state residents, therefore, indicates that the Court sees little value in states being such affective communities. This is not to say that state governments cannot encourage their residents to feel proud of being Hoosiers, Michiganders, and so on, in superficial and essentially trivial ways. There undoubtedly can be state festivals that celebrate the climate, culture, historical legacy, crafts, and agricultural products that are peculiar to a region or state. But, according to the Court, no state may say what every affective organization must be able to say—that newcomers are not fully members of the community until they have marinated for a significant period of time in the state's traditions and practices. For the Court, state citizenship must be as easily doffed and donned as the green bowler hat of a marcher in the typical St. Patrick's Day parade.

Why cannot state governments foster a deeper sort of loyalty to the state? This is something of a puzzle that the Court does not solve in its opinions. Indeed, the Court itself has suggested that states can reward citizens for remaining within the same locality for an extended period of time. In *Nordlinger v Hahn*, the Court held that California could give more favorable property tax assessments to homeowners who had owned their homes for longer periods of time, because such subsidies for long-term owners advanced the state's "legitimate interest in local neighborhood preservation, continuity, and stability."[98]

It is not easy to square *Nordlinger* with the Court's broad statements in *Zobel* that states cannot reward seniority. To be sure, the state law in *Nordlinger* did not facially discriminate against newcomers to the state, because intrastate migrants who moved within California would generally be reassessed at present value when they bought a new home within California.[99] But *Nordlinger*'s rea-

---

[98] 505 US 1, 13 (1992).

[99] By allowing property owners over 55 to avoid reassessment entirely when they moved to a new house and by allowing all property owners to transfer their homes to their children

soning seems to undercut *Zobel*'s argument that it is illegitimate
for states to reward seniority. Why is it illegitimate to reward state
seniority but legitimate to reward neighborhood seniority? If California can try to prevent "rapid turnover in ownership of homes
and businesses" in a neighborhood,[100] then why cannot Alaska reward someone for remaining in the same state for a long time and
preventing rapid turnover of the state's population?[101]

There is no easy answer to this question. I intend only to lay
bare what I take to be the implicit assumption on which such condemnation rests—the notion that state governments ought not to
be regarded as affective communities. With this assumption, it is
not hard to see why *Nordlinger* is distinguishable from *Zobel*: neighborhoods might properly be regarded as affective communities that
are benefited by low turnover that creates deeper bonds of mutual

---

without enduring a reassessment, California's assessment system became very close to a
facial discrimination against newcomers to the state. However, the Court avoided the entire
issue simply by noting that Stephanie Nordlinger lacked standing to assert the rights of
nonresidents of California. *Nordlinger*, 505 US at 11.

[100] Id.

[101] Clayton Gillette suggested to me that the distinction could be justified on the grounds
that the state legislature can be trusted to eliminate interlocal, but not interstate, discrimination, because state residents (and voters) are burdened by the former but not the latter.
Perhaps. However, one might respond by noting that the Court has consistently rejected
this argument. For instance, the *Hooper* Court rejected Justice Stevens's argument, See
Hooper v Bernalillo County, 472 US 612, 627–28 (1985) (Stevens, J, dissenting), that the
benefited class of old-timers in New Mexico—veterans resident in the state prior to May
8, 1976—was so small that newcomers could virtually be represented by other old-timers
who were not benefited by the state's tax exemption. Stevens's reasoning, of course, assumes
that the political power of a group increases with the group's size—an assumption that
might seem unreasonable. See Bruce Ackerman, *Beyond Carolene Products*, 98 Harv L Rev
713 (1985). For other instances in which the Court has refused to allow interlocal discrimination even where state residents were burdened and therefore could represent the interests
of nonresidents, see *Dean Milk Co. v City of Madison*, 340 US 349 (1951); *United Bldg Trades
Council v Mayor of Camden*, 465 US 208 (1984); *Brimmer v Redman*, 138 US 78, 82 (1891).
I tend to be skeptical that the Court could ever really figure out whether the burdened
state residents will suffice to represent out-of-state interests. After all, is there ever a case
in which burdened out-of-state interests like nonresident prospective home buyers have no
proxy—real estate brokers, home builders, lenders, and so on—for their interests? Such
"political process" arguments seem entirely too amorphous to bake any legal bread. For
similar misgivings about the "virtual-representation-of-outsiders" argument, see Donald
Regan, *The Supreme Court and State Protectionism: Making Sense of the Dormant Commerce
Clause*, 84 Mich L Rev 1091, 1160-67 (1986) (expressing skepticism about "political process" theories that base Dormant Commerce Clause decisions on the need to represent
nonvoting outsiders); *West-Lynn Creamery, Inc. v Healy*, 512 US 186 (1994) (Rehnquist, J,
dissenting) ("Analysis of interest group participation in the political process may serve many
useful purposes, but serving as a basis for interpreting the Dormant Commerce Clause is
not one of them".).

affection and trust.[102] Such bonds might contribute to the governance of neighborhoods by allowing neighbors to overcome collective action problems and sponsor litter pickups, crime watches, block parties, and so on.

By contrast, the Court seems to think that there is no analogous benefit from fostering such ties among all long-term state citizens. Why not? Perhaps the number of persons is too large and their opportunities for useful collaboration too small. Perhaps the sheer interstate mobility of Americans suggests that patriotic ties to a state as opposed to a neighborhood have no foundation in our political traditions. If this is the Court's view, then the efforts of old-timers to secure benefits exclusively for themselves at the expense of newcomers will look like selfish rent seeking by insiders at the expense of outsiders, a transfer of wealth that produces no collateral benefits to anyone.

In response to this argument, one might maintain that either the states' internal political process or interstate competition among the states for taxable wealth will adequately curb such rent seeking. Saul Levmore, for instance, has suggested that the Court should ask whether the state has some sort of power to exploit residents in other states by withholding some unique resource over which it has a monopoly.[103] But one might respond that such a test is judicially unmanageable, because it is extremely difficult to ascertain whether a jurisdiction enjoys a monopoly over some resource.[104] Why bother with such investigation if one is already con-

---

[102] Certainly, courts routinely uphold single-family residential zones on the assumption that cohesive household units will stick around longer than more fortuitous combinations of people. See, e.g., *City of Des Plaines v Trottner*, 216 NE2d 116, 119–20 (Ill 1966) ("In terms of permissible zoning objectives, a group of persons bound together only by their common desire to operate a single housekeeping unit, might be thought to have a transient quality that would affect adversely the stability of the neighborhood, and so depreciate the value of other property").

[103] Levmore, 69 Va L Rev at 570–75 (cited in note 97).

[104] For some studies suggesting the difficulty of determining whether local governments exploit monopolistic control over unique types of land with their zoning ordinances, see James A. Thorson, *An Examination of the Monopoly Zoning Hypothesis*, 72 Land Econ 43 (1996); William Fischel, *Zoning and the Exercise of Monopoly Power: A Reevaluation*, 8 J Urban Econ 283 (1980). Indeed, Professor Levmore's attack on *Zobel*, note 97 supra at 586–89, seems to have overlooked the possibility that Alaska's Permanent Fund, financed entirely by taxes and royalties paid by oil companies extracting oil from Alaskan territory, might constitute exploitation of nonresidents through state monopolistic control over oil reserves in the Prudhoe Bay area. In effect, the state was providing benefits to old-timers by taxing oil consumers and/or shareholders of oil companies throughout the nation.

vinced that redistribution of wealth to old-timers promotes no socially useful goal? A simple prophylactic rule against all such redistribution is defensible if one starts with the premise that states are not affective communities such that long-term commitment to them ought to be promoted.

In particular, the Court's refusal to regard states as affective communities entails the rejection of Mark Pauly's argument that local redistribution is a local public good.[105] The essence of this argument is that local redistribution of wealth satisfies taxpayers' altruistic desire to benefit familiar neighbors over alien strangers. Since *Hooper* and *Zobel*, such a preference will seem illegitimate to the Court, at least to the extent that "being a familiar neighbor" is defined solely in terms of residence within a single state. If states should not be affective communities, then selective regard for indigent old-timers may look like nothing more than an effort by well-organized insiders to reap a subsidy at the expense of politically disorganized newcomers.

C. SETTLEMENT AND RETURN REVISITED: DO LAWS DISCRIMINATING
   AGAINST INDIGENT NEWCOMERS THREATEN NATIONAL
   CITIZENSHIP?

But this account of national citizenship does not easily explain the result in *Saenz* and *Shapiro*. The difficulty is that the extra long residence requirements in *Saenz* and *Shapiro* have a fiscal justification that is completely independent of any theory of the state as an affective community or special regard for old-timers. As explained in Part IIA above, stringent tests for bona fide residence can help to preserve redistributive programs that, according to conventional wisdom, are socially useful. Extra long residence requirements for redistributive programs need not rest on any assumption that newcomers are less worthy than old-timers. Rather, the discriminating state might simply want to insure that other states bear their fair share of the burden of maintaining redistributive programs.

Why, then, should the Court strike down such residence requirements as offending the value of national citizenship? One answer is that Part IIA of this article is simply wrong: a state's interest

---

[105] Mark Pauly, *Income Redistribution as a Local Public Good*, 2 J Pub Econ 35 (1973).

in protecting its fisc from subsidy-motivated newcomers is simply not a legitimate interest. But, as I have already suggested in Part IIA, I think that this position is untenable. Assuming that my readers are convinced by this argument—or at least troubled enough by it not to reject it out of hand—I would like to suggest an alternative justification for *Saenz* and *Shapiro*, one that does not rest on the notion that states ought to be indifferent to the threat posed to their fisc by subsidy-motivated migrants.

To anticipate my argument, I argue in IIC that *Saenz* and *Shapiro* can be justified by the danger that discrimination against indigent migrants is motivated not so much by fiscal prudence as by cultural fear—in particular, fear of the mobile indigent as a stranger who is morally unworthy to join the state community. Such a fear squarely violates the principle outlined above in Part IIB that states are not affective communities: they may not aspire to social or cultural homogeneity. But why believe that discrimination against indigent newcomers is based on this impermissible purpose of excluding persons deemed socially unfit to join the state "club"? To understand why the Court would suspect such a cultural motive, it is useful to describe the regime of "settlement and return" that used to govern indigent migrants prior to the Court's repudiation of this regime in *Edwards v California*.[106] I recapitulate this history because it suggests that discrimination against the indigent migrant historically has not merely been motivated by fiscal concerns (which I deem to be legitimate) but also by cultural anxieties about the moral unworthiness of the mobile indigent. To the extent that discrimination against indigent newcomers continues to reflect such anxieties, the Court might rightly regard them as illegitimately attempting to transform the state into an affective community.

Prior to the New Deal, the law of poverty in the United States was dominated by the principle of "settlement and removal," a concept that traces its origins at least as far back as the English Statute of Settlement and Removal of 1662.[107] As the phrase implies, the principle of "settlement and removal" had two related components. First, the notion of "settlement" provided that each local community had a duty to provide public support only to "its

---

[106] 314 US 160 (1941).

[107] 14 Car 2, ch 12 (1662) (Eng.).

own," to "neighbors" as opposed to "strangers." Second, the notion of "removal" provided that localities could expel any "unsettled" indigent person to their proper place of settlement.

Like being a bona fide resident, being "settled" in a community
was a necessary condition for being eligible for public assistance.
But unlike the Court's brief and cryptic assertions about bona fide
residency, the legal definition of "settlement" was extraordinarily
detailed and complex: as one 1824 report stated, legal questions
surrounding settlement were "so technical, numerous, and complicated, if not obscure, that even eminent counsel [could not answer
them]."[108] One's place of settlement could depend on numerous
facts such as the location of one's real property; the residence of
one's parents, spouse, or master (if one were an apprentice); and
the jurisdiction to which one had paid taxes during some defined
period of time.[109] Different towns would frequently become en-
meshed in expensive and protracted litigation over which of them
owed a duty of support to an indigent person as that person's
proper place of settlement—litigation that had some of the flavor
of paternity suits. But these bewildering legal technicalities all
pointed to a simpler principle: one could claim support only from
that unique community in which one had spent a considerable period of one's life as a contributing taxpayer, family member, or
property owner. Under the traditional law of poverty, no one had
the right to rely on the kindness of strangers.

Related to the notion of "settlement" was the notion of "removal": indigent persons who were not settled in a community
were removed from it by force. The local sheriff would typically
escort the stranger to the edge of town with a warning not to
return on the pain of being whipped.[110] It was the accepted consensus throughout the nineteenth century, reflected not only in political practice but also judicial precedent, that local communities had

---

[108] Michael B. Katz, *In The Shadow of the Poor House: A Social History of Welfare in America*
21 (1986).

[109] William P. Quigley, *Reluctant Charity: Poor Laws in the Original 13 States*, 31 U Richmond L Rev 111, 142–43 (1997).

[110] For a quick summary of various removal statutes, see William P. Quigley, id at 115;
William P. Quigley, *Work or Starve: Regulation of the Poor in Colonial America*, 31 USF L
Rev 35, 42–81 (1996) (describing provisions for expelling poor in colonial laws). For a more
detailed account of the practice of "warning out" the "unsettled" poor, see Hendrik Hartog,
The Public Law of a County Court: Judicial Government in 18th Century Massachusetts, 20 Am
J Legal Hist 282 (1976).

the power to protect themselves from such unfamiliar "paupers" by expelling them. As the Court stated in *Mayor of New York v Miln* when upholding a New York law to prevent paupers from entering New York City on ships,

> We think it as competent and as necessary for a state to provide precautionary measures against the moral pestilence of paupers, vagabonds, and possibly convicts; as it is to guard against the physical pestilence, which may arise from unsound and infections articles imported, or from a ship, the crew of which may be laboring under an infectious disease.[111]

Miln's view of "paupers" as a "moral pestilence" was reiterated by several justices in *The Passenger Cases*.[112] Although *Shapiro* cites *The Passenger Cases* as authority supporting indigent persons' right to travel, the several opinions in *The Passenger Cases* repeatedly assert that "paupers and vagabonds" have absolutely no right to enter any state; in Justice Wayne's words, each state may "put [paupers] under all proper restraint, may carry them out, or drive them off."[113]

What explains this unanimous judicial and legislative endorsement of settlement and removal? In part, the concept of settlement served the same fiscal function as "bona fide residency" in modern welfare law: it insured that no single jurisdiction's resources would be overtaxed by the indigent from other jurisdictions. In other words, settlement was a device by which taxpayers could apportion responsibility among themselves for funding public assistance programs.

---

[111] *Mayor of New York v Miln*, 11 Peters 102, 142–43 (1837).

[112] 48 US (7 How) 283 (1849).

[113] *Passenger Cases*, 48 US at 426 (Wayne, J, concurring). According to Justice Wayne, "[t]he states have the right to turn off paupers, vagabonds, and fugitives from justice" and Congress lacked any power to interfere with these state powers. Justice Wayne stated categorically that paupers and vagabonds "have no rights of national intercourse; no one has the right to transport them . . . from where they are to any other place; and their only rights . . . are such as the law gives to all men who have not altogether forfeited its protection." Id. Justice Grier repeated *Miln*'s language about paupers being a "moral pestilence," id at 457, and Justice Catron concurred in Justice Grier's opinion. Justice Taney, whose dissent was cited by *Shapiro*, agreed wholeheartedly that states have the power to exclude paupers from their borders: he went even further, asserting that states must have discretion to decide "from what persons or description of persons the danger of pauperism is to be apprehended." Id at 469. In short, the notion that *The Passenger Cases* supports the right of indigent persons to cross state lines is wholly fanciful.

But settlement and removal had a cultural as well as a fiscal justification: until the New Deal, it was commonplace to regard indigent persons as not merely expensive but dangerous and morally undeserving, not only because they were poor but also because they were mobile. They were "hobos, scroungers, and would-be criminals,"[114] "locusts,"[115] a "moral pestilence" equivalent to convicted felons.[116] In the revealing epithet of the late nineteenth century, they were "tramps": their very "tramping"—walking across jurisdictional lines—showed that they had no legitimate claim on the community. It was a staple complaint of eighteenth- and nineteenth-century policymakers that public assistance to the indigent encouraged able-bodied persons to become idle at the public expense.[117] Accordingly, policymakers were obsessed with devising ways to separate the able-bodied indigent from the "impotent" (meaning any persons incapable of working, such as very young children, the physically or mentally disabled, or the aged).[118] To nineteenth-century policymakers, the "tramp" who migrated from one state to another seemed, by definition, to be able-bodied, because such a person was healthy enough to migrate across state lines.[119] Thus, "tramping"—that is, mobility—was itself blameworthy: such movement indicated that the indigent person was an able-bodied and lazy parasite on the citizenry in a way that "settled" indigent persons were not.[120]

---

[114] See William R. Brock, *Welfare, Democracy, and the New Deal* 167 (1988).

[115] Paul T. Ringenbach, *Tramps and Reformers, 1873–1916: The Discovery of Unemployment in New York* 3–4 (1973).

[116] In *The Passenger Cases*, both Justices Wayne and Catron compare paupers to convicted criminals.

[117] See William P. Quigley, *Rumblings of Reform: Northern Poor Relief Legislation in Antebellum America*, 26 Cap U L Rev 739, 756–63 (1997); Katz (cited in note 108) at 3–35; June Axinn and Herman Levin, *Social Welfare: A History of the American Response to Need* 45–53 (3d ed 1992).

[118] Katz (cited in note 108) at 19–20.

[119] Id at 95, 153.

[120] For descriptions of how "tramps" were regarded as the epitome of the undeserving poor, see Eric Monkkonen, *Walking to Work: Tramps in America, 1790–1935* (U Nebraska Press, 1984); Paul T. Ringenbach, *Tramps and Reformers, 1873–1916: The Discovery of Unemployment in New York* (Greenwood Press, 1973). For an account of how sixteenth- and seventeenth-century English opinion branded the vagabond poor as a special threat to the social order, see A. L. Beier, *Masterless Men: The Vagrancy Problem in England, 1560–1640* (1985). As one writer graphically put it, the mobile poor were like "rotten legs and arms that drop from the body." Don Herzog, *Happy Slaves: A Critique of Consent Theory* 49 (1989).

The mobile "unsettled" indigent were not only despised as lazy but feared as dangerous. Almost by definition, such persons lacked land or capital, and they lacked any long-term contract with property owner–employers. In short, they had nothing to lose. Anglo-American ideologies of property tended to regard such landless people as the likely dupes of demagogues, recruits for mobs who would easily be incited into rioting against property owners.[121] Since the mid-fourteenth century in England, the Crown had attempted to control the indigent by forcing them into long-term service contracts with property owners and barring them from migrating from their town, borough, or manor to search for better terms.[122] While these measures were apparently not enforced against most nonindentured labor in America after the eighteenth century,[123] settlement and removal served the same function by forcing indigent persons to return to a unique place of settlement where they could be monitored in poorhouses or auctioned off to labor contractors under systems of outdoor relief. When landless and masterless men began to march free from these restraints— whether as IWW organizers, Coxey's army, or Exodusters—property owners trembled.[124] In one revealing rant, a wealthy colonial property owner denounced "[t]he Sot, the Rambler, the Spend-thrift, and the Slip Season" as responsible for Philadelphia's economic decline.[125] According to eighteenth-century ideology, he was

[121] The view that propertyless persons were likely to be manipulated by wealthy persons was a standard trope of republican ideology. For an account of property owners' dread of riots by the propertyless in colonial America, see Gary Nash, *Social Change and the Growth of Prerevolutionary Urban Radicalism*, in *Race, Class, and Politics: Essays on American Colonial and Revolutionary Society* 211–42 (1986). The property owners' dread of rioting mobs composed of propertyless and masterless men had not abated by the late nineteenth century, as the U.S. government's treatment of Coxey's Army attests.

[122] Under the Ordinance and Statute of Laborers and the Statute of Artificers, those who lacked land sufficient to support themselves were forced to enter into long-term contracts of labor—typically for terms of at least a year—that could specifically be enforced against them if they ran away before the end of the term. Moreover, such landless laborers were barred from traveling to new employers without a "testimonial" stating that they had completed their past labor contract. See Robert J. Steinfeld, *The Invention of Free Labor: The Employment Relation in English and American Law and Culture, 1350–1870* at 16–37 (1991).

[123] Id at 50–52. Servants who had entered into labor contracts in return for payment of their passage across the Atlantic, however, could be held to labor for the duration of their agreement well into the nineteenth century. Id.

[124] For an account of how industrialists and reformers both blamed a "tramp army" for labor disturbances in the post–Civil War United States, see Ringenbach, *Tramps and Reformers* (cited in note 115) at 14.

[125] Gary Nash, *Social Change and Prerevolutionary Urban Radicalism*, in Gary Nash, *Race, Class, and Politics: Essays on American Colonial and Revolutionary Society* 217 (1986).

right: like the drunk or spendthrift, the "rambler" and "slip season" (i.e., migrant worker who "slipped" out of the jurisdiction before his seasonal labor contract expired) were guilty of fomenting social disorder, of violating norms of deference believed to be essential to the maintenance of private property.

But one suspects that dislike of the mobile indigent—"tramps" or "hoboes"—probably cannot be reduced to these worries about social revolution or idleness. Beyond these specific fears is a more psychologically basic suspicion of strangers and fondness for neighbors.[126] As Mark Pauly famously suggested, altruism might have a spatial dimension in that state voters may feel a greater sense of benevolence toward long-time residents. If so, requiring indigent persons to be settled allows state taxpayers to satisfy their urge to bestow tax dollars on familiar neighbors, whereas redistribution to newcomers does not provide such a benefit to state taxpayers.[127] Pauly cited no evidence to suggest that state redistribution to familiar "settled" families provides a special benefit to taxpayers, but there is some evidence that suburban taxpayers have a preference for redistributing affordable housing to long-term residents rather than new migrants.[128]

It is essential to see that this cultural preference for "settled" neighbors over the mobile indigent is essentially different from the fiscal justification for discrimination against newcomers defended above in Part IIA. As noted above, the fiscal argument does not depend on any belief that indigent newcomers are less worthy or more dangerous than old-timers: according to the fiscal theory, the distinction between old-timers and newcomers is merely a convenient way to insure that each state bears its fair share of the

---

[126] For an artfully ironic anthropological description of this fear of strangers and travelers, see chs I and II of Elsie Clew Persons, *Fear and Conventionality* 1–18 (Putnam's, 1914) (reprinted by U of Chicago Press, 1997).

[127] Mark Pauly, *Income Redistribution as a Local Public Good*, 2 J Pub Econ 35 (1973).

[128] Under the New Jersey Fair Housing Act of 1985, suburban communities tend to be eager to satisfy their obligations to provide a fair share of the regional need for affordable housing by providing housing to "indigenous" poor—namely, poor who already live within the suburban community. For a decision rejecting a suburb's attempt to satisfy its *Mt. Laurel* obligation by housing "indigenous" poor, see *In re Township of Warren*, 622 A2d 1257 (NJ 1993). This suburban eagerness may have an element of familial regard: the "indigenous" poor may often be the elderly parents or impecunious children of the local taxpayers. See David L. Kirp, John P. Dwyer, and Larry Rosenthal, *Our Town: Race, Housing, and the Soul of Suburbia* 187–88 (1995) (noting suburbs' desire to satisfy their obligation to provide affordable housing by building housing for "safe seniors" and their own grown-up children).

322   THE SUPREME COURT REVIEW

costs of supporting the indigent. By contrast, the theory of settlement and removal treated the state as an affective community that
was entitled to expel the stranger because such a rootless person
lacked sufficient ties to the state or loyalty to the state's social order. The theory of settlement and removal, in short, offends
against the Court's theory of national citizenship barring states
from acting like affective communities in a way the fiscal argument
does not.

Of course, the practice of settlement and removal has been
swept away by the Court since the New Deal. Why summarize
this defunct regime? I think that this summary is useful, because,
since *Edwards v California*,[129] the Court has defined national citizenship in opposition to the old practice of settlement and removal. *Miln* has joined the ranks of infamous precedents such as
Lochner v New York, *Plessy v Ferguson*, and *Dred Scott v Sanders* as
a precedent that is oddly influential even after its demise precisely
because the Court uses it as a benchmark for defining what is constitutionally illegitimate.

The Court's opening shot in its war against settlement and removal was fired in *Edwards v California*, in which the Court held
that California could not bar migrants from entering the state simply because they were indigent. While briefly noting *Miln*'s approval of such restrictions on the movement of "paupers," the
Court rejected the notion that such an ideology could still survive
the New Deal: "Whatever may have been the notion then prevail-
ing [in 1836], we do not think that it will now be seriously contended that because a person is without employment and without
funds he constitutes a 'moral pestilence'. Poverty and immorality
are not synonymous."[130]

Just as *Edwards* rejects the premise underlying the principle of
"return"—the belief that indigent newcomers are likely to impose
"depredations and evil example" on the state[131]—so, too, *Shapiro*
and its progeny can be seen as rejecting the fundamental premise
of settlement—the belief that communities owe a greater duty of

---

[129] 314 US 160 (1941).

[130] Id at 168.

[131] See *Prigg v Pennsylvania*, 41 US (16 Pet) 539, 625 (1842) (per Story, J) (state may use
police power to expel runaway slaves to prevent their "depredations and evil example, as
they certainly may do in cases of idlers, vagabonds and paupers").

benevolence to old-timers than to newcomers. *Shapiro* expressly noted that the extra long durational residence requirements for welfare were crude versions of "settlement."[132] *Hooper* also rejected the core principle of "settlement"—the notion that states had a special duty to take care of "their own."

In short, the Court began its jurisprudence attacking the vision of states as affective communities with its attack on the principle of settlement and removal: for the Court, state residents' cultural fear of the mobile poor forms the paradigm case of what it means for a state to regard itself as an affective community. The unsavory form in which the Court first confronted the idea of states as affective communities might help explain what was so puzzling in Part IIB—why the Court has so thoroughly rejected this model of state citizenship. If the "affective state" took its most familiar form when it was expelling the mobile poor as a "moral pestilence," then it is not hard to see why the Court would find such a vision repellent. It is worth noting that the Court's post–New Deal condemnation of settlement and removal is an extraordinary instance of disregard for precedent and tradition. As *Edwards* conceded, a long chain of precedents had expressly approved the practice of settlement and removal in dicta and holding.[133] Moreover, the practice had been commonly practiced by states from colonial times right up until the New Deal. When *Edwards* condemned the practice, it could cite nothing in support of its new position. Or rather, nothing but a radically changed political consensus about the social meaning of poverty and unemployment. As much as more famous judicial reversals of direction—*Brown v Board of Education*,[134] *Reynolds v Sims*,[135] and *Jones & Laughlin Steel*[136]—*Edwards* is a decision self-consciously rooted in changed popular values rather than traditional legal principles.

Given the opinion's own reliance on extra-legal values, it is worth asking whether *Edwards'* condemnation of the idea of settlement and removal makes functional sense. I think it does, but the question is complicated by the fact that *Edwards* embodies more

---

[132] *Shapiro*, 394 US at 628 n 7.
[133] *Edwards*, 314 US at 168.
[134] 347 US 483 (1954).
[135] 377 US 533 (1964).
[136] 301 US 1 (1937).

than one principle of constitutional law. In part, *Edwards* is rooted in the straightforward idea that hostility toward the indigent is constitutionally suspect, because "[p]overty and immorality are not synonymous."[137] Viewed in this way, *Edwards* constitutionalizes a new popular consensus about the poor epitomized by John Steinbeck's *Grapes of Wrath*, in which the Joads replaced the malingering "tramp" as the symbol of the migratory indigent. This version of *Edwards* is a forerunner to the argument pressed in the late 1960s that wealth-based classifications are constitutionally suspect under the Fourteenth Amendment's Equal Protection Clause.[138] Since this argument has been thoroughly rejected by the Court, one might regard *Edwards* as a curious vestige of a defunct doctrine rather than a foundational decision.

But there is another and more promising side to *Edwards* that is rooted in a different principle—the notion that states may not attempt to transform themselves into affective communities that pick their members based on the degree to which newcomers will add to the social cohesion of the state's population. This aspect of *Edwards* is best stated by Justice Jackson in his concurrence when he asserts that

> [s]tate citizenship is ephemeral. It results only from residence and is gained or lost therewith. That choice of residence was subject to local approval is contrary to the inescapable implications of the westward movement of our civilization.[139]

Under this theory, the flaw of the California statute in *Edwards* was not that it discriminated against the indigent but that it tried to exclude indigent *newcomers* to insure that its population maintained a certain social, cultural, or political homogeneity. In Justice Jackson's theory, states may not legitimately perpetuate their current population's dominance by excluding a new set of citizens who have different beliefs or values. Viewed in this way, *Edwards* is the forerunner to the Court's voting rights decisions in which the Court repeatedly held that states may not "fenc[e] out from the franchise a sector of the population because of the way they may

---

[137] *Edwards*, 314 US at 168.

[138] For an analysis of such arguments, Frank Michelman, *Foreword: On Protecting the Poor Through the Fourteenth Amendment*, 83 Harv L Rev 7, 22–33 (1969).

[139] *Edwards*, 314 US at 184.

vote."[140] If one assumes that states are not entitled to be affective communities—that they must, in Justice Jackson's phrase, be "ephemeral"—then it makes sense for the Court to bar states from using settlement and removal to insure a " 'common interest in all matters pertaining to (the community's) government.' "[141]

But settlement and removal are not the only practices that are suspect under the principle barring states' acting like affective communities. California's durational residence requirement, overturned in *Saenz*, is suspect under the same principle. The reason is that there is a high likelihood that California's residence requirement is based on the same social or cultural fears underlying the regime of settlement and removal—the fear that newcomers will change the character of the state for the worse. The durational residence requirement, after all, targets the indigent, who have historically been the object of the same deep social anxieties that motivated settlement and removal. Moreover, the durational residence requirement itself suspiciously resembles settlement: the law smells like an effort by California to insure that newly arrived indigent have some familial, occupational, or other deep and lasting attachment to California before they can collect public support.

Thus the suspicion arises that California is not really worried about other states' free-riding off of their tax effort or about the fiscal impact of subsidy-motivated migrants. Rather, California is worried that indigent migrants will change the social, cultural, or political character of the state by changing the state's demography. If states are not entitled to preserve themselves as affective communities, then this worry is not a legitimate purpose capable of sustaining the durational residence requirement against a challenge that it burdens the right to travel. Californians must reconcile themselves to the constitutional reality that their state's demographic character must remain "ephemeral" and cannot be en-

---

[140] See, e.g., *Carrington v Rash*, 380 US 89, 94 (1965); *Dunn v Blumstein*, 405 US 330, 356 (1972). I am indebted to Professor Laurence Tribe for this argument from *Carrington* and *Dunn*, which he insightfully elaborates in a forthcoming article, *Saenz Sans Prophecy: Does the Privileges and Immunities Revival Portend the Future—or Reveal the Structure of the Present?* 113 Harv L Rev 110 (1999). Although I read the article in page proofs shortly before entering the final revisions on my own article, I obtained the article too soon before publication of my own effort to discuss Professor Tribe's argument with the thoroughness that it deserves.

[141] *Dunn*, 405 US at 356.

trenched by a requirement that newcomers be subject to "local approval."

III. Should the Court Defer More to State or Federal Legislatures?

In sum, there are special reasons why the Court might be especially suspicious of state laws burdening indigent newcomers despite the sensible fiscal justification for such laws. Such laws have a greater likelihood of being based on the notion that states are affective communities that have no duty to help "rootless," mobile poor people. But it is not obvious how this suspicion of state purposes can be reconciled with the Court's normal presumption that the legislature is motivated by constitutional principles: the plaintiff normally bears the burden of showing an impermissible purpose.[142] Should the rule be different here?

A. DEFERENCE TO STATE LEGISLATURES

Suppose that one wanted to distinguish between state laws that discriminated against indigent newcomers for legitimate fiscal reasons and state laws that do so because of illegitimate cultural dislike of the indigent. In theory, this should not be difficult. The state might simply specify that indigent newcomers will not be regarded as bona fide residents if their sole reason for migrating to the state were to take advantage of the state's more generous subsidies to the indigent. As noted in Part IIA, *Vlandis* proffered something like this test of bona fide residence for determining eligibility for in-state tuition. Of course, *Shapiro* condemned such a test for welfare, but *Shapiro* erroneously assumed that such a test necessarily rests on the assumption that indigent newcomers seeking public assistance are undeserving of relief. No such assumption is necessary, as explained in Part IIA: States might merely want to insure that their extra generosity does not let other states off the hook of providing for their state residents. Therefore, without any hostility toward indigent migrants, a state might provide welfare only to those whose presence in the state was not a result of the state's generous welfare program. In this way, stingy states could

---

[142] See *Washington v Davis*, 426 US 229 (1976).

not increase the redistributive obligations of more generous states by encouraging their indigent citizens to migrate through miserly welfare programs. Why not allow such a test for bona fide residence to solve the "free-rider" problem raised by redistributive programs? In short, why not overrule this aspect of *Shapiro* and adopt *Vlandis?*

The difficulty with such a test is that there is no feasible way to know whether without the state's generous redistributive programs the indigent migrant would have entered this state.[143] This problem arises not only because of the usual difficulties of determining the causes of interstate migration but also because of the peculiar position of indigent migrants. The difficulty is that, for indigent migrants, every state program is redistributive. As Bruce Hamilton has noted,[144] states redistribute wealth to owners of low-value property with every public spending program whenever they finance those programs with *ad valorem* property taxes rather than lump-sum taxes or user fees: the owners of low-value property pay lower property taxes than the median taxpayer for the same level of services. But the same reasoning suggests why all state spending programs redistribute wealth to the indigent: like the owner of low-value property, the indigent will pay lower property or income taxes than the median taxpayer but receive the same services. Therefore, every state spending program—parks, public schools, police patrols, recycling, street sweeping, and so on—redistributes wealth to the indigent.

If redistribution to the indigent is ubiquitous, then it will be practically impossible to determine whether indigent migrants come to the state to take advantage of some redistributive subsidy. Because all state spending is redistributive as far as the indigent migrant is concerned, one could say that indigent migrants are motivated by the prospect of subsidies whenever he or she is attracted to the state by the quality of any aspect of its government, ranging from police protection to an aggressive program of downtown redevelopment. Taken to its logical extreme, the fiscal justification for durational residence requirements for welfare should also justify special barriers to indigent eligibility for *any* of a state's

---

[143] For an acute analysis of four different reasons that a community might have for excluding the indigent, see William T. Bogart, *"What Big Teeth You Have!" Identifying the Motivations for Exclusionary Zoning*, 30 Urban Stud 1669 (1993).

[144] Hamilton, 12 Urban Stud 205 (cited in note 83).

spending programs. If a state can discriminate against indigent newcomers to avoid becoming a welfare magnet, then why cannot they do so to avoid becoming a "parks magnet," a "police magnet," a "downtown revitalization magnet," or a "clean streets magnet"?

The obvious answer is that allowing such state discrimination against the indigent would effectively overrule *Edwards* and bring back the regime of settlement and removal. There is no other way to prevent an indigent migrant from taking advantage of the state's nonexcludable local public goods except by excluding the indigent altogether. (Indeed, some economists have made precisely such a fiscal argument in favor of exclusionary zoning). The fiscal justification for discriminating against indigent migrants, in short, proves too much, as *Shapiro* seemed to recognize.[145]

One could arbitrarily limit the scope of such discrimination to cover only welfare programs and not other redistributive benefits. But the question again arises: how *much* discrimination is appropriate to advance the (by hypothesis) legitimate fiscal goal? The answer is easy in theory but impossible in practice. In theory, states should discriminate just enough to insure that indigent migrants are not motivated to migrate by the new state's greater generosity in providing welfare benefits. In practice, however, it is impossible to determine how much discrimination will accomplish this goal. Moreover, states have powerful incentives to exclude indigent persons altogether, either because of cultural animosity or because indigent persons are generally a net fiscal burden even if they do not receive welfare. It will be natural, therefore, for the Court to infer that the residence requirement does not serve the purpose of avoiding a free-rider problem but instead serves the goal of excluding all indigent migrants, regardless of whether welfare was the cause of their migration.

California's durational residence requirement presents a case in point. By providing only those benefits that the welfare recipients would have received in their former state, California theoretically insured that differences in benefit levels could not influence any

---

[145] See *Shapiro*, 394 US at 632–33 ("Appellants' reasoning would logically permit the State to bar new residents from schools, parks, and libraries or deprive them of police and fire protection. Indeed it would permit the State to apportion all benefits and services according to the past tax contributions of its citizens").

migrant's decision to enter California. However, by failing to adjust welfare benefits by the higher cost of living in California, California insured that it was imposing a burden on new migrants from
states with lower cost of living far in excess of what was necessary
to deter subsidy-motivated migration.[146]

Moreover, California could not solve this problem by increasing
the migrant's benefit level to account for the higher cost of living
in California. For there might be a myriad of conditions in California that would require new migrants to receive higher benefits than
they received in their former state if the living conditions of the
migrant would not decline as a result of his or her decision to
migrate. The migrant's former state might provide lower benefits
but also have a lower crime rate, lower unemployment rate, better
public transportation, or better access to subsidized housing. Likewise, the migrant's former state might provide lower benefit levels
but also more job training or better access to day-care or greater
leniency in requiring welfare recipients to find employment. In
short, if California really intended to provide benefits equal to
those paid to migrants in their former state, it would have had to
provide adjustments in benefits reflecting an extraordinary variety
of circumstances.

Of course, devising such a formula would be practically impossible. But this means that the goal of protecting the state fisc from
subsidy-motivated migration founders on the sheer impossibility
of deciding which migrants are subsidy motivated and which are
not. The whole project of removing California benefits from the
migratory calculus of newcomers to the state is wrecked by an insurmountable problem of *dépeçage:* the entitlements provided by a
former state are mismatched with the economic conditions and
legal context in the new state where the migrant actually lives.
California adopted the legal fiction that indigent migrants from
other states were not really living in California, that they instead
were still in their former state and could therefore subsist off of
the former state's benefit levels. But this legal fiction obviously
would not pay the rents in, say, Los Angeles County or the Bay
area. By relegating the residents to a legal regime utterly inappro-

---

[146] For instance, the maximum benefit provided by fifteen states would not pay for half
of the fair market rent of even a one-bedroom apartment in California. *Roe*, 966 F Supp
at 981 n 10.

priate to the area in which they actually lived, California effectively imposed a tariff on all indigent residents migrating to California.

One could nevertheless argue that the Court should defer to California's legislation as a good-faith (albeit overbroad) effort to address the fiscal problem raised by welfare-motivated migration. But I suggest that such deference would be inappropriate given the cultural context of the United States and the fiscal incentives of states. All residence requirements, after all, are imposed in the shadow of a long history of settlement and removal during which "paupers" were habitually grouped with lunatics and convicts and treated as malingerers and criminals. When states discriminate against indigent migrants, it is natural to infer that the old regime of settlement and removal lives on under another name.

Moreover, as noted above, states have fiscal incentives to exclude *all* indigent migrants, regardless of whether they migrate to obtain higher welfare payments. As noted above, indigent persons always tend to burden the state fisc because their net tax payments tend to be lower than those of the median taxpayer. Therefore, the Court might justifiably suspect that state discrimination against indigent newcomers is really designed to exclude all such migrants rather than filter out migration caused by state generosity in welfare payments. Again, laws like California's durational residence requirement are well suited for such an impermissible purpose.

In short, *Saenz* is probably correct to reject categorically fiscal justifications for discrimination against indigent migrants. But this is not because such justifications are somehow illegitimate. On the contrary, both precedent and policy suggest that the proper function of residence requirements is to cabin states' fiscal responsibilities. The problem with fiscal justifications for discrimination against indigent migrants arises from problems unique to indigency. When discrimination against indigent persons is at stake, there is simply too great a risk that the state is motivated by cultural hostility or a global desire to exclude all indigent migrants.

The peculiar nature of indigency also distinguishes residence requirements for welfare from similar requirements for in-state tuition or divorce decrees. There is no reason to suspect that states have an incentive to exclude out-of-state college applicants because the state feared the effect that college applicants would have on the character of the state. The same can be said for persons seeking divorce decrees. Therefore, it makes sense for the Court to review

more leniently durational residence requirements for in-state tuition or divorce decrees: there is no reason to suspect that the state
imposed the requirement to maintain the social, cultural, or political character of the state. It is the greater likelihood that states
want to bar indigent persons from entering the state for the purpose of maintaining a particular affective community that makes
residence requirements for welfare suspect, not the fact that such
benefits are not "portable." In sum, *Saenz*'s holding was probably
correct, but its reasoning was inadequate.

To avoid being misunderstood, I emphasize that the argument
against durational residence requirements for welfare is not an argument that classifications burdening the indigent are generally
constitutionally suspect. Rather, I argue that the Fourteenth
Amendment prohibits all durational residence requirements designed to maintain the current demographic character of the state
against what the current population regards as socially undesirable
migrants. It so happens that, for specific historical reasons, states
have disliked indigent immigrants because they believed that the
mobile poor were socially disruptive and morally pernicious.
Therefore, judicial suspicion of durational residence requirements
targeting the indigent is a sensible way to enforce the rule against
states setting themselves up as affective communities. However,
were there any indication that states had similar reasons for imposing durational residency requirements on college students (or military personnel, bakers, lawyers, and so on), then the same suspicion
should apply.

B. CONGRESS'S POWER TO AUTHORIZE STATE DISCRIMINATION AGAINST INDIGENT NEWCOMERS

Congress apparently authorized California's discrimination
against newcomers by enacting 42 USC § 604(c), which provides
that "[a] State operating a program funded under this part may
apply to a family the rules (including benefit amounts) of the program funded under this part of another State if the family has
moved to the State from the other State and has resided in the
State for less than 12 months." Can Congress authorize states to
use a classification that would be barred to the states acting alone?

Saenz found that this question was "readily answered" by the
principle that "Congress may not authorize the States to violate

the Fourteenth Amendment." But, as Professor William Cohen has noted, this answer is "mirrors and smoke," for it ignores the possibility that Congress's power to define the constitutional right in question might be greater than the states'.[147] *Saenz* came close to addressing the question when it noted that "the protection afforded by the Citizenship clause of [the Fourteenth] Amendment is a limitation on the powers of the National Government as well as the States." But this assertion is too conclusory to be a satisfactory argument.

In *Saenz*, the constitutional right in question is the right to be free from discrimination based on the recency of one's arrival in a state. It is hard not to see this right as exclusively a protection against state parochialism. If so, then it is difficult to see why such a right should be enforceable against Congress. After all, newcomers to a state are just as much citizens in the federal union and just as well represented in Congress as anyone else. Why should the Court intervene to prevent the federal government from disregarding migrants' interests?

Consider a hypothetical scenario offered by Justice Breyer during oral argument of *Saenz*. Suppose that Congress had created a federal pilot program that served only the residents in a particular census tract. Suppose also that Congress had decided to conserve the program's per capita resources by barring persons from participating in the program who had migrated into the census tract after a certain date. It would seem peculiar to treat this limit on program participation as a burden on the constitutional right to travel or equal citizenship. Presumably, Congress can bestow a fixed amount of money on a group of people defined by their geographic residence without extending the benefit to other people who move next door after the program commences. How does this program differ from what Congress actually did—limit newcomers' access to generous welfare "pilot programs" by state governments?

Even if one assumes that the right in question was addressed to Congress as well as the states, why should Congress not have some power to determine the contours of the right? As Akhil Amar has observed, it is not obvious why this authorization could not be construed as an effort to enforce rather than violate the Fourteenth

---

[147] William Cohen, *Congressional Power to Validate Unconstitutional State Laws: A Forgotten Solution to an Old Enigma*, 35 Stan L Rev 387, 417 (1983).

Amendment.[148] Suppose Congress found that, absent durational residence requirements, states would compete to reduce welfare benefits drastically and irrationally, in that the reduction might not be desired by any single state but rather was a result of their individual strategic efforts to "free ride" off of the tax efforts of their neighbors. Under these circumstances, why cannot Congress's authorization of discrimination against newcomers be regarded as an effort to prevent indigent persons from incurring this collectively irrational reduction in welfare benefits? Like any other state classification, such a reduction in welfare benefits would be subject to review under the Fourteenth Amendment.[149] Why could Congress not find that such a reduction deprives indigent persons of the equal protection of the laws?[150] Moreover, why could Congress not also conclude that the best way to remedy this violation was to eliminate state incentives to engage in a race to the bottom?

Saenz does not discuss any of these questions. Nonetheless, *Saenz*'s holding was correct, for reasons that *Saenz* ignored. The problem with Congress's authorization of state discrimination in *Saenz* is that Congress did not seriously deliberate about the constitutional rights that it was allegedly enforcing.[151]

Consider the legislative history of 42 USC § 604(c). The record suggests that Congress was indifferent to the serious constitutional issues that the provision raised. The House Report on 42 USC § 604(c) simply acknowledged the holding in *Shapiro* and then observed that the Court "has not ruled on the question of paying lower amounts of aid for incoming residents."[152] The floor debate was similarly cursory. So far as I can tell, members of Congress were silent about the constitutional question in the debates over the TANF block grant program. In earlier debates over a similar provision introduced as a rider to the 1992 Omnibus Budget Act, supporters of durational residence requirements again merely noted that the proposed federal statute was different from the total

---

[148] See Akhil Amar, *Lost Clause*, The New Republic (June 14, 1999).

[149] See, e.g., *Lyng v Castillo*, 477 US 635 (1986).

[150] Compare Frank Michelman, *The Supreme Court, 1968 Term—Foreword: On Protecting the Poor Through the Fourteenth Amendment*, 83 Harv L Rev 7 (1969).

[151] For an intelligent exposition of this duty to deliberate on constitutional issues, see Paul Brest, *The Conscientious Legislator's Guide to Constitutional Interpretation*, 27 Stan L Rev 586 (1975).

[152] HR No 104-651, reprinted in 1996 US Code, Cong, & Admin News 2183, 2396.

denial of welfare benefits struck down by the Court in *Shapiro*, but no one explained why this distinction had constitutional significance.[153] Moreover, some members of Congress objected to even this trivial mention of the constitutional issue, arguing that "it is going to take a lot of time for a vote on constitutionality" and that reductions in federal spending alone did not themselves raise constitutional questions.[154]

The resulting legislation gave states carte blanche to discriminate against newcomers, ignoring all differences between the living conditions and legal context of the different states. In effect, Congress allowed states to impose tariffs on newcomers, a practice that, under any plausible view of the Fourteenth Amendment's Citizenship Clause, is unconstitutional. Given the impoverished state of the congressional record, it would not have been impossible for the Court to find that congressional authorization for state discrimination was constitutionally inadequate without making broad pronouncements about whether Congress could *ever* authorize such discrimination.[155] *Saenz*, however, preferred the cleaver to the scalpel: it dismissed federal legislation as practically irrelevant to the question of residence requirements.

This denigration of Congress's role in determining Fourteenth Amendment rights was unfortunate, given the complexity of the values implicated by state residency. Indeed, one can speculate that the formalistic flavor of the opinion is related to *Saenz*'s impoverished view of Congress's remedial powers. As noted above, *Saenz* seems to dismiss all complex empirical considerations as constitutionally irrelevant in favor of a categorical antidiscrimination rule. According to *Saenz*, it simply does not matter whether residence requirements are necessary to avoid a free-rider problem or sustain the state fisc from subsidy-motivated migration: all of those concerns are simply "unequivocally impermissible." As I suggested in Part IIA, this rejection of fiscal considerations makes no sense from a functional point of view: the whole point of residence is to define

---

[153] See Proceedings and Debates of the 102d Cong, 2d Sess (April 10, 1992), 138 Cong Rec S5413, S5474 (remarks by Senator D'Amato) (observing that "there is a distinction that can be made and should be made" between facts of *Shapiro* and lesser reduction of welfare benefits).

[154] See remarks of Senator Domenici, id at S5474–75.

[155] A classic defense of this position is Hans Linde, *Due Process of Lawmaking*, 55 Neb L Rev 197 (1970).

and cabin states' fiscal obligations. But, from the point of view of judicial manageability, this formalism makes sense: if one assumes that only the Court is permitted to enforce the doctrine, then one had better get a doctrine that the Court can enforce. Thus, the Court confines the institutions that are permitted to define constitutional rights and then prunes the constitutional doctrine to fit its Procrustean set of institutions.

IV. Conclusion

The essential purpose of bona fide residence is to define who is eligible for the benefits and burdens of state citizenship. But this purpose can sensibly be served only when benefits and burdens are linked to each other. Whenever states create a redistributive program, that link is broken. Contrary to the rhetoric of *Saenz* and *Shapiro*, there is nothing illegitimate about states' efforts to prevent other states from "free riding" off of their redistributive tax efforts by limiting access to the fruits of that effort. Text, precedent, and sensible policy certainly do not require such a result.

The problem with discrimination against *indigent* migrants is that states have too many reasons—legitimate and illegitimate—to keep indigent persons out of the state. As our legacy of settlement and removal indicates, states might exclude such persons out of a desire to perpetuate the state's current demographic composition for the sake of social or cultural cohesion. Because this purpose to foster an affective community through exclusion offends the central notion of national citizenship announced in *Edwards*, the Court must forbid such exclusion. But, because it is practically impossible for the Court to distinguish between legitimate and illegitimate motives for discriminating against indigent newcomers, it is appropriate for the Court to set out a prophylactic rule barring all such discrimination across the board. As crude and costly as this rule is, it is preferable to the alternatives. But *Saenz* would have done better not to make a constitutional virtue out of necessity and instead limited this categorical rule to the context in which it was most needed—to remedy discrimination against indigent newcomers and not newcomers more generally.

SAMUEL ISSACHAROFF

GOVERNANCE AND LEGITIMACY
IN THE LAW OF CLASS ACTIONS

After almost a decade of dormancy, the law of class actions has
emerged prominently in the Supreme Court's docket in the past
few Terms. In repeated confrontations with the relatively recent
emergence of the settlement class action, the Court has traced an
uncertain line between the efficiency mandates of aggregate dispute resolution and the fairness concerns of the absent class members. The fact that three recent major cases, *Matsushita v Epstein*,[1]
Amchem Products, Inc. v Windsor,[2] and *Ortiz v Fibreboard Corp.*,[3] all
arose in the settlement context complicates an already difficult
merger of what should be two distinct questions in the class certification context: the necessity of class treatment to overcome collective action barriers to the prosecution of perceived group harms,
and the question of who should control the class action and under
what terms. Because these two questions are addressed jointly as
part of the certification inquiry, courts have had great difficulty

Samuel Issacharoff is a Professor of Law at Columbia Law School.

AUTHOR'S NOTE: I received helpful comments from Steve Burbank, Jack Coffee, Cynthia
Estlund, Jill Fisch, Marcel Kahan, Henry Monaghan, Linda Silberman, and Charles Silver,
although as will be evident from the disagreements with many of these colleagues, the views
expressed are mine alone. Prior versions of this article were presented at workshops at
Columbia, Fordham, and NYU law schools, and the article benefited from critical commentary at these schools. Jason Golub and Xi Chen provided valuable research assistance.

[1] 116 US 367 (1996) (upholding a Delaware state court settlement of all class claims,
including federal claims over which the Delaware court had no subject matter jurisdiction).

[2] 521 US 591 (1997) (striking down settlement class that included both present and future
asbestos claimants).

[3] 119 S Ct 2295 (1999) (striking down use of limited fund settlement class of present
and future claimants).

separating their particular attributes. Such disaggregation requires both doctrinal and theoretical sensitivity, and will hopefully shed light on the difficult field of class actions.

The first inquiry concerning the need for collective action follows a well-trod path in political theory. Hobbes and others point out that in the absence of collective security, the pitiable state of nature, there is no individual incentive to industry.[4] Without assurance that each individual will secure the benefits of his or her own toil and initiative, all individuals are reduced jealously to warding off encroachments by potentially rapacious neighbors; each individual cannot invest in the development of property beyond that which can be immediately defended; and each individual is reduced to contracting only for what can be immediately exchanged as transactions into the future cannot be secured. While the existence of such a hypothesized state of nature may be questioned as a historical matter,[5] the antidote to such disorder has been fairly clear. The primary solution has been the creation of a centralized authority, the state, capable of securing to each citizen a security interest in the guarantees of property and the enforceability of exchange. The cost of this centralized authority is then distributed among all the citizens through a system of taxation.

Before moving on to the question of the governance of the state and the equity of the taxation mechanism, it is useful to draw the analogy to the class action. For present purposes, it is useful to think of the class action mechanism as fundamentally a centralizing device designed to accomplish some of the same functions as performed by the state, particularly in those situations in which the state has not or cannot perform its regulatory function, or it would be inefficient for the state to undertake such regulation directly. In such circumstances, the class action delegates to private individuals the power to lead a diffuse group in a collective endeavor, provide internal equity in the treatment of the group's members, and spread the burden of collectively financing the endeavor across the entire group. It is a mechanism that assures that each individual

---

[4] See Thomas Hobbes, *Leviathan* 89 (Cambridge, 1996) (noting that in the hypothesized state of nature, "there is no place for industry; because the fruit thereof is uncertain: and consequently no culture of the Earth; no Navigation, nor use of the commodities that may be imported by Sea; no commodious building . . .").

[5] See Matt Ridley, *The Origins of Virtue: Human Instincts and the Evolution of Cooperation* (Viking, 1998).

member will have his interests protected and that each will be taxed for the collective undertaking. The taxation assessed through the class action allows for the selection of an agent, just as the taxation of the polity underwrites the apparatus of government. As expressed by the Supreme Court two decades ago:

> The aggregation of individual claims in a classwide suit is an evolutionary response to the existence of injuries unremedied by the regulatory action of the government. Where it is not economically feasible to obtain relief within the traditional framework of a multiplicity of small individual suits for damages, aggrieved persons may be without any effective redress unless they may employ the class action device.[6]

The analogy to the state then points to the second part of the inquiry: the question of the forms of governance. For Hobbes, recognition of the need for centralized power yielded the assumption that sovereign power must take the form of a monarchy. Without belaboring the point, political theory has progressed quite a bit in the intervening centuries as Locke, Montesquieu, and generations of democratic theorists have pondered the issue of the legitimacy of various forms of governance. All such theories accept the need for collective discipline, but all recognize that this is only the beginning of the inquiry for political legitimacy. The legitimacy of any particular governmental arrangement then turns on the ability to curb oppressive, abusive, or self-serving behavior that may emerge from within the newly created governing class.

This analogy then follows as well into the field of class actions. The very purpose of the class action mechanism is to discipline the individualized members so that they may be regulated and taxed and a governor appointed. This is essentially the crux of what the Supreme Court recognized in *Amchem*:

> The policy at the very core of the class action mechanism is to overcome the problem that small recoveries do not provide the incentive for any individual to bring a solo action prosecuting his or her rights. A class action solves this problem by aggregating the relatively paltry potential recoveries into something worth someone's (usually an attorney's) labor.[7]

---

[6] *Deposit Guaranty Bank v Roper*, 445 US 326, 339 (1980).

[7] *Amchem*, 521 US at 617, quoting *Mace v Van Ru Credit Corp.*, 109 F3d 338, 344 (7th Cir 1997). *Amchem*, as will be developed below, is distinct from this classic rendition of the class action. While all class actions seek economies of scale, the newer, more aggressive

That such an agent is necessary, however, does not answer the question whether any particular agent is acting properly, or whether a presumption of legitimacy should attach to that agent's decision making, or whether the system of taxation and the burdens of sacrifice are equitably distributed. As in democratic theory more broadly, that separate question of governmental legitimacy is extremely problematic. In fact, as I will argue below, it is the governance question that is emerging at the heart of the most troublesome class action cases of late, even in cases in which the need for collective prosecution is relatively clear. The key to the recent class action cases, I will argue, is that it is the governmental structures of a class action that define whether representative litigation can satisfy the constitutional requirements of due process.

Unfortunately, disaggregating the collective action inquiry from the governance problem will not yield a bright line test for either the propriety of class certification or for the structure of administration of the class action. Instead, it will identify the complicated factors which need to be weighed in striking a balance between forging a workable group action and securing the precarious interests of nonparticipating litigants. Moreover, a specific focus on the governance of the class action brings into sharper relief the core difficulty in the functional analysis developed by the Court in *Amchem* and *Ortiz*. In attempting to control abusive class action practice from within the loose standards of Rule 23 of the Federal Rules of Civil Procedure, the Court identifies rather than fully explains the potential mischief in the class action settlements it condemns. By focusing more clearly on these cases as governance problems, the Court's analysis may be reconceptualized as a classic principal-agent problem in which there are insufficient checks on opportunistic or self-serving behavior by the agents.

The claim here is not that the Court is unaware of the problem of class action governance or that it does not comprehend the dangers of opportunism or outright betrayal of the interests of absent class members. Rather, it is that the Court's reluctant return to rules formalism at the end of the day in both *Amchem* and *Ortiz* obscures the otherwise extremely positive development of a due

---

23(b)(3) class actions, particularly in the tort context, are purely creatures of efficiency. In mass tort class actions, many if not most of the claimed injuries would warrant individual prosecution as conventional tort claims but for the overlap in trial presentation and the corresponding strain on limited judicial resources.

process–based analysis for the law of representative actions.[8] This due process approach rests the propriety of class certification on the guarantees of loyalty of the agents for the absent class members (first and foremost class counsel) to those whose rights must ultimately be adjudicated in absentia. By contrast to the rules formalism evident in both *Amchem*, with regard to the technical requirement of manageability for certification under Rule 23(b)(3), and *Ortiz*, concerning the requirement of a truly limited fund for certification under Rule 23(b)(1), both opinions also apply a highly functional analysis to the adequacy of representation determination of whether the absent principals were loyally served by their agents. In turn, while adequacy of representation is part of the rule-based certification inquiry under 23(a)(4), this article will suggest that once the governance issue is examined independently, it forms part of a robust due process tradition linking the current class action cases to more distant predecessors such as *Hansberry v Lee*[9] and *Martin v Wilks*.[10]

The remainder of my argument will proceed in three sections. The first will discuss the problem of virtual representation in the class action context and the strategies to curb its abuse. The most extreme version arises in any mandatory class action setting, in which class members are denied the ability to opt out, even as a purely formal matter. The denial of even a modicum of individual class member control over submergence in a collective action explains and fully justifies the Court's refusal in *Ortiz* to allow an easing of the standards for the invocation of Rule 23(b)(1) limited fund actions. But the problem is not limited to the mandatory class action setting, as the next section will illustrate. Class actions almost invariably come into being through the actions of lawyers— in effect, it is the agents who create the principals—and will not emerge without some protection of the entrepreneurial initiative of those lawyers. How then should the lawyer-entrepreneurs be checked? A number of commentators have proposed mechanisms that align themselves along the familiar continuum of exit (an in-

---

[8] The antecedents of this approach can be found in the requirement that a judgment is entitled to full faith and credit only insofar as it satisfies the "minimum procedural requirements" of due process. *Kremer v Chemical Construction Co.*, 456 US 461, 481 (1982). See also *Hansberry v Lee*, 311 US 32 (1940).

[9] 311 US 32 (1940).

[10] 490 US 755 (1989).

alienable right to opt out[11]), voice (a commensurate right to intervene and participate[12]), and loyalty (the view of the class action as
an "entity,"[13] or governed by the same terms as if there had been
an ex ante contract,[14] or a structured auction,[15] or as protected
through an intermediary[16]) as strategies to protect the absent class
members. While attentive to these concerns, the Court in *Amchem*
and *Ortiz* has nonetheless chosen a functional approach focusing
on the presence of conflict in the duty of representation. The final
section will look at the types of cases in which this conflict issue
is posed to suggest how the functional balance may be applied.

I. The Problem Presented: The Rise and Fall of the Mass Tort Settlement Class

A. THE LITIGATION MORASS

There is little doubt that courts are besieged by the "elephantine
mass of asbestos cases," as colorfully framed by *Ortiz*.[17] These cases

---

[11] See Mark C. Weber, *A Consent-Based Approach to Class Action Settlement: Improving Amchem Products, Inc. v. Weber*, 59 Ohio St L J 1155, 1193, 1201 (1998). See also John C. Coffee, Jr., *Class Wars: The Dilemma of the Mass Tort Class Action*, 95 Colum L Rev 1343, 1465 (1995) (noting the importance of the right to opt out in mass tort cases); Samuel Issacharoff, *Class Action Conflicts*, 30 UC Davis L Rev 805, 833 (1997) (endorsing the importance of the right to opt out as signaling rival lawyers that a deal is in the works, as well as avoiding illegitimate Star Chamber secrecy in judicial processes).

[12] See Patrick Woolley, *Rethinking the Adequacy of Adequate Representation*, 75 Tex L Rev 571, 602–03 (1997).

[13] See David L. Shapiro, *Class Actions: The Class as Party and Client*, 73 Notre Dame L Rev 913, 958–59 (1998).

[14] See Charles Silver and Lynn Baker, *I Cut, You Choose: The Role of Plaintiffs' Counsel in Allocating Settlement Proceeds*, 84 Va L Rev 1465, 1466 (1998).

[15] See Jonathan R. Macey and Geoffrey P. Miller, *The Plaintiffs' Attorney's Role in Class Action and Derivative Litigation: Economic Analysis and Recommendations for Reform*, 58 U Chi L Rev 1, 105–16 (1991).

[16] See Susan P. Koniak, *Feasting While the Widows Weep: Georgine v. Amchem Products, Inc.*, 80 Cornell L Rev 1045, 1092 (1995) (proposing use of a guardian ad litem to protect interests of absent class members against potential collusive behavior by class counsel); Eric D. Green, *What Will We Do When Adjudication Ends? We'll Settle in Bunches: Bringing Rule 23 into the Twenty-First Century*, 44 UCLA L Rev 1773, 1796–97 (1997) (advocating early appointment of ad litem, by a professor who served as the guardian ad litem for the class in *Ortiz*).

[17] 119 S Ct at 2302. Estimates of the number of workers occupationally exposed to asbestos range from 13 to 21 million. *Report of the Judicial Conference Ad Hoc Committee on Asbestos Litigation* 6–7 (1991). In dissent in *Ortiz*, Justice Breyer adds that 80,000 new federal cases have been filed in the past decade, 10,000 in the last year alone. 119 S Ct at 2324 (Breyer, J, dissenting). The spiral of new asbestos claims is not expected to peak for another decade.

are conceptually quite daunting. On the one hand, the various harms emerging from asbestos exposure are a classic individual tort claim arising from a defective product. Plaintiffs in such cases will claim all manner of individual specific harms, including not only the pain and suffering occasioned by asbestos-related disease, but also the full range of attendant injuries from lost income to loss of consortium. At the same time, the sheer volume of these cases yields a remarkably specific valuation of each new claim based upon the rich data set of prior cases. This experience of several decades of asbestos litigation makes individual trials in each new case generally superfluous and inevitably wasteful. In the new *lingua franca* of complex litigation, asbestos is the paradigmatic "mature tort"[18] in which all the theories of liability, defense, assumption of risk, state of the art, contributory hazards, and expert wizardry have been played out in trial after trial in courts across the country.[19] The difficulty for any kind of aggregative resolution of asbestos claims lies in the tension between the prototypically individual nature of the legal claim and compensable harm, on the one hand, and the volume of claims and predictability of the value of each claim on the other. The highly variegated, individualized nature of the harm runs counter to the requirements of claim cohesion required for class certification, while the volume of claims takes asbestos-related disease very far from the conception of a randomized harm that underlies customary tort litigation.

For a mature mass tort, of which asbestos is the prototype, there is a fundamental tension between the aggregate question of liability and the individualized issue of damages. In order to understand the difficulties encountered in *Amchem* and particularly in *Ortiz*, it is necessary to put the aggregate treatment of asbestos claims in context. The Supreme Court's confrontation with mass asbestos claims follows several frustrated efforts to cut through the mass asbestos docket by Judge Robert Parker, who at the time was a very able trial judge hailing from what has been termed the "fertile

---

[18] See *Castano v American Tobacco Co*, 84 F3d 734 (5th Cir 1996) (defining the concept of a mass tort and rejecting a cigarette smokers' class action, inter alia, on the basis that the claims and defenses had not matured through sufficient individual trials).

[19] Thus, by the time of *Ortiz*, Justice Souter could describe the valuation of asbestos claims in the Eastern District of Texas as being of "almost mechanical regularity." 119 S Ct at 2303.

crescent of asbestos litigation," eastern Texas.[20] The first effort in
Raymark v Jenkins certified a class of all asbestos plaintiffs with
claims pending in the Eastern District of Texas for purposes of
resolving several common issues that senselessly and repeatedly demanded trial time in each individual case, such as the defendants'
repeated (and unsuccessful) invocation of the state of the art defense. While this approach withstood appellate review,[21] it accomplished very little. The sheer number of individual specific issues
that remained to be tried overwhelmed any prospect of judicial
management of the docket.[22]

Building on the partial opening to class treatment in *Raymark*,
Judge Parker then tried to extend the class action model to bring
all the pending asbestos cases into one aggregate proceeding. In
Cimino v Raymark, the class action device was used to impose a
trial management plan on all cases in the Eastern District of Texas.
The plan structured the jury questions so as to fill out essentially
the same form of basic grid structure typically relied upon by
plaintiff and defense counsel in the settlement of asbestos cases.[23]
Plaintiffs were divided into subclasses based on their disease pathology, years of exposure, and whether or not they were smokers,
and a representative subgroup of each was set for trial, with the
results to be extrapolated to all members of the subgroup.[24] That
approach was quickly and unceremoniously overturned on mandamus by the Fifth Circuit.[25] Subsequently, Judge Parker attempted
to achieve the same result by ordering the consolidation of all cases
(as opposed to class certification) and the use of sample trials to

---

[20] Judge Parker now sits on the Fifth Circuit.

[21] *Jenkins v Raymark Industries, Inc.*, 785 F2d 1034 (5th Cir 1986).

[22] See *Cimino v Raymark, Industries, Inc.*, 751 F Supp 649, 651 (ED Tex 1990). Judge
Parker estimated that even under the unrealistic assumption that the trial court could resolve
thirty cases a month, it would take over six years to try the then pending docket, leaving
untouched the 5,000 additional cases that would have been filed in the interim. Id at 652.
Moreover, Judge Parker graphically noted that during the pendency of asbestos claims in
his court, 448 of the original plaintiffs had died awaiting a trial setting. Id at 651.

[23] Id at 651.

[24] This is a thumbnail sketch of a detailed trial plan. I must disclose that I served as part
of the special master task force assembled by Judge Parker (with my colleagues at the University of Texas, Jack Ratliff, the lead master, and Charles Silver) to implement this class
action approach. For my defense of the trial plan proposed in *Cimino*, see Samuel Issacharoff, *Administering Damage Awards in Mass-Tort Litigation*, 10 Rev Litig 463 (1991)

[25] See *In re Fibreboard Corp.*, 893 F2d 706, 712 (5th Cir 1986) (holding that the district
court's trial management plan would inappropriately change Texas's substantive tort law).

extrapolate judgments on the same grid formula; that too was over-turned on appeal.[26] In each case, defendants were able to overturn the procedural innovations by invoking idealized renditions of in-dividual trials of all claims, leading Judge Parker to bemoan the growing "disparity of appreciation for the magnitude of the prob-lem" between the besieged trial courts and the more formalistic appellate bench.[27]

But the strategic twists and turns of complex litigation are not to be underestimated. For while the class action device envisioned in *Cimino* may have appeared as a "sword" to break through the litigation thicket, it soon became apparent that a class action could serve defendants as a most welcome shield against future litigation, to borrow Professor Coffee's imagery.[28] As expressed by Judge Di-ane Wood,

> The vigor with which the defense bar has often opposed class certifications might cause one to think that defendants prefer to take their cases one at a time, but that would be too simplistic a view. In fact, the existence and incidence of another exception to the general rule, the doctrine of virtual representation, sug-gests that defendants sometimes like the benefits of a group result—because it is usually defendants who argue that a new group of plaintiffs is barred from bringing an action since the plaintiff in an earlier suit was its "virtual representative."[29]

Amchem and *Ortiz* in fact both emerge from the attempt to se-cure the secular equivalent of a plenary indulgence against future challenges through the class action settlement device. In each case, the asbestos defendants initiated negotiations with the established doyens of the plaintiffs' asbestos bar;[30] in each case the objective

---

[26] See *Cimino v Raymark Industries, Inc.*, 151 F3d 297 (1998). Because *Cimino* involved all cases on file in the Eastern District of Texas, consolidation and class actions serve essentially the same ends. They both aggregate a limited domain of already filed cases in which all individuals are represented by counsel. The major representation issues present in the cre-ation of class actions with either unknown class members or class members with no contrac-tual relation to counsel are not present.

[27] *Cimino*, 751 F Supp at 651.

[28] John C. Coffee, Jr., *The Corruption of the Class Action: The New Technology of Collusion*, 80 Cornell L Rev 851, 851–52 (1995).

[29] *Tice v American Airlines*, 162 F3d 966, 968 (7th Cir 1998).

[30] See *Ortiz*, 119 S Ct at 2304; *Amchem*, 117 S Ct at 2239. The *Amchem* negotiations followed the consolidation of all asbestos cases pending in federal court (except those against firms in bankruptcy) through the Judicial Panel of Multidistrict Litigation. 117 S Ct at 2238.

was to provide structured compensation that would resolve all pending and future cases. Whereas *Amchem* did so through the apparently consensual path of Rule 23(b)(3), in which all class members retained at least the putative right to opt out,[31] *Ortiz* innovated the use of the mandatory limited fund provision of Rule 23(b)(1) to compel the unitary litigation of all claims against a company that represented that it could not discharge all its litigation liabilities.

Notwithstanding the different bases for the requested class certification, the similarities of the cases are the most striking, particularly the prospect they held out for embattled defendants of a conclusive end to asbestos litigation. Each case sought certification of a class that could not possibly be certified for trial, particularly if forced to satisfy the manageability standard of Rule 23(b)(3); each class sought to bind personal injury claimants whose claims were not yet present and who had not filed suit;[32] each case sought to overcome potentially serious variances in state law governing the underlying claims through the use of a single, undifferentiated settlement structure; and each case sought to create a representative structure for the absent class members (including the future claimants) that placed their claims under the common stewardship of the attorneys handling the claims of the already injured.[33] On this

---

[31] Of course, the right to opt out for future claimants is largely a fiction. The *Manual for Complex Litigation, Third*, states categorically that future claimants "cannot be given meaningful notice . . . and their opt-out rights (in a Rule 23(b)(3) action) may be illusory." Federal Judicial Center, *Manual for Complex Litigation, Third* § 30.45 (West, 3d ed 1995). This point is well captured by Professor Coffee: "when a mass torts class action is defined primarily to encompass future claimants, defendants can expect 'rational apathy' on the part of most class members, who have little incentive to protect themselves (and no reason to opt out with regard to injuries they have not yet experienced). This, in turn, sets the stage for a collusive settlement." Coffee, *The Corruption of the Class Action* at 855 (cited in note 28). See also Todd W. Latz, Note, *Who Can Tell The Futures? Protecting Settlement Class Members Without Notice*, 85 Va L Rev 531, 568 (1999) (rejecting idea of meaningful notice to future class members and instead focusing on the adequacy of representation as critical due process protection).

[32] Professor Marcus describes the three categories of future claimants as those who have already suffered injury but have not yet filed suit, those who have been exposed to a potentially toxic product but have not yet developed any pathology that would occasion filing suit, and those who have not yet been exposed but who, if exposed, may be predicted to develop injuries into the future. Richard L. Marcus, *They Can't Do That, Can They? Tort Reform Via Rule 23*, 80 Cornell L Rev 858, 882 (1995).

[33] The presence of future claimants raised further Article III case of controversy problems since in many jurisdictions exposure without the onset of disease was nonjusticiable. In each case, the Court circumvented this troubling subject matter jurisdiction issue by allowing the case to address class certification even in the absence of a confirmed Article III case

last point, however, the paths differ somewhat. The *Amchem* litigation used a negotiation group drawn from the existing steering committee of those presently injured to negotiate the terms of the settlement, including the intraclass tradeoffs between the present and future injured class members. The *Ortiz* litigation developed a more elaborate structure that relied on direct involvement of Judge Parker in the negotiations, the appointment of a law professor as guardian ad litem for the absent class members, and the services of a highly respected sitting Fifth Circuit judge, Patrick Higginbottham, in the unusual capacity of mediator[34] of a case that was to come before his court.[35] Nonetheless, the common question in the cases was whether the claimed "fairness" of the resulting settlement structure could be accepted as sufficiently protective of the rights of the absent class members, or whether due process compelled other structural protections in representative actions.

B. THE RE-EMERGENCE OF THE DUE PROCESS INQUIRY

The Supreme Court reversed in both cases with opinions that uneasily combined a very stringent rules-based analysis and a less developed due process component. While the Court's attention may have started with the former, it is the latter that gives force to the Court's developing case law.

In *Amchem*, the Court held that the fact of settlement, standing alone, could not substitute for the Rule 23 inquiry into the appropriate bases for certification. Instead, the use of the settlement class device required no less attention to the procedural safeguards of Rule 23 than would the certification of a class for litigation purposes. Thus, the claimed fairness of the settlement was not a suffi-

---

or controversy. According to the Court, the class issues could be addressed because "their resolution here is logically antecedent to the existence of any Article III issues . . . ." *Amchem*, 521 US at 612; see also *Ortiz*, 119 S Ct at 2307. The Court, however, did note that it was "mindful that Rule 23's requirements must be interpreted in keeping with Article III constraints . . . ." Id. The Court also showed itself willing this past Term to allow federal courts to dispose of cases on other bases, such as personal jurisdiction, even where the existence of federal subject matter jurisdiction was in question. See *Ruhrgas v Marathon Oil Co.*, 119 S Ct 1563 (1999).

[34] 119 S Ct at 2295, 2304–05.

[35] Judge Higginbotham of course recused himself when the Fibreboard litigation reached the Fifth Circuit. There is more than a touch of irony in the fact that Judge Higginbottham had been a member of the Fifth Circuit panel that issued the per curium mandamus reversing Judge Parker in the first round of *Cimino* class litigation. See *In re Fibreboard*, 893 F2d 706 (5th Cir 1986).

cient guarantee of the rights of absent class members since, presumably, the protections present in Rule 23 had not been applied. The easiest application of this approach would have been to condemn the proposed *Amchem* settlement class because of both its internal divisions and its incorporation of highly idiosyncratic claims of individual harm, both of which would have precluded the case serving as a class action in the customary litigation setting. But the Court stumbled a bit in holding that lower courts need not address the manageability of class actions for trial, pursuant to Rule 23(b)(3)(D), since by definition there would be no trial of a proposed settlement class.[36]

This tension in reasoning was made worse by the Court's simultaneous admonition that the evil to be avoided in the settlement class context was an abstract valuation of a class settlement outside the testing of the claims through the adversarial process.[37] Since claims that cannot credibly be taken to trial cannot, of necessity, be tested in adversarial processes, the Court's opinion left some puzzlement. Any settlement class that does not emerge from an adversarial posture in which there is at least a threat of going to trial must, by definition, arise from the agreement of the parties. Taken one step further, a class that cannot be formed for litigation purposes and exists only as a settlement vehicle exists by the good graces of the defendant—almost the very definition of nonadversarial relations. Had the Court pursued this line of inquiry slightly further it would have followed that a class cannot be represented by an attorney agent who owes his leadership of the class to the acquiescence of the adversary rather than the zealous representation of the class. Instead, the Court halted the inquiry by stating that its construction of the Rule 23 inquiry was mandated by the Rule itself and that federal courts lack the capacity to alter this inquiry outside of the formal rule drafting processes.[38]

Despite the retreat to rules formalism, the key issue after *Amchem* remained whether under any scenario a class action that could not have been litigated would not necessarily result in "disarmed" class counsel. Perhaps, as I shall suggest in discussing *Matsushita* below, counsel would not be disarmed by the inability to certify

---

[36] 521 US at 620.

[37] Id at 620–22.

[38] Id at 621.

a litigation class *if and only if* they retained a credible trial threat in that or another jurisdiction, either in some aggregative capacity or through repeated individual trials. Under this approach, the issue would not turn so much on the fact that the class could not be certified for trial as the reason it could not be certified. An inability to certify because of a jurisdictional problem in the particular court before which settlement approval is sought would not necessarily doom the representation afforded as per se "disarmed." On the other hand, an inability to certify that revealed a fundamental tension in the treatment afforded different sectors of the class, or an inability to certify that reflected that portions of the class were unrepresented, would raise barriers to the approval of a settlement class. Such an approach would not have overcome the problem in the certification of the *Amchem* settlement class since prospectively injured class members could not maintain such an independent threat to defendants, and since they were unrepresented except through the creation of the settlement class. Regardless of the applicability to the facts of *Amchem*, the tension between certifiability for settlement and the ability to try a case as a litigation class remained unexplored through the *Amchem* decision.

Ortiz presented a slightly more complicated picture because of the invocation of the Rule 23(b)(1) limited fund. From the vantage point of proponents of a settlement, Rule 23(b)(1) holds two key advantages. First, there is no individual right to opt out, so that all claims may be extinguished with certainty. Second, Rule 23(b)(1) does not trigger judicial inquiry into the manageability of a class action at trial or the predominance of common issues over individual issues.[39] Because of the requirement that there in fact be a limited fund, Rule 23(b)(1) was rarely invoked until the rise of the settlement class action in the 1990s. The *Fibreboard* defendants offered two novel theories for the invocation of the mandatory participation of the class in a limited fund: first, that it could not possibly ever pay off all the asbestos claims that confronted the company, and second, that the company's main asset was its ongoing litigation claim to substantial but contested insurance coverage. Having struck a deal with its insurers, Fibreboard sought to offer

---

[39] These are required under Rule 23(b)(3) for class actions organized for efficiency reasons.

closure in exchange for the certainty of $2 billion worth of insurance coverage.[40] The purported benevolence of Fibreboard's ability to tender its insurance coverage was somewhat mitigated by the fact that the company would pay only $500,000 of its own money, despite a net worth in excess of $200 million.[41]

Justice Souter's opinion, like that of Justice Ginsburg in *Amchem*, proceeded along two fronts. First, Souter carefully traced the historical antecedents for modern Rule 23(b)(1) to find that three distinctive features of the Rule's pedigree were missing: the claims against Fibreboard were not liquidated, Fibreboard did not devote the entirety of its assets to satisfying its claimants, and the plaintiffs were not joined by a common theory of recovery that insured the equitable treatment as among themselves.[42] While not conclusively holding that such a limited fund could never be allowed, Souter opined that "the greater the leniency in departing form the historical limited fund model, the greater the likelihood of abuse. . . ."[43] The abuse is then defined, as in *Amchem*, by the fact that the class is hopelessly riven by internal divisions between present and future claimants,[44] and that the representation could not be presumed adequate since it lacked the essential elements of "parties of equal knowledge and bargaining skill agree[ing] upon the figure through arms-length bargaining, unhindered by any considerations tugging against the interests of the parties ostensibly represented in the negotiations."[45] This alone should have sufficed for the Court's holding since adequate representation under these circumstances would require, at a minimum, "independently represented sub-

---

[40] 119 S Ct at 2295, 2304–05. In what must surely be one of the most ornate, if not baroque, legal maneuvers ever attempted, the insurers in turn hoped to use their obligation to the Fibreboard class to claim limited funds of their own and in turn force a compelled class action of all present and future claimants against them. In effect, the *Ortiz* litigation was the opening salvo in an attempt to create a mounting edifice of limited funds that would close out all asbestos litigation.

[41] See *In re Asbestos Litigation*, 90 F3d 963, 993 (5th Cir 1998) (Smith, J, dissenting).

[42] *Ortiz*, 119 S Ct at 2308–11.

[43] Id at 2313.

[44] Id. Presumably this issue had been laid to rest in *Amchem*. Nonetheless, the Fifth Circuit reaffirmed its holding after a remand from the Supreme Court following *Amchem*. The Fifth Circuit nonetheless reaffirmed its ruling in a five paragraph per curium opinion, *In re Asbestos Litigation*, 134 F 3d 668 (5th Cir 1998), which prompted Professor Tribe's memorable opening in his petition for certiorari, "Some people just can't take a hint." *Ortiz v Fibreboard*, Petition for Writ of Certiorari 1 (1998).

[45] 119 S Ct at 2301.

classes,"[46] which were not present. If further pursued, as I shall argue below, this latter point should have subsumed the entire rule-based limited fund discussion. Instead, the Court retreated to a claimed inability to reform the standard for 23(b)(1) certification, a point driven home by the concurrence of Chief Justice Rehnquist, who stressed the Court's inability to act absent a formal amendment of the Federal Rules of Civil Procedure.[47]

The retreat to rules formalism in both *Amchem* and *Ortiz* is unfortunate because it implies that the failure to resort to the formal processes of rule amendment is what doomed the proposed settlement class resolution of asbestos litigation.[48] First off, the invocation of the failure of the Federal Rules to allow for the challenged procedures is somewhat disingenuous given that the rules amendment process is in fact as much the product of Court action as is case law.[49] The reliance on rules formalism undercuts the force of the Court's observations on the failure of representation in *Amchem* and *Ortiz*. This effectively opens the door to Justice Breyer's dissent in both *Amchem* and *Ortiz*, in which he treats the proposed settlement class actions as the functional equivalent of an administrative agency and fails to distinguish the presumed dispassionate administrative expertise of an agency from the self-interested behavior of the parties who put together the proposed asbestos settlements.

Second, the retreat to rules formalism implies that had the formal rules amendment process been followed, Justice Breyer's endorsement of the resolution in *Ortiz* would have carried the day— a proposition very nearly endorsed by Chief Justice Rehnquist. Reliance on the rules amendment issue deprives the majorities in both *Amchem* and *Ortiz* of the overriding ability to challenge the

---

[46] Id at 2323.

[47] Id at 2324.

[48] This is clearest in the concurring opinion of Chief Justice Rehnquist in *Ortiz*, in which he states, on behalf of Justices Scalia and Kennedy, that he would join the dissent of Justice Breyer, but for the failure of the rules to have been amended to allow for the proposed settlement class. 119 S Ct at 2324.

[49] See Charles Alan Wright and Arthur R. Miller, 4 *Federal Practice and Procedure* § 1001 (2d ed 1986) (noting that "[t]he existing situation . . . may be described as judicial rulemaking pursuant to a legislative delegation and subject to a congressional veto") and § 1008 (noting that "The federal courts now are largely self-governing in procedural matters, with rulemaking powers limited only by their own sense of justice, sensible considerations of public policy, and the possibility of congressional veto.").

legitimacy of the class action to assume the role of a state agency, rather than serving as a nonaccountable imposition of a resolution on nonparticipating and, in some cases, not yet existing class members. But more centrally, the rules formalism obscures what the Court has actually accomplished in *Amchem* and *Ortiz*.[50]

The fundamental strength of *Amchem* and *Ortiz* inheres in the subtle revisitation of the law governing due process in the resolution of representative actions.[51] The Court redefines due process to focus centrally on the faithfulness of the agent that has litigated on behalf of the absent class members, what Rule 23 terms the "adequacy of representation," and in turn addresses the conditions under which legal rights of nonparticipants in litigation may be conclusively terminated.

Contrary to the Court's invocation of the formal rules amendment process, what emerges is in fact a much more limited role for the rules-based certification inquiry. Instead, the rules inquiry is reconstructed as ultimately being best addressed to the conditions that call for aggregate treatment of the perceived class injury. This is entirely consistent with the formal structure of Rule 23, which directs the bulk of a district court's inquiry to the features of the dispute that occasion the need for collective action, as exemplified by the numerosity and common question inquiry of 23(a) and the predominance and manageability concerns of 23(b)(3).

---

[50] I leave aside for the moment the inconsistent result in *Matsushita*.

[51] There is a consistent though muted strain in class action law focusing on the attorneys as the guarantors of adequacy of representation. See, e.g., *In re General Motors Corp. Engine Interchange Litigation*, 594 F2d 1106 (1979) (trial court has continuing duty to undertake stringent examination of adequate representation by named class representatives and their counsel at all stages of litigation); *General Telephone Co. v Falcon*, 457 US 147, 158 (1982) ("The adequacy of representation requirement . . . also raises concerns about the competency of class counsel and conflicts of interest."); *Nilsson v Couglin*, 670 F Supp 1186 (SDNY 1987) (discussing necessity for adequate/qualified class counsel for class action). On several occasions, class action status has been denied because of inadequacy of counsel. See, e.g., *Shields v Valley Nat'l Bank*, 56 FRD 448 (D Ariz 1971); *Anderson v Moorer*, 372 F2d 747 (5th Cir 1967). See generally *Newberg on Class Actions*, ch 3 (". . . in the usual case when the plaintiff has no conflict with the class, courts focus primarily on class counsel, not on the plaintiff, to determine if there will be vigorous prosecution of the class action . . . . Apart from special circumstances involving the class representative, the primary focus of the vigorous prosecution aspect of the adequacy test is on counsel for the class."); Note, *The Class Representative: The Problem of Absent Plaintiffs*, 68 Nw U L Rev 1133, 1136 (1974) ("the single most important factor considered by the courts in determining the quality of the representatives' ability and willingness to advocate the cause of the class has been the caliber of the plaintiff's attorney. It is well settled that the lawyer must be 'qualified, experienced, and generally able to conduct the proposed litigation'.").

The issue that emerges at the forefront of the Court's recent cases, however, is the question of governance, and the requirement that there be adequacy of representation for absent class members before they may be bound to a proceeding in which the had no individual ability to participate. While this requirement is present in the Rules, it is in fact a restatement of a fundamental tenet of constitutional due process. There is no reason to believe, either as a matter of rules craftsmanship or case law or policy, that the concept of adequate representation present in the rules is anything other than the level of constitutional protection of absent class member interests necessary to deem their virtual participation in litigation fundamentally fair. If this thesis is correct, it follows that the Court's invocation of its claimed inability to modify the application of the Federal Rules through case law rather than the rules enabling procedure is misplaced. The Court is, in effect, explicating the constitutional standards for nonparticipant representation sufficient to bind nonparticipants to the outcome of litigation, by settlement or otherwise.[52] As expressed by Professor Owen Fiss, the emerging constitutional standard guarantees "not a right of participation, but rather . . . a 'right of representation': not a day in court but the right to have one's interest adequately represented."[53]

II. GROUPS AND THE LIMITS ON INDIVIDUAL SELF-DETERMINATION

A. THE CENTRAL ROLE OF REPRESENTATION

It is not simply the Court's misplaced reliance on the rules amendment process that clouds the issues in the difficult settlement class cases. Rather, the very structure of the Rule 23 inquiry distracts courts from what is significant in the representation of absent class members. Following the template of Rule 23(a), courts

---

[52] This is made express in *Hansberry*, 311 US at 42–43.

[53] Owen M. Fiss, *The Allure of Individualism*, 78 Iowa L Rev 965, 970–71 (1993). To formulate the inquiry in this fashion does not resolve what the level of adequacy must be. For instance, Professor Fiss and I disagree on the application of subsequent preclusion to non-class members whose claims were affected by a class consent decree in *Martin v Wilks*. Compare Fiss, supra, with Samuel Issacharoff, *When Substance Mandates Procedure: Martin v. Wilks and the Rights of Vested Incumbents in Civil Rights Consent Decrees*, 77 Cornell L Rev 189 (1992).

must first inquire under 23(a)(3) whether the named plaintiff is "typical" of the class.[54] This rather amorphous requirement either devolves into inquiring simply whether the named plaintiff has an interest sufficiently adverse to the defendant, or more characteristically merges into the 23(a)(4) requirement of adequacy of representation.[55] The focus on the named plaintiff then leads to a misdirected inquiry into the role of the named class representative in protecting the rights of the absent class members. This ignores the fact known to all participants in class actions (courts no doubt included) that "class representatives often are recruited by class counsel, play no client role whatsoever, and—when deposed to test the adequacy of representation—commonly show no understanding of their litigation."[56] Instead, "[c]lass actions often are lawyer actions. Adequacy of representation is measured first and foremost by the adequacy of counsel."[57] To the extent that the Rules direct courts to focus on the named class parties, they provide what is at best a distraction from the real source of legitimacy in class actions: the incentives for faithful representation by class counsel.[58]

The peculiarly resilient focus on the named class plaintiffs is not, however, simply a by-product of the rule-created menu by which the 23(a)(3) typicality inquiry is frontloaded by what the Rule defines as a "prerequisite" to class certification. Rather, there

---

[54] The better formulation is that the claims or defenses of the named plaintiff be representative of the class. See *General Telephone Co. v Falcon*, 457 US at 147 (1982) (rejecting across-the-board class certification and requiring that named plaintiff have claim common to absent class members).

[55] For a discussion of the limited case law success with defining 23(a)(3), see Issacharoff, *Administering Damage Awards* at 463 (cited in note 24).

[56] Edward H. Cooper, *The (Cloudy) Future of Class Actions*, 40 Ariz L Rev 923, 927 (1998). This theme was developed in the academic literature by Professor Coffee. See John C. Coffee, Jr., *The Regulation of Entrepreneurial Litigation: Balancing Fairness and Efficiency in the Large Class Action*, 54 U Chi L Rev 877, 899 ("From a policy perspective, the choice is between truth and illusion. We could continue to pretend that the class representative is the true party in interest, or we could recognize the reality of the attorney as entrepreneur."). See also Silver and Baker at 1489 (cited in note 14) ("Attorneys, not named plaintiffs, control what happens in class actions"); Issacharoff, *Class Action Conflicts* at 828–29 (cited in note 11).

[57] Cooper at 927 (cited in note 56).

[58] This is a theme that is emerging in some of the commentary on the recent class action cases. See, e.g., Shapiro at 958–59 (cited in note 13) ("the constitutional propriety of class action treatment . . . turns on the issue of adequate representation" which in turn must focus "on the adequacy of counsel (rather than worrying about the named representative))"; Coffee, *Class Wars*, at 1348–52 (cited in note 11) (analyzing reasons for class member passivity in class actions).

remains significant tension over the status of absent class members in representative litigation.[59] The core conception is that class actions are representative actions in which only the named parties are parties as that concept is traditionally understood. The Supreme Court in *Phillips Petroleum v Shutts*, to take the most notable example, appeared to protect the right of class members to remain independent of the conduct of the class action.[60] The Court held that, at least for purposes of establishing jurisdiction, absent class plaintiffs need not be given due process protections as rigorous as those afforded out-of-state defendants.[61] Absent class members may not be assessed costs should their interests fail in litigation and they are not automatically subject to discovery and other obligations of parties.[62] In sum, "an absent class-action plaintiff is not required to do anything."[63]

But this cannot possibly be the end of the inquiry. In other critical respects, absent class members must be treated as parties. If this were not so, then a class action would have no conclusive effects for any individuals beyond the named parties; as the Supreme Court held in *Martin v Wilks*, "[a] judgment or decree among parties to a lawsuit resolves issues as among them, but it does not conclude the rights to strangers to those proceedings."[64] Yet the very essence of the class action device is its capacity to bring closure to claims that stretch beyond the named parties. In effect, the class action must take on an existence apart from the named class representatives. Indeed, it is well established in the class action case law that the death or withdrawal of the class representative will not terminate the class action; the action survives following a right to substitute class representatives.[65] The key question in the class action context is what imparts legitimacy to the actions of the rep-

---

[59] For a leading early discussion of this point, see Diane Wood Hutchinson, *Class Actions: Joinder or Representational Device?* 1983 Supreme Court Review 459.

[60] *Phillips Petroleum Co. v Shutts*, 472 US 797 (1985).

[61] *Shutts*, 472 US at 808.

[62] See Charles Alan Wright, et al, 7B *Federal Practice and Procedure* § 1796.1 (2d ed 1986); *Manual for Complex Litigation, Third*, § 21.1–21.4 (cited in note 31) (summarizing judicial experience as requiring no automatic entitlement by a defendant to take discovery of absent class members).

[63] *Shutts*, 472 US at 810.

[64] 490 US at 762.

[65] See *Sosna v Iowa*, 419 US 393 (1975).

resentative who seeks judicial approval for a decree that will bind the nonparticipating class members. Somehow, the process of creating and monitoring a class action must distinguish it from the facts of *Martin*,[66] in which parties to a bipolar lawsuit sought judicial enforcement of a consent decree that would bind truly nonparticipating third parties.[67]

Thus, the rule-based initial focus on the typicality of the named parties does little to elucidate the overriding issue of due process. Rule 23 can certify that the named plaintiffs can stand as nominal representatives for the absent class members. But, it cannot treat these absent class members as genuinely independent from the proceedings, as the Court did with the third-party antagonists in *Martin*. At the end of the day, the question is whether it is fair to allow the actual representatives to speak for the absent class members, and thereby conclude the dispute. In turn, "[w]hether a class suit decree has binding effects on the class goes to the essence of the class suit device."[68]

To bind individuals not joined in their individual capacity requires imparting some organic quality to the class action. It is of course the case that "[t]he law can regard any person either as a member of a group or as a legally distinct individual."[69] But the law of class actions appears to attempt to do both at once. Absent

---

[66] In *Martin*, a civil rights challenge to discriminatory hiring practices in the Birmingham, Alabama, fire department ended in a consent decree between black firefighters and the city. The decree provided for a restructuring of promotional rules that were in force through a collective bargaining agreement between the city and the overwhelmingly white firefighters' union. The issue in the case was whether the consent decree would foreclose any union legal challenge to the continued enforceability of the union contract. The Court held that nonparties to the class action consent decree could not be bound to its outcome, even if they were offered the possibility of expressing objection at the approval hearing. *Martin v Wilks*, 490 US 755 (1989). For an extended defense of the Court's holding in *Martin*, see Issacharoff, *When Substance Mandates Procedure* (cited in note 53).

[67] I have previously argued at length that viewed in this fashion, the decision in *Martin* was compelled by fundamental due process concerns. See Issacharoff, *When Substance Mandates Procedure* (cited in note 53).

[68] Geoffrey C. Hazard, Jr., et al, *An Historical Analysis of the Binding Effect of Class Suits*, 146 U Pa L Rev 1849, 1850 (1998). Professor Hazard and his collaborators continue:

> The key legal question for the class suit therefore has been whether, where the judgment in such a suit is adverse to members who were actual parties, the judgment would be not merely discouraging to absentees, but preclusive against them as a matter of law—whether the rule of bar applies to absent class members.

Id at 1850–51.

[69] Id at 1852.

class plaintiffs are both members of a judicially approved collective body and yet stand apart in terms of actual participation and control over the management of that collective body. It is for this reason that recent scholarship has begun to gnaw at the underdeveloped concept of representative actions and has instead begun to view the class action as an "entity" once certified, to use Professor David Shapiro's term.[70]

What follows from the recognition that a class action, once created, takes on a significant institutional life of its own, much as do other legally sanctified entities ranging from corporations, to partnerships, to marriages, and so forth? Does it follow that the individual in the class must "tie his fortunes to those of the group with respect to the litigation, its progress, and its outcome"?[71] In light of the Court's emerging due process jurisprudence, the answer is that simply recognizing the class as some form of entity does not suffice to establish the legitimacy of how this newly created entity is governed. Rather, class action law must give further attention to the relation between the individuals who comprise the collective entity and their potentially wayward agents who may deviate from the interests of the principals.[72] As a result, it cannot be sufficient to limit the judicial inquiry to the conditions precedent for the formation of such an entity, any more than the law of corporations can be truncated to review only the corporate charter and the initial requirements for filing incorporation papers. As with any legally recognized entity, there will need to be a clearer articulation of the fiduciary obligations of representatives toward the collective entity that in turn legitimate the ability of the representatives to bind the entity. Just as with corporations, the problems of governance and managerial responsiveness to the interests of the affected principals take on a legal significance that oftentimes overshadows the question of the original creation of the corporate entity.

---

[70] Shapiro at 917 (cited in note 13).

[71] Id at 919.

[72] I will primarily address this due process concern using the language of principal-agent relations. It is also possible to speak of the "moral hazard" confronting an agent whose actions (*a*) cannot be monitored by the principal, and (*b*) can realize returns under conditions at variance with the interests of the principal. See Paul Milgrom and John Roberts, *Economics, Organizations, and Management* 169 (Prentice-Hall, 1992) (analyzing principal-agent relationship in terms of moral hazard problem).

The history of class actions reveals that the law has always been centrally concerned with the legitimacy and loyalty of the agent who purports to speak for the collective body, as it must be in any case where preclusion rests upon representation. But the history also reveals that the more limited class actions of old resolved this problem by looking to preexisting representative structures to confer legitimacy on the representation undertaken by the class agent or by restricting the authority of the class agent to bind absent class members to an adverse outcome. Unfortunately, that approach is insufficient for the modern class action.

B. IDENTIFYING THE LEGITIMATE REPRESENTATIVE

Historically, class actions were of two types. The first involved situations in which no individual's claim could be resolved without a final accounting of the proportionate claims of all interested parties. In such cases, finality of all potential claims was necessary for any rights to be secured. Examples include probate and the distribution of war booty among victorious seamen demanding their spoils. In either case a distribution had to be made and no distribution could be made without closing the account books. Whatever its terms, the distribution that resulted would affect many beyond the parties that initiated the proceeding. For example, the English government encouraged private actions at sea to seize the goods on board ships of hostile nations.[73] These actions were sufficiently prevalent to lead Professor Bone to characterize these privateer actions as one of the leading historic antecedents of the modern class action.[74] Once these ships returned to port, there were strict conventions governing the distribution of booty, and the seamen could claim a legal entitlement to an accurate distribution. The courts of equity were called upon to act as the final arbiters of the accuracy of the distribution of booty and did so in a binding representative proceeding. "Non-participating crew

---

[73] See Stephen C. Yeazell, *From Medieval Group Litigation to the Modern Class Action* 182 (Yale, 1987).

[74] See Robert G. Bone, *Personal and Impersonal Litigative Forms: Reconceiving the History of Adjudicative Representation*, 70 BU L Rev 213 (1990) (reviewing Yeazell (cited in note 73)). Professor Bone characterizes the three types of suits in equity as general right, voluntary association, and privateer. Id at 236–38.

members were not allowed to challenge the final decree's determination of the total crewshare fund or the proportion to which fellow crew members were entitled."[75] As with probate, the needs of finality overwhelmed any claim to hold out for a private action.

To apply this account to the modern class action it is necessary to recast mildly the historical record mined by Professor Yeazell. Prior accounts tend to focus on the development of the bill of peace as an aggregative mechanism that allowed for the joinder of multiple claims. While this is descriptively accurate, we should focus more on the rationale for the joinder. In any of these bill of peace aggregations, the driving force is the inability to adjudicate *any* claims without implicating *all* potential claimants. The compelled quality of the adjudication then comes from two sources. The first is the well recognized problem that the inability to find some potential legatees or victorious seamen could deprive all participants of the ability to secure a distribution of their claims to the recovery. The idea here is that no one can sue unless everyone is joined—something that as a practical matter can only be done by judicial compulsion, not by individual service of process. The second, taking a more modern tack, is the fear that potential holdouts could demand unjust shares as a condition to their joinder as necessary parties[76] to a final adjudication. This form of compulsory joinder—justified by the practical inability to avoid adjudicating the rights of all in the course of adjudicating the rights of any— is carried forth in the modern rules as the compelled participation in either the limited fund of Rule 23(b)(1) or the injunctive action characteristic of Rule 23(b)(2). In its current version, these compelled class actions carry no requirement of individual notice and do not provide for the right to opt out.[77] This is because the individual claimant has no separable claim, and would have no meaningful legal remedy should she attempt to opt out. The presumption is that under a 23(b)(1) limited fund, the corpus would be

---

[75] Bone at 267 (cited in note 74).

[76] Under Justice Story's summary of equity jurisprudence, this was known as the Necessary Parties Rule. Joseph Story, *Commentaries on Equity Pleadings*, § 72-238 at 74 (2d ed 1840). For a discussion of the relaxation of the Necessary Parties Rule in equity jurisprudence, see Hazard, et al at 1878–80 (cited in note 68).

[77] Under the federal rules, the right of notice and the ability to opt out are covered by Rule 23(c)(2), which is in turn triggered only by class actions certified under Rule 23(b)(3).

exhausted by the claimants and nothing would remain for the opt out.[78] Similarly, in a 23(b)(2) injunctive decree, should the plaintiffs prevail, the defendant will already have been legally coerced into a defined course of conduct that must be applied to all similarly situated individuals.[79] These cases are not representative actions in any meaningful sense since individual claimants have no choice but to have their rights fully adjudicated in this proceeding.[80] At the same time, although these cases are not truly representative actions, they nonetheless impose a form of virtual representation since the direction of the litigation will not be controlled by the individual claimants. They are compelled participation cases whose coerced quality is justified by the inability for any legal resolution to proceed absent complete resolution. Because of the extraordinary constriction of individual rights in these cases, courts are justifiably leery of expanding the conditions under which compelled participation class action may be invoked, under either Rule 23(b)(1)[81] or under 23(b)(2).[82]

---

[78] I have previously argued that the limited fund class action should be seen as the plaintiff's equivalent of an interpleader action. See Issacharoff, *Class Action Conflicts* at 820–21 (cited in note 11). The class is created not by the interrelation among the class members but by the confines of the limited stake that would leave a corpus devoid of funds facing ongoing similar claims. In like fashion, the injunctive action is defined by the conduct of the defendant's obligation, rather than the similarly situated posture of the plaintiff class; indeed, Rule 23(b)(2) takes as its core the idea that the class is defined by the fact that "the party opposing the class has acted or refused to act on grounds generally applicable to the class, thereby making appropriate final injunctive relief or corresponding declaratory relief with respect to the class as a whole. . . ."

[79] Thus, for example, in a voting rights class action challenging at-large municipal elections, a defendant municipality is either compelled to alter its system of elections or it is not. It would make no sense to order the defendant to hold districted elections for the victorious class members but continue its prior electoral system for those that opted out.

[80] At best, objecting class members may intervene through independent counsel. But that does not obviate the fact that their rights will be adjudicated as part of the class proceeding.

[81] This is well captured in *Ortiz*, in which the Court holds the "greater the leniency in departing from the historical limited fund model, the greater the likelihood of abuse in ways that will be apparent when we apply the limited fund criteria to the case before us. The prudent course, therefore, is to presume that when subdivision (b)(1)(B) was devised to cover limited fund actions, the object was to stay close to the historical model." 119 S Ct at 2313.

[82] The clearest example of this comes in *Allison v Citgo Petroleum*, 151 F3d 402 (5th Cir 1998). As a result of the Civil Rights Act of 1991, plaintiffs in employment discrimination claims were entitled to legal damages for harms that included emotional distress and other characteristically individual issues. The Fifth Circuit held that the introduction of these prototypically individual claims took a Title VII claim out of the mold of the civil right injunctive case that had routinely been certified under 23(b)(2) and required more fine-grained evaluation under Rule 23(b)(3). Id at 425.

It follows that the most difficult governance problems emerge when there is not the capacity, even in theory, for the principal to reject proposed representation by an agent. This is the consequence of the mandatory class action, in which the elimination of the right to opt out compels representation with only the difficult promise of the right to protest as a check on agent misbehavior. Nonetheless, this form of nonselective representation is not unique, but forms a subset of the broader problem of "virtual representation" that is present whenever a party is granted the right to bind another to the outcome of a legal decision. As defined in one leading case, such virtual representation is proper when a person "though not a party" is so situated that "one of the parties to the suit is so closely aligned with his interests as to be his virtual representative."[83] The concept of virtual representation in modern jurisprudence is most evident in fields in which the imperative need for finality overwhelms the customary presumption that each individual is entitled to his or her day in court.[84] Thus the concept of virtual representation emerges from the field of probate proceedings, in which "it is often necessary to establish a procedure that will bind persons unknown, unascertained, or not yet born."[85] While oftentimes invoked, the expansion of virtual representation would run strongly counter to the idea of a legal claim as a *chose in action* to which the right of ownership and control would normally attach.[86] Rather, the doctrine is invoked in extraordinary circumstances, as when one party actually controls the litigation efforts of another despite not having formal party status in the first proceeding.[87]

---

[83] *Aerojet-General Corp. v Askew*, 511 F2d 710, 719 (5th Cir 1975).

[84] See *Martin*, 490 US at 762 ("our 'deep-rooted historic tradition that everyone should have his own day in court'"), quoting Charles Alan Wright, et al, 18 *Federal Practice & Procedure* § 4449, at 417 (1981); *Hansberry*, 311 US at 40 (tracing the principle in "Anglo-American jurisprudence that one is not bound by a judgment in personam in a litigation in which he is not designated as a party or to which he has not been made a party by service of process").

[85] Wright, et al, 18 *Federal Practice and Procedure* § 4457 at 494.

[86] This is elaborated by Patrick Woolley into a defense of the right of participation for all individuals holding a legal claim, even in the class action context. See Woolley at 602–03 (cited in note 12).

[87] "All of the cases that in fact preclude relitigation by a nonparty have involved several factors in addition to apparently adequate litigation by a party holding parallel interests." Wright, et al, § 4457 (1998 Supp) at 420. As noted by the Seventh Circuit, "[e]xamples of these additional factors include control or participation in the earlier litigation, acquiescence, deliberate maneuvering to avoid the effects of the first case, or the close relationship

The prime modern exception is of course the class action, as it has been historically. But class actions continue to draw a very fine and problematic distinction between the nonparty status of the absent class members and their capacity to be subject to preclusion by the outcome of the litigation. Even the much invoked Supreme Court protection of absent class members in *Hansberry v Lee*[88] does not disturb this uneasy line between limited participation and potential complete preclusion. Rather, *Hansberry* compels greater attention to the procedural protections for the representation of the class, as now embodied in modern Rule 23, prior to allowing rights to be conclusively disposed of through class action litigation.[89] Indeed, courts rejecting the application of virtual representation preclusion outside the class action context invoke the procedural safeguards of Rule 23 as the precondition for permissible preclusion without participation.[90]

---

between the parties to the various cases." *Tice v American Airlines*, 162 F3d 966, 971 (7th Cir 1998). See, e.g., *Tyus v Schoemehl*, 93 F3d 449, 454–56 (8th Cir 1996) (adding that the doctrine is more appropriate in public law cases); *NAACP v Metropolitan Council*, 125 F3d 1171, 1175 (8th Cir 1997), vacated, 118 S Ct 1162 reinstated, 144 F3d 1168 (8th Cir 1998); *Bittinger v Tecumseh Products Co.*, 123 F3d 877, 881 (6th Cir 1997); *Collins v E.I. DuPont de Nemours & Co.*, 34 F3d 172, 175–78 (3d Cir 1994); see also Wright, et al, 18 *Federal Practice and Procedure: Jurisdiction* § 4457, at 502.

[88] 311 US 32 (1940).

[89] At other levels, *Hansberry* continues to be a problematic case. The issue before the Court was whether a racially restricting covenant would be enforced. The suit was brought on behalf of a prospective black purchaser of a home in an all-white section of Chicago. A previous attempt to rent to a black family had resulted in a class action by the homeowners' association, purporting to represent all homeowners seeking to enforce the covenant. That suit was successful, although there were apparently significant factual errors relevant to both the basis for class treatment and the enforceability of the covenant. Despite the Court's assumption that the covenant, if properly implemented, was enforceable, the Court treated the Hansberrys' interest in the purchase as an individual right rather than as an interest running with the land. In the former case, clearly the interests of the would-be black purchasers could not have been adequately represented by the all-white homeowners' association. But if the issue was the enforceability of the covenant as written, then both the seller and buyer in proposed later transactions would be bound by their predecessors in interest in the property. It is entirely possible that the Court finessed this point to avoid upholding an offensive racial covenant during World War II. But two parts of *Hansberry* survive nonetheless. First, the opinion makes clear that a proper class action may bind the absent class members to its outcome. 311 US 32, 41 (1940). Second, the potential misuse of the class action device requires greater procedural regularity in its application than that provided by equity practice of old. Id at 42.

[90] As expressed by Judge Diane Wood of the Seventh Circuit:

[T]he fact that virtual representation looks like a class action but avoids compliance with Rule 23 is a weakness, not a strength, of the doctrine. . . . In properly certified class actions, parties who have adequate notice and (at a minimum) an opportunity to opt out of an earlier case may, if their interests are sufficiently aligned with one

But the great modern innovation in class actions is the dramatic expansion of the efficiency-based use of aggregation under Rule 23(b)(3). Whereas early twentieth-century jurisprudence would recognize the limited fund cases as what were termed "true" class actions, the cases of similar personal claims against a common defendant were termed "spurious" class actions, although the term spurious carried over to injunctive actions as well.[91] Unlike the cases that are brought into being by the unitary nature of the relief sought, these "spurious" class actions are the product of a functional compromise between equity and efficiency. The justifications for compelled participation are not present: the parties to the litigation can have their claims satisfied in the absence of nonparticipating claimants, and, by extension, no nonparticipant can extort an unjustified surplus by threatening to withhold consent to participation.

What then is the source of legitimacy for a class action to be deemed the proper mechanism to resolve the claims of absent class members? Historic practice yields two answers that are inadequate for the modern 23(b)(3) class action. In the first instance, the historic record analyzed by Professor Yeazell reveals a significant body of cases in which the representative entity preexisted the class action litigation, as with local governors bringing suit as the named representative for their citizenry.[92] In teaching this area of law, I

---

of the earlier parties, be bound by the results of that litigation. See, eg, *Hansberry v Lee*, 311 US 32 (1940); and *Phillips Petroleum Co v Shutts*, 472 US 797 (1985). This is the theory on which Rule 23 is based. The class action cases allowing preclusion after adequate notice and the opportunity to opt out recognize a form of consent that is enough to justify binding the later parties to the earlier result (again, when the other criteria such as identity of issue and interest are also satisfied).

Tice, 162 F3d at 972.

[91] This distinction is well developed in Hazard, et al, at 1919–22 (cited in note 68) (relying on Thomas Atkins Street, *Federal Equity Practice* (1909), as the best contemporary exposition of this approach). The distinction between true and spurious class actions was formally adopted in the Federal Equity Rules in 1912. Id at 1923–24. In 1938 the first Federal Rules of Civil Procedure were adopted. The original federal rules carried forth the distinction between what were termed "true," "hybrid," and "spurious" class actions. In 1966, the modern form of Rule 23 was introduced which abolished these distinctions in favor of the Rule 23(a) common characteristics of class actions and the Rule 23(b) division along the lines of relief sought in the case.

[92] Yeazell at 40 (cited in note 73) ("most medieval group litigation involved groups whose organization antedated the lawsuit itself. . . . unlike some modern collective litigation, medieval group litigation did not overcome the difficulties of organizing a group for collective action. That task had already been done").

refer to these as organic class actions so as to highlight the fact that the organizational form of the legal action precedes the particular controversy and does not raise legitimacy concerns for the court's recognition of the class agent. Thus, for example, in one famous case, the mayor of York assumed the role of representative agent on behalf of the residents of his city in a dispute with citizens of other towns concerning fishing rights in a local river.[93] For a court to recognize this representative role for the mayor did nothing more than extend an already existing political authority into the jural realm. Other similar cases recognize the role of an unincorporated association assuming the role of protector of the interests of its members, as with the members of a freemasons' lodge suing on behalf of all lodge members in an action over legal title to the lodge's possessions.[94] The search for extrinsic sources of representational legitimacy is of limited application in the much more robust world of mass actions today, for two separate reasons. First, the medieval world lent itself far more readily to identifying individuals by their status as members of a village, parish, or fraternal order[95] than does contemporary law with its focus on individual rights. Second, the nature of the claims brought to courts has changed as well. In modern 23(b)(3) class actions consisting of consumer or securities fraud claims, for instance, looking to preexisting forms of governance is simply not a meaningful option.[96]

The other mechanism for avoiding the problem of the legitimacy of class leadership is limiting the procedural scope of the class action so as not to bind absent class members to the outcome of the litigation. In premodern class actions, the litigation was truly a representative action in which the claims of the class representatives were put forward as they would be if the case were adjudicated individually. In the event of a plaintiff's victory, the absent class members could, in effect, join into the law-

---

[93] *Mayor of York v Pilkington*, 25 Eng Rep 946 (Ch 1737).

[94] *Lloyd v Loaring*, 31 Eng Rep 1302 (Ch 1802); see generally Hazard, et al, at 1874–76 (cited in note 68).

[95] See Yeazell at 52–68 (cited in note 73); Bone at 220 (cited in note 74).

[96] I will return to the attempts to use some preexisting authority to monitor the class action, as with the proposed requirement of notice of statewide class actions to the attorneys general contained in the Class Action Fairness Act of 1999, S 353, 106th Cong, or the attempt to give large institutional investors the option of assuming the lead plaintiff role in the Securities Litigation Reform Act of 1995, Pub L No 104-67, 109 Stat 737 (codified in scattered sections of 15 USC and 18 USC).

suit[97]—what in modern parlance would be termed an "opt in" class action.[98] This procedure avoids the legitimacy of representation problem since the class representative does not assume any capacity to impart anything but a costless victory upon the absent class members. Should the named plaintiff prevail, each class member retains the individual option of joining in the judgment; should the named plaintiff fail, the rights of the absent class members are unaffected. But this legitimacy for the role of the named representative is bought at a tremendous cost for the defendant in the class action. In effect, in any such class litigation, the defendant is able to prevail only as to the named plaintiff, but can lose to the entire class. Should the defendant prevail, there is the potential for demoralization of potential future plaintiffs, but no prohibition on multiple suits. Indeed, subsequent cases may be benefited by lessons learned in the first case, and from the second, and the third, and so on.[99] But, for the defendant, a loss is conclusive as to all class members. Since the 1921 decision in *Supreme Tribe of Ben-Hur v Cauble*,[100] the Supreme Court has made clear that the object of class actions must be to bind absent class members and consequently achieve finality—thereby equalizing the stakes in the litigation.[101] This is reflected in modern Rule 23(b)(3), which provides for finality in properly certified class actions should individual class members not opt out at the onset of litigation.

---

[97] See 7A Wright, et al, § 1752 (cited in note 49) (citing cases in which courts "suggested that if the class were successful, the absentees should be notified and asked if they wanted to take advantage of the result").

[98] See 7B Wright, et al, § 1787 (cited in note 49) (noting that "[b]y requiring the absentee to take affirmative action to avoid being bound, the rule attempts to eliminated the common practice in 'spurious' class suits prior to 1966 of waiting to see if the adjudication was favorable to the class before deciding whether to enter the action"), and Charles Alan Wright, *Law of Federal Courts* 483 (West, 2d ed 1983) (arguing that if an absentee does " 'opt out', and the judgement ultimately is favorable to the class, he should not be entitled to rely on it as collateral estoppel," because to permit it would "make a mockery of the (b)(3) procedure, and would restore in a different form the 'one way' intervention that the amended rule was expressly intended to preclude"). Similar discussion can also be found in the *Manual for Complex Litigation, Third* at 224 (cited in note 31).

[99] See Jack Ratliff, *Offensive Collateral Estoppel and the Option Effect*, 67 Tex L Rev 63, 77, 79 ("The basic unfairness lies in the disparate risks taken by plaintiffs as a class and the defendant in the first case . . . . [t]he option effect forces the first-case defendant to play for low stakes if he wins, but for high stakes if he loses").

[100] 255 US 356 (1921).

[101] For an extended discussion of asymmetries of the stakes in litigation, see Samuel Issacharoff, *Group Litigation of Consumer Claims: Lessons of the American Experience*, 34 Tex Intl L J 135, 142–45 (1999).

The challenge of the modern sprawling class action is therefore to find mechanisms that confer legitimacy under two conditions that were relatively absent from historic class action practice: first, that there is no preexisting political or organizational vehicle that can claim an independent source of authority to speak for the collective, and, second, where modern conceptions of fairness and finality require that the nonparticipating class members be bound to the outcome of the litigation as if they were parties. So until the modern class actions with these two features arose, there was no need to police independently the adequacy of representation. The basic rule that emerges most directly in the modern context is that adequate representation is a prerequisite for binding individuals to the outcome of a case, and that this in turn requires that the class representatives "fairly represent them with respect to the matters as to which the judgment is subsequently involved."[102] The key issue is the guarantee that the agent be the faithful guardian of the interests of the class.[103]

III. Strategies for Policing the Governance of Collective Action

If the basic proposition asserted thus far is accepted, if indeed the propriety of class actions turns primarily on the proper governance of these aggregative devices, then the next issue is the mechanisms that can guarantee such proper treatment. This discussion will be divided into the next two sections of this article. This section will address the various strategies presented by commentators to guarantee faithful representation. The discussion will be presented along the familiar pathways of exit, voice, and loyalty as the framework for institutional design,[104] with concluding con-

---

[102] Restatement (Second) of Judgments § 42(1)(d) (1982).

[103] While it is possible to address this problem in the language of agency costs in game theoretic terms, see, e.g., Michael A. Perino, *Class Action Chaos? The Theory of the Core and an Analysis of Opt-Out Rights in Mass Tort Class Actions*, 46 Emory L J 85, 125, 141–42 n 235 (1997) (applying this analysis to the conflicts presented in *Georgine*, the lower court version of *Amchem*), this is simply a recasting of the classic discussion over due process.

[104] This is of course taken from Albert Hirschman's seminal work, *Exit, Voice and Loyalty: Response to Decline in Firms, Organizations and States* (Harvard, 1970). In the course of many discussions, Jack Coffee and I both fastened on Hirschman's typology to characterize the debates over class actions. The exact origin of the inspiration is as forgotten as it is unimportant. See John C. Coffee, Jr., *Class Action Accountability: Reconciling Exit, Voice, and Loyalty in Representative Litigation*, 100 Colum L Rev (forthcoming, 2000).

siderations based on the unique strategic frailties of class actions.
The next section will return more directly to the Court's steps
toward assuring faithful representation through the progress of the
case law leading to *Ortiz*.

A. THE RIGHT OF EXIT

The use of the mandatory class action in *Ortiz* brings to the
forefront the need for class members to have some escape vehicle
from a bad proposed class settlement. The mechanism of choice
is the right to opt out, and the sudden popularity of the 23(b)(1)
limited fund class action has everything to do with the ability to
impose finality on the absent class members without any right of
exit. This is a matter of particular significance in the mass tort
context. As Professor Coffee points out with regard to the silicone
gel breast implant class action, for instance, the opt out right can
be of great value in protecting individual claimants with substantial
personal injury claims.[105] An effective right to opt out must allow
the ability of objectors to get out at critical junctures, either at the
time the class is formed for litigation purposes or at the time of
the fairness hearing in a settlement class.

While the right to opt out may indeed offer protection to class
members in exceptional high individual value litigation, in most
class actions it is of limited utility for three reasons. First, in the
most "adventuresome"[106] of the current wave of class actions, the
class purports to bind future claimants who do not currently have
a claim, and who therefore have little reason to be on guard that
their potential future claims are at risk.[107] Clearly, without knowledge of the reason to opt out, the benefit standing alone offers
little. Second, in class actions in which the claims of individual
class members are low in value, there may be no incentive to opt
out even where a class member has notice and actually suspects

---

[105] Coffee, *Class Wars* at 1408 (cited in note 11).

[106] This is the Supreme Court's characterization in *Amchem*, 521 US at 617.

[107] I make it a practice to ask my procedure students how many had opted out of the
Amchem litigation. Given the scope of the class definition, virtually any twenty-something-
year-old American with a working parent was likely to have been a class member. The class
is defined as "exposed individuals who currently suffer no physical ailments, but who may
in the future develop possibly fatal asbestos-related diseases." *Georgine*, 83 F3d at 617.
"Exposure" is in turn defined to include anyone exposed by contact to the work clothes
of a parent or other family member.

that the settlement is insufficient. If the claim is not one that would ever have justified individual prosecution, the act of withdrawing from the class action is at best a self-harming symbolic protest; any recovery is better than nothing. By opting out, the individual class member retains the right to a claim that will never justify its private enforcement.[108] Third, in most class actions, the limited individual stake does not justify the acquisition of detailed information by class members. Although information is not so costly as proceeding with individual litigation, it is nonetheless a consuming undertaking, particularly where the information cannot lead to a meaningful decision to proceed individually. Thus, while many have written skeptically on the difficulty that individual class members have in assessing the information contained in legal notices,[109] there are nonetheless still proposals to place greater emphasis on the individual act of ratifying the terms of a class action settlement.[110]

Even if this ability to opt out may be of little practical utility, there is no reason to object to better notice as such. Notice to the class may serve some function if it dispels the notion that a court is acting secretively, or if it gives other sets of lawyers notice that an improper settlement is in the works.[111] The problem arises on the back side with the assumption that an individual's failure to opt out implies consent[112] and perhaps, by extension, exhausts the protective mechanisms that must be in place for absent class members. This invigoration of the opt out approach, which admittedly

---

[108] This may also be expressed in game theoretic terms as a product of the cost of defection exceeding the potential alternative payoff. See Perino at 127–29 (cited in note 103). In simple terms, there is no gain to be had from preserving the right to bring an action whose expected payoff is zero.

[109] See Arthur R. Miller, *Problems of Giving Notice in Class Actions*, 58 FRD 313, 322 (1973) ; Deborah Rhode, *Class Conflicts in Class Actions*, 34 Stan L Rev 1183, 1215 (1982).

[110] See Weber at 1193–1201 (cited in note 11) ("the class member must receive adequate notice of the settlement and have adequate time to reflect on the decision to accept or reject the settlement. Notice of the decision entails an adequate description of the settlement and its effects so that the person can make a choice that will maximize individual well-being.").

[111] I have previously argued for this functional approach to the right to notice. See Issacharoff, *Class Action Conflicts* at 833 (cited in note 11).

[112] For example, Professor Weber proposes a muscular notion of notice so as to place the emphasis in settlement approval "on the idea of individual consent." Accordingly, his approach "would stress . . . whether the individual class member has the opportunity to accept or reject the settlement. Consent should matter; the consent that matters should be meaningful consent; implied consent is no substitute for real choice; and the practical effects of requiring choice will be beneficial." Weber at 1193 (cited in note 11).

appears attractive in light of the extension of class action law to the current round of massive tort settlements, nonetheless introduces two distortions in class action law. First, and most clearly, it returns the law to a premise of individual autonomy within the class structure that is likely to be unrealistic for the reasons already discussed. Moreover, it has never been clear that the capacity to absent oneself has ever served as the key to due process protections in representative actions. As David Shapiro observes, in the early jurisprudence of class actions, due process was measured by the adequacy of representation, and the individual right to opt out was not even mentioned.[113] The ability to opt out rises to constitutional dimensions only with *Phillips Petroleum v Shutts*, in which the ability to opt out is considered a mild signifier of consent to jurisdiction—although not to adequacy of representation—in a forum that otherwise had no contact with the injuries claimed by some portion of the absent class members.[114]

But there is also a second concern that elevating the role of individual consent can create peculiar strategic complications to what is already highly complex litigation. Class actions depend on entrepreneurial lawyers not only for their leadership, as I have argued already, but for their formation. Large-scale class actions require significant investments of time and resources to be viable. Unfortunately for the plaintiffs' attorney, however, that investment remains unsecured throughout the litigation, in addition to being subject to the usual risks of nonrecovery in contingent litigation. Unlike a contractual contingent representation of an individual client, a plaintiffs' class action lawyer cannot place a lien on a file to secure a quantum meruit recovery in the case of discharge. Should the class not be certified under any particular lawyer's stewardship, there is nothing to show for the investment, regardless of the time and resources necessary to develop the claim. On top of the risk of being discharged as class counsel, however, is the risk posed by the developing practice of copycat and overlapping class actions filed on the heels of well-publicized class claims. These derivative

---

[113] Shapiro at 937 (cited in note 13) (focusing on the seminal cases *Ben Hur* and *Hansberry*). Moreover, these cases did not even mention notice to the absent class members. Id.

[114] See *Shutts*, 472 US 797 (1985); Henry Paul Monaghan, *Antisuit Injunctions and Preclusion Against Absent Nonresident Class Members*, 98 Colum L Rev 1148, 1170 (1998) (addressing the jurisdictional "fiction" of the *Shutts* implied consent approach).

actions threaten the ability of the lawyer-entrepreneurs to get a reasonable return on their investment,[115] as lawyers without a significant investment in the case may offer defendants a cheap settlement in exchange for any attorneys' fees that they may garner. The focus on the individual litigant unfortunately reinforces the threat of overlapping litigation, particularly since rival sets of attorneys "need only supply the name of a class member as their key to the courthouse door. . . ."[116] To the extent that the law of class actions is focused on a desire for universal approval of class leadership, there is an invitation not only to the strategic holdout class member, but to the rival class suit threatening to undermine the unsecured investment of class counsel.

Put another way, it cannot be that the failure of individual consent must terminate a class action or prevent a settlement from being approved. Such an approach would run counter to the premise of class actions as being able to discipline an inherently unruly body that is incapable of generating sufficient individual protections through consensual means. There are of course extreme cases in which courts must address objections by informed class members, but any requirement that the consent of all the governed is the prerequisite to judicial approval of the maintenance or settlement of a class action threatens the viability of this aggregative tool.[117]

---

[115] This is a topic of increasing concern in the commentary on class actions. See Marcel Kahan and Linda Silberman, *The Inadequate Search for "Adequacy" in Class Actions: A Critique of Epstein v. MCA, Inc.*, 73 NYU L Rev 765 (1998); Geoffrey P. Miller, *Overlapping Class Actions*, 71 NYU L Rev 514 (1996); Geoffrey P. Miller, *Full Faith and Credit to Settlements in Overlapping Class Actions: A Reply to Professors Kahan and Silberman*, 73 NYU L Rev 1167 (1998); Coffee, *Class Action Accountability* (cited in note 104); Issacharoff, *Class Action Conflicts* (cited in note 11).

[116] Miller, *Full Faith and Credit* at 1167 (cited in note 115).

[117] Consistent with the notion that in litigation anything can and does happen is the fact pattern in the recent *Lazy Oil Co. v Witco*, 166 F3d 581 (3rd Cir 1999). In that case, litigation was truly client-initiated by an informed major shareholder of a company who then opposed a proposed class settlement of antitrust litigation. Only one of the class representatives supported the settlement, and a surprising 384 class members objected to the terms of the settlement. Id at 583–84. The objecting class members then demanded that the class counsel be disqualified from the case for holding a conflicting position to individual class members who objected to counsel's continued representation. The Third Circuit affirmed the district court in finding that complete class approval was not a prerequisite either to settlement or to the continued role of class counsel, and approved the settlement. One may question whether the intensity of opposition by unusually informed class members should have been more heavily weighted in the decision to approve of the settlement, but the conclusion that individual class members, even named class members, do not have a veto on class counsel seems inescapable. Nonetheless, there are plenty of reported opinions of class settlements

B. GIVING VOICE TO CLASS MEMBERS

An alternative to exit is to enhance the participation of class members.[118] As expressed by Professor Woolley, for example, this would require an increased right of intervention and direct participation by class members in the conduct of a class action.[119] Such intervention is now presumptively necessary as a precondition for any individual class member pressing an appellate challenge to the governance of a class action. The majority of federal circuit courts, following the decision of the Eleventh Circuit in *Guthrie v Evans*,[120] have held that absent class members must affirmatively intervene in the district court in order to perfect a right of appeal.[121] This past Term, an equally divided Supreme Court affirmed the Seventh Circuit in denying shareholders opposing an antitrust settlement the right to appeal because they had failed to intervene below.[122]

The problem remains that the very reason there is a class action in most cases in the first place, the insufficient stakes of the class members, is the very reason there is insufficient incentive for individual class members to actively monitor class counsel[123] or to actively intervene on their own behalf. While there may be much to commend facilitating the ability of the absent class members to

---

being approved over the objections of substantial numbers of class members, including the class representatives. See, e.g., *Maywalt v Parker & Parsley Petroleum Co.*, 864 F Supp 1422, 1426–33 (SDNY 1994), affirmed, 67 F3d 1072 (2d Cir 1995) (settlement approved despite objections by nearly 2,700 class members, including the class representatives); *County of Suffolk v Long Island Lighting Co.*, 907 F2d 1295, 1325 (2d Cir 1990) (opposition by a majority of the class representatives insufficient to prevent settlement approval).

[118] For an early attempt to use voting rules and intervention to control conflicts in representations of multiple principals by one agent, as in class actions, see Lewis A. Kornhauser, *Control of Conflicts of Interest in Class-Action Suits*, 41 Public Choice 145 (1983). Kornhauser subsequently dubbed such representation "hydraheaded." Lewis A. Kornhauser, *Fair Division of Settlements, A Comment on Silver and Baker*, 84 Va L Rev 1561, 1562 (1998).

[119] Woolley at 629 (cited in note 12).

[120] 815 F2d 626 (11th Cir 1987).

[121] See *Walker v City of Mesquite*, 858 F2d 1071 (5th Cir 1988); *Shults v Champion International Corp.*, 35 F3d 1056 (6th Cir 1994); *In re Brand Name Prescription Drugs Antitrust Litigation*, 115 F3d 456 (7th Cir 1997); *Croyden Associates v Alleco*, 969 F2d 675 (8th Cir 1992); *Gottlieb v Wiles*, 11 F3d 1004 (10th Cir 1993).

[122] *California Public Employees' Retirement System v Felzen*, 119 S Ct 720 (1999), affirming 134 F3d 873 (7th Cir 1998).

[123] See Marcel Kahan and Linda Silberman, *Matsushita and Beyond: The Role of State Courts in Class Actions Involving Exclusive Federal Claims*, 1996 Supreme Court Review 219, 232 (noting that this further "creates the danger that unscrupulous class counsel will settle a class claim for a generous attorney fee, but a paltry recovery.").

intervene should they so desire, the reality is that in the broad swath of class actions such an offer of participation will be as illusory as the idealized form of an individual suit. Indeed, the right of intervention is *more* problematic than the ability to opt out, since the intervention seeks not to remove an individual from the class but asserts a different representative agent for the class as a whole. The strategic problem of raids on proposed (and legitimate) class settlements arises whenever rival attorneys may threaten to delay or disrupt a class settlement simply by intervening and threatening to tie up the case on appeal. As with the right of exit, the ability to intervene does little to resolve the ultimate difficult issue in modern class action law: what kind of structural protections are available for the range of class counsel decision making that must of necessity occur "without the informed consent of their clients"?[124]

A variant of the voice approach is presented by Professor Monaghan, who seeks to preserve not a right of participation in the initial litigation, but the capacity to revisit in a second forum. For Professor Monaghan, this translates into an elaborate due process right of collateral attack on the adequacy of representation.[125] While the Supreme Court has acted to protect the rights of non-class members to collaterally challenge a consent decree that purported to bind them,[126] a formal right to collateral challenge in class actions would require a significant reassertion of the view of absent class members as nonparties to the original litigation.[127] No doubt some of the unfortunate collusive class action practices may indeed prompt a strong desire for such secondary avenues of challenge, but it is not clear why direct appeal is not a sufficient route for challenge if the bases for proper class action governance[128] were

---

[124] See Silver and Baker at 1468 (cited in note 14) (emphasis omitted).

[125] See Monaghan, *Antisuit Injunctions and Preclusion* at 1148 (cited in note 114). This position has some support on the Court. See *Matsushita Elec. Indus. Co. v Epstein*, 516 US at 386–87 (Ginsburg, J, concurring in part and dissenting in part).

[126] See *Martin v Wilks*, 490 US 755 (1989). In particular, the Court distinguished class members from third parties for purposes of collateral attack. 490 US at 762 n 2.

[127] For an argument directly to the contrary, see Kahan and Silberman, *Matsushita and Beyond* at 264 (cited in note 123) ("[A]s long as the court entertaining a proposed class action affords class members fair opportunity to raise the issue, adequacy of representation should be raised directly, and not be permitted to be raised collaterally.").

[128] I stress this point because, since all class action settlements must obtain judicial approval, it is insufficient to rely on the fact of judicial acceptance of the settlement as itself the guarantor of fair treatment of absent class members. This is the approach that *Amchem*

more clearly established.[129] Indeed, it would be ironic if the restrictive development of recent habeas jurisprudence were to leave capital penalty defendants with highly constricted nonappeal routes of challenge,[130] but would afford that same opportunity to absent class action plaintiffs. So long as notice is sufficient and the opportunity to intervene and appeal is protected, it remains unclear why collateral challenge is the preferred mechanism to challenge abuse of class action practice. The major issue in the current class action controversies appears not so much the forum in which to challenge the terms of settlement as the conditions of adequacy of representation that go to the heart of the class action.

For this reason, it is difficult to avoid skepticism in the face of strategies to police class actions that require greater individual oversight, either through the ability to exit or through participation.[131] Certainly, there should be the right to monitor class actions, to opt out except in the most constrained definition of limited fund or injunctive cases, or to intervene in protection of an individual's stake in the litigation. But ex post individual challenges to a settlement are a poor substitute for good governance of class actions ex ante, just as a malpractice action is a poor substitute for adequate representation by an attorney in an individual dispute. By the same token, certainly there should be greater judicial scrutiny of the terms of settlement, and perhaps the imposition of trustees or guardians ad litem to oversee the interests of the absent

---

derisively referred to as the "chancellor's foot" standard of review in which a "disarmed" court makes an estimation of how reasonable a settlement appears based on limited information and potentially tainted incentives of the proponents of the settlement—and the reviewing court itself. The issue must be what are the standards for judicial scrutiny of settlements. Also, because of the danger that collusive class actions may be brought before courts suspected of being friendly, the proper legal standard is all the more important as setting up the basis for exacting appellate scrutiny of the faithful representation by the class agents.

[129] I leave aside the problem of overlapping class actions in which a race to the courthouse might lead to the inequities in forcing a certified class (or even one awaiting certification) having to present its claims as part of an objection, intervention, and appellate challenge in a rival forum. This leaves open the problem presented in cases such as *Matsushita v Epstein*, 516 US 367, in which the real controversy was over which forum would control the disposition of the litigation.

[130] Last Term's latest installment in this trend is *O'Sullivan v Boerckel*, 119 S Ct 1728 (1999) (requiring complete exhaustion of state appellate procedures, including disfavored discretionary review in state's highest court, prior to commencement of collateral habeas challenge).

[131] For a discussion of the disincentives toward individual monitoring of class action settlements, see Susan P. Koniak and George M. Cohen, *Under Cloak of Settlement*, 82 Va L Rev 1051, 1122–30 (1996).

class members. But it is difficult to believe that these will serve as meaningful protections for absent class members in the majority of cases. It is worth recalling, after all, that virtually all of these were present in some fashion in either *Amchem* or *Ortiz*, or both.

C. CLASS ACTION LOYALTY

At the other end of the spectrum from the individual rights approach to policing class actions stand various proposals that would impart a greater institutional legitimacy to class actions and, by extension, create greater legitimacy for actions taken on behalf of absent class members. Consistent with Professor Shapiro's enterprise theory of class actions, it is possible to view class actions as a subset of public law and assess whether from an ex ante original position approach, any class member would have had occasion to object.[132] The clear import of this approach is that the entity, once formed, should be able to command the affiliation of class members and may justifiably suppress individual objections. This view of class actions imparts great significance to the initial formation of the class action, akin to the initial articles of incorporation of a publicly held company, and then underplays the significance of post-creation decision making, in effect the class action equivalent of the business judgment rule. This analogy is flawed, in the first instance, because of the far greater role of legal compulsion in participating in a class action than in a corporation. More significantly, even if the analogy were accepted, the law of corporate governance speaks volumes about the inability to presume that managerial agents will faithfully discharge the interests of the shareholders and does little to dispel concerns over improper behavior by the stewards for the class. Even viewing the class as an entity does little to address the tension that may emerge between the interests of the principals and those of their agents.

This principal-agent dilemma is addressed in the highly intriguing approach of Professors Macey and Miller, who try to overcome the separation between ownership of the claims and control of the litigation by, in essence, allowing the attorneys to buy the

---

[132] See Bruce Hay and David Rosenberg, *The Individual Justice of Averaging* (Working Paper 1999) (arguing that class members with less than complete information would prefer a regime of damage averaging, rather than individual determinations of recovery).

claims and take the litigation private.[133] The idea is to create a market for class control that would then have the presumed moral authority of an adequate pricing mechanism for class governance. They propose a court-supervised auction in which courts would approve the certification of a class and appoint as class counsel those attorneys willing to pay the most for the claim. Once ownership of the class is auctioned to suitable attorney-entrepreneurs, there is no longer any principal-agent tension because the agents are the principals. While it is difficult to see such an approach succeeding, for reasons both practical and conceptual,[134] the proposal's strength is that it identifies the problematic relation between principal and agent as the key issue in class action legitimacy.

The prime area of development, however, is in the attempt to impose an overseer on the class action, in effect an agent to watch over the class's agents.[135] The most immediate candidates are the

---

[133] See Macey and Miller (cited in note 15).

[134] The problems are of four different sorts. First, in one variant of the proposal, and as some courts have tried to implement it, the winning bid is given to the lawyers willing to undertake the representation most cheaply. As with dentistry, there may be some pain associated with delivering yourself to professionals whose chief attribute is their willingness to work you over cheaply. See Macey and Miller at 113 (cited in note 15) (recognizing that "the competence or financial qualification of the low bidder might also be suspect"); see also Julie Rubin, *Auctioning Class Actions: Turning the Tables on Plaintiffs' Lawyers Abuse*, 52 Bus Law 1441, 1455 (1997) (criticizing proposal on these grounds). Second, there is likely to be a systematic bias toward undervaluing class claims because of the lack of information at the prediscovery auction stage. See Randall S. Thomas and Robert G. Hansen, *Auctioning Class Action and Derivative Lawsuits: A Critical Analysis*, 87 Nw U L Rev 423 (1993). Third, because of uncertainty over future control of the class, there will be a systematic bias toward underinvestment in discovery, compounding the problem of the systematic undervaluation of the class claim. See Thomas and Hansen; Jill E. Fisch, *Class Action Reform, Qui Tam, and the Role of the Plaintiff*, 60 Law & Contemp Probs 167, 182 (1997) ("the auction has the potential to undercut the incentive to commit resources investigating possible corporate wrongdoing . . . . Because the auction procedure allows an entrepreneurial lawyer to outbid the plaintiff or lawyer who files the initial suit, the financial reward of representative litigation do not go to those who search out wrongdoing."). Finally, in the mass tort context, the sheer size of the claims at stake would exceed the resources of even the most well-heeled plaintiffs' firms. The only realistic prospective bidders would be the defendants or their insurers. This would compound the problems of information asymmetries leading to undervaluation and would, in effect, recreate the problem in the settlement class context of the class being created through the contrivance of the defendant, rather than through the adversarial process.

[135] The phrase comes from Bernard Black's discussion of the use of oversight entities in the corporate governance context. See Bernard S. Black, *Agents Watching Agents: The Promise of Institutional Investor Voice*, 39 UCLA L Rev 811 (1992). For an extended discussion of the use of intermediaries as a governance strategy and the potential disruptions presented, see Samuel Issacharoff and Daniel Ortiz, *Governing Through Intermediaries*, 85 Va L Rev 1627 (1999).

courts[136] or independent guardians ad litem.[137] Under these approaches, the independence of either the court or the ad litem from the financial returns available to class counsel insures some greater measure of fidelity to the interests of the class. But what is it that the guardian or the court can reasonably be expected to monitor? There is a problematic faith that these procedures will generate greater substantive review of the merits of settlements in particular. Courts can never fully assess the full range of litigation decisions that go into the decision to settle,[138] and there is unfortunately more than a hint in the case law of friendly courts approving outlandish class action settlements. Nor can a guardian revisit such issues unless the guardian has the full range of information available to counsel—in effect doubling the costs of representation. Perhaps the cost of an overseeing guardian may prove worthwhile in some litigation, but I suspect that it will more likely prove expensive with little payoff. More significantly, these strategies are addressed to the role of third party oversight of the overall fairness of the resolution of a class action as opposed to focusing on the structure of class action representation by the direct agents. As I shall present in the next section, the Supreme Court significantly advanced the case law in *Ortiz* and *Amchem* by focusing on the internal structural incentives facing class counsel, rather than on external opinions as to "gestalt" or "chancellor's foot" assessments of fairness.[139]

The leading alternative candidates are intermediaries who may serve as more vigorous class representatives. The key example

---

[136] See Kahan and Silberman, *The Inadequate Search for "Adequacy"* at 782 (cited in note 115) (arguing that more exacting review of the adequacy of representation in the first forum is the best guarantor of the protection of the absent class members).

[137] See Koniak at 1092 n 216 (cited in note 16); Green at 1797 (cited in note 167). There is some judicial skepticism about the benefits of such an approach. As observed in *In re Intelligent Electronics, Inc. Securities Litigation*, 1997 WL 786984 (ED Pa 1997), "The appointment of a class guardian would only further increase costs, extend indefinitely the time before distribution to the class and further needlessly complicate the procedures." 1997 WL 786984 at * 10.

[138] For a discussion of this point, see Weber at 1213–15 (cited in note 11); James A. Henderson, Jr., *Comment: Settlement Class Actions and the Limits of Adjudication*, 80 Cornell L Rev 1014, 1020 (1995) (describing docket-clearing incentives for judges to approve "done-deals"); Charles Wolfram, *Mass Torts, Messy Ethics*, 80 Cornell L Rev 1228, 1233 (1995) (describing judicial incentives toward settlement as one of the sources of problems in modern mass tort litigation).

[139] See *Amchem*, 521 US at 594–95.

comes with the Private Securities Reform Litigation Act of 1995, which introduced the idea that the largest stakeholder among the plaintiff class should have a presumptive right to act as lead plaintiff and to have control over the selection of class counsel.[140] Similarly, the proposed Class Action Fairness Act of 1999[141] seeks, among its many proposals, to allow for a right of participation for state attorneys general in any statewide consumer class action. Each of these legislative attempts sought to control potential principal-agent tension in class actions by invigorating the participation of a representative plaintiff who has a sufficiently large stake to monitor the activity of the class counsel. While the idea has much intrinsic appeal, there are limits to the willingness of even substantial class members to assume the role of monitors if there is no direct gain for them. In effect, such class monitors are being asked to perform an uncompensated service on behalf of the class, with the remainder of the class being allowed to free-ride on their efforts. These efforts run into the problems faced by potentially self-interested intermediaries: they may be opportunistic[142] or they may impose a costly filter.[143] The latter is particularly problematic

---

[140] Under the Private Securities Litigation Reform Act of 1995, 15 USC § 78u-4 (1998), courts are directed to appoint the most adequate plaintiff as lead named plaintiff and to entertain a presumption that this most adequate plaintiff is either the plaintiff in whose name the case was filed or the plaintiff that has the largest financial interest in the relief sought by the class. Id § 78u-4(a)(3)(B)(iii)(I)(aa) and (bb). The bill was prompted by an article advocating the appointment of large institutional investors whose stake in the litigation would provide an incentive for effective monitoring of class counsel and who would faithfully represent the interests of all class members. See Elliot J. Weiss and John S. Beckerman, *Let the Money Do the Monitoring: How Institutional Investors can Reduce Agency Costs in Securities Class Actions*, 104 Yale L J 2053 (1995). But see Jill E. Fisch, *Class Action Reform: Lessons from Securities Litigation*, 39 Ariz L Rev 533 (1997) (challenging assumption that large institutional investors have interests identical to small stakeholders, and positing that there are significant dangers of collusive behavior between large investors and defendants).

[141] S 353, 106th Cong, 1st Sess (February 3, 1999).

[142] For example, there were recently allegations in New York that the state comptroller was using the lead plaintiff position of state pension funds to secure campaign contributions from lawyers seeking appointment as class counsel in securities fraud litigation. See *Donors to McCall Campaign Got Pension Fund Contracts*, NY Times (Oct 3, 1998) at A1.

[143] In one well publicized case in Texas involving the use of computational changes to allegedly overcharge purchasers of auto insurance, the Attorney General demanded that $1.5 million of the class's settlement fund be set aside for a public relations effort warning consumers of the risk of consumer fraud. There was widespread belief that this public education drive would take the form of showcasing incumbent state officials in the context of reelection campaigns. See Deborah R. Hensler, *Class Action Dilemmas: Pursuing Public Goals for Private Gain* (Rand, 1999) (describing factual background of *Zendejo v Allstate*). It must be disclosed that I served as a co-counsel for the plaintiffs in this litigation.

for those causes of action that allow for both public and private
enforcement; there is an inherent difficulty in giving public en-
forcers that have passed on the opportunity to litigate a further
gatekeeping function.

In sum, however, the intermediary approach is at best a partial
approach, much like the options for exit and participation. There
are elements of each that are likely beneficial: exit condemns
the extreme form of non opt out classes, probably the single
most suspect device in this area of law; voice requires some capacity to participate, as through intervention; and loyalty must
ultimately stand as a central highest value, if the properly represented class action is to have the ability to provide repose in mass
litigation.

But these gains must be weighed against the difficulty that in
nearly all cases (and the departures from the general rule are few
and far between) the class comes into existence only through the
intervention of counsel. Class actions may resemble corporations
in that there is a separation between ownership and control,[144] but
the operational capital in a class action comes not from the owners,
but from the managers. This in turn means that absent some presumptive return to counsel, such as the right to lead the class and
profit from any successes the class may enjoy, there will be no
investment in the development of the case. This is simply another
way of stating the problem that there is no security interest sufficient to protect the necessary investment for the discovery, development, and prosecution of a class action on behalf of individuals
with whom one has no independent contractual relation. Particularly in the unfortunate era of copycat class actions, uncertain powers of multidistrict litigation courts,[145] overlapping state and federal
actions, some protection of security interest must be had lest the
whole enterprise be doomed. For class actions to continue to be
viable, therefore, as much uncertainty as possible must be handled
at the threshold stage of litigation so that class counsel may invest
in the development of the case knowing the terms under which

---

[144] Silver and Baker at 1466 (cited in note 14).

[145] See *Lexecon, Inc. v Milberg, Weiss, Bershad Hynes & Lerach*, 523 US 26 (1998) (holding
that a district court conducting pretrial proceedings in a civil action transferred from the
Judicial Panel on Multidistrict Litigation could not assign the case to itself for trial, but
not defining the full range of power of the MDL court).

later returns would be realized.[146] This in turn further reinforces the point that the conditions under which class counsel may legitimately speak for the class must be the *primary* protection of the absent class members, and not post facto review by courts, ad litems, intervenors, or intermediaries.[147]

The importance of establishing concrete expectations of returns to investment in the prosecution of a class action is an independent reason to build the primary protections of the class into the initial structure of representation. As class action practice has expanded, there has emerged a new variant of lawyer-entrepreneur who arrives at class settlement fairness hearing representing one client and claiming to object to the settlement on the basis that class recovery is too low or class counsel fees too high. While each of these may be justifiable bases for objection to a class settlement, this lawyer will typically have no investment in the case and appear purporting to be the class litigation equivalent of the white knight from the world of corporate mergers. Since one such objection may tie up the settlement in further litigation and appeals, the objector entrepreneur is in a strong position to demand some form of compensation to drop his objection—the class action equivalent of greenmail. This is facilitated by the fact that the investment of class counsel is unsecured and that the need for only one client allows easy entry to claim to be the protector of the class against

---

[146] This is reflected in the suggestion in the *Manual for Complex Litigation, Third* that the form of compensation for class counsel (e.g., what percentage of any common fund generated will be set aside for attorneys' fees) should be determined at the outset under the full conditions of uncertainty when the decisions of how much to invest in the case have to be made, rather than ex post, when the outcome is already at hand. See id § 24.21 (cited in note 31). For an academic defense of this approach, see Charles Silver, *Unloading the Lodestar: Toward a New Fee Award Procedure*, 70 Tex L Rev 865, 902 (1992).

[147] This reflects a long-standing argument made by Professor Coffee that the basic approach to class action governance should be to structure incentives for class counsel so as to make the process as self-policing as possible. As stated by Coffee,

If one wishes to economize on the judicial time that is today invested in monitoring class and derivative litigation, the highest priority should be given to those reforms that restrict collusion and are essentially self- policing. The percentage of the recovery award formula is such a "deregulatory" reform because it relies on incentives rather than costly monitoring. Ultimately, this "deregulatory" approach is the only alternative to converting the courts into the equivalent of public utility commissions that oversee the plaintiff's attorney and elaborately fix the attorney's "fair" return.

John C. Coffee, Jr., *Understanding the Plaintiff's Attorney: The Implications of Economic Theory for Private Enforcement of the Law Through Class and Derivative Actions*, 86 Colum L Rev 669, 724–25 (1986).

the perditions of class counsel. Giving some protection to the investment of class counsel early on prevents excessive pressures on class counsel that serve as an invitation to the strategic holdup. Without such protections, and should the strategic intervenor practice grow, there will be additional disincentives to class counsel undertaking the risks of litigation.

IV. Defining the Role of a Legitimate Representative: The Law After Ortiz

Amchem provoked considerable consternation within the class action bar because of its apparently intractable opposition to any allocative decisions made by plaintiffs' counsel.[148] In an extreme form, this reading of *Amchem* would create a spiral of subclasses and sets of counsel that would not only swamp the incentive to invest in bringing a class action, but would impose tremendous transactional costs on an already vulnerable procedure that turned heavily on its ability to realize economies of scale. A number of proposals emerged in the brief period between *Amchem* and *Ortiz* to address this potentially destabilizing aspect of *Amchem*. For example, one approach was to divide prospective class actions by the amount of the individual stake and the extent of the variation in recovery among class members as a result of the allocative decisions made by counsel. As proposed by Professor Coffee, intraclass divisions by lawyers in high-personal-stakes cases would require separate subclasses and counsel, while similar decisions in small-value consumer cases would not.[149] This division is intended to not burden the low-value cases with divisions into "an unwieldy and balkanized coalition of contending subclasses"[150] that would condemn the economic viability of these cases. At the other pole is the approach of Professors Silver and Baker, who would allow lawyers in class actions, what they term "nonconsensual" joinders, to make the same allocative decisions that would be allowed in consensual or voluntary joinder cases, or even between the commit-

---

[148] For a defense of *Amchem* as a check on improper delegation of power to private parties, see Monaghan at 1165 n 73 (cited in note 114).

[149] John C. Coffee, Jr., *Conflicts, Consent, and Allocation after Amchem Products—Or, Why Attorneys Still Need Consent to Give Away Their Clients' Money*, 84 Va L Rev 1541, 1555–56 (1998).

[150] Id at 1543.

ment of resources to one or another case within a lawyer's personal docket.[151] Their approach would replicate the contractual consent of the voluntary attorney-client relation with a presumption that the same ambit of attorney discretion would best serve the class as a whole in the decidedly nonconsensual class setting. This approach is based on the presumption that whatever degree of discretion prevails in private attorney-client relations should equally serve nonvoluntary classes, even without the client retaining the power to fire a wayward attorney.

Both of these approaches, despite their manifest differences, build on the fundamental contribution of *Amchem* that adequacy of representation is the linchpin for proper governance of a class action. Combining the concepts of class governance from *Amchem* with the further development in *Ortiz* yields an alternative that neither excessively burdens the direction of a class action nor facilitates rogue agent behavior. Certain issues are easily resolved once the focus is on governance. When agents have external loyalties, such that they will profit off satellite dealings with the defendant, there is no basis for trusting their stewardship.[152] It may well be that counsel is serving as an agent, but not as the agent for the class,[153] as even a simple example from the world of corporate governance can show. Imagine a corporate representative who wishes to bind the company to a contract in which he or she stood to gain privately. This would be considered the very model of a conflict of interest that would violate the fiduciary obligations of the corpo-

---

[151] Silver and Baker at 1509 (cited in note 14) (concluding that "attorneys who manage class actions are trustees or guardians as much as they are agents or delegates").

[152] Professor Cramton points to the presence of side agreements as creating an impermissible conflict of interest between the representation of absent class members and the representation of those individuals with a direct contractual relation to plaintiffs' counsel. Roger Cramton, *Individualized Justice, Mass Torts, and "Settlement Class Actions:" An Introduction*, 80 Cornell L Rev 811, 832 (1995).

[153] Here I would take issue with Professor Coffee, who argues that in intraclass divisions of proceeds, "plaintiffs' attorneys have little economic incentive to make a 'fair' allocation, whereas they have a strong economic incentive to maximize the size of the settlement fund." Coffee, *Conflicts, Consent, and Allocation* at 1542 (cited in note 149). So long as attorneys are equally beholden to all members of the class, and will receive no change in remuneration depending on the intraclass allocation, the attorneys have no incentive not to make a fair allocation. Under these conditions, all sorts of administrative shortcuts that save money for the class as a whole are permitted under current law, as they must be if consumer and other low value class actions are to exist. In typical cases, "[d]istinctions are usually drawn among plaintiffs mainly on the basis of significant objective factors that are easy to apply, while smaller differences and subjective factors are ignored." Silver and Baker at 1481 (cited in note 14).

rate officer to the shareholders.[154] Or imagine a corporate officer who was paid separately by one class of shareholders and acted to advance their interest relative to that of other shareholders. This too would seem an obvious breach of the duty of loyalty. *Amchem* and *Ortiz* are simply variants of this scenario, and the Court rightly condemned these conflicts as undermining the ability of class counsel to serve as a faithful agent.[155] Similarly, mandatory classes must raise the strong presumptions against allocative decisions by counsel because of the absence of even the possibility of exit through the opt out, the lack of required notice, and the difficulty of rival lawyers mounting a challenge for class leadership.

But the fact remains that classes, like all organizations, require agents because of the need to make decisions that the principals cannot make for themselves.[156] The decision to pursue one claim and not another, to depose one witness but not another, to make all sorts of litigation decisions, must be entrusted to the agent. What then are the limits on the power of the agent? The most restrictive reading of *Amchem* as prohibiting all intraclass allocative decisions by the agent[157] does not survive *Ortiz*. This goes too far, for it would derail any settlement in a complex case.

If this is correct, what exactly were the infirmities in governance that the Court struck down? In *Ortiz*, the problem is presented in

---

[154] See, e.g., *Committee on Corporate laws, Section of Business Law, American Bar Assoc., Corporate Director's Guidebook* 12–13 (1994) (noting that "The duty of loyalty requires directors to exercise their powers in the interests of corporation and not in the directors' own interest or in the interest of another person"); Lewis D. Solomon and Alan R. Palmiter, *Corporations: Examples and Explanations* 315 (Little Brown, 2d ed 1994) (noting that "Directors, officers and controlling shareholders breach their duty of loyalty when they divert assets, opportunities or information of the corporation for personal gain").

[155] For a discussion of potential ethical difficulties for class counsel representing parties with divergent interests, see Carrie Menkel-Meadow, *Ethics and the Settlement of Mass Torts: When the Rules Meet the Road*, 80 Cornell L Rev 1159, 1214 (1995); Cramton at 833 (cited in note 152) ("The facts in a number of recent settlement class actions make it clear that the two sets of deals are interconnected. If the terms of the two deals are different, the court should presume that the representation of the class was inadequate"); Nancy Morawetz, *Bargaining, Class Representation and Fairness*, 54 Ohio St L J 1 (1993).

[156] See, generally, Issacharoff and Ortiz, *Governing Through Intermediaries* (cited in note 135).

[157] The strongest version of this argument is found in the initial remand to the Fifth Circuit of *Ortiz* in light of *Amchem*. In dissent, Judge Jerry Smith argued that *Amchem* required that "any real conflict, even if minor when compared to the interest held in common, will render the representation inadequate." *In re Asbestos Litig.*, 134 F3d 668, 677 (5th Cir 1998) (Smith, J, dissenting), rev'd sub nom. *Ortiz v Fibreboard*, 119 S Ct 2295 (1999).

a simpler form because counsel had an external conflict—that is, they stood to recover independently of their representation of the class. *Amchem* presents a more complicated picture because the major failing was not external, but in the internal disunity of the class—in particular, the agreement of counsel to a settlement in which certain class members would receive nothing and those class members least capable of expressing opposition (the unknown future claimants) were also the least well treated in the settlement structure. This was then compounded by the structural incentives of the plaintiffs' counsel to favor present claimants over future claimants.[158] This point remained unclear because *Amchem* continued to insist that, while the merging of such disparate claims within the same class violated due process, the cure lay in separate subclasses led by separate class representatives.[159]

Nonetheless, the fact that plaintiffs were ultimately treated differently at the remedial stage, or indeed that some received nothing, cannot by itself doom class actions—or at least it has not done so historically. In Title VII employment discrimination cases, for example, trials were routinely bifurcated between a Phase I proceeding that established the defendant's liability, and a Phase II that determined what specific relief should be accorded. Where an employer refused to consider any blacks in the relevant labor market for job openings and only a finite number of jobs would come open, the certifiability of the class was not defeated by the fact that some but not other class members would obtain the desired jobs. The key seems to be the extent to which the allocative decisions made by lawyers claiming to represent the whole class (*a*) conform to some preexisting division within the class (such as those class members that best meet the employer's other, non-race-based hiring criteria); (*b*) are amenable to justification on an objective basis;[160] and (*c*) do not alter the basis for attorney com-

---

[158] This is described at length in Koniak (cited in note 16). Among the sources of internal preferences for the present injured over the future claimants were the contingent arrangements that plaintiffs' counsel had with their inventory of clients and the prospect of continuing legal fees in representing the currently injured before the dispute resolution mechanisms set up as part of the settlement process.

[159] *Amchem*, 521 US at 623–25.

[160] This would correspond to a requirement of "horizontal equity" among class members by which a class action must "treat similarly situated people similarly," particularly in the settlement context. Menkel-Meadow at 1211 (cited in note 155). See also Kornhauser at 1578 (cited in note 118) (applying symmetry principle from bankruptcy to class action settlements).

pensation—that is, the attorney has no financial reason to prefer a reward to one part as opposed to another of the class.

From this perspective, *Ortiz* represents a significant step forward in the Court's thinking from *Amchem* in two regards. First, in *Ortiz*, the Court abandons the focus on class representatives and instead properly recasts its attention squarely to the incentives under which plaintiffs' counsel operated: "[I]t is obvious after *Amchem* that a class divided between holders of present and future claims (some of them involving no physical injury and to claimants not yet born) requires division into homogeneous subclasses under Rule 23(c)(4)(B), with *separate representation to eliminate conflicting interests of counsel.*"[161] Second, the Court did not condemn the fact that there were intraclass allocation decisions made as such, but instead found that the settlement certification was "deficient" and lacked "fairness" and "equity"[162] because of the incentive structures operating on class counsel as they undertook the process of negotiating the settlement:

> In this case, certainly, any assumption that plaintiffs' counsel could be of a mind to do their simple best in bargaining for the benefit of the settlement class is patently at odds with the fact that at least some of the same lawyers representing plaintiffs and the class had also negotiated the separate settlement of 45,000 pending claims . . . the full payment of which was contingent on a successful global settlement agreement or the successful resolution of the insurance coverage dispute . . . . As for the settled inventory claims, their plaintiffs appeared to have obtained better terms than the class members.[163]

Had any intraclass allocations been per se prohibited, there would clearly have been no need for a functional evaluation of the incentives operating in the crafting of this particular settlement. The defect was not that the agents participated in the division of the proceeds, but that the agents were disloyal. Further, under the facts presented in *Ortiz*, no combination of judicial scrutiny, extraordinary judicial mediation by a sitting appellate judge, oversight by a guardian ad litem, and claimed litigation exigency could

---

[161] 119 S Ct at 2319 (emphasis added). The Court fairly directly acknowledges the shift from *Amchem*'s focus on the named representatives. Id at n 31.

[162] 119 S Ct at 2319.

[163] Id at 2317–19.

overcome the due process right of absent class members to be represented faithfully by agents owing them an uncompromised duty of loyalty.

Ortiz thereby advances the ball significantly by refining the inquiry to focus functionally on the adequacy of representation. What then should be done about the inevitable intraclass divisions in complex cases? What about allocation decisions among class members? Again, the *Ortiz* Court is careful to avoid equating equity with the way that "[f]air treatment in the older cases was characteristically assured by straightforward pro rata distribution of the limited fund."[164] Acknowledging that "equity in such a simple sense" is not always going to be available in the complex cases before the courts today, *Ortiz* nonetheless holds out the prospect of a complex settlement passing judicial muster based on "procedures to resolve the difficult issues of treating such differently situated claimants with fairness as among themselves."[165]

Putting the two parts of the Court's analysis together would allow for even complex settlements with contestable intraclass allocation issues, so long as there are clear guarantees of attorney fidelity to the class. The key is that a supervising court must be assured at the threshold stage of the litigation that there are no structural allegiances of class counsel that would create incentives to favor one part of the class over another, or be biased against seeking the best possible return to a defined subset of claims. This is an important advance in the Court's treatment of class actions because it avoids collapsing the viability of legitimate class actions simply because of there having been issues of intraclass allocation. Some allocation decisions are inescapable because there is an inevitable rough-hewn quality to the relief provided by class actions.[166] This can take place overtly, as with the common decision to substitute imprecise damage estimates in cases where the administrative costs of fine-tuning individual recoveries would overwhelm the resources available to the class.[167] But it can just as easily take place

---

[164] Id at 2319.

[165] Id.

[166] See Coffee, *The Regulation of Entrepreneurial Litigation* at 919 (cited in note 56) (dubbing this feature of class actions as "damage averaging").

[167] See Silver and Baker at 1479–81 (cited in note 14) (giving examples from consumer class actions of using damage estimates to provide some recovery to all class members).

covertly when lawyers decide to forgo some claims, such as those arguably barred by a statute of limitations, or decide not to prosecute individual-based damages that would place the class action beyond the managerial control of one court. As summed up by Professors Silver and Baker, "fine-tuning is not the norm."[168]

The key that emerges is the incentive of counsel to faithfully prosecute the case on behalf of all class members, and this portends a revisitation of class action law through a more direct examination of the question of attorneys' fees. A number of lower court decisions have already confronted the problem of attorneys being compensated differently from their class clients. For example, many small-value consumer claims are settled for "coupons"—a form of in-kind compensation that may reflect the excessive transactional costs of providing cash for all class members, or may simply reflect the low value of the asserted claims.[169] Such claims should raise concern when the coupons are of uncertain value and the lawyers propounding the settlement are being paid a cash premium in fees, independent of the ability of the class to obtain the benefits purportedly secured through the coupon settlement.

Unlike most principal-agent relations, of which contracted-for attorney representation is a subset, the representation of absent class members does not involve any negotiation of the relation between principal and agent. It is therefore useful to identify what contractual relations would most likely have emerged had the transactional barriers to negotiation not precluded direct contracting.[170] Almost invariably in cases in which plaintiffs are unable

---

[168] Id at 1482.

[169] For cases expressing great skepticism over coupon settlements, see *In re GM Corp. Pick-Up Truck Fuel Tank Products Liability Litigation*, 55 F3d 768 (3d Cir 1995), cert denied 516 US 824 (1995); *Bloyed v General Motors Corp.*, 881 SW2d 422 (Tx Ct App 1994), affirmed 916 SW2d 949 (Tex S Ct 1996) (also rejecting coupon settlement in GM truck litigation, but suggesting that the case had little value). But see Geoffrey P. Miller and Lori S. Singer, *Nonpecuniary Class Action Settlements*, 60 Law & Contemp Probs 97 (1997) (arguing that coupon settlements may be efficient in certain cases).

[170] This point was persuasively made by Judge Posner in *In re Continental Illinois Securities Litigation*, 962 F2d 566, 568 (7th Cir 1992) in the context of setting an appropriate fee for class counsel: "it is not the function of judges in fee litigation to determine the equivalent of the medieval just price. It is to determine what the lawyer would receive if he were selling his services in the market rather than being paid by court order." He reiterated the point in *In the Matter of Continental Illinois Securities Litigation*, 985 F2d 867, 868 (7th Cir 1993), stating that "in accordance with the principle that a judge in setting a fee award should be trying to give the lawyers what they would have got in a voluntary transaction in the market for legal services."

to pay the costs of litigation and an hourly fee to lawyers, the result is a contingency arrangement in which lawyers obtain a percentage recovery based on what the clients actually receive.[171] Although principal-agent problems are notoriously difficult, tying the agent's recovery to the principal's is an important first step in insuring that the agent has a clear incentive to maximize the return to the principal.

Determining how attorneys are to be compensated, and under what circumstances, is an important first step in grounding the law of class actions in the quality of the representation afforded absent class members. The duty of faithful representation by the attorney for the absent class members may fail under a variety of circumstances, as most clearly when the attorney is compensated in some fashion independently of the recovery of the class, or as in *Amchem* and *Ortiz*, when class counsel has a structural incentive to favor one portion of the class relative to another. But this does not exhaust the circumstances in which counsel are structurally precluded from acting as faithful agents of the class, and *Amchem* and *Ortiz* should be read to place the duty of faithful representation as a central inquiry, independent of the other requirements of Rule 23. Apart from the issue of attorney compensation untethered to the recovery of the class, class action case law suggests that the duty of faithful representation would fail where attorneys represent class members that either do not have a viable claim or have a claim that those attorneys cannot prosecute. This is the case for two separate reasons.

---

[171] This is the traditional basis for compensating attorneys when settlements or judgments create common funds and there is no contract between the lawyer and the beneficiaries. See, e.g., *Trustees v Greenough*, 105 US 527 (1881), and *Central Railroad & Baring Co. of Georgia v Pettus*, 113 US 116, 124 (1885). The Supreme Court reaffirmed the percentage recovery method of compensating attorneys who generate a common fund in *Blum v Stenson*, 465 US 886, 900 n 16 (1984) (observing that "under the 'common fund doctrine' . . . a reasonable fee is based on a percentage of the fund bestowed on the class"). See also *Camden I Condominium Ass'n v Dunkle*, 946 F2d 768, 771 (11th Cir 1991) ("From the time of the *Pettus* decision in 1885 until 1973, fee awards granted pursuant to the common fund . . . were computed as a percentage of the fund."). The percentage approach is also routinely employed in common fund cases in the vast majority of federal circuits. See, e.g., *In re Thirteen Appeals Arising Out of the San Juan DuPont Plaza Hotel Fire Litigation*, 56 F3d 295, 304–08 (1st Cir 1995); *In re General Motors Corp. Pick-Up Truck Fuel Tank Products Liability Litigation*, 55 F3d 768, 822 (3rd Cir 1995); *Rawlings v Prudential-Bache Properties Inc.*, 9 F3d 513, 516 (6th Cir 1993); *Florin v Nations Bank of Georgia*, 34 F3d 560, 565–66 (7th Cir 1994); *Johnston v Comenca Mort. Corp.*, 83 F3d 241, 246 (8th Cir 1996); *In re Washington Public Power Supply System Securities Litigation*, 19 F3d 1291, 1296 (9th Cir 1994); *Gottlieb v Barry*, 43 F3d 474, 483 (10th Cir 1994); *Camden I*, 946 F2d at 771–74; *Swedish Hospital Corp. v Shalala*, 1 F3d 1261, 1267–71 (DC Cir 1993).

First, class counsel are necessarily "disarmed," as defined by Amchem,[172] where the sine qua non of their representation of the class is their selection by the opposing party or the acquiescence of that party. If, as was implicit in *Amchem*[173] and fleshed out expressly in *Ortiz*,[174] the normal adversarial processes are an important guarantor of noncollusion in binding class action settlements, then the absence of a truly adversarial relation between the parties dooms this important guarantee that representation will be adequate.

Second, and relatedly, the failure to insist on truly adversarial relations between the parties creates the perfect medium for the creation of a reverse auction[175]—a process in which the claims of the class will be sold to the lowest bidder. Without some threat of a trial in some forum on behalf of the individuals comprising the class, however remote the possibility may in fact be, there is nothing to impede the "settlement" of claims that are not even at issue in any particular class action.[176] This is the familiar practice in class action law of negotiating a broad release to accompany the final decree.[177] There is a strong pressure toward a race to the bottom when lawyers are negotiating to close out claims that they did not have any control over in the first place. Any fee generated from a low-value settlement is better than the prospect of no fee in the event that there is no settlement. Since multiple actions may be—and often are—brought over the same general course of conduct, a defendant may play the rival class counsel off against each other seeking to extract the broadest release at the lowest price.

This analysis is difficult to reconcile with the Court's deci-

---

[172] 521 US at 619–22

[173] Id at 619–20.

[174] 119 S Ct at 2317–18.

[175] See Coffee, *Class Wars* at 1366–67 (cited in note 11); Richard A. Nagareda, *Turning from Tort to Administration*, 94 Mich L Rev 899, 960 (1996); Kahan and Silberman, *Matsushita and Beyond* at 238–39 (cited in note 123) (referring to this problem as "plaintiff shopping").

[176] See Coffee, *Class Wars* at 1354 (cited in note 11); Kahan and Silberman, *Matsushita and Beyond* at 235–38 (cited in note 123). I want to stress, however, that the threat need not be trial in the particular forum as structured through the proposed class action. A trial threat is not necessarily less credible because it will involve multiple actions.

[177] This is discussed in Issacharoff, *Class Action Conflicts* at 811–13 (cited in note 11).

sion in *Matsushita v Epstein*,[178] which involved rival class action challenges to a tender offer by Matsushita for MCA, Inc., a film enterprise incorporated in Delaware. Both class actions claimed misconduct or conflict of interest by the directors and managers of the target company. A Delaware state court class action did so under state law; a rival federal court class action in California did so under the federal securities laws. After extensive procedural wrangling, a settlement was reached and approved in Delaware state court that released all claims, including the securities claims over which the state court had no subject matter jurisdiction.

The Court, per Justice Thomas, treated the case as presenting the narrow question whether the settlement of claims over which the state court did not have jurisdiction was entitled to full faith and credit in a subsequent collateral challenge to the effect of the settlement on the California federal litigation. The Court's narrow jurisdictional reading of the case allowed it to conclude that the application of state res judicata principles would extend finality to all claims released through a consent decree, regardless of the absence of subject matter jurisdiction. Assuming such finality, the Court held that collateral challenge in the federal courts was barred by full faith and credit.[179] It was left to Justice Ginsburg's separate opinion to separate the issue of *where* the representation could be challenged from the issue of adequacy of representation left unaddressed by Justice Thomas's narrow jurisdictional approach. Justice Ginsburg, by contrast, stressed "the centrality of the procedural due process protection of adequate representation in class action lawsuits, emphatically including those resolved by settlement."[180]

Independent of the forum issue concerning the availability of collateral attack, *Matsushita* treats far too lightly the potential consequences of a settlement in which not only does the supervising court have no jurisdiction, but the lawyers have no claim to speak as authoritative agents for the class. From the approach suggested by *Amchem* and *Ortiz*, the issue was not necessarily the state court's lack of jurisdiction over the federal claims in a technical sense, but

---

[178] 516 US 367 (1996).

[179] Id at 373–86.

[180] Id at 399.

rather the lawyers' inability to represent the class as to the claims not presented in Delaware, except through the complicity of the defendants. The same scenario would look much different if the lawyers from the federal action had been present in the Delaware negotiations and had decided to settle in that forum.[181] Although the court would still not have jurisdiction to try all the claims had settlement failed, all the lawyers involved on behalf of the class would have legitimately endorsed the resolution of claims that they had properly asserted. In effect, the lawyers would have had the power generated by a credible threat to resort to adversarial litigation if the settlement offer was insufficient. And, most critically, they would have had the legitimacy of deriving their power from the capacity to advance the interests of the class, rather than from the complicity of the defendants

V. Conclusion

The combined effect of the Court's opinions in *Amchem* and *Ortiz* is to return the focus of class action law to the two themes that have been present since at least *Hansberry v Lee:* the importance of a structured inquiry to insure that the preconditions for subsuming individual claims within a collective action are met, and the separate issue of the legitimacy of representational governance that protects the interests of the absent class members that will be bound to a final decree. Looking back at earlier case law from the vantage point of *Amchem* and *Ortiz* reveals that these two themes have always been present in the Court's class action jurisprudence. *Hansberry* refused to allow claim preclusion in a context where the informal aggregation procedures of Illinois equity practice provided no assurance that a purported class action actually met the threshold requirements of having sufficient common characteristics and common interests so as to be jointly bound through one proceeding. At the other pole, *Martin v Wilks* refused to allow nonparties to a class action to be bound by a consent decree entered into by parties with interests antagonistic to

---

[181] On this score I agree with Professors Kahan and Silberman. Although they are generally supportive of the Court's reasoning in *Matsushita*, see Kahan and Silberman, *Matsushita and Beyond* at 230 (cited in note 123), they argue for far greater deference to a settlement in state court if the federal plaintiff is present as well as a proponent of the settlement. Id at 260–61.

theirs.[182] *Amchem* and *Ortiz* build upon these two bases of class action law.

In the first instance, the new class action case law reinforces the importance of procedural regularity in the formation of class actions. The 1966 Amendments to Rule 23 created for the first time a formal structured inquiry that allows courts to determine when aggregate treatment is appropriate. *Amchem* refused to allow the desire for settlement to substitute for the steps required to assure suitable aggregate treatment of the dispute. *Ortiz* similarly rejected the use of a potential litigation recovery to create a limited fund that would vitiate the minimal procedural protection that would otherwise be available under Rule 23(b)(3) certification. Taken together, these cases are an important reaffirmation of the role of procedural regularity in the delicate business of binding nonparticipants in representative actions.

But, despite the Court's invocation in both cases of rules formalism, the significance of *Amchem* and particularly *Ortiz* lies with the extension of the second part of the class action inquiry: the preconditions for legitimate governance of class actions. Here, I suggest, the Court's holdings have little if anything to do with the formal processes of Rule 23, and everything to do with the fundamental guarantees of due process. The Court has now explained that binding a nonparticipant to a judicial decree requires, at the very least, capable representation by an agent who must be faithful to the interests of the nonparticipants that are to be so bound. That agent is effectively the lawyer at the head of the class action, and the faithfulness of that lawyer is determined by whether there are structural incentives that force the lawyer's interests to deviate from those of the represented class.

What emerges, therefore, is a bifurcated inquiry that must accompany the initial request for class certification. In the first instance, the structured Rule 23 inquiry addresses the preconditions for aggregative treatment of the class claims. The recent class action case law has done little more than reinforce the significance of the formal class certification that has emerged from the 1966 amendments to Rule 23. At the same time, the due process inquiry

---

[182] *Martin* also anticipates that the process of judicial review in a fairness hearing under Rule 23(e) is not a substitute for adequate representation in the underlying litigation. 490 US 755 (1989).

into the governance of the class has advanced dramatically by finally focusing on the incentives facing the true representative agent, the class counsel, as the prime guarantor of the interests of the absent class members. As in the domain of politics, proper governance is the best guarantor of legitimacy for the decisions that must follow.

DOUGLAS G. BAIRD AND
ROBERT K. RASMUSSEN

BOYD'S LEGACY AND BLACKSTONE'S GHOST

Great battles are often fought in unlikely places. Last Term, the Supreme Court entertained an ordinary commercial law dispute between a financing bank and a group of real estate investors over the ownership of fifteen floors of an office building in downtown Chicago.[1] At issue was the ability of the partnership to restructure the bank's loan in Chapter 11. The partnership offered a plan that, in its view, left the bank with more than it would receive through a state law foreclosure, yet allowed the prebankruptcy investors in the partnership to remain as owners and enjoy significant tax benefits. When the bank turned down the partnership's plan, the bankruptcy court had to decide whether the plan could be confirmed over the bank's objection.

On its face, it might seem that such a dispute would not occupy the attention of a Supreme Court that now hears only about eighty cases a year. The property was well run, and no one suggested

Douglas G. Baird is Harry A. Bigelow Distinguished Service Professor of Law, The University of Chicago. Robert K. Rasmussen is Professor of Law, Vanderbilt Law School.

AUTHORS' NOTE: We are grateful to Barry Adler, Richard Bendix, Rebecca Brown, Constance Fleischer, John Goldberg, J. Winston King, Richard Levin, Ronald Mann, Bruce Markell, James Millstein, Cass Sunstein, Todd Zywicki, colleagues at workshops at Chicago, Columbia, and Vanderbilt, and participants at the Bankruptcy Roundtable at the University of Pennsylvania Institute for Law and Economics for their help. One of us wrote an amicus curiae brief on behalf of a group of law professors supporting the position of the bank and the Solicitor General. The other worked with the debtor's counsel.

[1] *Bank of America National Trust Savings Association v 203 North LaSalle Street Partnership*, 119 S Ct 1411 (1999).

that its day-to-day operations needed to be revamped.[2] Uncertainty about the value of the building was not a source of dispute either; both the bank and the investors agreed that the remaining balance on the loan far exceeded the market value of the property. Similarly, no one doubted either the existence of substantial tax benefits for the investors or the willingness and ability of the investors to add several million dollars to the pot to retain them. The inability of two sophisticated parties to reach a mutually beneficial bargain had few effects on anyone else. Their failure to make a deal, however, gave the Court the chance to address the most important open question under the Bankruptcy Code.

Everything revolved around on a single clause in Chapter 11 of the Bankruptcy Code. With its statutory and case-law antecedents, the language of this clause addresses the pivotal controversy in the law of corporate reorganizations for most of this century. The interpretation one chooses shapes all of Chapter 11, and the choice among interpretations turns in large part on the interpretative methodology one uses. Hence, a two-party dispute over an ordinary office building in Chicago joins a major debate over statutory interpretation.

The precise legal issue can be set out simply. To the extent that it was owed more than its collateral was worth, the bank held an unsecured claim in addition to its secured claim. Every claim in Chapter 11 is placed into a class, and the bank's claim was of a sort that had to be put in a class by itself.[3] Hence, when the bank voted against the plan, a class of unsecured claims necessarily voted against it as well. Section 1129(b) of the Bankruptcy Code provides, in relevant part, that when a class of unsecured claims dissents from a plan of reorganization, the bankruptcy court can confirm the plan only if:

---

[2] Indeed, the bank was concerned because some of the debtor's employees were leaving and it feared that equally able replacements might not be found. See *In re 203 North LaSalle Street Limited Partnership*, 190 Bankr 567, 591–92 (Bankr ND Ill 1995), aff'd, 195 Bankr 692 (ND Ill 1996), aff'd, 126 F3d 955 (7th Cir 1997), rev'd and rem'd, 119 S Ct 1411 (1999). The bank also pointed to one prepetition tax payment that the debtor had mishandled, but the bankruptcy court rejected this complaint, as well as the complaint that the management fee was too high.

[3] We are oversimplifying matters somewhat. The question of whether the bank's deficiency claim ought to be classified separately from other unsecured claims is an issue on which the courts are divided. The question, however, is settled in the Seventh Circuit and was not before the Court in *LaSalle*. See *In re Woodbrook Associates*, 19 F3d 312 (7th Cir 1994).

> [T]he plan . . . is fair and equitable. . . . [T]he condition that
> a plan be fair and equitable . . . includes the following require-
> ment[ ]: . . . the holder of any [junior] interest . . . will not
> receive or retain under the plan on account of such junior . . .
> interest any property.[4]

In other words, to confirm the plan, the court had to find that the
plan was "fair and equitable," which, at a minimum, requires that
the old investors not receive any "property" "on account of" their
old interests. None of these words is defined in the Bankruptcy
Code, but the phrase "fair and equitable" had been used in two
previous bankruptcy laws and in judicial opinions before then.

In writing for the Court, Justice Souter examined the origins of
the "fair and equitable" language and concluded—on the basis of
this history—that Section 1129(b) required adherence to "absolute
priority."[5] Under a regime of absolute priority, old equity cannot
receive anything if a dissenting class was not being paid in full. If
old equity could participate at all, it would be required to contribute an infusion of new capital. Old equity could not be given any
breaks. Old equity had to pay "top dollar" for the new interest.[6]
The bankruptcy court had not taken sufficient steps to ensure that
this had in fact been the case.[7] Hence, the plan could not be confirmed and the Court remanded.

Justice Thomas, joined by Justice Scalia, wrote a concurring
opinion in which he argued that one could resolve the case without
recourse to history, the concept of "absolute priority," or anything
beyond the words in the statute. The plan, in substance, gave the
old equityholders the exclusive right to the equity of the reorganized entity. Such an exclusive right was a stock option, something
ordinarily regarded as "property" and hence "property" within the
meaning of the statute.[8] Because the plan gave this option only to
the old equityholders, they received it "on account of" their old
interest. Hence, the plan did not meet the specific requirement set
out in Section 1129. Justice Thomas concluded that the Court

---

[4] 11 USC § 1129(b)(2).

[5] 119 S Ct 1416–17.

[6] Id at 1423.

[7] Justice Stevens in dissent agreed with most of this analysis, parting company with the
majority only over the issue of whether the thorough and financially sophisticated opinion
of the bankruptcy court paid sufficient attention to this specific question.

[8] Id at 1424.

could reject the debtor's plan without having to ask whether, as a general matter, the plan was "fair and equitable." He never had to invoke the principle of absolute priority.

While Justice Thomas reached the same conclusion as Justice Souter, the methodology he advanced would require lower courts to apply the Bankruptcy Code differently as a general matter. For Justice Thomas, the obligation of a reviewing court in bankruptcy cases is to set out "a clear method for interpreting the Bankruptcy Code."[9] This method should eschew exploring the origins of words such as "fair and equitable" when the focus is the meaning of an ordinary word such as "property." Instead of importing the mysticism and uncertainty of common law judging into statutory interpretation, courts should allow the plain language of the statute to speak for itself. An interpretative approach that focuses on words and their ordinary meaning yields more certain outcomes and provides better guidance to lower courts than one that attempts to discover a seamless web woven through decades-old cases and repeated statutory enactments. For every case in which a nuanced common law approach sheds valuable insight, there are ten in which it leads judges astray. We live in a statutory era, and courts should not let open-textured language tempt them to wander about searching for principles immanent in the law. Judges should not chase Blackstone's ghost.

In this article, we examine these two different ways of interpreting the Bankruptcy Code. Similar questions, of course, arise whenever a statute contains fragments of old law. One can use these as landmarks that help organize a statutory regime and discover its internal coherence. Alternatively, one can treat these fragments as vestiges of the past that ought to be confronted only when they are squarely put in issue and not otherwise. Any coherence a statute has must come from a straightforward interpretation of the text. *LaSalle* provides the chance to study how this debate plays out in a specific context.

Many debates over statutory interpretation are debates about judicial restraint. The debate in *LaSalle* is different. Neither Justice Souter nor Justice Thomas is a judicial activist. Neither sees the judge as Hercules nor does either embrace dynamic interpreta-

---

[9] Id at 1425.

tion.[10] They both want to give guidance to lower courts, while recognizing that, as generalist appellate judges, they lack subject matter expertise. Neither has an interest in boldly reshaping the law. They both want a methodology that ensures lower courts implement faithfully the laws that Congress has passed. Their debate concerns the best methodology after one has made a commitment to judicial moderation.

From Justice Thomas's perspective, Justice Souter's methodology, relying as it does on history and common law precedent, is too uncertain and ignores the institutional and practical constraints under which judges operate. Implicit in Justice Souter's opinion is the belief that Justice Thomas's approach is simpler in appearance only. His methodology depends upon assumptions that, if not grounded in history, must be grounded some place else. Central to understanding Justice Souter's opinion in *LaSalle* and Justice Thomas's critique of it is the question of whether and to what extent history is necessary to interpreting this section of the Bankruptcy Code. We turn first to that history.

I. Boyd and the Equity Receivership

The modern law of corporate reorganizations begins with *Northern Pacific Railway v Boyd*.[11] In 1886, a man named Spaulding had supplied $25,000 worth of materials and labor to the Coeur D'Alene Railroad for which he was never paid. The assets of the Coeur D'Alene, after several restructurings, ultimately became part of the Northern Pacific Railroad. Spaulding believed he could hold the Northern Pacific Railroad liable for this debt. Before he acquired a judgment against it, however, the Northern Pacific Railroad became insolvent and went through a common law reorganization—an equity receivership—out of which emerged a new entity called the Northern Pacific Railway.

---

[10] For an argument that textualism by the Supreme Court would promote better outcomes than dynamic interpretation in bankruptcy cases, see Robert K. Rasmussen, *A Study of the Costs and Benefits of Textualism: The Supreme Court's Bankruptcy Cases*, 71 Wash U L Q 535 (1993).

[11] 228 US 482 (1913). For two excellent accounts of *Boyd* and the evolution of the absolute priority rule, see John D. Ayer, *Rethinking Absolute Priority After Ahlers*, 87 Mich L Rev 963 (1989); Randolph J. Haines, *The Unwarranted Attack on New Value*, 72 Am Bankr L J 387 (1998).

Spaulding's successor, a man named Boyd, did not participate in the reorganization of the Northern Pacific Railroad and instead sued the new entity. The dispute finally reached the U.S. Supreme Court in 1913. The Court found first that the old Northern Pacific had indeed been responsible for the obligations of Coeur D'Alene. Hence, the Court then had to ask whether the new Northern Pacific was responsible for the debts of the old. Shareholders of the old Northern Pacific remained shareholders of the new.[12] Boyd argued that a reorganization could not allow old shareholders to remain in place and at the same time extinguish his rights as a general creditor. As a general creditor he was entitled to priority over the shareholders.

The matter, however, was not this simple. Shareholders participated with the blessing of the railroad's senior creditors. These senior creditors enjoyed priority over general creditors like Boyd, and the court that oversaw the reorganization had found that they were owed more than the Northern Pacific Railroad was worth. Hence, one could argue, Boyd had nothing to complain about. These senior creditors were entitled to the entire firm. They thus were free to include the shareholders or not as they pleased.

Boyd v Northern Pacific Railway is perhaps the most important bankruptcy opinion of the last century.[13] The Supreme Court relied on a doctrine from the law of real estate mortgages to decide the case. This reliance raised the larger question of how many other principles of real estate foreclosure law should be imported into the law of corporate reorganizations. This larger question has still not been completely answered. *Boyd*'s legacy was to make this question the central focus of corporate reorganizations for almost a century.

Before addressing the larger issue, however, we should focus on the holding of *Boyd* proper. *Boyd* relied on a doctrine from the law of fraudulent conveyances. Fraudulent conveyance law voids transfers by a debtor that subvert the rights of creditors. Most significantly, it looks at substance rather than form. The relevant transaction to which it applied in the context of a real estate fore-

---

[12] The old shareholders could retain their interests only if they paid an assessment, but the shares they received were worth more than they were assessed.

[13] See, e.g., Randal C. Picker, *Designing Verifiability: Boyd's Implications for Modern Bankruptcy Law* (U Chicago, 1999).

closure takes the following form. First Bank holds a $100 first mortgage on Blackacre and Second Bank holds a $100 second mortgage. Owner defaults and First Bank forecloses. Owner makes the winning bid of $100 at the foreclosure sale. First Bank is paid $100. Owner now enjoys the property, not because of its old interest, but because it was the high bidder at the sale. At this point, Owner returns to First Bank, borrows $100 from it, and gives it a new mortgage on Blackacre.

Owner and First Bank argue that the foreclosure sale extinguished the claim of Second Bank. Once one pierces form and looks at substance, however, nothing has happened, other than the elimination of Second Bank's claim. Fraudulent conveyance law tells us First Bank and Owner cannot engage in a transaction that, in substance, does no more than wipe out the interests of a creditor. Hence, fraudulent conveyance law dictates that Second Bank's claim survives the foreclosure and Second Bank remains free to enforce its claim.

In *Boyd*, a divided court found that the same principle existed in the law of corporate reorganizations:

> As against creditors, [the sale] was a mere form. Though the Northern Pacific Railroad was divested of the legal title, the old stockholders were still owners of the same railroad, encumbered by the same debts. The circumlocution did not better their title against Boyd as a nonassenting creditor. They had changed the name but not the relation.[14]

Nor did it matter that the assets were worth less than what creditors senior to Boyd were owed:

> [T]he question must be decided according to a fixed principle, not leaving the rights of the creditors to depend upon the balancing of evidence as to whether, on the day of sale the property was insufficient to pay prior encumbrances . . .
>   . . . If the value of the road justified the issuance of stock in exchange for old shares, the creditors were entitled to the benefit of that value, whether it was present or prospective, for dividends or only for purposes of control. In either event it was a right of property out of which the creditors were entitled to be paid before the stockholders could retain it for any purpose whatever.[15]

---

[14] 228 US at 506–07.

[15] Id at 507–08.

The Court did not go so far as to say that all of real estate foreclosure law should be mechanically transplanted to the law of corporate reorganizations. In a real estate foreclosure, for example, it would not have mattered whether Boyd was actively involved in the process. Moreover, any continuing interest of the old owner after the foreclosure would allow the junior creditor to pursue its claim against the land. Importing this doctrine into the law of corporate reorganizations unmodified would radically unsettle the law of corporate reorganizations. *Boyd*, however, did not do this. The Court held only that a complete freeze-out of an intervening creditor was not permitted. Indeed, the Court itself was quick to note that its holding was narrow:

> [We do not] require the impossible and make it necessary to pay an unsecured creditor in cash as a condition of stockholders retaining an interest in the reorganized company. His interest can be preserved by the issuance, on equitable terms, of income bonds or preferred stock. If he declines a fair offer he is left to protect himself as any other creditor of a judgment debtor, and, having refused to come into a just reorganization, could not thereafter be heard in a court of equity to attack it.[16]

In contrast to real estate foreclosures, a plan of reorganization could include shareholders if the creditor were given a "fair offer" in a "just reorganization." Exactly what this meant, the Court did not explain. Lower courts had to identify on their own the contours of the "fixed principle" that should be at work. They had to decide on their own how much of real estate foreclosure law to use in assessing whether a plan satisfied *Boyd*.

Lower courts soon began to find their way. They found, for example, that old shareholders could participate if the old shareholders were the best source of new capital, if they were putting in new capital equal to the value of the stock they were receiving in return, and if the senior lenders blessed the plan.[17] As long as the general creditors were given a hearing, their interests could be wiped out completely.[18]

---

[16] Id at 508.

[17] For example, see *Oehring v Fox Typewriter Co.*, 272 F 833, 835 (6th Cir 1921) (general creditor could not obtain relief where "[e]very new stockholder paid cash in full for his new stock and received nothing in exchange for his old.").

[18] Henry Friendly's observation in a 1934 article reflected the thinking of judges and lawyers of the time:

The most important unanswered question after *Boyd* was whether the old shareholders could receive stock worth *more* than the amount of the new capital they put in. The real estate analogy would suggest that they could not. A real estate foreclosure is a day of reckoning in which the ownership of the property necessarily changes hands. The land is sold for a fixed amount. The creditors stand in line according to the order in which they recorded their interests. The first mortgagee is paid in full, then the second, and so forth until the money is exhausted. Under such a regime of "absolute priority" (as it came to be called[19]), one could not justify giving the shareholders any more than they contributed in new capital. In the wake of *Boyd*, however, lower courts found that the law of corporate reorganizations did not include the rule of absolute priority, but rather another rule, a rule that was eventually called "relative priority." This rule, one that courts were to use for twenty-five years, was shaped in large part by a single lawyer— Robert Swaine.

II. ROBERT SWAINE AND RELATIVE PRIORITY

Robert Swaine went to the Harvard Law School where he was president of the *Law Review* and awarded the Fay Diploma.[20] He was recruited to teach at Harvard by Dean Ames, but that plan fell through when Ames died unexpectedly. Swaine then joined the Cravath firm in 1910 as a litigator, planning to teach after some time in practice. Within a year, however, Swaine had lost his interest in both litigation and teaching. He turned instead to corporate reorganizations. In early 1916, a month before his thirtieth birthday, he was sent to Jefferson City, Missouri, and charged with the task of persuading the district court there to approve a reorganiza-

---

[A] few principles can be regarded as definitely settled. Stockholders who furnish new money required by the reorganized company may be permitted to retain an interest in the company, even though sacrifices from creditors are compelled.

Henry J. Friendly, *Some Comments on the Corporate Reorganizations Act*, 48 Harv L Rev 39, 75–76 (1934). See also James C. Bonbright and Milton M. Bergerman, *Two Rival Theories of the Priority Rights of Security Holders in a Corporate Reorganization*, 28 Colum L Rev 127, 132 (1928); John Gerdes, 2 *Corporate Reorganizations Under Section 77B of the Bankruptcy Act* § 1084 at 1733 n 7 (Callaghan & Co., 1936).

[19] The phrase "absolutely priority" appears to have appeared first in Bonbright and Bergerman, *Two Rival Theories* at 130 (cited in note 18).

[20] See Robert T. Swaine, 2 *The Cravath Firm and Its Predecessors* 162–65 (Ad Press, Ltd., 1948).

tion of the Frisco line.[21] Starting in this case, he began to develop a theory of priority quite different from the one with which real estate lawyers had long been familiar.

We need to look at the financing of railroads in the nineteenth century to understand Swaine's conception of relative priority. Railroads were the first giant privately financed corporations.[22] By 1860, however, private investment in railroads exceeded a billion dollars, and investment bankers such as J. P. Morgan, August Belmont, and Kidder Peabody had to turn to large commercial centers of Europe for the capital to finance the transcontinental railroads that were to be built over the next three decades. These investment bankers sat on the boards of the various railroads and represented the interests of their European investors.[23] Because they counted on repeated dealings with these investors, they had the incentive to represent them well. So too did the lawyers who represented them. Early on, among the most prominent was the Cravath firm.[24]

The period between 1865 and 1890 was one of enormous growth for the railroads. The period also saw the consolidation of different lines in haphazard and unpredictable ways. Over 75,000 miles of track were laid down in the 1880s alone. This was a time of increasing competition.[25] Moreover, there was at the same time increasing government regulation, the most important of which was the Interstate Commerce Act of 1887. Competition among the different lines intensified, cartels came into existence and then fell apart. At the same time, the early 1890s brought on one of the United States's worst economic downturns. All these factors created an industry that by the mid-1890s was insolvent. Most of the railroads that had been built could not meet their fixed obliga-

---

[21] For an account of Swaine's role in the reorganization of the Frisco line, see id at 169–75.

[22] For a discussion of the equity receivership and the role that lawyers played in shaping it, see Robert W. Gordon, *Legal Thought and Legal Practice in the Age of American Enterprise, 1870–1920*, in Gerald L. Geison, ed, *Professions and Professional Ideologies in America* 70, 101–10 (U North Carolina Press, 1983).

[23] See Alfred D. Chandler, Jr., *The Visible Hand: The Managerial Revolution in American Business* 146 (Belknap, 1977).

[24] Even in the 1880s, the railroad reorganization clients of Cravath's predecessor firm included the Deutsche Bank, as well as bondholders in London, Frankfurt, and Amsterdam. See Swaine, 1 *The Cravath Firm* at 377, 614–15 (cited in note 20).

[25] For a discussion of the competition among railroads connecting Chicago with New York during this period, see William Cronon, *Nature's Metropolis: Chicago and the Great West* 81–93 (Norton, 1991).

tions. Over half the railroad tracks in the United States went through reorganization during this period, some more than once.[26]

A paradigmatic railroad in need of reorganization took the following form. There were few general creditors. There were different classes of bonds, each widely held by diverse investors, many of whom were in Europe. One bond was secured by the track between point A and point B, another secured by track between point B and point C, a third between C and D, and so on. Points B through Y are in the middle of nowhere, and the terminals at points A and Z connect to solvent railroads owned by the shareholders.[27] The collateral of individual creditors adds value to the ongoing railroad. This value, however, could not be realized by foreclosing on the collateral; rather, only through the active participation of all parties could the value of the constituent parts be maximized.[28]

Bringing about a successful reorganization was hard. The value of the railroad had to be estimated against a background of rapid technological and regulatory change. The claim of the many different kinds of bondholders turned on how much their collateral contributed to the earnings of the railroad as a whole. Moreover, many of the investors lived abroad and could not actively participate in the reorganization. They had to rely on their investment bankers and their lawyers to represent them. While Congress had the power to enact federal bankruptcy law, it had not enacted a corporate reorganization statute. Faced with dispersed interests with uncertain value and no statutory guidance, the lawyers used the equity receivership to reorganize the railroads.

One of the powers of a judge sitting in equity is the ability to

---

[26] For a history of railroad reorganizations of the 1890s, see Stuart Daggett, *Railroad Reorganization* (Harvard U Press, 1908).

[27] For an account of the financial structure of one of the railroads that Swaine reorganized, see Swaine, 2 *The Cravath Firm* at 169 (cited in note 20) (the Frisco had thirty different issues of securities other than equipment trusts and terminal bonds, most of them secured by liens on single constituent lines).

[28] As one commentator noted:

> In arriving at the standard which the legislature should set, reasoning based upon the rights of security holders upon bankruptcy or foreclosure if they should insist upon their rights is . . . somewhat beside the point. That kind of argument opens the way to the discussion of what kind of right it is which in most cases the individual security holder in a large reorganization can never insist upon.

Edward H. Levi, *Corporate Reorganization and a Ministry of Justice*, 23 Minn L Rev 3, 19 (1938).

appoint a person (called a receiver) to administer assets over which there is dispute. A creditor, for example, could petition the court to appoint a receiver to gain control over the assets of its debtor and sell them. This device was reshaped to accommodate the nineteenth-century railroads that had obligations so inconsistent with their earnings that they needed a new capital structure. The insiders who ran the railroad, typically also owners of a substantial part of the stock, would find a friendly creditor and have that creditor petition the court to place the assets in the hands of a receiver, usually the same person then managing the railroad.

The receivership provided an umbrella under which those holding different classes of claims and interests could organize themselves. At the end of the process was a court-supervised sale. The period preceding the sale was a time of intense negotiation among the affected parties. Committees would be established to represent each class of claimants. Each committee would persuade individual claimants to deposit their claims with the committee. The committees would then form a reorganization committee, composed of members from the other committees.

The reorganization committee would decide how much each claimant should receive in the reorganized railroad. After negotiating this plan of reorganization, the reorganization committee would attend the sale of the railroad. The market was sufficiently illiquid that the winning bidder would inevitably be the reorganization committee, and the amount bid would typically be only a fraction of the value of the railroad, measured on a going-concern basis. Those who participated in the reorganization would receive what the plan awarded them; those who did not would only get their share of what the assets fetched at the court sale. As a result, anyone who did not participate in the process would receive nothing or only a fraction of the amount of his claim.

The equity receivership depended upon the active cooperation of the old shareholders because they were the ones who actively managed the railroad and kept its books. They would have no incentive to orchestrate the reorganization if its effect would be to wipe out their interests completely. The reorganization, at the very least, could not leave them worse off than if they did nothing other than pray that things would get better. Moreover, the old shareholders were one of the few sources of new capital. As a result, equity receiverships usually produced a plan of reorganization that allowed the shareholders to retain an equity interest in the rail-road, an opportunity often conditioned on their willingness to contribute new funds to the cash-strapped enterprise.

The equity receivership provided a way in which investors could organize themselves and overcome the collective action problem from holdouts. Crucial was the ability to conduct a sale in which the reorganization committee could make a winning bid for less than the going-concern value of the assets. It often had the effect of leaving shareholders in place, even though intervening creditors were not being paid in full. This vehicle worked because the judicial sale created a new owner who took the assets free of all pre-existing claims. The bargaining among the committees allowed people to sort out priorities that might not have been clear.

The investors, as a group, were sophisticated parties and repeat players who believed that the system worked to their benefit. A creditor with a nonrecourse junior lien on a spur line could not complain about the rights of the shareholders in the reorganized entity and indeed would not want to, given that its only chance of being paid anything was if it actively participated on a reorganization committee. Most of the general creditors were suppliers with ongoing relationships with the railroad. Several rules (such as the six-month rule and the doctrine of necessity) had the effect of paying such general creditors in full,[29] even though the railroads were typically worth far less than what the secured creditors were owed. Those who objected tended to be people like Boyd who possessed an off-beat claim.

Because the railroads were the first experiments in large aggregations of capital from diverse investors, many of the terms of the investment contracts were left blank or imported mechanically from real estate transactions. The law of equity receiverships had to supply the missing terms, and these had to respond to the distinct problems that arose when the firm needed a new capital structure. The equity receivership provided such a mechanism, but it could work only if the insiders, the holders of the equity, found it in their interest to start the process and provide the new money needed just to pay for the restructuring. The solution that emerged was one in which the shareholders could invoke the process and

---

[29] See, e.g., *Fosdick v Schall*, 99 US 235 (1878); *Miltenberger v Logansport Railway*, 106 US 286 (1882).

remain in control provided they contributed the capital necessary to pay for the reorganization.

This solution departs radically from current conceptions of debt contracts. Today, debt contracts are thought to include the right of the debtholders to wipe out the shareholders once a firm becomes insolvent.[30] Insolvency triggers an acceleration of the debtor's obligations and sorts out the rights of all the players by collapsing all future values to the present. When liabilities, fairly discounted, exceed assets, the shareholders should be eliminated. The equity receivership, by contrast, is a world that depends upon the old shareholders to take the lead in recapitalizing the insolvent firm and to continue to manage it afterwards. In such a world, we should not expect insolvency itself to trigger a day of reckoning.

Robert Swaine's central contribution to the law of corporate reorganizations was to show that the priority to which creditors are entitled vis-à-vis shareholders does not require that we extinguish the shareholder's interest when a firm's liabilities exceed its assets. An equity interest in an insolvent firm ceases to have value only after we decide to collapse all future assets and liabilities to their present value. In the absence of an event that recognizes gains and losses, equity always possesses an option value. It trades for a positive price *even when liabilities exceed assets.* Allowing equity to initiate a recapitalization and receive in return shares in the new firm that reflect the option value of their old shares is a coherent way to organize the world. Such a recapitalization respects the priority of the bondholders who have no practical ability to force a day of reckoning on their own.[31]

Boyd tells us that creditors cannot be wiped out in a reorganiza-

---

[30] For an economic justification of absolute priority, see Alan Schwartz, *The Absolute Priority Rule and the Firm's Investment Policy,* 72 Wash U L Q 1213 (1994).

[31] See Robert T. Swaine, *Reorganization of Corporations: Certain Developments of the Last Decade,* 27 Colum L Rev 901, 912–23 (1927); Bonbright and Bergerman, *Two Rival Theories* at 131–32 (cited in note 18). Relative priority turns centrally on protecting the option value of the equity and not treating the reorganization as a recognition event, a realization. Neither Swaine nor his contemporaries, however, presented their view explicitly in these terms, and attacks on relative priority gained much of their power from the belief that relative priority could not be rigorously defended, given the priority to which creditors were contractually entitled. See Address of Abe Fortas, Assistant Director of the Public Utilities Division, Securities and Exchange Commission, July 14, 1938, New York, NY, at p 8.

Modern scholarship, however, has shown that sound rationales might support departures from the absolute priority rule. See, e.g., Thomas H. Jackson and Robert E. Scott, *On the Nature of Bankruptcy: An Essay on Bankruptcy Sharing and the Creditors' Bargain,* 75 Va L Rev 155 (1989).

tion, and that their new interests in the firm have to reflect the value they had relative to the old equity. Nothing in *Boyd*, however, forbids taking into account the option value of equity. We do not have to treat the reorganization itself as a recognition event that collapses the value of all liabilities and assets to fixed sums. This idea of relative priority emerged in the lower courts after *Boyd*. It allowed investors to sort out their rights with a minimum of judicial interference, it ensured the survival of the firm as a going concern, and it provided enough judicial scrutiny at the end to ensure that the rights of dissenters were respected.[32]

In 1926, after these developments in the lower courts, the Supreme Court returned to the issues raised by *Boyd*. In *Kansas City Terminal Railway v Central Union Trust*,[33] the Court found that a reorganization had to recognize the right of all creditors "to be preferred to stockholders against the full value of all property belonging to the debtor corporation."[34] The opinion does not discuss what it means by "full value." It is as consistent with a regime of relative priority, one that recognizes the option value of an insolvent equity interest, as with absolute priority, which does not. At the same time, the opinion seems to endorse the universally accepted practice of allowing shareholders to participate in the new reorganization when they were willing to contribute new capital to the enterprise:

> Generally, additional funds will be essential to the success of the undertaking, and it may be impossible to obtain them unless stockholders are permitted to contribute and retain an interest sufficiently valuable to move them. In such or similar cases the chancellor may exercise an informed discretion concerning the practical adjustment of the several rights.[35]

---

[32] Less central, but nevertheless important, was the idea that we should also, to the extent possible, give creditors a type of interest in the firm, such as debentures or preferred stock, that is senior to the old shareholders. Doing this made it easier to value them relative to the equity and it made it hard to dilute their value subsequently. Bonbright and Bergerman, *Two Rival Theories* at 144–45 (cited in note 18).

[33] 271 US 445 (1926).

[34] Id at 454.

[35] Id at 455. The Court in its opinion was answering poorly framed interrogatories from the Circuit Court. Hence, the exact holding is hard to fathom. Ayer and Haines both conclude that *Kansas City* does not squarely adopt either absolute or relative priority. See Ayer, *Rethinking Absolute Priority* at 1001–07 (cited in note 11); Haines, *Unwarranted Attack* at 405–06 (cited in note 11).

The equity receivership under a regime of relative priority effectively allows creditors as a group to compromise their claims in accord with the realities of bargaining power as well as their nominal legal entitlements. Individual creditors could not, apart from the reorganization committees, insist on the rights they would enjoy in the absence of a receivership.

Such was the view of reorganizations that Robert Swaine put forward after *Boyd*.[36] This regime of "relative priority" was one in which sophisticated Wall Street lawyers and investment bankers occupied center stage. With a minimum of outside involvement, they protected the interests of their clients and ensured that railroads on which the economy depended continued to run. Lower courts continued to confirm plans of reorganizations in which shareholders remained in the picture either without contributing new capital or by contributing an amount worth significantly less than what they put in. A good example is *Jameson v Guaranty Trust*.[37] Holders of refunding bonds challenged a reorganization plan which scaled back their interests and, in exchange for a fresh capital infusion, allowed the old shareholders to retain the equity in the firm and receive bonds senior to those received by the dissenting creditors. In rejecting this challenge, the Seventh Circuit noted:

> As between the stock and the refunding bonds, the advantages of the plan to the latter, in our judgment, will approximately balance whatever concessions the plan requires of them, and, the stock remaining, as before, subordinate to the bonds, we do not see wherein the plan unfairly or inequitably gives material advantage to the stock over these bonds.[38]

III. Jerome Frank and Absolute Priority

As reorganization practice expanded beyond the railroads, a number of lawyers became increasingly skeptical of relative priority as the proper understanding of *Boyd*. These lawyers had a much less benign view of reorganizations than did Swaine. Chief

---

[36] See, e.g., Swaine, *Reorganization of Corporations* at 912–23 (cited in note 31).

[37] 20 F2d 808 (7th Cir), cert denied, 275 US 569 (1927). *Jameson* was included as a principal case is the leading casebook on corporate reorganizations. See William O. Douglas and Carrol M. Shanks, *Cases and Materials on the Law of Corporate Reorganization* 287 (West Pub, 1931).

[38] 20 F2d at 813.

among them was a reorganization lawyer who practiced in Chicago for many years before moving to New York in the late 1920s. His name was Jerome Frank.

Jerome Frank's initial experiences with the law were not at all like Swaine's. Frank's first job was as a secretary to a reform Chicago alderman. "Against the likes of aldermen popularly known as Hinky Dink and Bath House John, Frank honed a political style that was never to be known for its subtlety nor its reticence."[39] Frank soon turned to private practice in Chicago. Like Swaine, he focused on corporate reorganizations, but his practice involved not only the restructuring of great railroads, but also industrial firms that were financed with publicly traded securities. The debt tended to be diversely held while the stock was often in the hands of those who ran the firm.

The capital structure of these firms was simple and hierarchical. The corporation in reorganization might be a holding company that had issued a single class of bond. Each creditor held the same instrument and differed only in the amount that they held. Insiders would hold the equity of the holding company, and its sole asset would be the stock of the subsidiary. The subsidiary would be a manufacturer or some other industrial firm. The holders of the equity of the parent sat on the boards of both the parent and the subsidiary.

The crazy quilt capital structures seen in railroads in the nineteenth century had largely disappeared. Moreover, bondholders were no longer sophisticated European investors represented by major Wall Street law firms. Rather, in Frank's view, they were too often diverse members of the public with neither the time nor the expertise to protect themselves. They were largely at the mercy of the shareholders and a variety of professionals, ranging from indenture trustees to bankers to lawyers, who appeared once the reorganization began and who stood to profit from restructuring.

Frank believed that, by the 1930s, the receivership had become a vehicle by which the old shareholders and professionals could extract value at the expense of unsophisticated investors.[40] The le-

---

[39] Joel Seligman, *The Transformation of Wall Street: A History of the Securities and Exchange Commission and Modern Corporate Finance* 215 (Northeastern U Press, rev ed 1995).

[40] Jerome Frank, *Some Realistic Reflections on Some Aspects of Corporate Reorganization*, 19 Va L Rev 541 (1933). Frank's views were shared by fellow New Dealers. Max Lowenthal casts reorganization lawyers like Swaine in a negative light in his account of the Chicago,

gal system needed to protect the latter group. Frank rejected
Swaine's theory of relative priority. He argued that the paradigm
from real estate law should apply with full force. The reorganization of a firm should be a day of reckoning on which we establish
the value of the assets and sort out all the claims according to the
priority they enjoy upon default outside of bankruptcy. If the firm
is insolvent, the old equity should be wiped out. Priority for Frank
was absolute:

> If the property of the old company cannot on any conceivable
> basis be shown to be worth more than its debts, there is no
> excuse for allowing . . . participation by stockholders where
> essential new funds can be as advantageously procured without
> recourse to the stockholders. To hold otherwise would be to
> eviscerate the "law of fraudulent conveyances."[41]

Frank found the analogy to foreclosure compelling and thought
relative priority too vague. Lawyers could present a plan to the
court as a fait accompli and the court would be hard pressed to
find that the plan was not, in the language of *Boyd*, "just" if the
"fixed principle" at work was relative priority. While Swaine
thought relative priority was needed to ensure the cooperation of
the insiders who held the equity, Frank advocated absolute priority
because it best protected the public investors:

> Courts of equity have a tradition of aiding the helpless, such
> as infants, idiots and drunkards. The average security holder
> in a corporate reorganization is of like kind.[42]

Milwaukee & St. Paul Railway. See Max Lowenthal, *The Investor Pays* (Knopf, 1933). Thurman Arnold paints the following picture:

> Large fees in such situations are the rule rather than the exception. Generally
> counsel fees in reorganizations constitute the largest single item for all service
> and usually exceed the compensation of the officers or groups which the attorney
> represents. The fees represent high-class boondoggling and bureaucratic red tape
> of so complicated a nature that it is almost impossible to say at what point they
> are unjustified. Moral judgments can scarcely be made. In addition to fees, key
> places in any reorganization offer opportunities for distribution of valuable patron-
> age. The stakes of participation in reorganization have become so high that they
> often are a greater objective that the reorganization itself.
>   The situation is very similar to the control of a municipal government by a
> political machine, with the possible exception that the public opinion does not
> permit politicians to take any such percentage of the income of the municipality
> which they control.

Thurman W. Arnold, *The Folklore of Capitalism* 258–59 (Yale U Press, 1937).

[41] Frank, *Some Realistic Reflections* at 560 (cited in note 40).

[42] Id at 569.

Swaine, the establishment Wall Street lawyer, saw negotiation and compromise among professionals like him as the essential feature of corporate reorganization. Frank, the zealous New Deal lawyer, saw the need to recognize legal entitlements and regulate the entire process so as to ensure that small investors were protected. Swaine cared most about preserving going concern value; Frank cared about respecting the rights of individual investors through government regulation. Swaine thought that the process could be lawyer-driven with a judge arriving on the scene after the fact to confirm that the overall process was fair. Frank thought that a lawyer-driven process was too cozy and too easy to manipulate at the expense of the unsophisticated.

The differences between Swaine and Frank rarely surfaced in court. The entire process was one in which the players avoided valuations and other mechanisms that would require the issue to be confronted. In many cases, the lower courts were not squarely faced with the obligation to find that a firm was insolvent. As long as the court did not find that the firm was insolvent, one could argue that a plan that included shareholders still complied with absolute priority. Moreover, a plan that includes shareholders complies with absolute priority when the shareholders are contributing new capital needed for the reorganization and their new stake is reasonably tied to their contribution.

Against this ongoing struggle over the continued evolution of reorganization practice, Congress enacted a reorganization statute in 1934.[43] The statute required, inter alia, that two-thirds of each class of claimant approve the plan, and that the plan be "fair and equitable." The Supreme Court had never used "fair and equitable" in *Boyd* or in any other opinion. The courts that used "fair and equitable" and similar language had, for the most part, adopted relative priority. These courts, however, were using *Boyd* and *Kansas City* as their benchmarks. One could argue that if these courts were told that *Boyd* mandated absolute priority, they would agree that only a plan that satisfied absolute priority was "fair and equitable." By using "fair and equitable," neither this legislation

---

[43] For David Skeel's fine account of the emergence of modern reorganization law out of the equity receivership, see David A. Skeel, Jr., *An Evolutionary Theory of Corporate Law and Corporate Bankruptcy*, 51 Vand L Rev 1325, 1353–76 (1998); David A. Skeel, Jr., *The Rise and Fall of the SEC in Bankruptcy*, University of Pennsylvania Law School Institute for Law and Economics Working Paper No 267, 5–12 (Nov 1999).

nor its successor in 1938 resolved the different interpretations of *Boyd* put forward by Swaine and Frank.[44]

IV. William O. Douglas and Los Angeles Lumber Products

The Supreme Court did not face the question of whether "fair and equitable" required absolute or relative priority until the end of the 1930s.[45] At issue was the reorganization of a holding company whose principal asset was the Los Angeles Shipbuilding & Drydock Corporation. This shipyard had built ships for the Navy during World War I, but had languished during the isolationism of the 1920s and 1930s. The only creditors were holders of twenty-year bonds issued in 1924 and due in 1944. Over 92% of the face amount of the bondholders voted in favor of the plan. The plan of reorganization gave 23% of the stock in the new corporation to the old shareholders. They planned to continue to play a managerial role in operating the business, but they were not contributing any new cash.

The District Court had held that the plan was "fair and equitable." It noted that only two bondholders had objected to the plan, and the court did not want to give a few dissenters the ability to hold up a reorganization approved by a substantial majority of the bondholders. As to continued participation of the old equityholders, the district court justified their inclusion on the ground that they were willing to assume managerial responsibilities in the company and they were "the only persons who [were] familiar with the company's operations and who [had] experience in shipbuilding." In addition, the Court noted:

> Most of the present bondholders are widely scattered with small holdings, and their position would be benefited by being

---

[44] Commentators faulted the legislation on exactly this ground. See, e.g., Levi, *Corporate Reorganization* at 3, 6, 18–19 (cited in note 28). After rehearsing how the fair and equitable test leaves "uncertainty as to how much the intermediate class may demand," Levi later notes that the "failure of chapter X further to elaborate the standards for a 'fair and equitable' plan seems a mistake."

[45] *Case v Los Angeles Lumber Products Co.*, 308 US 106 (1939). The Court had already found that shareholders of an insolvent firm could not insist upon being included in the new firm as a right. *In re 629 Church Street Building Corp.*, 299 US 24 (1936). Hence, the Court had already decided that shareholders could not insist upon relative priority as of right, but it had not established the converse, that creditors had a right to insist on absolute priority.

associated with old stockholders of financial influence and stability who might be able to assist in proper financing.[46]

The reorganization was brought about, it seems, from the need
for additional capital, not the threat of foreclosure by existing
creditors. Due to a previous workout, interest payments were owed
only if earned, and the creditors lacked the power to foreclose until
1944.

From Swaine's perspective, the approval of the plan by 90% of
the creditors would have been sufficient.[47] Requiring unanimity
was unreasonable, and the old equity had to be given some of the
going-concern value or they would not cooperate in reorganizing
the firm. Nor did including the shareholders violate the terms of
the debt contract, given that the creditors' contract did not give
them a right to reach the assets until 1944. From the vantage point
of early 1938, when the District Court confirmed the plan, the
expected value of the shipyard in 1944 was less than what the creditors were owed. If, as expected, the economy remained much the
same, there would be nothing for the shareholders. But one could
not be sure. The world was at peace, but war clouds loomed in
Europe. An increase in the demand for naval vessels or an unex-
pected decline in the existing stock was possible and, if the shipyard were in the right hands, it might increase in value enough to
pay the creditors in full and still leave something for the shareholders. Giving the shareholders a small minority interest in the stock
of the new firm was a sensible way to account for this possibility.
The dissenting creditors may have thought the amount of equity
given the old shareholders was too large, but they had had a full
opportunity to voice their objections during the reorganization.
Moreover, the overwhelming majority of those in the position of
the creditors favored the reorganization plan.

Those who accepted Jerome Frank's view saw the case altogether differently. Modern firms are no different from parcels of

---

[46] *In re Los Angeles Lumber Products Co.*, 24 F Supp 501, 513 (SD Calif 1938), aff'd, 100
F2d 963 (9th Cir), rev'd, 308 US 106 (1939). The District Court's opinion tracked practice
in the lower courts. See Bonbright and Bergerman, *Two Rival Theories* at 154 (cited in note
18).

[47] See also *Jameson*, 20 F2d at 815 ("While in such matters majorities do not govern, the
approval thus signified by this vastly greater number, whose interests are identical in kind
with those of the objectors, is entitled to much weight in determining whether or not the
plan is equitable and fair.").

real estate. Defaults justify having a day of reckoning in which the equity should be wiped out if the firm has liabilities that, at fair valuation, exceed the assets. Allowing the old shareholders to continue was a source of mischief that took away from public investors value that properly belonged to them. If the old shareholders could sabotage the reorganization, then the solution was not to pay them off, but rather to empower the judge or others to step in and remove them. In large firms, the shareholders would not control the day-to-day operations in any event. Professionals could be brought in to do the job. Government regulators such as the S.E.C. (of which Frank was then chair) could assist the court in ensuring the process was fair. Only in the narrowest of circumstances should old equity continue in the face of any dissent. There was no threat to the going concern remotely comparable to those a railroad faced when it had dozens of different kinds of secured debt scattered across many jurisdictions.

The opinion in *Los Angeles Lumber* was among the first opinions assigned to William O. Douglas. Indeed, as he had never sat on the bench before, *Los Angeles Lumber* may have been the first opinion he ever wrote. The controversy turned on the merits of absolute and relative priority, and courts had never addressed the issue. Indeed, at the time Justice Douglas wrote his opinion, none ever even used the words "absolute priority."[48] Justice Douglas, however, was no stranger to the controversy over the "fair and equitable" standard. After law school, Douglas worked on corporate reorganizations at the Cravath firm for Robert Swaine.[49] He then took his expertise in corporate reorganizations to the Columbia and Yale law schools where he taught corporate reorganizations, wrote the leading casebook in the field, and did path-breaking empirical studies of equity receiverships and business bankruptcies.[50]

---

[48] *In re Utilities Power & Light Corp.*, 29 F Supp 763 (ND Ill 1939), rather than *Los Angeles Lumber*, is the first reported opinion we have found that uses the words "absolute priority" in assessing the rights of creditors and shareholders. It was decided only ten days before *Los Angeles Lumber*, however, and hence was very likely unavailable to Justice Douglas.

[49] In his autobiography, Justice Douglas recalled that Swaine thought well of his work and, just before he left, tried to persuade him to stay. "He had a full expectation that in a few years I would be a junior partner, and from there on, the world was my oyster." William O. Douglas, *Go East, Young Man* 156 (Random House, 1974).

[50] See William O. Douglas and John H. Weir, *Equity Receiverships in the United States District Court for Connecticut: 1920–29*, 4 Conn Bar J 1 (1930); William O. Douglas and Dorothy S. Thomas, *The Business Failures Project—II. An Analysis of Methods of Investigation*,

Douglas then went to Washington where he wrote an eight-volume report on corporate reorganizations. He drafted Chapter X of the Bankruptcy Act and pushed it through Congress. (Chapter X was the reorganization law that succeeded the statute involved in *Los Angeles Lumber*. It carried forward the language "fair and equitable.") In short, along with Robert Swaine and Jerome Frank, William O. Douglas was the country's foremost authority on the meaning of the words "fair and equitable."

Writing for a unanimous Court, Justice Douglas acknowledged that the plan in *Los Angeles Lumber* complied with relative priority,[51] but went on to hold that this was not enough. The words "fair and equitable" required adherence to absolute priority. The approval of the plan by the vast majority of security holders "was immaterial on the basic issue of [the plan's] fairness."[52] "Fair and equitable," Justice Douglas asserted, were "words of art" that had taken on a settled meaning in *Boyd* and *Kansas City Terminal*.[53] This meaning was the "rule of full or absolute priority." "The fact that bondholders might fare worse as a result of a foreclosure and liquidation than they would by taking a debtor's plan . . . can have no relevant bearing on whether a proposed plan is 'fair and equitable'. . . ."[54] When the firm is insolvent, the interests of old equity must be extinguished:

> [W]here the debtor is insolvent, the stockholder's participation must be based on a contribution in money or money's worth, reasonably equivalent in view of all the circumstances to the participation of the stockholder.[55]

The plan of reorganization before the Court could not be confirmed because the shareholders retained their old interests and were not putting in any new cash.

The words "fair and equitable" were, however, very far from

---

40 Yale L J 1034 (1931). Indeed, these studies brought Douglas to prominence and led him to Washington. See Douglas, *Go East* at 258 (cited in note 49).

[51] 308 US at 119–20; see also *Consolidated Rock Products Co. v Du Bois*, 312 US 510, 527 (1941) ("And we indicated in [*Los Angeles Lumber*] that the ["fair and equitable"] rule was not satisfied even though the 'relative priorities' of creditors and stockholders were maintained.") (opinion per Justice Douglas).

[52] 308 US at 115.

[53] Id.

[54] Id at 123.

[55] Id at 122.

being "words of art." They were simply one among a number of different phrases that had been used to identify the *Boyd* legacy. The Court itself had never used the words "fair and equitable" in *Boyd* or any other case. Justice Douglas for his own part had used a different formulation when he testified about the law in front of Congress as the chair of the S.E.C.[56] Justice Douglas asserted that "fair and equitable" and its alternative formulations had come to mean "absolute priority." But a number of the lower courts he cited for this proposition had actually adopted "relative priority." These include *Jameson*, a leading case on relative priority that Justice Douglas himself had used in his own casebook on corporate reorganizations.

The opinion on its face gives no trace of it, but Justice Douglas set out an interpretation of "fair and equitable" that was controversial and ideologically charged. Nothing separates William O. Douglas's view of "fair and equitable" from Jerome Frank's. Indeed, *Los Angeles Lumber* tracks the brief submitted by the United States that had been prepared by the S.E.C. under Jerome Frank's supervision, who at the time had just become its chair.

That Douglas's views tracked Frank's should not have come as a surprise. Douglas's list of the people who most shaped his view of the law at the start of his career contained only six names. On this list, one that included the likes of Franklin Roosevelt, Louis Brandeis, and Hugo Black,[57] was Jerome Frank. Moreover, William O. Douglas had already written an article with Frank on *Boyd* and the absolute priority rule.[58] Douglas and Frank were longtime colleagues, kindred spirits, and close friends.[59]

Before *Los Angeles Lumber*, the idea that "fair and equitable" meant absolute priority was at best only one of several defensible interpretations, but as soon as the opinion was issued, the competing interpretations disappeared. What was an open question prior to *Los Angeles Lumber*—whether "fair and equitable" meant rela-

---

[56] He used the formulation "fairness, soundness, and equity" when he testified before Congress on Chapter X. See Hearings Before the Committee on the Judiciary, House of Representatives, on HR 6439, 75th Cong 182–83 (1937) (statement of William O. Douglas).

[57] See Douglas, *Go East* at 182 (cited in note 49).

[58] See William O. Douglas and Jerome Frank, *Landlords' Claims in Reorganizations*, 42 Yale L J 1003, 1012–13 (1933).

[59] See Seligman, *Transformation of Wall Street* at 214–15 (cited in note 39).

tive or absolute priority—was settled decisively. Nevertheless, readers of this opinion today who are unfamiliar with the evolution of the law of corporate reorganizations, something that exists largely outside of reported opinions, are left with the distinct impression that the absolute priority rule was settled long before.[60]

V. ABSOLUTE PRIORITY AND THE BANKRUPTCY REFORM ACT

For purposes of understanding present law, however, the uncertainty that existed before 1939 no longer matters. *Los Angeles Lumber* pushed corporate reorganization law toward the real estate foreclosure model by forging a link between the words "fair and equitable" and absolute priority, a link that lawyers, judges, and Congress itself accepted during the decades between *Los Angeles Lumber* and the Bankruptcy Reform Act of 1978.[61] When one interprets Chapter 11, one can therefore read into Section 1129(b) the idea of absolute priority through its use of "fair and equitable." This interpretation in turn affects how we should interpret the requirement that old equity not receive any "property" "on account of" their old interests.

Section 1129(b)(2) does not say: (1) a plan has to be fair and equitable, *and* (2) that old investors cannot receive any property on account of their old interests. Rather, it provides: (1) the plan must be "fair and equitable," and (2) "fair and equitable" *"includes"* within it the idea that old investors cannot receive property on account of their old interest. The structure of the clause invites us to see the specific requirement that equityholders receive nothing on account of their prior interest as an integral component of

---

[60] Because of the way it is written and the way it characterizes its largely inaccessible antecedents, *Los Angeles Lumber* is often characterized as the opinion that introduces the new value exception to the absolute priority rule. In fact, it is better characterized as the source of the absolute priority rule itself. Several scholars have written about this peculiar state of affairs. See Ayer, *Rethinking Absolute Priority* at 974–76 (cited in note 11); Haines, *The Unwarranted Attack* at 407–14 (cited in note 11); Bruce A. Markell, *Owners, Auctions, and Absolute Priority in Bankruptcy Reorganizations*, 44 Stan L Rev 69, 84–85 (1991).

[61] Justice Douglas's interpretation was implicitly accepted by Congress. Chapter XI, which dealt with the reorganization of smaller firms, had never been thought to embody the absolute priority rule, yet it too contained the requirement that a plan be "fair and equitable." In 1952, Congress deleted this requirement from Chapter XI to ensure that the absolute priority rule would not be imported into it. See Act of July 7, 1952, ch 579 §§ 35 & 43, 66 Stat 433 & 435. Reconciling other legislation with the holding of *Los Angeles Lumber* reenforced Justice Douglas's judicial gloss equating "fair and equitable" with absolute priority.

a "fair and equitable" plan. The most straightforward way of doing this is to read this clause as a mandate that the "fair and equitable" language, notwithstanding its inherent malleability, retains the gloss that the Court placed upon it in *Los Angeles Lumber*. However much judges continue to refine the "fair and equitable" standard, they cannot return to a regime of relative priority. If a firm does not have sufficient assets to pay its creditors in full, the shareholders cannot receive property simply because they had once been shareholders. A relative priority regime would allow shareholders to receive property without more because it permits the option value of the shareholder's interest to be recognized.

Justice Souter's opinion for the Court in *LaSalle* recognized the historical pedigree of the "fair and equitable" requirement:

> [Section] 77B (and its successor, Chapter X) of the old Act [required] that an reorganization plan be "fair and equitable." The reason for such a limitation was the danger inherent in any reorganization plan proposed by a debtor, then and now, that the plan will simply turn out to be too good a deal for the debtor's owners. Hence the pre-Code judicial response known as the absolute priority rule, that fairness and equity required that "the creditors . . . be paid before the stockholders retain [equity interests] for any purpose whatever."[62]

The Court then made its own addition to the *Boyd* tradition by finding that it was not enough, when shareholders are given exclusive rights to the equity, for the bankruptcy judge merely to find that the value the shareholders received was equal in value to their new contribution:

> [It would be] a fatal flaw if old equity acquired or retained the property interest without paying full value. It would thus be necessary for old equity to demonstrate its payment of top dollar, but this it could not satisfactorily do when it would receive or retain its property under a plan giving it exclusive rights and in the absence of a competing plan of any sort. Under a plan granting an exclusive right, making no provision for competing bids or competing plans, any determination that the price was top dollar would necessarily be made by a judge in

---

[62] 119 S Ct at 1417 (citations omitted). The Court also considered and, while it called it "starchy," did not decisively reject an approach advanced by the bank and the government as *amicus curiae*. Id at 1420. That approach would find that the Code's prohibition of retaining "property" "on account of" a prior interest dooms any plan where there is any causal relationship between the prior interest and new one.

bankruptcy court, whereas the best way to determine value is exposure to a market.[63]

Boyd told us that nonparticipating general creditors cannot be excluded when old shareholders remain in place. *Los Angeles Lumber* told us that old shareholders cannot participate, at least if they are not contributing an amount equal in value to the equity they receive. *LaSalle* tells us that, at the very least, the bankruptcy judge must use the market or some other test to establish that the old shareholders are in fact paying more for the equity than anyone else. The majority's opinion exemplifies common law judging in a statutory age. It looks to a chain of precedents because of statutory text that is itself derived from them.

True to the spirit of common law judging, *LaSalle*'s contribution to the absolute priority rule is both small and process oriented. Adherence to the absolute priority rule requires that any shareholder participation be no more than justified by the amount of new capital contributed. Moreover, an objective mechanism must be put in place to ensure that this is so. A judicial finding that the two are equal is not enough. The exact mechanism is one that the lower courts must now discover, just as they had to shape the contours of a "fair" offer and a "just" reorganization after *Boyd*. With *Boyd*, the Court provided general principles to protect creditors that lower courts then had to refine and develop. *LaSalle* continues that tradition.

This modest advancement, complete with its failure to resolve definitely the continued role of "new value" in corporate reorganizations, comports with the Supreme Court's institutional role. Our legal system relies upon generalist appellate judges to interpret statutes and ensure consistency across types of cases. An interpretative methodology is sound only if it reflects the competence of the typical generalist appellate judge and the constraints under which she operates. A generalist appellate judge, aided only by the submissions of interested parties and the assistance of newly minted lawyers, cannot hope to become a master of the antecedents of the Bankruptcy Code (or indeed the antecedents of any intricate statutory regime). An interpretative methodology is suspect if it points most judges toward lines of inquiry that they are ill-equipped to conduct and empowers others in ways that are hard

[63] Id at 1423.

to control. Justice Souter's opinion avoids these flaws by articulating the general principle distilled from the prior cases, extending this principle to resolve the case at hand, and leaving for further development the ultimate fate of "new value."

Contrast *Los Angeles Lumber*. No one else on the Supreme Court at that time possessed an understanding of corporate reorganizations remotely comparable to that of Justice Douglas. The perceived comparative advantage that Justice Douglas had may have led the rest of the Court to be too inclined to take what their new colleague wrote at face value. A bold judge, ostensibly hewing to the signposts already laid down, can reshape the law in ways that are hard to detect and control, especially when the judges who must review the opinion are generalists.[64] Judges who believe that their common law powers entitle them to shape boldly a dynamic and evolving law are hard to rein in. Justice Douglas reshaped corporate reorganization law in *Los Angeles Lumber*. By purporting to follow law already established in other cases, Justice Douglas may well have been able to obscure from his colleagues on the Court the dramatic step that they were taking.

One should not, however, measure the potential of a measured common law approach solely by the performance of Justice Douglas. If the opinion had been assigned to a different Justice and were written in the same spirit as *LaSalle*, it likely would have focused only on the matter at hand. It could have reached the same outcome by clarifying that *Kansas City Terminal* and *Boyd* require that whenever old equity participates in a reorganization, it had to bring something new to the table. Such a modest extension would have disposed of the reorganization plan before the Court, and would have been agnostic on the relative priority/absolute priority debate.

Justice Douglas, however, held an a priori commitment to the ascendancy of the absolute priority rule over the competing theory of relative priority. Given this commitment, any interpretative methodology might have brought as unyielding an opinion. Moreover, we no longer live in a world where the path to the Supreme Court is through becoming an expert in bankruptcy law or other area of private law. Most Justices today are more likely to enjoy reputations as generalist appellate judges. They see their mission

---

[64] See, e.g., Grant Gilmore's description of Benjamin Cardozo's tenure on the New York Court of Appeals. Grant Gilmore, *The Ages of American Law* 75 (Yale U Press, 1977).

in private law cases as giving guidance to other appellate judges and to experts in lower tribunals.

For the Justice who does not have an intellectual stake in bankruptcy law, a common law approach can offer a way to guide lower courts, impart coherence to the law, and yet not require a subject matter competence that she does not have. This careful and measured form of common law reasoning insulates the judge from mistakes. As have many before him, Justice Souter misunderstood *Boyd* and *Kansas City Terminal*. He assumed that they held what Justice Douglas asserted they held—that "fair and equitable" had by 1939 become terms of art meaning absolute priority. Nevertheless, the guidance that emanates from the Court's opinion in *LaSalle* depends only on the idea that absolute priority had become part of *Boyd*'s legacy at the time of the 1978 Bankruptcy Reform Act. The principle extracted from the history is so central to it that, even when much of the history is wrong, the principle that is abstracted from it is still sound.[65]

None of this, however, is to suggest that looking toward history in the wrong way or at the wrong time insulates judges from error. Justice Thomas in his concurring opinion in *LaSalle* rightly points to *Dewsnup v Timm*[66] as an example how pre-Code antecedents can lead courts astray, even when the Court focuses upon narrow questions. To understand the force of this objection, it is necessary recount the problem presented by *Dewsnup*. Debtor borrows $100 from Bank, uses it to buy Blackacre, and gives Bank a mortgage on Blackacre. Real estate values collapse and Debtor files a bankruptcy petition. The bankruptcy court finds that Blackacre is now worth only $60. Debtor, having procured funds from another source, wants to pay Bank $60, and leave Chapter 7 as the owner of Blackacre free and clear.[67] The question under the Bankruptcy Code is whether debtors can "strip down" liens in this fashion.

---

[65] See Cass R. Sunstein, *One Case at a Time: Judicial Minimalism on the Supreme Court* 46–60 (Harv U Press, 1999).

[66] 502 US 410 (1992).

[67] Alternatively, Debtor may, after a judicial valuation, seek to end the Chapter 7 case, and then file a Chapter 13 case before Bank can foreclose. To the extent that Blackacre is not a personal residence, and to the extent that Debtor can strip down Bank's lien to judicially determined value of the property, Debtor can use Chapter 13 to force a payment plan on Bank. See Barry E. Adler, *Creditor Rights After Johnson and Dewsnup*, 10 Bankr Dev J 1, 4–5 (1993–94). This strategy, like the one in text, disadvantages creditors in that it allows debtors to take advantage of low judicial valuations.

Stripping down a lien in bankruptcy has the effect after the fact of benefiting debtors at the expense of creditors. If the bankruptcy judge places too high a value on the land, the debtor can always surrender the land to the secured creditor. If the bankruptcy judge errs on the low side, the debtor can pay the bank this amount and keep the land. In other words, debtors can systematically take advantage of those judicial valuations that are too low, but not be stuck with those valuations which are too high. Lien stripping also runs contrary to established practice in bankruptcy before the 1978 Bankruptcy Act. Finally, it runs contrary to the notion in real estate law that, when a debtor defaults, the value of the land is set through a foreclosure sale rather than through a judicial valuation. But one cannot say that the result is absurd. Statutes passed in the 1930s involving moratoria on mortgages often used such devices to protect debtors,[68] and consumer advocates have long promoted lien strip-down.

Against this background, we look at the language of the Bankruptcy Code. All agree that Bank has an "allowed secured claim" for the amount the judge sets (or $60 in our case). Similarly, there is an "allowed unsecured claim" of $40.[69] The controversy is over what happens to the lien that supports the "allowed secured claim." Section 506(d), the relevant provision, reads:

> To the extent that a lien secures a claim against the debtor that is not an allowed secured claim, such lien is void.

This language seems to provide that Bank's lien is void to the extent that it is more than the amount of its secured claim. Debtor owes Bank $100, but Bank's secured claim is for only $60. Hence, the lien is void to the extent it exceeds $60. Debtor could thus pay Bank $60, and remove the lien on Blackacre.

Bank, however, argued that this section was not aimed at lien strip-down at all. Rather, the provision was designed to prevent liens from surviving bankruptcy if the underlying claim was disallowed. To see this, consider the following. Lawyer provides legal services at an exorbitant fee and secures it with a lien on Debtor's property. Another section of the Bankruptcy Code disallows Law-

---

[68] These statutes were not always constitutional, but there was no colorable constitutional objection to lien strip-down in *Dewsnup*.

[69] See 11 USC § 506(a).

yer's claim, but only this provision voids Lawyer's lien. Under this view, the purpose of Section 506(d) was not to strip down liens, but rather to make sure that a creditor's lien fares no better than her claim. Section 506(d) ensures that Lawyer is both denied a pro rata share of Debtor's assets in bankruptcy and prevented from seizing collateral after the bankruptcy is over. The language, aimed at this specific kind of abuse, was never intended to deal with the ability of a debtor to reduce the amount of an otherwise valid creditor's lien and should not be read to do so.

The Court adopted this interpretation in *Dewsnup*. The majority's opinion noted that, had it simply looked at Section 506 "on a clean slate," it would have agreed with the debtor and stripped down the lien to the value of the property. However, in light of the historical practice of not stripping down liens in bankruptcy, and the fact that the Bank could make a plausible argument that the text was aimed at an altogether different problem, the majority concluded that strip-down was not allowed.

In his dissent, Justice Scalia rejected the interpretation Bank offered for Section 506(d). To have the effect that Bank claimed, it should have been written differently. It should have provided:

> To the extent that a lien secures a claim against the debtor that is not an allowed claim, such lien is void.

We should not treat the "allowed secured claims" of creditors like Bank as if they were the same as "allowed claims." The result here may be undesirable from the perspective of creditors and unsound as a matter of bankruptcy policy and contrary to pre-existing practice, but it was not beyond what some had advocated or what other insolvency laws had done. It might be a bad idea with dubious pedigree, but this should not be enough to deny the statutory language the meaning that both makes sense on its own and is consistent with the way the language is used elsewhere in the Code.

Justice Scalia faulted the majority in *Dewsnup* for repairing to pre-Code law without a sufficient justification for doing so. Nothing in the text of the law suggests recourse to history. "Allowed secured claim" is a concept unique to the 1978 Act and has no statutory or caselaw antecedents. These words are carefully defined and repeatedly and consistently used in other parts of the 1978 Act. There was a pre-Code tradition of how liens were treated in bankruptcy, but there is no landmark in the Code that invites a court to draw upon this history. The drafting of the Act was exceedingly careful, and these provisions were not last-minute additions. Courts should assume that drafters knew what they were doing, especially with respect to a term that has a consistent meaning every other place it appears. Competent drafters are unlikely to make such mistakes with terms that are a fundamental part of the architecture of the statute. (The chance that a judge would attribute an error when none occurred might be as great as the chance that an error would remain unchanged.)[70]

It is this complaint that Justice Thomas carries forward in his concurrence in *LaSalle*. The job of a generalist reviewing court is to ensure consistency in the lower courts. Insisting that lower courts follow the dictates of statutory text gives them clear instruction about what they should do and makes it easy to tell whether they have done it. This approach both respects the institutional role that Congress plays and recognizes the constraints of the institution that a reviewing judge oversees. If a judge attempts to engage in a more searching inquiry without a clear reason as to why she is doing it, she may be wrong more often than not.

The objection raised by Justices Scalia and Thomas to *Dewsnup* has force in that case, but it does not extend to *LaSalle*. One must not confuse the use of common law methodology to interpret Section 1129(b) and the departure from plain meaning in Section 506. In *Dewsnup*, the words at issue had never been used by anyone before 1978. In *LaSalle*, the words had a history stretching back many decades. In *Dewsnup*, the language is best seen as a case in which the Court mistakenly thinks it has found a drafting error.[71]

---

[70] For a similar point regarding legislative history, see Adrian Vermeule, *Legislative History and the Limits of Judicial Competence: The Untold Story of Holy Trinity Church*, 50 Stan L Rev 1833, 1857–77 (1998).

[71] Justice Scalia seems to admit the possibility of "scrivener's errors," but he defines them narrowly. See, e.g., *Union Bank v Wolas*, 502 US 151, 163 (1991) (concurring opinion). There were some provisions of the 1978 Bankruptcy Reform Act that might nevertheless qualify even under the narrowest conception of a "scrivener's error." For example, the bill as passed by the House and the Senate provided that "stockbrokers" could not file Chapter 11 petitions. (This provision ensured that cases involving stockbrokers would be heard using the special rules designed specifically for stockbrokers set out in Subchapter III of Chapter 7.) The enrolled bill, however, provided that "stock*holders*" could not file Chapter 11 petitions. This mistake was made by someone in the congressional printing office and was not caught before the enrolled bill was transmitted to the President. Read literally, the version of the Bankruptcy Reform Act actually signed by the President provided that no corporation with a subsidiary could ever file in Chapter 11. Whether a committed textualist would admit the reading of "stock*broker*" for stock*holder*, however, is not clear, given the primacy she is likely to give to the enrolled bill.

If the Court interpreted the language correctly, everyone would agree that it would have been better if the drafters had written it differently. Not so with *LaSalle*. The language is open-textured, and there are a number of reasons why Congress may choose to use such language.[72] While one can decide *Dewsnup* merely by exploring the internal structure of the Bankruptcy Code, one cannot do so in *LaSalle*.

Hewing to statutory text provides clear guidance to the lower court judges with respect to words like "allowed secured claim." Nevertheless, it does little with respect to open-textured language such as "ordinary course,"[73] or "reasonably equivalent value."[74] One needs to find benchmarks against which to ask whether something is "ordinary"; to know whether something is "equivalent," one must know what to compare it with.

Cases like *LaSalle* demand an interpretative methodology that allows one to choose among competing interpretations. To make a critique of Justice Souter's opinion in *LaSalle* compelling, a textualist must confront provisions of the Bankruptcy Code that are subject to competing interpretations. Textualists who fail to understand how such provisions work can embarrass themselves as much as the Court in *Dewsnup*.

VI. Judicial Minimalism and the Common Law Tradition in Bankruptcy

In his concurring opinion in *LaSalle*, Justice Thomas believed that he could resolve the case without exploring the common law background to the "fair and equitable" language. The exact contours of the "fair and equitable" test were unimportant because we can find that the old investors received "property" "on account of" their old interest without reference to the more general requirement that the plan be "fair and equitable."

Justice Thomas criticized the majority opinion for its long review of the history of the "fair and equitable" principle. The plan of reorganization in *LaSalle* in substance gave the old equityholders the equivalent of an exclusive option to acquire equity at a fixed

---

[72] See Sunstein, *One Case at a Time* 219–27 (cited in note 65).

[73] See *Union Bank v Wolas*, 502 US 151 (1991).

[74] See *BFP v Resolution Trust Corp.*, 511 US 531 (1994).

price the day the plan of reorganization was confirmed. The majority found that this option was "property." Once it reached this conclusion, the Court had only to use a common sense interpretation of the words "on account of" to resolve the case. Hence, its discussion of the "fair and equitable" standard was not only unnecessary, but suggested a methodology for interpreting the Bankruptcy Code that was confusing and rudderless.

The matter, however, is not so simple. The majority's conclusion that the equityholders were receiving "property" depended crucially on the link it made between the common law background of the "fair and equitable" standard and the absolute priority rule.[75] Without this link, it is much harder to conclude that the equityholders were receiving "property" under the plan.

Section 1129(a) requires that plans of reorganization be "feasible." Hence, anyone who proposes a plan has to be able to show that it will work. Some claims, principally administrative expenses, need to be paid in cash. In *LaSalle*, the plan also provided that debt other than that owed Bank would be paid in cash. Hence, for the plan in *LaSalle* to be "feasible," it had to identify the source of the cash needed to implement it. The old investors were willing to make a binding commitment to fund the plan in the event that it was confirmed, and the debtor took advantage of this willingness. Indeed, the debtor had to, given that the plan had to identify the source of the funds needed to implement it and no other source was available. Far from giving something of value to the old investors, the debtor was getting something from them. After all, when third parties commit themselves to funding a plan of reorganization before it is confirmed, they are typically paid a fee. To induce new investors to commit capital in advance, one must ordinarily pay them something.

From this perspective, the old investors did not receive an option or "property" of any sort. Indeed, it was the other way around. Under this view, far from giving property *to* the old investors, it was the debtor that had acquired a valuable asset—the com-

---

[75] Some courts have found that an exclusive option is property without relying on history. These courts have justified their interpretations by invoking the absolute priority rule. See, e.g., *Kham & Nate's Shoes No. 2, Inc. v First Bank*, 908 F2d 1351, 1360 (7th Cir 1990). But if one invokes the idea of absolute priority and does not link it to history, one must ground it in some other source. This is no easy task as the words "absolute priority" appear nowhere in the Bankruptcy Code.

mitment—*from* them. The old investors incurred an obligation to the debtor, while the debtor made none in return. The obligation was a *liability* to the old investors and an *asset* to the debtor.[76] For this arrangement to count as "property" in the old investors' hands, exactly the opposite would have to be true. The only "property" the old investors received were the interests in the new partnership they received after the plan was confirmed. These they received not on account of their old interests, but on account of the $4.1 million they contributed.

To decide a case such as *LaSalle*, a judge needs some way of choosing between these competing characterizations. The principle of absolute priority, as implemented in the text of the statute through the words "fair and equitable," is one way of doing this. This history attached to "fair and equitable" is replete with skepticism of any reorganization, regardless of how it is implemented, that is likely to leave old equity with a special deal. But this route is not available once one adopts a methodology that refuses to draw links to the past in interpreting words like "property." The text of the Bankruptcy Code does not provide for "absolute priority." It becomes easy to conclude that the old investors received property only *after* one accepts the idea that the Bankruptcy Code favors a theory of absolute priority over relative priority.

A statute like Chapter 11 that regulates the conduct of commercially sophisticated parties has to take account of their ability to adjust to whatever interpretative methodology the Court adopts. *LaSalle* is a good example. Lower courts had already noted that old investors received "property" if a plan gave them the exclusive option to buy equity at the value the bankruptcy judge set. Hence, the debtor in *LaSalle* structured things such that the old investors were not explicitly given an option. They made commitments in advance of plan confirmation. Hence, they had no "option" to exercise at the time the plan was confirmed. Justice Thomas recognized, quite correctly, that what the plan provided investors was substantively no different from what the shareholders would have received if they had been given options explicitly. Yet whenever

---

[76] Note that this characterization depends crucially on maintaining the legal distinction between the debtor and the old investors in much the same way that the equity receivership depended on maintaining the fiction that it was the creditors, and not the old shareholders, who were running the process.

one adopts a rule that looks to substance rather than form, one needs to know when such recharacterizations are permissible and when they are not. Recharacterization is simple in *LaSalle* once one is committed to the absolute priority rule, but not if one is committed to relative priority. Again, the text, separated from history, provides no way of choosing between them.

Ideas such as the absolute priority rule provide organizing principles that offer a way of seeing each of the provisions of the Bankruptcy Code as part of a coherent framework. A minimalist common law judge is cautious about choosing any organizing principles. Such a judge, for example, would not have written *Los Angeles Lumber*. Once such an opinion exists and the principle of absolute priority had been ratified by Congress, however, the principle ceases to be controversial. It has become part of the warp and woof of the law. Ignoring it is to discard a useful tool that may make the Bankruptcy Code easier to interpret, not harder.

The usefulness of this tool can be seen by considering the question that remains open after *LaSalle:* Are there any circumstances where old equityholders could participate in a reorganization over the dissent of a class of unsecured creditors? To explore this question, assume that on remand in *LaSalle* the bankruptcy court were to terminate the debtor's exclusive right to file a plan of reorganization and the bank were to offer its own plan of reorganization. This plan provides that, on the day of plan confirmation, the bank will deposit $90 million in cash with the bankruptcy court. These funds would, of course, be distributed according to the absolute priority rule, which would give the bank the entire $90 million. The bank votes in favor of the plan, and the general creditors and the former equityholders dissent. The plan, however, can be confirmed under the Code because it does not run afoul of Section 1129(b).

The debtor again files its plan. Recall that this plan gives the bank the entire economic value of the real estate, a set of promises valued at $4.1 million, and pays off the general creditors in full. No one else submits a third plan. To the extent that the debtor's plan can be confirmed, Section 1129(c) instructs the bankruptcy court to confirm one of the plans. In doing so, "the court shall consider the preferences of creditors and equity security holders . . . ."[77]

---

[77] 11 USC 1129(c).

The bank, however, argues that the court cannot get to Section 1129(c) because the debtor's plan does not comport with Section 1129(b)(2) because it gives "property" to the former investors "on account of" their prior equity interest. The debtor responds that the plan gives equity to the former owners only in exchange for the new capital infusion, and not "on account of" their old interest. *LaSalle* is satisfied because the debtor's plan has been exposed to the market, and, the debtor argues, it provides "top dollar" to the creditors. After all, both the bank and the general creditors receive more economic value under the debtor's plan than under the bank's plan. Moreover, the ability of the bank to offer a competing plan means that the old partners are not receiving property because of their old interest; rather, it is because they submitted the better plan.

The textualist cannot get a purchase on these facts. *LaSalle* no longer dictates that the old owners are receiving "property" under the debtor's plan. The conclusion that the debtor's plan, in effect, gave an option to the old equityholders turned on the exclusive nature of the process. On our hypothetical, however, that exclusivity has been removed. Moreover, is what the old partners seek to acquire "on account of" their old interest, or is it "on account of" the capital infusion that allows the debtor to offer the better plan? We see no way in which the text can offer any legitimate guidance on this issue.

Compare this linguistic dead end with the avenues available to the judge who approaches "fair and equitable" in a common law fashion. The history of "fair and equitable" makes one think twice about embracing a blanket prohibition against such shareholder participation. From shortly after *Boyd* was decided until the adoption of the Bankruptcy Code, there was one aspect of "fair and equitable" on which everyone from Jerome Frank to Robert Swaine agreed. A plan could be "fair and equitable" and yet still allow old equity to participate. Hence, a court ought to hesitate before finding that Section 1129(b) prohibits old shareholders from participating altogether. Such an interpretation would create the odd result that the "fair and equitable" standard "includes" a prohibition that no one ever thought it had.

The history of "fair and equitable" thus suggests caution before concluding that shareholders cannot participate over the dissent of a class of creditors; it does not, however, mandate that conclusion.

The enactment of Chapter 11 significantly changed the voting rules governing the approval of a plan of reorganization. Earlier legislation required that all classes of creditors approve a plan of reorganization *and* that the plan be "fair and equitable." In other words, "fair and equitable" became an issue only after all classes of creditors had approved the plan. By contrast, under Chapter 11 a court never has to probe whether a plan is "fair and equitable" unless a class of unsecured creditors has voted against it. By allowing creditor classes to approve a plan of reorganization, Chapter 11 allows for plans to be confirmed that are not "fair and equitable" even in the face of the objection by a isolated creditor. When every class approves the plan, the fair and equitable test is not reached. The Code thus allows creditors, by class, to approve equity participation in the reorganized firm. Hence, the plan in *Los Angles Lumber* would have been confirmed under today's Chapter 11 notwithstanding the dissenting creditors and no matter how one interpreted "fair and equitable."[78]

This change of when creditors can invoke the "fair and equitable" test is combined with the fact that today the disputes over whether a plan is "fair and equitable" arise for firms that are altogether different from the paradigms of either Swaine or Frank. In the typical case, a single creditor will hold all the claims in a particular class. Indeed, many are cases such as *LaSalle* in which one creditor has a claim that dwarfs all the others.[79] This claim vests the creditor with control over the class of which it is a member. None of Frank's concerns about protecting unsophisticated creditors are implicated, as the only creditor is itself a large bank or other investor. But Swaine's concerns are not implicated either. Because there is only one creditor, there is no danger that a small creditor will thwart the entire process. Even if there were a small creditor, as long as its claim was classified with others, it will be bound by the majority. These differences present a set of risks that neither Frank nor Swaine had to confront.

---

[78] Such participation by former shareholders seems to be the norm in the reorganization of publicly held enterprises. See Lynn M. LoPucki and William C. Whitford, *Bargaining Over Equity's Share in the Bankruptcy of Large, Publicly Held Companies*, 139 U Pa L Rev 125, 142 (1990) (creditors agreed to allow shareholder recovery in 21 of 30 cases).

[79] In 51 cases involving the new value question since 1986, 25 were single-asset cases, and four more were Chapter 11 cases involving farms. Three cases involved plans confirmed by bankruptcy courts which allowed old equityholders to participate, over the objections of a class of creditors, based on fresh capital contributions.

There is another way of making the point that pre-Code doctrine cannot be transplanted wholesale into the Code. The question in *Boyd* was the extent to which the real estate foreclosure rules should apply in railroad reorganizations. Today, most of the cases under Section 1129(b) are like *LaSalle*. The underlying asset is a piece of real property. Arguing that ordinary foreclosure rules should not apply in this environment is necessarily harder than making such an argument in the case of nineteenth-century railroads.

For all these reasons, we want to be precise in our claims about the potential of common law methodology in bankruptcy: it provides guidance, not guarantees. On the question left open after *LaSalle*, it tells us that Section 1129(b) mandates absolute priority, and it also suggests that a court should hesitate before banning participation by old shareholders completely. We do not claim, however, that this approach relieves a judge from making judgments. The virtue of this approach is that it allows a generalist judge to understand the commitment to absolute priority, and to make a judgment as to how that commitment is implemented in the Code.[80] The common law approach frames the choice; it does not force it.

Minimalist common law judging in bankruptcy directs the court's attention to the relevant decision to be made. An added virtue is that it may also respond better to the institutional relationship between Congress and the courts. Congress faces a budget constraint in monitoring the evolution of bankruptcy law. It can pass a limited number of laws each session, and imposing coherence on a statutory scheme is a time-consuming endeavor. Congress amends the Bankruptcy Code almost every year. By contrast, systemic revisions to the bankruptcy law occur roughly every twenty years. There were major revisions in 1938, 1952, and 1978. A similar large-scale revision is now before Congress.

The systemic reforms address a central failing of individual amendments. Individual amendments tend to tear at the fabric of the system. They often reflect the pressing needs of a certain interest group. In the early 1980s, for example, some courts found that when a firm entered bankruptcy it had the power to cancel con-

---

[80] On history as providing a guide to judgment rather than inescapable answers, see Rebecca L. Brown, *Tradition and Insight*, 103 Yale L J 177 (1993).

tracts that licensed its technology to other firms.[81] Firms were soon tempted to use Chapter 11 to renegotiate technology licenses. In response, firms became reluctant to acquire licenses from start-up firms or those in financial distress. In response to heavy lobbying, Congress quickly amended the Bankruptcy Code to straighten out this disruption.[82]

Finding that firms had the right to rid themselves of unfavorable technology licenses and other contracts did no violence to the text of the Bankruptcy Code. Nevertheless, these interpretations were hard to square with the conception of "rejection" of executory contracts that had been developed in the caselaw before the 1978 Act.[83] When opinions are sufficiently out of step with commercial practice, Congress often amends the law, and it did so here. But the congressional response focused on a narrow problem is imperfect. Congress's amendment addressed technology licenses only, the arena in which the interpretation caused the greatest problems. The interest groups that pushed the amendment had little incentive to ensure that its provision handled related problems, such as trademark licenses, franchise agreements, or covenants not to compete. Nor were they likely to be attentive to the way in which their amendment interacted with other parts of the Bankruptcy Code with respect to issues that did not affect them.

Such amendments make a statutory regime increasingly unwieldy over time. When courts focus on text to the exclusion of the principles that animate them, statutory regimes tend to lose their coherence more quickly. The provision that gave rise to the technology mess provides a good illustration. Courts, for the most part, have interpreted the section governing executory contracts in light of a handful of principles firmly rooted in bankruptcy precedent. (The most important one being that the trustee's power to "reject" an executory contract is merely the nonbankruptcy power to breach transplanted into the bankruptcy environment.) As a result, the section is more coherent and considerably less controversial than it might have been otherwise. An unyielding textualist

---

[81] See, e.g., *Lubrizol Enterprises Inc. v Richmond Metal Finishers Inc.*, 756 F2d 1043 (4th Cir 1985), cert denied, 475 US 1057.

[82] See 11 USC § 365(n).

[83] See Thomas H. Jackson, *The Logic and Limits of Bankruptcy Law* 105–21 (Harv U Press, 1986); Michael T. Andrew, *Executory Contracts in Bankruptcy: Understanding "Rejection,"* 59 U Colo L Rev 845, 931–32 (1988).

approach to the same section could not have done the same work. It could not have pointed in a consistent direction.

The Bankruptcy Code may be more likely to retain coherence over time when appellate judges adopt a minimalist common law methodology. Congress cannot monitor systematically judicial interpretation of the Bankruptcy Code. Its attention is focused on other matters. Given two interpretative methodologies that are equally easy to apply, we are better off with one that best maintains the coherence of the Code as a whole during the interregnum.

Finally, a minimalist common law method may perform better than textualism in our hierarchical judicial system. Such a methodology by appellate courts may also allow better oversight of lower tribunals over the course of many cases. When we tell a bankruptcy judge that the principle of the absolute priority rule is to be meticulously observed, we keep her in tighter check than when we tell her to focus upon the text of the statute. At the same time, we take advantage of her expertise. She has the ability to implement a procedure that ensures adherence to absolute priority in a way that the appellate court does not. Indeed, Justice Souter's principal contribution in *LaSalle* was to ensure not only that absolute priority will guide the bankruptcy judge, but also that the bankruptcy judge will implement the idea of absolute priority in a way that allows generalist appellate judges to review it.

To be sure, when an appellate judge uses common law methodologies to interpret the Bankruptcy Code, she may reshape the law in the process. Justice Douglas dramatically transformed our understanding of *Boyd* without many people, perhaps not even his fellow Justices, knowing it. But other methodologies may prove no more able to check strong-willed judges. Moreover, a methodology that insists on history and the articulation of general principles requires the strong-willed judge to make a large target. The absolute priority rule could not have been a bad rule and still found such ready acceptance in so many quarters so quickly. In other words, this methodology may be, to some extent, self-correcting. When one is forced to articulate general principles (such as the absolute priority rule) and show how they flow from words such as "fair and equitable," there is a limit to how far one can stray without drawing attention. As aggressive as Justice Douglas may have been in *Los Angeles Lumber*, he nevertheless still put forward an interpretation that was sufficiently sensible to win general acceptance. The deficiency of textualism in bankruptcy cases is that it sets out too few landmarks. In its hands, bankruptcy law can become both diffuse and inaccessible, and it may be harder to hold judges accountable.

LaSalle tells us that Section 1129(b) embodies the absolute priority rule and that bankruptcy judges must implement that provision in a way that allows generalist appellate judges to ensure that former equity holders have not evaded the strictures of capital structure that they have created. This, we now know, is *Boyd*'s legacy. Such a holding offers guidance that, while sensible, clear, and uncontroversial, is simply not available to the textualist judge. At least in bankruptcy cases, the common law tradition illuminates.